W9-CNA-030

$2195

Social and Psychological Research in Community Settings

Designing and Conducting Programs for Social and Personal Well-Being

Ricardo F. Muñoz
Lonnie R. Snowden
James G. Kelly
and Associates

Social and Psychological Research in Community Settings

Jossey-Bass Publishers

San Francisco • Washington • London • 1979

SOCIAL AND PSYCHOLOGICAL RESEARCH IN COMMUNITY
SETTINGS
by Ricardo F. Muñoz, Lonnie R. Snowden, James G. Kelly,
and Associates

Copyright © 1979 by: Jossey-Bass, Inc., Publishers
433 California Street
San Francisco, California 94104
&
Jossey-Bass Limited
28 Banner Street
London EC1Y 8QE

Copyright under International, Pan American, and
Universal Copyright Conventions. All rights
reserved. No part of this book may be reproduced
in any form—except for brief quotation (not to
exceed 1,000 words) in a review or professional
work—without permission in writing from the publishers.

Library of Congress Cataloging in Publication Data

Main entry under title:

Social and psychological research in community
    settings.
    (The Jossey-Bass social and behavioral science
series)
    Bibliography: p.
    Includes index.
    1. Sociological research—Methodology—Addresses,
essays, lectures. 2. Community life—Psychological
aspects—Addresses, essays, lectures. I. Muñoz,
Ricardo F. II. Snowden, Lonnie R., 1947–
III. Kelly, James G.
HM48.S56   301.34'07'2   79-88107
ISBN 0-87589-423-2

FIRST EDITION

Code 7928

The Jossey-Bass
Social and Behavioral Science Series

We dedicate this book

To Pat Marine Muñoz

*To Lonnie and Sylvia Snowden
and Fran Snowden*

*To Cosmo Belle Kelly
and the memory of James G. Kelly,
and to Sue Rombach Kelly
and Jim, Maureen, Ann, Sharon, and Kay*

*and to the mission and success of
The Lila Acheson Wallace School of
Community Service and Public Affairs*

Preface

This book is about research projects in community settings. We became interested in this project while collaborating on a chapter in the 1977 *Annual Review of Psychology* titled "Social and Community Interventions." It became clear to us that community psychology was evolving toward a stronger identity. Strategies, methods, and foci of intervention were being conceptualized in terms of communities and being applied in community settings. Our decision to put together this book stemmed from a desire to contribute to this process of self-definition.

Our primary emphasis is on research-oriented interventions. The process involved in bringing about change experimentally in nonlaboratory settings needs to be described and highlighted, both because of its intrinsic interest and because of its practical use for future workers in the community. The focus of the book is twofold: to showcase model research studies of change in community contexts and to present the process of carrying out such studies—the "behind the scenes" material that is usually omitted from formal research reports.

Contributors were selected from the pool of authors whose material we reviewed for the 1977 *Annual Review* chapter (publications appearing between January 1972 and January 1976). Criteria for selection included having completed a successful community-oriented research project and being willing to speak candidly about what it took to carry it out. The nature of the project was more important than the author's identification with the area of community psychology. Indeed, some of the contributors had not considered their work to be within this area until we contacted them. We looked for prototypic studies that illustrated issues of particular significance in a manner that would encourage further investigation. The result, we hope, is a report of exemplary research projects done in social and community contexts with the purpose of measuring or bringing about change.

Part One consists of two introductory chapters by the editors. Chapter One places the book and the contributed chapters in the context of contemporary community psychology. Main concepts and issues touched on by the eight projects are discussed. Chapter Two expands on the notion of process as it relates to research-oriented community interventions.

Parts Two, Three, and Four include the eight contributed chapters. Each of these chapters consists of two sections. The first is a report by the researcher on the nature of the project—its origins, design, results, and the process of carrying it out. The second is an interview with the researcher, which is designed to give the reader a glimpse into the personal and informal factors that help bring about a successful community project.

Part Two is devoted to prevention. Chapters Three and Four are examples of projects that have demonstrated primary prevention effects. Shure (Chapter Three) recounts her work with teaching young school children cognitive skills for interpersonal problem solving and its impact on both preventing and reducing maladaptive behavior. Maccoby and Alexander (Chapter Four) describe their Three-Community Study, a quasi-experimental design that compared the effects of a social-learning-oriented media campaign on heart disease risk in three California towns. They have documented the fact that people will use health-promoting knowledge when specific action-oriented suggestions are presented in a professional way. Chapter Five is an example of a successful secondary prevention program for juveniles. Besides presenting the basic data about the project, Rappaport, Seidman, and Davidson also recount their experiences of what happens when the original researchers pass on an innovative program to established agencies.

Part Three focuses on characteristics and effects of the environment as they pertain to successful coping and adaptation. Moos (Chapter Six) discusses his development of scales to measure the climate of social environments. Gottlieb and Todd (Chapter Seven) present their insights on social support networks based on their research on components of social support and identification of personal support network. And Holahan (Chapter Eight) reports on the effect of physical design of the environment on the interactional patterns in a psychiatric inpatient ward.

Part Four deals with documenting and producing pervasive change. Leighton (Chapter Nine) describes a small Stirling County community, The Road, which showed remarkable positive change during a ten-year period, to illustrate the hypothesis that the level of community integration affects levels of psychopathology in the population. The use of early epidemiological techniques to document change in community mental health is depicted clearly, raising questions about how they could be used today. Fairweather (Chapter Ten) contributes a methodologically exciting discussion on bringing about change experimentally. Using the concept of the lodge (an alternative to hospitalization) as the innovation, he randomly assigned hospitals throughout the United States to different dissemination approaches to determine which were most effective. Implications for social policy are discussed. Fairweather's attempt at change is not merely a proposal for a new therapy but rather a new institution, an autonomous social setting that provides new roles for patients and service-delivery systems.

In the concluding chapter, the editors bring together some of the common themes of the preceding chapters, point out major differences among the contributors' approaches, and discuss their implications for further research.

We hope that this book will spark greater interest in students who want to apply their training in psychology, social sciences, and related mental health professions to issues of concern to society and its institutions. We also hope that this book serves as a catalyst to rigorous thinking about community psychology and as a resource book to psychologists and social scientists who are willing to take the plunge into community work. We feel that our contributors are models for the professional who wants to pursue both research-based inquiry and social impact.

We would like to express our appreciation to the many people who have been instrumental in helping us complete this book. Special thanks go to Ed Lichtenstein for his detailed, frank, and constructive comments on earlier drafts of the manuscript. Guillermo Bernal, Michael Rossi, and Rhona Weinstein also read and commented on parts of the book. Their suggestions were most welcome. Susan Evans and Margie Rodriguez were extremely helpful in preparing the manuscript. Anna Fabiani, Albert Lainoff, and Angelina Rutledge were also involved in various stages of the typing.

August 1979

RICARDO F. MUÑOZ
San Francisco, California

LONNIE R. SNOWDEN
Berkeley, California

JAMES G. KELLY
Eugene, Oregon

Contents

xiii

Contributors

RICARDO F. MUÑOZ is assistant professor in residence at the University of California, San Francisco, School of Medicine, in the Social and Community Psychiatry Program located at San Francisco General Hospital. Muñoz, who immigrated to San Francisco at age eleven from his native Peru, was awarded the B.A. degree in psychology at Stanford University (1972) and the M.A. and Ph.D. degrees in clinical psychology at the University of Oregon (1975 and 1977, respectively).

Muñoz did his clinical-community internship at the South Sacramento Community Mental Health Center, part of the Medical School at the University of California, Davis. In the clinical area, he has done work in social learning approaches to self-control and has a special interest in the treatment of depression. Muñoz is coauthor of *How to Control Your Drinking* (with W. R. Miller, 1976), and *Control Your Depression* (with P. M. Lewinsohn, M. A. Youngren, and A. M. Zeiss, 1978). He has also contributed to the literature in community psychology, especially in the area of primary prevention, and is on the editorial board of the *American Journal of Community Psychology*. As a bilingual, bicultural psychologist, he is involved in the development of mental health services for the Latino community.

LONNIE R. SNOWDEN is assistant professor in the School of Social Welfare at the University of California, Berkeley. He was awarded the B.A. degree in psychology at the University of Michigan (1969) and the M.A. and the Ph.D. degrees in clinical psychology at Wayne State University (1972 and 1975, respectively).

Snowden began his career as an assistant professor of psychology at the University of Oregon and has been a visiting assistant professor of psychology at the University of California, Berkeley. He has published articles in the areas of social and community interventions, the psychology of effective behavior, and assessment and treatment of drug abuse. Among his contributions were two chapters in the *Annual Review of Psychology*. He has served on the Psychology Education Review Committee of the National Institute of Mental Health, been named a consultant to the National Institute on Alcohol Abuse and Alcoholism, and acted as an editorial consultant for the *American Journal of Community Psychology*.

JAMES G. KELLY is professor in the Department of Psychology at the University of Oregon, where he has also served as dean of the Lila Acheson Wallace School of Community Service and Public Affairs (1972 to 1978). He was awarded the B.A. degree with honors in psychology at the University of Cincinnati (1953), the M.A. degree at Bowling Green State University (1954), and the Ph.D. degree at the University of Texas (1958), both in clinical psychology, and the M.S. degree in hygiene from Harvard University (1960).

Identified with the development of community psychology, Kelly has developed research and theoretical contributions in ecological psychology. He is past president of the Division of Community Psychology and of the Division of Psychologists in Public Service of the American Psychological Association; in 1978, he received the Distinguished Contribution Award from the Division of Community Psychology. He has served on the faculties of the University of Michigan and Ohio State University and on the staff of the National Institute of Mental Health. In addition to numerous articles and three books, Kelly has collaborated with R. F. Muñoz on *The Prevention of Mental Disorders* (1975) and with Muñoz and Snowden on "Social and Community Interventions" in the 1977 *Annual Review of Psychology*.

JANET ALEXANDER is senior research associate at the Institute for Communication Research at Stanford University in Stanford, California.

WILLIAM S. DAVIDSON II is associate professor in the Department of Psychology at Michigan State University.

GEORGE W. FAIRWEATHER is professor in the Department of Psychology and director of the Ecological Psychology Program at Michigan State University.

BENJAMIN H. GOTTLIEB is associate professor in the Department of Psychology at the University of Guelph, in Guelph, Ontario, Canada.

CHARLES J. HOLAHAN is associate professor in the Department of Psychology at the University of Texas at Austin.

DOROTHEA C. LEIGHTON is lecturer in the Department of International Medicine at the University of California, San Francisco.

NATHAN MACCOBY is professor emeritus in the Department of Communication and director of the Institute for Communication Research at Stanford University in Stanford, California.

RUDOLF H. MOOS is professor and director of the Social Ecology Laboratory at Stanford University and the Veterans Administration Medical Center in Palo Alto, California.

JULIAN RAPPAPORT is professor, associate department head, and director of clinical training in the Department of Psychology at the University of Illinois at Urbana-Champaign.

EDWARD SEIDMAN is professor in the Department of Psychology at the University of Illinois at Urbana-Champaign.

MYRNA BETH SHURE is head of Child Development Studies at the Hahnemann Community Mental Health/Mental Retardation Center.

DAVID M. TODD is associate professor and director of clinical training in the Department of Psychology at the University of Massachusetts in Amherst.

Social and Psychological Research in Community Settings

Designing and Conducting Programs for Social and Personal Well-Being

1

Research-Oriented
Interventions
in Natural Settings

Ricardo F. Muñoz
Lonnie R. Snowden
James G. Kelly

In 1965, a group of psychologists who actively supported
the application of social science to community contexts dubbed this
area of research and action *community psychology*. In 1967, a growing number of interested participants formed the Community
Psychology Division (Division 27) of the American Psychological
Association. By 1977, the division was 1,272 strong (Dorr, 1977).
Prompted by the accumulation of published material on this subject, *The Annual Review of Psychology* began periodically devoting
one of its chapters to Social and Community Interventions in 1973
(Cowen, 1973; Kelly, Snowden, and Muñoz, 1977).

Even with this obvious interest, the precise nature of community psychology has been a source of much debate. Many of its

descriptions are made in the form of comparisons with previously defined areas of research and intervention. For example, it is said that clinical psychology deals with treatment of disorders, whereas community psychology deals with prevention of disorders and promotion of health. Rappaport (1977) emphasizes a political perspective—he compares community psychology with community mental health, and he states that community mental health focuses mainly on making clinical services available to a wider population. Therefore, community mental health implicitly focuses on helping individuals to adapt to society as it is. Community psychology, Rappaport argues, focuses away from traditional clinical work and toward preventive interventions, which embody an ethic of reshaping social structures to serve individuals.

Another dimension that is sometimes cited in defining community psychology is the integral role of research. Although both social activists and community psychologists could be involved in effecting social change, the latter would be expected to have a greater respect for and commitment to empirical evaluation of their efforts. Questions that arise regarding community research include the relative importance given to research aspects of the task versus the actual impact of the intervention, that is, the emphasis placed on the role of the scientist or change agent. For the social activist, of course, the question is one of energy expenditure—are research people useful, or are they merely a drain on change efforts?

However one may choose to define community psychology, the enthusiasm behind its issues and concerns provides evidence of an unfilled need in the work of mental health professionals—the need to build a psychology that functions in natural settings and permits the professional to be simultaneously a participant, a systematic observer, and a change agent. At present, the work of most community psychology professionals is probably far from this ideal, but the search and struggle to bring this goal to fruition continue.

Goals of Community Psychology

The three goals we have alluded to—preventive interventions, empirical evaluation, and professional engagement in natural settings—often mix in seemingly contradictory efforts. A preventive intervention may disturb traditional community processes and start a chain reaction with unpredictable effects. Rigorous evaluative methodology may require so much control over structural practices as to make the results nongeneralizable, even to the environment in which the innovation was tested. The reactivity of observational techniques presents difficulties, even in purely descriptive studies of community practices.

The nature of the research enterprise needs to be redefined as psychologists move into settings where control over experimental variables may be undesirable or impractical. The preciseness of laboratory work may be inapplicable when dealing with multiple open social systems. Yet, we feel that the use of social science research methods is what sets community psychology apart from the many other efforts to promote human well-being. Other forces, such as politics and religion, intervene in human affairs to produce behavior believed to be beneficial and to diminish behavior believed to be harmful. The introduction of evaluative technology, which adds a self-critical step to the process of community interventions, produces the particular blend of scientific endeavor and humanistic ideals that community psychology aspires to.

Of course, community psychology does not hold a monopoly on using scientific methods to produce and evaluate social change. Public health, applied anthropology, social psychology, social work, and social and community psychiatry, for example, have focused on similar goals. Our purpose here is not to draw sharp distinctions among these disciplines; indeed, we encourage contact and collaboration among them. We feel that no one of these disciplines can claim exclusive ownership over its products, since the theoretical and methodological debts inherent in any such endeavor are bound to overlap disciplinary boundaries. Therefore, although we will continue to discuss the projects in this book in terms of community psychology, we hope others will evaluate them from their own points of view.

Community research would ideally combine the value of helping people to achieve psychological well-being with the value of empirically evaluating results. One way to achieve this objective would be to (1) introduce empirical tests at each step of the intervention planning phase, (2) employ a collaborative style in the planning phase, and (3) focus conscious attention on the process of implementation.

Empirical tests can enter the process at three stages—theory formulation, intervention, and monitoring long-term effects. During theory formulation, the researcher advances a hypothesis, which purports to describe a cause-and-effect relationship. For example, Shure and her colleagues (Chapter Three) proposed that interpersonal maladjustment is causally related to the inability cognitively to generate alternative ways of interacting. This hypothesis was carefully tested prior to planning their intervention. They were able to find supporting evidence, and only then did they take the next step of devising a procedure to teach the missing skill to children. In doing so, they entered the second stage, the intervention phase. Here again, they evaluated their procedure. Specifically, they tested the immediate effects of their intervention by ascertaining that, after undergoing the training program, children were able to generate more alternatives to specific problem situations than control children.

The third stage involves monitoring long-term effects. Given that one has intervened to provide for hypothesized needs of participants, does this intervention produce the predicted increase in positive behavior and the decrease in dysfunctional behaviors? Shure and associates were able to document both therapeutic and preventive effects on maladjustment after as long as one year following intervention. Tests of theoretical relationships, of the immediate effects of the intervention, and of the long-range outcomes are essential in maintaining the scientific values of community research. The more humanistic values are embodied in what we have called *style* and *process*.

The informal ethic of community psychology favors a style of openness to community participation at all stages of intervention. Although this ethic of close collaboration with the community is more of an ideal than a well-established tradition, we can trace its effects at each stage of research. In formulating theory, value would be placed on whether the community in which the researcher works either generated the focus of study or influenced the choice of hypotheses to be tested through formal or informal representation. The nature of the intervention would preferably be decided in consultation with members of the target group. In measuring both immediate and long-term effects, one would include those that seem most important to the affected individuals. A more prevalent style is that of the researcher who conscientiously tries to learn about a community's attitudes and self-defined needs and then works to respect them and to respond to them. The style of the self-absorbed researcher who manipulates whatever he or she can, regardless of public sentiment, is becoming less popular, largely because communities refuse to permit it.

Whatever the style chosen, however, the process of research-oriented community interventions is sufficiently different from processes required by other kinds of research to be studied on its own merits. One of the aims of this book is to contribute an experiential base for the study of community research. We want to highlight the strategies and procedures involved in carrying out projects designed to change naturally existing groups. The chapters and accompanying interviews are designed to provide insights into community work from the views of experienced researchers.

The concept of process used in this book is further elaborated in Chapter Two. We devote the remainder of Chapter One to a discussion of some of the contemporary issues of community psychology, using the contributed chapters as sources of specific examples. We shall follow the format of the book, covering prevention issues, the role of the social and architectural environment, and issues involved in producing and documenting change.

Issues in Community Psychology

Prevention. Prevention is usually divided into three levels — primary, secondary, and tertiary. The first level refers to reductions in the incidence of new cases; the second level refers to early detection and amelioration of dysfunctions to forestall disabilities; and the third level refers to services rendered to identified cases to minimize the length of disability and to reduce the probability of recurrence. We have only included examples of the first two levels in Part Two, but examples of the third level may be found in Chapters Eight and Ten. The remaining chapters also have implications for prevention, of course, such as the role of social climate (Chapter Six), social support systems (Chapter Seven), and levels of integration-disintegration in a community (Chapter

Nine). We will point out preventive aspects in the section on environment and change, since prevention is so central to community psychology.

We are particularly pleased to have two examples of primary preventive projects, those of Shure (Chapter Three) and Maccoby and Alexander (Chapter Four). There is a dearth of empirical evidence for primary prevention, and we hope that more will appear in the next decade. Let us examine some of the obstacles associated with this endeavor.

In talking about primary prevention with people who espouse the concept, we have found a general commonality of attitudes regarding its intent. Primary prevention refers to efforts aimed at "reducing the incidence of new cases of mental disorder and disability in a population" (Caplan and Grunebaum, 1972, p. 128). But, when we have requested more detailed descriptions, we have found that definitions vary from professional to professional. Cowen (1973, p. 433), for example, states that "Primary prevention activities are targeted impersonally to groups and communities; once individual distress is identified, intervention is other than primary."

Such a definition implies that the population must be defined demographically—that is, by characteristics other than individual behavior. Thus, a group defined by sex, age, ethnic background, and socioeconomic class would be a proper focus of primary prevention. A group defined by individual truancy records, evidence of thought disorder, violent behavior, or other prodromal signs would more clearly fit the secondary or even tertiary level of prevention.

Our impression is that the motivation for definitional rigor stems from at least two sources. One is a desire to advance the study of preventive intervention, a goal that can best be accomplished if we limit our focus of study to programs clearly at the preventive end of the prevention-treatment continuum. The second source is related to the first but is more economically minded—if individuals who show signs of trouble can be receivers of preventive services, then funds for such services may be used for early treatment or therapy. In both cases, the result could be a neglect of prevention, which sorely needs all the resources that it can find. To reduce the excessive use of the label *primary prevention,* Kelly, Snowden, and Muñoz (1977) have suggested that professional journals restrict use of the term to reports specifying what they are intending to prevent and how such impact can be assessed. Only then will we be able to evaluate prevention efforts clearly.

The possibility of achieving primary prevention has been a source of much debate. The comments made by Freymann (1975) about preventive medicine help shed some light on preventive psychology. He observes that curative (clinical) services have been in demand since humans became tribal animals, and this demand has never abated. Setting the stage for preventive work, however, involves three prerequisites (Freymann, 1975, p. 526):

- The body politic must be able to see beyond the problems of immediate survival. Preventive measures have no place in a society overwhelmed by the present.
- There must be a positive attitude toward health as an asset. Preventive measures have no meaning, if disease is considered either inevitable or irrelevant to the general welfare.
- There must be a community conscience that places value on individual life and health. Preventive measures are inconsistent with the spirit of "every man for himself."

Launching preventive public health programs requires three additional prerequisites (Freymann, 1975, p. 526):

- Epidemiologic and demographic data that define the health problems of a society.
- An effective administrative organization.
- Personnel qualified for the task.

The greatest lack in our society is probably in the last two categories. There is no agency charged with delivering psychological primary prevention services to the public, and most professionals get little if any training in this area. Our belief is that this will continue to be the case until cost-benefit studies show the financial advisability of this approach. However, since no one is specifically charged with carrying out such studies, we may be a long time waiting.

Freymann's comments raise the question of whether these necessary (but not sufficient) conditions can be created. For example, can we help to establish an agency charged with delivery of preventive services? Can we begin to train professionals in this area? It is clear that the agencies that are popularly thought to be charged with these tasks, the community mental health centers, are not (and may have never been) mandated to do this (Muñoz, 1976; Snow and Newton, 1976). The result is that the bulk of the preventively oriented community work must be carried out by independent research groups, which are laying the groundwork for what will hopefully become a valid area of public health programming.

One of the main arguments for lack of support of primary prevention efforts is that the evidence for true preventive effects is minimal. It is difficult to know if an intervention caused something not to happen, especially if such an intervention is very global in nature and attempts to affect general levels of well-being. Social learning clinicians have long been advocating the need to devise specific treatment procedures to deal with specific disorders— more efficient and effective results can be produced and evaluated in this manner. The same argument can be made for prevention. After pinpointing deficiencies found in people with the same type of dysfunction, we could devise specific preventive strategies that would provide target populations with the skills thought to be useful in warding off the dysfunction. The next evaluative step would consist of testing the procedure to see if it indeed produced the desired skills. The third step would be to follow the target group and compare its incidence rates with a control group. If the target group's incidence rates were significantly lower than those of the control group, replications and dissemination of the findings would be in order.

The work of Shure and her colleagues (Chapter Three) is a good example of this paradigm. Another exciting example is the Stanford Heart Disease Prevention Project (Chapter Four), which attempted to teach a set of competencies that correlated with low risk of heart disease. They included mainly self-control skills, concerning diet, smoking, and exercise, which were reflected in a numerical risk score on the Cornfield Scale, a composite of such data as weight, smoking rate, and blood pressure. Using techniques from communication theory and applied social learning theory, such as the modeling of specific skills, Maccoby, Alexander, and their colleagues were able to affect significantly the average risk scores of target towns through the use of mass media and face-to-face instruction.

Dissemination of information about this approach is already taking place, and the model for preventive research at the community level is now being adapted to other problems. For example, the Office of Alcoholism of the State of California is funding an alcohol problem-minimization experiment using a similar quasi-experimental design (Wallack, 1978). The need for more empirically tested primary prevention projects is great. We hope these examples will generate the enthusiasm to continue work in this area.

Secondary prevention is well represented by Rappaport, Seidman, and Davidson (Chapter Five). Their experiences show how an active advocacy relationship can be combined with specific intervention techniques to minimize further difficulties with the juvenile court system. The implications of their argument regarding true adoption as opposed to manifest adoption are of significance to any research project that is to be taken over by naturally existing systems, whether in the same community or elsewhere. The central question is whether the program becomes altered in some essential way when it is passed on. The evaluation already performed may be irrelevant to the new program; its effects may be diminished or even negated. Issues of responsibility also arise—does the original investigator have the duty to make periodic checks on the program? Chapter Five clearly touches on the unfinished nature of community work. No program or intervention can be seen as static. The changing aspects of a living system imbue any structure superimposed on it, such as a new intervention program, with the same fluidity that characterizes the system.

The Environment. Another elusive concept in community psychology is that of the influence of environments on people. We have devoted three chapters to examples of different approaches to this topic. The role of the social and physical environment on psychological well-being as well as physical well-being has long been assumed to be of great importance. The factors that produce specific results and mechanisms to mediate these effects are still far from being adequately identified. The interaction of environmental factors with individual characteristics are even more difficult to pinpoint.

The contributors to Part Four are in the vanguard of this scientific endeavor. In Chapters Six and Seven, they illustrate the process of analyzing and labeling specific environmental elements, quantifying them, and thereby providing the tools needed to describe and to experiment with these elements. The work of Rudolf Moos (Chapter Six) begins this part of the book, because it represents a major step in the quantification of the atmosphere of interpersonal settings—what he calls the *social climate*. His scales to represent climates of different environments can be used to compare diverse settings and to distinguish between healthy and noxious ones. It may be possible in the future to develop an empirically validated taxonomy of settings that prescribes the kind of setting most conducive to specific human activities. The scales can serve as measures of planned change, thereby helping people to exert more control over their living and working conditions. The scales can also assist in efforts to develop predictive models of person-environment fit, which can serve as warnings to individuals not to enter particular environments.

Whereas Moos deals with geographically definable social settings, Gottlieb and Todd (Chapter Seven) have tackled an even more rapidly shifting phenomenon—social support networks. The role of such networks in providing stability and strength to individuals has long been assumed, and such networks are one of the major targets for preventive interactions, whether in the form of self-help groups, indigenous care-givers, or community development.

The specific factors that promote the formation of social support networks and produce beneficial results are still far from being clearly understood. Gottlieb and Todd provide a schema for identifying the kinds of helping behavior that are found in natural interactions, and they give an example of how individuals can be assisted to become aware of and to use their support networks. The careful manner in which sole-support mothers were contacted, the self-conscious modification of methodology to match gradually changing perceptions of the participants' responses, and the concern for providing at least an attentive ear in return for the information obtained make this chapter an example for conscientiously planned community psychology research projects.

In Chapter Eight, Holahan describes an intervention that gauged the effects of modifying the *built environment*—in this case, the physical layout of an inpatient psychiatric ward. The positive results of the physical changes on interactional patterns of patients suggests many more applications of systematic architectural and interior design modifications to encourage adaptive behavior. However, the process of entering and working with the ward staff, as described in the chapter, is at least as important as architectural modifications for the researcher who wants to implement similar procedures.

Preventive implications of environmental interventions abound. The creation or modification of social climates that produce health can be investigated, once we have such tools as those provided by Moos to quantify our observations. The next challenge becomes pinpointing the kind of expectations or behavioral patterns that produce a certain kind of climate, devising techniques to influence them, and assessing the effect of this change on the people in the environment. The kinds of skills identified by Gottlieb and Todd could be taught. The results would affect both groups and individuals. The helping behaviors specified by Gottlieb would be useful in increasing supportive interaction in general. The process devised by Todd of learning to describe and augment one's own support network could serve as a self-help strategy based on using available resources to enhance one's well-being. Whether the application of these skills reduces maladaptive reactions to difficult situations could be the object of formal experimentation. Use of the built environment to increase adaptive constructive behaviors, as exemplified by Holahan, could be adapted to a myriad of settings. The combination of these techniques with social climate assessment and social support building could produce a powerful synergistic effect, increasing the environment's potential as a preventive force.

Change. As may be clear by now, each of the chapters brings up many issues that are presently in the forefront of community psychology. The chapters in Part Five deal with what may be the central issue, change—how to document it, evaluate it, and produce it.

In Chapter Nine, we have the fortunate opportunity to have recounted for us one of the many stories from a classic epidemiological study, the Stirling County Study. Dorothea Leighton, one of the original researchers, shares with us the fate of a small community called The Road. The historical perspective of this early attempt to determine the mental health levels of entire towns is sensitively captured in her account. We discover the first tentative attempts to gather data, the pervasive inroads made by the research staff into the community to try to understand fully the meaning of the data, and the commitment of the staff to continue monitoring the county for decades. The surprising change in the condition of The Road and the accompanying reduction in signs of mental disorder serve as a natural source of support for the integration-disintegration hypothesis. The ability to document and, to some extent, to quantify the changes that occur in communities is one of the immediately obvious contributions of epidemiology to community psychology. The apparently informal relationship that sprang up between the researchers and the caregivers or patients is very much in tune with present values, although perhaps less in tune with present practice. It appears that the Stirling County staff was ready to become more involved with the communities it was working with than would be the case for most contemporary researchers. Leighton's chapter serves as a reminder of the change that has occurred in community psychology and the relatively short span of time that these ideas and methodologies have been in use.

Fairweather's contribution (Chapter Ten) gives us a particularly fresh view of the role of the experimental tradition on dissemination. Once the work has been done, the information gathered, and conclusions drawn, the work of the community psychologist is not yet over. The question of assimilation and implementation in other communities remains a major goal. After having tested the Lodge program and finding it more effective and less expensive than traditional treatment, Fairweather found that his research findings went unused, even at the hospital where he performed his investigations. Turning frustration into creative energy, he proceeded to use the mental hospitals of the United States as a large subject pool. His question was how most effectively to disseminate an already tested idea. Assigning the hospitals to predetermined experimental conditions, he was able to determine differential rates of adoption according to method of approach. Fairweather exemplifies the activist wedded to strict experimental rigor. His experiences provide unique insights into the problems of doing community psychology, especially the impact (or lack of it) that experimental findings have on decision making. Rappaport's warning regarding manifest adoption of programs is in order here. Even after Fairweather or his associates receive assurances that their idea will be adopted, the process is not finished. The adopting agency could inadvertently modify essential elements in the program, which would necessitate beginning the state of evaluation anew.

Of the many preventive implications of these two chapters, we will focus on those stemming from their particular methodologies, namely epidemiology and the experimental study of disseminations. The technology derived from epidemiology must complement any large-scale preventive project. The focus of assessment could then be not only on the target problem being prevented but also on other problems that may unknowingly be affected by the intervention. Longitudinal epidemiologic studies, such as the Stirling County Study, are probably the best type to detect unplanned effects, both positive and negative.

The experimental study of dissemination could very well be the fulcrum needed to raise primary prevention to a more significant position in mental health care. Identification of the factors that increase the probability of adoption of a preventive innovation could improve the cost-effectiveness of dissemination efforts. As tested programs become more common, the demand for such projects will increase. Standards of quality and evaluative guidelines for prevention could then be more widespread, and the development and dissemination of such projects could become a much more frequent endeavor.

The constant tug between the conscientious researcher-evaluator and the conscientious change-agent remains a basic part of the community psychologist's life. At some point, all of us are faced with the question of whether knowing is better than doing. The same question holds for matters of science versus politics or reason versus power. Ideally, of course, both alternatives would be balanced and would rarely compete. In reality, most of us prefer one alternative to the other and neglect the less-preferred role. The following chapters can serve as models for a good balance of methodologically respectable intervention and community impact.

2

The Process
of Implementing
Community-Based Research

Lonnie R. Snowden
Ricardo F. Muñoz
James G. Kelly

By tradition, formal presentations of research are restricted to formal manipulations and end products, and discussions of what goes on behind the scenes is relegated to casual social encounters. As community psychology strives to clarify its values, concepts, and methods, a systematic look behind published outcomes seems particularly timely.

Special hazards confront community-based research. In contrast to researcher-controlled environments, community settings demand accountability, may be naturally unstable, make the researcher's perspective that of an outsider, require prodigious investments of time and energy, and possess priorities that differ from those of the researcher—for example, preferring action to research (Cowen, Lorian, and Dorr, 1974). Researchers must

14

therefore consider not only the theory and design of successful projects but also the implementation process.

The editors have asked the contributors to this book to explore how they accomplished their research goals. This chapter discusses the concept of *research process* by developing its meaning, applications, and relationship to other ideas. Thus, we offer here an orientation to the research process and attendant issues; Chapter Eleven summarizes the handling of these issues by our contributors.

The Research Process: Meaning and Implications

What are the experiences that make up the research process? Certain steps are common to all research. A discussion by Bailey (1978) presents these well-known activities as a five-stage cycle: (1) choosing the problem and stating the hypothesis; (2) formulating the research design; (3) data collection; (4) coding and analyzing data; (5) interpreting results. Since interpretation of results stimulates new research problems, the process forms a continuous loop.

Outlining the research sequence in such a straightforward manner belies the complications at every step. Each decision is complex, demanding a grasp of sophisticated theoretical and methodological issues. Any researcher will recognize that certain nonscientific practices are also involved. One must identify sources of funding, arrange for adequate research space, recruit staff and subjects, and attend to many other logistical concerns. Although these activities merely support the basic scientific endeavor, they are essential to its success.

When research must be conducted in a community context, the complications mount. Not only are the physical impediments increased, such as distance and numbers of participants, but also the ethical, psychological, and political aspects become questions of added substance. For example, to the degree that researchers identify with a community psychology perspective, problem selection is no longer determined solely by the professional interests and personal tastes of the researcher. Community priorities affect problem selection in social community research (Price and Cherniss, 1977). Moreover, the nature of the definition that is reached may itself have significant social and psychological consequences. As critics

(Caplan and Nelson, 1973; Rappaport, 1977) have emphasized, habitually attributing causes of social problems to persons rather than to social institutions can strengthen undesirable mechanisms of social control. For the community researcher, selecting and defining a problem can have unexpected political implications.

Generally, working in the community introduces additional concerns and stages to the research process. This occurs in part because community researchers do not have the same ability to control their circumstances that laboratory-based researchers have. Community researchers' ability to collect the preferred data with adequate controls depends on the consent and cooperation of unobligated citizens. The agents in control of community systems have little vested interest in research. Hence, they may demand more payoff than the creation of knowledge and may adjust their commitment with changing circumstances.

We do not highlight the differences between laboratory and community-based research to belittle the ingenuity of noncommunity research. All good research is difficult and demands a serious commitment in time and talent. It is equally true, however, that community researchers encounter distinctive challenges. Moreover, the perspective for viewing these added tasks is itself an issue. As we shall see, these unique circumstances may be regarded not only as vexing annoyances to be overcome but also as opportunities to understand important phenomena.

Thus, in conducting community-based research, complex processes of arranging for research implementation are superimposed on issues of theory and method. To give a view of the spectrum of activities involved, we have depicted sequentially some tasks of community-based research. Table 1 presents ten stages in the life of a hypothetical community-based research project. Within each stage is listed a series of steps that would advance the project. Each step is presented with the potential influences and issues affecting the course of development taken by the project at that particular step. Not every project will follow this exact path, and the sequence in Table 1 should be regarded as a general or idealized model.

Often, events comprising the research process are dismissed as "political hassles." A careful look, however, reveals an interplay of social influence that may significantly affect the character and outcome of a project. Researchers attempt to induce cooperation

**Table 1. Natural History of a Successful Community-Based
Research Project**

Sources of Influence	Project Stage	Process Issues
Training Current literature Personal values Institutional forces: pressure to publish, norms concerning independence, cooperation	Focusing interest	Clarifying concepts and methods Resolving value conflicts Finding colleague support Establishing professional priorities
Ongoing responsibilities Institutional, community wealth Personal preferences for joint versus individual undertakings Interest, accessibility of colleagues and citizens	Early planning	Allocating time and energy Identifying needed resources Engaging potential collaborators Soliciting ideas and feedback Identifying community settings
Larger social history, zeitgeist Prior community-investigator, or community-institution contacts Investigator skills, values, sensitivities Community openness, innovative spirit	Community soundings	Entering community settings Clarifying mutual interests and goals Establishing trust and credibility Recognizing resources and opportunities
Professional literature Acceptance by community settings Investigator administrative and methodological skills	Pilot testing	Crystalizing research procedures Allocating staff responsibilities Monitoring staff and community obligations Determining whether results justify larger-scale replication

Table 1. (Continued)

Sources of Influence	Project Stage	Process Issues
Policies and budgets of funding agencies Institutional and community interest, priorities, and wealth Investigator resourcefulness and commitment	Assembling resources	Arranging funding Confirming, renewing community interest Arranging for space, personnel, supplies
Availability of interested people Investigator recruiting, managerial skill Investigator style and values (such as preference for trust, privacy, control)	Expanding staff	Devising a structure Recruiting new members Orienting, training new staff Establishing mechanisms giving feedback, maintaining involvement, solving problems, supplying needed materials
Adequacy of planning Stability versus change of circumstances	Project implementation	Obtaining promised cooperation Coping with unforeseen and overlooked problems
Investigator managerial skill Investigator values and priorities Stability of community settings	Project monitoring	Correcting drift from prescribed procedures Maintaining morale Coping with unexpected disruptions Noting effects on social equilibrium (such as alliances, conflicts, norms in the setting) Giving and receiving community feedback
Professional literature Research data	Interpreting results	Processing, organizing, and analyzing data Evaluating indications for replication, modification, and dissemination

Table 1. (Continued)

Sources of Influence	Project Stage	Process Issues
Investigator commitment to dissemination	Disseminating findings	Preparing reports, manuscripts
Relative advantage of new procedure		Advocating to potential consumers
Communicability, philosophical compatibility of new procedure		Consulting on implementation

with an existing plan; citizens reject the plan or attempt to modify it to suit their purposes. Researchers think it well justified temporarily to suspend or interfere with usual operations; agency staff think it well justified to bend research procedures for the immediate needs of people. After the project ends, researchers discover new ways to work with agencies or community groups and may also think differently about their research problem; citizens may work together differently and may change their usual view of outsiders. The process of research in the community, then, involves strategies of influence and values about desirable circumstances. Since each party may successively affect the other, the process can be a reciprocal one. Often, this process cannot be entirely anticipated, revealing alternative directions and outcomes only as it unfolds.

As presently conceived, the major concerns of the research process are those values, strategies, and social systems that affect performance of community-based research. Included are both the planned arrangements for implementing research procedures and the often unplanned consequences of fulfilling these arrangements. This process is intertwined with, but often distinguishable from, the formal operations and objectives of research. As presented in Chapter Three, the research experience of Myrna Shure provides a useful example. Shure discusses a program of empirical inquiry into the role of interpersonal problem-solving skills as mediators of social adjustment among young children. By a series of investigations, Shure and colleagues demonstrated that instruction in cognitive interpersonal problem solving effectively boosted children's ability to conceptualize alternative solutions to problems. This skill in turn produced both improvements in current social adjustment and prevention of later social maladjustment. Implementing these formal procedures involved negotiating in the educational systems with several levels of administrative personnel. Shure's goals in these contacts were approval of the project and participation by teachers in learning to present her curriculum. Once established, these arrangements had consequences apart from the impact on subjects of training in interpersonal problem solving. Among these effects were the creation of a supportive context for the project, which stimulated her to develop a continuing service program for training in interpersonal problem solving. Also, teacher's aides showed greater job commitment after having been engaged by the project. Many other steps and consequences of establishing the project are described in the chapter.

Narrative accounts such as Shure's document the importance of what may seem to be simply routine interactions. How may such accounts be placed in perspective? Appropriately, literature on research emphasizes operationalizing concepts and formulating rigorous research designs. In so doing, this literature provides little basis for understanding social processes in the performance of research. For consideration of the psychological import of how psychologists work, we turn to those disciplines that are concerned with interpersonal process as a context for delivering psychological services.

Traditionally, attention to how psychologists work has been largely associated with study in two disciplines—psychotherapy and organizational and community consultation. The literature in these areas reveals a lively interest in the process of providing help and recognizes that relationships must become potent sources of leverage in the service of psychological change. A distinction enjoying wide acceptance is that between the process of an intervention and its ultimate outcome. These more familiar concepts for discussing the working process can be transferred to analysis of the community research process.

Psychotherapy has a long research tradition of investigating the therapeutic process. Accurate empathy, warmth, and genuineness, as experienced by the client, have been correlated regularly with a degree of therapeutic success (Truax and Mitchell, 1971). In both theory and research, the therapeutic triad of empathy, warmth, and genuineness have been at least implicitly regarded as flowing unilaterally from the therapist. Recent commentators (Gomes-Schwartz, Hadley, and Strupp, 1978) have emphasized the joint nature of the therapeutic endeavor. Thus, an effective working relationship may be the consequence of an interaction between therapist and patient.

Published views of consultation reveal general agreement on the outlines of strategic practice. One widely accepted analysis has identified four broad procedures: (1) building an effective relationship, (2) adequately defining the problem, (3) identifying alternatives for action, and (4) addressing the affective reactions of consultees (Altrocchi, 1972). The first of these procedures, developing a consultative relationship, has been emphasized as a fundamental precursor for consultative work. Cherniss (1978) defined the consultation readiness of a relationship in terms of a six-level continuum, ranging from no relationship at all to one in which the consultee advocates consultation to other prospective consumers.

Technical expertise enters the helping process in enabling the psychologist both to establish a constructive relationship and to apply specific techniques for particular goals to be pursued in that constructive relationship. In proposing a general model of psychotherapy, Strupp (1973) formally distinguishes these two elements. He characterizes technical procedures, ranging from systematic desensitization to transference interpretation, to be one of the two ingredients. The context of the procedures—an enveloping social relationship—defines the other element of psychotherapy. Constructive relationships are those that enable therapists to perform technical operations in a manner that is readily accepted by clients. Strupp's distinction is easily extended to the process of consultation. Whether the approach is consultee-centered, group process, social action, or ecological (Dworkin and Dworkin, 1975), the consultant performs technical procedures based on psychological principles in the context of an ongoing relationship with the consultee.

The distinction between a relationship and specific procedures can be usefully extended to the research process in a social context. The designated operations of research are analogous to specific technical procedures, and the process of research is analogous to the relationship context. Applied to the work of Myrna Shure, this scheme would differentiate her research design, training, curriculum, and criterion measures from her negotiations, cohesiveness-building, and provision of feedback.

A worthwhile reason for seeking principles of interpersonal process in the applied areas is to find guidance in enlisting and maintaining community cooperation. In addition, an understanding of the research process may also be valuable for those researchers who are consciously trying to honor an ethical commitment to provide service while conducting research.

A hallmark of community psychology is its commitment that psychologists should make constructive contributions, instead of merely furthering their research in their contacts with community settings (Price and Cherniss, 1977). These contributions occur in two forms. First, as a primary goal, the community psychologist's research should pursue information or procedures that can help a community to meet its needs and objectives. A second, less frequently cited benefit involves the by-products or repercussions of the research. The manner of the community psychologist's work can serve to undermine or to encourage constructive practices within the setting. For example, by respecting self-determination, involving all administrative levels in decision making, or providing specific, usable feedback, even when these are not the expedient courses of action, the community psychologist may be advancing the well-being of a social setting. However, by trying to overpower sources of resistance or to play off competing factions against each other, the community psychologist may be exacerbating troublesome tendencies. The researcher is better equipped to be sensitive to such possibilities if he or she understands the social dynamics of various institutional arrangements.

Theoretical Perspectives

This book intends to stimulate theoretical development of the research process in a community context. The authors have identified three broad conceptual approaches—organizational psychology, ethical stances and priorities of researchers, and historical analysis. Although considered separately in the following discussion, these points of view should be regarded as complementary.

One useful approach to the research process is implied by George Fairweather in Chapter Ten. In discussing the process of community-based experimental research, Fairweather highlights the problems in bargaining for research agreements and coordinating the activities of diverse social agencies and interest groups.

Rudolf Moos (Chapter Six) implies something similar in describing the care and forethought necessary to approach an agency that might participate in research. To succeed, the community-based researcher must be an adept administrator of complex organizations.

Another useful approach to the research process lies in considering the project, the setting, and their social matrix to be interacting organizations. An area of organizational psychology has evolved for understanding institutional effectiveness and quality of life in human systems (for example, Alderfer, 1977).

In one of the few studies of the research process, Glaser and Taylor (1973) illustrate and encourage the application of organizational theory to understanding successful applied research. These authors conducted a study that contrasted five successful projects to five unsuccessful projects funded by the Applied Research Branch of the National Institute of Mental Health. Located both within and outside of direct-service agencies, the projects they examined had been deeply involved with community-based organizations in the conduct of their research. Glaser and Taylor's criteria for a successful outcome included attainment of project objectives in either original or appropriately modified form, presentation of results in a clear and cogent report, and adequate dissemination of findings.

Successful projects were indeed distinguished by several procedural features, and Glaser and Taylor (p. 145) summarize these findings by sketching generalized portraits of more successful and less successful projects: "Throughout the life of the [successful] project there was ample evidence of adequate project structure (that is, committees, liaison, linkage). There was leadership capability, with consensus among those involved regarding priority of goals. Dissemination was planned for, and a higher level of utilization was achieved. The communication component paid off again and again; when severe problems were encountered by successful projects, their base of involved supporters was sufficient to cope with the problems." Less successful projects were: "Characterized by calm during the idea, design, and funding stages (in contrast to the successful projects, which were dynamic and laden with conflict), these projects erupted soon after the research stage began. Problems developed suddenly and often were unanticipated. Coping efforts were hindered by the fact that part-time principal investigators did not have the time to devote to resolution efforts. Nor did they have an invested group of supporters to help and share responsibility. Each problem reverberated throughout the project, causing extensive shock" (1973, p. 145).

Several of Glaser and Taylor's success-fostering characteristics for applied research are found in the work of Charles J. Holahan, which is described in Chapter Eight. Holahan's research evaluated the hypothesis that physical redesign of a psychiatric ward would increase the level of social interaction among patients. To arrange the remodeling, the researchers engaged the ward staff in a collaborative planning process. Researchers and staff openly explored criteria of patient mental health and agreed strongly to endorse less withdrawal and more sociability as important goals for patients. Thus, Holahan's project exemplifies several of the features found by Glaser and Taylor to characterize the more successful projects—an ongoing dialogue assured opportunities for communication, and consensus for several pivotal goals was sought. Holahan initiated and managed this process, giving evidence of effective leadership.

What Glaser and Taylor refer to as *adequate project structure* is important for relations not only within community settings but also among project staff. In Chapter Four, on the use of mass media to reduce risk of heart disease, Maccoby and Alexander discuss the potential barriers to an effective group effort when staff have diverse training and disciplinary affiliations. As described by Maccoby and Alexander, maintaining cooperation between social and biomedical researchers and media producers requires facilitating ongoing communication. This continuing dialogue enables each group to appreciate the other's perspective.

Yet another feature of successful human systems is their ability to maintain a direct path to goal attainment. Changing conditions require corrective adjustments. Chapter Four also presents a useful feedback mechanism for community interventions. The aim of Maccoby and Alexander's research was to evaluate the impact of a mass media campaign—presented both alone and in conjunction with intensive face-to-face instruction—on knowledge, attitudes, and behavior related to cardiovascular risk. Interestingly, the researchers did not plan a complete mass media campaign in advance. Built into the process of research were *mini-surveys* of public reaction to trial media spots. This method of process evaluation allows for informed decisions in an evolutionary, adaptive approach to intervention design.

For many of the projects in this book, the research process produced incidental benefits. Often, these side effects grew not from the self-interest of the investigator but rather from a general sense of fair play or implicit ethical code. Indeed, the researcher's scheme of personal values may also affect theoretical and methodological preferences. A second approach to analyzing community-based research involves identifying the values and guiding concerns expressed in the research process. Chapter Five by Rappaport, Seidman, and Davidson probes similar intangibles. To explain those aspects of an intervention that may be easily overlooked in the process of implementing research findings, these authors propose a characteristic they call *essence*. The essence of a project is said to lie in the values, goals, ideology, and spirit that guided its conception and enactment. Since these qualities transcend concrete operations, it is possible to mimic an intervention procedurally while missing the intervention's essence. However, according to Rappaport, Seidman, and Davidson, neglect of essence has operational consequences. Operating from a different sense of propriety, those carrying out an intervention will use it eventually in ways that, although technically correct, are nevertheless unacceptable to the intervention's originators.

An ethical sense to combine service with research in community settings has much in common with the notion of essence. Both attempt to capture belief systems or personal philosophies that are important to a comprehensive understanding of our work.

The central figure in any discussion of research philosophy is the principal researcher. As the researcher lends impetus, justification, and direction to a project, the researcher's sensitivities and interests may be as influential as what is technically correct or administratively functional, if not more so. Accordingly, our emphasis now shifts from the principal investigator's role requirements to his or her personal qualities.

The impact on research of investigator priorities, both intellectual and personal, is evident in the work described by Benjamin Gottlieb and David Todd (Chapter Seven). Their paradigm for studying social support features a more balanced relationship be-

tween subject and investigator than is usually found in social research. Informants and interviewers become coinvestigators, as
both the conceptual framework and empirical methods for understanding social support arise from helping subjects to analyze their
supportive experiences. Also, Gottlieb and Todd are determined
that the research process enhance the social support of subjects.
Their choice of this more anthropological stance reveals serious
misgivings about imposing frames of reference on behavior, which
may ultimately prove inappropriate. Another commitment of both
investigators concerns the utility of research to subjects. By giving
useful feedback about sources of support, researchers can work
toward improving the well-being of participating subjects.

Chapter Nine by Dorothea Leighton presents another
example of the influence exerted by ethical commitments and work
styles. Leighton describes an unplanned adjunct to a major
epidemiological study, where community-development activities
were started in response to high levels of community disintegration. Upon reevaluation a decade later, the investigators found that
community integration improved and psychopathology declined.

This worthwhile project of measuring and participating in
social change arose because of two characteristics of the researchers. Like Gottlieb and Todd, Leighton felt a sense of obligation to
repay those who had cooperated in implementing the procedures
for research. Responding to this commitment with another valuable quality, the ability to improvise, Leighton was able to document
that, as residents organized community action and began to obtain
added economic resources, community mental health improved.

Influences affecting and emanating from the research process often change over time. As with other relationships, agreements established to conduct research may shift as they are
enacted; some functions are added or accentuated, some clarified,
and others eliminated. A completely cross-sectional perspective is
insensitive to qualities of longitudinal development.

The authors consider it important to broaden one's scope
beyond formal methods and research outcomes, not only to include
other activities but also to include other points in time. The usual
writings of psychologists show little attention to either general social history or the particular background of particular social systems becoming the clients of community psychologists. Among

those urging greater historical sensitivity has been Seymour Sarason (1972), whose ideas have explicitly influenced Rappaport, Seidman, and Davidson's chapter in this book. Sarason argues that, by having limited our study of social settings to mature ones, we have risked a biased and incomplete understanding.

Reppucci and Saunders (1977) have advocated a historical perspective for approaching organizational analysis and change. Both specific organizational history and general social history are depicted as valuable conceptual tools for understanding institutional problems and implementing programs of organizational change. Reppucci and Saunders have asserted that "the systematic investigation of history can aid understanding by providing a broader conceptual context for the change-oriented psychologist. Moreover, it can facilitate understanding in at least three concrete ways: (a) it provides new information and questions the permanence of present knowledge; (b) it helps to illuminate the changing character of intervention strategies over time by emphasizing the importance of social context; (c) it provides a relative perspective for interpretation of present events" (p. 403).

In their reference to a relative perspective, Reppucci and Saunders are arguing that the present can be profitably regarded as a phase rather than as a discrete, discontinuous instance. The trap of a detached present easily ensnares researchers because of their preoccupation with results. What trends are embodied or challenged by the research enterprise and what revisions in its interpretation have occurred already and are likely to be required later are part of a broader inquiry, which is easily ignored.

In Chapter Ten, George Fairweather invokes a historical perspective to justify revising the commonly accepted model of the researcher role. Noting that insulation from social problems is usually considered necessary for scientific work, Fairweather argues to the contrary, advocating an involved, problem-solving stance. In part, Fairweather's position rests on a historical understanding of scientists' need for social passivity. Thus, Fairweather advances the cause of a more socially active research process by placing the accepted style of research into its historical context. Also, Fairweather sketches a clearly longitudinal model of social research. Only in part does Fairweather direct our attention to his residential lodge per se as a helpful, efficient response to the problem of chronic mental disorder. His larger aim, promoting the experimental solution to social problems, involves a long-term, multiphased process: selecting and defining a social problem, developing alternative programmatic solutions, translating these into tangible programs, experimental evaluation of impact, and disseminating effective solutions. Each phase presents a somewhat independent challenge, but the significance of the process is a function of all phases.

Chapter Five by Rappaport, Seidman, and Davidson is presented as an example of the knowledge to be gained from a longitudinal appraisal of research. Their program for adolescents in legal jeopardy had important philosophical underpinnings that were formed prior to the design of their intervention. The historical developments of interest were certain experiences in the local black community, which persuaded the investigators of the necessity of emphasizing autonomy, diversity, and strengths. By following the project after completion of apparently successful research, the authors observed an enlightening but troubling outcome—although adopted by the agency where it was tested, the project's actual implementation proved incomplete. Its basis in value and ideology had been left behind, so that the adopted version was felt by the investigators to reflect a seriously compromised set of aims and procedures.

Reppucci and Saunders, in their reference to corresponding changes in intervention strategies and the social context, propose that the zeitgeist serves to brighten the reception afforded certain modes of intervention. Rudolph Moos in Chapter Six traces how the rediscovery of environmental determinants of social problems created a favorable environment for his work. The enthusiasm he reports for a collateral area of research, the feedback of environmental measurement to facilitate constructive organizational change, may reflect the prevailing interest in a social rather than an individual locus to solutions to problems. However, as Reppucci and Saunders have cautioned, trends in social ideology are prone to cyclical swings. Hence, questioning the limits and propriety of organizational reform may enjoy a resurgence in the foreseeable future. By proceeding cautiously and preparing a sound methodological base, Moos may be serving to insulate himself from the buffeting of changing climates of opinion.

Field Research

Increasing numbers of psychological researchers are disenchanted with the laboratory paradigm, arguing that laboratory analogues provide precise but incomplete and distorted approximations of social events (Levine, 1974; Sommer, 1977). This renewed concern with the correspondence between laboratory events and their natural counterparts is often expressed as an affirmation of external validity, a neglected methodological criterion.

The search for greater external validity is prompting an increase in research conducted under natural conditions. Alternative naturalistic paradigms have (1) retained experimentation as the preferred method (Rieken and Borouch, 1974), (2) relied on observational and descriptive procedures associated with other disciplines (Lazarus and Cohen, 1976), or (3) even adapted modes of inference from outside the social sciences (Levine, 1974). In such cases, the researcher must be prepared to face problems similar to the problems discussed in the following chapters.

As researchers attempt to work in a new social context, it will be important for them to shift perspective in accordance with their new circumstances. As attested by the many successful field projects reported here and elsewhere, good community research can be done. However, this work places a heavy burden on one's understanding of social processes and one's facility in social interaction. These skills allow the researcher to relate to nonresearchers sometimes as collaborators, sometimes as bargaining agents, and sometimes as adversaries. In some cases, the outcome of this relationship will be more than a completed research project. The researcher and the community may learn unexpected lessons. Studying the research process can enable us to ensure that these experiences are profitable.

3

Training Children to Solve Interpersonal Problems: A *Preventive Mental Health Program*

Myrna Beth Shure

Our program for primary prevention introduces concepts of problem solving to four- and five-year-old children. The program is an outgrowth of six years of research and controlled intervention projects, which have demonstrated that, as early as age four, (1) some children are significantly more capable than others to think through and solve typical interpersonal problems, (2) efficient problem-solvers display significantly better-adjusted behaviors in school as compared with their more deficient problem-solving peers, (3) exposure to interpersonal cognitive problem solving (ICPS) training significantly increases ability to solve problems with peers and adults, and (4) whether children are trained by their teachers or by their mothers, youngsters who most improve in the trained-thinking skills are the same as those who most improve in social adjustment as observed at school. The effects of training occur within a wide IQ range (70–120+) and last at least two years following its termination. Trained youngsters not showing behavior problems in nursery are significantly less likely to begin showing them a year later in kindergarten (highlighting implications for prevention).

To date, more than 900 nursery and kindergarten children have been trained by 49 teachers, and, in a two-year time span, 40 children have been trained by their mothers. Training scripts are similar in content; they were upgraded in sophistication for use in kindergarten and modified for use with a single child at home.

Although our focus is on work with young children, the ICPS approach is applicable to any age in a variety of settings. Our experiences in training mental-health workers and child-abuse hotline staff are described in Shure and Spivack (1978). By using age-appropriate content, the approach has been adapted for use by teachers of normal elementary school-aged children (Elardo and Cooper, 1977; Gesten and others, 1977; Kirschenbaum and others, 1977; Allen and others, 1976; McClure, 1975). ICPS training has also been adapted for use with hyperaggressive seven-year-olds (Camp and Bash, 1975) and with retarded-educable six to twelve-year-olds (Healey, 1977). In adults, the approach has been used with varying degrees of success with short-term inpatients (Coché and Flick, 1975) and with chronic schizophrenics (Siegel and Spivack, 1973). Using a program designed by Platt and Spivack (1976), Intagliata (1976) has found significant change in the thinking and behavior patterns of alcoholics (see Spivack, Platt, and Shure, 1976).

The training programs for young children were first set into motion as formal, controlled, research-demonstration projects, then as service delivery within federally funded day-care programs in Philadelphia, and finally to staff of the division of Consultation and Education at Hahnemann Hospital for further dissemination for use by community agencies. In the first part of this chapter, I will describe the research, its background, and findings; in the second part, I will discuss the process of implementing ICPS programming under conditions of controlled research as well as service to the community at large.

Background Research

The study of ICPS began in the early 1960s, when George Spivack and Murray Levine found marked differences in the way normal and disturbed adolescents thought about and solved interpersonal problems. These investigators found that, regardless of IQ and mere verbal production, disturbed youngsters were prone to jump immediately to the end goal, whereas normals conceptualized sequenced means to obtain it. Also, relative to normals, the disturbed were less cognizant of potential obstacles to reaching the goal and were less prone to appreciate that goal attainment may take time. Another skill that distinguished between adjustment groups was consequential thinking, as measured by the spontaneous tendency to weigh the pros and cons when tempted with transgression, such as going to a party and staying up beyond the time limit set by the football coach (Spivack and Levine, 1963).

Contrasts in problem-solving ability occurred in other age groups as well—in adults (Platt and Spivack, 1973), in adolescents (Platt and others, 1974), and in children ten to twelve years of age (Shure and Spivack, 1972). Not only were differences clear when normals were compared with clinically disturbed individuals, but differences were clear in more homogeneous samples of ten-year-olds displaying varying degrees of behavioral difficulties in regular school classrooms (Shure and Spivack, 1970a) and among institutionalized dependent-neglected youngsters nine to twelve years of age (Larcen, Spivack, and Shure, 1972).

Since deficiencies in ICPS ability were consistently related to a variety of adjustment levels from age group to age group, the next question was, how early could such relationships be discovered?

Using a procedure modified and supplemented with pictures to meet the abilities and interests of a still younger age group, such differences were found as early as age four (Shure and Spivack, 1970b; Shure, Spivack, and Jaeger, 1974; Shure, Newman, and Silver, 1973). Instead of a story-telling technique, which proved to be too demanding for this age group, youngsters were presented with age-relevant interpersonal problems (such as a child wanting to play with a toy another child has), the sole requirement being to think of types or categories of solution ("ask him," "be his friend," "take it"). In one study (Shure and Spivack, 1970b), we found a relationship between an ability to conceptualize alternative solutions to interpersonal problems and both school behavioral-adjustment and socioeconomic level (SES). Children of low social class (in contrast to middle social class) as well as the less well adjusted within each SES group emitted fewer possible solutions to problems and fewer categories of solution. The better-adjusted youngsters in both SES groups thought of forceful ways to obtain a toy from another child ("snatch it," "hit him"), and the middle-class group thought of more nonforceful ways ("ask," "say, 'you can play with my truck,'" or "take turns").

In subsequent studies of lower class four- and five-year-olds, three other ICPS skills have been identified: (1) consequential thinking, defined as the ability to conceptualize what might happen next, if, for example, one child grabs a toy from another; (2) causal thinking, defined as ability to link one interpersonal event to a previous one with regard to the cause that might have precipitated an act; (3) sensitivity to interpersonal problems, defined as the cognitive ability to perceive a problem when it exists and the tendency to focus on those aspects of interpersonal confrontation that create a problem for the individuals involved. Regardless of measured IQ (PPVT, Slosson, Stanford-Binet) and mere test verbosity, alternative-solution thinking has consistently related most strongly to overt adjustment, particularly the degree to which youngsters display impulsivity or inhibition in the classroom. Consequential thinking has consistently been second in strength in distinguishing adjusted from less-adjusted youngsters. Causal thinking and sensitivity have only borderline relationships to behavior, although each relates to alternative and consequential thinking and no doubt plays a role in the overall problem-solving thinking of the young child. (For a further description of ICPS research, see Spivack and Shure, 1974; Spivack, Platt, and Shure, 1976; Shure and Spivack, 1978).

Implicitly assumed in all these studies was Spivack's theoretical position that ICPS skills are an antecedent condition for healthy social adjustment. Spivack (1973) asserted that an individual who can think through and solve problems, weigh the pros and cons of an act, and appreciate underlying causal dynamics of an interpersonal solution will be less likely to make impulsive mistakes, and will suffer less frustration from failure and circumstances leading to less maladaptive functioning.

To test this theory, we decided to design interventions that would enhance ICPS skills and to observe whether such changes would relate to improvement in social adjustment. We assumed that the earliest feasible age is optimal to enhance positive mental-health functioning (and support optimal cognitive development). Having discovered that four-year-olds were the youngest age group for which our measuring tools could effectively evaluate such training, attention was focused on lower SES children who, at this very early age, showed clear interpersonal cognitive problem-solving deficiencies relative to their middle-class age-mates (Shure and Spivack, 1970a, 1970b). If richness of available problem-solving strategies plays a significant role in determining success in adjusting to the world of other people, the results of all these studies have significant implications for early childhood intervention and primary prevention programs for the disadvantaged preschool child.

The Training Program

The background research provided us with a springboard from which to design the contents of the training curriculums. Children's ability to think of multiple options to interpersonal problems and consequences of acts is most intimately related to school behavioral adjustment in young children. We therefore took the approach that children can learn to think for themselves what and what not to do and why. To accomplish this, we designed a sequenced series of lessons, in game form, that begin with certain language and thinking skills judged to be prerequisite for learning major ICPS skills found to be related to adjustment before training. For example, such words as *not* and *same-different* were taught, so children could later decide whether an idea is or is *not* a good one and then think of a *different* idea. Listening to people, watching them, and discussions of ways to find out about people's feelings and desires were included. Having learned to take emotions and preferences of others into account, children are encouraged to think about hypothetical interpersonal problem situations, why the problem came to be, all the things the child having the problem could do or say to solve it, and what might happen next, if particular solutions are carried out. By extracting from children their thoughts about the problem and what to do about it, the children are taught how, but not what, to think.

Based on the formal lessons, conducted twenty minutes daily in small groups (by teachers) or with a single child (by mothers) for approximately three months, the problem-solving approach is extended to real problems as well. Teachers and mothers learn to encourage the child to tell them his viewpoint of the problem and how he and others involved might feel (or have felt) and to help the child think through new solutions and their consequences.

Finally, a new element was added to the training of mothers. In addition to teaching them how to administer the formal games of the program script and how to guide their children to think about real problems, one group of mothers was given ICPS training of their own. These mothers were given exercises to sensitize them to other people's thoughts and feelings (including their children's), which may differ from their own; they were taught that there is more than one way to solve a problem and that it is important to think about the potential consequences before taking action. One purpose of this training was to provide for the child a model of problem-solving thinking, on the assumption that a thinking parent might inspire a child to think. In training, neither children nor parents were told or advised about specific solutions to specific problems. The value was not what they think but that they think. (The childrearing curriculum, the third in a series of program scripts developed by Shure and Spivack, is presented in full in Shure and Spivack, in press; the nursery-teacher script is presented in Spivack and Shure, 1974; the kindergarten script is presented in Shure and Spivack, 1974a).

The Research Setting

All research with four-year-olds was conducted in classes of the Philadelphia Get Set Pre-Kindergarten Project (a year-around Head Start program). Since the program's inception in 1965, the public school system of Philadelphia has administered the program, regardless of its funding. During our early pilot background research in 1968, Get Set was funded by the Office of Economic Opportunity (OEO), and, when we began our pilot intervention in

1969, the Department of Public Welfare contracted with the school district. At the time of the pilot investigation, funding was provided by Title IVA of the Social Security Act (Title XX in 1974), and Get Set became a total daycare program, extending its hours from 9:00 A.M.–3:00 P.M. to 7:00 A.M.–6:00 P.M.

At the time of our first major intervention project in 1971, Get Set maintained 106 centers, mostly in churches located in federally designated pockets of poverty throughout the city. Get Set served over 5,000 three- and four-year-old children, 88.5 percent of them black, 7.4 percent white, 3.9 percent Puerto Rican, and 0.3 percent Asian. The program has always provided health, nutritional, educational, and social services as well as psychological services for children who need special testing or attention. I made my first contact with the chief of psychological services, who was also responsible for research. My experiences with him and other administrative personnel (director and assistant director) will be discussed with the process of implementation later in this chapter. Other personnel, with whom I also negotiated prior to intervention, consist of field supervisors, whose responsibilities include administrative duties as well as instructional supervision for clusters of centers within a particular school district, and a lead teacher within each center, the on-site overseer of the center's activities. Unlike teachers in national Head Start programs, Get Set teachers were required to be college graduates and presently are also required to have certification in this field. Some teachers had credits toward a master's degree. Each classroom also had a full-time assistant teacher (some college required) or a teacher's aide (high school or equivalency), and, during the peak of the day, when teachers conducted our training program with the children, both an assistant teacher and teacher's aide were generally on hand.

Without question, Get Set was and is perceived by both poverty and nonpoverty communities as a beneficial preschool educational program. When funding difficulties almost closed the entire 106 centers in 1968, parents and community leaders city-wide teamed up with the Policy Advisory Committee (a policy board of Get Set parents) and the League of Women Voters; together, they created the mechanisms whereby the funding was quickly changed from OEO to Title IVA of the Social Security Act, thus saving the Get Set program.

The kindergarten research was conducted in regular public elementary schools the Get Set children would enter.

Controlled-Intervention Research

Selection of Teachers. Our nursery research took place in twenty Get Set centers, located in three of the city's eight school districts. Ten teachers to be trained were recruited from a random selection of those meeting the following criteria: (1) the center would be geographically convenient to Hahnemann Hospital; (2) no other research or special programs would be conducted; (3) the building would be equipped with at least one room suitable for individual testing; (4) all children in the class would be entering kindergarten the following fall; (5) all teachers would have received top evaluation for their teaching ability from their field supervisor; (6) the children would be entering kindergarten classes in schools that (by prearrangement) would cooperate in the follow-up research.

After the training teachers were recruited (all volunteers), ten additional control teachers meeting the same criteria were recruited. How both nursery and kindergarten teachers were approached will be discussed in the section on process of implementation later in this chapter.

Research Children. The major four-year period of research that followed the initial pilot work began with all children in each class of the twenty teachers. Those available for pre-post nursery testing were:

Teacher Trained, Nursery	*Teacher Controls, Nursery*
Boys 47	Boys 50
Girls 66	Girls 56
113	106

All the children were black. At pretest, training and control children averaged four years and three months of age and were equated with respect to Binet IQ, all ICPS skills, and behavioral-adjustment group.

When the children entered kindergarten, the nursery-trained and controls were divided into four groups. Children available the entire two-year period were:

	Trained Nursery and Kindergarten	Trained Nursery Only	Trained Kindergarten Only	Controls, Nursery and Kindergarten
Boys	15	12	15	12
Girls	24	18	20	15
Total	39	30	35	27

To train all twelve kindergarten teachers promised the previous year, new children were added to replace nursery youngsters lost through attrition, and they were analyzed separately (see Shure and Spivack, 1975a).

In years three and four of our research, Get Set children were trained by their mothers.

	Nursery Mothers: I Pilot Training	Nursery Mothers: II Training	Control
Boys	13	10	10
Girls	7	10	10
Total	20	20	20

Mothers in the pilot group were recruited from a total of ninety-four interviewed for correlational purposes at pretest (see Shure and Spivack, 1975; Spivack, Platt, and Shure, 1976; Shure and Spivack, 1978). During this year, any twenty mothers could be included, as the purpose was primarily to determine the feasibility of training inner-city mothers and to experiment with readapting the program script for use with a single child at home.

In the second year of training mothers, twenty (of eighty interviewed for correlational purposes) were again recruited. This time, however, the purpose was to test the maximum impact of training mothers as ICPS agents, and we chose mothers of youngsters who showed observable behavioral difficulties at school or were ICPS-deficient. Twenty controls were selected, matched for ICPS ability and school behavioral adjustment. Seventeen trained and sixteen control youngsters met the criterion of displaying school behavioral problems. All youngsters came from centers ✓ in which teachers were not trained, so as to evaluate effectively the training by mothers alone.

Teacher and Parent Training Procedures

Teachers and parents met with me and a research assistant in small groups for ten three-hour meetings held once a week. Each meeting was devoted to demonstrating the lesson, and each teacher and mother acted it out to ensure familiarity with the games and dialogues before conducting them with the children. After a few weeks, not every lesson needed to be acted out, but every lesson was demonstrated. Time in each meeting was devoted to discussion of any problems the teacher or parent had with specific lessons or to difficulties created by the children. Tape recordings of actual training sessions with the children were heard and discussed. At the end of each meeting, the teachers and parents were given techniques for informal dialoguing when problems came up.

For the teacher-trained groups, three separate meetings were held for their aides. Our purpose was not to teach them how to apply the formal lessons (although some were taught to do so by their teachers) but rather to apply the informal dialoguing throughout the day. Such training was necessary to keep the style of talk consistent within the classroom.

To test the effects of systematic training of mothers' own ICPS skills on the ICPS skills and behavioral adjustment of the children, the second group of twenty mothers was given additional exercises designed to give the mothers a greater problem solving orientation.

Child Training Procedures

Teachers divided their classes into small groups for the formal lessons—six to eight in nursery, ten in kindergarten. Each group consisted of boys and girls, responders as well as nonresponders. Most of the mothers worked individually with their four-year-olds at home, although some included older siblings who sometimes helped to teach. Initial lessons lasted about five minutes, building to twenty minutes per day. Given holidays, illnesses, and other interfering factors, teachers and mothers generally took about twelve weeks to complete the formal training.

Pre-Post Evaluation Measures: Children

Each measure described in this section was administered immediately prior to and following training and, for nursery-teacher trained and teacher controls, six months and one year later. All cognitive tests administered individually by the research staff are described in Shure and Spivack, 1975. Those yielding the greatest results were:

Preschool Interpersonal Problem Solving Test (PIPS). PIPS measures ability to conceptualize alternative solutions to two interpersonal problems: (1) ways for one child to obtain a toy from another and (2) ways to avert mother's anger after having damaged something of value to her. This test is available in a complete manual (Shure and Spivack, 1974b).

What Happens Next Game (WHNG).   WHNG measures ability to anticipate multiple consequences to acts when: (1) one child grabs a toy from another and (2) a child takes an object from an adult without first asking.

Hahnemann Preschool Behavior Rating Scale (HPSB).   HPSB measures school behavioral adjustment via teacher ratings. The scale consists of items analyzed into three factors: Impatience (nags, demands, grabs toys), Emotionality (shows anger or upset behavior to peers or adults when things go wrong), and Aggression (physical or verbal). Teacher ratings allowed the child to be classified as adjusted, impulsive (showing more than average amounts of behaviors described), or inhibited (showing significantly less-than-normal amounts of the behaviors described). For teacher-trained nursery and kindergarten youngsters and their controls, behavior was also rated at the end of first grade.

Pre-Post Evaluation Measures: Mothers

Pilot mothers were interviewed individually prior to training, and, in the second year, training and control mothers were interviewed prior to and immediately following the period of intervention.

Problem-Solving Childrearing Style.   Each mother was asked to relate how she typically handles real problem situations brought to or created for her by her child. A scale was devised to score the reported extent to which a mother helped her child to articulate a problem and to see possible solutions and their consequences or the extent to which mothers guided or encouraged the child to explore these in his own mind. Problems included the child refusing a mother's request, the child taking something from a peer, and the child reporting he was physically or verbally attacked by a peer.

Six situations were given at pretest during both years of research with mothers, and eight were given at posttest in the second mother-training study. For each category of problem given, the mother could substitute content that actually occurred.

Means-Ends Problem-Solving Test (MEPS): Mother-Child Stories.   This test measures the mother's ability to plan sequenced steps to solve hypothetical problems between a mother and her child.

Program Evaluation

Because each of the four years of research constituted separate studies, the results will be presented here in summary form. Comprehensive descriptions and analyses of all pretesting and posttesting procedures, results, and discussions are presented in Shure and Spivack, 1975.

1. Each year, there was a significant training effect in ICPS skills for youngsters who began as adjusted and an even more significant training effect for those initially displaying impulsive or inhibited behaviors.

2. ICPS skills most affected were alternative-solution and consequential thinking (see Tables 1 and 2).

3. Immediate effects of training on behavioral adjustment were similar for youngsters trained in nursery and for youngsters trained in kindergarten, and effects were not significantly different for those trained one year from those trained both years. All training groups had a significantly greater improvement in ICPS skills as well as behavior than the never-trained controls (see Table 3). Therefore, it became clear that, if youngsters were not trained in nursery, kindergarten was not too late, although nursery-trained youngsters did begin kindergarten with a better behavioral base.

Table 1. Means and SDs of Two ICPS Skills and Percentage of Adjusted Ss For Teacher- and Mother-Trained Ss During Nursery Year

| | PIPS Solutions[a] | | WHNG Consequences[a] | | Percent Adjusted | |
	Fall Nursery	Spring Nursery	Fall Nursery	Spring Nursery	Fall Nursery	Spring Nursery
Teacher-Trained						
X̄	4.74	10.04	4.74	6.90	36	71
SD	(2.79)	(3.03)	(2.24)	(2.15)		
N	113	113	113	113		
Teacher-Controls						
X̄	5.34	6.09	5.28	5.52	47	54
SD	(2.61)	(2.75)	(2.37)	(2.18)		
N	106	106	106	106		
Mother-Trained						
X̄	4.00	8.85	4.25	7.30	15[b]	75
SD	(2.58)	(3.23)	(1.97)	(2.03)		
N	20	20	20	20		
Mother-Controls						
X̄	3.95	4.95	4.80	5.65	20	40
SD	(2.37)	(2.04)	(2.19)	(1.79)		
N	20	20	20	20		

[a]No ceiling in scores.
[b]Deliberate choosing of few adjusted Ss at pretest.

Table 2. Means, SDs and F-Ratios of Two ICPS Skills and Percentage of Adjusted Ss for Four Groups of Teacher-Trained Ss in Spring of Kindergarten Year

Measure[a]	Group				df	F
	Trained $Nu + Ki$	Trained Nu	Trained Ki	Control $Nu + Ki$		
ICPS						
PIPS Solutions						
$\overline{X}$	16.46_{xy} [b]	11.53_x	12.34_y	8.33_{xy}	3; 127	31.79^c
SD	(4.66)	(3.13)	(2.75)	(2.08)		
N	39	30	35	27		
WHNG Consequences						
$\overline{X}$	10.74_x	9.03_x	9.74_y	6.59_{xy}	3; 125	18.79^c
SD	(2.58)	(2.43)	(2.06)	(1.74)		
N	39	30	34	26		
Behavior						
Adjusted						
N	33	23	29	8		
Percent	85	77	83	30	$X^b = 28.81$ df = 3 p <0.01	
Impulsive + Inhibited						
N	6	7	6	19		
Percent	15	23	17	70		

[a]There were no significant pretest differences between any groups at the first measuring period of Fall, Nursery, one year earlier.
[b]Within each row, means with the same subscript are significantly different at at least 0.05, Newman-Keuls.
[c]P <0.001.

Table 3. Mean Gain in Two ICPS Skills for Initially Aberrant Training Ss Who Did and Did Not Improve in Behavioral Adjustment

PIPS Solutions	Behavior Improved			Behavior Not Improved			t	df	p
	$\overline{X}$ Gain	SD	N	$\overline{X}$ Gain	SD	N			
Nursery-Teacher[a]	7.83	(2.14)	43	4.14	(2.46)	29	6.78	70	.001
Kindergarten-Teacher[a]	6.36	(2.87)	14	2.51	(1.64)	6	3.05	18	.01
Nursery-Mother[a,b]	5.58	(1.88)	12	3.20	(1.09)	5	2.62	15	.05
WHNG Consequences									
Nursery-Teacher	3.12	(2.92)	43	1.97	(2.05)	29	1.61	70	.06[d]
Kindergarten-Teacher	4.38	(3.18)	13[c]	1.00	(1.26)	6	2.54	17[c]	.05
Nursery-Mother	3.85	(1.73)	12	2.60	(1.95)	5	1.03	15	ns

[a]Nursery-Teacher, trained in school; Kindergarten-Teacher, trained in school; Nursery-Mother, trained at home, attended school.
[b]Second group of trained mothers only; first group (pilot group) did not have enough initially aberrant Ss for analyses.
[c]One child did not receive the consequences test.
[d]One-tailed test.

ICPS effects measured one year later maintained holding power, and behavioral effects of training were still evident two years later.

4. Independently of measured IQ and mere test verbosity, youngsters who most improved in the trained-thinking skills were the same children who most improved in behavioral adjustment. This direct linkage was especially true of alternative-solution thinking for both age levels and it was true whether the child was trained by his teacher or by his mother. Consequential thinking as a behavioral mediator was particularly impressive in the kindergarten year (see Table 3).

5. In addition to helping youngsters already displaying impulsivity and inhibition, a preventive effect of the program was evident. Among youngsters normally adjusted throughout the nursery year, significantly more trained than nontrained youngsters maintained that good adjustment throughout kindergarten and first grade.

6. Both teachers and mothers could learn to become effective ICPS agents. Boys and girls benefitted equally, regardless of training agent. This finding was especially important among mother-trained youngsters, as pretest correlational data twice indicated natural relationships of ICPS between mothers and their daughters but not their sons. Children of mothers given additional training exercises relevant to their own thinking skills improved in solution thinking more than did children of mothers who administered the formal games and dialogues but were not given special ICPS training of their own. Importantly, mothers who most improved in both childrearing style and in child-related means-ends thinking had children who improved in their ICPS skills, again true of both boys and girls.

7. The improved behavior of children trained at home generalized to the school, as evidenced by behavior ratings completed by the child's teacher. The improved behavior was related to improved problem-solving ability and was not situation-specific. This result is attributed to the approach of the program, which was to teach children how to think, not what to think.

Validity of Training Effect

Questions may be raised concerning the effect of possible teacher bias in making the post-behavior ratings and whether or not ICPS improvement or behavioral improvement might have been a function of attention given to the children by their teachers or mothers. Evidence clearly suggests that neither of these factors significantly affected the results.

1. Those ICPS skills that most strongly related to adjustment measures before training also showed the strongest linkage after training. Consistently, youngsters who improved most in alternative-solution thinking also improved most in behavior, followed by consequential thinking—the same order of strength of relationships to behavior at pretest. Teachers were unaware of the child's ICPS test scores, which were administered by the research staff. Had teachers rated behavior on the basis of training-session performance, the thought-behavioral linkages would also have occurred for other skills tested, namely, interpersonal causal thinking and cognitive sensitivity to interpersonal problems. In addition, feedback to the nursery teachers indicated that they were indeed more interested in the children's IQ change than in ICPS change. No relationship occurred between change in behavior and change in measured IQ.

2. Teachers rated nineteen additional behavioral items, and only those related to ICPS ability at pretest showed a significant training effect. Had teachers rated behavior on mere training performance, they would likely have judged responsive youngsters as having higher scores on items describing verbal skills, comprehension and general effectiveness, irrelevant-responsiveness, and others, but such was not the case.

3. Independent ratings by teachers and their aides yielded agreements of over 85 percent all four years of the research.

4. Kindergarten teachers rated the nursery youngsters remarkably similar in the fall of the year to nursery teachers' ratings the previous spring. Nursery-trained youngsters not receiving further reinforcement, whose behavior was rated to have improved at the end of nursery, were consistently rated similarly by different teachers throughout the first grade.

5. Children trained by their mothers at home were rated by their teachers in school, who remained unaware of children's ICPS scores and which children were trained and which were not. Thus, these teachers were not in a position to evaluate the child's training performance.

6. During our pilot years, a placebo-attention group did not improve ICPS skills or behavior in the same way as did trained youngsters (Shure, Spivack, and Gordon, 1972). Had mere attention been a key factor, improvement would have occurred for all skills tested in a random way and not in direct proportion to the strength of relationships to behavior at pretest. In this regard, the finding is important that children of mothers given ICPS training of their own improved in ICPS skills more than did youngsters of mothers who were not trained. In administering the program script, both groups of mothers gave equal attention to their children.

7. Interestingly, teachers who were given ICPS training as a service and who were not part of the research years were told of the behavioral goals (unlike the research teachers) as well as cognitive ones (see the later section on ICPS as service delivery). Their ratings of children's behavioral improvement showed percentages remarkably similar to those in the research years. This finding suggests that, even if research teachers had inferred behavioral goals, the results would likely not have been different from those obtained.

Clearly, teachers rated the children honestly and objectively, and results support our position of ICPS as significant mediators of behavioral adjustment. We believe the efficacy of a theoretically based intervention procedure with broad mental-health significance has been confirmed. It appears that both teachers and poor inner-city mothers can learn to become effective ICPS agents for four- and five-year-old children, especially when these mothers are given special ICPS training of their own. The emerging data have theoretical significance for our understanding of early childhood development. The data indicate an intimate relationship between specific identifiable interpersonal cognitive problem-solving skills and overt behavioral adjustment among four- and five-year-olds, and direct manipulation by training these cognitive functions affects overt level of adjustment.

Process of Implementation

First, I will describe the steps we took to develop and maintain the support of school personnel and citizen groups, including the planning involved to stage and validate the intervention, as well as how we dealt with service versus research priorities of key personnel. I will also discuss how the intervention has been and is being maintained and its flexibility for application with new groups. Stresses encountered along the way were caused by what seemed at times to have been insurmountable obstacles, but we were able to circumvent them, and our perseverence was largely due to the almost daily satisfactions and rewards we could not help but feel. Based on our experiences, I will also pinpoint principles of process management that have been successful for us.

ICPS as Research Project

Initiating, Planning, and Staging the Intervention. My first step was to meet with the chief of psychological services of Get Set, an introduction facilitated by previous contacts by Hahnemann staff. First, I explained the project and the extent of teacher involvement and that the research would be paid for through Hahnemann and would therefore involve no cost to them. He was informed that my colleague, George Spivack, had developed a theory about interpersonal cognitive problem-solving ability and adjustment and had found marked differences in this kind of thinking in adjusted and maladjusted adolescents (Spivack and Levine, 1963). I explained that my own training and interests involved preschoolers and that I had begun to pilot measures to test these relationships in youngsters as young as four years of age. It was suggested that, if ICPS skills could distinguish Get Set youngsters showing behavior problems from those who were not, then we could develop a curriculum to improve these skills and test whether such training would also enhance school behaviors. This administrator was very receptive to such research, because it would provide new training techniques for some of the teachers, because a large number of children were showing behavior problems, and probably because it would involve no cost to Get Set. Programs being implemented at that time had impersonal cognitive goals, such as language development and learning colors and shapes, but none were having significant impact on behavior. To him, the idea of ICPS training seemed unique and challenging.

The chief of psychological services then introduced me to other administrative staff (director and assistant director), to field supervisors (middle-level administrators), and to center lead teachers, as it was necessary to gain their approval before approaching classroom teachers. The latter two groups had the authority to disallow our efforts, but acceptance and clearance by top administration reduced that likelihood, and it never happened.

In our first two centers, further testing was administered, and some of the lessons designed for the ICPS curriculum were prepiloted. Then, in 1969, a formal pilot was set up in these same centers. To do this, Hahnemann gave us $500 in seed money (to buy materials, pay teachers for completing behavior ratings, and provide transportation expenses). At the same time, arrangements were made for students from the Psychology Department at Temple University to work with us and receive credit for a research practicum. In that pilot year, the students and I worked directly with the children, a step I felt was necessary for us to feel the subtle dynamics of how children would respond to the lessons as well as to increase our sensitivity to what teachers and mothers might later experience. During this time, we kept administrative staff abreast of our activities, with the assurance that, once the research was over, both they and the teachers would be given complete feedback about our findings. The subject of feedback will be taken up later, but it is extremely important in developing and maintaining relations in the schools.

Having obtained encouraging results from our pilot (Shure, Spivack, and Gordon, 1972), I applied for and received a small National Institute of Health (NIH) daughter grant from Hahnemann. I then trained four volunteer teachers; four teachers served as controls. All recruited teachers were introduced to me personally by the Get Set chief of psychological services. After completing the pilot, I perfected the training procedures and then, with George Spivack, applied for a large grant from the Applied Research Branch of the National Institute of Mental Health (NIMH) to conduct a full-scale controlled-research project to test the theory of ICPS skills as behavioral mediators.

The NIMH grant lasted from 1971 through 1975. The first year was slated to continue in Get Set. By now, I had learned how best to approach teachers. The chief of psychological services suggested supervisors and centers, and I began my first independent recruiting effort. All contacted teachers enthusiastically volunteered to participate. They were looking for new teaching techniques, and these would not interfere with their ongoing program (the lessons were conducted for five to twenty minutes per day, usually during story time). Realistically, we recognized that part of their enthusiasm might also have been due to remuneration they would receive for their training time.

Interest of the teachers, trained in two groups of five each, was maintained throughout. They were told of the cognitive goals (but not the behavioral goals), and they found the interest level and responses of the children rewarding. Teachers were free at any time to offer suggestions for change in technique or content (but not concepts). They felt that they were an integral part of a team to develop techniques that would both teach the concepts and hold maximum interest of the children. During this year, we added training for the classroom aides. Training these aides (as described previously) proved to be extremely fruitful, not only because it increased continuity of style in dealing with the children but also because it made them feel important, and their work attendance became dramatically more regular. This, however, could not have accounted for improved behavior, because children trained at home showed the same behavior change in classes where such continuity did not exist.

In anticipation of the second (kindergarten) year, we talked to the executive director of research and the director of early childhood programs of the Philadelphia school district. All principals and teachers were contacted prior to selection of nursery centers to prepare for a smooth follow-through in the second year. Had any principal or kindergarten teacher chosen not to participate, we would have had to select nursery youngsters from centers feeding different elementary schools. After many negotiations with principals and teachers, it was decided in advance which kindergarten teachers would train or serve as controls and the kindergarten placements of the children. The crucial considerations in planning were to ensure that children trained for the second time would not be in the same class with those first receiving training and that children slated to be controls would not be placed in a training class. Because achievement tracking does not occur until the first grade, this kind of placement presented no difficulties. Two teachers slated to train left before the kindergarten study had begun, but fortunately their replacements agreed to participate.

In the third year of our research, we returned to Get Set to learn how mothers naturally play a role in the development of their children's ICPS skills and to set up a pilot to study whether these mothers could also be trained to become effective ICPS agents. Get Set administrators introduced me to a new group of field supervisors, who helped me distribute flyers to inform mothers about the program. But first, I had to obtain clearance from the Policy Advisory Committee (PAC). This committee consists of parent groups from each of twelve administrative areas, each area represented by six to eight Get Set centers. Functions of PAC include providing input on all aspects of programs, operations, policies, and procedures as related to delivery of services to parents and children. Having selected our centers, I appeared at individual centers and talked with mothers in center meetings and as I could catch them when they brought their children to school. In year four, mothers were recruited the same way, except that the Department of Public Welfare, the primary Get Set funding agency, required that, for daycare eligibility, parents must either be employed, enrolled in a job-training program, or in school. Some mothers could not train, and, for most who could, it was necessary for us to make arrangements with their employer. For those interviewing only (pre- or pre- and posttesting), we had to see some on Saturdays or in the evening. We were able to recruit enough mothers, but it did take much time and effort.

The research phase of implementation did require careful long-range planning. Contact was made with every level of administrative personnel, not only for clearance but to assure all participants that we had the support of their superiors.

Feedback: Research versus Service Priorities. At appropriate times, we provided complete feedback to administrative personnel and to teachers, and we assured them that no information about any child would ever be included in his or her school records. Providing personal feedback might have been the single most important thing we did, not so much because they were concerned about specific research results, but because it indicated our interest in them. As one principal said, "So many psychologists come here and test the kids, and we never see or hear from them again." As more schools became involved, we called group meetings for feedback, one with administrative personnel, one with training teachers, and one with controls. Those who could not attend were

seen individually, but the number of sessions was markedly reduced. Each of these three groups had quite different interests
regarding feedback. Administrators and principals were most concerned about the training for their teachers—that is, the benefits
for staff development. Trained teachers were interested primarily
in individual children's progress, as reflected by their ICPS test
scores and especially IQ. Control teachers' major concern was how
IQ changed, a measure we used for research control purposes, but
IQ was no doubt seen by both training and control teachers as a
reflection of their teaching. None, however, showed overwhelming
enthusiasm to learn more about our theoretical framework or research goals. No one was in any way against our doing research.
The point here is that, in maintaining the support of anyone involved in such a project, it is absolutely essential to focus on what is
important to them and not merely to present a prepared speech
emphasizing what is important to the researcher.

ICPS as Service Delivery: Maintaining the Intervention

In 1973, a contract to the board of education was written
and planned with the help and advice of the Get Set administrative
staff, particularly the assistant director. We were accepted to train
more teachers as a service to incorporate the program into more
Get Set centers. Training was conducted only during school hours,
which made it unnecessary to pay the teachers. Classroom aides
were given in-service credit, which accumulates toward salary increase. Contract expenses were limited to purchase of materials for
twelve new teachers, other miscellaneous expenses (such as dup-
licating), and token payment to Hahnemann for our services as
consultants. It is therefore possible to implement programs as service with very little money, and even less would be needed, if some
of the materials were made instead of bought.

In our first year of service delivery, our plans were to set up
three home centers of participating research teachers, who would
now function as key trainers. The trainers contacted others they
knew in nearby centers and interested them and their aides in
learning the program. By the time we were to begin, Get Set
employees joined the teachers' union, and the law required that
any teacher in the system could volunteer and would be chosen on
the basis of seniority. Because we were, however, simultaneously

conducting our mother-training research, we were allowed to stipulate that teachers in those centers could not be eligible at that time (to avoid contaminating our research evaluation of children trained by their mothers). Having already set up plans for service implementation, it was fortunate that not too many teachers signed up that year (other than those already contacted), and we were able to proceed with our originally selected group.

By the second year of service delivery, many more teachers had heard about the program, and those who signed up were now from centers scattered all over the city (again, except for those from centers involved in our mother research project). Our contract, planned and written with the help and advice of Get Set administrators, now provided for expenses for fourteen additional trainees and their aides, and most of the newly trained teachers desired to serve as key trainers. This contract also paid for transportation costs, so that trainers could visit trainees in their classrooms to demonstrate, observe, and consult on all phases of program application. Additional expenses were provided for travel to a central location for six two-hour workshops, which I led during the course of the year—three for teachers and three for aides. Get Set curriculum staff attended these workshops, so that they could continue implementation in future years. We learned that, with relatively little supervision from us, teachers could train their peers. In addition, a questionnaire indicated high enthusiasm for both the children and themselves.

With regard to community implementation, it is important to recognize that, even though the program script is written clearly enough for teachers to follow themselves, as are examples of dialoguing techniques for use during the day, small-group weekly meetings provide the most desirable training model, for four reasons: (1) they provide a group feeling, an important support system for mothers who may feel insecure, at least initially; (2) they provide an opportunity for the trainee to role play the games to ensure familiarity with them; (3) it gives the trainee a reassurance that any problems experienced during the week can soon be discussed; and (4) it is possible to concentrate on small portions of the program at a time, making easy absorption possible. As I learned later, Get Set administration was very pleased with the amount of time spent with teachers and parents, which increased their enthusiasm for the program as time passed. Yet, if weekly meetings are not feasible, the alternative models that we used are still beneficial.

Stresses and Satisfactions

Implementation was not always smooth. Stresses at times caught us quite unexpectedly, especially during the research years, when time restrictions were greater because of individual ICPS pre- and posttesting requirements. Between November and February of each year, individual child or child-and-mother pretesting had to be completed, as did teachers' behavior ratings. Three months were allocated for training (February through April), so that posttesting could be completed by the end of the school year, late in June. We did not want to begin testing before November for two reasons—it took time to train the testers, who joined us from Temple University in September of each year, and teachers had to know the children sufficiently well to rate their behaviors, as children entered on a staggered schedule well into the month of October. With these time restraints, any delays produced inevitable anxiety (these restraints, of course, are considerably relaxed when ICPS training is a *service*).

The first problem arose when Temple University changed their school schedule. Christmas vacation was extended to five weeks, right in the heart of our pretesting, and the school year ended near the beginning of May, just after we would start our posttesting. The students could learn the testing procedures earlier in September, and we could begin testing a few weeks earlier than originally planned, but it would not have been good research to test too far in advance of the teachers' rating of the behaviors, so we had to redistribute our grant funds and pay those who would be willing to test outside the period of their school term. For both educational and reliability purposes, students also coded at least some of the data, which was made more difficult by this change in their schedule. In subsequent years, we were prepared for this, and we recruited enough students who would promise to test for us at least two of the five weeks of their Christmas break and also test and code data until the end of June.

Each year, we calculated how many college students would be needed in addition to our own research assistants for ICPS testing. After having recruited the needed number of students for kindergarten testing, we were confronted with a three-week school strike in the fall, which, still unsettled, was anticipated to be resumed in January. To complete pretesting by that time, additional students were recruited, and, that year, the schedule of pretesting did have to be moved up to begin at the end of October. This worked well, because, unlike Get Set, where enrollment was staggered until the end of October, all children had entered kindergarten by the end of September, so that teachers could rate them while we pretested. The strike did resume in January for eight more weeks. Training took place March, April, and May, and, had it not been for our additional student testers, it would not have been possible to complete our posttesting before the end of that particular school year.

When schools did open at the end of the first three-week strike, we were faced with still another problem. In addition to dealing with the stress of time delay, we learned that a new principal had been assigned to one of our training schools. When I called to make an appointment, he told me I could talk with him but that he probably would not permit any research to be conducted in his school (even though the previous principal had approved). His belief was that psychologists just use the schools for their own ends and contribute little or nothing to the school or to the children. Racing through my mind were thoughts of losing almost twenty children slated to be trained for the first time, children who had been studied for a full year as nursery controls. Since we already lost some children to our study due to natural attrition, then still more because of the first (three-week) school strike, this was a group we could ill afford to lose. Fortunately, this was to be a training and not a control school. I stressed the value of our approach—what we had learned about it the previous year, reactions of nursery teachers, and its effects on children. I particularly stressed the value to teachers and not the continuity of our research, because I had learned that, to principals, staff development was of more concern than our own research interests. He did allow us to proceed, and later he became one of our greatest supporters.

Problems came up during our research with mothers as well. Making an appointment for the pretest interview was one thing, but actually showing up was another. Approximately 25 percent of the mothers did not follow through. This wasted much time and pressured us, because we wanted to interview as many mothers as possible for correlational-research purposes before we began our training. Most of the mothers finally did come, but, in many cases, three or four appointments were necessary to accomplish it. This apparent lack of concern about keeping appointments was perhaps understandable, in that they did not yet know us well or fully understand what we would be doing. Nonetheless, having learned that many inner-city adults have little regard for keeping appointments and have too many daily pressures to be concerned about them, we were aware that it would be necessary to make special efforts to motivate training mothers not to drop out in the middle of the program.

Mothers selected (according to criteria described in Shure and Spivack, 1978) were asked if there was anything they knew that could prevent them from completing the ten-week program, and we explained the importance of not dropping out. Also, we called them for the first couple of weeks, gently reminding them of the meeting; in doing this, we developed a joking, happy rapport. We also put our telephone number on the program script, and, unlike the first interview, when we paid them after they arrived, we gave them car fare for five meetings and every third week paid them $10.00 for each attended meeting. As it turned out, these mothers looked forward to the meetings. They liked the program, the pay, and the materials they would be bringing home to their children. Of forty mothers, twenty each year, only one dropped out after the first week, and there was time to replace her.

During the second year that we trained mothers, we encountered a new problem. In the fourth week of training, we were faced with a mass-transportation strike that lasted for two weeks. We did not want to interrupt the momentum, so we picked them up and took them home, and here again we stressed the importance of being on time, lest one mother would keep another waiting. The mothers showed up on time, for which they were highly praised, and perhaps this experience brought us all still closer together. This positive secondary effect, however, was not what improved the children's behavior. Our mothers did feel good about themselves, and this could have had an effect on their children. But, as in the teacher-training research, not all children's behavior improved, only those who improved in the trained ICPS skills (see the program evaluation section). Again, mere attention to mothers and children would have produced random results. I mention this togetherness to point out how a crisis can be turned to advantage instead of defeat.

The major stress was the rather frequent necessity to readjust our plans, whether because of difficulties within the schools, schedule changes of staff from supporting institutions, laws regarding recipient eligibility, changing staff in the program itself, or outside intrusions, such as a mass-transportation strike. Perhaps it is useful to summarize, from our experiences, some principles of process management.

1. Personal contact must be made with all levels of administration, not just those most visible.
2. All personnel, administrators, staff, and recipients (for example, parents) must understand the relevance of intervention to them, not just to the researcher.
3. Flexibility and openness to suggestions by all personnel at all levels is crucial.
4. All levels of participating staff and recipients must feel they are an important part of the project.
5. Willingness to spend time with and show interest in the participants is essential throughout all phases of the project.
6. Although planning is necessary, flexibility must be maintained.
7. Working through the inevitable stresses and strains together as a team is optimal.
8. Feedback, when feasible, must be promised and delivered.
9. When reasonable and feasible, participants should be volunteers paid in money, in-service credit, or a suitable substitute.

Stresses and strains notwithstanding, activating these principles clearly paved the way for the satisfactions and rewards we experienced. It was evident that everyone involved was enthusiastic about the experience, and not only because of the effect it had on the children. Teachers and mothers felt it had real benefits for them. One very shy teacher became more confident, and a mother reported that she used the dialoguing techniques with her coworkers, when interpersonal problems would arise at her office. It was satisfying to hear from both teachers and mothers that the programs were received enthusiastically. Because recipients are not taught what to do but rather are taught a set of skills that allowed them to solve their own problems in their own way, the programs do not require a readjustment of teaching or childrearing philosophy, a major shift of habits, or a change in values held by any group. We were told that the curriculum, a step-by-step building process, is easy to learn and can be implemented without lengthy preparation. The goals and relevance to the concerns of the user are quickly recognized, the materials are readily available and usable for many purposes, and users quickly see the children's enthusiasm and progress. Some trainees appreciated the opportunity to create new games and dialogues relevant to their own group or child (within program goals), especially teachers who did not wish to be restricted to word-for-word program scripts. Others were happy to have the organized script before them, as it gave them a sense of structure.

But our greatest satisfactions came from the children. After having provoked us to do this and not to do that in their own inimitable way, they were the ones who really made the program what it is today. Their responses (or lack of them) made us add, subtract, and substitute content and techniques to which they could, and would respond.

Watching behaviorally aberrant children learn to solve problems and become less impulsive or less inhibited was particularly gratifying. In a teacher-training classroom, for example, I observed Tammy, a painfully shy child who just watched other children play. If the teacher helped her into the group by suggesting she might "help dress the doll baby," Tammy would become more frightened. She was not ready to enter into group play. After training, Tammy once announced, "I just cooked a cake." A child yelled, "Can we have a party?" Tammy was in business. She was now able to think of her own way to move forward. Children who frequently push, hit, or otherwise forcefully impose themselves on others learn there is more than one way to get what they want, and, when they cannot have it, they are able to think of other ways to satisfy their needs.

This kind of behavior change was our ultimate goal and unquestionably our greatest reward.

INTERVIEW WITH MYRNA BETH SHURE

Snowden: Myrna, would you talk about your involvement in the work? Give some history and an idea of what the experience has been like for you.

Shure: I arrived at Hahnemann in 1968, as a research associate, a year after the Division of Research and Evaluation had been created. George Spivack, the director of that division, wanted to continue the research in interpersonal cognitive problem solving that he had begun with adolescents in the early 1960s. My first project involved testing ten-year-olds' ability to think through and solve real-life problems and to see if such ability related to various measures of social adjustment. As I was working with the ten-year-olds, I mentioned that I would be interested in seeing whether it was possible to measure such skills in four-year-olds (the age group I specialized in during my graduate training). George and I both knew that the process we were measuring in older age groups would not be appropriate for such young children, because that process involved a story-telling procedure of sequenced step-by-step planning to reach a goal, a spontaneous tendency to foresee obstacles that could interfere, and a spontaneous tendency to recognize that it often takes time to reach a goal. Knowing the test measure would have to be changed to fit the cognitive capacities of four-year-old children, George gave me free reign to experiment.

I went to a school I had previous contact with in downtown Philadelphia, a middle-class urban school. To see if a range of problem-solving skills existed in children that young, I started showing them some pictures—that helps to keep four-year-olds interested. Some of them could tell stories, but there wasn't much range. As one child I tested was talking, it occurred to me that, instead of asking these children to tell stories, I could get them to tell what they could do to solve a problem, and then to name different ways. For four-year-olds, one very important problem is seen when one child has a toy another wants. So I would say, "What could Johnny do to get Jimmy to let him play with his truck?" The child would give some answer like, "Ask him for it," and I would ask, "O. K., what else could he do? Let's think of lots of things he could do." The children typically looked at me and said, "I told you already!" Or, they would look very upset, as if to say, "You didn't like my answer," and the most I would get was three solutions from the most efficient group of children. I felt frustrated, because I knew I was close to something, but I didn't have it yet. And then I remembered that, when I did my Ph.D thesis, I had pictures of toys on different cards, and I wondered if showing them one at a time and asking for only one solution per picture would help us get a range of solutions. To the child, each new toy might seem like a new story, but we were really asking for more than one solution to the same problem. This procedure did hold their interest, and we were able to get the range we were looking for.

Snowden: And that's how you developed the Preschool Interpersonal Problem Solving or PIPS Test?

Shure: Yes. Then, another story problem was added to the test—how to keep mother from getting mad after a story child damaged something of value. We changed the object damaged, when a solution was given. We saw that some four-year-olds could do better than others; we didn't know what kind of score was good or deficient yet, but we knew there were differences. So, the next step was to go back to the theory. Now that we had this range, we asked if it would relate to behavior in the classroom. That was the next thing we tried to determine. George had developed a behavior-rating scale with Marshall Swift that was applicable to kindergarten on up. We took some of the behavioral items that seemed appropriate for nursery, like hitting, grabbing, and getting overemotional. Then, we had the teacher rate many behavior items, and we saw that some of them did relate to this problem-solving skill.

From there, we determined other skills we could measure. We knew that adolescents and adults could weigh the pros and cons before choosing to act, but, again, that was measured through a story-telling procedure. For four-year-olds, we discovered that the best way to measure consequential thinking was to ask for alternative consequences, just as we had asked for alternative solutions. We simply asked, "What might happen next if a child grabs another child's toy?" Of course, we kept changing the toy after each new consequence was given. And we went on like that, piloting new measures, until we came up with our test battery.

Snowden: While being adapted from the adult level to a level suitable for four-year-olds, the project underwent another transition— from theory to application. Could you tell us about that?

Shure: Back in 1968, the chairman of our mental health center told George that he was free to pursue his problem-solving interests because of its relevance to mental health. He and I agreed that, since there appeared to be a relationship between problem-solving skills and behavior, the next question was, what would happen to the behavior of deficient problem-solvers, if we could train them how to think and solve problems? Training would allow us to test the theory of interpersonal problem-solving skills as behavioral mediators by trying to alter thinking and then observe whether those who most improved in the trained-thinking skills would be the same as those who would most improve in behavior. We agreed that would entail very exciting discoveries in mental health, and that was the beginning of the thought processes for our venture.

Snowden: It sounds as though an important factor was the institutional mission of Hahnemann Mental Health and Retardation Center. What personal factors caused you to devise an intervention instead of merely elaborating on the theory?

Shure: When the idea to do intervention was mentioned, I jumped at it, because it allowed me the opportunity not only to be with children but also to apply my research interests I had developed in graduate school. Because of the nature of our program—teaching kids how, not what, to think—I had no qualms about conducting intervention in schools.

Snowden: Then the project blended ingredients you had found exciting for some time. Might that have sustained you through this truly major effort? In terms of number of schools, time, and other parameters, this has been a project of impressive scope. It must have taken a lot of personal commitment.

Shure: I was very fortunate, in that Hahnemann gave me the time to do it. They saw it as important, even though we did not know yet that it was going to have preventive effects, as we later found in our research. One thing that was exciting to me from the very beginning was the way that administration and teachers whom I didn't even know responded to what I was going to do. In a great deal of research, people like me are often seen as intruding, whereas their reaction was just the opposite. Their attitude of "When are you going to start?" really got my adrenalin going.

Snowden: Perhaps their reactions stimulated you, and your enthusiasm stimulated them.

Shure: The concept of the program is almost self-selling, as soon as I say, "We're going to teach children how to think, so they can solve real-life problems." I didn't go into our long research, because they wouldn't relate to that anyway, but the way I approached it was, "We want to develop a curriculum, and we need your help to see if we can teach kids as young as four how to think, so they can solve their own problems." Being a developmental psychologist, I knew what kinds of thinking skills four-year-olds did and did not have—not specific problem-solving skills, but how to go about developing a curriculum for that age group. At first, the director of Get Set brought me into the schools. I should interject that, by now, we had decided to work in the inner city with economically disadvantaged black youngsters, and I made my first contact with the personnel of these schools for training. I discuss this in detail in the chapter. After piloting the training curriculum with some of these children and perfecting the measures of problem-solving thinking, I could talk about these experiences with administrative personnel and teachers in new schools. They were impressed with the fact that I had given effort to trying out the program with children before trying to train teachers to apply it.

Snowden: Do you think another factor might have been your background as a nursery school teacher?

Shure: That wasn't a selling factor, but it was, I'm sure, important in what made me feel pleased about what I was doing. I got across the perception that I had worked with children, that it meant a lot to me to work with them, and that I wasn't doing it because it was a job or because it was something somebody told me to do. I don't think that helped sell the program, but it might have helped sell me.

Snowden: What you are describing is a relationship with several advantages. The program, as you mentioned, sells itself; it sounds very appealing. But it is also put across by a person who is perceived as understanding and knowledgeable about the teacher's point of view. Would you agree?

Shure: There's another factor to the intervention. Teachers mentioned that they liked how the program had distinct goals, which, for purposes of research, were, as far as they knew, only the cognitive ones. We didn't talk about the behavioral-outcome goals at that time. Many had commented that, in their training, they had bits of Piaget and bits of other theorists and scattered strategies for teaching. When they got into the classroom, they didn't know what to do with these bits of information. In our program, they could see how the prerequisite lessons were built toward the final concept goals, and they liked that. I also made it clear that they could be flexible with the content, as long as they kept to the concepts, which gave them a chance to be creative.

Snowden: One thing that comes through in the chapter is the cohesiveness displayed by teachers, mothers, and others. What helped to engender this spirit?

Shure: I just can't stress enough how important I think it is to tell people from the beginning that you are not going to tell them what to do or what to think but help them decide for themselves—that really hits a chord in people.

Snowden: I'm wondering too about the way you interacted with participants—the kinds of relationships you built.

Shure: Well, I think, before they knew me, they may have seen me as not particularly authoritative. I'm not sure, but I was told later by the assistant director of Get Set that people appreciated how I didn't come into the schools with an "I'm-going-to-take-over" attitude. It's important to let people know that we are all learning together, that one person doesn't have all the answers.

I really believe that had a lot to do with it, but, on the other hand, I'm not totally naive. We did have a government grant, and we did pay the teachers and parents to train. Plus, we provided them with puppets, pictures, and trinkets for the kids—things I'm sure they were happy to receive. So, there were a lot of factors that contributed to everyone's participation.

Snowden: Let's talk for a few minutes about your research design. How did the final evaluation design evolve?

Shure: Well, one thing about research design is the idea of having a training group and then having a control group to evaluate the effects of training. By the way, there were two aspects of research to this program. One was to test the theory of interpersonal problem-solving skills as behavioral mediators. For that, you would not really need a control group, because you could just do within-group correlations of those given problem-solving training, comparing those whose behavior improved with those whose behavior did not. But if you are looking at it from the point of view of program evaluation, then you need a control group, because, if trained children improve as a group from their starting point, you don't know whether it is because they are a year older or whether your giving them attention was a factor or what.

We also had a placebo group the year we trained children ourselves. Here, the teachers didn't know what each child was going out of the room for. Some of the children went out for training, and some got mere attention; for that, we still had teacher-led games, but it was animal imitations and the like, not problem-solving training. For placebo children, improvement was significantly less than for the training group, although it was slightly more than the complete no-treatment group. Attention alone has some effect on behavior in children, but it didn't affect their thinking, and the behavioral improvement was not nearly as consistent as the program-trained group. Given that, plus the internal within-training-group correlations, the fact that teachers didn't know their cognitive scores and rated all kinds of behaviors, plus other changes that I have mentioned in the chapter, we were able to demonstrate the validity of our design. I emphasize this, because, although we had cohesiveness, that was not what caused the positive results of our research.

Snowden: Could you talk about how you wound up using the entire class—that is, in teacher training?

Shure: During our very first pilot year, when we took children out of the classroom, we wanted to include every teacher in the school (four of them). We wanted to get different teachers' ratings on the children, because we didn't want ratings to be affected by the personality of any one teacher. Some children in each class were in the no-treatment group and did not go out. After a while, some of them got upset, because they wanted to go out for games, too. That was one reason. Another reason was that, later, we added informal dialogues to the training. The dialogues are our way of teaching teachers and parents how to extend the language of this formal training program to situations where children are really having a problem or creating one. The teacher is going to say in the formal part of the script, in the problem-solving section, "What can this child do to solve this problem?" and then ask him what might happen if he tries that. If, ten minutes later, when the children are back in free play, the teacher says, "Johnny, I told you not to hit— you should ask!" she would be undoing the very thing that she just did. So we said, "Why not extend the same kind of talk when the child is really having a problem?" For that kind of dialoguing, to have the teacher think, "Well, this is a control child, and I can't talk with him, and this is a training child, and I can" is ridiculous, and so we decided to take whole classes in another school for our control, where the teacher wouldn't even know about the training program.

Snowden: The dialoguing, or the practice of problem-solving skills outside designated instruction, suggests that the culture of the classroom may have been changed as a by-product of training. Were pervasive changes evident in characteristic modes of classroom interaction?

Shure: From the research point of view, somebody can say, "How do you know it isn't just the way the kids started talking to each other; how do you know it's your formal script?" I don't really care which one it was; to us, it was the total package. There was no point in the teacher undoing informally what she did formally. So, after it became obvious to us that it made sense to extend the dialoguing, we made the informal dialogue techniques part of the training program. The point is that, even though I am a researcher and am concerned about whether what we are training is what is mediating the behavior change, I am not concerned about whether it's page 6 of the script or page 8 of the script that's doing it, or whether it's the informal dialogues or the formal lessons. To me, it's the total package, and we made the informal dialoguing part of the training program. We've never done one without the other; that would be an interesting study someday. It just doesn't make any sense to me to think that twenty minutes of formal training without extended application in the classroom would have the same effect.

Snowden: And what about the way the children interacted?

Shure: It was very interesting, because, in talking with the teachers about their impressions of the program when they finished training, one brought out a very enlightening viewpoint on it. He said that, after a while, they don't have to apply the whole dialogue. Once they start it, the kids finish it themselves. A whole dialogue consists of asking the child for alternative solutions, what might happen next, how each child feels about the situation, and so on. After a while, all the teacher has to say to a child who grabbed to get a toy, is, "Grabbing is one way," and the child will say, "And I can ask him, that's another way." Sometimes they use concepts taught in the program by themselves, such as when they are reading a story book.

By the way, a very important point, so I don't mislead anybody—we are not trying to make six-year-olds out of four-year-olds. We are just trying to bring deficient kids up to the level of efficient ones—what we know from our pretesting that efficient four-year-olds can do. Nontrained, efficient children before training can think of solutions to problems, if given the opportunity. So we are not training skills that some four-year-olds don't have.

Snowden: Perhaps another aspect of changed classroom culture would be differences in teachers' methods for handling problems with children.

Shure: You know, it's interesting, because a lot of teachers think they apply problem-solving techniques with children already, and the reason is because some teachers do talk to children about the way people feel. And it is very common for a teacher to ask, "Why did you do that?" But very few carry it the one step further and include the problem-solving steps in the process.

Snowden: What do you see as the theoretical significance of your work?

Shure: That problem-solving skills mediate social adjustment. Instead of saying that, if one could be relieved of tension and conflict, then one could think straight, one could also say the opposite. If one could think straight, one might be relieved of tension and conflict. We are not claiming that ours is the only way to change behavior. We just claim that it is another way, and it works, and it seems to be well received by those who do it. But it is a different technique from those used by other kinds of theorists. The main thing for us is that children develop a style of thinking, so they can evaluate what they do and turn to another way to solve a problem if need be.

Snowden: It seems also possible that, if the child thinks of alternatives and decides that this is really what he wants to do, and you end up disagreeing, it's because there is a genuine disagreement, not because the child is stymied and got fixed on this one course of action.

Shure: In the initial part of the training, a child might say or do something you don't like, and it might be because he can't think of anything else. Your immediate tendency is to suggest something. But we don't (unless, of course, there is possibility of real harm), because our whole philosophy is that children have to learn to think for themselves. Also, we don't say a parent or teacher should never get angry with a child. That would be abnormal and unhealthy, and anger is a problem the child has to learn to deal with. You can ask for solutions when things are emotional, but, when things get too hot, you have to wait.

Snowden: It's a long project, and it has accomplished a fair amount. I'm wondering what its biggest accomplishments are.

Shure: It depends on who you are. If you're a researcher, you have one set of ideas; if you're a teacher, you would see it from a different perspective; if you're a school administrator, well . . . it depends on whose point of view you're talking about.

Snowden: How does it sort out for you?

Shure: To me, the most important accomplishment is that I think we contributed a new approach to working with children that works. And people like it. People may disagree, but I really feel strongly about not telling children what to do. Adults have to learn patience, just as the children do.

Snowden: What do you think it would take to do this with different kinds of children? Do you think there are differences among socioeconomic classes?

Shure: As a group, yes. Middle-class children come out with higher group means on scores. But I found a lot of overlap. A lot of our inner-city children were very well adjusted and were very good problem-solvers. And lots of them did better than some of the children in the central city. People who use our program with middle-class children go through the early games a little faster than we did, but all games should still be included because of their needed association for later lessons. Having fun with the word *different,* for example, by tapping your head, then doing something different (patting your knee), rings a bell when children are later asked if they can think of a different idea. And regardless of social class, the approach is still the same—teaching children how, not what, to think.

Snowden: The school system and teachers have shown a lot of interest in the program, as evidenced by their willingness to carry forward into the service-delivery phase. I'm wondering if you can comment on some of the differences between you and many of these people—racial differences, socioeconomic differences, and so on.

Shure: I was never aware of any racial problems. The only problem I had was in one particular Get Set Center the very first year. I did not meet the supervisor, which at that time, I didn't realize was so crucial. When she found out I was in the school, she said, "Who is that Dr. Shure? Is she taking over my center?" So, it wasn't a racial issue; it was a "who-is-that-stranger-in-my-school" issue. That taught me a lesson. I never let that happen again. By the way, Get Set had white teachers as well as black ones, so I wasn't the only white person in the building. Maybe that had something to do with it.

Snowden: Let me ask, as a final question, something about what the project has meant to you personally.

Shure: Besides the fact that I really felt good about changing the behavior of impulsive and inhibited children, it gave me other satisfactions, too. After the training was done, and we had the numbers, we would look at the results, and it was like election night. We would run something through the calculator wondering "Does it work?" "Doesn't it work?" And when we saw it did, what a moment! It's a thrill to take my program into the community, have it work, and have people respond to me both as a professional and as a person.

4

Reducing Heart Disease Risk Using the Mass Media:
Comparing the Effects on Three Communities

Nathan Maccoby
Janet Alexander

The initial impetus for the Three-Community Study and its parent organization, the Stanford Heart Disease Prevention Program (SHDPP), came from a recognition of cardiovascular disease as a major public health problem. In the 1950s, cardiovascular epidemiologists were learning that heart disease had reached epidemic proportions in the developed world. In the 1960s, over one-half of all deaths in the United States were due to some form of cardiovascular disease, with coronary heart disease affecting younger and younger age groups (American Heart Association, 1972). In 1970, despite great strides on many medical fronts, a forty-five-year-old U.S. male had only a slightly greater life expectancy than did his forebears at the turn of the century (Lew and Seltzer, 1970).

In the report of the Inter-Society Commission for Heart Disease Resources (1970), the preponderance of evidence indicated that the epidemic of premature coronary heart disease in the United States (in the under-sixty age groups) resulted principally from three widely prevalent risk factors—smoking, high serum cholesterol, and hypertension. Their view was that "the relationship between these risk factors and the development of coronary heart disease is probably causal." As consensus formed around the three primary risk factors, there was debate, which continues still, on their relative importance and that of other risk factors, such as age, sex, genetic predisposition, perceived stress, or harmful emotional life-styles. Also, differences of opinion were openly expressed within the medical profession as to whether risk status could be modified through behavior change (for example, by fat modification in the diet).

By 1970, the National Heart, Lung, and Blood Institute was laying the groundwork for an ambitious effort of mounting several long-term clinical trials. But they would take a decade to complete, and a question would remain as to what degree one could generalize the effects obtained with high-risk groups in a clinical setting to free-living, apparently healthy populations. Another view was that of the necessity for educating the population at large as soon as possible. From the primary prevention perspective, the nature of atherosclerosis and its widespread distribution across large segments of the population called for a new kind of preventive medicine (Hatch, 1968). The prevention perspective advocated that the flow of knowledge to the public should not be inhibited by the debate over how much was known, what was ultimately knowable, how final were the conclusions about its application to human behavior, and how much more research would be needed for definitive conclusions.

The Stanford group decided that they could best contribute by participating in the clinical trials while also undertaking parallel research in risk reduction through behavior change for the population at large. If, ten years hence, the clinical trials were to conclude that risk reduction was effective in reducing the deaths from coronary heart disease, then proven methods would be needed immediately to help people change the antecedent behavior.

John W. Farquhar, M.D., and Stanford Medical School coresearchers Peter D. Wood, Byron W. Brown, Jr., William Haskell, and Michael Stern joined in a decision in early 1970 to develop a research plan to explore efficient means of risk reduction in the population at large and to participate in the clinical trials. In Farquhar's view, it would require a broadly interdisciplinary team of biomedical and social scientists to address the wide range of questions raised by the research problem. This led him to reach beyond medical science and to consult with Maccoby and the Department of Communication and other behavioral scientists. In early 1970, this group began to assess how best to go about a public education program in cardiovascular disease risk reduction.

Since the primary risk factors of smoking, diet, and hypertension were distributed across large segments of the total adult population, techniques that would reach large numbers of people were called for. At this point, the idea of intervening in total communities via mass media was introduced. Reviewing the projected limitations in resources and manpower, the decision was reached to limit the target population to all adults ages thirty-five to fifty-nine.

As a result of interaction between the communication researchers, psychologists, communication specialists, and others, Farquhar and the biomedical scientists made a basic change in the research plan. They turned the planning from a medical model, concerned with high-risk populations and key health professional opinion leaders, to a more complex but potentially more effective community model, relying principally on communication as the basic intervention tool. Discussion then shifted to considering a research design appropriate to this model and a behavior-change strategy appropriate to the target population.

Since the media campaign was to be directed at entire communities, random assignment of individuals to the treatment or control condition was not feasible. An equally rigorous experimental method, treating a large number of entire geographically defined populations as single units and randomly assigning some of these communities to treatment and some to control conditions, was not administratively possible. We concluded that the most realistic compromise between feasibility and rigor was a quasi-experimental research approach (Campbell and Stanley, 1966) on a small number of experimental units.

The basic intent of the study design, as it finally emerged, was to discover the magnitude of change in attitude, motivation, and behavior that may be achieved by mass media alone. We wanted to provide public health policy makers with a demonstration of cost-effective methods of community-wide public health education. The basis of our thinking was the assumption that mass media had the potential to reach many more people than would methods of personal contact and would be inherently less expensive per unit of population reached.

In addition, our plan was to apply personal contact to a subset of individuals in one of two communities to add interesting dimensions to the basic and primary question of the effectiveness of mass media. These dimensions were: (1) the maximum likelihood of change that we assumed to result from the combined treatment of mass media plus intensive instruction; (2) in the town with the combined treatment, we would be able to see evidence for the catalytic effect of the intensively instructed participants on others and to note the degree to which such diffusion enhances effects or generates its own effects; (3) by organizing and carrying out intensive instruction at the community level, within the context of a media campaign, we could gain more experience in the intensive-instruction group process, which we hoped would lead to new ideas on the topic; and (4) the instructional process would act as a community laboratory to locate particularly effective elements that could be subsequently applied to mass media to help make the campaign more effective.

The design was limited to the three conditions of no treatment, treatment by media only, and treatment by media plus intensive interpersonal instruction. The fourth logical experimental condition, that of a town with only the intensive instruction as intervention, was given the lowest priority. It was not incorporated into the design, as it appeared extremely unlikely that such a labor-intensive educational program could ever be adopted as a public health program for the population at large. Thus, after discussing many alternatives, the choice was a before-after design (with a small after-only group) to involve three communities. Resource limitations led to this three-city design, an admitted compromise of the more desirable (many units, randomly allocated to treatment or control) with the feasible.

From the early planning stages of the project, we were faced with some fundamental problems that, all too often, most of us ignore when working in the laboratory. First, we were confronted with the fact that our ultimate goal was neither attitude change nor education. In this study, the bottom line was behavior change. And, to make the problem just a bit more challenging, it required long-term change of behaviors that are very important to people—basic life-style behaviors. For the intensive-instruction component, a model drawing primarily on the theory and technique of behavior modification and based primarily on the work of Bandura (1969, 1971) and others was devised. This method focuses on the specific behaviors to be changed rather than on global attitudes, psycho-dynamic constructs, or information alone. The final objective was for these new behaviors to become self-rewarding. The client would learn to derive positive value from the practice of the new behaviors—to want to do them for their own sake or to be rewarded without the instructor's intervention. The plan that emerged used social learning and behavior modification theory in a group-dynamic framework. Combined with the media campaign, participation in the group would trigger additional risk reduction over a several-month period. The group would provide subject interaction, the modeling of new behaviors, and self-report feedback systems. The plan of action was worked out and pretested with the cooperation of the nearby Varian Corporation (Meyer and Henderson, 1974).

When preparing our mass-media component, our knowledge of the prior research showing its limited effectiveness in modifying behavior gave rise to concerns and misgivings (Bauer, 1964; Griffiths and Knutson, 1960; Hyman and Sheatsley, 1947; Klapper, 1960; Katz and Lazarsfeld, 1955; O'Keefe, 1971; Star and Hughes, 1950; Udry, 1972). Nevertheless, we felt that, learning from the work of others (Cartwright, 1949; Mendelsohn, 1973) and from new research, we could devise a mass media campaign that would have a reasonable chance of success. To increase those chances of success, we concentrated on designing a program that, at a minimum, met the following criteria:

1. Establish specific objectives. Objectives must be set for both the total campaign and the various parts of the campaign, over time.

2. Define audience segments. Specific messages with specific

goals must be sent through channels used by each specific target audiences. The audience is not a homogeneous group.

3. Create clear and useful messages. Messages must relate to specific objectives and be readily comprehensible to the audience; provide clear directions for the audience to take action.

4. Utilize creative scheduling. Audience segments can only be reached by scheduling messages when and where they are most likely to be attending. Usually media time or space offered gratis as a public service precludes such careful placement, but effective work with the media gatekeepers can sometimes get around this problem.

5. It is necessary to make the messages important and salient to the individual and to create motivation for some behavioral action.

6. Stimulate interpersonal communication. Social comparison and social-influence processes are critical supplements to the mass media.

7. Advocate appropriate kinds of behavior change. Simple, well-defined courses of action to be done in the short term are more likely to be implemented in the target audience than are complex, diffuse, or poorly defined courses of action to be carried out over the long term.

8. Obtain regular feedback through process evaluation to assess campaign progress.

9. Obtain long-term commitments for campaign support. Short-term campaigns often lead to no substantial effects. Also, delayed effects are likely and need to be observed well after the end of the campaign.

These and other considerations were molded together into the design for the Three-Community Study. In October 1970, the proposal was submitted to the National Heart, Lung, and Blood Institute (NHLBI). In June of 1971, notice was received of project approval and funding; Farquhar became the principal investigator of a five-year research project in community cardiovascular risk-reduction methods and principal investigator of one of the seventeen collaborative centers in the Lipid Research Clinic's cholesterol-lowering trial. Thus, the Stanford Heart Disease Prevention Program (SHDPP) was launched.

Research Methods and Results

Three roughly comparable communities in northern California were selected for the study (Maccoby and Farquhar, 1975). Tracy was chosen as a control, because it was relatively distant and thus isolated from media in the other communities. Gilroy and Watsonville, the other two communities, shared some media channels (television and radio), but each town had its own newspaper. Watsonville and Gilroy received different strategies of health education during the two campaign years (C1, C2), with a reduced or maintenance program presented in the third year (C3). Gilroy received health education through the mass media alone; Watsonville received education through the mass media and, for a selected high-risk group, intensive instruction. The timing of the surveys and community educational campaign and instruction, from 1972 to 1975, is presented in Figure 1. Surveys were conducted in the fall of the year: Watsonville, September-October; Gilroy, October-November; Tracy, November-December. Media campaigns were directed at all participants in the two treatment communities. Intensive instruction was conducted among two-thirds of the high-risk participants in Watsonville and their spouses.

To assess the effects of these interventions, data were gathered at a baseline survey (Survey 1 or S1) through interviews and medical examinations of a random (multistage probability) sample of persons aged thirty-five to fifty-nine from each of the three communities. Follow-up data were obtained at yearly intervals from the same group over the subsequent three years (S2, S3, S4). Baseline data were gathered by home interviewers, but the initial medical assessment took place in temporary survey centers set up in each town. In subsequent surveys, all measures were taken during one month in temporary community facilities (churches, gyms, city halls). An additional sample (the after-only sample) was surveyed in each community only in 1973, after the end of the first campaign year, to observe the effects of the measurement process itself. Table 1 shows selected town characteristics and response rates.

The annual interviews in the three communities were de-

Figure 1. Survey and Campaign Sequences in the Three Communities[a]

	1972 →	1973 →		1974 →		1975 →	
Watsonville (W)	Baseline Survey (S1)	• Media campaign • Intensive instruction (II) for 2/3 of high risk participants	Second Survey (S2)	• Media campaign • Intensive instruction (II) for 2/3 of high risk participants	Third Survey (S3)	• Maintenance (low-level) Media campaign • II: Summer Follow-up	Fourth Survey (S4)
Gilroy (G)	Baseline Survey (S1)	• Media campaign	Second Survey (S2)	• Media campaign	Third Survey (S3)	• Maintenance (low-level) Media campaign	Fourth Survey (S4)
Tracy (T)	Baseline Survey (S1)		Second Survey (S2)		Third Survey (S3)		Fourth Survey (S4)

[a]From Farquhar, 1978.

**Table 1. Demographic Characteristics and Survey
Response Rates in Each of Three Communities**

Characteristics of the Community Groups	Tracy	Gilroy	Watsonville
Total population (1970 census)	14,724	12,665	14,569
Population (35–59 years of age)	4,283	3,224	4,115
Mean age of 35–59-year-old group (years)	47.0	46.2	47.6
Male/female ratio of 35–59 age group	0.96	0.88	0.86
Random Sample (Ages 35–59)			
Original sample	659	659	833
Natural attrition (migration or death)	74	79	107
Potential participants for all three surveys	585	580	726
Percent of original sample	88.8	88.0	87.1
Refusals and dropouts over two years	201	183	303
Participants completing first and third survey	418	427	449
Percent of potential participants	72	74	62
Mean age at October, 1972 (years)	46.9	45.8	48.4
Male/female ratio	0.84	0.78	0.75
Spanish speaking (percent)	3.1	8.3	7.8
Bilingual (percent)	6.0	17.9	9.5
Completed high school (percent)	68.5	63.5	64.7
Annual family income above $10,000 (percent)	68.9	65.3	62.2

signed to observe both initial levels in knowledge, attitudes, and individual behavior related to cardiovascular risk. The end point of greatest interest was the overall summation of risk of coronary heart disease. The risk score, based on the longitudinal data from the Framingham Study (Truett, Cornfield and Kannel, 1967), predicts a person's probability of developing coronary heart disease within twelve years. The person's age, sex, plasma cholesterol concentration, systolic blood pressure, relative weight, smoking rate, and electrocardiographic findings enter into the equation. This measure allowed us to identify a high-risk study group in each town and to monitor changes in the estimated risk of coronary heart disease. Also, the surveys covered demographic information, knowledge, attitude, and behavioral variables. Knowledge of risk factors was measured with a test of knowledge about dietary and other risk factors associated with coronary heart disease based on twenty-five variables. Of these twenty-five items, three were concerned with the role of smoking in heart disease, fourteen with eating habits and heart disease, four with physical activity, two with body weight, and two with general information about heart disease.

Eating habits were assessed to allow estimation of regular intake of cholesterol, saturated and polyunsaturated fats, salt, sugar, and alcohol. The physiological data required to compute the overall risk status were obtained. Plasma insulin concentration, plasma renin concentration, and urinary sodium were also determined. Participants' self-reports on their daily rates of cigarette, pipe, or cigar smoking were validated through an assay of plasma thiocyanate concentration (which indicated that only about 4 percent of those reporting abstinence may have given inaccurate reports).

The risk-reduction program recommended dietary habits for all participants, which, if followed, would lead to reduced intake of saturated fat, cholesterol, salt, sugar, and alcohol. Also, it focused on reduction in body weight through caloric reduction and increased physical activity and on smoking cessation or how to reduce the daily rate of cigarette consumption. The basic risk-reduction messages were transformed into formats or vehicles appropriate for distribution through the mass media (television spots, direct mail, booklets, radio spots, newspaper columns and ads, bus cards, and so on). Because of the sizable Spanish-speaking population in the communities, both a Spanish campaign and an English campaign were presented. The media campaign began in January 1973 (at the close of the initial survey period) and continued for nine months in 1973. It stopped during the second survey (October-December 1973) and then continued for nine more months in 1974, until the third survey period (S3). A low-level campaign (C3) began several months after the third survey for the April-September 1975 period and was followed by the fourth and final survey (S4) of the study cohort.

From the baseline survey data, we identified those 113 Watsonville participants in the top quartile of risk of coronary heart disease according to the multiple-logistic formula. A randomized experiment among this subsample of persons at higher levels of risk for cardiovascular disease was designed. Intensive face-to-face instruction occurred for two-thirds of this group (N = 77); the remaining people (N = 56) from this group (exposed only to health education through the media) became the reference group. High-risk subsamples were also identified in Gilroy and Tracy and observed as separate study groups.

The intensive-instruction educational effort was launched in the spring of 1972, six months after the first baseline survey, and was conducted intensively over a ten-week period. These individuals and their physicians were informed by letter of their relatively high-risk status and were invited with their spouses to participate in the group sessions. One hundred seven of 113 participants originally assigned to receive intensive instruction were successfully recruited for treatment, and seventy-seven high-risk individuals (and thirty-four spouses) completed all three interviews and examinations.

The baseline data from the three communities are compared with those obtained one and two years following. Demographic characteristics and response rates for the samples are presented in Table 1. Analyses of characteristics of refusals and dropouts revealed these groups to be slightly younger and to average less income and education. The magnitude of possible biases in projecting sample effects to the total community populations are readily estimated, if one assumes no effect of our campaigns on these individuals.

The main finding is that both the media treatment and media plus face-to-face instruction treatment (as represented by results for Gilroy and Watsonville total participants) show evidence of positive risk-reduction effects after two years, as compared with the reference group in Tracy. At the end of the second year, the level of estimated coronary disease risk decreased by 17 to 18 percent in the treatment community samples, but it increased by more than 6 percent in Tracy (Farquhar and others, 1977). Information levels, attitudes, and behaviors changed more for the people in the two treatment towns than for those in the control town. In general, subject groups in Watsonville changed more than their counterparts in Gilroy, particularly during the first year. Furthermore, those in the high-risk intensive-instruction group changed more quickly and more substantially than those exposed only to the general mass media campaign. However, in the second year, the groups exposed only to the media show important further gains; the apparent difference between the effects of media and media plus face-to-face instruction on overall risk is diminished and is no longer statistically significant. The media plus intensive instruction created effects more quickly, but similar reductions were achieved through mass media alone after an additional year.

At the end of the first year, the Watsonville high-risk participants in intensive instruction outperformed the control group in reduction of smoking, systolic blood pressure, plasma cholesterol, and overall risk. However, by the end of the second year, only the difference in smoking reduction remained. For smoking in the full samples, face-to-face instruction plus mass media resulted in greater decrease in smoking than Gilroy's mass media treatment alone and an even greater difference, as compared with the control city. Media alone, although less effective than the combined media and instruction, was effective in producing modest changes in self-reported smoking behavior.

Several other publications contain more extensive reports on campaign results after one and two years. Maccoby and others (1977) present details on changes after the first year. The results of the campaign on dietary behavior after two years are reported by Stern and others (1976). The article includes a more complete description of the sampling methods, the composition of the twelve study groups, and measures of effects for those groups on diet and overall risk. For diet, the main findings were substantial, and significant reductions often occurred in cholesterol consumption and saturated-fat consumption for men and women in the two treatment towns. Again, we find that the Watsonville groups showed much greater initial reductions, as compared with Gilroy, but, in some cases, differences that were significant at the end of year one were not significant at the end of year two, whereas others held up strongly. Mass media cohorts tended to outperform the Tracy study groups. Also, we observed that the more the participants learned, the more they changed their behavior and thus their estimated overall risk of heart disease (Maccoby and others, 1977). In both treatment towns, increases in activity and relative decreases in weight were not noted, but changes in smoking (particularly for Watsonville), in dietary practices, and in blood pressure led to the improvements in overall risk status.

The data presented in this and other reports are interesting in many ways, but we must acknowledge some uncertainties and possible artifacts in interpretation of our results. Our participants were randomly selected from open populations to provide a better basis for generalization to future public health education efforts. But, since we were able to recruit only about two-thirds of the total sample of eligible participants selected in the three surveys, the generalizability of our results may be limited by that ratio. The fact that refusals and drop-outs tended to be younger, of lower income, and of lower education may bias results somewhat. Also, we must acknowledge that we did not produce, or we were unable to measure accurately, any increase in physical-activity level in the treatment communities, nor were we able to help participants learn to achieve sustained weight loss.

Despite reservations and shortcomings, we are encouraged by the results that we have observed. Finding that media and face-to-face health education can affect knowledge and behavior has confirmed our most hopeful expectations. Beneficial changes in risk factors that might be considered of relatively minor degree individually can combine to yield a sizable reduction in overall cardiovascular risk. We tentatively attribute much of the success of the community education campaigns to the synergistic interaction of multiple educational inputs and to interpersonal communication stimulated by application of these inputs in a community setting. Of particular interest is the finding that, in general, the changes in knowledge, behavior, and physiologic end points observed in the first year of treatment were maintained and even improved in the second year of study.

Processes of Research in the Community

In this section, we focus on several background areas of interest to researchers, as they go about putting theory into practice and research in the community. The central idea is that the plans of researchers become the initial blueprints, from which the project then unfolds. Researchers may be the architects, but the final product also requires the work of many builders, craftsmen, and journeymen.

Design Changes.   Some changes were anticipated from the inception of the project. In our view, the media education program was planned to be evolutionary in nature. Formative evaluation and feedback systems were built in from the beginning to provide planners with information that was in turn used to direct subsequent actions. But some changes were the result of new funding and staff additions. Plans shifted considerably, when professional staff was added (J. Alexander as media coordinator and director of media and, later, James Cusenza as Spanish language producer and Kent Gibson as English producer). After obtaining supplemental funding, we added a second year to the media campaign and were also able to add an equally intensive Spanish language campaign.

Community Cooperation.   Community reaction to our project was another factor to consider. A community must see some import in the problem area to be motivated to want to do something about it. Passive tolerance of the research may not be sufficient. After funding was secured, our first step was to establish acceptance and support of the project from the local physicians, health professionals, medical society, hospital staffs, and key civic leaders. Initial contact was made with the county medical society and key physicians and hospital officials by telephone and letter. Appointments were made for initial visits by a team (Farquhar, Stern, Wood, and Maccoby) to present the Three-Community Study plans. During these meetings, SHDPP investigators would explain the study purpose and design, answer questions, and request an expression of consent or agreement in principle to the project. After these initial contacts, Breitrose, Haskell, Maccoby, Alexander, and others visited with the city mayors, key media gatekeepers, and other civic leaders.

As a result of the early meetings, the media people perceived the immediate importance and utility of the subject matter to their audience or readership and its general importance to others in the long run. In a sense, they responded to the "public good" issues involved and evidenced a sincere sense of civic responsibility in their roles as media gatekeepers. Beyond that, the materials we provided were not only free and of high professional quality but also, from their point of view, had impeccable credibility. They were happy to have Stanford University's School of Medicine as a source for health education materials; they were glad to use them if (and only if) those materials were an easy fit with their existing formats and program needs and were at least up to local professional standards. One way we were able to thank each of the cooperating broadcast outlets was to let the Federal Communications Commission (FCC) know the important role media managers had played in program success and the important public service they had performed for their community.

Campaign Design.   An evolutionary approach to intervention design requires a constant flow of evaluative data. Our annual surveys were therefore supplemented with a series of systematic but informal small-scale information-gathering efforts or *mini-surveys.* Each was designed to provide media planners with immediate feedback on the public's awareness, acceptance, and response to specified sets of media events as well as to gauge the progress to date. The way such mini-surveys were analyzed and put into action is of some interest. Usually, no formal tabulations and reports were made at the time. The favored reporting method was for the campaign staff to sit around a table and each code a section of the questionnaires, make a draft table, and note the main results on the table. When this was done, we talked over what we had observed, what we thought it meant, and what it indicated to us in terms of action. Within days, the data were translated into decisions; within a week or two, new plans were underway. This information was so useful and timely and was obtainable at such reasonable costs (for the first mini-survey, about fifteen days of staff time and about $1,000 in media kits, forms, interviewer training, and expenses) that we became dedicated to process evaluation. This approach to evaluating and planning the campaign became a permanent feature of campaign management.

The Spanish Campaign.   In the Three-Community Study, we found that a significant segment of the population spoke only Spanish. The 1970 census data indicated that approximately 30 percent of the total population would have Spanish surnames; we found 10 to 15 percent Spanish-speaking and about 15 to 20 percent bilingual. These facts led us to design and mount two distinct campaigns, one in English and one in Spanish.

The existence of such a large ethnic group within both towns had both theoretical and action relevance for media planners. It suggested that there would be styles of culturally determined behavior, which had implications for the kind of behavior changes needed and the barriers to that change. Differential dietary and other risk-factor behavior (less smoking, greater relative weight), as compared with the Anglo population, appeared to exist. These facts had to be taken into account in the design and production of a media campaign for the Spanish-speaking population. Even if one assumed that Mexican-Americans who speak Spanish develop heart disease at equivalent rates with Anglos (although that was unclear in 1972), it was posited as quite unlikely that the patterns of risk-related living habits would be similar for Spanish-speaking and English-speaking persons. Later data analyses revealed that, in fact, the overall risk for those speaking only Spanish was higher but was constituted in quite different ways (Stern, 1975).

Also, we were concerned about the distribution of effects—the equity with which all population segments would be treated by the campaign. Tichenor, Donohue, and Olien (1970) had brought attention to the possibilities of creating even larger knowledge gaps due to varying patterns of media usage among various socio-economic groups.

Media selection was based on an analysis of the reported media-use patterns of the Spanish-speaking. Radio seemed to be the most effective means of reaching the Spanish-speaking target audience. We ascertained that almost all the Spanish-speaking radio listeners could be reached through the three local radio stations that broadcast a significant amount of programming in Spanish. Accordingly, production and budget priorities were given to Spanish radio, and, as it turned out, approximately 90 percent of our radio production dollars and energy were spent on Spanish radio productions. We needed to gain the confidence of all the managers of Spanish-language media channels, not only as representatives of a worthwhile program that needed free airtime, but also as media and health professionals sensitive to the ethnolinguistic differences of that audience. There was extensive personal contact between our program's representatives and the individual radio station personnel. This resulted in very successful scheduling of our public service announcements and programs. Our contacts in the Spanish-language radio stations brought these issues to our attention: (1) If they were to be given air time, public service announcements had to be of the same quality as commercial announcements; (2) Programs should be sensitive to the regional linquistic differences within the Spanish-speaking population; (3) The most usable media formats would be thirty- or sixty-second public service announcements and five-minute public service programs.

One problem in producing Spanish-language media is that the producers must work within a predominantly English-speaking environment. In our case, almost all the scientists were monolingual (English) and monocultural. Thus, the campaign content was specified in English, argued out in English, written down in English, and conceived in terms of the academic Anglo experience. The job of producing a Spanish campaign was not so much one of translation but rather of transforming the whole conceptual scheme, as well as the content, aims, and specific objectives, in ways that were appropriate and useful to those who spoke only Spanish. The difficulty was multiplied by the lack of expert bilingual consultation readily available within the scientific team.

Much effort went into locating media producers, advisers, counselors, and content experts who were professionally trained in the subject matter of the campaign (nutritionists and physicians, for example) and who were also fluent in Spanish and English. The project's success in reaching the Spanish-speaking audience in a way that was meaningful and effective for them is largely due to the multicultural expertise of James Cusenza and the bilingual team he recruited and trained. Although not Chicano himself, his multicultural world-view and fluency in six languages made him highly effective in achieving SHDPP goals in the Spanish media campaign. Cusenza shaped project content in quite different ways for Spanish than for English. For example, during the first year of the campaign, he developed a five-minute *radionovela* — a series of radio programs with a soap-opera format, which has had great popularity with a Spanish-speaking audience. These dramas enjoyed success not only with their listening audience but also with the cooperating radio stations. Much of the success of our intervention program goes to our good luck in recruiting a few such talented and dedicated people, a critical aspect of applied community research that is often overlooked and underrated.

Standardizing the Independent Variables. In the design of field experiments, the selection of communities often cannot be on a random basis. Thus, one does not have a true experiment at all, and a number of threats to validity arise (Campbell and Stanley,

1966; Cook and Campbell, 1976). For example, the problem of standardizing the independent variables proved somewhat trouble-some for the media planners. Although we did our best to have functionally comparable media inputs into the two intervention towns, we sometimes were faced with unequal cooperation from media outlets. In particular, in the first campaign year, the news-paper in one town provided far fewer column inches per week to our newspaper columns than did the paper in the other town. Addi-tional discussions with the managing editor and the publisher did nothing to increase the regularity and amount of exposure for the SHDPP columns. Thus, we had to take a number of actions in an attempt to balance the input between towns. We requested and received permission from the cooperating newspaper editor to re-print the newspaper columns. We designed a booklet containing these printed columns in both Spanish and English. Then, we purchased a city-wide mailing list of addresses from a commercial direct-mail firm. We mailed a copy of the booklet to city residents and set up a call-in service that provided a tape recording with Phyllis Ullman, SHDPP nutritionist, giving the same recipes and food advice as in the newspaper columns.

Controls.   If given a chance, probably no community would choose to become the control or reference group. In a longitudinal study design such as ours, ethical issues are raised by the necessity of withholding the intervention from the control community. Our method of dealing with this concern was to provide risk-reduction materials to Tracy participants after the close of the fourth and final survey in 1975. We made up a print-media information pack-age for each survey subject in Tracy and sent it to them via direct mail, with a letter from Dr. Farquhar thanking them for their par-ticipation. Although perhaps less than the ideal, this was the most practical line of action for us at that time. A better solution for future studies, if possible, would be to design the study with a delayed or staged intervention with the early control communities targeted to receive the treatment at a later stage. Costs of such a study design may present a problem to most sponsors, however.

Teamwork.   In any endeavor involving people with highly trained, diverse talents, it is natural that conflicts of opinion and judgment will occur. Our concerns were how to balance the work-ing relationships between the social and biomedical scientists and the whole scientific team against the media team. Media producers typically resent the intrusion of aesthetically and technically untrained behavioral researchers. Conversely, researchers tend to feel frustrated by the lack of use of their findings in shaping campaign strategy or in targeting the communications to obtain specific outcomes. Not working together can lead to annoying problems in the development of instructional and persuasive media, where it is inevitable that content experts and media producers work closely together. In our case, this proved to be less of a major difficulty than is usual, for several reasons. First, we maintained day-to-day control over the mass media design and production through the organization of a core in-house staff. Second, the media producers were themselves trained in both media and evaluation techniques (at Stanford) and had an appreciation of the importance of evaluation and the research constraints within which we all worked. Thus, the problems of communication and lack of shared values between researcher-evaluator or content expert and media producer were not extinguished but kept at a minimum. Finally, we found, as we worked together on productions, that the quality of work improved as we all became more familiar with each other's style of work, limitations, and area of expertise.

Interdisciplinary Research. Interdisciplinary research has much to offer, but it also has its frustrations. Research of the sort we have been conducting simply could not be done without a variety of skills. Medical researchers with various specialties, such as in lipid metabolism, cardiovascular epidemiology, exercise physiology, biochemistry, and biostatistics, as well as interdisciplinary behavioral scientists and media experts, were all important contributors to the research. As noted previously, one of the requirements was that each specialist learn a great deal about the others' specialties—otherwise, the situation of the blind man and the elephant would apply. In an effort to reduce the number of specialists required for this type of work, we now have a postdoctoral training program in which young M.D.s learn about behavioral science and communication and young Ph.D.s learn about cardiovascular medicine.

Initially, one of the chief frustrations was the slow pace with which consensus was reached in research decisions because of the sheer number of researchers such work requires and the differing methodologies employed in various areas of research. As time went on and the staff learned a great deal about each other's work, this source of frustration was reduced somewhat. Another serious problem, at least at Stanford, was that there was no administrative home for such interdisciplinary work. Furthermore, the standards of scholarly accomplishment in our respective disciplines tend to be along intradisciplinary lines. Preventive medicine research has as yet neither the prestige of laboratory research, or bench research, as they call it, nor the status of clinical research. Thus, young people are offered little stimulation to enter this type of work.

Impact of Research. If one of the major purposes of a field study is to discover ways of helping people in a community to change their life-styles more or less permanently, a means of achieving such long-term behavior change must be found. Clearly, a highly important ingredient of such a process must be a system of self-help and self-control (Bandura, 1978). In our future research, we plan to recruit and train community members to perform the training. Thus, the very nature of an important aspect of the intervention method should serve as a way of helping to maintain a long-term new habit. We can see no reason why the model adopted by us for heart-disease prevention could not be adapted to other problems of disease prevention, such as some forms of cancer, drug and alcohol abuse, and immunization. There are important differences. Although cigarette smoking may be a form of addiction in some people, it apparently has nothing like the addictive powers of some other drugs. However, prevention among the young may be the best solution to such problems, and organized community efforts with professional guidance may well be a promising means for achieving prevention.

INTERVIEW WITH NATHAN MACCOBY
AND JANET ALEXANDER

Muñoz: Dr. Maccoby, how did you become involved in this work?
Maccoby: I became involved through a historical accident, I suppose. In the fall of 1970, John W. Farquhar, M.D., director of the program and this project, and Peter Wood, a biochemist, came to visit Henry Breitrose, then head of the Film and Broadcasting Division and now chairman of the Department of Communication. I happened to come by, and I saw these two gentlemen. I said, "Oh, excuse me, Henry; I didn't realize you had company." He said,

"No, you better come in, because what we're talking about is more down your line than mine." So I came in and met Farquhar and Wood. They were planning a community research project on reducing the risk of cardiovascular disease and thought that the project would need a film to help people make the kind of changes in life-style required for risk reduction. Farquhar had recently returned from a sabbatical year spent with Sir Geoffrey Rose at the London School of Tropical Medicine. While there, he had become interested in cardiovascular epidemiology and came back resolved to get out of the laboratory and into the field of primary prevention of cardiovascular disease.

As to the film, I said, "Well, I'm afraid, gentlemen, that creating the changes you're talking about is going to be a little more complicated than making one film." They asked me to explain that, and I did so in terms of theory and research in attitude and behavior change and what we knew about the role of mass media in this process. That was the beginning of my involvement in this project.

Muñoz: How about you, Jan? How did you get involved?

Alexander: Dr. Maccoby brought me into the project in 1971 as media coordinator. Previously, I had been on the department's broadcasting and film faculty to teach production design and writing, among other things. Also, I had put in some time working on a Ph.D. in communication research. Knowing that my ambition was to combine production and research in one job, Dr. Maccoby offered this job to me. I jumped at the chance, of course, and have been at it ever since.

Muñoz: How would you summarize what you found in the Three-Community Study?

Maccoby: We found that the mass media alone were slower to achieve comparable results than were the mass media plus face-to-face intervention. However, at the end of two years, they were equally effective. In terms of the durability of the change produced, we found after three years some evidence of fading in the mass media alone group, more so than in the mass media plus face-to-face group. But we had every reason to feel from our results that mass media alone would be virtually as effective as mass media supplemented by group face-to-face intervention.

Muñoz: Would you summarize what you think are the most important things you've accomplished?

Maccoby: The accomplishment of greatest importance, in my view, is that we have demonstrated that it is possible to achieve changes in behavior sufficient to achieve substantial reductions in cardiovascular risk in communities as a whole. It is most important to note that, in one community, we did it entirely via an exportable method, the mass media. Even the more intensive and expensive combination approach used in another town, mass media supplemented by face-to-face instruction, can probably be modified to be more exportable, we think. This will be a major facet of our new project. Of course, mass media programs have an enormous advantage in their potential to reach vast numbers of Americans at risk; intensive instruction or group counseling of millions of people does not seem feasible.

Alexander: The research literature, at the time we developed the campaign, was quite confusing and contradictory as to what role media might be expected to play in mass health education in a highly developed industrial society where the media are essentially controlled by the private sector. We were able to demonstrate that media have the potential to be an effective teacher and potent force for knowledge gains and behavior change in the health area.

Another point I think our research demonstrates is that people deserve a good deal of credit for their capacity for self-education. We see that people respond in self-helping ways to information coming to them directly through the media. When previous campaigns failed to produce effects, researchers developed a generalized notion that the media audience was passive, obstinate, unyielding, resistant to ideas incompatible with those presently held, and in other ways was a rather hopeless bunch of passive do-nothings. We doubted that this was generally true and based our campaign on the opposite point of view—that people can and will help themselves when given the necessary information and tools.

As a result of the media campaign, we see that people did respond in great numbers with significant effects—not all people on all risk factors, but the results are encouraging. This suggests to me that the responsibility for the lack of significant effects of the past should not just be blamed on the target audience but also to some extent on the source or sending system. The Three-Community Study results suggest that, if it is feasible to provide health information on a systematic basis, the public will respond.

The problem then becomes one of access to the system. Right now, there is an incredible amount of information available to people who can assess it, or purchase it, or spend large amounts of time browsing in bookstores, libraries, and the like. However, that leaves out large numbers of the general public, whose life constraints do not permit such luxuries. And these, of course, are the people who could benefit most from a more public system.

Muñoz: What made the difference? Why did you succeed with media where others had not?

Alexander: We should recall that the research environment in which Dr. Maccoby and I worked was the Institute for Communication Research at Stanford, not the Medical School. We had worked with Wilbur Schramm and had become familiar with the research and practice centering around the uses of mass media for both formal and nonformal educational purposes in the U.S. and in developing countries. Dr. Maccoby was heavily involved with this research, in which media was the central element in some program of behavioral and social change. For example, in the 1960s, he headed an evaluation project in Colombia, through the Peace Corps, on the introduction of television for classroom education. In this milieu, the question was not "Do media work?" but rather how to make them work in this country for the purposes in mind.

Maccoby: We recognized a widespread pessimism about how much media might accomplish in terms of attitude change and behavior change. However, my belief was that we were on firm ground. In my view, there is a substantial body of communication and other research findings that demonstrates the feasibility of a mass media approach. I was convinced myself, in part from my own previous research, some of which goes all the way back to World War II. During the War, for example, I worked with Carl Hovland. We did systematic experimental research and were able to observe that various media were effective tools in many important persuasive and learning tasks. Evidence of the effectiveness of media was found in a whole series of studies we did on the uses of newspapers, magazines, army publications, educational programs, and correspondence schools to influence information, attitudes, and the behavior of American troops. Also, in the 1950s, I worked with Lumsdaine, Sheffield, and others and measured how such factors as audience participation influenced skills learned from film and audiovisual materials. I had every reason to believe, from all this previous psychological and communication research, that films and other media had a great potential to change people's attitudes and to teach people information and skills. We were on sound footing in terms of the selection of mass media as the intervention tool; we knew it had a good chance for success at the theoretical level. We were reasonably confident that the idea had a good chance, but the question was how to do it and how to measure it.

Alexander: The practical aspects of the situation were where we had to concentrate our efforts. What are the barriers to effective communication through the mass media? What are the contingent conditions for success? How can we apply the findings of communication research to avoid as many mistakes as possible and to enhance the effects of media? In one sense, it was a systems problem—how do you put together all the pieces and all the players in the appropriate balance and relationship? How do you command and allocate all the resources, put the forces in line, integrate and manage them, sequence events, and stage the actions? Further, how do you integrate and apply sound psychological and other learning principles in ways that show up in the media product? How do you organize the campaign structure to use state-of-the-art technology and innovative communication, advertising, and marketing principles within a university research context?

Muñoz: Let's go back to that first question—how do you stage the research? What have you learned that you can pass on to students who are reading this?

Alexander: Shoot for the moon. Don't ask for $100,000 to do something for six months or a year; ask for a million dollars to do it for two, three, or five years. In field demonstrations of complex programs, the researcher must recognize that there is a threshold problem in terms of the stimulus. The point to consider is "What are you really trying to test?" What if you don't have adequate resources to produce the stimulus needed to give the idea a fair test? What if you try with only half of what you need? What if the stimulus does not go on long enough or intensively enough, or a necessary piece is missing? Or perhaps the observation and data collection may be inadequate. Then what have you really tested? You've probably found out that, without enough money to do it properly, long enough, completely enough, and so on, the project failed. Such structural constraints on the research situation, rather than the quality of the idea or hypothesis itself, often can be the very factor that gives you no significant differences or no important impact. It's my judgment that much of the conflicting findings in the mass communication literature spring from inappropriate or inadequate choice of intervention actions, inadequate stimulus duration, measurement problems, or other structural defects in design and implementation.

Maccoby: Let me illustrate a point. If you look at a good deal of research in attitude change over the years, you will find that most researchers have used dittoed pieces of paper as their communications. And, even when films or radio programs were made, they were, generally speaking, very amateurish. There are exceptions—for example, during World War II, there was an experiment reported by Hovland, Lumsdaine, and Sheffield on the effects of presenting one point of view alone versus introducing the point with some potential counterarguments. Sheffield worked on that. They produced what they used to call *electrical transcriptions* in Hollywood with a professional radio producer. These were not pieces of paper or some psychologist talking into a microphone. These were professionally produced programs, which varied only in that one of them simply states the point of view being advocated and the other one precedes the statement of this point of view by some potential counterarguments. And that worked beautifully and led to a whole host of research, principally by McGuire. The point is that the history of psychological research in this area is strewn with amateurish communications. And, in our case, we integrated media professionals into the research team and worked together to do it.

Another point, from the measurements perspective, is that, if you don't get detectable change as a result of your intervention, you don't have a chance to compare the relative effects of two or more treatments. We tend to emphasize the independent variable more, since, in this kind of research, researchers are usually much more familiar with the problems and pitfalls associated with measurement and analysis, but this is not so with media programs and the like. You have to have a stimulus that evokes a response of a measurable sort, if you plan to measure whether or not a particular stimulation is more effective than some other stimulation. And that's what is missing from much of the previous research in this field at the community level.

Muñoz: Something that I found personally very interesting was your emphasis on the Spanish-language programming. Could you tell us how you first thought about doing that?

Maccoby: If you go back to the original proposal, there is no mention of Spanish. Before the cities were selected, a Spanish campaign was not in the plans. That was an oversight on our part.

Alexander: Once we found out that we had a sizable Spanish-speaking group in the target population, we began discussing what to do. We asked ourselves, how could we leave out 15 to 20 percent of the population in a community health study like this? But there was no budget allocation for a Spanish-language campaign. We had little enough money to mount a campaign even in one language. So, there was some tearing of hair and gnashing of teeth. Very soon, however, we realized that we simply had to find a way to do a Spanish campaign. Then the problem became one of finding the people to plan and do it. We also went back to the sponsors to say, "We need more money to do this." And the National Heart, Lung, and Blood Institute came through with a supplemental grant for this and other purposes.

Muñoz: Obviously, this comes from a set of personal values that you had, which makes a lot of sense to me but apparently has not made a lot of sense to other people who have done this kind of work before. Where do you think those values came from?

Alexander: In this case, personal values and the project's overriding goals were congruent. After all, we wanted to demonstrate the effects of media education in an equitable way, across the board, for all population segments in a community.

Maccoby: By then (1972), most of us felt that it was very important to do a Spanish campaign. The problem was that someone had to take it on and see to it that it had a high priority, to care about it and to push it along. If Janet had not made up her mind that this must be done and done well, then things might have gone differently. She (and, later, Jim Cusenza) managed the media resources to make this happen, and they demonstrated the need for an equal Spanish effort.

Alexander: If you look at the results of our media campaign in English and Spanish, you will see that the two convey similar messages but are quite distinct. The Spanish campaign is not simply a translation of the English campaign into Spanish. Most materials were produced directly in Spanish, taking into account the different cultural norms and values, different cultural interests and images, different perspectives on health and disease, and a different configuration in life-style relative to cardiovascular risk. The aim was to adapt the content in ways fitting for the Spanish cultural concerns and interests and the local Chicano life-styles and traditions. If personal values play a part, for me the challenge was essentially to be equitable. Those views spring from my personal values of what's right and fair, I suppose. If the campaign didn't work for one group or another, then it was a great failure on my part.

Maccoby: We felt that if we left out the Spanish, we would also be leaving out a disproportionate share of the poorer people. It would not be just leaving out a language group or an ethnic group, it would be leaving out a large proportion of the poor. And that's not fair, that's all.

Muñoz: But it sounds like what it took, given the economic difficulties, was for at least one person in the project to say "This has got to be done." That's what it sounds like.

Maccoby: And Janet was that person.

Alexander: Jim Cusenza and I did push it, and I think we did a good job. We hope others will take this approach in the future. But doing the campaign in Spanish was a challenge at another level. About half way through the second campaign year, we found ourselves the target of a political action on the part of campus Chicano students.

Maccoby: It was well into the second campaign year. We had the Spanish campaign going strong, and we felt pretty good about it. Yet, in the late winter and early spring, we found ourselves being attacked in the campus newspaper by several Ph.D. candidates within our department, along with other Chicano students on campus. Essentially, they challenged the project's right to address the Spanish-speaking. We did not want to counter publicly, because we wanted them to become our graduating Ph.D.s. Incidentally, they all did, and all occupy good positions.

Alexander: I felt their allegations were politically motivated. Even though we had been in production and distribution for nearly two years and were well acquainted with several of these people, they had evidenced very little interest in the Spanish campaign plans. So, we didn't see a point in engaging in a shouting match and mounting a defense in public.

Maccoby: As far as we could see, their main concept was that our research provided a further basis for the economic and psychological exploitation of the Spanish-speaking people. After some debate, and after finding out more about what the Three-Community Study was really all about, this view shifted to an acknowledgment that, although our goals might be perfectly good, our results would be published, and marketers would learn how to manipulate Spanish-speaking people and particularly the poor people, who presumably could not effectively resist. We wanted the research program to go forward with their support, so we discussed it with the students and with representatives of the Spanish-speaking in the community. Eventually, it was resolved by setting up a campus committee of faculty and students to review the Spanish media campaign materials. Of all the media in Spanish, they were able to find only one television spot about which they could mount a specific objection. We withdrew it from the campaign, and, from that time, everything else went forward in a normal fashion. They also later proved helpful in the analysis of the data. Also, by that time, it was summer; the campaign year was coming to an end, and so was the academic school year.

Alexander: Another thing we've observed from past research and our experience in the Three-Community Study is that a media campaign has to be much more pervasive and much more enduring than had been originally thought. This clearly implies that there must be a long-term commitment of resources, a public health commitment, to the prevention concept.

Muñoz: Just as there is now a commitment to treatment, there should be a commitment to prevention?

Maccoby: Yes, exactly. We now see the beginnings of a visible national movement in this direction. Some of the talk is beginning to turn into action. For example, Senator Kennedy and others are promoting a disease-prevention policy with hearings on legislation designed to launch a national program of preventive health services. Among other things, one bill proposes to set up centers for health promotion and five comprehensive community-based programs to demonstrate and evaluate optimal methods for organizing and delivering comprehensive preventive health services to defined populations. We have talked to people in government and in the private sector whose mandates are in various other health areas—cancer, drug and alcohol abuse, and nutrition education, in particular. They have all shown great interest in attempting to apply this kind of model to the study of their problem areas. In that sense, we feel we've helped to open up a whole area of research and action possibilities in public health and prevention.

Muñoz: That's why we were so interested in having your contribution in our book, because we really do feel that it has done that.

Alexander: And our doors are open. The number of people who write, call, and come is truly amazing. We need another grant to support our open-door policy! It seems to be an idea whose time has finally come. Given the number of people we hear from all over the United States and other countries, it almost seems, by virtue of our timing as well as anything else, we've become the touchstone of a movement in cardiovascular disease prevention—or prevention in general.

Maccoby: Various agencies in Canada are very interested in this at both provincial and national levels. At the state level in the U.S., Pennsylvania is launching a project, as are Minnesota, Idaho, Rhode Island, and so on. Besides Pekka Puska's work in Finland, there is activity of this kind in Great Britain, Germany, the Soviet Union, South Africa, Australia, and Israel, just to mention a few. We've been in touch with people from all these places who are in various stages of planning or implementation of projects of this sort. We have either visited them, or they have visited us here, or both. So, we feel that we have helped to open up this whole area of interest. For decades, many people have said that prevention was a good thing; nobody has known quite how to go about it.

We don't think we had the first word or the last word on this; presently, we seem to have some of the most visible words! We are delighted to discover a great interest in our project in a great many other places, and we are gratified to find so many other people getting interested in doing this type of research. It seems that a whole new tradition of research, akin to that of the Three-

Community Study and Puska's Finland study, is getting under way in the U.S. and internationally. We would like to think we helped to get that movement started, and we certainly plan to help it along.

Alexander: We recognize that many types of health professionals have been in this field for a lot longer than we have. However, we can see the important thing about our study is its touchstone qualities. This is certainly not the first time that community-wide health behavior changes have occurred as a result of intervention, but it is the first time that cardiovascular behavior-change programs through mass media education have been successful at a community level within an experimental framework. Thus, the findings can be assessed and evaluated for their generalizability to other areas. In a sense, what was known and believed and done for years about public health is now being recreated into the kind of knowledge that can form the basis of health policy and legislative action in a way that commands resources. It was very interesting for us to develop the knowledge and attempt to report it to the world. Now, it is extremely interesting to watch the policy shifts and actions rippling off from those "pebbles in the pond" reports.

You may be interested to know that a lot of media or marketing people say to us, "Ho Hum, what's new? Media works? We knew that all along." So they did, but that view of media was not at all accepted in biomedical circles and health policy circles. It doesn't become knowledge within a discipline or power center until it's done properly as research, reported, and discussed in meetings. Then, program officials and legislators can say, "Look—here's a scientific basis for doing what I've been wanting to do all along." If the first Three-Community Study report, when it emerged, was the pebble, I'm not sure what the pond is. It's a lot bigger than Dr. Farquhar and Dr. Wood or any of us ever anticipated, as we went through six years of the Three-Community Study.

Muñoz: What implications does your experience have regarding methodology?

Maccoby: Well, I think, for example, that, although it is clear that the controlled experiment is ideal, the controlled experiment often has to be modified, if one is going to find out anything important in the real world. In my experience, at least in the earlier days of psychology, there were people who insisted on the controlled experiment, and I typically was one of them. We said, "The other stuff doesn't tell you anything about cause and effect." Meanwhile, there were some who denigrated the role of the controlled experiment. Now, obviously, psychologists and others have helped lead the way to methods that are in between "hard" and "soft," through use of the field experiment and quasi-experimental designs and the development of statistical techniques, such as time-series analysis, cross-lag panel correlation, and so on. I find that both what the psychologists have to contribute and what the epidemiologists and biostatisticians have to contribute are all important there.

Muñoz: Is there anything else you would like to tell us?

Alexander: It was difficult to get published, and it has been difficult to get re-funded. That may be hard to believe, but it is true. Being multidisciplinary has its distinct drawbacks also, it should be noted.

Maccoby: We've had some problems getting published; it's been interesting.

Alexander: We should probably say that, in part, it might have to do with our writing abilities and our abilities to describe this complex study, but one suspects there's more to it than that.

Maccoby: This is a problem worth mentioning. It's not just the writing or the publication problem—that's only part of it. There is a problem in getting peer review of both the research process and the research product. It relates back to what we just said about the different standards that different kinds of scientists follow. On the one hand, some people feel that the research is not precise enough; for example, we should be sticking to one risk factor at a time. We should be working on smoking and nothing else, or we should be working on certain aspects of nutrition and nothing else, and so on. And we feel that, because the problem is so urgent and because of the synergistic nature of risk factors and the environmental influences on life-style, a multiple-intervention method applied in a field setting was necessary. It also turns out that, once you get people into the role of changing, it's easier for them to change in a number of ways. It's like learning how to learn; the skills involved apply to all risk factors. So, there's a very important rationale for *not* doing a piece at a time as a controlled experiment or clinical trial.

Alexander: Discussions of design and methods in the multidisciplinary realm become, as I observe it, a kind of value battle among types and kinds of scientists based on "what goes" in their fields. We are often the subject, for example, of criticism by a type of social or medical scientist who chooses to believe that nothing can be learned with enough clarity in the dirty field setting to make it worth the effort. That is, we are criticized pretty heavily by some for the quasi-experimental design, and, going beyond that, for dipping into the community, for trying it out for size, before some specified sets of prior research questions have been answered. And, there are others who almost philosophically seem to believe that you cannot tear the warp from the woof and still have a piece of cloth; in their view, you have to implant the main features of the whole system and monitor it as best you can through formative evaluation and other statistical techniques for the idea to have a fair test and to obtain a glimpse of the factors that interact in reality. So, the debate derives from two ways of looking at the world and assessing where it's important to begin: with the state of the art of basic science or with the reality of human needs.

Maccoby: I like to put it this way: You can either work on only the most important problems that you can handle *with precision,* or you can work on the *most important problems* with the best of inadequate research methods.

Alexander: And, for each person, that is a value choice, a personal choice and a professional choice. And, for each problem or re-search topic, there is a basic scientific approach or a social needs approach. Take your choice.

Maccoby: We are in the middle of that one; I think we are right down the middle of it. And I like to be there—I'm comfortable with it. I think one of the great attractions of this kind of research, beyond the stimulation of the multidisciplinary collegial working groups, is the opportunity to work in part in the real world with real people on real problems. To advance knowledge while at the same time seeing it effectively applied to social needs is, to us, the best of all possible worlds.

5

Demonstration Research and Manifest Versus True Adoption: *The Natural History of a Research Project to Divert Adolescents from the Legal System*

Julian Rappaport
Edward Seidman
William S. Davidson II

All researchers know that what goes on "before the beginning" influences their research. We all know how, in ways that are rarely reported, certain events, attitudes, values, and experiences influence what actually takes place during a project's formal conduct. Those who are familiar with the work of Seymour B. Sarason

Note: The work reported here was supported by Grant #22336 from the National Institute of Mental Health and a Fulbright-Hays Award to the second author. Thanks is extended to the editors and to our colwill recognize that the phrase "before the beginning" is taken from his book *The Creation of Settings and the Future Societies* (1972), where he notes that "a major obstacle to our understanding of the creation and development of settings is the surprising lack of detailed descriptions of their 'natural history' " (p. 26). Sarason goes on to note that, with the thousands of professionals who devote themselves to the study and change of organizations, it is surprising there is so little understanding about how such settings are created and developed. *"What must be recognized . . . is that (their) ideas derive almost exclusively from observing and working with chronologically mature settings"* (p. 26, italics in original). The same may be said for demonstration projects, which are almost universally described in the literature as if they were created and ended during the project's actual conduct. There is no past and no future.

In this chapter, we describe the natural history of a research and demonstration project, which spans a long enough period of time to enable us to take a unique perspective; it includes not only information on "before the beginning" but on "after the end" as well. What we present is in one sense a case study, but, as we shall argue, it is so typical of correctly done demonstration research as to be quite representative of the paradigm. We will try to persuade that social and organizational change require conceptualization, research, and understanding beyond that which is obtained in such experiments. Furthermore, we will distinguish between *manifest adoption* of a demonstration project by other than its originators and *true adoption*. True adoption requires that the essence of a program be maintained. By *essence*, we mean the essential rules of the game that govern relationships among program participants as well as the spirit, ideology, values, and goals of the original project. These things are difficult to write about and to maintain in a given setting, and they are even more difficult to transpose from one setting to another. In describing the natural history of one demonstration research project, we hope to illuminate some of these difficulties and their implications for planned social change. The last portions of this chapter suggest a number of conceptual-

league, Kenneth Maton, for their helpful suggestions. An earlier version of these ideas benefitted from the thoughtful questions of faculty and students in the University of Michigan Community Psychology Program and the College of Human Development, Pennsylvania State University.

theoretical heuristics for thinking about such problems, with implications for action.

Communication of Essence and Tacit Understanding

Before we begin our description of the natural history, we first reflect on the idea of trying to write about the essence of a program rather than simply about its outcome. We want to describe those aspects of our work that do not fit conveniently into the methods sections of research reports. The aim is to get at the process of doing the work, to tell why we did what we did and what ideas and actions might not be apparent to someone who might want to do the same thing after reading about our results. We also wish to communicate certain observations that are not directly reflected in the data but represent our tacit understanding, which has developed as much after the formal research project was concluded as while we were engaged in it.

To argue that one knows something worthwhile, simply because it is more consistent with one's expressed values than are current ways of doing things, is not likely to be terribly influential, yet, in many ways, values guided the work described here, and values may be crucial to its essence. One of the problems in dissemination following a successful demonstration of effects may be that the *value base* on which the work was conceived is easy to dilute with other motives.

It is undeniable that description and interpretation based on tacit understanding are of limited influence in contemporary psychology unless broached in the context of hard data. Within the norms of social science, it is easier to convince people that you have something to say if you have experimental data that can be impressively displayed in graphs and tables, which show that you are a good scientist. Data allow one to have a platform from which to speak about what one knows, even if it is not reflected in the data. Frankly, that is why we were invited to do this paper. Although the editors specifically wanted to get beyond the data to the process of doing the work, they also wanted us to talk about a project for which we already have hard data.

It is simply a statement of reality that one must speak in the language of the listener in order to be heard. In contemporary psychology, data talk. That seems reasonable to us, except that, once the data leave one's own home, it is not always clear that they say the same thing they said at home, nor is it clear that they say what is most important. Numbers that reflect program outcomes are far more ambiguous than they are thought to be. And, it is very risky to assume that a demonstration project with a good outcome will be carried out in its essence when it is disseminated to other settings or even that the program itself, continued in the same setting, will continue to be what it was when the data were collected.

Anyone familiar with the Ayllon and Azrin (1968) book on token economies and with the large number of behavior modification units of state hospitals, which it and other similar demonstration projects helped to create, will know that something is amiss. While the words are the same, somehow, what goes on in settings labeled *behavior modification* is often so different in intangible ways (words like *excitement, expectation,* and *atmosphere* come to mind) as to be very different from the original, although they may objectively be the same. Certainly, such units have been widely *adopted,* in the jargon of dissemination research, but have they really been adopted if they have lost their essence? We are not speaking here of simply sloppy or technically incorrect programming, although that is a part of the problem, but rather of the elements of a human service program that are impossible to quantify or to put into program manuals (see Reppucci and Saunders, 1974). Goldenberg (1974) has made a similar observation with regard to reactions to his own work with hard-core delinquents. "The process of development as well as the results of the Residential Youth Center (RYC) have been presented in a variety of different publications . . . although a book recently published about the RYC has been rather favorably reviewed in a number of different journals (including some of our traditional "liberal" ones), I have been struck by how little attention reviewers have paid to some of the issues . . . even though (they) easily comprise two-thirds of the book's contents. It seems, rather, that reviewers . . . feel much more comfortable focusing attention on questions concerning clinical results for and on the target population than on the institutional and political implications of a setting developed, as the RYC was, as a reaction against the prevailing conceptions and internal processes that characterize most of our university departments and community agencies" (p. 169).

What Goldenberg is referring to is the fact that his data on program participants showing reduced likelihood of getting into legal difficulties and increased likelihood of employment has been widely acknowledged, but the essence of his program—a largely attitudinal set on the part of staff and participants alike vis a vis their relationships with one another and their implicit rules of the game—has been ignored (Rappaport, 1977).

Similarly, our observation of several halfway houses for chronic mental patients, which claim to be based on the lodge model of Fairweather and his colleagues (1969, 1974), has led us to wonder what those researchers would feel if they were to see such projects, which claim that model as their source. Often, these new programs, based in name on an autonomous alternative setting, are so different in intangible elements as to be only an illusion of the original idea. The original data were impressive enough to create an atmosphere of apparent national interest, but dissemination in essence is often more apparent than real.

What data cannot convey is the underlying sense of what a program is all about. That is beyond the data and can only be captured in experience and conception. It requires really understanding that, for example, both Fairweather and Goldenberg were talking about true *autonomous* alternative settings. Rappaport (1977) has distinguished between a *subunit,* a *new unit,* and a *true autonomous alternative setting.* In either of the first two variants of alternative settings, there *may be* a change in the status of the target people with regard to their autonomy, decision-making power, and role in the organization. The third variant of this strategy, the *autonomous setting,* is one in which the autonomy, power, and control of the organization are placed directly, overtly, and specifically in the hands of the people who are supposedly served by the setting. The role of the professional change-agent is ideally one of catalyst, facilitator, guide, or consultant.

If a successful program is a true autonomous alternative setting, and, in its adoption by others, it becomes something less, then it is reasonable to ask "Has the change been adopted?" We think not. This is what we mean when we distinguish between manifest adoption and true adoption.

Short of massive national experiments, one can legitimately address such questions as the impact of a demonstration project in a number of ways. One way is simply to count the number of other settings that adopt the project. Another, but relatively rare way, is to stay with a project *after the end* to see what impact it has on the setting in which it was initiated and to see how the program itself changes as its original essence is absorbed into the setting. What we mean by "after the end" is quite literally when the researcher's formal involvement is over. At that time, the researcher is in a unique position to assess impact—after the excitement and enthusiasm of research and the anticipation of something new is replaced by the routine of day-to-day work. In some ways, this is a more representative condition than the one that is created by dissemination experiments, wherein the researcher remains very much involved. It also goes beyond the question of "Did the innovation get adopted?" and asks "Did adoption of the innovation change the organization of which it is a part?"

The following sections of this chapter are an attempt to get beyond the data of a successful research project and to understand the values that motivated it, how it came about as a functional reality, and what happened to it after it was a successful demonstration project. We believe that such attempts to report the natural history of a project are too rare in psychology and that they are required if we are ever to get out of the state of demonstration research as a means to understand change. Although our work has used experiments, we have not experimentally examined this specific question. Rather, we have a case study of what is probably typical of much of the successful-outcome research in our field; therefore, it may be a generalizable experience with implications for planned social change, dissemination, and true adoption.

The Context

Several years ago, we began a program of research to evaluate the use of college students in helping roles in a variety of human service settings. Despite the widespread use of students and other nonprofessionals in such roles (Cowen, 1973; Gruver, 1971), there had never been a systematic look at the impact of such programming by direct comparison across settings (for example, schools, courts, mental health agencies, nursing homes), problem areas (school adjustment, delinquency, mental health, aging), or levels of analysis (individual, organizational, institutional). The general outlines of our research design are described in a previous publication (Seidman and Rappaport, 1974), and a detailed report of four simultaneous longitudinal-research projects is in preparation (Seidman and others, in press). Although the details need not concern us here, to provide a context for what is presented, it is useful to have an overview of the kinds of research questions to which we have been addressing ourselves: (1) What are the effects of supervised nonprofessionals (in this case, students) on target individuals? (2) What are the effects of participation on the helpers themselves? (3) How should we select and train potential helpers? (4) Do we have an impact on the culture of the settings in which we work?

Each of these general questions contains a number of sub-questions and is linked in a complex set of relationships that requires comparison *across* projects (Seidman and others, in press) but the purpose of this chapter is considerably more limited. Here, we focus primarily on selected aspects of the last question: "Do we have an impact on the culture of the settings in which we work?" We shall use one of the projects mentioned previously as a case example; it was selected, because, based on hard outcome data on the targets of the intervention, the project has already been judged to be very successful. As will be seen, the data-based evidence is compelling. Indeed, reports of this work have been awarded first prize in the Division of Consulting Psychology annual research awards competition, and it was selected by the Department of Justice as an "exemplary project." It has been visited and written about in a lengthy monograph commissioned by the Justice Department (Ku and Blew, 1977) and distributed to hundreds of juvenile justice workers. Many have contacted us to let us know that they have begun similar projects and to ask for information and advice. We are obviously pleased with our outcome results. Nevertheless, we also have a sense of uneasiness about these dissemination developments and a real concern about what they mean.

Before we address the question of our impact on the culture of the setting in which we worked and raise questions about the dissemination of demonstration projects, we present a description of how we became involved in this particular project "before the beginning," an examination of the values and goals that motivated us, and an abstract of the actual project and its results.

The program was developed to provide an alternative to the juvenile justice system for adolescents in legal jeopardy. The aim was to divert them from involvement in a juvenile court system, which we believe to be more of an impediment than an aid to their future. We also hoped that it would change at least the local court's ways of dealing with juveniles and perhaps have a more widespread impact.

Before the Beginning

Our involvement with a project to divert youth in difficulty with the legal system was more a result of circumstances than a before-the-fact planned intervention resulting from a calculated analysis of research literature. It is indeed one of the mystiques of planned intervention that such activities are supposedly developed by scientists dispassionately reviewing the literature, diagnosing the situation and the people in it, selecting from a bag of tricks the right prescription, and applying it with the seasoned expertise of a woodsman stalking his prey. If that is not the correct metaphor, perhaps one more familiar is the applied scientist moving from what he knows (in the verified sense—from the existing knowledge base) to an applied problem, much like the engineer who designs a bridge. In our experience, a much better analogy would be the artist struggling to bring out in visible images what he both feels and sees in his intuitions, which are shaped by knowledge of technique and knowledge of what others have done but are often independent of that knowledge, because this time, this place, and this activity are not quite the same as any other.

Our work began as early as 1968, when one of us, in an effort to provide graduate students with the kind of experiences to which they would be subject if they were to enter the world of community action as opposed to clinic-based psychology, established a year-long practicum. In this course, six to ten graduate students, often in pairs of Professional Degree (Psy.D.) and Research Degree (Ph.D.) students, were told to "go out to the local community and see what is happening." That meant to visit social service agencies, but it also meant "talk to people on the street," spend time walking around, visit homes, stores, and street corners; observe, interview, and befriend people and think about what resources we and they have that could be mobilized toward some end consistent with our shared values.

By 1971, the students had tried perhaps a dozen or so different kinds of projects. Some were relatively successful (O'Connor and Rappaport, 1970). Some were complete failures. For example, one student worked with a local job-training program in the black community (The Opportunities Industrialization Center) to help establish a credit union. We developed a fine plan and learned a great deal about economics but were never able to get it going.

Because part of this practicum involved bringing graduate students together each week for shared reporting, critique, and idea exchange, we all learned a great deal from comparing those projects that were not successful with those that were. One of the projects that did seem to work, in the sense of actually becoming a viable ongoing program, was developed by three graduate students (Irving Bieman, Jacob Herring, Michael Tallman) who had read about volunteer-in-court (VIC) activities in Denver, Colorado. These programs involved the use of various volunteers working on a one-to-one basis with teen-agers on probation. Beginning with their interest in VIC programs and the little bit they had read about such experiences, the students went to the local probation office to sell the idea.

One of the requirements for our graduate practicum was that, after one semester of planning, the program should bring in undergraduates, who would register for an independent study course during the second semester. There was a very simple reason for this: We were committed to providing experience for undergraduates, because we had started a practicum course for them. We did this, because we had become convinced that the work of such nonprofessionals could be quite valuable to both themselves and to others, but, in a sense, the requirement that our graduate students involve undergraduates in their programs was quite arbitrary. It clearly limited the nature of their community projects to those that could conveniently incorporate undergraduates. For students interested in working with adolescents in legal jeopardy, the nature of the community program they were permitted to develop was constrained in this way from the outset, not because we necessarily knew that students would be the best service deliverers for this population but because of prior decisions about involving undergraduates in applied work and providing supervisory experience for graduate students.

Our sales pitch to the probation office was simple: You have a huge case load, we have supervisors (graduate students and faculty) as well as an almost unlimited pool of undergraduate volunteers. We can together select, train, and supervise these volunteers in a systematic fashion and perhaps provide useful services for you and your clients, free of dollar cost. What is in it for us? A good training experience and perhaps even a chance to be helpful to kids in trouble. What needs to be remembered, however, is that we were selling a program before we had any basis for knowing if it would work. We offered it purely on faith, not on data. Given constraints on our resources and our previous commitment to under-graduates, this seemed like a reasonable way to work with youth in trouble with the law.

As might be expected, things were not quite that simple from the probation office's viewpoint. On the one hand, they are always required to justify their staff to the local county that supports their activities. Overworked case workers may be a less than desirable situation, but at budget time, it is a very useful one for arguing in favor of increased funds. On the other hand, most of the staff (other than the supervisors) were both young and bachelor's level people not terribly different, except for a few years of experience, from the student volunteers we wanted to provide. As one might imagine, this meant some careful feeling out of relationships. Nevertheless, after a year of tentativeness, the project seemed feasible.

We are not really sure why we were able to overcome the fears of the probation office. One reason that occurs to us is something called persistence. We simply did not go away. Perhaps it was because the graduate students needed to come to a class where everyone was very unsympathetic to the report that "they do not want to cooperate." Rather than accept such excuses, the class members and the instructors were often brutally unwilling to believe that anyone could not get anything going if they stayed with it. We developed a kind of expectation of "there is no reason why any agency, or any set of people, should be unwilling to work with you." The students believed in it, and, although for some it was painful, in most cases, they stayed with it.

We began with the referral of twelve adolescents from the probation office, each with a history of legal problems. In several months of working on a one-to-one basis, there were no catastrophes. As confidence increased, we got tougher cases. In some instances, we were not particularly useful in keeping the youth out of trouble; in others, there were few problems, but clearly we could not conclude that success was due to our activities. What was clear, however, was that the local adolescents and our undergraduates were getting along with each other. They seemed, in most cases, like a natural match. Each undergraduate kept a diary, and they met in a small group with the graduate students every week to go over each case. Our general orientation was a social-learning, problem-solving one. Our graduate students had been trained in the techniques of a social-learning approach, and this was the most natural one for them to teach to undergraduates. The strategy was first to get to know the youth and establish rapport and next to work out a plan together with the youngster. The plan had to be specific, goal-oriented, and behaviorally specifiable. We emphasized work with significant others.

At this point, our impression was that we were in an arena in which resources and needs might be profitably brought together, and we planned, with the probation office, to do it again a second year. Before that second year, we also tried to convince the probation office that it might be profitable, since we were only able to handle between twelve and twenty probationers, to identify more than that number to have a control group for comparison purposes. We were never able to do that in a very precise way (there always seemed to be a good reason to violate randomization), and we were never quite sure about differences between those who did and did not get into further difficulty.

In the next year of the practicum, we began to get the idea that, for these youngsters on probation, there was already, despite their ages (10 to 17), an established set of relationships with school, legal system, peers, and significant others that fostered the persistence of legal difficulties. There seemed to be no basic personality differences between the youths who continued to get into difficulty and those who did not. Looking back, those who continued to get into trouble were no more or less likable than those who did not, and we seemed to be good for both sets of people, in the sense that there was often a genuine interpersonal relationship established, where there were shared experiences of the kind that most of us would want in our own lives. But, as far as we could tell, these experiences were randomly related to whether or not a youth continued to get into trouble with the law.

By this time, we had also developed, out of our practicum, a second stable program. In this one, we were assigning college students to work with elementary school students experiencing behavioral or academic problems (Alden, Rappaport, and Seidman, 1975). This and a number of other service contacts with local mental health agencies and nursing homes led us to consider creating a more systematic evaluation of our practicums. We developed a proposal for a longitudinal-research study and submitted it to the National Institute of Mental Health. In this proposal, we first began to raise in a systematic way the sorts of questions listed in the section on context.

In the time between the conclusion of our early work with the local legal system and the onset of our work sponsored by NIMH, who funded us beginning in 1972, we were able to think through both our observations and our social values. That led to major changes in the focus of our work with youth. Several concerns seemed to emerge from our experience, and, probably because they were consistent with our values, we acted on them to change the nature of our program.

One thing we began to notice was that, to the extent that a youngster is engaged in the legal system, so too will significant others in his or her life, including those who would help the youth, be entangled in that system. Our own tacit knowledge was enhanced in a very real sense by the kind of thinking Edwin Schur in his book *Radical Nonintervention* (1973) was able to bring to bear. Schur's basic argument is that so-called delinquency can only be understood in the context of the labelers as well as the labeled and that many children so designated might be better off if simply left alone. We began to realize that even the questions we were asking about delinquency prevention were unknowingly a function of where and why we were asking them, and the answers were often determined by the questions. We have written about the details of this rather cryptic-sounding observation elsewhere (Seidman, 1978; Rappaport, Lamiell, and Seidman, in press). Here, the point is that a very real part of the essence of our program became our commitment, before the beginning, to keep children from being labeled as delinquent and thereby drawn into the juvenile justice system. This commitment, we have discovered, requires as much or more work with the labelers as it does with the adolescents themselves. It may be central to the essence of our project.

Essence: Values and Goals of the Diversion Project

It is most important, if one is to understand the Adolescent Diversion Project that finally emerged, to keep in mind that, as a consequence of our "before the beginning" experiences with probationers, we realized that it was going to be necessary for us to intervene earlier than at the time of probation in the process of adolescent involvement with the legal system.

Equally important, at the same time, we learned during the pilot phases of our work with the police that there was a real danger in overidentifying so-called predelinquent youth. In general, police were often willing to use their discretionary powers to warn and release both first offenders and status offenders (those who were in trouble for committing an act that would not be illegal were they an adult, such as a runaway, a curfew violator, a truant, and the like). Unfortunately, most social service agencies, including so-called Youth Service Bureaus, have tended to encourage police to refer these children to their agency for counseling. Such referrals are often simply an imposition of middle-class morals or an over-psychologizing of nonpsychological problems. For such offenses to be crimes is perhaps totally absurd, and it is often equally unreasonable for children and their families to be forced into social services "for their own good." In many cases, such forced treatment is simply a rationalization of social service agencies' own need to grow and to expand their sphere of control.

This problem has been discussed by us in detail. For a full consideration of the conceptual and ethical issues, the reader is referred to a recent report prepared for the American Psychological Association Task Force on Psychologists in the Criminal Justice System (Rappaport, Lamiell, and Seidman, in press). Here, we simply point out that, as a consequence of our experience "before the beginning," our intentions were to aim our intervention at a very narrow set of children: those for whom the police had already used a warn and release option and for whom the juvenile officer now felt that there was no choice but to file a petition with the State's Attorney's Office. If a petition were filed, it would have meant the formal engagement of the youth in the court system, complete with a formal trial, in which the child would almost always be represented by a public defender and in most cases be placed on probation. He or she would then be officially labeled as delinquent. Our first and foremost aim was to prevent this from happening, because from both our experience and our reading (Gold, 1970; Schur, 1973), we were convinced that it made things worse rather than better for the youth.

The program results described in this chapter pertain entirely to youths for whom the police were about to file a petition for court action but referred to our program instead. The program provided a true alternative to adjudication. If the children were to be warned and released, we did not take them in the program.

In addition to aiming our intervention at this very specific group of children—those not likely to be one-time offenders but rather those likely to end up in court at a later date—we targeted our goals for each youngster around a uniform major aim: keep them out of legal difficulties. In every case, as we worked out goal-setting by means of goal-attainment scales, although there were individualized subgoals, we all knew that the major focus was simply to keep the youth out of legal difficulty.

Our values also brought to bear a number of other considerations. We were committed to the notion that not only does labeling a child as delinquent create more harm than good but that the most sensible way to approach such problems is from an *environmental resources social advocacy* point of view. As we have written elsewhere (Davidson and Rappaport, 1978, pp. 76–77):

> In contrast with other approaches, the environmental resources conception does not concern itself with the eradication or amelioration of differences in individuals or target groups. At the very heart of the environmental resources conception is the notion that a wide variety of differences do exist in this society. From a statistical standpoint, given two comparison groups of sufficient size, there will be differences observed on a multitude of individual and environmental variables. Finding problems such as crime, poverty, etc., disproportionately represented in various social groups

has in the past led to the conclusion that, to eradicate the observed differences, the major characteristics of the groups or individuals had to be altered. Within the environmental resources conception, group differences are viewed as the assets of a pluralistic society, and such differences are to be supported rather than used as a basis for exclusion from resource availability. Some (Triandis, 1976) have even suggested that the special assets of "out groups" should be taught to the majority as a means for creating a true multicultural society.

The environmental resources conception takes a universalistic rather than an exceptionalistic approach to social problems (Ryan, 1971). The universalistic approach assumes that the variety of unmet needs displayed by various groups in our society are not exclusively housed within those identified groups and individuals. It is recognized that the very process of identification of "problem groups" often sets in motion a series of events which exacerbate rather than remedy the situation while placing responsibility for failure on the individuals in question. The alternative suggested by the environmental resources conception is that all people of this society have a right to have their collective and individual needs fulfilled. The vehicle of advocacy is suggested as a means of focusing intervention efforts on resource stimulation and generation rather than on individual repair.

This conception, together with the sense that the youths with whom we were dealing often have a variety of strengths and competencies that need encouragement and development rather than therapy (Rappaport, 1977), led us to emphasize an intervention based on both social advocacy and behavioral contracting with significant others. Both of these approaches require that the youth be regarded as a full-fledged active participant rather than as a case. (For a detailed description of this approach, see Davidson and Rapp, 1976; Davidson and Rappaport, 1978.)

We next summarize the hard data accumulated over a period of several years after the formal onset of the research. The aim is quite simply to affirm that we had a project that really worked, so that the non-data-based observations that make up the remainder of this chapter can be put in perspective.

Summary of the Research Data

The first year of the Adolescent Diversion Project was primarily a pilot study, in which relationships, agreements, and working procedures were established in consultation with the local police officers.* A variety of measurement devices were also selected and pilot tested.

During the second year, thirty-seven apprehended youth were assigned randomly to either a college student who worked with the youth on a one-to-one basis (N = 25) or a "treatment as usual" condition (N = 12) in lieu of juvenile court referral. The training (and supervisory orientation) received by the nonprofessionals involved developing a combination of relationship, child-advocacy, and behavioral-contracting skills.‡ Each student met weekly with other students and a graduate student supervisor, who in turn met with the authors.

Examination of archival data at several intervals (one year preproject, five months during, and both one and two years after the program conclusion) indicates highly significant decrements in police contact, seriousness of offense, and juvenile court referral for experimental as opposed to control-group children (see Figure 1). We also found that the diversion project reduced the proportion of *all* youth petitioned to court by the cooperating police departments during the time of the project's operation.

Despite the powerful effects of the major outcome data, standard self-report questionnaire measures at the pre and post time points from the perspective of the targeted youths, their parents, and nominated peers show no statistically significant effects or trends.

In year three, the behavioral-contracting and child-advocacy training and supervisory orientations were separated to ascertain the relative efficacy of each. Here, a new group of thirty-six youths who were about to be petitioned to juvenile court were referred to the program and randomly assigned to either a behavioral-contracting (N = 12), a child-advocacy (N = 12), or a control condi-

* For greater detail, including more complete data analysis and descriptions of program activities, see Davidson and others (1977); Ku and Blew (1977); Seidman, Rappaport, and Davidson (1976); Seidman and others, in press.

‡ Very detailed case examples and program descriptions are available in a report distributed by the U.S. Department of Justice titled "The Adolescent Diversion Project—A University's Approach to Delinquency Prevention." The report may be obtained by sending $2.00 to the Superintendent of Documents, U.S. Government Printing Office, Washington, D.C. 20402, Stock Number 027-000-00471-7.

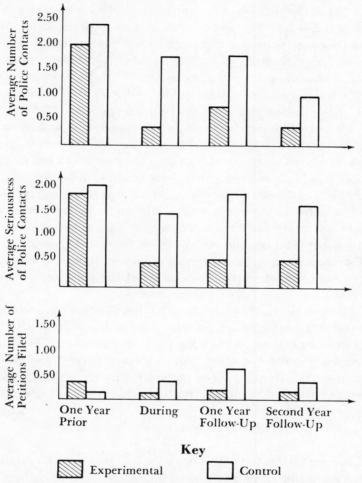

Key

Experimental   Control

Figure 1. Police and Court Record Data for First Year of Research

tion (N = 12). The research and supervision process followed a format similar to the prior year in terms of design and measurement. An additional component involved the construction, analysis, and administration of *process interviews* aimed at ascertaining critical life events, critical intervention components, and performance in training and supervision. Interviews were conducted at six-week intervals with the target youth, their parents, the volunteer student, and the student's supervisor.

As in the previous year, police-court data indicated significantly less delinquent behavior for each of the experimental groups in contrast to controls (see Figure 2). In addition, analyses of school data indicated that the experimental youth were more likely to continue attending school, whereas the control youth decreased their school attendance dramatically. Analyses of questionnaire data again failed to yield changes from any perspective.

The relationship between process dimensions and outcome was also examined. Successful cases were much more likely to maintain positive interactions with significant social systems (family, school), less likely to report deterioration on change dimensions, more likely successfully to initiate their respective intervention package (advocacy or contracting), and more likely to receive a broad band intervention (focusing on more than one social system). Those youth who became reinvolved in the justice system did so almost immediately after referral and were unable to extricate themselves from the system. This led to relatively narrow interventions focused on the justice system alone.

Based on this research, we have felt justified in concluding that our alternative to the traditional juvenile justice system has demonstrated efficacy in reducing the rates and severity of official delinquency in two successive years with two independent groups of youngsters. These changes endured through a two-year and one-year follow-up point for the first and second set of participants, respectively.

Four things should be emphasized in our results:

1. The youths referred to this program and kept out of legal difficulty are not from an "easy" population. In twenty-three of twenty-four cases, the control youths (referred to the program and randomly assigned to "treatment as usual") were found to have further legal difficulty.
2. The youths referred were, in all cases, those for whom formal court action was about to be initiated. We did *not* take first or minor offenders for whom a warn and release action might be effective, nor did we wait until they were officially in the system and on probation.
3. Although we were successful in ending further contact with the law, it is not the case that we turned these children into funda-

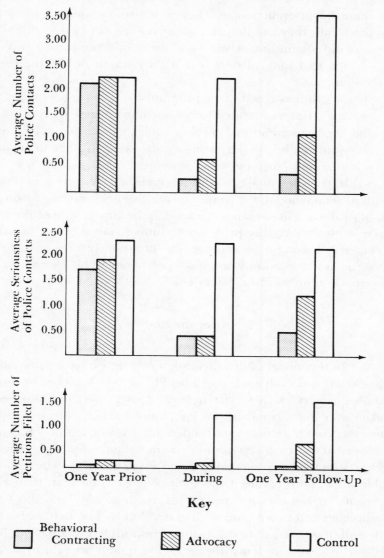

Key

Behavioral Contracting   Advocacy   Control

Figure 2. Police and Court Record Data for Second Year of Research

mentally different people. They may have attended school more often, but they did not necessarily do any better academically, nor did significant others view them differently. The major change that took place was that they stayed out of the legal system.

4. Those youth assigned to the program but for whom we failed to make a difference tended to become immediately reinvolved in the legal system and to envelop quickly both themselves and our students in the intricacies of that system rather than with school, family, or other social systems.

In the later phases of this intervention, we were concerned with dissemination of the project to local agencies, and we involved local professionals, whom we trained in the supervision of the college students. As this program continues, cooperation has developed between police and the new program professionals such that the local community now has a potentially viable alternative to court action on youthful offenders.

After the End

In the model of demonstration research, once a program is developed and evaluated, one must plan for its takeover by those whose primary job is service delivery. Our project has now been taken over in exactly that way. We planned for this by generating interest from a local county-funded agency, whose sole job is the delivery of outreach services to prevent delinquency. They agreed to carry on the program and to assign a staff member to be responsible for it, even before it was their own. For one year, that staff person worked in our project as cosupervisor, learning the techniques and procedures we had developed. The first year after the end of our research, she assumed responsibility along with two of our graduate students; the second year, she brought in a new staff member, whom she trained and who took over the supervisory duties the following year.

Not only are we now in the third generation of supervisors, but we also find the original juvenile officers responsible for referral in different jobs and the agency head that sponsored our program's adoption replaced. The agency head is the one who must maintain contact with the police to keep appropriate referrals coming in. The original plan was for the agency head to visit weekly with the responsible juvenile officer. As both parties were replaced, one of the original researchers explained the program to each of them, they read all the project materials, and they were both interested and enthusiastic. The police and the local agency professionals each identified with the program and regarded it as their own.

Our relationship to the project has now shifted from one of researchers to consultants. Each year, we help to recruit interested undergraduates and provide advice and assistance to the local agency that has assumed program responsibility. They maintain relationships with the police and make administrative decisions.

Because of our unique association to the program, we have been in a position to observe (from the inside) what happens when a project developed as a demonstration is actually disseminated. What we are talking about now is not how it was disseminated but what the program became after it left the original researchers and was adopted by others. The consultant role has enabled us to observe, with the same closeness that we were permitted "before the beginning," what takes place "after the end" of the formal research and program adoption.

At this time, the formal research has been concluded for almost three years. Normally, one would not expect to follow up what happened next. Usually, demonstration projects simply end. Sometimes, if they are successful, they are written up for journals or books or government reports. More rarely, they are actually implemented elsewhere, either as a research project to be replicated or as a service project picked up by various agencies independent of its originators. Even more rarely, the original authors may take responsibility for dissemination, as in the case of Fairweather, Sanders, and Tornatzky (1974). In rare cases, the program may be observed by its originators in new settings, but usually demonstration projects simply become "the literature."

In our case, two unique things happened. One of us (Davidson) left to take a job at another university and applied for and received a grant to replicate and extend the research in another community. That work is going on now. At the same time, Rappaport and Seidman have continued to observe the project. We are discussing a project that already has collected data on participants as much as two years after their involvement in the program. But that is not what we are referring to here—rather, we are talking about observing how the program has continued to operate after the research team exited from it, after the original supervisors have gone, and after the original responsible police officers have been replaced.

This situation provides the rare opportunity to observe directly what happens to an experimentally validated program when it is disseminated. At issue is what happens to a carefully developed program when it is turned over to a social agency or group, which must: (1) operate with the demands of ongoing research, (2) negotiate and maintain the funding relationships necessary for a local human service agency, (3) operate as a survival-oriented entity rather than with the excitement-oriented independence of a research project, and (4) operate in the face of changing political and procedural pressures. Our impression is that the situation described here accurately represents a common phenomenon. As such, it calls into question the current assumptions, scope, and methods of contemporary social innovation, which assume that a program, once established, remains a stable entity.

At this writing, when none of the principals who were present at the creation, during the formal research, or at the end of it are directly involved, we are able to compare this time with a time that existed earlier—before the beginning—to see if there have been any changes in the juvenile justice system that might be attributed to the project. Does the program's adoption make a difference in the way the setting operates now as opposed to before it had adopted this program?

What we see is instructive. Officially, the program is functioning very well. Four years after conclusion of formal research, the local agency continues to operate it. The program provides careful supervision of college students, who work in a one-to-one relationship doing advocacy and behavioral contracting with referred adolescents. It operates at full capacity and is supported by county funds; the police cooperate and express pride in it, and undergraduate students wait in line to sign up for participation. Indeed, the project still goes on and provides useful services to youths and to undergraduates. But we also see that something has changed. Perhaps what has changed is the essence of the program, which has to do with values, reasons for doing what one does, and what one thinks a diversion program is all about.

One overt change is in the nature of the referred population. Despite the fact that this aspect has always been a key element in written as well as verbal agreements, over the years, the police, under pressure from a newly elected judge, have tended to refer fewer and fewer youths for whom they are actually about to file a court petition. They have instead become increasingly willing to refer adolescents for whom they would normally use a warn and release procedure. At the same time, the county agency, under pressure to show a significant number of cases, has tended increasingly to accept referral from the State Department of Children and Family Services and from mental health agencies, school counselors, and social workers. The problems handled are more and more problems of mental health adjustment rather than legal problems. It is not so much that the youths are intrinsically different but rather that a program with a reputation for success among the social service and school community is now expected to solve all sorts of problems for which it was neither designed nor has any empirical evidence of success. (Recall the results reported previously with regard to what the program was shown *not* to do as well as what it did accomplish).

The county agency is willing to accept referrals wherever it can get them, be it from the police or anyone else. They must show a case load. The university has a similar problem. To operate the program, students must register for a course in August for an entire year. If the police are not referring appropriate cases, then the students will have no work to do. At some point in the school year, the university, like the service agency, is willing to accept referrals from anywhere, so that it can keep its obligation to the students.

The crux of the matter is this: What the adoption of the project failed to accomplish was a change in the local juvenile justice *system* and in the norms of social service agency survival. Such a change would have meant that referral to the project prior to filing a petition would have become the *normal procedure*. Similarly, a systems change would have meant that the county agency would not take as referrals youths for whom warn and release is sufficient or those referred by schools and social workers for other than legal problems. Instead, decision making in the system remains at the discretion of the juvenile officer and the social service agency's intake worker. This means that the adopted program's *appropriate* use (or nonuse) is a function of the good will and understanding of individual people rather than being automatic. People change, people forget, and, more importantly, different people *understand* what the program is in ways that violate the original essence. The juvenile officer is subject to political winds, and the program is used more as a function of these influences than as a function of rational decision making about what is best for the youth, as demonstrated by experimental data.

The social service community, represented in the county agency that runs the program, is always ready to expand services and is quite willing to use its resources to get referrals, even if they are for school problems, family problems, or some other difficulty that supposedly makes the child "predelinquent." This does not mean that they are necessarily doing a poor job but that the program is not what it was intended to be, even though it looks from the outside as if it is. Indeed, despite the fact that our research showed that, *during* the operation of the research, the number of petitions filed by police for court action on juveniles was reduced, recent reports of the number of petitions filed now show an increase.

The Adolescent Diversion Project is no longer a diversion project. It is now, as many have warned that such programs may be (Rappaport, Lamiell, and Seidman, in press; Rutherford and McDermott, 1976; Scari and Hassenfeld, 1976), a place for referral of children who would ordinarily be left alone, as Schur (1973) and others (Institute of Judicial Administration/American Bar Association, 1977) suggest they should be. At the same time, the courts continue to involve in their jurisdiction those children for whom we have good evidence that involvement in the legal system not only does not help (and may actually hurt) but for whom a viable alternative is not only demonstrated and available but was supposedly adopted!

Manifest Versus True Adoption

Tracing the natural history of a research project has taught us a number of things. Some of them, we suppose, we should have known before we started. Yet, as the phenomenologists have so often suggested, to know about something is not quite the same as to experience it. Perhaps the same will be true for readers of this natural history. One might say, "The reason your demonstration project has ended up this way is because you failed to maintain personal contact with police and court to keep them referring the right sort of cases." Perhaps this is correct. But then again, perhaps not, or, more precisely, perhaps that is not the issue.

We could go back and intervene in the court system and try to reestablish appropriate referrals, but what is crucial to understand is that doing that is necessary. What it means is that a *successful demonstration project is not enough to create genuine systems change, and program adoption does not necessarily mean that systems change has been created.*

Objectively, we are convinced that we did all the right things vis-à-vis the model of demonstration-research experiments. Our results are quite satisfactory, when viewed by the usual criteria. We have excellent outcome data, including follow-up on the targets of the intervention. The program systematically planned its own adoption and provided manuals, forms, supervision techniques, and reading material. We established good relationships. The local court has viewed the program as theirs. Program information has been nationally disseminated through the Justice Department, and a number of settings are manifestly adopting the procedures. Although we have not systematically encouraged national program adoption or followed it elsewhere, one of us is replicating the project in another location.

What we have reported here as "after the end" is distressing at best; for most demonstration projects, there is no "after the end," or, if there is, it is never examined. It seems reasonable to assume that none of the places in the juvenile justice system where this program might be adopted by others is likely to be doing it as close to the way it was originally designed as in the local setting. As we have observed, the essence is gone. On the surface, the program looks the same, but in reality the underlying intention—to keep children out of contact with the legal system—has been severely violated. Instead, referrals that seek to help children adjust to school or to behave in a more socially appropriate way or to cope with their disrupted family life are now accepted. These are not bad things in and of themselves; they are simply different things.

The original aim, to divert youth from the legal system, has been lost, while the local county and court can claim that it is funding such programs. What has clearly, and perhaps predictably, happened is that the culture of the court and the social service systems in which we tried to embed our program so as to change *them* has instead changed the *program*. We may be more confident about what we know, because we have conducted a successful experiment. However, that may have very little to do with creating social change. This is, in our view, a powerful case study of the impossibility of creating social change by demonstration projects alone.

Implications for Action and Understanding

We have seen that demonstration projects alone are insufficient for creating genuine system change. Social innovations are unlike technological innovations, which are rapidly disseminated and adopted to the extent that they require minimal changes in social relationships (Fairweather, 1972). Technological innovations usually make work easier and more rewarding, financially and otherwise, for the consumer as well as for the producer. Thus, it is in the best interest of most parties to adopt the innovation. Social innovations, on the other hand, have few immediate or tangible benefits for many of the involved parties (organizations); the promise of greater social justice and a better world seem to wither in comparison with the threat to the immediate interests of those who work day to day in society's organizations.

Perhaps this will become clearer, if we unfold the scenario that might have resulted if the changes in the juvenile justice system that we believe should have rationally followed from our successful social experiment had actually occurred. These changes included an automatic voluntary referral of all alleged offenders to the Adolescent Diversion Project prior to filing a formal petition and refusal to accept referrals for whom warn and release is sufficient or those referred by schools or social agencies for other than legal problems.

If these procedures were followed, the juvenile officers would find themselves with less and less to do. Instead, they would find themselves defending their refusal to accept cases from the school and other social agencies (few of whom seem to have much confidence in dealing with problematic adolescents). They would not have the usual case overload as an explanation. The probation office would be "breathing down their necks," because so few youths were having petitions filed, and consequently very few would have been placed on probation. The lack of large case loads for each probation officer might eventually jeopardize their job security. The various social service agencies would likely apply similar pressure for similar reasons. As this scenario unfolds, we would see increasing tension at the interface of police and other organizations that have a vested interest in the growth of the juvenile justice system. These agencies would view themselves as moving with increasing speed along a pathway of self-annihilation. Instead of this fantasy scenario, however, the successful demonstration program became part of several of the organizations, as planned, but, in the process, *they transformed the very essence, values, objectives, and nature of the project* into something that helped them expand or maintain the scope of their functions.

While engaged in this research, we foresaw this outcome, although we had difficulty verbalizing it. But we were already caught in our own experiment and its established procedures. *We are no different from those we study, in that we also found it too costly to change.* We too are slaves to established procedures and requirements of our organizations (the culture of the university and the acceptable practices of social science). We simply continued to follow our experimental procedures and to collect data, despite our growing awareness of what was happening. Perhaps one reason we did not stop is because we did not know what else to do. Our discipline and our experience have provided us with few guidelines for doing anything other than completing our research as designed.

We had hoped for changes in decision-making between problem youth, police, and social organizations, but our intervention focused primarily at the level of individual youth, and our attempts to measure change were also restricted to either the individual or the organizational level. In other words, our implicit goals were for second-order change—that is, change in the pattern of transactions between levels of social organizations—but the nature of our intervention and our measurement devices were concentrated within a single level of social organization, that is, at the first order (Rappaport, 1977; Seidman, 1976; Watzlawick, Weakland, and Fisch, 1974). We did spend some time trying to develop a schema to measure these potential changes in social relationships, but the press of developing and implementing adequate psychological measurement devices at the individual level was so time consuming that we were distracted from fully realizing what we were beginning to understand was a critical need. We were responding to the implicit demands of our granting agency to complete our research and to our own internal sense that we should not interrupt our experiment and that somehow we needed first to gather data at the individual level of analysis.

We are implying that our values and goals were not congruent with our intervention strategies and measurement techniques. Consequently, it is not surprising that, "after the end," we are uneasy about what we see. These comments are not meant to represent an apology on our part. They are intended for those interested in understanding and facilitating social change, so they can benefit from our experience and can more clearly see the tasks before them.

How to act on these observations is not a simple matter. It probably requires, if psychologists are to be serious about such intentions, a great deal more attention to understanding social policy than we have given in the past. It also means more work at understanding organizations, cultures, customs, and traditions of settings as well as individuals and their interrelationships. Implicit in these comments is a broadened temporal perspective in both retrospective and prospective terms. To date, most of the problem-solving models that we have employed are static, making observations at only one or two points in time. Not only do we need to expand our models to include the study of patterns or transactions between different levels of social organization over time, but we need to incorporate other methods for understanding social-psychological phenomena as well, such as social history (Gergen, 1973, 1976).

In part as a function of our desire to be like natural scientists and engineers who are esteemed as problem solvers, we psychologists have a tendency to think in terms of solutions to social problems by means of *packaged interventions*—tested, approved, evaluated. Given the internal characteristics of human service organizations (let alone the larger social environment with which such open systems must have commerce), it may not be sensible to strive for the selling of experimentally sanctioned interventions as supermarket-style cellophane packages of supposedly transportable programs for adoption. It is not that it is impossible to have such a package adopted but rather that adoption of a package does not guarantee adoption of its essence. Sometimes, in dissemination research, it is easy to confuse these two quite different problems.

Most of the efforts of social scientists to disseminate innovations have assumed that, like the technological innovations of natural science and engineering, the essence and the physical reality of the package are identical. If, as we have suggested, the transactions between participants, the values, rules of the game, ideology, and metacommunications are a significant portion of the essence of a program, then the assumption that this may be expressed in simple physical terms, transportable in some automatic fashion, is a faulty one. Psychologists know relatively little about this problem, although in many ways it is a very psychological problem indeed.

Among psychologists, the most intellectually acceptable method for understanding and for bringing about change is to do experiments or quasi-experiments to test the effects of a given planned program of action and to argue for dissemination and replication by others, which hopefully leads to widespread development of successful programs. Theoretically, if a successful program is widely disseminated, it would mean the drastic reduction and perhaps even eventual elimination of the problem for which the program was developed. The model is one borrowed from the physical sciences. It suggests that, once we figure out how to get to the moon, it becomes possible to do it. Once we can do it, the problem moves from scientific to technological interest. Science solves problems; provides understanding; technology applies that understanding to the solution of problems. The scientist moves on to a new problem.

Seymour Sarason (1977) has recently argued most cogently that the problem-solving model adopted by the natural sciences may be, to put it mildly, inappropriate as a means to social change. He asserts that there is a fundamental difference between scientific problems and social action. The position we take is similar but not identical to Sarason's. The function of experimental data in the realm of social action is as a language for convincing. The key is to convince first yourself and then others to adopt a particular way of doing things by showing them that it will accomplish their aims. In some ways, the task is similar to the way in which Maskelyne, in his comprehensive book of magic (undated), refers to the task of the magician: "I cannot overestimate the importance of a persuasiveness where the magician is concerned!" We cannot overestimate the importance of persuasiveness where the change-agent is concerned. Experiments are probably a useful but incomplete way to be persuasive in the modern world; more is required, and what *more* means is where the future of research in social change must lie.

There are a variety of conceptual-theoretical heuristics available for thinking about such research. One way to conceptualize the issue is to take a kind of *anthropological perspective*, in which one views social organization as local culture. Here, the need to understand the values, regularized rituals, and modes of thinking and behaving that are normally unnoticed and unquestioned in a given setting where people regularly come together steps from ground into figure. This local culture may be most difficult to change and may be at the center of an organization's essence. If the essence of an adopted program and the essence of an organization are at odds, it is likely that the one with the most powerful culture will absorb the other. For most packaged programs developed as demonstration research projects, the culture of the settings into which they are placed may be far more powerful than the culture of the program itself. This fact suggests that we may need to develop research strategies for understanding the culture of the settings into which we intend our work to go. It may require what anthropologists call *emic* units of analysis (those that are determined by discovery through careful and detailed descriptions and emerge out of that description) as opposed to *etic* units, based on information available and effects predicted beforehand (Pike, 1967; Bloom, 1974).

The implications of such a view suggest that one may need to progress from etic to emic to etic research in longitudinal fashion. It may also turn out that one setting may not be just like any other setting, which makes transportation of programs from one place to another problematic. If this indeed is the case, then we will need to develop our skills in descriptive and emic research, because each setting we wish to influence will necessarily require its own analysis. This thinking is similar to what Mehan (1978) and Mehan and Wood (1975) refer to as *constitutive ethnography,* or description of the processes by which participants create structures in a given setting.

A second way to think about this problem is by application of the *ecological analogy* (Kelly, 1977; Trickett, Kelly, and Todd, 1972). Each environment may be thought of as having a local ecology. Although the general principles of ecological relationships may hold across settings (for example, cycling of resources, adaptation, and interdependence), each setting is unique. The introduction of something new into that environment must take into account the local resources and available niches and their interrelationships. As any amateur ecologist now knows, we must be alert to the unintended consequences of our interventions.

Another analogy that is useful for thinking about such problems is the organ transplant. Even though human bodies are reasonably similar to one another (more so than human service settings, such as hospitals, courts, and schools, are to one another), on many occasions, the host organism will reject an organ transplant—even when it was the right organ and performed the necessary functions. To do successful transplants, one must know a great deal about the particular body into which it is being planted. In this case, possible rejection of the transplant is only part of our problem (manifest adoption), and that part may be addressed by dissemination research (see Fairweather, Sanders, and Tornatzky, 1974). The other part of the problem, to which typical dissemination research does not speak (true adoption), is that *the program transplanted may be absorbed into the system without changing the system at all.*

A fourth way to conceptualize this problem, which we have already mentioned, is by *levels of analysis* and *first and second-order change* as a function of the rules of the game. This is taken from the thinking of Watzlawick, Weakland, and Fisch (1974) and Bateson (1972); we have written about it ourselves elsewhere (Rappaport, 1977; Seidman, 1976).

We need to develop more sophisticated conceptions of second-order processes and change. Different intervention targets, strategies, and tactics should logically follow from these newer conceptions as well as more appropriate methods of assessment and measurement (Seidman, 1976). Such developments, particularly the emphasis on change in pattern and form as opposed to substance (Bateson, 1972), will hopefully provide a new direction for social-change experiments and quasi-experiments. This approach should provide an increment to our current understanding, but it would be naive to suggest that quantifiable data available from such experiments will ever be sufficient to create social change. We will need to continue to face future social issues anew. The solution of problems, even if generalizable across locations, would undoubtedly lead to a set of new and different problems. All we can reasonably quest for is that our conceptions, interventions, and assessment and measurement techniques coincide with our implicit values and goals, so as to capture the essence of our projects.

INTERVIEW WITH JULIAN RAPPAPORT

Snowden: I would like to start, Julian, by asking you about some of the contributors to your work. What kinds of organizational, personal, and historical influences got you going and gave the work its character?
Rappaport: I guess I probably should begin by talking about who I'm speaking for. The project is very clearly a product of Ed Seidman and Bill Davidson as well as myself; and, I guess the things that we have written about and the ideas generated are pretty much a shared experience. I don't know where my own contribution begins and somebody else's ends, because there has been a fair amount of transaction among us. At the same time, I see this interview as a little more personal, since Bill is in East Lansing and Ed is in Greece for the year. I don't know exactly how they would react to your questions. I'm sure there would be a lot of overlap on some of the things, but I think it would be a fair guess to say that, on other things, we might violently disagree. All I can be sure of is that 100 percent of the interview will be me.
Snowden: I was interested in the sorts of contributions from institutions, personal life events, and experiences that were important in getting this work going and giving it its particular character.

Rappaport: One of the things that we try to say in the chapter is that the project grew out of the experience of trying to teach and work with graduate and undergraduate students. It was an early recognition that really grew out of the community mental health movement, which was an attempt to involve people not usually delivering services in service delivery, somehow to teach graduate students that one legitimate part of their role might be to supervise, mobilize, and facilitate those people who don't normally serve in helping roles; and, of course, when you're in a university, one huge source of such manpower is undergraduates. My dissertation, for example, was on that topic, back in Rochester in 1967–1968, when Jack Chinskey and I worked with Emory Cowen in using undergraduates in a mental hospital. After I arrived at Illinois, Ed Seidman and I set out to provide graduate students with some kind of experience that would begin to prepare them for the growing community mental health movement. Getting them involved in supervising undergraduates was a convenient way to do that.

Snowden: One characteristic of this intervention is that you have a very clear value stance. You come down on the side of competence, environmental resources, and diversity, which often isn't the point of view from which interventions are designed. I'm wondering how that point of view came to be yours?

Rappaport: Well, probably that whole point of view comes from our experiences outside of trying to deal with juvenile delinquency. By the way, I should say we don't really like the term *juvenile delinquency*. I guess what we usually talk about are youth in legal jeopardy. The notion of juvenile delinquency implies that somehow it's an entity, a thing, and that somehow these kids are different from other kids, and they possess this as a trait. We don't believe that.

I guess the point of view and the value system have a long history; some of it comes from just trying to go out into our local community and relate to people, together with our graduate students, and discovering while interacting that there was something wrong about our conceptions. There was something that just wasn't working right. When, for example, I would go to the local black community and talk to people about what services we could provide for them, they often didn't understand what I was talking about. In their view, they knew that they had all kinds of things they could do or things they weren't allowed to do because they lacked the resources. What they always wanted were things like jobs— everybody wants a job; everybody wants a job for their brother-in-law, for their son, for their mother-in-law, or for themselves. If you take what they say at face value, what you might conclude is what they want is just some "piece of the action"—they want something for themselves. But when you stay with it over several years, you discover that what people are really talking about is that they need simple resources and options, not services. What they need are opportunities to be who they are, do things that they know they can do but for which they either can't get hired or for which there is no place in their community, because there are no resources in their community. When I first got to Champaign and tried to develop this university's community mental health program, it became clear to me after a short time that the university had a long history of taking from the black community and giving nothing back to it. And, as the black community began to protest, as everybody was protesting in the 1960s, the kinds of responses they got from the university were to appoint a person for Affirmative Action or to hire a local leader to head up a phantom program that created a job with no substance for somebody who talked a lot. One of the things that we didn't want to do was set up a program that would only be a training program for graduate students and be based primarily or solely on federal research grants that enable you to complete the three-year contract, and that's it, you're done and you're gone. What we wanted to do was to get the university into an ongoing relationship to the community. I spoke to the chairman of our department, Mort Weir, who was extremely helpful in helping me figure out ways to ask the university for funds of that nature; and we wrote a proposal, which took another four years before it finally got implemented. It was always approved by the university, but there were never any funds for it. As the fates would have it, Mort Weir eventually became the Vice-Chancellor for Academic Affairs here, and he was able to help. He stayed with me and helped to reorient internal funds for a program that would be ongoing.

The kind of program that I'm talking about is something like the way we usually think about the Agricultural Extension Service. It's perfectly legitimate for a university to have that kind of program to deal with the farming community, and nobody raises any eyebrows about it; it seems like a perfectly reasonable service-teaching-training-research relationship. It's funded by ongoing university funds. Another example is the counseling centers or the psychological clinics, which serve a whole different community. That's the way I conceptualized our program to the university. When we got some understanding of what we wanted and when we got a commitment to an ongoing program was when I was able for the first time to go into the local community and talk to people with a different kind of promise. It was the promise of an ongoing commitment over time, not just for jobs but for legitimacy, for resources, for ongoing mutuality.

At that point, I began to learn a great deal about the community; what I learned was that a lot of people who look on the surface like they are in great need of everything are not in great need of everything; they're in great need of some things but not all the things that we imagined. Some of them have just absolutely tremendous unused talents and skills—artists, people with fantastic abilities to talk and think and relate to people and to care for kids and to do all kinds of positive things for which there are no vehicles for expression. And I don't mean *expression* in some vague, humanistic sense; I mean it in a genuine productive sense.

Many of these people did not want to go outside of their neighborhood to use their skills in the white middle-class community, to move their family, and to take their work skills away from home. They do not enter the mainstream culture, either because they are excluded or, often, for reasons of personal comfort—avoiding cultural discomfort, or for ideological reasons, or for—it could be a million reasons, maybe for reasons of just not knowing where they could go to use their skills.

I don't mean this to sound like the "noble savage" or the notion that somehow it's all in there and just has to be brought out; I'm just saying that most people, and there are very few exceptions, have competencies that they've had to learn in growing up and in living, and they need niches in which to actualize the competence. Well, we learned that in a setting that had nothing directly to do with this project.

Snowden: But it sounds like it had a definite and rather clear bearing on the project, in that you learned something about putting resources at people's disposal and how that, rather than focusing on problems, can be very useful, can help people be what they can become.

Rappaport: Yes, in some ways, we came to view our job as "there are kids who have all kinds of skills and assets, and they don't need 'help' in the usual sense of what that means; they don't need that kind of helper-helpee relationship as much as access routes for resources, niches, places to function."

If we conceptualize people—and I mean this as more than words—as literally having strengths and skills and competencies and simply needing access routes, that's very different than conceptualizing them as people who need competence training or people who somehow need skills that we'll teach them or people who need to have their behavior modified. Just think about the metacommunication in those words. Now, I don't mean that it's magic; but I do mean that there are all kinds of implicit communications and messages that become understood between people, and what I was learning and what Bill Davidson—who was very instrumental, along with people like Mel Wilson, then a graduate student who's now teaching at Houston, in helping me set up our programs in the black community at the time—what we were all learning was that what we began to understand there about the wrongheadedness of our relationship to the people we thought we were trying to help would generalize to anybody we got into this helping relationship with. Bill Davidson wrote a paper with a fellow named Charlie Rapp, who is in social work, in which he began to conceptualize things like "What does it mean to have an environmental resources conception of helping instead of all those other kinds of conceptions that we usually have?" The environmental resources conception basically says that the difficulties that people have are a function of their access to resources. That seems pretty straightforward; but it's tremendously different than saying the difficulties that people have are a function of their lack of competence. It's very different to say "What we have to do is teach people skills" than it is to say "What we have to do is allow people to figure out how to contract with significant others and advocate for themselves to obtain the resources that they need to live their life well." Now, one might argue that that's a verbal distinction. Maybe—but I think it's more than a verbal distinction; it may even be that, if you look at the precise descriptions of what you do with a person in the outward behavioral sense, it looks like you're doing the same thing. But I'm convinced that what is communicated to the person is just as real as any skill; what it says is "you're damned good." "You're very competent; the only problem you've had is that you haven't—other people haven't, or the environment hasn't—recognized that you require access to those things you need in order to function at your fullest." That to me is a very different view than the one helpers usually present.

One of the things we found difficult to counteract was that the undergraduates coming into this project—and remember, this project is one of four that was going on simultaneously—all come in, I'd say 95 percent of them, with "good psychological heads." I put "good" in quotes. It's incredible how much individual psychology is a part of our culture and certainly the culture of college students. The idea of being psychologically minded pervaded the undergraduates who came into our projects. In general, their thinking was: "We need to understand the deep meanings that a given event has for these kids, the underlying motivations." So, partly what we were operating against was our own history, the history of psychology, convincing people that their individual psychologies are the most significant thing about them and then our tendency to do what Ryan calls *victim-blame* on that basis.

We found that, for many of these individuals, it was very difficult to think in other than individual causal terminology. Actually, my recollection of this data, which I haven't looked at now for a while, is that, in this project, as opposed to our projects with the elderly in nursing homes or with mental patients or with kids in schools, was relatively more successful than the others in getting around that kind of person-blame ideology. I think, partly because, in this project, there was not that much difference in age, we often found ourselves working with teenagers. Once they got to know the kids, maybe they were more able to see that they weren't so different. They were also operating in a system that was not confined, as compared to a school system, for example, or a nursing home. This was a more open system. What I mean is that it was difficult to communicate something other than the individual psychology person-blame ideology, because that is so much a part of our culture; we've gone too darned far in "psychologizing." What we have to begin to do is to counteract culture. We have got to offer a different way of thinking. Now, I think what we're talking about in terms of strengths is not the whole different way of thinking, it's just a part of it. It's a beginning to turn around our view. I mean, I don't believe that it's anywhere near sufficient, but it's a piece of it. We need to think in terms of different frameworks for research, perhaps of the sort we mention in the last part of our chapter.

Snowden: What did you learn about the kids—their social settings and coping styles; were there differences between successful and unsuccessful kids?

Rappaport: All the measures of the kids, in terms of their attitudes and the attitudes of their significant others, and all the self-report data, and so on, for our successful kids and our unsuccessful kids, showed absolutely no differences—they were perfectly stable. That finding first of all floored us. We really thought that we'd get attitude change, but who knew if we'd keep the kids out of trouble? And we found exactly the opposite, which is totally counterintuitive, given the history of psychology and juvenile justice interventions. You almost always get kids to tell you what you want them to say and you almost never get them to behave the way you want them to behave! The fact that we replicated the findings, the fact that we found the same thing in two different years, convinces us that it's real. Now, maybe we have poor self-assessment, self-report measures, but I don't think that's the problem. I don't think the kids became different people. I think they simply figured out how to stay out of trouble with the law; and I don't think you have to be an all-American boy or girl to stay out of trouble with the law. I think a lot of all-American girls and boys do stay out of trouble, and some don't.

Basically, I think the reason you find rates of so-called delinquency going down with age is that almost everybody learns how to stay out of trouble with the law, given the time, and they don't really change who they are psychologically. They may or may not be engaged in the same activities that were called illegal before. From the process interviews that Bill Davidson developed, we began to see that the kids who were failures, whether they were in the experimental group or the control group, were kids who were getting back in trouble with the law almost right away, within a couple of weeks of the time that we picked them up. If we could keep them out of trouble for about a month, they would tend to stay out of trouble throughout our two-year follow-up. But, if they got right back in trouble, what tended to happen was that they and the undergraduate and anybody else involved with them would spend all their time hassling in the criminal justice system, talking to probation officers, and working out whether or not they were going to jail, and really being obsessively involved in that system. The kids who were most successful ended up simply spending more time in other places; they actually attended school more often, although that was not a consistent or major finding; many of them would spend more time with family and friends and away from actions in the criminal justice system. You can go into a whole labeling theory kind of explanation. The child not only gets labeled, but he begins to think of himself as somebody who is a criminal; all his time and energy are focused on that.

Snowden: Well, let me move over to another area that's somewhat related and ask about lessons that people in the project and people in the juvenile justice system might have learned, apart from the intervention itself. How were they affected, and how were you affected by working together?

Rappaport: I don't know how it affected them. I mean, part of me says it's because I didn't collect the right data; but I don't know if that's completely it. I think we did the wrong things in some ways. I mean, we did what it seemed like one should do, if one wanted to affect that system; Bill Davidson especially spent hour after hour at the police station; they even wrote some jointly authored papers in police journals. There was a real sense of shared identification with the project; we did involve people in it, so it was theirs, not just ours. I don't know if you've ever had any contact with juvenile officers or policemen, but I think you could say this about any profession: There is a set of implicit ways of being in the world that pervades it, and I don't think we made one little dent in that. I don't think that our ideology got communicated to that system. I think our intervention was focused on the individual kids, and certainly we tried and probably were partly successful in communicating it to the undergraduates who worked with the kids, but we didn't even try to understand the culture of the police station; what I'm now saying is that we should have. Before you can try to change something, you have to understand what it is you want to change. I'm not even sure I understand in any systematic way what it means to a juvenile police officer when he picks up a kid and what he thinks when he refers them to a project, even one that he likes; I mean, I think the police probably liked it for different reasons than we liked it. In some ways, it was seen as better than some of the other agency programs that they were already mad at, or, in some ways, we were seen as better than those bleeding-heart social workers who were running around. We did a lot of non-bleeding-heart things, a lot of "You're right; these kids are—"; "There's no use in mollycoddling these kids"; and that's true, I think; I mean, I don't think they need a lot of that. In a lot of ways, the police could understand this kind of project, one where you talk about contracting, you talk about advocacy; that made sense intuitively, but I'm not sure that the underlying ideology made a lot of sense. Probably, the way to do it is to study, understand, and intervene directly in that system. The fantasy we have is "Well, if we can just show a useful program, then by rationality, once it's demonstrated, anyone will see that that's the right way to do it; the ideology along with the program will be communicated; everybody's logical—it's the experimenting society, right? And we all want to do good, right?" I mean, I think we may just have intervened in the wrong place. I know we did. Although I feel very confident that we did good for the kids we worked with, I don't think we did the same kind of good for the kids that came in afterward, and I certainly don't think that we affected the system in any long-term way. I think that we could have made a very strong empirical case that we did affect the system—look, the program's running right now; you can count the number of kids that were in it, you can see what they're doing, you can collect the statistics on them; and we could say, "Now, that sounds like an effect, I know it does." And that's what we mean in the chapter about the difference between manifest adoption and true adoption. I'd be willing to bet the same is true about most adopted demonstration projects.

Snowden: Let's move to questions of method. What do you think is the role of various ways of learning about things, and what do you think is the role of experimentation?

Rappaport: Well, I think there is no danger that American psychology will abandon experimentation as the idol, before which all other things shall be sacrificed. Experimentation has its place; there are a lot of things you can learn from doing an experiment, but you can't learn a lot of other things, and I really think that doing experiments is simply not adequate for the kinds of tasks that community psychologists are going to want to engage in. I actually question whether or not doing experiments is adequate for psychology more generally. I am not saying one should not do experiments, but I really think that there is an overfascination with experiments. It's almost a magical belief that, if you have an experimental group and a control group, you'll somehow know the answer to your questions. First of all, that's not at all clear; all it does is bolster some kind of inferences and tells you absolutely nothing about others. One place to cut into it is to understand that a lot of the research that people do in social interventions—similar to what we've done—is to have a pre and a post and a follow-up, because you're supposed to, but that doesn't tell you at all what's going on in between. Now, we tried to compensate for that somewhat by doing those process kinds of interviews. There's a whole lot of other things going on in the lives of people that we know nothing about; there's a whole lot in the social situation, in the context in which the research is taking place, that one knows nothing about. You might be willing to make some inferences on the basis of outcome data, but there are certain other things that you know nothing about, such as what's the mechanism, how does it work? Well, I'm not saying that you can't do experiments to find out how things work, or at least to add to your information about how things work. I am saying that there are some things, especially in social context, for which you need very careful and detailed description to know how they work. It may be that, when description is adequate enough, that's when you call it explanation. I mean that we have got to spend a lot more time describing the step-by-step things that go on in a given setting, a lot more time than we now spend. I guess, to be concrete about it here, it ties back to what I was saying before about why I couldn't answer your question about what changes took place that I either expected or didn't expect. I don't think any did; maybe I just don't know, because we didn't describe enough. How to pull it off is another problem. I'm inclined to think that what we should be doing is hanging around the police station a lot more and describing what goes on in the transactions between the policemen and the kids, maybe even describing what goes on when the kids aren't there. What are the conversations like? What are the implicit personality theories that the policemen have? What are the explicit things that they say?

We have a new juvenile judge in town; he was elected not too long ago, and he takes a hard line; he says we should punish the kids. How much does that affect what the policemen do when they interact with a child, when they arrest him and have him at their discretion? Think about this: Here's a policeman who picks up a child for maybe the second time, and he has gotten into some minor trouble, but it's clearly a violation of some law. Well, the policeman has a lot of discretion; he can warn and release, or he can file a legal petition; he can do that at any time. How much does what the judge is communicating in the newspapers about his stand on delinquency influence the way the policeman interacts with that child and the decisions that he makes about use of this discretion? We don't know anything about that at the moment, but we could make some guesses. My guess is that, if we did things like a time-series analysis of petitions and looked for critical events over time in the political sphere, we would probably find some fluctuations related to those political events. That's not quite where I want to go, but that's part of it. It's a kind of research that I think is worth doing.

Snowden: It sounds like you're saying that it's important to be sensitive to and to come to terms with what you're doing in ways outside the formal—

Rappaport: Outside the formal research, yes. If I'm optimistic at all about community psychology it would be—maybe I mean this about psychology in general—it would mean that we could reach a place where we're open enough to be able to integrate our so-called sophisticated statistical methodologies, our ability to do things like use time-series analysis and multidimensional scaling and multivariate data analysis, together with the methodologies, the patience, the descriptive skill of the anthropologist, to go to the level of what the anthropologists call the *emic* analysis, where one lets the variables be determined by the people in the setting and then goes from hypothesis test to hypothesis generation and back again.

You know, as I'm talking about it, one of the things that occurs to me is that we probably publish too damned frequently; and maybe what we really should do is require ourselves to study whatever it is we're studying over time and generate a series, in which one step influences the next step, in which we go from description to experimentation to new description to maybe doing some self-report phenomenological kinds of information gathering and combine that with independent observers, and combine that with being a participant in the setting that we're interested in; and, of course, it would take a very long time.

I think what I want to argue for is a broadened sense of what it means to be a scholar in psychology. That may mean that some psychologists might methodologically look like anthropologists, when they ask their psychological questions; others might look like highly quantitative methodologists; and others might look like novelists. What I want to make a plea for, I suppose, is a plurality of method; or maybe it's what Feyerabend calls, in that wonderful book *Against Method,* anarchy in methodology. Let's test methods by seeing what they produce rather than writing them off because the physical sciences have not used a given model for doing research. What I would want to argue for is a plurality and openness, with a sense that there is no single best way to get at the truth. I think what we have to begin to recognize is that we need a whole multiplicity of methods and viewpoints and what many people are now calling a dialectic. People usually talk about dialectics in terms of points of view or two different value systems or two different conceptions with totally opposite assumptions and then look at what happens when they see the same information from one view as opposed to the other. I think we need that kind of dialectic in methodology as well as in content.

Snowden: What are your feelings about education and training?

Rappaport: Well, I think it's usual to make the distinction between training and education. I think, at the graduate level, we should educate our students very early in an understanding of philosophy of science. I would start with philosophy of science; I actually think that psychology is absurdly unaware of philosophy of science. We don't even discuss that which sets so much of the basis for what follows and for our assumptions, which are never examined, so my preference would be that the prime root of our education be in philosophy of science and multiple methodologies for doing research and asking questions, ranging from highly quantitative to qualitative. I think that content, the specific subject matter, is something that, for almost any content area, any reasonably intelligent graduate student can learn in a month or two. If you want to enter a new area of content, you go to the library, and, in a month, you can probably read everything that's worthwhile. But what you can't learn so quickly, and the habits that you can't break so easily, are how to think—how to think about your preconceptions, about your philosophy of science, about ways to ask questions; I think that's what graduate school should be about as an educational experience.

When it comes to training, it depends on whether or not you see yourself as training people with very specific skills to deliver services or whether you see yourself as training—well, what else? I'm not sure what else. I guess what I want to say is that, unless we're planning on training our graduate students to provide a very concrete service, like psychotherapy, for example (which, as far as I'm concerned, is not unimportant but is just a lower priority), I think what we really ought to be concerned about is education rather than training. And, I guess what I want to talk about is social scientists rather than professional helpers; if we're talking about social scientists, I would emphasize education as opposed to training.

Snowden: Any final thoughts?

Rappaport: It's been a broad enough interview so that I feel comfortable saying this as a part of it: I think that psychology, maybe social science, is in a time of transition. I don't want to use that hackneyed word *crisis,* but that sort of captures some of the flavor of it. I think what we're beginning to realize more and more is that we may have, as Leon Rappoport has said recently, reached the limits of the usefulness of the positivistic model of science. We're reaching a place where there's an increasing understanding of the influence of our values and our beliefs and our political ideologies and a decreasing sense of the naive use of numbers as reification. We have an increasing sense of the limits of traditional normal science. A lot of that, I think, is a reflection of the kind of impact that Kuhn has had. It's ironic, in some ways; writing about revolutions, he may have stimulated a revolution. I guess I welcome all that; I think that we're very rapidly coming to a place where it's going to be harder and harder for us to be satisfied with the limitations of the narrow view of science. And, we are beginning to recognize that psychology is basically a moral and ethical endeavor; it can have as much to say about how people ought to live as about how people do live.

6

Improving Social Settings by Social Climate Measurement and Feedback

Rudolf H. Moos

In extensive work on assessing and evaluating social settings, my colleagues and I have used survey feedback to help people understand and change their environments. We have found that information about social settings may help people select and cope with the settings in which they function. In this chapter, I describe the conceptual framework we use to understand how social environments function, provide an overview of our experiences in giving feedback and of some of the problems that arise thereby, illustrate the concrete steps and procedures involved in facilitating change, and discuss some ideas about how knowledge of

Note: An earlier version of the chapter was presented at a symposium entitled "Community Psychology: Managing the Tensions Between Inquiry and Impact" at the annual convention of the American Psychological Association, San Francisco, August 1977. The work was supported by NIAAA Grant AA02863, NIMH Grant MH28177, and Veterans Administration Health Services Research and Development Service Funds.

the psychological properties of social environments can help people develop environmental competence.

Our work has been carried out within a social-ecological perspective, which provides a distinctive framework by which the transactions between people and their environments and the impacts of these transactions on human functioning can be conceptualized. This perspective, which is being integrated into developmental psychology (Bronfenbrenner, 1977), gerontology (Lawton and Nahemow, 1973), and health psychology (Moos, 1979a), is also relevant to clinical and community psychology (Holahan, 1978). I call this framework *social-ecological* to emphasize the inclusion of both social-environmental (for example, social climate) and physical-environmental (that is, ecological) variables.

An Integrative Conceptual Framework

My interest in human environments developed from a clinical perspective rather than from a perspective of social action or of environmental or social psychology. This background led me to a certain focus on human environments—on how they should be measured and on the practical implications that follow from this approach. I have commented elsewhere on the personal and professional influences that helped to shape my thinking in this area (Moos, 1976a, 1976b).

When I began my work, over fifteen years ago, I did not know how to characterize social settings. Although many theorists had emphasized the importance of the social environment, the only detailed conceptualization available was that of Henry Murray (1938), who formulated the notion of environmental press. But the specific press Murray thought might characterize environments developed from his description of personality needs rather than from empirical studies of social environments. C. Robert Pace and George Stern (1958) had used Murray's conceptualization to construct a College Characteristics Index, composed of thirty environmental press dimensions, which paralleled thirty commensurate need dimensions.

With this background and an initial focus on treatment settings, my colleagues and I began extensive naturalistic observations in a wide range of social environments. This eventually led to the development of a set of Social Climate Scales, which assess similar underlying patterns in different social settings. I have conceptualized these dimensions in three broad categories: Relationship dimensions, Personal Growth or Goal Orientation dimensions, and System Maintenance and System Change dimensions. These categories of dimensions are similar across many environments, although vastly different settings may impose unique variations within the general categories.

Relationship dimensions assess the extent to which people are involved in the environment, the extent to which they support and help one another, and the extent of spontaneity and free and open expression among them.

Personal Growth or Goal Orientation dimensions assess the basic directions along which personal development and self-enhancement tend to occur in a particular setting. These dimensions vary among different environments, depending on their underlying purposes and goals. For example, in psychiatric and correctional programs, we have autonomy, practical orientation, and personal problem orientation, whereas, in family settings, we have independence, achievement orientation, intellectual-cultural orientation, active recreational orientation, and moral-religious emphasis.

System Maintenance and System Change dimensions deal with the extent to which an environment is orderly, is clear in its expectations, maintains control, and is responsive to change.

These overall concepts hold as well for scales developed by other investigators as they do for our Social Climate Scales. For example, Stern (1970) identified several major types of dimensions, based on extensive research with the Organizational Climate Index. The first two dimensions—closeness and group life—appear to be Relationship dimensions. Three of Stern's dimensions seem to reflect Personal Growth: intellectual climate, personal dignity, and achievement standards. Stern's last two factors—orderliness and impulse control, or constraint—are System Maintenance factors. Other investigators have found conceptually similar dimensions in other types of environments (see Moos, 1974a, 1974b; Walberg, 1976).

I have dealt with some of the criticisms of this formulation elsewhere (Moos, 1975, chap. 13). Suffice it to say that I am not arguing that the dimensions I conceptualize are the only ones by which social environments can be characterized. I simply believe that it is necessary, although it may not be sufficient, to assess these three types of dimensions, if one wishes to have a reasonably complete picture of a social environment.

One other point must be mentioned here. Some people have argued that certain dimensions of social environments are positive or growth-producing (anabolic), whereas others are negative or growth-inhibiting (catabolic). There is some evidence that Relationship and Personal Growth dimensions are growth-producing and that the System Maintenance dimension of control is growth-inhibiting. However, strong emphasis on certain Personal Growth dimensions (for example, autonomy, competition) may relate to maladaptive physiological arousal, physical and emotional symptoms, or increased drop-out and absenteeism rates. Also, some people react positively to control, and some social environments need high control to function adequately. We must make value judgments in evaluating and changing social settings, but we must be careful not to confuse these value judgments with dependable data regarding the actual impacts of these settings on different outcome criteria (Moos, 1976a, 1976b; 1979b).

Constructing Environment Assessment Procedures

I am often asked whether my conceptual framework was empirically developed, or whether the social climate scales were constructed from prior theoretical convictions. Neither, and both, are true. As much as possible, my work represents an interaction among conceptual, methodological, and practical criteria. For example, we are currently constructing a Multiple Environmental Assessment Procedure (MEAP) to evaluate sheltered-care settings for the elderly.

The five parts of the MEAP follow a conceptual approach, in that they represent five of the basic sets of dimensions by which human environments have been characterized and related to human behavior. From a methodological point of view, the MEAP items must empirically discriminate among sheltered care settings, must be amenable to reliable observation or judgment, must link to other items to form coherent clusters or scales, and so on. From a practical point of view, we want to characterize the environment along dimensions that are meaningful to staff who work with the elderly and are useful for continued self-assessment and quality control of the sheltered care setting.

The development of an environmental assessment technique is not simply a methodological exercise. I often find it necessary to choose among alternative strategies in situations in which methodological, conceptual, and practical criteria are in conflict. One typical problem relates to item format and wording. We use true-false items, even though most respondents would prefer to answer items on three or four (or more) point scales. Our pretest evidence indicated that a true-false item format obtained as much information as other formats and avoided problems related to personal styles, such as preferences for middle-of-the-road, undecided, extreme, or deviant response tendencies. Thus, in this case, we followed methodological rather than practical (respondent satisfaction) criteria.

A related item format problem was recently highlighted in our attempt to develop a new social climate scale, the Sheltered Care Environment Scale (SCES), to assess the social environments of sheltered care settings for the elderly. Many of the respondents in these settings cannot understand the kinds of negatively keyed items we included in our other scales to control for acquiescence response set. Practical criteria dictated the development of simpler items (for example, "Do residents ever talk about illness and death?" rather than "Residents hardly ever talk about illness and death"). In this situation, we decided that item understandability (the practical criterion) should take precedence over the complete control of acquiescence response styles. (Recent evidence indicating that agreement acquiescence is a relatively minor determinant of responses to structured questionnaires suggests that the response style issue has been somewhat overemphasized; see Bentler, Jackson, and Messick, 1971; and Rorer, 1965.)

Another issue relates to the choice of items to include in each subscale. At this stage of scale development, we have used primarily empirical criteria, such as high item-subscale correlations, reasonably good item splits (that is, not everybody answers true or false), and significant item discrimination among settings. However, each item must also have conceptual validity—that is, participants in a particular setting must feel that the item is a reasonable indicator of the particular dimension on which it falls.

At the next stage of development, it is necessary to decide on the specific subscales to be included in a scale. To what extent should this decision be made on empirical (for example, factor-analytic) versus rational-conceptual grounds? We have used empirical criteria to reduce the number of subscales. For example, although affiliation and involvement can be conceptually distinguished, their high intercorrelations in several samples of respondents resulted in our combining them into one subscale in the Ward Atmosphere Scale (WAS). However, although factor analysis suggests that it is possible to combine cohesion items (Relationship dimension) and some organizational and clarity items (System Maintenance dimensions) into one subscale, I believe they are conceptually distinct, have different practical implications, and tend to be changed by somewhat different procedures and thus should be kept separate, even though they may be moderately highly intercorrelated.

Factor-analytic solutions are themselves determined in part by rational-conceptual considerations and, perhaps more importantly, by the specific statistical procedures and criteria employed, the characteristics of the sample included, and so forth (Walberg, 1976). In this connection, various factor analyses of the Social Climate Scales and their derivatives have already resulted in two-factor (Wilkinson, 1973; Kohn, Jeger, and Koretzky, 1979), three-factor (Alden, 1978), four-factor (Lawton, Lipton, and Cohen, 1976a; Manderscheid and Koening, 1977), five-factor (Edelson and Paul, 1977), and six-factor (Lawton, Lipton, and Cohen, 1976b; Trickett and Quinlan, 1977) solutions. Although the attempt to develop a smaller number of dimensions by which social environments can be characterized is laudable, the proliferation of different sets of factor dimensions may lead to endless conceptual disagreements and retard the development of dependable knowledge about the effects of specific, consistently defined environmental characteristics.

A final point relates to the decision about whether to use the same scale dimensions for different respondents in an environment, even though the empirical characteristics of their responses may differ somewhat. For example, it might be most faithful to the data to develop a six-subscale Sheltered Care Environment Scale for residents and an eight-subscale version for staff. We use practical criteria to make this decision. Specifically, it seems much more useful to be able to directly compare the perceptions of different sets of respondents with the same dimensions than to adhere rigidly to the exact details of certain statistical and empirical procedures (see Buros, 1977, for a similar perspective on ability and aptitude testing). This decision has made feedback considerably more useful and involving, since different groups of respondents can more meaningfully evaluate the similarities and differences in their perceptions of the environment.

Although there was considerable serendipity and luck involved, we followed four relevant principles in constructing our scales, which helped to make them practically useful: (1) item development through naturalistic observations and interviews; (2) inclusion of a representative variety of settings in initial standardization samples; (3) utilization of dimensions and concepts that generally make sense to people concerned with the particular settings evaluated, and (4) the interactive use of conceptual, psychometric, and practical criteria in scale development.

Giving and Taking Feedback

Since we began our work primarily from a research perspective, our original intent in giving people feedback was to enhance their participation in and enthusiasm for our research. This was a good strategy, since we managed to obtain and maintain a high level of cooperation. It quickly turned out, however, that the process and dynamics of giving feedback became as interesting and as time consuming as the process of collecting and analyzing the data.

In brief, we provided people with information about how they perceived their social environment, how different groups compared with each other (such as patients and staff, teachers and students, parents and children), how their setting compared with other similar settings, and, in some cases, how their current setting compared with what they considered ideal.

One practical problem is that people sometimes feel that particular items or subscales are not relevant to their setting. We have usually not accepted this criticism, because we know that items that are perceived as not relevant in one setting (often meaning that everyone answers them either true or false) empirically discriminate among settings. Respondents who are familiar with one group home, sheltered care setting, or correctional facility are often unaware of the extensive differences that exist among different group homes, sheltered care settings, or correctional facilities. Feedback can sensitize them to the ways in which their setting compares with other similar settings and with the innovative practices successfully implemented elsewhere. In this connection, there is growing evidence that the Social Climate Scales may be useful in comparative cross-cultural studies of social settings (Espvall and Astrom, 1974; Friis, 1974; Menard, 1974; Moos, 1974a, chapters 3 and 10; Paige, 1977; Skalar, 1974; Schneewind and Lortz, 1976).

In general, people are quite interested in what their setting is like, and they tend to find this kind of feedback useful, although the recipients of our feedback coped with it in a variety of ways. One major coping style was for people to show active interest and to indicate that they wished to use the data to enhance their setting. Although this was generally a good sign, it sometimes took a surprising turn.

In one case, we evaluated two psychiatric programs in one department. We gave feedback individually to each program, and the psychiatrists in charge of the programs independently stated that they were pleased with the results and wanted to reevaluate their program over time. About a month later, I received an irate letter from one of the psychiatrists (Dr. A) accusing me of giving feedback about his program to his department head and making it look bad in comparison with its counterpart.

It took a considerable amount of time and intuition to discover what had actually happened. Dr. A, convinced that his program's profile looked good, had placed it on the ward bulletin board. Staff members from the other ward heard about this, and, because of their interest in comparing the two wards, obtained a copy of the profile. The ward chief of the second program (Dr. B) thereupon forwarded the two profiles to the department head, requesting additional funding for his ward, because it had a better treatment milieu. When Dr. A heard about this, he concluded that we had violated our agreement of confidentiality, but, in reality, Dr. A was guilty of the lesser crime of naivete. One positive aspect of this experience was that it provided an unusual example of psychiatrists taking psychologists' test results too seriously!

In another case, we were involved in giving feedback on the Classroom Environment Scale (CES) to several high school classes. Two students in one class printed a fake letterhead, composed a fake feedback letter ostensibly signed by our research assistant, and produced a fake but highly authentic-looking computer printout of the CES results, all of which they mailed to the hapless teacher and to the school principal, using the return address of a recently rented post office box.

The letterhead read *Educational Environment Testing Service,* and the feedback letter stated: "We are led to believe from student answers on the surveys that your classroom is far from ideal. The students want an immediate change of classroom structure, whereas your answers indicate a very well organized and likeable classroom atmosphere." Also included were such pithy statements as "This teacher is still competing with rookie teachers but is out of his league. The class is obviously bored with the work, and a definite change of atmosphere is needed. Although it will be hard to undo the damage that has been done, we are giving you a list of reforming methods that we urge you to use."

The ruse worked. Everyone thought it was authentic feedback from us. You can imagine the anger, the mistrust, and the excitement aroused in trying to cope with this situation, which threatened our relationships with all the schools in the area, and the number of explanatory meetings necessary to resolve the situation (of course, the particular research assistant involved was away the day this happened). Although I would not suggest this as a general strategy by which to implement change, we did successfully resolve the situation, and, so far as I know, the learning environment of the classroom involved changed radically, although we did not attempt to reassess it!

Implementation of data-based feedback involves a number of complex issues, such as: (1) who should get the feedback (only the administrator of a program, all the staff, all the participants, only those people designated by the administrator), (2) should the higher echelon administration also obtain feedback, and (3) to what extent can or should specific settings remain unidentified? If there are only a few programs in an institution, as is often the case in a small hospital or school, can feedback be given and anonymity maintained? Should one only give feedback to a high school principal, for example, after all the teachers have been given individual feedback and have agreed to share the results? I cannot go into these and other related issues here. Suffice it to say that they are complex and need to be raised and resolved before data collection takes place. (See Moos, 1974a,b, for a discussion of respondent anonymity and other relevant scale-administration procedures).

Contrary to first impressions, there is no single answer to any of these questions. We have been in settings in which the administrator of a hospital would accept no feedback, unless ward staff agreed that feedback should be given. We have also worked in a correctional facility in which staff decided to have a joint meeting, where feedback on each individual unit was given to the entire staff and administration of the facility. Of course, conflicts sometimes arise between administrators' desires for identifiable feedback from the programs under their administration (such as all the wards in one hospital, all the classrooms in one school) and our usual procedures, which are to ensure confidentiality of the results, unless the setting participants wish to share them. Despite these and other problems, my overall conclusion is that feedback is generally worthwhile, both in training the person giving it and in increasing the understanding of the people receiving it.

Facilitating and Monitoring Environmental Change

In some of the settings in which we gave feedback, interest developed in using the information to facilitate and monitor environmental change. A number of studies have been carried out in this area in the past few years. For example, the WAS has been used to assess the change related to the development of group-therapy (Leviege, 1970) and token-economy programs (Gripp and Magaro, 1971; Jeger, 1977) and to plan humanistically oriented changes in an ongoing behaviorally oriented program that patients and staff were dissatisfied about (Curtiss, 1976).

The Community-Oriented Programs Environment Scale (COPES) has been used to facilitate change in two alcoholism treatment programs (Bliss, Moos, and Bromet, 1976) and to evaluate change and stability in a community-based residential treatment program for acute schizophrenic patients (Mosher, Menn, and Matthews, 1975). Other studies have involved the Correctional Institutions Environment Scale to assess change related to the development of token-economy and transactional-analysis programs in correctional facilities (Jesness and others, 1972); the University Residence Environment Scale to evaluate the differences between novel living-learning environments and traditional dormitory units (Schroeder and Griffin, 1976) and to contrast the social milieus of high-rise and low-rise university dormitories (Wilcox and Holahan, 1976); and the Group Environment Scale to help residence hall staff focus on milieu management and design better social settings (Schroeder, 1979).

We have been involved in three demonstration studies in which the treatment milieus of three psychiatric programs were successfully changed. Two studies were carried out in small, heavily staffed, hospital-based programs. The WAS served as a teaching device for program staff, and, after intensive discussion of real versus ideal program discrepancies, attempts were made to formulate specific change goals. Relatively large overall changes in the social milieus of the programs demonstrated that assessment and intensive staff discussion could function as a stimulus for positive change.

Changing the Milieu of an Adolescent Residential Center. A third study was conducted in an adolescent residential center. The center was a coeducational home for teenagers referred from hospitals or the juvenile courts. The youngsters were diagnosed as having primarily mental or emotional difficulties; many also had drug problems and a history of school failure. With a capacity to serve fourteen adolescents, the program had four live-in house managers and a director, who was a research psychologist. Residents stayed in the program for about four months and progressed through as many step levels, each level having increasing responsibilities and privileges. Residents were rated weekly on a point system by other residents and staff. At these meetings, progress was evaluated in such areas as personal care, money management, interpersonal relationships, and meeting step level expectations.

The COPES results showed that residents felt encouraged to be spontaneous, to freely express their feelings (including angry feelings), and to discuss and understand their personal problems.

They believed there was above average emphasis on preparing them for release from the program (practical orientation), but they reported below average emphasis on support and order and organization (see Figure 1). Residents and staff basically saw the program similarly, although staff saw more emphasis on support and autonomy and less emphasis on involvement and spontaneity than the residents did.

Figure 2 compares the degree of change the residents and staff wanted in the program. The amount of change desired was calculated by subtracting the score the residents (or staff) gave the actual program (Form R means) from the score they gave an ideal program (Form I means). The profile shows the amount of increase or decrease needed in each area for the program to become an ideal program, as envisioned by residents and staff. The line marked *zero* in the center of the profile indicates no change desired—that is, there is no discrepancy between real and ideal sub-

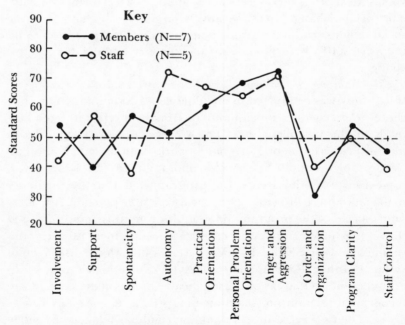

Figure 1. COPES Form R Profiles for Members and Staff in an Adolescent Residential Center

scale means. For example, neither residents nor staff desired any change in the emphasis on personal problem orientation. Positive scores indicate a desire for more emphasis in an area—for example, residents and staff wanted fairly substantial increases in involvement, spontaneity, and program clarity.

The COPES profiles were discussed with residents and staff, and both groups showed an interest in systematically changing the program's social environment. A change facilitator met with residents and staff over a four-month period, initially suggesting possible changes and later helping to implement specific new procedures. For example, new positions of food manager (responsible for assisting and supervising meal preparation) and crew job leader (responsible for supervising and checking all work around the house) were instituted. The sphere of authority of the resident coordinator, who supervised the food manager and crew job leader, was clarified. The coordinator was given the authority to

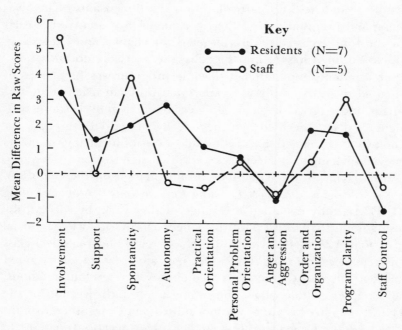

Figure 2. Real-Ideal Discrepancies, as Perceived by Members and Staff in an Adolescent Residential Center

call resident group meetings whenever problems arose and was placed on the screening committee, which decided about accepting new residents into the house.

Additional attempts were made to clarify expectations, by giving a resident the responsibility of teaching new residents their job obligations in the house, instituting a clearer structure in the process of individual goal-setting, and establishing a new peer-rating procedure, by which each resident rated the others on certain personal characteristics. As might be expected in an adolescent residential center, autonomy and staff control issues were quite complex and were discussed in considerable detail.

The Real and Ideal Forms of the COPES were readministered to residents and staff about six months after the initial testing. The residents generally felt that the treatment milieu was closer to their ideal in the second testing. The largest changes occurred on the dimensions of involvement, support, autonomy, and program clarity. Staff also saw the program as closer to their ideal at the second testing, particularly on the dimensions of involvement and program clarity. Specific changes thus occurred in each of the four areas that were targeted for change and extensively discussed following the initial feedback sessions. Significantly, however, residents and staff felt that the program was further from their ideal in its emphasis on personal problem orientation and anger and aggression. This shift occurred mainly because residents and staff decided that they ideally wished less emphasis on the two areas named, illustrating that views of ideal environments may also change with feedback and discussion sessions (see Moos, 1974a, chaps. 4 and 11, for more information on these studies).

Changing Classroom Learning Environments.   Alan DeYoung (1977) recently extended the range of this work, by successfully using the CES to effect positive change in a college sociology-social psychology class. He used information regarding real-ideal class discrepancies from one class, which indicated that students wanted more involvement, greater stress on innovative teaching methods, and clearer notions about the organization and direction of the class, to modify his approach in a subsequent class. Students indicated a desire to "get a group together for a project" (affiliation), to have the instructor "spend a little time just talking with students" (teacher support), to "engage in unusual projects," and to "do different things on different days" (innovation). Students also reported that they were confused about classroom policies and procedures. Therefore, teams of students were formed to report on specific topics, and efforts were made to see students individually, to discuss class subject matter and organization, to clarify grading policies and appeal procedures, to encourage innovative projects and alternative classroom delivery and participation techniques, and so forth.

Although the social climate desired by the students in the two classes was virtually identical, there were large differences in their actual learning environments. Students in the second class perceived more emphasis on all three Relationship dimensions (involvement, affiliation, and teacher support), on rule clarity, and on innovation. These differences, which represented the specific areas the instructor had attempted to influence, indicate that one can change the learning environment along lines suggested by the CES, given an understanding of the salient features of the classroom setting. Importantly, the differences were linked to greater student interest and participation and a higher student attendance rate.

One of the problems that may occur, when one allows the participants in an environment to indicate the extent and direction of change they desire, is illustrated by the fact that students wanted less emphasis on task orientation. The instructor decided that decreasing the emphasis on this dimension would jeopardize overall learning objectives, and thus no attempt was made to alter the amount of attention given to course work. This disregard of students' wishes was demonstrated in the similarity of task-orientation scores in the two classes, indicating that it is possible to restructure and improve a class without sacrificing attention to course content.

There are basically four steps involved in this process of facilitating and monitoring environmental change: (1) systematic assessment of the environment, (2) feedback to participating groups with particular stress on real-ideal setting differences, (3) planning and instituting specific changes, and (4) reassessment. Since there is no specific end point to this process, continual change and reassessment often occur.

Some benefits that may occur in the process of planning and facilitating change include: (1) Participants can untangle and analyze the multiple dimensions of setting functioning. (2) Important characteristics that are often overlooked are systematically called into awareness, such as the clarity of expectations regarding policies and procedures. (3) Participants' input is comprehensively obtained in a manner that makes them feel comfortable and competent. For example, although many junior high and high school students do not feel qualified to criticize a course, they do feel able to act as reporters about its current functioning. (4) In some settings (treatment and correctional programs, social science classrooms), issues surrounding the utilization of social climate feedback can provide relevant discussion topics, such as an analysis of patient versus staff roles or of institutional sanctions and sources of resistance to change. (5) Supervisors may subtly change their perceptions of their own role—that is, they may begin to emphasize their role as facilitators of learning in addition to their administrative role. (6) Since participants can concentrate their attempts to change their setting on a few commonly defined areas, the possibility of confusion or conflicting behavior is reduced, and the likelihood that change can take place in an orderly manner is enhanced. (7) Involvement may be increased, simply because people are engaged in the common task of changing their own social environments.

Resistance to Change and Other Problems. These procedures are no panacea, and serious resistance to change and other problems may occur during the evaluation and change process (Ellsworth, 1975; Gurel, 1975). Resistance tends to arise when existing social relationships are ignored, when people feel that changes may lead to an increase in disruptive or uncontrollable behavior (such as by students in classrooms) or cause staff to be uncertain of what is expected of them, when the need for change is not adequately understood by setting participants, and so forth. Although resistance to change is a formidable issue, it should not be used as an explanation to mask such problems as lack of coherent training, inadequate knowledge of environmental conceptualizations, unwillingness to commit the required amount of time to successfully monitor and resolve ongoing difficulties in change attempts, and the like.

Different concepts of ideal environments and resulting disagreement regarding the direction of change can be a serious problem. Nevertheless, feedback and discussion of social climate information may help to identify common values and to clarify the exact nature of the differences in value orientations. Although teachers, principals, parents, and school board administrators may disagree about the ideal amount of emphasis on classroom competition, for example, they usually agree that an emphasis on involvement, affiliation, teacher support, and clarity is important. Whereas some people feel that classroom structure and organization are essential, others are convinced that an emphasis on these dimensions retards the development of independence and intrinsic motivation to learn. To complicate matters further, people may not know what is best for them and, for example, may wish to function in settings that maximize immediate satisfaction and comfort rather than the development of basic learning skills and long-range social competence.

Another general issue involves the emergence of unintended consequences. Patients in two of our studies perceived decreases in program clarity after change attempts were instituted. Implementing new policies and procedures may be accompanied by initial confusion (particularly on the part of the people not directly involved in planning change) and a consequent decrease in clarity. Differences in perceptions on this dimension indicate that the change process is incomplete, and such differences point to the need for better communication and greater involvement of all the participants in the setting.

Since most changes are implemented through structural or organizational means (such as new rules or better channels of communication), efforts to increase cohesion, support, or autonomy may be confounded by people's reactions to greater emphasis on system maintenance (the degree of control is an important indicator here). For example, the initial changes in one alcoholism program led to greater structure and a concomitant decrease in the quality of interpersonal relationships, particularly spontaneity (Bliss, Moos, and Bromet, 1976). The continuing development process eventually brought about the desired changes, but a temporary unintended decrease in cohesion and spontaneity can occur when attempts are made to increase program structure.

Another potential problem is that change may continue beyond the originally desired goals. Changes may take place within a generally consistent ideology; that is, a setting can institute a series of carefully thought-out and graduated changes while still retaining its essential overall direction. However, it may be difficult to control or stop change, once it has been initiated. The effects of attempts to change programs often lead to changes in the ideals valued by program participants. In a follow-up of one of our studies, it was found that subsequent program changes led to predictable changes in staff ideals (Cooper, 1973), which in turn led to a desire for further change. Feedback of information is a dynamic ongoing process that may result in changes in the concept of an ideal social environment as well as changes in perceptions of the real environment.

A final issue is the maintenance of an innovation, once it has been successfully implemented. The two most common problems involve a gradual decrease in the motivation of participants and, usually more importantly, changes in the overall setting (such as the hospital or school) that impinge on the particular subsetting (such as the ward or classroom) involved (Sarata and Reppucci, 1975). There is no wholly satisfactory answer to these problems; however, easily administered assessment procedures, such as the Social Climate Scales, are reasonable short-term information-gathering techniques for busy staff lacking extensive facilities or personnel for evaluation. The administration and analysis of these scales is a useful service that a hospital or university psychology department or counseling center can provide to interested settings (Daher, Corazzini, and McKinnon, 1977; Kish, 1971). If this kind of procedure were instituted on a regular (annual or semiannual) basis, it would at the very least provide dependable information on the longitudinal life-cycle characteristics of social settings.

Determinants of Successful Innovations. McKeachie's (1976) cogent analysis suggests that feedback works best when three basic conditions are met. First, the feedback must provide relevant information to the learner (consultee). McKeachie points out that studies of student ratings of college teachers and of videotaped feedback, which are based on the assumption that teaching will improve if teachers get feedback, often fail to show positive effects. One problem is that the feedback may not provide useable information. As McKeachie (p. 824) states, "anyone who has watched an English professor's eyes glaze over as she or he looks at a computer printout of means and standard deviations of student ratings on an eighty-item form is likely to have some doubts about the information communicated. . . . We can fail to understand because of *too much* information as well as too little."

Second, the recipients of the feedback must be motivated to change. Competing motivations, such as reducing perceived threats to organizational control, maintaining traditional prerogatives and role status, and fear of external scrutiny have been cogently discussed elsewhere (Ellsworth, 1975; Gurel, 1975). Initial feedback regarding dysfunctional behavior (high absenteeism rates, sick-call rates, drop-out rates, and so forth) is usually perceived as highly relevant to program functioning and may enhance the relative strength of motivation toward constructive change. The characteristics of the social environment become more relevant once the connections between them and the dysfunctional behaviors are clarified.

The third condition for enhancing change is that respondents must perceive the practical availability of better alternatives. Participants may feel that the feedback is relevant and may be motivated to change, but change may be impossible due to the types of people in the setting, constricting bureaucratic policies, stringent cost constraints, and so forth. A recurring issue here is whether providing printed feedback or one feedback session is sufficient to produce change. Although printed feedback may be useful under certain conditions (see Rokeach, 1975), it is generally not very effective in implementing social systems change (see McKeachie, 1976, for similar conclusions regarding the impact of printed versus personal feedback on teaching effectiveness). Outside motivational support and specific suggestions about ways to implement change are usually necessary in using social systems feedback to foster long-term change.

In general, I believe our methods are promising and work reasonably well, because they are consonant with the three principles for determining successful innovations and for three additional reasons: (1) They concentrate on relatively small social settings (classrooms instead of schools, wards instead of hospitals), which are usually highly salient to their members. (2) They focus on those aspects of settings that tend to be under local control (that is, teachers and students *can* change the emphasis on involvement, affiliation, teacher support, task orientation, and rule clarity in their own classrooms). (3) They speak directly to each individual's need for personal efficacy, which includes actively helping to mold his or her social environment.

Fullan and Pomfret (1977) have recently presented an overview of four sets of determinants of the success of innovations. They focus primarily on curriculum and instruction innovations, but most of the issues are more generally relevant. First, in terms of the characteristics of the innovation itself, the important aspects are the degree of explicitness of the plans and the simplicity or ease of implementing the change required by the innovation. Second, in terms of methods employed to introduce and implement the innovation, feedback mechanisms that stimulate interaction, problem identification, and participation in decision making are helpful. Continuous interaction between teachers and consultants seems to be better than single workshops or preservice training. Change agents must also recognize the need for adequate time for people in the setting to familiarize themselves with new materials and methods and to reflect and work on implementation problems both individually and collectively. The time perspective for adequately implementing innovations is often unrealistically short, primarily because the complexity of the process of implementation is insufficiently understood or the immediacy of the perceived need for change is too great.

The third set of relevant factors involves the characteristics of the adopting units (such as an adolescent residential center or a classroom). The organizational climate and degree of environmental support are crucial factors here. High morale of teachers at a school and active support of principals and superintendents increase the chances of educational change and perceived success. This consideration raises the possibility of using the Social Climate Scales to increase cohesion and morale and thereby facilitate the later introduction of a broader, more comprehensive innovation.

The fourth set of factors are macrosociopolitical. Does the degree to which political agencies promote large-scale programs increase the likelihood of adoption but decrease the likelihood of effective implementation? Does the political context inhibit the identification of problems in implementation, due to the emphasis on rapid payoff and the focus on outcome? Changing social settings involves a very complex process, and it must be remembered that most successful innovations themselves undergo gradual but continual change during the implementation phase, reflecting a process of mutual adaptation between the change-advocate and the host setting.

Corwin (1972) notes that organizations can be more easily changed if they are staffed by young, flexible, supportive, and competent boundary personnel, or gatekeepers, and if their members have positions that are reasonably secure and protected from the status risks involved in change. He points out that it is important to have liberal, creative, and unconventional outsiders with fresh perspectives but that change-agents with these characteristics may be a source of friction and tensions, and their presence often arouses defensive reactions and reduces the probability of successfully implementing innovations. The attempt to combine the change-agent role with an apprenticeship system (for example, psychology interns who attempt to facilitate change in schools) places interns in a precarious position between two powerful organizations. They are representatives of the outside organization that is attempting to facilitate change (that is, the university) but can count on little direct support from remote university professors, whereas they are directly supervised by resistant school personnel.

Finally, the issue of how to evaluate the success of an innovation needs to be addressed. Hall and Loucks (1977) have presented a developmental model to help determine the extent to which an innovation has actually been implemented. They introduce the concept of *levels of use* of an innovation and describe eight such levels. These range from level 1, in which the user has little or no knowledge of the innovation, through orientation (level 2), preparation (level 3), and mechanical use (level 4), in which the focus is on the short-term, day-to-day use of the innovation with little time for reflection. At this level, changes are made primarily to meet user rather than client needs, and the user is engaged in a stepwise attempt to master the tasks required to implement the innovation, often resulting in disjointed and superficial use. This indicates that it is not sufficient to evaluate an innovation by examining only behavioral changes, since these may represent superficial or mechanical use. An exclusive focus on behavior may result in users evidencing change without fully understanding the principles underlying it.

Level 5 is routine use, in which the innovation is stabilized, but little preparation or thought is given to improving it or its consequences. The next levels are refinement (level 6), intregation (level 7), and, finally, renewal (level 8), in which the user reevaluates the quality of the innovation, seeks major modifications or alternatives to it to achieve increased impacts on clients, examines new developments in the field, and explores new goals for the self and the system. The logical end of an innovation is thus the development of still another innovation, in a continually changing and never-ending process.

Practical Utility of the Social Climate Concept

My recent work has led me to identify several related areas in which a focus on social environments may be useful for enhancing individual environmental competence. For example, information about social environments can help to implement institutional consultation to formulate ecologically relevant clinical case descriptions (Eichel, 1978), to optimize person-environment congruence, and to test and expand on conceptual and theoretical propositions regarding the differences to be expected among social environments (Hearn and Moos, 1976; Moos, 1979b, chaps. 4 and 8; Trickett, 1978).

From the broadest perspective, the social climate approach can sensitize us about what to look for in analyzing social settings. The three types of dimensions—that is, Relationship, Personal Growth, and System Maintenance and System Change—provide a useful way of understanding the confusing complexity of social settings. These dimensions may help individuals select a wide range of environments in which to participate in their everyday lives. In addition, those responsible for selecting the environments of others, such as children or the elderly, can do so with better awareness of the personal traits that alternative environments foster.

I have described other major uses of information about social environments elsewhere (Moos, 1976b), but three brief examples may serve to further illustrate the range of possibilities. First, there is considerable current interest in environmental resources or supports that may buffer environmental stress. Since family cohesion and support are related to positive treatment outcome for alcoholism (Bromet and Moos, 1977), it might be useful to assess the family environments of patients just before or immediately after release, to identify those families in which preventive intervention and after-care services could be most helpful. Similar considerations apply in the treatment and rehabilitation process in major physical illnesses, such as severe burns, heart attacks, strokes, and organ transplants (Moos, 1977).

More generally, information about social environments can be used to identify those social settings in which preventive intervention might be particularly useful. Studies conducted in quite different types of institutions (such as classrooms, student living groups, psychiatric treatment programs, and military basic training companies) have suggested that settings perceived to be low in involvement, support, or autonomy and high in competition, strictness, and control tend to be characterized by dysfunctional reactions, such as high complaints of physical symptoms, sick call, absenteeism, and drop-out rates (see, for example, Moos and Van Dort, 1979). It might be useful for us to focus on identifying and changing these high-risk settings. Since the work environments of health care staff (for example, intensive-care units or terminal cancer wards) can be highly stressful, community psychologists might also consider attempts to evaluate and change these settings.

Another intriguing way to better evaluate community settings is to focus on how people cope with environmental stress and transcend environmental pressure. Many people conform to their environments, but some people do not. Studies of these environmental resistors and of the coping methods they use would be particularly informative. For example, we identified the personal characteristics that distinguished university students whose level of physical symptoms conformed to the symptom level of their living unit from those whose symptom level did not. Low symptom females living in high symptom living groups who did not themselves increase in symptoms (environmental resistors) were higher in dominance and religious concern and lower in social participation than those who increased in symptoms (Nielsen and Moos, 1977). Further specification of the personal variables that relate to the degree of conformity or resistance to environmental influence is central to understanding the differential impact of community settings.

A third, more general notion involves the need for environmental educators—that is, people who can help individuals or organizations to maximize the use of existing environments. Environmental educators could teach people about their environment, about how to conceptualize its component parts and their interrelationship, and, most important, about how to understand and control its potential impact in their everyday lives. For example, some organizations have developed a realistic job preview to increase the amount and accuracy of information given to job candidates in an effort to enhance the overall quality of their organizational choices.

The effects of the usual job-selection process are that expectations held by newcomers are almost always inflated and that increasing experience in an organization is associated with a less favorable view of it. Realistic job previews change people's expectations but neither drive away prospective employees nor reduce the favorability of the selection ratio for the organization. These previews may enhance job tenure by facilitating more effective organizational choices by the individual, by communicating an air of honesty to applicants (who then feel a greater degree of freedom in their organizational choice), and by lowering individual expectations to a level more congruent with the actual organizational climate, thereby preparing newcomers for the unpleasant aspects of a new environment. In general, there is a need for a more integrated conceptual view of the entire joining process, one which approaches the process from both sides—that of the individual and that of the organization (Wanous, 1977).

Current emphasis on competence building, self-control and self-esteem, and the importance of perceived control over the environment support these notions. Cohen, Glass, and Phillips (1977) have suggested that feelings of helplessness and an inability to control environmental stimuli may be more important than the actual characteristics of the environment itself. Langer and Saegert (1977) found that the consequences of crowded environments could be ameliorated through cognitive means. Providing information that explained and validated the experience of arousal resulted in reducing the emotional and behavioral consequences of crowding.

This information even had a beneficial influence in an uncrowded setting, suggesting that it would be useful to teach skills for coping with different kinds of environments.

Although these areas are promising, I do not wish to minimize the inherent problems and contradictions involved. Willems (1977) has pointed out that seemingly promising interventions may have unintended negative consequences. For example, De-Shong (1976) assessed students' expressed satisfaction toward their campus environment before and after participation in small-group discussions that focused on formulating recommendations for change to be presented to the university president and administrative council. Contrary to predictions, overall satisfaction with the university environment was not altered, and, in fact, students' satisfaction with administrative policies decreased. Students probably felt that the administration was responsible for immediate action that was not forthcoming. The group sessions led students to expect that they would have an influence in changing the environment, but these expectations were not met. Participation in change-oriented groups may increase students' feelings of alienation in the absence of visible changes resulting from their participation.

A second example comes from a recent study of the mentally ill in community-based sheltered care. The COPES was used by residents and operators of facilities to evaluate the social environments of 234 sheltered-care settings in California. An ideal psychiatric environment was defined as one that is involving, supportive, spontaneous, independence-fostering, oriented toward dealing with practical and personal problems, permitting open expression of anger, and organized with clearly defined procedures. This type of environment related positively to social integration in the community. Importantly, however, the ideal environment seemed to act as a social insulator for more severely disturbed or symptomatic patients, promoting social integration within the facility but having no effect on integration into the community. A very positive sheltered-care environment may inhibit certain types of patients from extending their social contacts outside the facility (Segal and Aviram, 1978).

In another study, retirement home residents, who had initially benefited from a short-term intervention that increased the control and predictability of the environment, exhibited precipitous declines in health and psychological status, once the study was terminated. The residents who gained most as a result of the interventions also declined most later on. Further work indicated that an intervention to effect a permanent increase in the predictability of the environment (through establishing an individualized orientation program, which included detailed information about facility procedures, available services, directions on how to get to different areas of the facility, and the like) had a positive impact that persisted over time (Schulz and Hanusa, 1978).

The best we can do is to try to understand when unintended effects may occur, to monitor their emergence, and to attempt to use the resulting information to develop more effective interventions. One general problem is that increased control for one person may lower that of another and lead to a decrease in cohesion and support. In addition, too strong a need to control the environment may lead to sustained elevation of catecholamines, serum cholesterol, and blood pressure and thus may lead to a greater probability of coronary heart disease (Glass, Snyder, and Hollis, 1974). These considerations underscore the necessity for caution and moderation.

We need people who can understand environments, the kinds of reactions people have in them, and the environmental dimensions and psychological and physiological mediating mechanisms involved. When this information is combined with information about how people generally cope with and adapt to social environments (see Holahan, 1978, for an extended discussion), then the role of environmental educator can be more fully implemented. Although there are some examples of the use of information about social environments as an aid in teaching people about their settings (for example, the use of the Ward Atmosphere Scale in teaching interns and residents about treatment settings and the use of the Family Environment Scale as a teaching aid in a marriage and family living class), the general utility of this area remains largely unexplored. Since the role of environmental educator will enhance the efficacy of community psychologists, we should develop these ideas as rapidly as possible. I hope they can contribute to helping us improve the everyday social settings in which we function, as well as to solving broader environmental problems, by enhancing our perceived—and actual—adaptation to our environment (see Moos and Brownstein, 1977, for a discussion of these broader issues).

INTERVIEW WITH RUDOLF H. MOOS

Snowden: I would like to begin by asking you about some of the facilitating influences on your work, some of the circumstances in your environment that have proven helpful.

Moos: The intellectual stimulation during my undergraduate and graduate days in the Psychology Department at the University of California in Berkeley was initially most important. There was a scientific and scholarly tradition in the department that affected me — people as diverse as David Krech, who was an exciting and critical teacher and demanded the best of a student, and Mark Rosenzweig, from whom I took some difficult but excellent courses in physiological psychology, embodied this tradition. At the time, I was trying to explore the whole range of psychology, since I had not yet formed any specialized interests. After entering graduate school, I decided to seek clinical training and to become a clinical psychologist.

My early clinical work had an important influence on me. I was asked to evaluate patients, using the Minnesota Multiphasic Personality Inventory (MMPI), the Rorschach, and other similar assessment techniques, and to make predictions about what those patients were going to do — for example, whether they would function adequately when they left the hospital. I found that it was very difficult to make such predictions accurately. I learned that the social settings in which patients functioned after they left treatment had an important impact on them. If, for example, family and work settings strongly influence patients' posttreatment functioning, which I think they do, then a clinician cannot make accurate predictions based only on information about the patient. These considerations sparked my interest in environmental effects on behavior.

Snowden: It sounds as though both academic and applied work settings gave direction to your thinking. What other influences can you identify?

Moos: My next experience was an internship at Langley Porter, during which I became interested in psychosomatic and psychophysiological research. At the time, I did not envision that this would eventually lead me into community psychology. Bernard Engel, who is now a psychophysiologist with the National Institute on Aging, influenced my intellectual development at this point. I learned about the psychophysiological concepts of individual response specificity and stimulus response specificity. I saw these as analogous to personality traits and social setting influences. The idea of individual response specificity proposes that people react to varied stimuli with a consistent set of autonomic responses. Thus, for example, a hypertensive patient would be expected to respond consistently with a rise in blood pressure to different stressors. The idea of stimulus-response specificity proposes that certain stressors elicit specific autonomic responses from most people. For example, the stress of being pressured and overburdened at work may generally elicit increases in blood pressure. Bernard Engel and I collaborated on a paper illustrating how these psychophysiological concepts were relevant to the issue of the relative amount of variance attributable to personal and situational factors in making predictions of behavior.

Snowden: Psychophysiology is an unexpected source of ideas for ecology. What was your next step?

Moos: The next step in the development of my work included a set of studies in which I compared the importance of personal and situational factors in forecasting behavior. My first research in this area stemmed from my interest in psychosomatic problems. In the early 1960s, I conducted several studies on the personality characteristics of rheumatoid arthritic patients. I focused on whether one could accurately describe these patients in terms of personality traits or whether such so-called traits varied, depending on the situation. Accordingly, I developed a questionnaire to assess how these patients felt and behaved in different settings. About that time, Norman Endler and J. McVicker Hunt were carrying out similar studies on anxiety and hostility. This background led me to conduct a set of studies on the proportion of variance in behavior that could be accounted for by persons, settings, and their interactions.

Snowden: Please discuss these studies. In doing so, could you describe facilitating aspects of your own work environment?

Moos: Those studies, as well as all my subsequent work, were conducted after I came to the Department of Psychiatry at Stanford University and the Palo Alto Veterans Administration Medical Center. I was very fortunate, in that our department chairman was David Hamburg, a psychiatrist with a broad view of behavioral science and research. He established a social environment in which I felt both maximum freedom and support. With his support, I conducted a set of studies in which I observed people in different settings and analyzed the extent to which they varied their behavior across settings. In one such study, I had four therapists see each of six patients in a counterbalanced design. I was interested in the degree to which therapists were empathic regardless of the patient they were seeing (empathy as a therapist trait), versus the degree to which some patients elicited more empathy from therapists than other patients did (empathy as situationally or patient-determined). Surprisingly, the results showed that therapist empathy was largely determined by the patient; that is, it was much easier for the therapists to empathize with some patients than with others.

Taken together, these and my other studies convinced me that people vary their behavior considerably as they move from one setting to another. As I look back on it, I feel good about these studies, although I wish I had completed them more quickly. In retrospect, I probably should have assumed that people vary their behavior across settings and not spent so much time trying to demonstrate it. But the dominant idea in personality theory at that time was that personality traits and motives determined behavior and that situational influences were relatively unimportant. Given that zeitgeist, it was difficult for me to trust my instincts and jump ahead to develop measures of environments.

Snowden: How did you proceed from conceptual appreciation of environmental influences to developing standardized assessment procedures?

Moos: All this eventually led me to begin my work on evaluating treatment environments. I began in 1965 with the straightforward idea that, if people varied their behavior in different settings, the obvious next step was to develop measures of such settings. I focused on treatment environments, because I was in a Department of Psychiatry and was located in a Veterans Administration Hospital. Given the ideas of Maxwell Jones about the therapeutic community, which had a strong effect on me, I set myself the task of trying to develop a measure of psychiatric ward atmosphere. An important influence here was the assessment and statistical training that I had received in the Psychology Department at Berkeley from people like Harrison Gough, who taught me about the MMPI and CPI. From my experimental, statistical, and methodological background, in conjunction with my clinical experience, I was prepared to devise psychometric measures of social settings. Support, in that I had a congenial faculty to work with, was essential in actually carrying out the work. It was possible for me to talk to staff, to go to the wards, to collect pretest data, and so on.

Snowden: Again, it sounds as though the social climate was important. What was your next step?

Moos: The most important next step was obtaining grant support. During the first few years, I did most of the work myself. George Coelho of the NIMH helped me to obtain my first significant grant support. George Coelho visited, just as Peter Houts and I were completing the initial work on the Ward Atmosphere Scale. He became quite excited about my prospective instrument. At the time, he was trying to establish epidemiology field stations to systematically collect data about the social-environmental conditions in metropolitan areas throughout the country. Unfortunately, these field stations were never developed in quite the way that Coelho envisioned, although one was begun in Kansas City. His idea was to go beyond prevalence studies to focus on how specific personal and environmental factors combined to produce illness. For example, many studies have found a high concentration of mentally ill patients in inner-city areas. Why is that so? How much is due to the person; how much is due to aspects of the environment? To answer these questions, one must have procedures for systematic measurement of the environment. Although my work was on psychiatric wards rather than in cities or neighborhoods, Coelho saw the potential applications of the basic idea and helped me develop a proposal, which led to a three-year grant to construct and validate the Ward Atmosphere Scale.

Snowden: Your work involves contacting and maintaining relationships with a vast number of social settings. I wonder if you could talk about how your style of relating to settings has evolved?

Moos: As I mentioned, the first part of the work was easy, because I already had good relationships with those local psychiatric programs that were administered by the psychiatrists on our faculty. Through my relationship with these people, I enlisted help with observations, interviewing, pretesting items, reliability, and the like. This is essential but often rather dull work that involves a considerable amount of time. My main reason for branching out was that I thought it was necessary to obtain data from a varied and representative sample of psychiatric wards to develop a scale that would adequately measure all types of treatment milieus. Researchers sometimes forget the need to sample settings, when doing research on environments, leading them, for example, to develop a scale based on data obtained in only one setting. I thought that it would be necessary to test many wards and that my sample should be reasonably representative of the types of programs that exist.

Snowden: Could you give an example of how you enlist and maintain cooperation?

Moos: I recruited fourteen wards for the initial development of the Ward Atmosphere Scale by making a list of all the potentially available programs in the area and working primarily through personal contact. A community hospital in which our residents went to be trained supplied a ward. People whom I knew at Langley Porter gave me access to a ward. There were some state hospitals in which I knew people who helped me collect data on several wards.

How does one actually obtain cooperation? Every case is different. I will use the Veterans Administration as an example. I thought that backing from the central administration of an organization such as V.A. would facilitate entry into a large number of programs. I wrote to the Chief of Psychology, Cecil Peck, explaining my project and requesting his help in identifying interested hospitals. We eventually got the V.A. Central Office to send out letters requesting statements of interest in participating. Hospitals were selected to be reasonably representative of V.A. facilities around the country. We followed up by contacting the hospital Directors and then usually the chief of the psychology service. We previously found that the psychologists were usually interested in facilitating our work. These procedures helped us to obtain data on fifty-five wards in Veterans Administration hospitals.

Snowden: Would you recommend the strategy of approaching top echelons as a general strategy with large organizations?

Moos: Although there are potential advantages, I prefer not to approach a large organization in the manner just described because of the possible complications concerning feedback. Once one has information about a program's social environment, the question of feedback inevitably arises. Many feedback procedures are possible, depending on the arrangement one makes, but one must be careful to be quite specific about the details. The more levels of administration involved in obtaining cooperation, the more difficult this problem becomes. If one goes to a central federal or state government administration, there is a question about whether they will get feedback. Will the director of each participating hospital or the principal of each school get feedback? Will the chief of the psychology service in a hospital or the head guidance counselor in a school system get feedback? Since these people are almost always interested in comparing the programs under their jurisdiction, this can be a complex problem. The problem is that the people who are responsible for the setting being studied feel they are being evaluated and may or may not wish to share the results of the evaluation with their administrative superiors. A less obvious but just as frequent problem is that some program directors do not wish to share results with the staff or patients on their unit. Solving these problems successfully can be time consuming, especially when people at several administrative levels, each of whom has different and often competing interests, are involved.

Snowden: How did you cope with these problems?

Moos: Since these issues continually arose, I eventually developed some flexible guidelines about how to handle them. I believe that my most important decision was to guarantee confidentiality to each setting (such as a ward or classroom), much as a therapist guarantees confidentiality to each patient. We will not identify the results for a particular setting, unless we have permission from the director of that setting, and, in general, we prefer to let the responsible people in the setting provide feedback to others, if they wish.

Let me give you one more example of our data-collection procedures. We are currently conducting a study of sheltered-care programs for the elderly. The purpose is to develop a comprehensive way to assess environments. This will cover not only social climate but other features derived from our conceptual framework—physical and architectural dimensions, program and policy dimensions, and human aggregate dimensions. To begin our project, we needed to obtain a sample of nursing homes, residential care facilities, such as life-care contract homes, and congregate apartment facilities, that is, facilities in which meals and other types of services are available. I did not personally know any administrators of such facilities, so I had to start from scratch.

We made a list of facilities and initiated contact with a letter, since a phone call seemed too intrusive. Our letter described the sheltered-care project and noted that we had institutional and financial support for the research and that we were interested in assessing the facility. We followed this letter with a phone call; that is, we took the next step. We did not wait for the facility administrator to act. The idea was to approach the facilities gradually. First, somebody went there to discuss the general ideas with the staff. We next discussed the amount of time that would be involved and covered other practical concerns.

Using these procedures, we were able to obtain cooperation from a large number of facilities for a comprehensive two-day program of data collection. I think four main factors were involved. The first factor is the manner of approach, which I just explained. The second factor is the issue of confidentiality. By now, we know all the facets of this issue to which administrators will be sensitive. When they do not ask the relevant questions, we focus on them before they arise. The third factor is the provision of feedback. After working in the same region, the San Francisco Bay Area, for almost twenty years, people get to know us. They know that we can be trusted to deliver the feedback we promise.

The fourth factor is that we were funded and could pay small amounts of money when an added incentive was required —for example, for difficult aspects of data collection. One such situation occurred when we wanted to measure the human aggregate—that is, the characteristics of the people in the setting. Because of the necessity to examine the facility's files, we became concerned about maintaining confidentiality. We handled that by paying someone in the setting who had access to the files to collect the information for us. We were not interested in information on individuals, only on groups. I should emphasize one additional point. We do not get every setting to cooperate with us. Some administrators are simply not interested and are unwilling to cooperate. There are always facilities with which satisfactory collaboration cannot be achieved, and beginning investigators should not be discouraged by some refusals to participate.

Snowden: I would like to turn now to your interest in using the procedures as a basis for systematically guiding and evaluating organizational change. How did that develop, and how do you see it further developing?

Moos: That was a serendipitous development. I wanted to construct measures of social environments, and my interest was primarily in conducting and facilitating research. Edison Trickett, who was very important in this development, was a postdoctoral fellow in my laboratory at the time. He knew Bill Pierce, who was in San Francisco working as a psychologist on a small psychiatric inpatient unit. The three of us planned and conducted the first change study using the Ward Atmosphere Scale. Bill Pierce was responsible for administering the scale—for giving feedback and for developing ideas about how the resulting information could be used.

Snowden: What were your reactions to that experience?

Moos: The idea intrigued me, so I decided to conduct a second study, which was carried out here at the Social Ecology Laboratory in collaboration with one of our research assistants, Jean Otto. People liked the idea of using the social climate scales in a practical way to facilitate change, and I was pulled along by the social and intellectual environment. The original idea was just to monitor the environment of a social setting, but this was later expanded to include sharing the information with the setting's inhabitants. Initially, we could not give feedback until several weeks after data collection, because our computer technology was not as efficient as it is now. Hence, if we gave feedback in a setting in which the climate did not look particularly good, staff would say that it had changed. This prompted us to begin reassessing environments. The other important innovation was to begin measuring the ideal environment. I should give credit to Carl Rogers, since the notion of comparing the real and ideal environment stemmed from the real-ideal Q-sort.

Snowden: Can you envision ways in which the use of the scales might be harmful?

Moos: Yes. Probably every potential beneficial impact could be matched with a potentially harmful one. The scales themselves are neither beneficial nor harmful; it is the use to which they are put that counts. As we have learned from the identification of deterioration effects in psychotherapy, any technique that can facilitate change can change things for better or for worse. The most likely sources of harmful effects include the possible need to confront widely divergent value systems in a setting, the emergence of such unintended consequences of change as decreases in cohesion and spontaneity, the potential stress on deviant individuals who espouse unpopular suggestions for change, the fact that change may temporarily result in a decrease in clarity and satisfaction, and the problem that people may choose to change their settings in ways that maximize short-term satisfaction rather than long-term personal growth.

Furthermore, an overly zealous change-advocate can have detrimental effects. A person may try to increase cohesion but end up facilitating overly intense relationships that restrict and inhibit people's independence. It is also possible to create a setting in which people are encouraged to perform beyond their capabilities (too much personal-growth or goal orientation) or a setting with structured and controlling relationships that leave little room for spontaneity and self-expression (too much system maintenance). For example, some highly symptomatic patients (such as some acutely ill schizophrenic patients) are likely to show an exacerbation of symptoms when they are pushed to perform beyond their capabilities. Change-advocates need to be sensitized to these and other similar factors and to try and minimize their effects. Our attempts to change settings must also be tempered by the fact that we lack dependable information on the differential effects of different types of social environments on varied groups of people.

Snowden: What about the future? In what directions will your work proceed?

Moos: We are planning several new types of studies for the next few years. In the past, I was primarily concerned with developing methods by which the social environments of settings could be measured. I talked about physical and architectural variables, program policies and procedures, and the aggregate characteristics of the people in a setting as other general domains by which environments could be characterized. We are now actually developing methods by which these environmental domains can be measured systematically.

Our next step will be to develop some integrative conceptual frameworks for our work. We are currently focusing on two such frameworks with respect to social environments. We know that such social environmental factors as the degree of support and cohesion among people, the extent to which people are encouraged to exercise responsibility and self-direction, and the clarity and organization of policies and procedures are particularly important characteristics of settings. But what factors influence the type of social environment that emerges? To what extent do the physical and architectural features influence the social environment that develops in a setting? To what extent do the policy and program characteristics affect the social environment? Do the aggregate characteristics of the people who function in a setting affect the social environment that emerges in it? We are developing a conceptual framework that focuses on the extent to which physical and architectural, policy and program, and human-aggregate characteristics influence the social environment of a setting. We are also working on a broader framework to illustrate how treatment experiences and the social environments of treatment settings may affect treatment outcome. In brief, we are looking at how personal factors affect the types of settings people enter and create and how these settings in turn affect people's morale and functioning. Although we know that there is reciprocal causation between people and environments, we still need to create conceptual frameworks that are adequate to handle this reality.

Finally, we are going to focus more on the coping responses people use that serve as the mediating links between environmental factors and indices of outcome. Many investigators are studying environmental impact in a simple input-treatment-outcome model, but I believe that one cannot understand the connection between environmental variables and outcome unless one focuses on the factors, such as people's coping skills, that mediate the influence of environmental factors on outcome. This is an area I have been interested in for many years and plan to address more systematically in the future. I also intend to continue our work on the practical utility of the social climate scales for such uses as facilitating environmental change and providing people with more accurate information about their settings.

Snowden: I would like to ask you about education and training. What experiences are important for doing this kind of work?

Moos: If you want to train young investigators to develop conceptual and methodological research, the training and role models should be primarily university based. I was fortunate in obtaining a strong academic background. I would counsel someone just entering psychology to take basic courses that provide a solid grounding. Role models are also important, but it is not necessary for the role model to be someone in the specific area in which the student intends to specialize. Anyone who has a scholarly interest in intellectual and research areas can fulfill the role-model function, since primarily general values and ways of approaching problems are being transmitted. I see enormous development over the next decade, not necessarily in environmental or community psychology per se, but rather in conceptual advances that can help to pull these and selected other fields together. Students with conceptual and research interests and skills will be needed to further this development.

   With respect to practical or field training, I like the idea of placing students into a setting for a minimum period of two or three days a week for six months. I think brief, very limited training is a poor strategy. It is better for students to be exposed to an in-depth experience in a setting where they can spend at least half-time for a minimum of six months. If we are going to train students to see how things work and to get deeply involved in a setting, they must invest time. In the case of practical training, the role model ought to be someone who is actually working in the field. In clinical and community work, specific interpersonal skills and knowledge for approaching practical problems are being transmitted. Much of what a student needs to learn is related to a style of approaching people and settings. The mentor must be doing that kind of work, so that he or she can actually observe the student perform. It is similar to watching a videotape of someone doing psychotherapy; the trainer witnesses the performance to give feedback.

Snowden: You've worked with many, many social settings. I'm wondering if you have had opportunities to see some secondary effects of your contacts, things that have come out of them unexpectedly; for example, people having more awareness of their environment and their ability to control it than before.

Moos: This certainly does happen, but people also become more aware of their *inability* to control their environment. In my experience, increasing awareness actually has contradictory effects. Let me put it personally. Carrying out in-depth studies of social settings has helped me to understand more clearly how different factors facilitate or hinder the functioning of institutional environments. I probably have increased my control of my environment somewhat—but it is mainly a kind of passive control. One learns which environments to stay out of. This is very important, possibly the most important issue in controlling the environment. It is very popular these days to say that we can control our environments. If you really think about it, however, an individual's control is quite limited. I would like to believe we can control our environment, but I think we have much less control than most textbooks in environmental psychology suggest.

Snowden: How important is selecting the right environment?

Moos: I believe that the best way to control your environment is to choose the right environment in the first place: The basic issue is to learn about what type of setting to enter and what type to stay away from. I have found the dimensions on the social climate scales to be very helpful in my own thinking in this respect. For example, my wife and I were unhappy with the school our children were attending. We had to face the problem of how to select a new school setting. My experience with evaluating classrooms helped me to avoid characterizing them undimensionally, like open versus traditional. An open school is fine, provided there is a reasonable amount of clarity and organization. And a back-to-basics school is also fine, provided that it emphasizes involvement and support in addition to task orientation. I find the concepts of the three types of social-environmental variables, that is, Relationship, Personal Growth, and System Maintenance and Change, quite helpful in thinking about environments, and I believe they can be helpful to other people as well.

7

Characterizing and Promoting Social Support In Natural Settings

Benjamin H. Gottlieb
David M. Todd

Informal social support is a pervasive and integral aspect of everyday life. People solve personal problems, accomplish tasks, develop social competencies, and address collective issues through an ongoing exchange of resources with members of their personal community. This exchange of resources, whether tangible goods like information or money or intangible resources like emotional nurturance, can be viewed broadly as social support. There is increasing evidence that social support mediates life stress (Cobb, 1976), and it is likely that the vitality, richness, accessibility, and sensitivity of natural support systems have significant impact on personal and collective adaptation. This perspective suggests a major shift from views that have been dominant—that coping with stress is an individual and largely psychological process and that help, when needed, is best provided by a trained professional. Although professional services have an important role to play, they should be understood within the context of natural support systems, as ways of supplementing and strengthening the ongoing social processes that are an inherent part of people's lives. This position expresses a central premise of an ecological perspective—that resources should be used not only to solve specific problems but also to preserve and develop the continuing capacity of the system to sustain vigorous life (Kelly, 1968; Trickett, Kelly, and Todd, 1972; Trickett and Todd, 1972). A focus on natural support systems offers an approach to the prevention of psychosocial disorder that capitalizes on the strength of existing ties among people in a community and can therefore lead to improvements in the well-being of individual members and to a sense of collective esteem and power.

　　The research discussed in this chapter represents two efforts to contribute to ecologically valid theory and knowledge about social support in natural contexts. First, Benjamin Gottlieb provides an account of research on the kinds of resources that are exchanged in primary-group helping relationships. Then, David Todd discusses research on structural features of social networks and their interaction with individual characteristics as they affect social support. These projects have not involved a direct collaboration between the authors, but they do reflect shared assumptions, not only about the importance of informal social support but also about the process of developing theory and knowledge. Our methods have been naturalistic, involving intensive and direct interactions with the people and settings we wish to understand. Gottlieb has used individual interviews, and Todd and his associates have developed a workshop format, which involves network analysis and peer-group discussion. These methods allow dialogue and the exploration of the personal and social contexts in which social support occurs. The use of such methods is especially justified by the uncharted nature of the territory, but it also reflects a value for collaborative modes of inquiry. We both view our research as a partnership with persons who are native to the culture we are studying. This partnership opens the research to a wide variety of influences from the setting and gives us the opportunity to take part in the self-assessment and problem-solving efforts of the participants. Under these conditions, the research process itself can contribute to the development of natural support systems. We shall address these issues in terms of our respective research efforts and then comment on further implications of the similarities and differences in our work.

Characterizing Social Support Among Single Mothers

Imagine, if you will, the following scenario: The setting is a playground in a municipal park. The props include a couple of slides, a set of swings, a large sandbox, and a jungle gym. The actors include three toddlers and their respective mothers. Although they all live nearby, this is the first time these mother-toddler pairs have seen one another. The action centers around the sandbox, in which the toddlers have settled themselves, alternating between parallel and joint play activities typical of their age. The mothers also follow a predictable pattern. First, they avoid direct eye contact with one another, favoring instead to monitor their own child's play. Inevitably, the icebreaker occurs when one mother suggests to her child that he share a toy with another child. This gesture is reciprocated by a second mother, who compliments a child on a sand sculpture he has just completed. Moments later, the third mother offers cookies all around, and the second mother now directly compliments the first mother on her son's creative sculpture while confessing that her own child contents himself with repetitive bulldozer maneuvers. Mother three interjects sentiments about her boy, adding that the paintings he brings home from preschool are like photographic duplicates of one another. Typically, conversation then enters a new phase, marked by a flurry of questions about comparisons among the children—their ages, their stage in toilet training, the preschool they attend, the number and ages of their siblings, and so forth. And, finally, each mother's more intimate and pressing issues may emerge in the form of statements of exasperation about some aspect of her child's behavior or direct requests for information about when and how another child was helped to master an unhappy phase or where the family went to get extra resources. The scenario terminates either with a noncommital expression of optimism that the three pairs will meet again or a more deliberate comparison of one another's schedule of park visits.

This is only one of dozens of scripts that I have experienced on an outing to the park with my son that have frequently led me to engage in the process of social comparison and the attendant provision and receipt of informal help. Furthermore, this setting is only one instance of numerous natural social contexts in which people who perceive themselves in similar circumstances begin by comparing notes, proceed to a more intimate level of self-disclosure, and culminate by reciprocating both instrumental acts and verbal expressions of support. I have witnessed such spontaneous helping transactions among persons waiting together for their scheduled appointments with dentists and physicians, among couples participating in prenatal education classes, among next-door neighbors in my condominium community, and among my own family members at times when each of us faced difficult decisions or achieved important successes.

Yet, it was only through retrospective analysis that I came to view these situations as exemplars of informal social support. At the time of their occurrence, my participation in these interactions appeared routine, even mundane. The parties to the transactions rarely used words like *problems* or *anxieties* or *help,* and I never left these occasions with the impression that I had added myself to someone's "caseload" or had enlarged my own. No one signalled an awareness that new coping strategies had been aired or that he felt less deviant as a result of an empathic exchange. Yet, in the absence of these attributes, which one normally associates with helping relationships, what evidence was there for my conclusion that others experienced these interactions as supportive? Healthy skepticism suggests that my attributions regarding the support that others received reflect a severe case of selective perception compounded by retrospective myopia. Others simply may not share my definitions of the substance of supportive behaviors, or they may include a broader range of behaviors than I had perceived. Furthermore, my personal construction of the reality of social support may have been strongly tainted by my prior participation and socialization in a professional and middle-class culture. These reflections lead me to conclude that my initial efforts to document systematically the forms of informal helping behavior would have to be grounded in the perceptions of the actors and in this way minimize the risk of definitional bias on the part of a detached observer. The task before me was to generate a classification scheme of informal helping behaviors that would show fidelity to the actors' own phenomenology in the situation.

Other difficulties cropped up as I began to examine the possibility of conducting rigorous research in any of the open settings I have catalogued here. If, indeed, informal helping transactions occur spontaneously in the natural environment, if they occur irregularly and in multiple settings and among diverse groupings and in response to contrasting agendas of the parties, how would it be possible to conduct an orderly, much less controlled and standardized, investigation on the topic? Reflexively, my thought ran to the social psychology laboratory as the ideal setting for ordering chaos, manipulating conditions, and quickly controlling my own intolerance for ambiguity. After all, Schachter (1959) was able to use a laboratory setting to induce fear in a group of subjects and show that they preferred to affiliate rather than to remain isolated under such conditions of anxiety. He was able to discover the importance of social comparison as an informal helping behavior among his subjects. I realized also that his purposes were not at all similar to mine. First, the laboratory places strong restrictions on the range of helping behaviors that occur in everyday life; second, there is little commonality between the circumstances under which laboratory subjects are convened as contrasted with people's natural participation in human milieux; however, the fundamental limitation of the laboratory method hinges on the fact that I did not want to induce any condition among the participants. It is obviously a contradiction in terms to study natural helping behaviors in a contrived place under an artificial pretext using a prepared script.

I next considered the possibility of conducting a field study, which would rely upon systematic social observations as the primary research tool. Perhaps observers stationed near a sandbox and covertly recording the verbal and behavioral interactions of the adult caretakers might serve my purposes. The parents could be asked for permission to use the recording for analysis after their interactions have been documented, and the analysis would also yield data about the topics of discussion. Furthermore, the parents could provide a limited amount of demographic data to characterize the study sample. Although this design might satisfy the naturalist's concern with minimizing subject reactivity, it, too, was discounted for several reasons. The notion of presenting the participants with a recording of their natural activities and then asking for permission to use the recording seemed unduly coercive and conformed all too closely to the image of the social scientist who engages in covert operations. Second, the study was too inefficient in its use of observers. A few random visits to the municipal parks confirmed my suspicions that the observation rate would be too low to justify the time and expense of deploying observers in this way. Finally, and most importantly, without the involvement of the parents in the analysis phase, it would be impossible to capture the phenomenology of perceived helping behaviors. Coders would simply be unable to distinguish between helping behaviors and other forms of social influence.

The method that was finally adopted was based on an interview approach, in which respondents described to me three problems they were currently experiencing, citing the persons who had become involved in helping them deal with these problems and providing detailed accounts of the helping behaviors and supportive qualities of these persons. The interviews were tape-recorded with the prior permission of the respondents, and the rich qualitative data were transcribed and subjected to content analysis by a team of three independent coders. Details of our procedure and the resulting classification scheme, composed of twenty-six informal helping behaviors, are presented elsewhere (Gottlieb, 1978). I would first like to highlight some of the major features of the scheme and then concentrate on several subterranean aspects of the research process.

Based on conceptual distinctions, I have organized the twenty-six categories of helping behaviors into four classes of influence (see Table 1). The first class, Emotionally Sustaining Behaviors, includes twelve categories that describe personal qualities and behaviors of the helper that promote emotionally supportive conditions for the helpee. Seven of these closely resemble the core of facilitative behaviors associated with constructive client change or gain in the classical counseling literature. Three of the categories converge with the processes underlying companionship therapy and reflect the importance of the simple presence of the helper as an antidote to the isolation compounding the stressful episode. The second class of influence, Problem-Solving Behaviors, includes

Table 1. A Classification Scheme of Informal Helping Behavior[a]

Category	Definition	Example
A. Emotionally Sustaining Behaviors		
A1 Talking (unfocused)	Airing or ventilation of general concerns without reference to problem specifics	"She'll talk things over with me."
A2 Provides reassurance	Expresses confidence in R as a person, in some aspect of R's *past* or *present* behavior, or with regard to the future course of events.	"He seems to have faith in me."
A3 Provides encouragement	Stimulates or motivates R to engage in some *future* behavior.	"She pushed me a lot of times when I was saying, 'oh, to heck with it.'"
A4 Listens	Listening only, without reference to dialogue.	"He listens to me when I talk to him about things."
A5 Reflects understanding	Signals understanding of the facts of R's problem or of R's feelings.	"She would know what I was saying."
A6 Reflects respect	Expresses respect or esteem for R.	"Some people look down on you; well, she doesn't."
A7 Reflects concern	Expresses concern about the importance or severity of the problem's impact on R or for the problem itself.	"Just by telling me how worried or afraid she is" (for me).
A8 Reflects trust	Reflects assurance of the confidentiality of shared information.	"She's someone I trust and I knew that it was confidential."
A9 Reflects intimacy	Provides or reflects interpersonal intimacy.	"He's just close to me."
A10 Provides companionship	Offers simple companionship or access to new companions.	"I've always got her and I really don't feel alone."

Table 1. (Continued)

Category	Definition	Example
A11 Provides accompaniment in stressful situation	Accompanies R in a stressful situation.	"She took the time to be there with me so I didn't have to face it alone."
A12 Provides extended period of care	Maintains a supportive relationship to R over what R considers an extended period of time.	"She was with me the whole way."
B. Problem-Solving Behaviors		
B1 Talking (focused)	Airing or ventilation of specific problem details.	"I'm able to tell him what's bugging me and we discuss it."
B2 Provides clarification	Discussion of problem details, which aims to promote new understanding or new perspective.	"Making me more aware of what I was actually saying other than just having the words come out."
B3 Provides suggestions	Provides suggestions or advice about the means of problem solving.	"He offered suggestions of what I could do."
B4 Provides directive	Commands, orders or directs S about the means of problem solving.	"All Rose told me was to be more assertive."
B5 Provides information about source of stress	Definition same as category name.	"She keeps me in touch with what my child's doing."
B6 Provides referral	Refers R to alternative helping resources.	"Financially, he put me on to a car mechanic who gave me a tune-up for less than I would pay in a garage."

B7	Monitors directive	Attempts to ensure that R complies with problem solving directive.	"Making sure that I follow through with their orders."
B8	Buffers S from source of stress	Engages in behavior that prevents contact between R and stressor.	"He doesn't offer it (alcohol) to me anymore."
B9	Models or provides testimony of own experience	Models behaviors or provides oral testimony related to the helper's own experience in a similar situation.	"Just even watching her and how confident she seems has taught me something."
B10	Provides material aid or direct service	Lends or gives tangibles (food, clothing, money) or provides service (babysitting, transportation) to R.	"He brought his truck and moved me so I wouldn't have to rent a truck."
B11	Distracts from problem focus	Temporarily diverts R's attention through initiating activity (verbal or action-oriented) unrelated to the problem.	"Or he'll say, 'Let's go for a drive,' some little thing to get my mind off it."
C. Indirect Personal Influence			
C1	Reflects unconditional access	Helper conveys an unconditional availability to R (without reference to problem-solving actions).	"She's there when I need her."
C2	Reflects readiness to act	Helper conveys to R readiness to engage in future problem-solving behavior.	"He'll do all he can do."
D. Environmental Action			
D1	Intervenes in the environment to reduce source of stress	Intervenes in the environment to remove or diminish the source of stress.	"She helped by talking to the owners and convincing them to wait for the money a while."

Source: Gottlieb, 1978.

eleven categories that describe ways in which the helper supplements the helpee's coping resources by providing new information or a new perspective on existing information and by personally intervening in the problem situation. Some of the more provocative categories include "Models or provides testimony of own experience," a behavior that those studying mutual-aid groups have elaborated on; "Monitors directive," a behavior that has been the subject of much attention in studies of therapeutic compliance, and the most active and direct problem-solving behaviors, "Buffers S from Source of Stress" and "Provides material aid or direct service."

The third class contains two behaviors, which most vividly depict instances of informal help that are predicated upon the helper's natural participation in the life of the helpee. The categories reflect indirect forms of influence stemming from the S's conviction that the helper or the helper's resources are unconditionally available. Each of their titles, "Reflects unconditional access" and "Reflects readiness to act," captures a different aspect of the importance of *milieu reliability*. One final helping behavior in a class of its own stands for a variety of advocacy behaviors taken by the helper to reduce the source of stress on the helpee's behalf.

The decision to sacrifice the *ecological validity* (Bronfenbrenner, 1977) of naturalistic observations in favor of interviews was primarily prompted by my need to ensure that the respondents, not the observer, define instances of interpersonal support. Although I was aware of the potential distortions that arise when people are asked to report on highly charged interactions with members of their social networks, I felt that I could minimize these biases in several ways. First, as a hedge on retrospective bias, I insisted that my respondents only discuss the concerns they were currently experiencing; second, I developed a number of interview probes, which were intended both to encourage the respondent to describe the help she had received in behavioral terms and to minimize global, evaluative statements. For example, instead of asking, What helpful influence did X have on you?" the question was worded "What did X do, say, or give you that helped?" Finally, in an effort to supplement the interview data with behavioral specimens, my original proposal called for a behavioral log of all helping transactions to be completed by each respondent over a period of five days.

The sample of forty sole-support mothers was selected for two important reasons. First, to identify those helping behaviors that uniquely characterize informal social support, I required a sample of people who would be likely to use both professional and lay helping resources. In this way, it would be possible to assess whether the respondents distinguish between the supportive tactics of these two classes of helpers. In short, without documenting the respondent's perceptions of professional behaviors, conclusions about the unique qualities of informal support are unwarranted. Since sole-support mothers maintain ties to the welfare system through social workers and other counseling professionals while also participating in a distinct lay culture, I predicted that they would provide sufficient data to allow for comparative analysis of informal and professional helping behaviors. Second, I selected sole-support mothers, because they experience multiple problems in living that potentially call forth an equally broad range of helping responses from others. Since my work represents an initial exploratory attempt to document informal helping behaviors, I placed a premium on comprehensive reconnaissance on the topic.

The motives for my choice of sole-support mothers were only partially fuelled by a zeal to discover how lay persons define the substance of social support. My involvement with this group was also prompted by my interest in taking future action on the creation and development of more effective natural support systems among low-income groups. There is little need here to reiterate details of the numerous reports attesting to the fact that traditional mental health services are not acceptable and are unaffordable and ineffective for low-income populations. Hence, my agenda in the long run was to gain a better appreciation of the ingredients of healthy support system functioning so as to inform future practice and, in the short run, to challenge the local professionals who provide services to sole-support mothers. I expected that the study would highlight several ways in which professional interventions weaken or supplant the work of natural support systems, and I hoped to use this evidence as a springboard for effecting changes in the professionals' stance toward the social milieu of their clients as well as in their repertoire of helping skills.

The decision to interview sole-support mothers posed two immediate problems, both stemming from the fact that I was estranged from the social networks of these women. This meant that

I would have to overcome certain barriers to the recruitment of respondents, and, on an interpersonal level, I would have to calibrate my own style of communication to enhance rapport and dispel suspiciousness among my interviewees. It so happened that, at the time I was formulating my thoughts about these matters, two sole-support mothers were participants in a small seminar I offered on the topic of "Ecological Considerations in Community Health." These two women agreed to act as informal consultants to me in regard to all aspects of the study's design, and they ultimately suggested the technique of *natural sponsorship* as my recruitment strategy. Recognizing that I had no natural entry to the social networks of their membership group, they offered to introduce me to one or two other mothers, who in turn would sponsor further introductions, the process continuing until my quota of forty had been attained. Since there was no need for strict random sampling, this technique seemed ideally suited to my purposes of gaining entry in a way that would minimize, if not entirely neutralize, the stereotypes associated with my formal roles as psychologist and academic. Furthermore, I felt that the brief and casual introductory visits in which the natural sponsorships would take place would allow me to explain my research agenda, work on reducing mutual inhibitions, and sample the environment prior to preparing the final interview schedule.

This technique of gaining entry was not implemented, however, because the initial student nominators who had devised the procedure felt that their nominees would be suspicious of their motives for selecting them as participants; hence, personal relationships would be jeopardized. Specifically, they felt that the nominees might assume that they had been chosen as persons who had a great many problems and that the consequences of participation would entail yet another professional effort to reform their lives. This marked the first of several occasions in which I learned about the sense of distrust and alienation that characterizes the responses of sole-support mothers to the incursions of most professionals in their lives. The second occasion was on the evening when I awaited telephone responses to a letter addressed to all sole-support mothers in the community. Over 200 letters had been mailed to eligible candidates by the local welfare office explaining the study's purpose, offering a payment in return for participation, indicating that their government benefits would be unaffected by their participation, and calling for volunteers. That night, two hesitant callers responded to the invitation, and, on subsequent evenings, only fifteen additional calls were received. I concluded that my second entry strategy was no less intimidating than the first. The medium had changed, but the hidden message had not.

With less than half my quota, I began to plot the residences of those who had called, and I quickly recognized that many were neighbors or at least lived in the same low-income townhouse developments. Realizing that "ghettoization" of low-income persons was a common phenomenon, I speculated that those neighbors who had received my invitations may have conferred with one another, some receiving support for the decision to participate and some for the decision to opt out. On the basis of several return calls I made to my existing list of participants, I was able to confirm this hypothesis and subsequently capitalize on it for the purpose of meeting my quota of respondents. I discovered, however, that the informal influence that had encouraged the calls of my initial group of volunteers had not been generated through a collective process of decision making—I had imagined a group of five or six women discussing the costs and merits of participating—but through the influence of one or two key influentials in each locality. These opinion leaders had been consulted individually and had given their nod to participation. My return calls enabled me to identify the persons who had sanctioned my study, explain my purposes to them in greater detail, and encourage them to take the initiative in tapping their networks more broadly in search of persons who met my criteria for participation. Hence, my final strategy of sample recruitment evolved slowly and painfully but serendipitously came full circle to a modified form of *natural sponsorship*. In retrospect, it seems to me that my original student sponsors may have sensed that their participation in university life had removed them from the culture of the sole-support community of their origin and had weakened their bonds to former associates. At the time I adopted them as collaborators and informants, however, I had no yardstick for measuring their affiliative orientations and would not have presumed to do so.

It should be obvious that my attraction to the original strategy of recruiting participants was based on my desire to build a bridge between myself, a culturally distant observer, and the local community of sole-support mothers. Another researcher might characterize that approach as naive, suggesting that, instead, I remain one step removed and deploy someone akin to the target population—an indigenous worker, who could be trained to function as a surrogate census taker. I considered but rejected this technique on the basis of two fundamental values guiding my research. First, I believe it is important that the researcher appreciate the ecological validity of the data that have been gathered. Social support cannot be fully understood if it is viewed simply as a function of two actors exchanging resources in some neutral space, since the occurrence of this transaction is itself conditional on the wider social and physical milieux in which the two participate. For example, one helping relationship may be predicated upon the actors' common involvement in the local chapter of Parents Without Partners; another may have evolved through repeated contact in a neighborhood laundromat. In either case, wider knowledge of the settings in which the respondents routinely participate can help one to understand the properties of their social networks, such as their density and heterogeneity, which affect the availability and diversity of social support.

Similarly, my domestic observations of family dynamics in the single-parent home and my exposure to a variety of housing and neighborhood conditions helped me to recognize the role of informal social support as a critical resource in people's accommodations to their milieux. Without direct participation in data collection, I would have assigned less weight to such ecological factors in my conceptualization of this domain of inquiry. Furthermore, especially where action research is undertaken, direct participation is a necessary element in the researcher's role obligations. Hence, I knew I would have little credibility in my follow-up visits with the workers in the local welfare office if I had only the results of an elaborate content-coding scheme as the basis for my remarks about the life experiences and support needs of their clients. Anecdotes based on my informal observations of family and neighborhood relations during my visits to the homes of respondents together with their off-the-record accounts of frustrations about being home-bound and stigmatized by the larger community might have more impact in stimulating reconsideration of current professional practices than all the finely tuned classification devices employed in the formal research.

My decision to participate directly in data collection also reflected the fact that I placed a premium on activities that would enhance my skills in communicating effectively with a diversity of social groups in the community. I felt that the interview process would present an opportunity for learning to manage the tensions that are inevitably produced when cultural differences exist between the researcher and the participants.

I conducted all but two of the interviews in the respondent's homes. Contrary to my expectations that I would have to tease information from them, my problems during the interview had to do with placing restrictions on the amount of biographical material, which they were eager to reveal. My introductory remarks, which emphasized my interest in problems the women were experiencing as well as their coping strategies, prompted too much detail about the former and insufficient attention to the latter. I was able later to alter this pattern by using the tape recorder as a cue to the respondents, turning it off at those times when I wanted to signal that problem details were belabored and turning it on when their comments turned to the topic of primary interest. This adaptation of my interview technique represents one instance of a more general dilemma, which had to do with my efforts during the interviewing process to attain a balance between reflecting sensitivity to the needs of my respondents and ensuring that my own research agenda was covered.

There was simply no denying the fact that many of my questions led the respondents to reexperience painful feelings that had not been resolved. Discussions of their marital separations brought back memories of abuse and feelings of abandonment; concerns about their children aroused guilty sentiments and doubts about their worth as parents; financial pressures provoked feelings of frustration and accounts of humiliations at the hands of sales clerks and taxi drivers.

I felt a responsibility to deal with these natural by-products of the interview, and I did so in a number of ways. On those occasions when intense emotional reactions were triggered, I simply dropped my interview schedule and attempted to respond empathically. On those occasions when the respondent's feelings closely paralleled experiences I had encountered, I found myself disclosing the feelings that had been aroused in me. On many occasions, a two-hour interview was followed by an extended visit, in which mutual attempts were made to deal with the interview's emotional fallout. At times, I was able effectively to settle the respondent by letting her know that other single mothers had described similar experiences and feelings, thus "normalizing" her reactions. Several women asked me if I could suggest an appropriate service for a problem they were facing. My referrals always included at least one professional agency and one informal source of help, since I was cautious not to betray an investment in a single style of helping.

The most stressful of all situations I encountered were those in which the respondent described critical choices she perceived in her life (for example, whether to return to work or school and sacrifice the welfare of her children and the security of the dole), listing the pros and cons of each alternative and then turning to me for an opinion. In these situations, I was easily swept up by the anxiety that inevitably accompanies ambivalence about important decisions, and therefore my first inclination was to ally myself with one of the alternatives. I did not act on this impulse for two reasons. First, although I was able to develop good rapport with the women, I was still outside the support system they routinely consulted and thus did not want to risk contradicting or supplanting the influence of their social network. Second, since many of the choices faced by these women were linked to the current patterning of local human services and to the welfare regulations surrounding their lives, I felt that their dilemmas ought to be (anonymously) aired and addressed during the follow-up workshops, which would be attended by the respondents and agency delegates. I hoped that these sessions would address their collective concerns, placing them in a perspective that emphasized their connection to institutional constraints rather than to personal circumstances. For these reasons, I rarely came down on one side of the respondent's dilemma, favoring instead to point out some of the potential long-term outcomes of each course of action and drawing the respondent into a discussion of alternative perspectives on her situation. At those times when I did endorse one course of action, I was sure to state that my preferences were purely personal and intuitive and were not based on academic professional expertise. It is likely, however, that these disclaimers augmented my credibility.

Considered together, these experiences shook my beliefs regarding the interview method as a situation in which an interviewer emits stimuli to guide and control the respondent behaviors of the interviewee. Instead, I now see interview-based research as a process of mutual influence, in which the interviewer is as much affected by the interactional context as the respondent.

Although I was able to calibrate my own interview style both to meet the emotional fallout of the issues I probed and to attain my informational goals, I was forced to abandon one major component of my research plan and to reorient my thinking about another as a result of my direct exposure to the lives of my respondents. My original proposal called for a behavioral log, which the respondents would use to record all their social contacts during the five days following the interview as well as a summary statement of the content of these interactions. The log was intended as a substitute for direct observation. According to my original grant application, the log would "provide current behavioral data about social contacts and will be inspected and coded for instances of helping transactions."

Although scientifically credible as a rough reliability check on the interview data, the log proved to be totally unworkable within the human context I entered. Besides the fact that many of my respondents had trouble with writing, the first few who learned of my request expressed two major reservations about completing the log. First, they felt they simply did not have the time to record such details of their daily lives and that the task would become burdensome and disruptive. More important, they were unwilling to subject intimate details of their life to the scrutiny of others. When I inquired about how they justified this position in light of the disclosures I had recorded during the interview, they did not recognize an inconsistency. The interview was an acceptable method of inquiry on two counts: first, they felt the interview situation allowed them to portray the context in which they experienced stressful events and to express their feelings about these events and the supportive people in their lives; second, although they had found the interview an occasion for meaningful dialogue and rapport, the log aroused familiar feelings of anonymity, since it suggested that my true interests were the exterior events in their lives and not the interior meaning of their experience. In short, they perceived me as taking away through the log what I had given through the interview.

Taken together, these considerations prompted me to disqualify the log as a strategy for data collection in this study. In future research, however, I hope to reinstate the use of a log in modified form. Specifically, with the development of the classification scheme, the respondents will no longer be burdened with the task of completing detailed descriptions of their helping transactions. Instead, with a short orientation to the classification scheme, they will be able to jot down the code number of the helping behavior that occurred. In addition, since the code is only a pale reflection of the respondents' experiences in the helping transaction and since the researcher ought to ensure that the code has been appropriately assigned, the researcher should meet with the respondents to review the events that underlie the written summary. This process should reflect greater fidelity to the respondent's experience, an increase in the reliability of the code assignments due to the researcher's check on the data, and a continuity in the personal style of the researcher.

The second aspect of data collection that was designed without sufficient regard for the respondents' perspectives and needs related to my method of evaluating the efficacy of the help extended to the respondents. My original research plan called for respondents to rate on a seven-point Likert scale the usefulness of the help provided by each source. I planned to use these ratings to assess which helping behaviors were most effective and ultimately to determine whether the effectiveness of a given helping behavior was contingent on the nature of the problem, the helper, or some interaction of the two. Here, too, however, my reductionistic perspective was contradicted by the respondents' own phenomenology when confronted with the task. They were simply unable to segment the person from the helping behavior that the person extended to them. My question "How useful was X's help?" was met with quizzical responses, such as "I always feel better when I see my mother" or "She's my closest friend, so she must be pretty useful." Furthermore, the fact that most help sources extended more than one type of helping behavior compounded the problem, since I had requested a single evaluation for each source and not for each behavior the source displayed. Finally, since I was inquiring about *current* problems, it was unrealistic to expect my respondents to know how useful a particular intervention had been. After all, some helping exchanges do not have an impact until the individual has an opportunity to reflect about them or even to experiment with suggested problem-solving strategies, whereas others have little effect alone but only cumulatively. My simple evaluative tool clearly did not reflect the complexity of the phenomenon of judging a helping transaction.

The foregoing analysis of several subterranean issues involved in research on the topic of informal social support among sole-support mothers is incomplete without a sketch of the feedback process, which we are about to implement. From the outset, an explicit contract was made with the staff of the local welfare office to the effect that a workshop based on the results of the study would be held. The workshop will be attended by front-line workers from a number of local agencies, which provide services to single-parent families, including the Welfare Office, the Children's Aid Society, Parents Without Partners, the Municipal Housing Authority, the Big Brothers and Big Sisters Organizations, and the Family Counseling Service. We also hope to include representatives from the care-giver sector of the community, including the principals of the two schools that serve the catchment areas of our respondents, teachers, two clergymen, and two physicians. The workshop will be planned and co-led by myself and a sole-support respondent, who will also take responsibility for encouraging the other respondents to attend.

The workshop design includes two main stages: feedback of the results and small-group sessions, in which action and policy implications will be generated. The two main items reviewed within the data feedback stage are the findings regarding the relative proportion of professional, gatekeeper, and informal agents who are utilized as help sources and, subsequently, the final classification scheme of informal helping behaviors. Each category of help will be explained through the use of brief vignettes excerpted from the transcribed protocols. The small groups of eight will be composed of equal numbers of respondents and human services people, and, in each group, one member will be assigned the role of recorder and one the role of facilitator. The facilitator's job will be to ensure that channels of communication are open to and used by all members of the group and to clarify the content of the messages. The groups will be asked to address themselves to three main issues regarding the content and style of delivering local human services: (1) ways in which organizational policy disrupts or weakens informal helping relationships, (2) ways in which organizational policy can be modified to strengthen natural support systems, and (3) recommendations regarding the desirability and substance of continuing exchanges between formal and natural support systems in the community.

Finally, one additional aspect of my method of investigation deserves reemphasis because of its bearing on the development of a comprehensive theory of social support. By involving myself so immediately in the lives of the sole-support mothers I interviewed and by leaving myself open to their "off the record" impressions of the community life of welfare recipients, I enlarged my understanding of social support to include a panel of social and ecological variables. At the outset, I had not anticipated that the social fabric of their lives was so intimately interwoven with such factors as their economic status, their limited involvement in the voluntary associations present in the community, their reliance on public transportation, and their concentration in low-income housing settlements, which lacked any semblance of community organization. In short, I had not considered the bearing of social-structural variables on the form and substance of support at the time I undertook this research, but the naturalistic method of inquiry that I adopted prompted their discovery. Consequently, my approach to future research will involve the exploration of both the person-to-person helping process and the ecological factors on which these transactions are predicated. In the following section of this chapter, David Todd presents one approach to the study of a set of situational and social-structural variables affecting the strength of personal support networks.

Social Support, Social Networks and Personal Adaptation: Support Development Groups

In addition to describing and conceptualizing informal helping, we would like to understand why such interactions take place and vary in their form and impact. The research discussed in this section explores social support as a function of social structure and individual styles of adaptation. Social structure, which refers to enduring patterns of interaction, is addressed in terms of the social or personal network—the system of interpersonal relationships in which an individual is involved (see, for example, Barnes, 1972; Bott, 1971; Mitchell, 1969). A structural analysis suggests that the pattern of such relationships, such as the degree of interconnectedness among network members (*density*), may affect the nature of those relationships. An interactional analysis considers the interplay of such structural factors with individual modes of coming to terms with the social environment. The action-research method to be discussed here, the Support Development Group, is designed to examine social support in a way that is simultaneously useful for informants in assessing their own support systems and to researchers in the development of theory.

The basic premises of the Support Development Group method were derived from several years' work with doctoral students in clinical and community psychology. This work took the form of intensive small-sample studies of coping and social support in a variety of settings, including a married student couple functioning well under high stress (Kinder, 1975), beginning psychotherapists in a training clinic (Rubenstein, 1976), graduate students entering a clinical psychology program (Sodano, 1977), and informal helpers in university dormitories (Walker, 1976).

One contribution of these studies was to clarify the value and limits of intensive case-oriented methods of research. We wanted to explore personal adaptation and social support in terms of the complex interplay of personal, interpersonal, and social-structural variables. There was little conceptual or empirical basis for selecting variables for controlled study and little sense of how such variables might be interrelated. The intensive study of individuals seemed appropriate for clarifying these issues but had little legitimacy within academic psychology as a research method (despite its acceptance as a basis for clinical practice). Our early studies, guided by reading in the field method literatures in sociology and anthropology, helped us clarify the value of qualitative methods for the kind of work we wanted to do: generating comprehensive, empirically grounded theory (Glaser and Strauss, 1967) and exploring the "systems character of the context" of personal adaptation and social support (Runkel and McGrath, 1972). The rich integrative descriptions produced by these interview studies were limited as a basis for generalization and the verification of specific hypotheses, but they were very useful for identifying critical variables and developing theory.

A second implication of our early work is similar to a conclusion reported by Gottlieb earlier in this chapter; the in-depth, integrative exploration of adaptive processes was often experienced by informants as satisfying, informative, and helpful. We began to think of this kind of research as a mutually beneficial collaboration between us and the people whose lives we were trying to understand. The dialogue of the interview seemed often to help people formulate aspects of their own lives that had been implicit; this was not only useful to them but also yielded more complete information than a more focused and passive research method would have generated.

Finally, these studies suggested the particular value of the social-network concept for understanding social structure in relation to personal adaptation and social support. Before we became aware of this concept, we drew on selected concepts from group and organizational theory to address issues of social structure, but this was problematic on several counts. First, these concepts were limited to a defined group or setting, and we were often interested in the person's adaptive efforts across settings. Secondly, most informants had a very limited sense of the structure of their groups or organizations, and we were not sure how to translate these phenomena into personally meaningful terms. Consequently, our analyses of social structure were sketchy, anecdotal, and based more on our understanding of the setting than on informants' comments. The concept of social network provides a structural view of the immediate comprehensive interpersonal environment of the individual, representing what Jules Henry (1958) aptly called the *personal community*. This unit of analysis seemed especially appropriate for understanding natural support systems and personal adaptation as well as being potentially meaningful to people in examining their own lives.

There was a small amount of theory and research relating social networks to social support. Much of this had been integrated by Wellman and his associates at the University of Toronto into a hypothesis about network density and the availability of two kinds of support (Craven and Wellman, 1973; Wellman, in press). They suggested that integrated (dense) social networks may be relatively small and homogeneous with intense and multifaceted relationships, which could provide strong nurturance or emotional support. In contrast, less integrated networks may have more numerous, heterogeneous, and single-function relationships, which provide less nurturance but strong access to instrumental resources, such as information and assistance with tasks. A dissertation by Tolsdorf (1975, 1976) incorporated this kind of structural-network analysis into an intensive study of two small matched groups of medically and psychiatrically hospitalized veterans. He was primarily interested in comparing the networks of the two groups and relating structural differences to the availability of social support; his data suggested some such differences, although not in overall density. However, Tolsdorf's interviews suggested that the impact of network structure on social support was strongly influenced by individual differences in willingness to seek or utilize support. This research suggested that the continued intensive study of network structure and individual coping style in relation to social support might be productive in identifying significant variables and ways in which they might interact. During the same time, other work of a more applied nature suggested that network analysis might help people conceptualize their own natural support systems as a basis for problem solving. If so, we thought that it should be possible to design a collaborative process of inquiry that had simultaneous value for personal exploration and the development of theory. The method we designed to explore this possibility is the Support Development Group.

The Support Development Group has taken different forms, but it incorporates several essential features: (1) an introduction to the topic of social support and the concept of social network as a systems view of relationships; (2) an exercise in which participants represent their own social networks in the form of a map or a matrix; (3) an opportunity to discuss network patterns and social support with a group of peers; and (4) techniques for retaining much of this information for research purposes. The most systematic use of this method to date has been with two small groups of first-year college students and in a study of work-life integration among university human service professionals. Discussions of these two projects will illustrate the Support Development Group method, provide an initial basis for evaluating its potential as an integrated action-research technique, and demonstrate the adaptation of the general approach to varied objectives and settings.

The introduction of support-development groups for first-year college students was based on the expectation that social network and support issues may be especially salient during times of transition. To create an integrated action-research approach, we used a three-session small-group workshop focused around network mapping, with individual follow-up interviews. The mapping involves a graphic representation of the person's significant others, their interrelatedness, and their psychological closeness to the informant and to each other. The participant locates network members (with small circles containing their initials) at appropriate distances from the center of a piece of paper, depending on their psychological closeness to the participant. Network members are clustered on the paper according to life sectors (such as family, work, or friends), and lines are drawn between network members who know one another. These lines can be made lighter or darker to represent closeness, and other qualities of the relationship, such as positive or negative valence, can be represented in other ways. The extent and pattern of lines provide an indication of structural properties of the network, such as overall density or segmentation between different sectors.

Our objective was to make these qualities of the network explicit, so that participants could examine their relationship to issues of social support. We used a peer-group discussion format, not only to provide a supportive context for personal exploration but also to generate issues we might not anticipate. The maps were supplemented with tape recordings of the group discussions, written journals kept during the three weeks, and individual interviews a few weeks after the completion of the workshops. These supplemental materials were useful to the research, and they were also intended to help participants review and integrate their experience. To ensure a continuation of this dual action-research focus, the interviews were conducted jointly by the participants' group facilitator, who was primarily responsible for the value of the interview to the participants, and a research assistant, whose primary task was to obtain relatively standardized information about the network map, perceptions of support, and evaluations of the workshop.

Participants were recruited from an introductory psychology class on "The College Experience." This course was designed explicitly to help new students cope with the academic and social challenges of the university. The Support Development Group was offered as one project students could choose as part of the course. From those who selected this project, we formed two groups of four and five participants each. Of those who began the workshops, three men and five women completed all phases.

These eight participants provided diverse examples of social networks, concerns about support, and responses to the workshops. In particular, they show the complex ways that network structures and personal characteristics can interact over time to affect social support. This dynamic process is most easily and fully portrayed through a case example from the project.*

> Initially quiet, Angela soon communicated clearly and easily in the group, and she worked hard on her journal notes and network map. Her map included over 130 people in four large clusters and four smaller ones. The largest clusters were of friends from four different places where Angela had lived and/or gone to school, including the university. The small clusters included her immediate family and close relatives, two geographically distant groups of relatives, and friends from a summer job. Angela seemed to maintain consistent contact with one person in each of the remote clusters, with limited contact with others. She described her network as large, complex, highly disconnected, and—largely as a result of her repeated moves—segmented.

> Angela was satisfied with her instrumental support. She was mostly self-sufficient financially and called on her parents for advice about major decisions. In her academic life, she gathered information from appropriate offices and peers but preferred to make decisions independently and then seek "moral support" from others.

> The dilemma of Angela's network concerned intimacy, which she defined as being known and understood across the seg-

*This summary was prepared by Ester Shapiro, who conducted this interview and played a major role in the project. Names and other identifying information have been changed to ensure confidentiality. Other participants in this project were Anne McComb, Andrea Sodano, and Rudy Chatlos.

ments of her life; this rarely occurred in her unconnected network. Angela found it difficult, and apparently threatening, to give people the information (or direct contact) they needed to understand her outside the segment in which they knew her. She even mentioned putting away letters from "outside" friends and making sure no one at school saw them, so she would not have to explain about other parts of her life. She actively kept her worlds separate and then felt "spread out" and lacking in intimacy, in a circular and self-defeating way.

During and after the workshop, Angela engaged in what she described as "spring cleaning" to move her network toward the intimate, interconnected group she wanted. Before she left for the summer, she concentrated her time with her closest friends at school and made plans to correspond. She planned a trip to visit old friends whom she hadn't seen in five years. Also, she decided to spend the fall semester on a farm with people she met through a university friend, where she hoped to experiment with more open self-disclosure in a close-knit group. If she could be more comfortable with this process, she hoped to be more able to connect her more selective relationships into a more intimate and emotionally supportive "core" network.

Angela described her experience with the Support Development Group as very helpful. She had already felt dissatisfied with her relationships, and the workshop gave her a more systematic understanding as a basis for change and a supportive base for some initial steps.

Of the eight participants, Angela was probably the most explicit and differentiated in her thinking and one of the most active in using the experience as an opportunity for self-assessment and change. However, each of the participants provided a complex and informative example of support functions within a social network, and all reported that the Support Development Group was personally useful. The areas of knowledge and impact produced by these Support Development Groups will be summarized in terms of four general categories: the identification and legitimization of needs for support, qualities of relationships that affect support, network structure and its impact on support, and change.

All participants identified aspects of support that they found lacking. Unlike Angela, most wanted more instrumental assistance in dealing with the university and career planning. Needs for nurturant support were more varied. Some, like Angela, desired a greater sense of integration or intimacy. Others, in contrast, wanted more variety or anonymity in their social lives. Specific problems with parents or dating relationships were mentioned by some people. The discussion of these needs with peers seemed to serve several important functions: it illustrated the varieties of support and individual differences in their availability and importance; it provided reassurance that support in some form is needed by most people; and it indicated that it is not only legitimate to accept support but even to seek it actively. These issues may have strong implications for whether the supportive potential of a network is utilized.

Other areas of impact were more directly related to the social network mapping. For example, simply looking at the full array of significant others and the closeness of these various relationships was a novel and informative experience to most participants. Mapping usually produced generalizations about the aggregate qualities of these relationships. Angela, for example, saw more clearly that her relationships were extensive, distant, and specialized and that she was lacking in intimate contacts. Other participants saw that they were closer to more people than they had realized, that they needed a great diversity of contacts, that certain people played unique roles in their lives, or that they had been neglecting important relationships. Some, like Angela, could see patterns in the way they had formed relationships in different settings or directions in which their networks seemed to be developing. These realizations often fell short of structural analyses, but they did extend an interpersonal view to consider the aggregate set of significant relationships.

Mapping the connections between network members provides a direct basis for considering structure. Our expectation was that awareness of structure would be generally limited and difficult to develop but that it would prove useful if achieved. We introduced two structural concepts into the discussion: *density* within the total network or a subnetwork and the *segmentation* of various life sectors. Density is the most commonly studied variable in the literature and was of some value to participants, but the notion of segmentation seemed more readily grasped and useful. Everyone found some degree of segmentation between life spheres, but people differed in the number of sectors, the extent of contact between them, and the impact of such segmentation (or integration) on their personal experience. Although the origins of segmentation were often ascribed to geography and mobility, psychosocial functions were often described as well. Angela, for example, attributed her highly segmented (and dispersed) network to geographic moves but saw her continuation of this pattern as a way of protecting herself from continued cycles of involvement and loss and as a means of controlling the flow of information. In the course of the workshop, she saw that these same structural factors inhibited the formation of intimate relationships, which she desired. For some people, the disintegrative impact of segmentation seemed to be moderated by the presence of critical *boundary-spanners.* For two participants, having old friends or siblings at the university was an important source of continuity as well as guidance. Angela's introduction of her roommate to her family and home served a related function. Overall, five of the eight participants reported insight into the impact of network structure on social support, with interesting variations. Like Angela, two other participants felt a need to reduce the segmentation of their networks to enhance nurturant support and personal integration. In contrast, two others felt excessively bound by interconnected networks and saw that a greater separation of sectors and an expansion of certain subnetworks might foster autonomy and change.

For all participants, either aggregate or structural analysis of their networks suggested changes that might enhance social support. For some, these changes simply involved adding (or subtracting) certain kinds of relationships. For a few others, the changes were more directly structural. Angela was taking active steps to consolidate a more integrated core network. Another participant was encouraged by his group to talk with his parents about aspects of his university life that might meet their disapproval to see if he could reduce the segmentation between those spheres of his life. (He found his parents more understanding than he expected and felt free of a major source of concern.) Other participants did not report such active steps during the course of the workshop, but all identified changes they would like to make.

The results of this study are encouraging. The participants reported that the experience was useful, and they showed an increased awareness and understanding of network factors in social support. From a research perspective, the data highlight several aspects of network structure and individual differences that may affect social support. Individuals differ in their needs and preferences for high or low network integration, and these needs and preferences change over time. Also, there is additional support for Tolsdorf's (1975, 1976) conclusion that people vary in their orientation to social support; some will seek social support, even when the network does not readily provide it, and others are reluctant to accept support, even when it is offered. Another critical and neglected dimension that is evident in these data is the active way in which people often engage their social worlds, as seen in Angela's maintenance of a segmented network as a defensive coping strategy and her new efforts to create a more nurturant structure. These issues of reciprocal interaction between social structure and personal qualities are central to an ecological view of behavior, and these data suggest aspects of such interaction that may be important for the study of social support.

This project suggests that the Support Development Group is a viable action-research method, but its potential and limits must be clarified through research with other settings, sampling strategies, and techniques. One such extension was made in a dissertation by George Brennan (1977). A brief discussion of this study will illustrate the adaptation of the general method to a specific issue and to a different population and set of objectives. Brennan was interested in the relationship between work and nonwork as an issue in contemporary culture and personal well-being, and he wanted to focus on human service workers. What patterns of integration or separation between work and nonwork exist in this population? What is the personal impact of such patterns, and how do people cope with their negative consequences? Brennan expected that such impact would be mediated by social network patterns and social support.

As an initial step, Brennan wanted to develop social network measures of work-life integration and to assess their relation to instrumental and nurturant support. Consistent with the Support Development Group method, he wanted to gather his data in a way that would be useful to participants in exploring these issues in their own lives. However, he wanted his data to provide more precise and efficient measures of network structure and social support than we had obtained in the college student project. Instead of network mapping, Brennan developed a matrix format for gathering network data. Participants were asked to list significant others, clustered according to their primary identification as coworkers, family, and friends. To form•the network matrix, the participant listed, next to each name, all the other network members who knew that person. Each network member was also rated on the extent to which they provide work-related collaboration and socioemotional nurturance. These data were generated in a one-session workshop, which began with a brief presentation of network and work-life integration concepts, followed by the matrix procedure. Attention was then directed to the distribution of collaborative and nurturant support in work, family, and friend sectors of the matrix and the extent of connectedness between these subnetworks. Finally, participants were invited to compare patterns, discuss their varied functions and limitations, and explore ways that network structure might be changed to promote desired relationships between work and the rest of their lives.

These workshops were conducted with four diverse groups of university human service professionals, with a total of forty people completing all aspects. Although the network matrix is a less graphic representation than the maps used in the college student project, it was easier for participants to indicate relationships between network members clearly, and most people found the completed matrices informative, interesting, and interpretable. As in the other project, these participants also reported that the workshop helped focus existing concerns more clearly and in some cases to bring new issues into awareness. Group discussions emphasized several topics: conceptions of work and its relation to the rest of life; needs for support in the work setting and in general; varied styles of managing the work-nonwork boundary; the advantages and costs of different styles; and the development of networks over time. Variations in network density and segmentation were related by participants to personal preferences, geographic mobility, length of stay, and the nature of the community or work place. On the whole, these workshops seemed to provide a relatively unique, involving, and nonthreatening forum for discussion of these issues among groups of coworkers.

From a research point of view, the matrix data allowed a quantitative examination of relationships between network structure and social support. Overall network density did not correlate significantly with support measures. Instead, more complex relationships were suggested between the density of subnetworks, the extent of segmentation, the varied functions of different clusters, and patterns of social support. Specific findings will not be discussed here, but some tentative conclusions can be stated: (1) subnetworks (family, friends, coworkers) differ significantly in their patterns of nurturant and instrumental support; (2) different subnetworks show different relationships between density and social support, possibly reflecting the unique functions and norms of the respective clusters; and (3) patterns of support within a cluster may vary with the degree of connectedness between that cluster and other subnetworks. Findings such as these, if validated through further research, allow a highly differentiated view of social network structure in relation to social support.

In both projects discussed here, data generated by participants as a basis for self-assessment were also useful for research. The intensive, qualitative data of the college student project provided examples of the complex interplay between personal and social network factors in social support. These examples show how the impact of network structures may vary according to individual needs and may change over time. They also demonstrate that people take active steps to maintain or to change the structure of their social worlds in relation to their needs. Both studies suggest that the segmentation of social networks, more clearly than overall density, may have important consequences for social support and personal integration, privacy, autonomy, and change. The study of human service professionals further suggests that the structural and functional qualities of subnetworks may vary and that segmentation between subnetworks may be related to the nature of support within the separate clusters. These findings suggest important ways in which our views of network structure can be refined for the study of social support and personal adaptation.

Differences between the two studies reflect the necessity to adapt a basic method to particular objectives and settings. The open-ended format of mapping and interviews in the college student workshops allowed a broad view of the interplay between personal and social network qualities for particular individuals, and it allowed considerable latitude for participants to explore varied aspects of their networks. The matrix format of the work-life integration workshops allowed the quantitative measurement and statistical analysis of selected variables and provided participants with detailed information around a specific issue of interest to them. Other variations and combinations could be used, but there are also trade-offs and limitations inherent in the general method.

The use of the group format, for example, confirmed our belief that discussion among peers in a supportive atmosphere can enhance personal exploration and mutual problem solving. The dialogue in these groups was also helpful in identifying issues that had not been previously suggested by our own thinking and reading of the research literature. However, the dynamics of these groups represented strong confounding factors in assessing the impact of network analysis. In the first-year college student study, for example, the two groups differed markedly, despite the fact that assignment was based solely on scheduling factors and a relatively standardized format was followed. Not only did one group seem generally more outgoing, but it also included a woman who modeled self-disclosure by reading a love letter in the first session to illustrate social support. Other members cited this incident as a positive factor in their willingness to use the group to practice being more expressive. These variations add complexity to an already complicated situation and make the research task more difficult.

Other limitations of the method are more inherent in network analysis as a basis for personal problem solving. Among the college students and professionals who volunteered for these studies, network analysis was seen as interesting and useful. Other work suggests, however, that such analysis may be less meaningful for other populations, including people seeking immediate support for crisis (Berman, 1977; Gelinas, 1975) and those who are less oriented to self-analysis and social interchange (Leavy and Lekisch, 1975). Another general limitation is that the data are based entirely on individual perceptions of complex relationships, with unknown correspondence to objective social network characteristics. Although these data may reflect the phenomenological network, they provide an uncertain basis for intervening in the actual social world. These limitations, combined with the focus on changing the awareness of individuals in a temporary workshop setting, suggest that the Support Development Group as it has been used is a very limited basis for social intervention.

The limitations of this method, like the differences between the two studies, are reminders that a particular method involves a variety of judgments and trade-offs. It is designed to address a specific problem defined in a given way and to provide certain forms of information with selected populations and settings and perhaps with explicit objectives for impact on the participants. When these choices are left implicit, it is difficult to keep a proper sense of perspective about the findings and method; chances are increased that the findings will be misinterpreted or misused, and methods may be extended to purposes and situations for which they are not appropriate. In these respects, our methods of inquiry and action are as complex and dynamic as the psychosocial phenomena we seek to understand and affect. For this reason, the active dialogue of action-research is as important for assessing the validity of our findings as it is for being useful to those who participate in the process of inquiry.

Integrating Substance and Structure

We composed this chapter in the belief that our respective research efforts were complementary in substance and reflected shared assumptions about method. We view them as variations on several common themes. The differences in our substantive foci are a matter of figure and ground. Benjamin Gottlieb has primarily concerned himself with the substance of informal helping exchanges, but he has tried to study and interpret these interactions within the social milieux in which they occur. David Todd has focused more directly on the structural characteristics of the social network as they affect the occurrence and form of social support. Ultimately, a highly differentiated conception of supportive interactions and a systematic structural view of the social environments in which they occur should be integrated into an ecological theory of social support. Our research also represents variations on several methodological themes—a view of the research process as an intervention, the researcher as participant-observer, and a problem-centered rather than a method-centered approach to research design.

In using methods that involve intensive probes into our respondents' lives, we were both confronted with the fact that the research process itself constituted an intervention. The data-collection process may be structured to limit and take account of reactive effects, but this does not eliminate them, and the investigator must assume some responsibility for them. Furthermore, although respondents' reactions complicate the interpretation of data in some respects, they also enrich the data and give the investigator a more adequate basis for understanding the respondents' experiences. In Todd's case, an integrated action-research approach was taken with the intention of making implicit issues more explicit for participants as an aid to problem solving.

A closely related theme in our work is our adoption of the role of participant-observer. This role is a valid one in sociological and anthropological research, and it is closely related to the kind of clinical interviewing in which both of us were trained. It involves entry into the phenomenological world of the respondent while retaining an important measure of objectivity. We have attempted to manage the tensions between the insider's experience and the outsider's calibrated observations in varied ways. We have both used semistructured formats for data collection and tape recordings to ensure standardization and accuracy. We have checked the fidelity of our perceptions and the reasonableness of some of our inferences with our respondents. In addition, Gottlieb used a team of three content-coders and Todd used dual interviewers as checks against interpretive prejudice. Such checks made it more reasonable for Gottlieb and for the interviewers and facilitators in the Support Development Groups to make judicious use of their own reactions as a basis for empathic response and for eliciting additional information. It is in this sense that participant-observation has its fullest meaning.

Finally, our research designs were developed from the nature of the problems and the objectives of our work rather than from methodological predispositions. The differences between our approaches reflect our contrasting research agendas. Gottlieb wanted to describe accurately and to categorize forms of helping in a particular population, and his more focused methods of collecting and analyzing data were appropriate to that objective. Todd had an explicit action objective of enhancing participant awareness of structural factors in social support, and the workshops were designed to provide conditions that facilitated the accomplishment of that purpose. Even within the Support Development Groups, methods were varied, depending on whether the focus was on broad exploration of interdependencies or on more precise measurement of particular variables.

The similarities in our methods reflect shared values and motives. Both of us wanted to understand and describe complex social processes in natural settings, and both of us had little prior systematic knowledge to draw on. We both focused on a topic—social support—that is personally significant in our lives. And we both held a commitment to developing knowledge as a guide for preventive intervention.

INTERVIEW WITH BENJAMIN H. GOTTLIEB

Kelly: Ben, could you elaborate on how your research ideas have evolved? Your current work features your research with forty sole-support mothers. How did you become interested in this particular kind of research?

Gottlieb: I think my interests in the topic of informal support began to jell when I was an undergraduate at the University of Michigan. I took a course on the effectiveness of clinical interventions, and I was always intrigued and mystified by the research in which a random sample of people who were candidates for therapy was divided into an experimental and a control group, with persons in the experimental group involved in traditional armchair psychotherapy and the persons assigned to the control group left to wait their turn. When outcomes were assessed, there was about as much progress made by the people in the control group as there was by the people in the experimental group. I was always mystified by those findings, because the class never received an adequate explanation as to how it was possible that the persons in the control group recovered spontaneously.

I think at the time I toyed with various ideas about this topic. One of those ideas related to the possibility that people availed themselves of informal resources by way of mobilizing family members and friends who helped them. Once these people realized that they were not going to be receiving treatment immediately, they turned to others in their everyday lives and sought some assistance from them. I should add that, when I say they sought assistance, we shouldn't think of that as a very conscious and deliberate effort to approach people and say "I have a problem; can you help me to resolve this problem or discuss it with me?" The helping process works in a more spontaneous and natural way. So I think that, if I were to mark the beginning point of my interest in this area, I would date it back to those days when I was so befuddled by that research and tried to put together some ideas of my own.

My thinking about the topic did go into hibernation for a while and then reemerged when I was considering a thesis topic. I decided that an important issue for me to investigate was aspects of the way youth seek assistance for their concerns. That study basically involved looking at four different subcultures in a high school. I did not concentrate on how they were helped by people—that is, the means of assistance—but rather tried to discover some systematic preferences among these youth for different helping resources. The results of that study revealed that there was a relationship between the place these students occupied in the overall status hierarchy of the school system—the particular informal status they held in the school's social system—and the kinds of people whom they preferred to engage and who preferred to engage them for help. So I think the study prompted my interest in informal helping behavior and made me more aware of the relationship between informal support and where people are in a given social structure.

I think there are also some important personal issues that prompted me to engage this research topic. I certainly have been aware over the years of the importance of kin and kith supports as I faced important transitions in my own life; specifically, I think about the diverse stresses associated with taking on a thesis and some of the important people who were there and who were available for me to talk to. I also think about the important role my wife Lois played in helping me adapt to a new position I took following completion of the Ph.D. degree. Even more than that, a bit more dramatically, I think about the importance of social support in my sister's life. Some years ago, she was diagnosed as having multiple sclerosis. At that time, she naturally had to go through a great deal of personal trauma in coming to terms with that diagnosis. The effects of that diagnosis were to disrupt some of her former social relationships, to strengthen others, and to catalyze the formation of new ties. By looking at the importance to her of people in her immediate social surrounding, I can really appreciate some of the health-protective effects of informal support.

Just as an anecdote, she has told me on a number of occasions about people in the building where she lives who have established very close relationships with her. Strangely enough, people who are normally viewed as relatively distant individuals, such as the mailman or the doorman in her building, have become very important in her social world, partly because her world has shrunk and because these are people with whom she has very regular interactions. She tells me about the mailman not dropping her mail in the slot downstairs but rather coming upstairs especially to bring it to her. He comes in, and they sit down together and have a cup of coffee and chat a bit. But he is just one of many people in her building, such as the doorman and other residents, who have played a critical role in giving her feedback and monitoring her condition on a regular basis, all within their ongoing friendship.

In terms of the specific question of how I became involved in studying sole-support mothers, I think that the first ideas I had about focusing on this group really stemmed from my involvement with a couple of sole-support mothers through a seminar called "Ecological Considerations in Community Mental Health" that I gave here at the university. At the time, we were talking about some of the factors that affect individuals' abilities to get help for resolving problems. These two women talked a great deal about their own situations—some of the constraints on women who are receiving welfare payments, some of the restrictions having to do with the need to spend a great deal of time within their own home, the fact that they do not participate in a number of different settings in the community because their main responsibility is with their children, and some of the effects of these constraints on the likelihood of their developing new relationships with other people. They were concerned with the fact that their world has contracted, so that they are limited to interactions with people who are neighbors or with people whom they may come across in their everyday neighborhood activities. I felt that it was important to understand a bit more about the situation of women like that and to try to appreciate how they defined informal support and how some of the restrictions on their lives affected the sources and kinds of support they received.

Finally, I think that, after having conducted a study of relatively privileged adolescents—I would describe these youth as middle-class boys in a middle-class community—I felt that it was important for me to understand how help was defined by people in a lower socioeconomic status. I think all those factors converged on the decision to undertake this research and to adopt this particular sample for the purposes of my study.

Kelly: With refreshing candor, you discuss the feelings you had in the initial part of the research design when you had sent out letters for participation in the study. As a result of the small return, you began to revise your procedures and methods in order to create a relationship with the informants that would give you more authentic information. Could you talk about any other factors that you may not have presented in your chapter that affected the choice of methods or the procedures in order to accomplish what you wanted to do?

Gottlieb: When I first set out to recover information about what the substance of informal social support was, I toyed with a number of different approaches. One of the things I did early was to go to the literature and try to locate information that addressed the generic characteristics of help—What is help? How is help defined? And I think the literature in the counseling area, the work of Carkhuff, Berensen, and others and that whole tradition of humanistic counseling was very important in terms of informing me of what the core characteristics of a helping relationship really are. I was basically interested in understanding how help is defined in lay, as opposed to professional, ecologies, and I felt that I had some preconceptions about what I would find, both from my own personal experience and my reading of the counseling literature.

I considered for a while the notion of trying to generate a rough classification scheme of informal helping. That is, by culling the literature and pulling out common themes about the helping relationship, I felt that I might be able to construct a classification scheme, which I then could take to my respondents, asking them to describe problems that they were experiencing and then to use my classification scheme and check off the categories that they felt applied in the helping relationships they had established. As I thought about that a bit more, however, it became clear to me that I would in some way be guiding their perceptions. I would be limiting their definitions to the categories that I had generated. I even said "Well, let's begin with some categories that they can refer to with regard to helping, and then they can add others of their own." But I still felt dissatisfied with that, because the existing categories might still predispose them to define their experiences in a way that paralleled my construction of reality. I was very reluctant to do that and decided to reject this approach in favor of an approach that was entirely grounded in their own perceptions. Basically, then, what I did was to record verbatim their descriptions of how they had been helped by people, and, from that, I generated a classification scheme.

But I think there are a couple of other reasons why I decided to adopt the particular design. It was very important for me really to participate with these women in their own homes, really to try to understand their phenomenology of helping. What I mean is that, in many cases, the women were able to explain to me how certain situational factors really did affect the availability of support for them. For example, as I mentioned earlier, the settings in which these women participate have a very clear effect on the opportunity to form new relationships. They have a clear effect on the diversity of people that they encounter in their lives, and, in turn, that diversity will have an effect on the norms that people express and the kinds of helping they express. I felt as though it was important for me, not in terms of documenting informal helping, but in terms of getting a contextual understanding of informal support, to participate with them and allow them to speak in an unrestricted way about factors that they felt had an influence on the availability of support. That's why I entered their homes and took a phenomenological approach to understanding their experience of help.

At the same time, I think my status as a newcomer to the community also affected my choice of an intensive and open-ended mode of inquiry. I undertook this study approximately a year after I arrived in this community, so naturally I wanted to get to know people. But more than that, I wanted to speak to citizens about their perceptions of the support systems—both informal and formal—in the community. Therefore, I felt that, in the course of my conversations with these welfare mothers, they would have a chance to describe helping relationships they have with family physicians, pediatricians, ministers, taxi drivers, the whole host of people in the community besides professionals working in the formal agencies. I also wanted to understand a bit more about how women in this status in the community understood and evaluated the formal human services that were being delivered to them. So again, my purpose was also to understand more about local helping patterns through the eyes of this particular sample.

Finally, I think that it was very important to me, and this goes back to the notion of a style match, to adopt a style of inquiry that really was respectful and reflected my concern about the lives of these women. I didn't want to go in there, grab the data, and run. I wanted to establish a relationship with them. I wanted to develop some rapport, and I wanted to give them an opportunity to talk about their lives with respect to the quality of support that they had available.

Kelly: As a result of your investment in this approach, which has taken about two years, beginning with your preparation, then the recruitment phase, then data collection, analysis, feedback, and so forth, how has this work changed your impressions of those people, revised your theory, and elaborated your methods? In what way has the research process affected you in your work?

Gottlieb: One of its effects has been to strengthen my own conviction that it is possible to obtain rich data through a method that is very open-ended in nature, through a method that does not have controls built into it, and through a method that calls very much on my own ability to calibrate my style of communication, my mannerisms, my own ability to relate to a diversity of types of individuals in the community. I think that, above all, the work has convinced me that one can in fact retrieve rich, scientifically credible information through an approach that is phenomenological. That certainly is one important outcome for me.

With regard to your question about how my perceptons of my respondents may have changed over time, I must say that my contact with them forced me to abandon a stereotype of these women as needy and dependent people. In my portion of the chapter, I highlighted the ways in which I tried to help my respondents to deal with the emotional aftermath of the issues I probed; however, there were many occasions when *I* was the beneficiary of their help and sensitivity.

Kelly: You talk about a proposed follow-up workshop that you are planning in several months. It is my mpression that many investigators would not plan such an occasion as part of their research design. You apparently feel that this is an important procedure. I gather that the rationale is to test out what you have learned and to provide feedback. But, since this seems to be an integral part of the research process, I wondered if you would comment on what led you to think about this kind of format and what your thoughts are today as you look ahead to the workshop.

Gottlieb: As I thought about the entire design of my study in light of my special interest in trying to document forms of informal helping behavior, it seemed natural to use that information to inform both my respondents and other people who had any informal, as well as professional, involvement with these women of some of the ways in which lay help is perceived and defined as effective. It seemed as though the research would simply not have come full circle, but would have been short-circuited, had I not somehow included feedback within the entire loop. I also felt as though the workshop would be an appropriate forum for sharing some of the secondary data I had uncovered about the specific needs of these particular women in this particular locale.

Furthermore, I had been told some things about how welfare regulations can restrict the range of settings that recipients participate in and can restrict the possibility of forming new social ties. So, in many ways, I felt that it was important to get back to people who enforced welfare regulations and in some way relate to them, through the perceptions of their clients, the constraints that are a function of the institutional arrangements in the community. For example, through the course of my conversations with the respondents, I was able to discover that there were one or two family physicians in the community with whom they could really sit down and discuss personal problems. In other cases, the respondents would tell me that they felt very rushed when they were with their physician; they would look around, see all the other individuals in the waiting room, and feel that there was no possibility at all for taking up the physician's time with anything other than purely medical symptomology. Consequently, I felt as though here was another domain where feedback could be provided, such that some examples of healthy relationships with gatekeepers could be described to other physicians in the community. In short, I felt as though I was getting a lot of information, not only about how these women defined informal helping behavior but also about how institutional regulations and the behavior of certain gatekeepers in the community affected the availability of help. I could then use this information as a tool for change. When I say a tool for change, I mean, through the medium of small-group workshops, assembling people from the gatekeeper sector, from the social welfare sector, and from the community of sole-support mothers and encouraging them to share perceptions of one another, review the research information, and make decisions about how modifications in the community could better serve the needs of these women. I'm saying that I certainly didn't see this work as a purely academic mission but one that also involved the recovery of data that could be fed back for the purposes of social change.

Kelly: In this format, do you see a way in which the workshop and the small-group discussion and your relationship with the informants can have some positive effects on the mothers' ability to create and elaborate their own informal social support systems?

Gottlieb: I certainly do. I think one of the most dramatic findings I came across during the research was that, in these pockets of the community where low-income people live, there is an aura of suspiciousness that develops. People are observing one another, noting who comes to someone's door and what is going on around the neighborhood, in a way that somehow has the effect of insulating people from one another as opposed to strengthening relationships between people. In another neighborhood, this surveillance might reflect a high level of social interdependence among residents and serve prosocial functions, such as watching out for potential burglars or protecting property values. But, in the locales I entered, the surveillance had a demoralizing effect, prompting residents to lower window shades and stay indoors. Yet, I feel it might be possible to counteract their relative isolation from one another by providing an opportunity for them to discuss the commonalities in their lives and to share their concerns and their ambitions. My optimism is based on the fact that many of my respondents were astonished to hear that other women I had interviewed had said exactly what they were saying about some aspect of their interaction with people in the community, about some aspect of the stresses they were facing in their everyday lives, or about some major decisions they were confronting. They seemed very relieved when they heard me say that it wasn't the first time that I had heard that opinion. So, it seems very important to me that these women hear one another saying very similar kinds of things in the workshop, partly because I think they would get a sense of normalization through the process and because it might be the first step in the process of creating a block club, a mutual-help group, or some other type of informal association among sole-support mothers. Together, they might also stand a better chance of wresting needed services from community institutions and changing some of the regulations that currently hamper their lives to the point where those regulations disrupt social relationships rather than fostering their development.

Kelly: Ben, thinking about your work with adolescents, the creation of the classification scheme, your theoretical ideas on social support, and the relationship of professionals and clients, and considering your work with these mothers, what are your most important accomplishments so far?

Gottlieb: I see the accomplishments on two levels: on the level of personal learnings that I have made as well as the knowledge, the information that I have been able to generate. I would add a third component, which is the notion of effecting some changes. Since the workshop has not yet occurred, I have only a promissory note here.

I think on a personal level I developed some new skills. I think I sharpened my own interviewing skills and developed a new appreciation of the interview as an occasion for data collection. I also was exposed to an entirely new methodology, that of content analysis. I had never received any training in that area—in fact, it had never been touched on in any of the graduate level courses that I took. So I had to begin right from the start familiarizing myself with the literature in the area and in fact learning by doing—going through the literature, understanding what the main elements of content analysis are, looking at studies that had used the method, looking particularly at critical articles on those studies, and ensuring that, in my own method, I was as thorough as possible in the content analysis that we conducted. So, certainly, there is a quantum leap in terms of my new understanding and new skill in content analysis.

I think also, on a personal level, I was able to satisfy my curiosity about developing a more complete contextual or ecological understanding of social support. I think I was able not only to identify the microscopic processes that constitute informal helping but also to understand how restrictions on the opportunities to form relationships with others have implications for the availability of informal help.

In terms of the product of the work, we now have available a classification scheme, which can be tested and used to document helping processes in naturalistic settings, ranging from very unstructured settings of the sort that I described at the outset of the chapter—playgrounds, nursery schools, student lounges—to more structured settings, such as mutual-help groups. I am sure the classification scheme will be modified as it is applied in future cases, certainly as it is applied within different subcultures from the one in which I initially generated the scheme.

Kelly: The editors have operated on a premise that, when you invest yourself in a research area that requires adaptation, either in the relationship with informants or in the methods, it requires a lot of extra help and support, either through organizations, people, or events. You've touched on some of those themes. Could you comment on those organizations or people that have been helpful to you so far in your work?

Gottlieb: I must say that, for the most part, I felt as though this was a solo venture. Certainly, the study could not have been done without the formal approval and help of the local Ministry of Community and Social Services, nor could the study have been undertaken without the financial assistance of the Canada Council and the very useful remarks that I received from the Council's grant reviewers.

During the design of the study, a graduate student who had been working with me was very helpful. He had spent the summer working for the local Children's Aid Society, where he had many opportunities to involve himself in the lives of sole-support mothers. When I say "involve himself in their lives," I really mean that, because he refused to sit behind his desk in the agency and favored instead spending time with the women and their children and working in a collaborative way between the home, the school, and the agency in order better to meet his clients' needs. He was very important to me, because he constantly reassured me about the suitability of the phenomenological approach that I was going to take and because he emphasized the importance of my interacting with these women in a very spontaneous way rather than taking a distant and structured approach. So I think that he was very important in terms of reassuring me about the suitability and the decency of the approach that I was adopting.

I certainly feel that the two sole-support mothers in my seminar were very helpful, to the extent that they worked with me on generating questions that would be as concrete as possible, that would be easily understood, and that the women would respond to. *Kelly:* There probably were some stresses and strains involved with this research. I would like your comments on the help you received as you tried to create a new method to study a problem that had not been studied before and as you tried to establish a relationship with people who were not convenient subjects.

Gottlieb: There is no doubt in my mind that Lois, my wife, played a very important role, especially during the critical time when I had sent out letters inviting respondents to participate in my study and assuring them that the study would have no bearing on the welfare payments they received. At that time, I had received about three or four calls. It was very difficult for me to understand why I was not getting much response. She played a very important role in helping me to contain my zeal to initiate the study after all the investment I had made in the planning and design phases, and, at the same time, she reassured me that there would, in fact, be a larger response in time.

Beyond that, she played a fundamentally important role in helping me to deal with the after-effects of many of the interviews. I recall many an evening when I would return from a session and recount to her some of the experiences that the women had described in an attempt to come to terms with the fact that our experience was so qualitatively different than their experience. The respondents' children were not indulged and stimulated with educational toys. In many cases, they had to rely on their own resources to find entertainment and stimulation. Yet, these children seemed to be coping well. I raised questions with her about our heavy investment in what I characterized as nurturing and mollycoddling our son. She again was able to help me put these emotions in perspective and was able to temper some of my very quick judgments about our own entire life-style.

Kelly: As you think about your research at this point, do you have some specific recommendations regarding how research of this type could be better designed or revised?

Gottlieb: I think in retrospect I am satisfied with the inductive approach that I took. I feel very confident that the categories that exist in this classification scheme do closely reflect the experiences of these women. During the entire coding process, the team of raters were very diligent about labeling categories in a way that closely reflected the everyday experience of the women. I think taking this naturalistic approach—conducting the study on the phenomenology of helping behavior—was the most appropriate way of proceeding, given that this was the first effort to document comprehensively categories of informal helping behavior.

As a beginning point, we have obtained a wide range of behaviors that likely generalize to a large number of different settings. My recommendations regarding the design of research in this area would be for others to also adopt, in the initial stages, an inductive approach that is grounded in the perceptions of the informants. Naturally, questions do arise as to the extent to which the categories that we generated correspond to actual behavior. It's important that the reader understand that we are discussing the *phenomenology of perceived helping behaviors.*

I think next steps would include the application of the scheme to ongoing helping transactions, to apply this scheme through observations of people negotiating their problems together. I think that would be the task—to test the reality of the categories. I have no doubt that they reflect perceptions of respondents.

Kelly: What recommendations do you have regarding the processes of doing this type of research?

Gottlieb: Again, I feel that, wherever people are interested in discovering the substance of social support, there must be a readiness on their part to immerse themselves in the everyday experience of the respondents. I think it's very important that we initially go to those settings where people are exchanging resources and try to find ways of documenting their behavior faithfully. I think that this is an area that is difficult to probe, because people are often not aware of the fact that informal help is occurring. People take mutual help for granted in their everyday lives, and it is up to the researcher to find ways of parceling out such phenomena and recording them with high fidelity.

Kelly: On reading your work and talking with you, one of the implications I am developing is this: If it is possible for the behavioral scientist to understand the informal processes of helping and social support, we can then learn more about some of the ingredients of mental health. It sounds as if your work can help clarify how professional help is offered. Am I reading too much into the implications of your work? Could you comment on that?

Gottlieb: First of all, it's important to make clear that I believe that informal help and professional help are not mutually exclusive. I think the importance of understanding informal support is that people naturally turn to primary-group helpers as the first recourse, when problems or concerns or stresses arise. All but the most isolated people first enter what I have described as a lay treatment network. Only after they have engaged that lay treatment network in an effort to understand and resolve their situations might they turn to professional resources. Sometimes they will turn to professional resources, because a primary group member has in fact referred them. Sometimes, the problems will become so severe that, after the individual has been cycled through the informal network, he or she will turn to professional resources, simply because the lay network itself defines the problem as requiring professional support.

But it's clear to me that there are certain aspects of informal helping that would be useful information for professionals. For example, I think that, if we understood more about how healthy support systems function, that kind of information would be very valuable to the clinician, because he can use his understanding of health support systems as a yardstick to assess the networks of clients that do come to him. To some extent, network therapy itself is a version of what I am talking about, where there is an attempt to realign the entire network of relations, so as to make it more productive and resourceful for the individual. But beyond that, I'm talking about informing the professional of the elements of healthy support-system functioning, partly through giving the professional insight about useful helping behaviors as well as about the range of primary-group helpers who are potentially available to the individual.

I think there has been a tendency on the part of professionals to colonize informal helpers, and by that I mean that, in some instances, professionals operate on the assumption that nobody knows how to help as effectively as someone who has been trained in helping. In programs of mental health consultation, there is often an implicit judgment that the consultee is in need of training in helping techniques. I think that, although that may be true in some cases, before the decision to train is made, there is an obligation on the part of the professional to do an assessment of the strengths of the consultee. We risk ruining or undermining some of the natural helping talents of community caregivers, if we simply fashion the consultee's role in our own image. I think there are some implications of this research for changing professional practice. Conversely, I think the professional can contribute toward strengthening primary-group helping if he or she has some greater knowledge of the elements of healthy primary-group support systems.

Kelly: In your description of the research, you mentioned that you had worked in this research with two undergraduate students and a graduate student. You already commented on how the graduate student had helped you. What recommendations do you have for training people to do similar work? Is there a legacy from the Gottlieb tradition that you can pass on to the next generation?

Gottlieb: I think students of community processes who are interested in exploring informal helping networks should have a sound grounding in methods of field research and naturalistic research. I think that courses I took in field-research methods at the University of Michigan had an important impact on my own preferences for research. I think that we need to strengthen such courses and make them as rigorous as courses emphasizing experimental methods.

At the same time, I think it's important for the researcher to be prepared to adopt a role that reflects involvement, spontaneity, and participation in the lives of the people he or she is working with. It was important in my own research that I involve myself with these women and adopt a collaborative approach, rather than simply act as an observer who was relatively remote and who had preconceived notions about the particular elements of behavior that were important to study.

INTERVIEW WITH DAVID M. TODD

Kelly: First of all, Dave, I think it would be very helpful to know how you became involved in this particular research topic.

Todd: This research really developed as an integration of research and applied interests I have had since graduate school. I had done research on informal helping. I had also done mental health consultation and organizational development work in schools as ways of approaching preventive intervention. But these two parts of my work were pretty separate. I decided I wanted to understand helping even more from a systems point of view; I wanted to go beyond formal organizations as the social context, and I wanted to do research that was integrated with preventive intervention. Just at the right time, I heard Carolyn Attneave give a colloquium on network therapy. The social network concept seemed like a powerful way to understand a person's social world across various settings. I wondered how it could be used in a preventive approach, and my attention turned to how people develop their natural support systems — how they create them, maintain them, use them, or don't use them.

Kelly: Could you give some examples of the way you have tried to use different methods and settings to understand the concept of social network?

Todd: When you are moving into a new area, to understand complex social processes in natural settings, it is important to develop ecologically validated guidelines for posing questions and choosing variables. To do that, you need a rich, integrative picture of those processes. You need to see the context in which things occur and not just isolated phenomena. You need to expose yourself to new possibilities and expand your frame of reference. You need, in short, to involve yourself in a dialogue.

Kelly: Could you illustrate this point from your work?

Todd: Well, Cris Tolsdorf's (1975) dissertation provides a good example. He was primarily interested in differences in network structure that might be related to psychiatric impairment and hospitalization. Much of his interview was designed to gather specific, detailed information about network structure. Still, his interviews were open-ended enough to gather important information we had not anticipated; the men Chris interviewed showed strong differences in their expectations that support would be offered, that it could be trusted, and that they would take it, even if it were available. These views seemed somewhat independent of structural patterns. Three men might describe very dense networks, but one would see his as nurturant, another would experience intrusiveness, and the third might suggest that support was being offered but refused. The individual's orientation to the network seemed to interact in very complex ways with network structure and norms to determine whether the support potential of a network was actualized. Although this was not surprising in retrospect, neither the existing research literature nor our own thinking had given these interactional factors the importance they seemed to have in these interviews.

Kelly: When you are working in a new area that has not been traditionally a research topic, it implies that the investigator has a commitment to the problem and then embraces knowledge where it derives. If knowledge comes from applied anthropology or social theory and requires improvisation, the investigator accommodates to the problem. Isn't this role both exhilarating and quite anxiety provoking? Could you comment on your reactions and those of your doctoral students as they have immersed themselves in this new research tradition?

Todd: Yes, it has required a lot of exploring and soul searching. We knew that intensive interviews produced very rich information and that they evoked and helped us to conceptualize many of our own experiences. This seemed extremely useful for developing our thinking. It seemed important to capture and communicate the complexity and integrity of the lives and social worlds of the people we were talking to. But this kind of work had little legitimacy or context within the conventional methodology of our discipline. How could we be objective and how could we give others a basis for evaluating our objectivity without randomization and statistical analysis? And yet, that is exactly what we tried to do in our psycho-

therapy and consultation work. We did a lot of reading in anthropology, sociology, and philosophy of science, and we found
important guidelines. For example, Rosalie Wax talks about how
the anthropologist gains in-depth, personal knowledge by becoming partially socialized into a new culture. This personal experience
becomes an additional important source of data. This kind of *reflective assimilation* was very similar to our processes of inquiry in
applied work, and her guidance for using such information in research was extremely useful. I developed a graduate course on
field methods to help integrate these ideas, and we had a de-
partmental debate on quantitative versus qualitative methods. It
was a very lively process! Our initial efforts were pretty intuitive
and global, and these dialogues were very important for identifying
fundamental issues and putting our concerns into some broader
perspective. The issue is not qualitative-naturalistic methods versus
experimental-laboratory methods. The important questions have
to do with the strengths and weaknesses of various methods for
different purposes.

Kelly: It sounds as if the result was to put aside some of the conventional canons of research procedure for a preference to engage, as
you said, in reflective assimilation. It would seem to me that this
creates a lot of ambiguity from the interviewer's point of view. I was
wondering how the colleagues and students with whom you have
worked have been able to deal with the ambiguity. As I think about
it, it must be essential to be clear about the phenomenon you are
after, and you must be willing to try different methods to get it. If
that clarity is not there, then the interview may become a projective
device. How do you balance these issues?

Todd: I agree that it is very important to be clear about your objectives and expectations. There are also many things you can do to
check the accuracy of your data and the validity of your interpretations. We try to share our understanding and interpretations with
respondents as we go along, while trying not to bias their statements. This requires an atmosphere of trust and openness and a
genuine expression of interest in understanding what they think.
We give most weight to interpretations that are supported by a
variety of statements made by the respondent. Where we can, we
try to use multiple methods of gathering information. In the Support Development Groups, for example, we had maps, journals,

group discussion, and individual interviews, which were conducted by two people, who could compare impressions and watch out for each other's blind spots. We base our analyses on a careful and systematic review of the information, and we try to be very explicit about the basis on which we make any inference. These are all ways of trying to assure that we have accurately understood and reported what the repondent said. But we also address an issue of validity that is often slighted in other methods: We try to make sure that the respondent is speaking out of a well-developed understanding of his or her own experience. Since we are studying issues that we expect are often *implicit* for people, this is a critical concern, and we must use a method that involves active dialogue.

Kelly: You point out that you use a variety of methods. You've talked about your network mapping, workshop format, journals, and interviews. What observations do you have about the relative efficiency of one kind of inquiry versus another for different aspects of the topic? Is there an intrinsic complementarity that you've uncovered?

Todd: Well, decisions about these things have often been more intuitive than I'd like to admit! But I think I can identify some important dimensions of the choice of methods. One dimension is the kind of information you want from people. As I mentioned, we wanted information that is not only somewhat personal but also probably implicit. Intensive interviews or workshops allowed for dialogue about such matters within a supportive atmosphere. Journals provide a record of experience outside a research setting and give quieter participants a voice, but they do not involve dialogue with an interested person to draw out implicit issues. A survey questionnaire would be even more limited in this respect. We also wanted expansive responses rather than narrowly restricted ones, so we needed methods that would generate information we might not have guessed we would want.

Another dimension is the form in which you want your data. We were not satisfied with maps as a complete source of social-network data—they were not detailed or precise enough. Our interviews, starting with a review of the person's map, allowed much more detail and accuracy. Brennan's matrix format allowed even more precision.

Considerations like these affect the design of any research.

In action research, you have the added questions of what impact you want to have on participants and what will be useful to them. George's matrix gave his participants enough information to look at the connections between work and nonwork spheres of life. In the Support Development Groups, maps provided a visual basis for looking at a wider range of network qualities. From an action standpoint, the use of groups in these studies was important for legitimizing social support, providing models, and giving people a chance to experiment with giving and receiving support. Every method has its advantages and limitations. You have to choose the combination that best suits your purposes.

Kelly: What about the sequencing of methods? Putting myself in the role of an informant, it would help me first to participate in an individual interview, then the group interview, then . . . be asked to do a journal, and then to collect log reports. Each one of those stages stimulates an increasing commitment on my part to be an active participant in the study.

Todd: Sequencing is important. In the Support Development Groups, we had people share thoughts and feelings about social support to give them some useful interaction and group cohesiveness before the more demanding task of network mapping. Then, we had them talk about their own reactions to mapping, before we focused discussion on the issues *we* were interested in. After the workshop, which was heavily focused on the usefulness of information to participants, we used the interview to get detail, which was more important to us. This sequence encouraged involvement, developed trust, and allowed us to get increasingly focused information.

Kelly: Your research has emphasized nonexperimental methods. Can you foresee a time when you would use a control group—an experimental laboratory setting—to test ideas that have been derived or accumulated as a result of your nonexperimental methods?

Todd: More controlled methods, including experiments, are very important to help untangle complex relationships, to evaluate alternative hypotheses, and to generalize results. My point is that they are not *sufficient*. We have an extensive experimental laboratory literature on altruism, but we have hardly *any* systematic descriptive studies of helping in natural settings. We also have little empirically grounded theory as a basis for integrating and extending the knowledge we have.

Personally, I enjoy the formative, intensive stages of research and the development of theory, so I'll probably continue to emphasize topics and methods that are appropriate to such work.

Kelly: In doing formative research on social support, a topic that could be perceived as faddish, do you and your colleagues have an extra responsibility to point out to the reader that these ideas are, in fact, a result of a reconnaissance in contrast to verified facts accumulated through control-group procedures?

Todd: Any researcher should be explicit about the basis for making statements—that's an essential condition of science. Questions of accuracy, completeness, and objectivity are always important. It's not that formative research is without controls or criteria or standards, but they may take different forms from experimental research. We have concentrated on getting a valid understanding of complex social processes under natural conditions for particular individuals and groups. To do that, we have limited our ability to make generalizations about the representativeness of those processes for a larger population. Other methods reverse these priorities. Ultimately, we need both. The problem is that specific criteria for experimental, hypothesis-testing research have become conventional wisdom, and we have little shared understanding about how to evaluate other forms of research. This does make it necessary for the researcher using unconventional methods to try to communicate appropriate criteria and frames of reference as well as providing a basis for evaluating the work against those criteria.

Kelly: How has your research had an impact on both the informant and the staff? How have these effects endured to stimulate new research to clarify the integrative sense of self?

Todd: Social-network concepts have had a significant impact on the staff's thinking. These ideas provide a language for explicit analysis and problem solving in our lives about issues that were generally implicit before. That's our hope for participants as well, and they usually report such effects following the workshops. We can't say yet how enduring or enacted these effects are in their lives.

Kelly: Can you illustrate the impact of doing the research on your colleagues and your students? Do they look at themselves differently in their pursuit of their graduate careers, the way in which they spend their time, their sense of connectedness? Are they more self-willed about creating a social connectedness?

Todd: I believe those things are often true. The work helps develop a sense of perspective. Some of us—myself included—come into academic departments wishing to find a sense of community and social integration as well as a place to do work. But the structural qualities of such an environment often act against social support. Many of us have used social-network concepts to get a personal sense of the issues George Brennan studied in his dissertation: needs for nurturant and instrumental support in and out of work, the relationship between work and the rest of life, and ways of finding some balance that is personally satisfying. Such analysis has often been helpful in realigning expectations, making decisions, or trying to effect some change.

Kelly: At this point in your work, what's your most important accomplishment?

Todd: I think the most important accomplishment is to have developed a set of methods that are meaningful and interesting to participants and at the same time allow us to focus on particular questions and to obtain relatively specific and detailed information about research questions.

I think another accomplishment that is also very important is to have evolved a more complex theoretical view of the personal and social-structural factors that affect social support. I think that, now that the theory is more developed, we can proceed to investigate it more systematically and verify or modify specific aspects of it. I feel that we are now closer to an ecologically valid framework and set of questions.

Kelly: What have been some of the events, people, or organizational resources that have sustained you in this work?

Todd: You mean, what are my personal, professional, and institutional support systems around this work? I would first say that the most important influence has been the graduate students with whom I have worked. It has been a very collaborative venture, with graduate students and myself having a mutual interest in a particular topic. As you mentioned, this style of research has certain unique anxieties that go with it. The mutual support and dialogue with the graduate students has been very important.

There was also important support from colleagues. In one

case, the setting for such support had to be actively created. As a community psychologist, I felt relatively alone in my own department. But there were people with similar interests in applied settings throughout the university, so we created a professional support group. We dealt with questions of professional identity and work-life integration, and we also collaborated in some work. And there were important colleagues in the Department of Psychology, especially Harold Raush, who were actively involved in trying to explore alternative research methods. Their presence was very valuable to me.

Kelly: What recommendations would you have regarding the design of research on social support systems and social networks? If you had to do it all over with the benefit of your experience, what would you recommend?

Todd: I'll start with a general point. I think one of the things that's crucial—you said it a little bit earlier—is starting with a clear problem orientation rather than a particular method. We stumbled around with that at first, as we thought about trying to fit our interests with traditional research methods. But we came to a simple belief that it is necessary to start with a very clear conception of the problem you want to study and what you want accomplished by studying it. Do you have certain action objectives? What is the state of knowledge? The design of the research must flow from the answers to these questions.

There are some things that we have learned along the way, too, that maybe are too specific to be detailed here. I used to watch my grandfather do carpentry, and he had a million shortcuts he had learned over the course of doing his work; there were certain quick ways to do things and certain ways that were too inefficient and weren't worth the effort. We have learned some of that. For example, we went through a long period of transcribing very detailed interviews word for word and finding that, if we had more carefully formulated what we wanted to know and taken selective notes, the whole process of intensive transcribing would have been unnecessary. So there are a lot of things on that order that I have learned.

I think probably the most general, most basic advice I would have about approaching this kind of research methodology is extensive contact with methods that are used in other disciplines. The anthropological literature and sociological literature on field work, and especially participant observation, are very instructive. Sociologists have more directly addressed the distinctions and the relative merits between quantitative and qualitative methods than we have at this point in psychology.

Another thing is that the development of personal awareness and self-reflexiveness is an essential quality in doing this kind of work. Much as is true in clinical interviewing or counseling interviewing, you need to be able to involve yourself empathically with what someone is saying to help them explore their own phenomenological world and yet keep enough perspective and distance to see it relatively objectively. A simple solution is to recommend that people doing this kind of research should be clinically trained. That suggestion misses the point, because there are some real liabilities in clinical training for doing this work as well. But the particular qualities of being able to listen carefully, to help someone explore, and to help them expand their awareness are critical. I think it goes back to your original point. It's not simply taking information that is ready-made and readily formed. It's helping the person develop his or her awareness of something without imposing your own expectations. It takes both a personal sensitivity and knowing how to structure the research process to help keep yourself honest.

Regarding mapping specifically, I think I have talked about some of the strengths of this method. It also has some very important limitations. Mapping is a very phenomenological tool; it's a tool for looking at an individual's perceptions of his or her social world. A lot of work is needed at this point to understand how accurately, and with what kinds of distortions, people view the realities of their social world.

Kelly: What about the process of doing the work? What would you recommend to a person who shared the same goals as you? What would you tell them about creating the relationships for the research to be done and to have impact?

Todd: One of my concerns is that the design of the support-development group as an intervention has some disturbing similarities to the one-shot T-group. The workshop format is more involving than typical data collection would be, but it is still a very limited action method. One of my major concerns would be to design a support-development group so that direct links are made to the natural support structure that people go back into. Very often, we found that couples or friends or coworkers who take a workshop together use it as an opportunity to explore issues of mutual support and to take their learnings back to their natural environment. I think that's a very important direction to pursue. It means that you have to begin with settings and people and social structures to which you have some direct and meaningful access. That was why we got involved with first-year college students. Ted Slovin, who was in the support group with me, taught a course called "The College Experience," in which first-year college students were already looking at their experience of coming to college in a number of ways. Looking at support and social networks was a meaningful extension of that for the students who participated in our study. I think other researchers would have to look for analogues in their own settings, where they could have that kind of integral involvement.

Kelly: It seems to me that you have just said something very important. You embedded yourself in a natural context, and you revised it. You adopted a classroom setting. There were certain natural expectations of the students in that class not to be in a didactic role but to learn by doing and by self-clarification. You then built the research around that. What I'm inferring from your comments is that the adaptive process is critical for research on the topic of social support. For example, an individual who was interested in the social support of persons who were over sixty-five would have the responsibility to design a relationship with older people in a context that would be authentic and reasonable and would have an easy fit. Did I get the point?

Todd: Yes, you got the point. In fact, there is a good example in one of the other projects that I mentioned, a bereavement group. We had hoped to apply the same support-development group method with mapping and interviews and to embed it within the context of a bereavement group. It became apparent that the methods we developed in the other situation took on different meanings and had different utilities in this group. In this situation, many of the people reported that what was missing in their natural environments was something that would be difficult to develop there. What they needed was a place to talk about intensely personal and emotional issues with people who had also experienced them, so that the support group in this situation became the important issue. Mapping and interviewing were something they were willing to do and found somewhat interesting, but it was not, at that point in their lives, a very powerful intervention. They were at the point of dealing with the issue of bereavement and not at the point of reconstructing a broader supportive social network. Although people varied a lot in their responses, those who were really looking to reconstruct their lives after the death of a loved one found the mapping useful and wanted to talk about it. But the usefulness of the method varied a lot, depending on what the participants were looking for.

Kelly: The recommendation that you are stating is that the investigator is as much involved in the design of settings as in the design of the methods of inquiry and that the two must be organic to the topic. That is why· you have used the word *ecology* in different points in your interview.

Todd: Yes, I have stressed identifying settings in which you have some access and awareness and personal involvement. I think Ben Gottlieb makes the important point in our chapter that, if you choose a setting that is relatively alien to you, then you need to go through an extensive and explicit process of acculturation, of really coming to terms with and making sure that you have a genuine involvement with and access to that new culture. I think you have to respect and familiarize yourself with and locate yourself within the setting and the population that you want to know something about. If you don't already have personal access, you have to develop that as an explicit part of the research process.

Kelly: What recommendations do you have about the education and training of persons who can design research and settings and go through acculturation and improvise? It sounds to me as if it takes an unusual, alert, relaxed yet intense, informal role. If so, that is not easy either to make or to create.

Todd: That's right. A half-facetious suggestion would be that all curriculums ought to be abolished at the end of every year and reestablished in the fall. Unfortunately, that would mean nothing could be done except trying to create curriculums! But an important part of my own training was creating my own educational experiences and developing a sense of responsibility and involvement in learning how selectively to utilize resources.

A second thing, I think, is some attention to the support processes within a training program. I don't necessarily mean creating a family. I think what ought to be a simple issue of doing collaborative work is often not modeled, not encouraged. People don't learn how to do it. It's possible, in the format of a research team, directly to address issues of collaboration and mutual planning. I think, again, that exposure to diverse disciplines is a very important part. Most of the practicum and research teams that I have directed have had some mix of people from different disciplines. The kind of dialogue that develops is a very critical part of the educational process. I think that any experience that helps people to develop a clear sense of themselves and an ability to engage people genuinely and at the same time to be accurate, perceptive observers is very important.

The other thing I think of immediately that is very important is an appreciation for diverse methods and their cost and benefits. In many training programs, the impression is given that all research flows from certain statistical models. That is a backward way of looking at research. There are a variety of methods, and particular methods are called for by particular problems, settings, or stages of investigation. Those methods in turn require certain techniques for data collection and analysis. I think it's absolutely critical that training focus on the derivation of methods from an analysis of the problem and the goals of the research. Education should give people the flexibility to use and adapt a variety of methods to the particular situation.

8

Redesigning Physical Environments to Enhance Social Interactions

Charles J. Holahan

Behavioral scientists have traditionally viewed the environment as the passive background of behavior, which is determined by programming that people carry around within themselves, rather than as a dynamic shaper of human events (Barker, 1965). In fact, it is only very recently that behavioral scientists have demonstrated a concern about the social and psychological impact of the built environment. In the mid 1960s, a small handful of architects and designers, realizing the need for a broadened appreciation of the human dimension implicit in architecture and design, turned toward the behavioral sciences for answers (Sanoff and Cohn, 1970). Although answers were initially few, persistent

Note: This chapter is based on an extensive revision of a paper previouly published in *Human Relations,* 1976, *29,* 153-166.

243

pressure from the design professions, along with increasing societal concern about environment issues, generated a marked change in this state of affairs. The ensuing decade saw a growing number of investigators from a diversity of disciplinary backgrounds, including psychology, geography, sociology, architecture, and planning, join to develop environmental psychology. Proshansky, Ittelson, and Rivlin (1970) have advanced the following functional definition of *environmental psychology:* it is concerned with the built environment, it has emerged from pressing social problems, it is multidisciplinary in nature, and it includes the study of people as a vital part of every problem.

A fundamental premise behind investigations of environment and behavior involves the assumption of a systematic interrelationship between architecture and patterns of human behavior. Izumi (1965) offers a diagram useful in understanding the meshing of human and nonhuman components in the architectural fabric. Imagine a rectangle to represent environmental design as related to buildings, with a diagonal separating the human and nonhuman factors. At the left are buildings designed essentially to contain objects, machinery, equipment, and other inanimate objects. At the right are buildings designed solely to contain human beings—for example, nursing homes, penitentiaries, psychiatric hospitals, and housing in general. Between these extremes are buildings used to contain both people and objects in varying proportions. These include libraries, laboratories, stores, and offices. As we move from left to right in the diagram, the evaluation of buildings becomes progressively more weighted toward performance as a social setting and against exclusively visually aesthetic properties.

A central thrust of research in environmental psychology has concerned a functionally based analysis of the performance of architectural settings. Our common-sense notions of the relationship between architecture and activity are often erroneous. For example, empirically based evaluations in hospital settings have demonstrated that bedrooms serve a wide range of personal needs in addition to sleeping, dining rooms are used more for social games than eating, and dayrooms are typified more by sleeping than recreation (Proshansky, Ittelson, and Rivlin, 1970). Thus, an adequate appreciation of the human impact of architectural settings needs to be founded on a systematic empirical evaluation. Environmental research involving this type of assessment has been conducted in a range of different settings, with a number of studies focused particularly on investigating the relationship between physical milieu and psychopathology in psychiatric treatment settings.

The need for this type of research has been pointed to by Watson (1970), who has underscored the need for the physical design of hospitals to meet the requirements of their dynamic activity systems. The physical environment of psychiatric hospitals has been the focus of vigorous criticism (Osmond, 1957; Sivadon, 1970). Osmond (1957) describes a well-known British mental hospital, which "welcomes its new arrivals in a richly painted and gilded hall. Among the intertwining leaves covering the walls, goblin-like creatures are concealed. Sometimes a whole head can be seen, sometimes only an eye gleams malevolently at the arrival." It is indeed ironic that of all building forms, the hospital is one of the most resistent to change; "visual patterns persist like vestigial characteristics long after their functional needs have changed" (Lindheim, 1966).

Sivadon (1970) has expressed strong theoretical beliefs concerning the therapeutic design of psychiatric hospitals. His impressionistic evaluation of the Marcel Riviere Institute, where his views were employed in designing the hospital, suggests the possible utility of his orientation. In a more systematically empirical attempt to understand the psychological impact of the physical environment of psychiatric settings, Ittelson, Proshansky, and Rivlin (1970b) have compared various psychiatric hospitals and found that behavioral options differ dramatically over types of hospitals. In both a city and a state hospital, patients exhibited significantly more passive, withdrawn behavior than in a private hospital, although, of course, physical environment was but one factor that distinguished the hospitals in their study.

Design variations within hospitals also have been shown to affect patient behavior. Ittelson, Proshansky, and Rivlin (1970a) reported more social interaction and more active isolated behavior in single-patient bedrooms than in two-, three-, or four-patient rooms. Sommer and Ross (1958) succeeded in doubling social interaction between patients on a geriatric ward by rearranging the furniture in the dayroom. Holahan (1972) furthered this line of research by using an experimental dayroom to demonstrate the relationship between contrasting seating arrangements and social processes for small groups of psychiatric patients.

The investigation of existing psychiatric wards usually has precluded controlled manipulation of the environment beyond the rearrangement of furniture. One exception is a study by Ittelson, Proshansky, and Rivlin (1970b). After observing behavior on a psychiatric ward for some time, the authors remodeled an underused solarium. As a result, not only did more active and social behavior occur in the solarium itself, but patterns of behavior on the entire ward also were affected. The isolated, withdrawn behavior typical in the solarium before renovation did not disappear from the ward but instead appeared in another place. Thus, the overall levels of social, active, and passive behavior on the ward did not change, but rather, specific behaviors were redistributed.

Planning a Field Experiment

The small scale of the solarium study leaves many interesting questions unanswered. For example, if the entire ward had been transformed, could overall levels of behavior have changed rather than merely the distribution of behavior? Could desirable behavior have been selectively increased? Answers to such questions are critical in evaluating the therapeutic potential of the physical environment in psychiatric hospitals.

Our recent work in the psychiatric pavilion of a large municipal hospital provided a unique opportunity for investigating further the psychological effects of the *ward physical environment*. To test the effects of variation in ward physical environment at a large-scale level, the Environmental Psychology Program at the City University of New York (CUNY)* received permission to plan, finance, and direct the extensive remodeling of an admissions ward

*The ward remodeling was supported by a grant from the National Institute of Mental Health to William Ittelson. The initial planning of the remodeling changes was coordinated by William Ittelson and Susan Saegert.

in this hospital. In addition, there was an opportunity to employ an experimental control in this hospital, since a second admissions ward was available that was identical to the remodeled ward before change. This situation was especially ideal, because the hospital followed a policy of randomly assigning patients to these two wards.

Observations of patient behavior on the two wards were conducted using the *behavioral mapping* procedure developed by Ittelson, Rivlin, and Proshansky (1970). Twenty-five patients were randomly selected for observation on each of the two wards. Experimental measures were initiated six months after the remodeling was completed, to allow sufficient time for enduring ward routines to become established, and were collected in an identical manner on the wards during a simultaneous five-week period. Five patients were studied per week on each ward. Observation sessions of seventy-five minutes were conducted on both the morning and afternoon of Mondays and Thursdays. A time-sampling procedure was used, in which an instantaneous recording of each patient's behavior was performed at five-minute intervals. There were fifteen intervals per observation session, resulting in a total of sixty observations per patient over four sessions.

The observations on which the process analysis of the ward system is based consisted of a detailed record kept by the principal experimenter of events on the ward throughout the planning, remodeling, and postchange periods. The following three categories of observations were recorded:

1. Formal and informal interactions between CUNY investigators and ward staff—for example, cooperative planning sessions for design decisions, casual sharing of personal reactions to the environmental changes.
2. Daily ward routines: (a) Process and content of ward staff meetings. (b) Role behavior of different staff groups—for example, habitual ward duties carried out by each group, typical interpersonal contacts between staff groups. (c) Unobtrusive measures—for example, personalization of space, arrangement of new furnitire by ward staff, occurrence and repair of damage to the new environment.

3. Critical incidents—for example, staff resistance to an environmental change, a flare-up between staff members.

Entré

Acquiring permission from administrators and staff to manage and effect environmental change in an ongoing naturalistic setting confronted us with a formidable interpersonal and political challenge. In conducting the field experiment, our first task involved an effort to establish an atmosphere of mutual respect, confidence, and trust between ourselves and the hospital administration at Bridgehaven. This was essential, because the decision-making process in the hospital was highly bureaucratic, with each ward relating to the central administration through a fixed hierarchy of authority. We found ourselves reminded repeatedly of "traditional channels" and "established procedure." Building a cooperative relationship with hospital administrators required punctilious accord with established channels for decision making in the hospital, respect (occasionally feigned) for the wisdom of the hospital's chief administrators, and patience. During this period, we were able to rely on the positive reputation and recognized expertise of CUNY's Environmental Psychology Program, which had been involved in environmental research in the New York City hospital system over a five-year period. In addition, our willingness to provide the economic backing for the project was critical in lining up administrative support for the study. In achieving a positive working relationship with ward staff, we were able to depend on the familiarity and trust the program had established with the ward during two years of observational research in the setting. The relationship we inherited was characterized by collaborative effort, openness to mutual need and interest, and interstaff respect. Finally, we were able to utilize, in addition, the facilitative benefits of friendship, in that the architect working with our team was a personal friend of the ward director.

Unfreezing

Kurt Lewin (1947) wrote that, for permanent change to be achieved, the change-agent must first unfreeze the old level of performance. One of the most compelling phenomena we observed on first entering Bridgehaven was a "petrification" of the ward environment. For example, over time, the established structure of the physical environment had become rigidly set, with both staff and patients viewing these established patterns as practically unalterable. This petrification pervaded the entire physical environment, including standard ward design, the usual types and arrangements of furnishings, and typical color preferences. Sommer and Ross (1958) have referred to this phenomenon as *institutional sanctity*. In fact, however, such petrification extends far beyond an inflexibility in physical setting and pervades the character of the entire institution, including standard ward routines and behavioral norms (see Goffman, 1961). In the remodeling study, we realized that productive environmental change would be possible only after the prevailing philosophy of stagnation had been altered. This involved replacing the existing body of expectations that militated against change in the ward system by new expectations that viewed change as both possible and desirable. Lippitt, Watson, and Westley (1958) propose as essential in the unfreezing process that individuals in the setting must be aware of existing problems and they must have confidence in the possibility of a more desirable state of affairs.

At Bridgehaven, we realized both of these factors were of importance. Ward staff did not at first consider the lethargic behavioral style on the ward as a therapeutic problem. Also, after having experienced repeated frustrations in initiating change through the hospital bureaucracy, staff evidenced only minimal faith in the prospect of real change. We thus accepted, as our first task, instilling problem awareness among ward staff. To this end, we met with representatives from all ward staff levels in a series of informal sessions to discuss potential ward needs. At these meetings, we presented, in a simplified summary form, data from a pilot behavioral mapping as feedback demonstrating the markedly passive and unsocial quality of daily life on the ward. Since these data clashed sharply with the staff's expectation that the ward provided an acceptable social atmosphere for patients, they helped to achieve problem awareness, along with a desire for improvement. Our second challenge was to establish confidence in the possibility of change. For this purpose we used an initial change—delivering new equipment to the game room—which was easily effected, highly visible, and likely to produce immediate behavioral effects.

After these initial efforts, we were able to proceed with a cooperative planning effort, which involved agreeing on specific remodeling features and selecting appropriate contractors. This does not convey that unfreezing was completed through our initial strategy. Despite the fact that CUNY funds were available to execute the changes, we worked throughout the planning period against recurring pessimism, bureaucratic entanglements, embedded competitiveness between staff groups, and a diffusion of decision-making responsibility in the hospital. During this period, we played a facilitative role with ward staff, sharing encouragement and listening openly to fears and grievances. Although we operated within the established power structure in the hospital, we made a concerted effort to keep all levels of staff interested and involved in all phases of planning.

Collaborative Planning

The changes we made were based on the preferences and dissatisfactions expressed by patients and staff in interviews and on our observations of behavior on the ward. Especially important in determining the kinds of changes we would make were the criteria ward staff employed in determining the degree of disturbance of a patient.

In initial discussions with ward staff, we found that staff considered successful social behavior to be the most significant indication that a patient could cope with the world outside the hospital. Conversely, extremely passive and withdrawn behavior was considered a sign of maladjustment serious enough to prevent the patient's discharge. Given the heavy pressure of constant new admissions, both wards had explicit policies of returning patients to the community as soon as possible. Our own observations had revealed that several aspects of the physical environment of the wards discouraged the very behaviors the staff desired the patients to engage in. Thus, we decided that the design we would suggest should encourage successful social interaction and discourage withdrawal.

Our own understanding of mental health, shared by most staff members, also entered into our decisions. For example, we expected that a positive emotional state would be encouraged or, at least, that depression would not be exacerbated if the ward environment were more attractive. Thus, our second major goal for the remodeling was to make the ward more attractive. The staff, the patients, and the CUNY investigators all found the wards to be extremely dismal in appearance. Many felt this aspect of the environment contributed to depression and lethargy.

A third goal we held for the remodeling, the provision of more varied alternatives for activities, arose from patients' complaints about boredom and staff's negative evaluation of patient inactivity. Both groups agreed that the tedium of ward life had undesirable psychological consequences. This goal seemed the least amenable to a design solution, because the organization of meaningful activities would have required new patterns of interactions between the staff and patients as well as new props for such interaction.

On first entering Bridgehaven, we were forcibly struck by the negative physical appearance of the ward. Before remodeling, the walls on the ward were dirty and peeling and were marred by scribbling that was rarely cleaned. Furniture on the ward was old, worn, and rather uncomfortable. The remodeling was designed to improve the ward atmosphere and to achieve a number of specific behavioral effects. The changes concerned with improving ward atmosphere included repainting the ward and the addition of new furniture. A range of bright colors was chosen for the repainting, and attractive, modern furniture was added in the dayrooms and bedrooms. A number of additional changes on the ward were concerned with creating areas that afforded a range of social options—from a high degree of privacy to a high level of social participation. A private sector was created in the bedrooms by installing six-foot-high partitions, creating a number of two-bed sections in each dormitory. A table and two comfortable chairs were installed in a screened-off area of each bedroom to allow for private conversations. Small-group interaction was encouraged in one dayroom, where new tables and chairs were arranged in small social groupings. Larger group socializing could occur at large tables in the dining room.

Resistance

A particularly surprising and unexpected aspect of the change process was the level of resistance to change we confronted on the part of ward staff. Although some resistance to the proposed changes on the part of staff probably operated covertly even during the prechange period, clear resistance surfaced only as real change began and the full implications of change were suddenly felt or imagined. The period during and immediately after the actual renovation of the admitting ward was not the emotionally positive phase we anticipated. Instead, the period was characterized by a general feeling of tension on the part of the ward staff and by a sense of reserve, coldness, and emotional distance in ward staff's behavior toward us. In part, this behavior probably reflected the staff's perception of us as outsiders who, despite the best intentions, could never fully appreciate the insider's intimate knowledge of ward life. In addition, we were especially impressed by how greatly change was feared and how unwilling staff members were to take personal responsibility for change. Resistance was particularly evident when obvious role changes were involved, as when an environmental change clearly implied a new staff behavior toward patients. Both the administrative structure and peer pressure militated against innovation on the part of staff members. For example, when the ward activity therapist proposed a new treatment philosophy during the change period, he was reprimanded by a supervisor for overstepping his bounds. Simply initiating environmental change on the ward was not enough, since the impact of change could be undone behaviorally, administratively, or politically. Katz and Kahn (1966) discuss this phenomenon more generally, noting that systems attempt to preserve their character through a quasistationary equilibrium, where a movement in one direction is countered by an approximate adjustment in the opposite direction.

A particularly dramatic example of resistance developed around our effort to install partitions in the large dormitories to create a more private atmosphere for patients in the bedrooms. Although all parties had agreed to the plan in advance, the nursing staff abruptly decided against it on the day carpenters arrived to implement the changes. The staff complained that partitions would make it impossible to survey the bedrooms from the hall as was previously possible. They harassed the unwitting carpenters to such an extent that they quit the job and refused to return until we contacted them directly. A compromise was reached by lowering a number of smaller partitions to facilitate surveillance. However, we later discovered that, for two weeks after the changes, the evening staff had not assigned any patients to the new bedrooms, choosing instead to put patients in alcoves and the hallway!

Personalization

In retrospect, it appears that resistance to the environmental changes was inversely related to the degree of perceived control staff members felt in producing changes. Resistance decreased dramatically when the ward staff was able to increase its feeling of control over the remodeling by personalizing the changes in their surroundings. For example, an open-house party on the newly completed ward was initiated and organized by ward staff themselves and served as a clear public notice that the changes were their changes. Also, staff extended the planned changes by adding touches of their own, as when the nursing assistants made curtains for the dayroom and dining room with money they raised on the ward. An interesting aspect of personalization was also observed in the behavior of patients on the ward. Whereas, before renovation, no personalization of space by patients occurred on the ward, after the change, personal articles, such as books, magazines, towels, powder, and flowers, were observed on the window ledges of the newly partitioned bedrooms. To some extent, we facilitated this personalization process by encouraging participation in design decisions across all levels of staff, although much of this phenomenon operated outside of our control and beyond our expectations.

Effects on Patients

We predicted that, after the remodeling, patients on the remodeled ward would engage in more social behavior and be less passive and withdrawn than patients on the unchanged control ward. These hypotheses were supported. Table 1 depicts mean behavior per subject in each behavior category on the remodeled

254   Social and Psychological Research in Community Settings

Table 1. Patient Behavior on the Remodeled and Control Wards[a]

Behavior Categories	Remodeled Ward X̄	S.D.	Control Ward X̄	S.D.
Social				
Social with patients	7.3	6.99	5.1	6.00
Social with staff	3.8	1.28	2.6	2.88
Social with visitors	3.2	4.96	1.1	3.60
Total social	14.3	11.56	8.8	7.50
Nonsocial				
Engaged in activity	9.5	7.44	9.9	6.74
Observing activity	5.6	9.24	3.5	3.39
Walking	6.7	6.63	8.3	6.97
Total non-social active	21.8	14.54	21.7	9.22
Isolated passive awake	7.1	5.47	11.5	7.51
Isolated passive sleeping	11.8	13.65	15.8	14.93
Total isolated passive	18.9	14.91	27.3	14.33

[a]*Source:* Holahan, 1976.

and control wards. The mean difference between the two wards in total social interaction was statistically significant at the 0.05 level with a directional test ($t = 1.78$, $df = 40$). The mean difference between the two wards in total isolated behavior was statistically significant at the 0.05 level with a directional test ($t = 1.84$, $df = 40$).

Unanticipated Social System Effects

An especially exciting dimension of the environmental-change process was a range of fascinating social-system and human repercussions of the remodeling that we had not anticipated. In effect, openness to change at one level provided an impetus for a simultaneous openness to change at other levels. For example, as the remodeling was being completed, ward staff began meeting on their own initiative to discuss for the first time the development of a ward treatment philosophy. These meetings offered, in addition, an opportunity for the open expression of long-standing resentments between different levels of staff. For example, one aide confronted the physician who headed her staff team and demanded to know if he even knew the names of the aides who were on his team. He did not. As a result of these meetings, staff members began to perceive the previously ignored needs, concerns, and frustrations of members of other staff groups.

Before the environmental changes, we observed that role behaviors on the ward were rigidly defined, affording little role latitude or flexibility for individual interpretation of role obligations. In addition, role relationships were strictly hierarchical, with implicit norms severely restricting both feedback and the exertion of social power from lower to upper staff echelons. During the six months following environmental change, we discovered marked changes in the role behaviors of ward staff. The previously tight hierarchical structure characterizing role relationships and the use of authority on the ward were considerably relaxed. Direct and open communication between different-level staff groups was enhanced and included implicit permission for open negative feedback from lower- to upper-echelon groups. In addition, roles for the various staff groups demonstrated greater role latitude, permitting individuals to interpret role obligations on the basis of their personal level of competence, interest, and skill. Ward physicians became more open to feedback from other staff members and better in touch with staff and patient needs. Nurses' aides gained the right to contribute suggestions to therapeutic planning and to express openly negative feedback toward other staff members at all levels.

We feel that new *expectations* were developed by the physical changes. The improved physical environment implied a greater interest, hope, and involvement in a therapeutic philosophy. Thus, ward staff felt expected to play a stronger role in therapeutic planning and programming. The feeling of increased self-importance the ward staff perceived as a result of the environmental improvements was significant in this process. In addition, the remodeling task itself demanded a new level of *competence* on the part of ward staff at all levels. Ward staff was forced to demonstrate and practice a range of highly competent behaviors in planning for the changes, from selecting color preferences to determining an optimum number of beds for the new bedrooms. Competence was also demanded from ward staff in executing the changes, from arranging new furniture in the dayroom to keeping painters and patients from interfering in one another's activities. We encouraged this process across all levels of staff by soliciting, facilitating, and legitimizing input from all staff groups throughout the change process. It appears that the increased feeling of competence and effectiveness on the part of ward staff learned in the environmental change process generalized to other role behaviors involving therapeutic planning, interpersonal staff relations, and more healthy contacts with patients.

We were surprised to find that the ward remodeling also triggered unanticipated reverberations at the level of the hospital's central administration. In fact, even before the remodeling had been completed, the hospital administration voluntarily added a substantial sum to our financial resources for the project in order to capitalize on the favorable impression created by the project. After the remodeling, the new ward became a showplace for hospital administrators, and it became customary for administrators to lead official visitors on a tour of the remodeled ward. Also, within a year after the project was completed, hospital administrators decided, on the basis of the perceived benefits of the remodeling, to repaint the control ward and later two additional admitting wards. These events are particularly noteworthy, due to the fact that the admitting wards at Bridgehaven had not been painted in well over ten years.

The Limits of Lasting Change

As I reflect on these dramatic unanticipated social-system effects of the change process, I am also poignantly aware of the very real limits of the environmental change, particularly as it affected the lives of patients. For example, although the remodeling encouraged ward staff to initiate a consideration of a ward treatment philosophy, the discussion eventually subsided with no lasting commitment to a defined treatment approach. In fact, the prevailing mode of psychiatric care after as before the remodeling remained essentially custodial. In priding ourselves on the benefits of environmental change, it is imperative to remember that no manipulations in physical environment will alone constitute a total therapeutic regime. Most essential to patient care is an articulated and effective philosophy of treatment. Only then can a thoughtfully planned physical milieu be designed with definite treatment objectives in mind.

In viewing ward life retrospectively, I believe that the physical design changes failed to improve noticeably the character of staff attitudes toward patients. In fact, the improved atmosphere on the ward immediately after the remodeling can be explained in terms of enhanced self-perceptions on the part of ward staff rather than as a result of a more positive attitude toward patients. From the outset, staff perceived the remodeling in terms of their personal comfort and ego enhancement rather than as an effort to create a better atmosphere for patients. In fact, one impact of the remodeling was to accelerate staff expectations for career advancement. For example, after the remodeling, one nurse sought an administrative position, an activity therapist decided to earn a graduate degree, and an aide planned to enter nursing school. Even the ward janitors became so involved in the new ward's upkeep that their work was held up as a model in the hospital's housekeeping unit.

Especially sobering, in considering the limits of the change process, is the realization that the physical-design changes within the hospital context left totally unaltered the patients' life prospects after discharge. For most patients at Bridgehaven, who were characteristically poor, educationally deficient, and from minority backgrounds, the aspiration for a decent life in society remained blocked by the plight of slum housing, prejudice in employment, and a family constellation typified by strife and discord. In fact, we came dishearteningly to feel that many Bridgehaven patients, who had originally been picked up on city streets by the police, were on discharge simply returned to the streets. In one deeply disturbing incident, a newly released patient accosted me at the hospital gate, claiming to have been released penniless and asking only for subway fare to return home. Clearly, intrahospital change needs to be complemented by community intervention strategies at a societal scale, oriented toward improving the quality of patients' lives in housing, employment, educational opportunity, and family life.

The Role of the Environmental Change-Agent

One might wonder how the change process here might be compared with the type of change discussed in the organizational change literature. We would propose that the two change processes are quite similar. Essentially, both represent structural changes in the social system of an organization initiated through change efforts by an outside agent. In fact, when environmental intervention is viewed as one strategy oriented toward social change, it becomes clear that other techniques, such as direct administrative or behavioral change, may sometimes more efficiently achieve the same ends. The phases of environmental change analyzed here are in fact somewhat similar to those of unfreezing, moving, and refreezing proposed by Kurt Lewin in discussing organizational change tactics at a more general level. In addition, many of the basic social-psychological issues involved in the environmental change at Bridgehaven are identical to those considered in the organizational change literature—for example, establishing organizational goals, clarifying group decision making, improving the communication network, and resolving intergroup conflict.

We believe that the systematic shift from resistance to personalization discussed here also bears an important similarity to current views of organizational change. The traditional organizational change model accepted the point of view of the change-agent as rational and assumed the resister's view to be irrational. A more current view enhances the role of the resister as vital to the system's survival and underscores the value of the change-agent's making positive use of this energy during the change process (Klein, 1969). Our discussion of resistance has stressed our original egocentric view as frustrated change-agents. The personalization process represented the involvement in the change process of positive adaptive capacities within the system, which we were forced to respond to and to make use of. The similarity between the personalization of the change process at Bridgehaven and current views of organizational change is especially evident in Watson's (1969) summary of the causes of organizational resistance. He says resistance will decrease when (1) participants feel that the project is their own, (2) participants feel that their autonomy is not threatened, and (3) the project is kept open to revision based on experience.

In reflecting on the demanding role of the change-agent, we must credit the considerable professional, physical, and emotional resources available to us from CUNY's Environmental Psychology Program throughout this project. For example, staff in the program included a number of investigators engaged simultaneously in large-scale field projects in other settings, including urban playgrounds, a preschool, a children's hospital, and an urban renewal neighborhood. Informal advice, suggestions, and support between staff members represented an essential ingredient in the program's social climate. At a more formal level, a monthly program meeting provided an opportunity for staff to present, discuss, and receive feedback on ongoing projects. In addition, the program offered motivated and energetic graduate students who were available as field observers and interviewers. Finally, the program's extensive and well-organized library presented a ready access to available expertise in the field of environment and behavior. It is truly impossible to contemplate the development and execution of the present project without the daily nurturance supplied to us from the rich resources of the Environmental Psychology Program.

Finally, let us reflect on some of the ideal qualities of the environmental change-agent in terms of both professional competencies and personality characteristics. At the level of professional competencies, the environmental change-agent requires training in the techniques of action research. In part, these involve interpersonal skills essential to establishing a collaborative working relationship, facilitating open communication, and dealing effectively and sensitively with resistance. Also included are research talents appropriate to evaluation research in field settings, including a familiarity with multivariate statistical techniques, quasi-experimental and correlational design strategies, and survey and observational methods of data collection. In terms of personality characteristics, the environmental change-agent must be able to work in a multidisciplinary, collaborative relationship, see alternative aspects of a problem, tolerate ambiguity, and accommodate innovative science; in short, he or she needs to be a flexible, egalitarian, patient, curious, and risk-taking person.

INTERVIEW WITH CHARLES J. HOLAHAN

Kelly: Josh, to get things going, I would like for you to elaborate on how you got involved in this particular research.
Holahan: In my own training as a psychology trainee at a Veterans Administration hospital, I became more and more impressed with the fact that, in many ways, the physical design of the psychiatric hospital actually fostered and maintained the very behaviors for which we had originally incarcerated patients. And, as I began, at a

very personal level, to reflect on what type of skills would be necessary to try to deal with the range of problems that went outside of the traditional boundaries of psychology, I realized that I would need a facility for studying field research; I would have to know something about how to collect data, how to conceptualize field situations, how to design research studies that make sense in naturalistic environments. So I began to look around for a setting where I could begin to pick up some skills that would go beyond what I had received in a traditional graduate training program in psychology. I found the Environmental Psychology Program at City University an exciting and attractive environment, because they were dealing with just these questions; they were learning to do field research, they were learning to develop designs that were appropriate to naturalistic settings, they were attacking the economic and political problems inherent in field research. I was as much interested in the process of how to conduct field research as I was in the specific content of environmental studies.

Kelly: In reading over your two published pieces and also your chapter, I was impressed with the fact that you were able to carry out a posttest-only control-group design. It occurred to me that it would be important, to the extent to which you care to do so, to bring out the type of administrative support at the hospital and within the environmental psychology program that made it possible for you as an outside investigator to plan and direct this remodeling, conduct unobtrusive observations on the ward, and randomly assign patients to your experimental ward and your control-group ward.

Holahan: In terms of the administrative support from within the City University of New York, it's probably not accidental that Harold Proshansky, one of the codirectors of the Environmental Psychology Program, happened also to be the president of the Graduate Center, in which the Environmental Psychology Program was located. From the top administrative level, we had support at the university that was saying, "Get outside of the walls of the academy; find out what's happening outside." I remember Hal Proshansky once mentioning to me that we had to keep reminding ourselves that the disciplinary boundaries that we are confronted with do not reflect the way social problems arise in the natural environment but rather reflect the traditional administrative categories within universities. He believed that we had to fight beyond those constraints constantly. So, there was always support from within the Graduate Center to get involved in real-world problems and to study them, which I think in many ways was a rare and unique academic setting.

In terms of the hospital, in many ways, I am grateful to the long history of trust and confidence that people in the City University of New York, such as Ittleson, Proshansky, Maxine Wolfe, Lee Rivlin, Gary Winkle, Sue Saegert—a superb team of investigators—had developed between themselves and the hospital system of New York City, so that the hospitals trusted the competencies of the investigators. The hospital staff felt that CUNY faculty were people who knew what they were doing and who would deliver. Second, Ittleson was prepared to deliver some funds. He did get a grant of $5,000 and said, "I will turn this money over to you to remodel one of your wards"; that exchange was extremely important. It was very different from the typical situation with the social or behavioral scientist. We were demonstrating that we had something we were willing to give that was very important. In addition, we were willing to be patient and to work with administrators in terms of their own time frame and in terms of their feeling that they had some control of the entire process. One of the aspects of working in a naturalistic setting, such as a psychiatric hospital, that really impressed me was the extent to which people within the setting need to feel in control and need to feel that the pace of change and the pace of involvement by social scientists is congruent with their own style of change within that setting. They constantly needed to be assured and comforted in terms of their important roles, in terms of their ability to change things if they needed to, and, maybe most importantly, in terms of our being willing to step back at those times when they wanted to be in the limelight, so that, if they wanted to announce to a newspaper or a visitor from another hospital that this project was going on, we were willing to sit back and let them present this in a way that they got the credit for it.

Kelly: What you stated very nicely is that, as an outside investigator develops a contract with a group to carry out an experiment, the investigators, the designers, have to be prepared to give up their sole right of creativity and to participate actively in a directly collaborative way with the people who are going to be living the experiment.

Holahan: Yes. This is very true, and, in fact, this runs counter to two traditional aspects of the psychologist's role. The first is the notion that we control all the variables that we don't want to affect the dependent variable. That simply doesn't work in naturalistic settings—they are not ours to control! Second, they are too complex to control. This idea also runs counter to the professional elitism whereby the scientist says, "This is my idea, I'll do it my way, I'll collect the data my way, and I'll write it up my way." That also doesn't hold in a naturalistic setting, because it happens to be somebody else's setting, and they have a right to decide who's going to be there and when they're going to be there and what's going to go on. These are some aspects of the psychologist's characteristic professional role that one does have to yield, and the process of doing it, at least in my own experience, is a very conscious and essential one.

Kelly: What were some of the other factors that were involved in the choice of the research design and the determination of research procedures?

Holahan: Part of that, I suppose, would deal with my own style as a psychologist. I wanted to prove at an empirical level that something was happening; that was important to me. On the one hand was my concern to do it in a naturalistic way, so that it would mean something in a real-world setting, so that it would be more than just a published study sitting on a library shelf collecting dust. So, I was interested in doing something in an effective way but, on the other hand, doing it in a manner that meaningfully affected some real-world setting. Second, in all the environmental psychology research that I have conducted, I have been convinced that there is no standard research design, no standard research strategy, no standard research measures that are appropriate to all naturalistic settings. Each new setting, in effect, speaks for itself. The demands of the setting will dictate the appropriate research design, the appropriate research tools, and the appropriate research measures. I think part of the excitement and creativity of being involved in environmental psychology is precisely this confrontation with a new environment, which, because of its physical characteristics, history, and people, demands to be dealt with in a unique way. The experimental design is a response to the particular parameters of the situation we were dealing with. For example, the fact that there was a second ward within the hospital that was similar to the ward we wanted to change allowed us to have a control. In another setting, we might not have been able to do that. The fact that we didn't have enough money or time to go into the setting to do preobservations dictated that we would have to do observations after the changes took place. The fact that the hospital was already randomly assigning patients to all their admitting wards allowed us to have a posttest-only control-group design, which is a true experimental design. Often, one is able, in a naturalistic setting, to be scientifically rigorous without distorting the naturalness of what one is doing. To me, that is the essential challenge—how can you do research that is as scientifically sound as possible without losing the richness of the naturalistic setting—and I think we were able to do that in this particular case.

Kelly: As an illustration of this point, I noted that your research procedures involved observation sessions of seventy-five minutes on Monday and Thursday mornings and afternoons and thirty-minute patient interviews during a five-week period. Listening to your portrait of the context that you were working in, I was wondering if in fact the choices about the time and the days of the week and the extent of the observations were a result of the effort to be both scientific and sensitive to the milieu of that ward.

Holahan: Yes. In fact, the particular procedures are a balance between the effort to be scientifically sound and at the same time to be responsive to a whole range of situational pragmatics. The specific amount of time was a concern with having enough information about the ward, so that we could be sure we were getting a reliable measure of what was happening on the ward, and, at the same time, being responsive to the daily routine in the hospital. Thus, we needed to do observations at a time that patients would likely be on the ward, so that we wouldn't interfere with natural ward routines. It would, for example, be quite disruptive if we pointed out to a head nurse, "So-and-so can't leave the ward now, because we're in the middle of our seventy-five minutes of observation." We tried to avoid that. The interest in doing the interviews with patients toward the end of the week was to make sure that the kind of reactive influences that can take place in interviews didn't alter the behavior we were observing on the ward.

Kelly: In your chapter, you have outlined some of the very clear consequences of the research for both the patients and the staff, and you have done it by looking at some processes about change. I was wondering if you would comment about at what point you began to conceptualize these processes that you have outlined in your second publication. Was that conceptual effort developed after the study, or did it emerge during the study, or did you have these implicit ideas before you began?

Holahan: While conducting the actual observations during the change period, I was not conscious of the model of change that was discussed in the chapter. My own feeling throughout the process was simply that we were missing something, that there was more going on than what we had originally entertained. Our initial notions of how the physical environment affects people seemed too simplistic. I actually began to formulate the model of change a year later, when taking a walk on the beach at Prince Edward Island in Canada. I began to think about the amount of energy in a system and the way action research in effect capitalizes on the natural energies within a system, and I began to think about ways of formulating a model of change that was congruent with this kind of natural energy within a system. In some way, it was the notion of the sea and its effect on the surrounding beach that gave me the feeling of slow natural processes within all systems. I began, at that point, a full year later, to put some balance and order into the record of observations that we collected at the hospital one year before. It didn't emerge as anything like a clear notion. I put it together, then I put it down and came back to it. Only after some period of time did those gut impressions begin to formulate in somewhat of a formal manner.

Kelly: I have the impression that your design was a deliberate choice that was appropriate for that occasion, that you thought very carefully about the research procedures, but then you accommodated the implementation of the research procedures. I think it would be important to point out how much thought and explicit commitment there was to the methodology of the research task. Immediately before you began the documentation, what was the nature of the improvisation and accommodation of research procedures?

Holahan: We were particularly concerned with gathering behavioral data that would offer a reliable picture of what was happening on the ward. Behavioral-recording techniques had been developed both by people within City University at the previous hospitals where they had been involved and also by myself in my work in Massachusetts. But, when we looked at the behavioral techniques that were already established, none of them was appropriate to the demands of this particular hospital. Thus, we had to develop new behavioral-recording techniques. There was a commitment to the technique, but there was also a willingness to adapt the technique to the unique demands of this setting. One concern was that the behavioral techniques as developed previously would likely influence what was going on in a ward—they would be too reactive. So we developed techniques where we became more a part of the daily routine on the ward, changing as little as possible the natural processes that were ongoing.

At the same time, I was very interested in getting some self-report from patients as to how they perceived the changes. The patients were extremely eager to have somebody talk with them. Most of them in fact were far more articulate than any of us had envisioned. I remember talking with one patient who discussed his impressions of the control ward that had not been remodeled. He said, "Boy, this has to be one of the most depressing environments in the world. All I do every day is either pace up and down this corridor or lie in my bed awake. There is simply nothing else to do." I remember I found a patient in bed in back of the control ward. He told me that, two days before, he had been pulled out of the East River after jumping off a bridge, that nobody had talked to him since he had been brought to the hospital, and that he was vigilantly lying awake, afraid to come out of the bed. I remember also talking with a woman on the ward that had been remodeled who had been to the hospital six or seven times before. She noted, "It's entirely different than it's ever been before. The walls are painted brighter colors, the furniture is more comfortable. It makes you feel better about yourself."

Kelly: You indicated that one of the consequences of your research was that there emerged a clearer philosophy about the psychological treatment on the remodeled ward and that you and your staff had been consulted regarding the hospital's decision to repaint the controlled ward and two additional admissions wards using the hospital's own funds. That sounds to me like a compliment; the hospital administration saw something in your work and adopted some of your principles. As you think back, what were the important properties of that environment that were the cues to enhance your ability to have impact?

Holahan: That's a very interesting question. I'm not so sure that we didn't just stumble into doing some of the right things. We could not clearly foresee that a lot of moves we made were, in fact, beneficial. The psychologists from the Environmental Psychology Program had a strong commitment to being responsive to the manner in which people within the setting saw their environment, the way they felt changes should be made, and how they felt about the change as it was carried on. There was, at a human level, a general responsiveness on our part to the people in the setting. But, in fact, they often were probably educating us. I could not say that we went in knowing exactly what we needed to do. I think it was simply a matter of being responsive to staff and letting them move us in some of the right directions.

Kelly: Josh, are you saying that the faculty members in the postdoctoral training program were implicitly serving as role models, that there is an organizational contagion about how you behave as an environmental psychologist when you enter a system to do research?

Holahan: Yes, absolutely. We had a very strong value base that promoted respect for the orientation and the needs of individuals within the setting. We thought that we were working for them, that the hospital staff would educate us as to what needed to be done, the way it needed to be done, and the way it shouldn't be done. I think that this value base had a lot to do with the way we approached the hospital, and it was probably quite important in shaping the history of good relationships between the Environmental Psychology Program and the hospital systems throughout the city, which allowed us to move so efficiently into this particular hospital.

Kelly: This work was done from June 1971 to August 1972, a fifteen-month period to carry out the entire procedures. It is now a little more than seven years later. As you think about this particular

part of your own research career, what are some of the most important accomplishments that you initiated in this work?
Holahan: Let me answer that in two ways. One is in terms of my own
reflections on what I personally learned from this work, and the
other is in terms of the kind of impact that we had within the
setting. Personally, it was an incredibly meaningful educational experience for me. My own implicit hunch in approaching the Environmental Psychology Program was that I could learn something
more about the dynamics of doing research in naturalistic settings
than I had learned in a traditional training in psychology. This
turned out to be absolutely true. It's difficult for me even now to
state and be fully aware of the number of things I learned. The
extent to which changes of the physical environment went beyond
what we originally envisioned and affected levels of activity within
the hospital at points far beyond simply altering the physical environment was really astounding. It was exceptionally surprising, a
real reeducation for me, to see the impact that we had at levels
beyond the original effort to change the physical environment. In
terms of how we affected the hospital itself, I would say that probably most important was our willingness, after the environmental
change, to go back to talk with people on the ward and administrators about how things were going. Were there any problems, was
there anything to be learned? I think in many ways this process of
following up on the original change was as important as the initial
changes.

     The changes on the control ward were fascinating. Appar-
ently, in the process of being used as a control ward, the staff
director began to realize that other things would be possible to
make this ward better. He began to reason that, if he was in a
control ward, then there must be somebody else who was in an
experimental ward. So, the director of the control ward checked
and found out that somebody else had had their ward repainted,
and he decided he would request it, too. We found out later that a
number of the wards in this particular part of the hospital had been
repainted after our initial changing of the remodeled ward, based
on the good feedback people had gotten in the hospital. So, there
were a number of effects within the hospital. If we could do anything else to improve the hospital, I would want to go back and
follow up on it considerably more.

Kelly: In describing some of the positive and negative side effects of this work, you commented that some of the ward nurses and nurses' aides resisted the effort initially. Then, later, the same nurses or the same aides began to feel more confident and express more commitment in their own work setting. They seemed to have been willing to learn new competences. In retrospect, do you think that your ability to deal with the resistance of the nurses or nurses' aides initially helped you to achieve a positive result?

Holahan: The resistance that you are referring to occurred when carpenters arrived to build partitions in the dormitory, where we wished to change a rather large open-space dormitory into an area that allowed semiprivate sleeping arrangements for the patients. The night staff became upset, because it would require more work in terms of their surveying patient behavior during the evening. We did, in fact, spend some time talking with staff. That was a very important stage. We didn't go in and simply say, "No, we designed it so there were going to be partitions, and we're going to do it that way." We said, "You people are far more upset than we thought anybody could be about this kind of thing. We're obviously touching on some nerves we weren't aware of."

We began to realize that they were talking about perceived changes in their own role behavior that were uncomfortable to them—probably not the changes in their own right, but rather the manner in which they perceived they were being brought about. To be honest, we had been insensitive—certainly not sensitive enough—to the perceptions of the night staff at the hospital. We had worked during the day with the day staff with the assumptions that the night staff would feel the same way and that the day staff talked to the night staff. Those assumptions were incorrect. It turned out that the night staff was an isolated, low status group, who felt constantly dumped on. I suppose our response at that point was to catch up. We were trying to provide some kind of facilitative arrangement with people, which we had failed to provide earlier. I think the manner in which we did this was really instrumental in terms of the way things developed from then on. I think a major thing we did was to encourage them to feel that, in fact, it was their change; they had a right to protest. We had an obligation to come back and talk it through with them, and they began to feel more confident and more comfortable. Most importantly, they were willing to relax a little bit and let their own excitement and energy get involved.

Kelly: It seemed that this was an important turning point. It gave you a chance to declare your basic values—that you were very sensitive to the fact that there was more to that social organization than you had thought. This allowed you to work in this reciprocal manner. It was my feeling in reading the chapter that there must have been a contagion or authenticity to communicate. During this next phase, people began to have a sense of shared commitment. You in fact were interested in the ward and not just in your experiment.

Holahan: Yes, I think that it was a very pivotal turning point. It was a demonstration on our part of respect for the staff, of responsiveness to their needs, of willingness to slow up and change things, if they could be made more consistent with the needs of the particular staff in that setting. That was very important to them. As I think back to what went on, they were at that point standing back and watching very closely our response to them. Our willingness to talk it through, to work out a compromise solution, was, I think, critically important. I think, more broadly, that probably in any consultation process or action-research process, there is a natural stage at which the researcher needs to step back, to relinquish control, to give over something to the individuals who are actually in the setting. I suppose there is the same kind of difficult weaning as there is with anything that one feels some personal responsibility and control over. In some ways, I think the process here was more dramatic, in that the kind of confrontation that evolved with the carpenters is not typical of all action research or consultation processes. But there is a natural stage in applied research where the scientist needs to step back and give over what's been done to the natural inhabitants of the environment. This is a critical and fundamental point, and I think that, unless these actions take place, it really hasn't been a good project.

Kelly: Josh, you have mentioned several of the people who contributed to the completion of the work. Are there other important individuals or organizations or events that not only contributed to the conception of the work but also sustained you while you were involved in this fifteen-month action expedition?

Holahan: I can think of two important types of emotional sustenance. One was within the Environmental Psychology Program, where the willingness of people to talk with one another—a free and open atmosphere in terms of discussing problems—created a setting where people could give one another a high level of support. In addition, within the hospital environment, there were two particular staff members who were critically important to our understanding of what was happening within the environment and who were also very important in giving us emotional sustenance when we occasionally became depressed about whether we could effect what we had hoped to. One of them was the nurse clinician on the ward, and the other was the activity therapist. It's interesting, because both of these people were individuals whose roles were somewhat ambiguous on the ward. Both of these people were really excited about outsiders coming in who were going to do some things that were exciting and interesting to them. From the start, they gave us an insider's view of what problems we were going to run into. They would let us know on a weekly basis what was going on. They would let us know what needed to be dealt with or if we were going to run into further problems. They were a constant source of information and support throughout the process.

Kelly: In talking about these two key informants, I have the sense that you are saying that the nurse clinician and the occupational therapist were very competent in their work; they cared a great deal about their work setting. They had access to other people, yet they had a marginal status; they were on the fringe. What I detect from your comments is that the combination of those properties makes that kind of person a very critical resource to the outsider. Does that sound right?

Holahan: Exactly. I think it's extremely beneficial in moving into an action-research situation to look for and to be aware of individuals who are competent, who have expertise in the particular areas of change that you're interested in, and who at the same time have an optimum level of frustration. They are willing to take a risk; they are willing to step outside the daily perimeter of their job. In fact, in this case, the activity therapist was scolded by his director for stepping outside his bounds, when, in the process of discussing the therapeutic philosophy, he came up with an organizational scheme of how each patient would be dealt with on their admission to the hospital. But he was willing to do it, because he was frustrated. He felt nobody else was doing it, and it needed to be done. That combination of expertise and an optimum level of frustration is extremely beneficial as a key source of natural energy within the system that can be tapped into by any change-agent moving into the system.

Kelly: As a result of doing this work, what recommendations and ideas would you have to the next generation of investigators in your field about the technical aspects of the research design?

Holahan: Most importantly, one needs to be extremely flexible; there are not going to be any simple answers in terms of research design. In fact, you need to engage in a process of developing research strategies in response to the demands of naturalistic settings. That process of learning how to develop new research strategies and new techniques congruent with the demands of the setting is far more important than memorizing any experimental designs that somebody else has used in different settings. In this sense, there is no "cookbook" for action-research designs. In fact, there is a need to be quite facile and flexible in developing strategies that are particularly responsive to the settings that you're dealing with.

One particular point that I think all of us could learn is to make better use of individuals within the setting as consultants to us in developing the research strategies. I think so much action research and environmental psychology research comes up with results that are difficult to make sense of, because the design is totally out of step with the life-styles and perspectives and daily routines of individuals within the setting. Had the staff been consulted in the first place, they would have said, "Oh, you're looking in the wrong place. We don't do such-and-such there. We don't do it at our formal meeting. We do it actually in a coffee clatch on Wednesday morning, so that's what you want to observe."

Kelly: If you were about to do this again, knowing now some of the things that you've uncovered, what would you do differently?

Holahan: Well, that's a big question. I think I would move even more slowly in developing a working relationship with staff in the hospital. I would probably work out some kind of format such as meeting on a weekly basis or maybe over coffee for an informal discussion of what's happening on the ward. I would do that in such a way that I was sure I was in touch with staff at all levels and through all shifts. So, for example, I would be sure to come in, at least a few times, to meet with the night staff very early on in the process, long before there was any commitment to any particular type of change.

I would build strategies for monitoring the kinds of social system changes that occur. I would build strategies for informing staff as to what some of our observations are as we go along, so that they begin to notice ways that they as a group and as individuals are being affected by the environmental change, so that they can give us feedback about how they feel about that. We could then put more attention into furthering the kinds of change that seem beneficial to us and to the staff. We could then also do something about correcting some of the areas in which tension might be developing between staff members that were part of the change process and that were not beneficial.

Kelly: Josh, the purpose of this book is to illustrate, for faculty, citizens, and students who are doing action research, alternate methods and processes for doing community-oriented research. As a result of your work, what recommendations do you have regarding training to do this kind of work?

Holahan: One recommendation is the very strong need to develop training in research strategies, research design, and measurement techniques that go well beyond traditional training in psychology programs. I can't emphasize enough the need to entertain new strategies and new types of measures within each setting and to possess a wide repertoire of potential strategies and potential measurement techniques, plus a facility in knowing how to choose between them.

In addition, I'm struck more and more by the extent to which action research always dovetails with consultation. In every setting where I've conducted a field action-research project, there has never been a case where some degree of organizational consultation was not necessary. At the very first stage, where one sits down to talk with members of an organization—a hospital staff, members of a neighborhood organization, a school district—a consultative role is necessary. You quickly discover that, in a lot of settings, individuals don't have clear objectives. Or, when they do have objectives, they're vague, they vary, and not everybody in the system has the same goals and objectives. You find people over here are expecting A, and people over there are expecting B, and it becomes essential to get these people to sit down together to talk.

Also, it becomes critical to have some skill as an organizational consultant in helping organizations, to be in a position where they can make use of your feedback as an action researcher. Very often, it turns out that, either the organization is not used to responding to change, so that change itself presents a new dimension, or there has been no delegation of responsibility for making decisions about bringing change into the environment. Maybe communication channels around the issue of bringing change into the organization aren't very clear. It thus becomes essential to prepare the organization to deal effectively with feedback. Either of two things may happen, if that's not done. You may stir up a hornet's nest, or, probably more likely, the feedback you give may end up gathering dust on a shelf, because the organization simply wasn't prepared to make use of the feedback.

So, I would really stress the combination of very flexible research strategies and training in that area and very flexible training in the area of consultation, organizational dynamics, and organizational consultation. It becomes essential to develop modes of training that capitalize on the learning of interpersonal sensitivity. One's ability to bring about change by working on a person-to-person basis, by listening to feedback, and by knowing one's own gut feelings is a fundamental aspect of the task.

Finally, I would have to emphasize the importance of the individual characteristics of the action researcher. What works effectively as good action research has a good deal to do with personal qualities of the change-agent, such as a willingness to listen and a willingness to know when you're not hearing, to step back and say, "I'm making some mistakes; I'd better find out where I'm going awry." You must be willing to listen, even when staff gives negative feedback, when people come along and say, "We're upset about this." You must not become defensive but instead say, "I'm missing something that clearly is of concern to you." At the same time, we need to pay attention to select individuals for change-oriented psychology programs, to make sure that, in addition to having 1450 in their Graduate Record Examination scores that they are also individuals who can listen, who can learn, who can be responsive, who are willing to take risks and get into something new.

Kelly: You ended your chapter by emphasizing this point. You offered the personal qualities of being flexible, egalitarian, patient, and curious and of taking risks. Do you think it is possible for any of us mortals to aspire to those qualities? Those qualities seem like basic characteristics that we would like in our family, friends, and our work environment. It also seems very difficult to locate persons with these qualities or to educate them. Have you been able to identify ways in which such qualities can be enhanced?

Holahan: Yes, they are basic human traits that are essential to good human communication and high quality interaction between people. I mention these qualities not as traits that one tests on a scale and says, "We've got four students coming in who are at the 80 percent level in risk taking, open-mindedness, and creativity." Rather, they are standards that we all need to work on. Our willingness to admit our limitations and our willingness to struggle to overcome them are essential. What I would emphasize is our willingness to treat these qualities as equally important to the academic and intellectual properties that we pay so much attention to within the academy. In retrospect, an especially meaningful part of this work has been the process of occasionally getting in over my head, of finding out that some of the skills that were needed weren't there yet and realizing "I'd better pay some attention to that and develop it along the way." So, for me, it's more a process of working toward ideals rather than being there. As long as we are open and honest about the fact that we are working toward these ideals, this kind of work can be a tremendous amount of fun.

9

Community Integration and Mental Health:
Documenting Social Change Through Longitudinal Research

Dorothea C. Leighton

Some explanation of the title of this chapter seems to be the first order of business: What is meant by *community integration, mental health,* and *social change*? *Community integration* implies a sociocultural cohesiveness within a community. Usually, there would be a common language, common traditions, and a complementarity of needs and resources, including human resources. Interpersonal relations would tend to be positive and helpful. There would be a few leaders, who would keep the good of the community in mind in making decisions. Effective communication would keep people in touch with each other. Ideals of behavior would be well enough observed that there would be little crime or delinquency. This need not be a static state, but too much or too rapid change will strain the equilibrium.

High community integration is usually found only in small communities or in city neighborhoods that differ from those around them in ways that tend to set the residents apart from outsiders but bind the insiders closely. Possibly, integration could exist in large communities, if they were sufficiently homogeneous, but usually the homogeneity is diluted as the population increases.

Mental health means the level of adaptation of a person to his life situation. It can be good or bad or somewhere in between. Those at the bad end will usually report a variety of physical or psychological symptoms, which are believed to represent the organism's reactions to the stresses it perceives. Ordinary functioning may be impeded by the symptoms. At the good end, there will be few symptoms to report and abundant evidence of satisfactory coping behavior. There is often an inverse relation between the number of symptoms the person reports and his ability to function adequately, although there are exceptions to this.

Significant changes in the life situation are usually accompanied by alterations in the mental health level, which may achieve a permanent new level or return to the original level after a period of readjustment. There are, of course, innumerable brief shifts in mental health level as a person moves through his life span. It is only recently (since World War II) that much attention has been paid to mental health levels that are better than those for which individuals seek professional help for their symptoms or impairment of functioning.

Social change refers to the pervasive weakening of traditions and the development of new ways of managing various aspects of the business of living and of relating to one another. Urbanization and industrialization have been aspects of change, as has the mechanization of farming, mining, transportation, and housekeeping. Each change leads to other changes, and, for some time now, changes have occurred so rapidly that mankind has experienced difficulties in adapting to them.

For example, country people moved their families to the city and continued a country style of family life. All too soon, it became necessary for mothers to work to maintain the standard of living, which made the old style of family life impossible. Many slight alterations, which might have eased these changes, were never made, because both parents were too busy to think or do much about them. Family life continued to fragment and lose its cohesiveness. If thought was given to finding substitute sources for the kinds of support that families used to supply, it might be possible to preserve the benefits of the pre-WW II family.

Perhaps, however, change has to continue until a new plateau is attained, when it will be more feasible to think of appropriate substitutes of wide application. Meanwhile, efforts at coping go on all around us.

Background of the Research

The research experience reported here was a part of the Stirling County Study of Psychiatric Disorder and Social Environment (Hughes and others, 1960; Leighton, 1959; Leighton and others, 1963), which was funded in 1950 and continued until a third and final survey in 1969. Analysis of the accumulated data still continues, but this chapter will be limited to the study's first ten years. The approach in this study was multidisciplinary: case finding was done by psychiatrists and psychologists, and the description of the sociocultural environment was provided by anthropologists, sociologists, and historians.

The research site was a rural county in the Canadian Maritimes with a population of 20,000, one half of whom were English-speaking and the other one half French-speaking. The population lived mostly in small villages of 200 to 500, although the county seat numbered 3,000 citizens, and there were a good many scattered homes.

The theoretical basis for the research was derived from a number of sources. The first of these was training in psychiatry under Adolf Meyer, whose holistic approach to human behavior and mental illness emphasized taking into account the person's life situation and his abilities and successes as well as his disabilities and failures (Meyer, 1957). Abram Kardiner's seminars concerning personality development in various cultures also contributed useful ideas (Kardiner, 1945), and many impressions of the interrelations between man and society as well as between man and culture were formed during a year's anthropological field work among Navajo Indians and Alaskan Eskimos.

When requested to propose an approach to psychiatric epidemiology, these influences helped us to shape a rough scheme, which was refined and improved by advice from a multidisciplinary faculty seminar at Cornell University during the academic year 1950–1951. Meanwhile, summer research done by graduate students (who examined the fishing and lumbering industries) and an opinion survey of local attitudes toward a school innovation provided information regarding the research site and experience in social research techniques.

The population distribution of the county, plus previous partial knowledge of some of the characteristics of small communities, led us to think of each small community as *the* important social setting for individuals within it, who would be influenced for better or worse by the ability of the community to supply their biological, sociological, and psychological needs. We hypothesized that communities well able to supply these needs would show residents with less psychiatric disorder than communities that were not able to do this. Originally, these two kinds of communities were labelled *organized* and *disorganized*. Later, these descriptive terms seemed too superficial and were shifted to *integrated* and *disintegrated,* to take better account of the depth effect we wanted to indicate. (Since civil rights activity has made use of *integration* in another meaning, this term is sometimes misunderstood but is still useful.)

Since we wanted to study the relationship between the quality of the community environment and mental health levels, we chose representative communities at the ends of a best-to-worst continuum, using the parameters of poverty/affluence, secularization/religiosity, and cultural confusion/cohesion. Particular villages were selected by asking knowledgeable people to rank-order all the communities of the county from best to worst on these parameters. Excellent convergence was obtained for the ends of the scale, from which we took the best French and the best English communities and three small, ethnically mixed, worst communities, one of them the subject of this chapter.

Principal techniques for data gathering were: (1) a structured questionnaire interview of male or female (alternately) heads of household; (2) participant observation within the representative communities; (3) key-informant interviews of leaders, knowledgeable people, and doctors; and (4) a search of hospital records. Within the selected communities, the sampling rate was adjusted to population, so that there would be adequate subjects for statistical purposes; in the balance of the county, every tenth household was sampled. Most of the investigators were faculty members or graduate students (and their spouses) from Cornell, Laval, Acadia and Dalhousie Universities, chiefly from the social science departments.

Our Focus Community, The Road

During the pilot period (see Table 1), which *preceded* the start of the main thrust of the larger research, in return for the excellent cooperation we had experienced from county residents, it was decided to study a small community that had been nominated by county officials as one of their "sore spots." They characterized its inhabitants as lazy drunkards, always fighting and stealing, amoral, mentally inferior due to inbreeding—"the worst place in the county"—a problem for the Mounted Police, and a heavy welfare burden. It was known to its neighbors by a pejorative term, which we will call *Monkeytown*, but we have named it *The Road* because of its geographic layout, straggled out along an unpaved road.

A psychology graduate student in need of a thesis topic (Allister M. Macmillan) undertook the investigation of this settlement of twenty-nine families (118 individuals) with the intention of testing the accuracy of the officials' description and deducing the implications for interventions of some sort (Macmillan and Leighton, 1952). Using a low-key conversational approach, he first made the acquaintance of each family. From his life-long experience with Maritime families, he was shocked to find that the second topic of conversation in each house (the first being the weather) was what terrible neighbors lived in the houses on each side. Subsequently, to get a grip on the accusation of mental inferiority, he tested the intelligence of all the resident school children, while a fellow graduate student tested children in communities of better reputation. They used the Chicago Non-Verbal Examination, because the psychologist had learned that The Road had not had a properly qualified teacher for about ten years. Both groups showed a normal distribution of IQs at a slightly lower level than urban norms (a common finding with rural children).

Table 1. Approximate Chronology of Events on The Road and in its Parent Study

	Stirling County Study	The Road	Constructive Events
1944			Canadian Family Allowance begun
1945			World War II ends
1946			
1947			Economic cycle to industrial center begun by pioneer Road couple
1948	Pilot studies begun (summers) Historical survey	Nominated troublesome community by officials	
1949	School attitude survey	Preliminary study continues	
1950	Fishing, lumbering study Micmac Indian study		Officials informed of findings Adult educator's movies
1951	Intensive research funded Planning, Full-Time Faculty Seminar		
1952	Family Life Survey of county	Included as representative community	Qualified teacher hired
1953	Data analysis		
1954	Reporting On-going special studies		Admitted to consolidated school district
1955			
1956			
1957		Greatly improved appearance noted	
1958			Improved local economic opportunities
1959			

1960
1961
1962 County resurvey

Retrospective study begun

Included in survey
Improvement found to average
level of county

Well accepted in county

Another important matter, the question of economic status and employability, revealed conditions of severe poverty. The main occupations were irregular laboring jobs at low wages. The men cut trees for woodlot owners, did odd jobs for neighboring farmers, and dug clams. Some women went fifteen miles to a clam packing plant to shuck the clams. Road residents were the last to be hired and the first to be fired, but they were said to work hard when employed. Housing was poor and dilapidated, without electricity or running water. All the families with children received the Family Allowance (which Canada instituted in 1944), and a couple of army veterans got disability pensions. No other welfare funds reached The Road.

As to the charges of amorality, fighting, stealing, and drinking, the psychologist had already noted the high level of disparagement of each other and soon found extensive interpersonal hostility. The hostility took the forms both of verbal animosity and of fighting on little provocation, which, of course, reinforced the mutual disparagement. There appeared to be few leisure-time social contacts, although there was some visiting of relatives by the women, and the men gathered at times at a gas station to drink, swap jokes and stories, and eventually to fight. Otherwise, they were quite guarded toward each other, practicing a mutual isolation, which was not at all like the neighborly social scene in the rest of the county. They were viewed as amoral and untrustworthy by most of the surrounding population, while Road residents saw outsiders as hypocritical, hostile, and exploitative. The Mounted Police disclaimed any concern for this group, not interfering unless the fighting spilled outside the community.

This whole picture is quite familiar nowadays, due to civil rights activities and efforts at community and economic development, but it is usually thought to be characteristic of overcrowded cities rather than of small rural groups.

A few years later, the 1952 questionnaire survey of the county confirmed the psychologist's findings and added evidence that there was very little affiliation with any outside social organizations, that its economic status was considerably worse than the county average (but about the same as the two other similar communities), and that its mental health rating was the poorest of any community in the county. Principal symptoms were psychophysiological, psychoneurotic, sociopathic, and personality disorder (Leighton and others, 1963).

A comparison of the five selected representative communities can be seen in Table 2, where the 1952 column indicates their status with respect to integration/disintegration, psychiatric symptomatology, and impairment of functioning related to the symptomatology. This is, of course, somewhat *after* the time of the original investigation. The statistical figures used, called *ridits*, are an index *r*elative to an *iden*tified distribution. Bross (1958) devised this measure in an effort to overcome some of the problems of interpretation that arise when arbitrary scores are assigned to the different categories of a subjective scale, such as the one for psychiatric status. Ridits have a maximum range of 0 to 1, with a mean of 0.5 in the identified distribution that serves as a standard of reference. It has a rectilinear distribution, with a standard deviation fairly close to 0.29 in the reference distribution. The ridit of a single individual is interpreted as the probability that this individual is worse or better off than an individual selected at random from the reference distribution. The average ridit of a group is interpreted as the probability that an individual selected at random from this group is worse or better off than an individual selected at random from the reference distribution.

Values *above* 0.5 for a given group indicate that there is a more than average chance that an individual in the group will have worse than average Psychiatric Status or Functional Impairment or that the community in question is tilted more toward disintegration than the county average.

As can be seen, all the selected communities showed some improvement in integration over the ten-year period, but the difference reached statistical significance only in the case of The Road. When these ten-year comparisons became available in 1965, there was great excitement that observed changes (especially in The Road and the French community) were thus reflected in the data analysis.

Added to the Integration change, the Psychiatric Status figures show a change toward poorer mental health in the French community, essentially no change in the English and Disintegrated I communities, and an improvement in Disintegrated II and The Road. Similarly, the Functional Impairment rose slightly in the

Table 2. Ten-Year Change in Sociocultural Integration, Psychiatric Status, and Functional Impairment in Five Selected Communities

Communities	Integration Ridit			Psychiatric Status Ridit			Functional Impairment Ridit		
	1952	1962	Difference[a]	1952	1962	Difference[a]	1952	1962	Difference[a]
French integrated	0.295	0.241	−0.054	0.393	0.493	0.100	0.414	0.455	0.041
English integrated	0.429	0.313	−0.116	0.467	0.482	0.015	0.437	0.449	0.012
Average integrated	0.368	0.274	−0.094	0.434	0.488	0.054	0.427	0.452	0.025
Disintegrated I	0.632	0.598	−0.034	0.514	0.529	0.015	0.549	0.502	−0.047
Disintegrated II	0.616	0.531	−0.085	0.548	0.480	−0.068	0.540	0.470	−0.069
The Road	0.627	0.468	−0.159[b]	0.594	0.503	−0.091	0.591	0.408	−0.183
Average Disintegrated	0.626	0.523	−0.102	0.551	0.504	−0.047	0.561	0.453	−0.107

[a]Negative values indicate an improvement.
[b]The only ridit difference in this column that is statistically significant.
Source: Staff memorandums, Cornell Program in Social Psychiatry, 1965.

French community and dropped in all the Disintegrated communities, especially The Road.

In other words, the French community scarcely changed in integration level but showed a deterioration in Psychiatric Status and a very slight increase in Functional Impairment. By contrast, The Road improved significantly in Integration; its Psychiatric Status improved about as much as the French community deteriorated; and its Functional Impairment was markedly reduced. (Except for the Integration ridits, the statistical significance of these other ridits is not available. I assume that The Road's Functional Impairment ridit change would be significant.)

In work with small numbers of subjects whose data are abstracted into multifactored indices like these, it is not very common to be able to demonstrate statistical significance. When, however, as in the case of The Road, the outcome agrees with the prediction, confidence in the meaning of the data is strengthened. The deterioration of the French community was not anticipated in the hypothesis specifically, yet the logic would cover it. Its occurrence is entirely congruent and provides additional strength, even though the difference is small.

The Intervention

As soon as the psychologist was sure of his findings, which he felt provided a number of possibilities for aiding The Road, he informed the county officials. They became interested in initiating some helpful action and selected educational improvement as within their scope. Although they were unable to find a qualified teacher for the school immediately, they secured the part-time services of an adult educator. In consultation with the psychologist, this man saw his role as helping the community adults improve their employability by (1) reducing hostility and social isolation, (2) developing cooperation and social skills, and (3) practicing some joint problem solving (Leighton and others, 1963).

Continuing the psychologist's low-key approach, he began showing movies to the children at the school, inviting adults to come for a repeat showing in the evening. In the absence of television or any other form of recreation, an audience began to grow, even though the performance was often interrupted temporarily when the portable generator would stop. As interest continued and increased, he got the audience to choose a committee to select the next movie, and he eventually reported that the school board was willing to provide half the cost of wiring the school, if the audience would raise the rest. This was the first such challenge Road residents had even received as well as the first suggestion that they should spend their own money on a public project. In spite of their low economic status, they managed to raise the $50 needed plus enough to pay the electric bill for a year.

After a time, a qualified teacher was found, who took over the school and worked closely with the women, trying to further the trend the adult educator had started. She suggested that they hold a series of bingo games to raise money for some new school desks, a more ambitious project than wiring the school and one requiring a considerably higher order of organization. This, too, succeeded.

Looking to the future, the teacher suggested that they attempt to get the community into a nearby consolidated school district, so that education beyond grade eight would be feasible. Besides taking steps to get the proposition on the next ballot, this necessitated persuading community outsiders in the larger school district to vote favorably—in other words, to get their worst disparagers to help them. This also succeeded, so that the older children were soon being bussed to school. Although, at the beginning, they looked noticeably different from the other pupils, after three to four months (without any suggestions or advice), they had become indistinguishable from the other students. As a result of the election success, the school board had resigned, and a resident of The Road was elected to the new board, another important step toward integration into the larger society.

Opportunity Knocks

Although, from time to time, many individuals had attempted to leave the community to seek a better fortune, most had returned to meet the jeers of their neighbors, discouraged by the unfamiliar ways of other places and the lack of friends or relatives. They had felt as out of place as the children had looked in their first weeks at the consolidated school. Shortly before the research began, however, a couple had succeeded in establishing themselves in an industrial area in Ontario, securing employment and finding a better life. A visit home by them started a succession of job seekers to the industrial area, where they stayed initially with the couple, found jobs, and saved money for some home project. As they satisfied their own needs and left, they would recommend to their employer some other worker from their community as replacement. At one point, there were twenty-one community members in the industrial center at the same time. Most stayed from six months to a year for any given trip, and, as far as is known, no one except the first couple migrated permanently. Living in the city, they, like the school children, learned to behave like those around them and noted how people with regular incomes lived. Much of their savings went into housing improvement back home, and some was used to buy property there or to start small businesses.

It should be explained that many people of all socioeconomic levels in the Maritimes have found it difficult to make an adequate living at home. At the same time, they have usually developed a strong attachment for the place where they grew up and feel very reluctant to pull up stakes, sell their property, and move away. A common resolution of this problem has been to seek employment in New England or Upper Canada for a period of years, meantime keeping up their taxes and paying an occasional visit for repairs and other upkeep. Thus, the residents of the rural slum were following a familiar and respected pattern, modified in a way that shows that their goals were shorter term than those of some Maritimers, in that working for half a year or a year at a time served their more immediate purposes.

The second economic opportunity came when a hydroelectric dam was constructed near The Road. Laborers were needed, and they were paid a standard wage, if they worked regularly, rather than the substandard wage that Road residents usually received.

Benefits Accrued

Both these opportunities had far-reaching effects. One, of course, was the influx of money to the community, which made it possible for nearly every family to buy material goods that had previously been beyond their means. This in itself would have raised morale and improved self-esteem. In addition, they had discovered that, away from the home county, they appeared to be quite acceptable to the kind of people who disparaged them and called them *monkeys* at home, and they were quite capable of doing a level of work that no one had offered them before.

Within only five to six years after the questionnaire survey, The Road had changed its appearance to such an extent that it was difficult for a researcher to be sure that he was in the right place. Houses had been enlarged and repaired; all had electricity, and many had running water; each was topped by a TV antenna. Lawns and gardens had appeared, and a car could be seen in most driveways. This was an extraordinary alteration from the former appearance of the smaller houses, covered with battered shingles or tarpaper and placed desolately among scrubby trees and bushes with little sign of care.

On the social side, the change included the presence of several card-playing groups that met regularly and an occasional party, which included the whole community. Several people were taking part in neighboring churches, and one family provided a place for catechism classes to be held. They were no longer willing to accept unskilled, underpaid work. They felt more sure of themselves in dealings with outsiders, and the outsiders treated them with much more respect. One outsider remarked with surprise, "You know, we don't call them 'monkeys' any more."

As was seen in Table 2, the Resurvey findings showed that The Road had improved with respect to the three indicators used. Table 3 compares The Road with Disintegrated I, the settlement that changed least of all in Integration and hardly at all in Psychiatric Status. So far as could be determined, Disintegrated I had neither experienced any such events as had occurred on The Road nor benefitted very much from the general socioeconomic improvement that had taken place in the county as a whole. Thus, Disintegrated I can serve as a contrast in expectable outcome, when neither intentional nor accidental intervention occurs. These findings in a "control" community tend to increase confidence that the changes in The Road reflect the relationships stated in the hypothesis.

The research team was immensely pleased to be able thus to document an improvement in mental health, along with improve-

Table 3. Effects of Constructive Change on Disintegrated Communities

Community	Integration Ridit[a]		Psychiatric Status Ridit		Functional Impairment Ridit	
	1952	1962	1952	1962	1952	1962
The Road (most change)	0.627	0.468[b]	0.594	0.503	0.591	0.408[c]
Disintegrated I (least change)	0.632	0.598	0.514	0.529	0.549	0.502

[a]See text for description. 0.5 is the mean ridit value for the entire county sample. A decrease in ridit indicates an improvement.
[b]Statistically significant.
[c]Probably statistically significant.
Source: Staff memorandums, Cornell Program in Social Psychiatry, 1965.

ment in sociocultural integration, in accordance with the basic hypothesis, even though it was too early to state that a causal relationship existed. As a result of this partial confirmation of the basic theory, a project was then initiated to see if constructive change could be brought about in a better-controlled manner and to see if it would also be accompanied by improvement in mental health. The Disintegrated II community was chosen for this effort, and Disintegrated I was retained as a control. Kern (1972) reports the development of this project, although 1969 survey findings are not yet available.

Conclusions and Speculations

The psychological, social, and economic improvement had taken place so gradually and with so little intentional outside assistance that considerable time passed before people began to talk about it. Even the residents appeared to take it in stride without feeling a need to boast or express surprise. The research staff has been wondering ever since whether the modest effort at social organization made it possible for the residents to take advantage of the economic opportunities or whether the chance to make more money by itself would have had the same effect. Was it the increased affluence or was it the improved interpersonal relations? Or was it perhaps just a "Hawthorne effect," where the attention given the community by outsiders had a stimulating influence? Was there, perhaps, more incipient leadership present in Road residents than had been noted?

The events we have described were by no means a main concern of the research staff at the time they were occurring. The original offer to study a troublesome community antedated the funding of the larger project; Macmillan's investigation also took place in the pilot phase (see Table 1). The county officials found the adult educator and, later, the teacher. There was some minor consultation with Macmillan and others and occasional progress notes from people in the consolidated school and in neighboring communities who knew of our previous interest in The Road. It was included in the main project, because it qualified and there were not many communities to choose from at the worst end of the scale. Only after we later heard of changes (between the first and second surveys) and paid The Road a belated visit did we realize how much had happened, and we then hired an anthropologist to discover the chain of events. There was no chronological record in our files nor any special information beyond what was collected in the first survey. The whole experience constitutes an excellent example of serendipity.

A few points seem to stand out:

1. The former bad reputation of the community was due to the fact that the residents were expressing their suffering in ways that irritated the larger society. The other two worst communities, by contrast, were suffering more passively. These differences were indicated by the difference in mental health levels; the symptoms were indicative of the frustration felt from not being able to satisfy basic needs. It appears that the presence of a high symptom count can be taken as evidence that the struggle is still going on, apathy has not set in, and there is some energy for a change-agent to work with. Although a *low* level of symptoms can be a sign of good adjustment, of course, it can also indicate a giving up of the struggle or a lack of awareness that a struggle is needed. This was demonstrated in a symptom survey of state mental hospital patients, in which the long-term patients reported almost no symptoms, whereas the new admissions with acute types of disorders reported high levels of symptoms (Leighton and Cline, 1972).

2. The early research was undertaken to assist the county officials to understand more adequately what a group of troublesome citizens needed. Quite clearly, it served a useful purpose, in that it helped dispel prejudices and open the minds of the officials. It also helped them select a feasible starting point for helping the

community. As far as I know, no harm came of working with the officials, even though it was later learned that researchers must be wary of sharing their findings with representatives of political power. In the early 1950s, such a possibility had hardly occurred to social scientists. The fact that officials and Road residents were near neighbors with the possibility of face-to-face interaction probably made this a very different situation from the misuse of knowledge where officials are remote from the people to whom the knowledge pertains.

The effect of the research itself on the community residents can only be speculated about, since most of the subjects were not accustomed to philosophical consideration and would not have found it easy to discuss various influences. It seems probable, based on opinions expressed by other subjects in the county, that the interest shown by Macmillan and the kind of questions he asked may have led the residents (like the county officials) to get a clearer view of their situation and to begin to understand some of its factors. This is quite similar to what happens when someone with a problem consults a professional and, in telling his own story to another person, begins to comprehend his predicament better.

3. Although it may never have been stated by anyone, the implicit goal of the officials and of those who intervened was to make the community self-supporting at a higher level. The research was needed to determine the various factors that contributed to its poor status. Once these were known, the officials could then initiate some positive action.

Maritimers have always had to live thriftily and to make use of what was at hand to solve problems. They have also tended to hold a high regard for the benefits of education. Thus, it was quite in keeping that the officials would hire an available adult educator and later an available qualified teacher and that each of them, in turn, would work within the existing social framework with whatever opportunities occurred to lead the community toward the county norms. Although the economic opportunities were unquestionably important in the happy outcome described, the industrial opportunity had been there for many years. It had been essentially unavailable to community members, however, until the constellation of other factors began to work together to enable them to benefit. Thus, the quite small input by the adult educator, which was designed to increase cooperation, to practice joint decision making, and to set goals, plus the teacher's carrying forward the practice in joint enterprises for the common good, can be seen as an important enabling mechanism (Kardiner, 1945).

Perhaps the broadest summary of what happened would be to say that the reduction of helplessness by a demonstration of what group action could accomplish served to greatly reduce hopelessness. This in turn inclined individuals to try harder and to take heart from small successes to go on to achieve greater ones. Perhaps they were able to see at last a slight opening crack in a formerly closed door.

Was the organizational input the most important factor? It may well have had the kind of effect that skillful psychotherapy can have with a person exhibiting self-defeating behavior—by itself, it is not sufficient for improvement, yet it may provide the essential impetus for constructive change by the individual himself.

How important was the successful couple who induced the circular migration pattern and provided welcome and guidance far from home? In my opinion, they were of great importance, particularly in making possible the economic improvement at the same time that the organizational stimulation was applied. It must surely have had a reinforcing effect in convincing the subjects that they could succeed if their peers had been able to do so.

Finally, was money really all that was needed? This is an extremely difficult question to answer with certainty. One would have to know more than I do about prevailing attitudes regarding charity, supposing that money had simply been provided by some outside source (a possibility truly inconceivable in the Maritimes in the early 1950s). A substantial handout would almost surely have further blackened their reputation in the county, even if not in their own eyes. The fact is that money certainly helped, probably all the more because it was acquired in acceptable ways.

Success was thus achieved not through the agency of a single factor but through the fortuitous synergy of all of them (see Table 4). A really crucial implied factor was, I think, the ability of the subjects to accept and utilize both intentional and accidental help when it appeared. Without their readiness, it seems unlikely that they would have progressed any further than the other two depressed communities in the study.

Table 4. Interaction of Road Characteristics and Constructive Events

Events	Road Characteristics	Effects	Overall Outcome
Economic opportunities	Poverty	Diminished	Greater self-esteem
Near	Low Education	Increased	
Far	Low Skills	Improved	Social and financial success
Official concern	Self- and other-disparagement	Diminished	
Study	Interpersonal hostility	Diminished	Satisfaction of basic needs
Adult educator	Poor cooperation	Improved	
Teacher	Little social interaction	Improved	
Admission to Consolidated School District	Helpless, hopeless	Diminished	Better mental health
Political Participation	Isolated from rest of community	Diminished	

INTERVIEW WITH DOROTHEA C. LEIGHTON

Muñoz: Dr. Leighton, as you know, the purpose of this book is not only to have examples of what we consider a model kind of project in the area of community interventions but also to get an idea of the process involved. These interviews are designed to give us a more personal insight into what went on. So, I would like you to begin with the personal background that got you involved in this particular kind of work.

Leighton: Well, I suppose that it goes back to medical school and then deciding to go into psychiatry, largely because I decided to marry my husband, who had his mind set on psychiatry. From his earlier acquaintance with Indian guides in Nova Scotia, he began raising the question, "Wouldn't there be some point in trying to see what anthropology could tell us that psychiatrists really ought to know?" It was a time when there was a growing interest among anthropologists in the personality aspect of humanity. In 1938 or 1939, Abram Kardiner, a psychoanalyst, and Ralph Linton, a well-known anthropologist in New York, began holding weekly seminars to discuss such matters. Linton would describe some culture that he had studied, and Kardiner would then try to sketch out what the "basic personality" of that culture would be. Many people thought this was a crazy undertaking, but it was very interesting and stimulating to us. We began looking for an anthropologist with whom we could discuss our interest, and we were put in touch with Clyde Kluckhohn.

Kluckhohn was particularly committed to Navajo Indians, and he made arrangements for us to spend a winter with them. We lived in a hogan next door to the hogan of an interpreter (few Navajos spoke English at that time). We traveled around with the interpreter, observing, questioning, and participating as opportunity offered. We were not looking for people with psychiatric problems at all, but rather, we wanted to see what kind of life problems were experienced by people of a very different culture from ourselves and how they dealt with them. It was an advantage for us that we were physicians, because Navajos have high health and illness concerns and welcomed us for our skills. It also provided a reason to visit medical facilities provided by the Indian Service and to converse with native healers. As a result of our contacts, medicine men or "singers" appeared to us to be in a better position to deal with functional illness of the Navajos than did the Anglo physicians provided by the government.

In the spring, we went to Alaska to stay with some Eskimos to broaden our non-Western cultural exposure, and we continued the type of work we had been doing with the Navajos. In each of these cultures, we observed examples of how cultural deprivation can adversely affect people, even where lack of money is not the main problem. Both cultures were very poor economically, by white U.S. standards, yet, for the most part, they were functioning very well, and the small groups we judged to be suffering from cultural deprivation in each culture were scarcely poorer in money than their more successful fellows. Yet, the two deprived groups shared the position of outcasts from their society and disparagement by their neighbors, like rural or urban slum dwellers in Western societies.

Without doubt, these observations, added to our subsequent cross-cultural work, were very important in the development of the idea of the crucial part played in a population's mental health status by the level of integration or disintegration of the sociocultural milieu.

Soon after our return from this adventurous year, we were asked by the Indian Service to give them any advice we might have regarding their responsibilities toward the people we had visited. At an evening meeting of a group of top Indian Service administrators, we reported that it seemed to us they were wasting an excellent medical resource, especially in the case of the Navajos, by not utilizing the skills and knowledge of the medicine men. It surprised us to see how such advice astonished this intelligent group, which was committed to doing whatever they could in the best interest of native peoples. We further advised them that a prime necessity, currently lacking, was an interesting and readable account of each of their diverse native groups, so that professional whites, coming to work with them, would be able to learn something about their charges. The group requested us to prepare such a book for the Navajos, as a starter, and we spent some time doing this.

Shortly after, World War II engulfed the U.S., and we were caught up in it. My husband was assigned to a Japanese Relocation

Center to study it as a developing community, while I worked with a research team testing Indian children for dimensions of their personalities. Following the War, we went to Cornell.

A few years later, my husband was invited to attend a conference of the Milbank Memorial Fund in New York. This Fund had invested most of its money in promoting epidemiological studies. Its director, Dr. Frank Boudreau, had reached the conclusion that it was time to turn attention to the epidemiology of chronic diseases. He was personally interested in mental health and illness and felt that investigation in this area had received short shrift. He had invited to the meeting the small number of people whom he thought to be interested or experienced in epidemiologic psychiatric research. The outcome of the conference was a request from Dr. Boudreau that my husband propose a manner of studying psychiatric epidemiology, as a first step in better understanding the requirements of mental health.

Muñoz: So, then, the Stirling County Study began with the suggestion from the Milbank Fund?

Leighton: Yes, that's right. I don't know whether we would ever have come to such an idea, otherwise. When the letter about the proposal came, we just laughed—it seemed such an unlikely undertaking. We were pretty vague about the details of epidemiology and hadn't really thought of it as applying to noncontagious illnesses. But we grew sober as we began to wonder how, indeed, you might do psychiatric epidemiology.

The big question in our minds was how you could distinguish and measure psychiatric disorder in people who had not complained of it or gone for help. Searching for clues in the literature, we came across a recent study by two psychiatrists in Williamson County, Tennessee, in the 1930s (Roth and Luton, 1942). This study had pioneered imaginative case-finding methods, including the search of general hospital records and the questioning of lay leaders and caregivers. Working at a time when medical people knew little about any type of research except case studies, this research was still a very good first try. It had a strong influence on us, partly because it was the only model we found for the sort of research that had been requested.

Until that time, psychiatric epidemiology had dealt only with treated cases. Malzberg had analyzed characteristics of patients in the New York state mental hospital system (Malzberg and Lee, 1956), and Hollingshead and Redlich were doing their study of people in New Haven who were receiving any type of psychiatric treatment (Hollingshead and Redlich, 1958). It seemed as if the time had come to try out the Williamson County ideas in a different area with improved methods to see how many people living in a community had recognizable psychiatric symptoms, whether or not they were being treated.

Social science and survey techniques had developed rapidly during and after the War. Although we had not been much involved in this, excellent advice was readily available and led us to a decision to do a population survey of the area we had selected as a site. In addition, we went through the steps of the Williamson County study with some modifications. It seems important to warn here that we found the use of hospital records an almost complete waste of time. Once in a while, there would be a valuable nugget, but they were rare. We gathered many file drawers full of records concerning county residents, but, in the end, even to count them became burdensome. It is possible that improved standards of record keeping in hospitals may have increased their usefulness.

We also found that interviewing knowledgeable people in the county in a general way about possible psychiatric disorder of residents was of limited value. We talked to the nine doctors as well as to many others, and they all told us about the same people—mainly those who were well known for "being crazy" (at least some of the time). None of them were ready to talk about minor problems that had not interfered seriously with the business of living. They all tended to view a person who might be labeled as having a personality disorder as just a neighbor with a quirk that had to be taken into account. Even the doctors had had very little psychiatric instruction. Conversely, after we determined who would be the subjects of our survey and went to the doctors with a list of names, they were extremely helpful. We used only general questions: Do you know him or her? How is his or her health? Does he or she have any psychological problems? How does he or she get along in the community? Because the doctors were closely involved in the community as well as medical affairs and took an active part in what went on, they knew many of our subjects from a number of points of view. Our only problem then was to convince them that what they regarded as gossip was useful behavioral data from our point of view.

Muñoz: How did you convince them of that?

Leighton: We just keep asking them the same questions and expressing gratitude for the kind of material they provided.

Muñoz: Why would they tell you some of those things?

Leighton: I think it was because we were also doctors, and they felt it appropriate to cooperate with us. I doubt that they would have been willing to confide in non-M.D.s. Perhaps it had something to do with their trust that we would treat their information confidentially. Their remarks were most helpful when it came to understanding the meaning of the medical and psychological questions of the questionnaire, which we used in evaluating everyone's psychiatric status.

Muñoz: In your chapter, you mention intervening in at least one other community after noting the improvements on The Road. I wonder if there were any questions in your mind about an epidemiological study intervening and thereby changing what was happening. Was this ever discussed?

Leighton: By that time, we had already made two surveys ten years apart, and we looked upon that intervention as action research, I think. We were not much concerned about the earlier intervention on The Road itself. This was very early in the history of this sort of research, since our first survey was in 1952. Community action had scarcely begun, and I think that everyone was naive about such matters. We didn't really think of what happened on The Road as our intervention, in any case, but rather as an exchange. The county officials and many other people whom we had consulted had been very helpful, and so it seemed only decent to give the county something in return. The original investigation of The Road was an effort in that direction.

Looking backward from where we are now (1979), it seems strange that we did not take this into account, as you suggest, but I don't think it occurred to us at all. By the time of the second survey (1962), we were very much aware of the need to keep things clean. We went so far, for example, as to get communities for comparison in distant parts of the province to minimize the ripple effect. As for The Road, it was really the local government people who did whatever intervention there was. Our contacts were the original investigation, the various surveys, and the later study to determine what had caused the remarkable change on The Road.

Later, we became very much interested in the effects of the research itself, because many people had something to say about what they thought was happening, more or less as a result of the surveys. Of course, all kinds of other influences were impinging at the same time. When television began in Nova Scotia, for instance, that naturally opened a whole new world for practically everybody. But I think there is little doubt that to have outsiders going around asking questions on selected topics has some effect on the way people are going to think about themselves. Our county did not have a very high opinion of itself as compared with the rest of Canada or the eastern U.S. In fact, the county felt about itself very much the way The Road felt about itself as compared with its neighboring communities. The very fact that people from big universities would come and ask local opinions about a good many matters and show an interest in the answers inclined the residents to conclude that maybe they were not as unimportant as they had imagined, after all.

Muñoz: Do you think that any of that has remained in the county —the long-term effects—or were the effects only short term?

Leighton: Well, I think that it reduced the feeling of helplessness to quite an extent. They had imagined that they could not do anything worthwhile to help themselves—they would have to wait until the Province or the Dominion took a hand. But they supported a Mental Health Center that was started and a Mental Health Association, and a few other things got going—not exactly instigated by the research project but certainly encouraged. Outsiders can do only so much. There were also several other innovations, some of which were quite accidental, so far as the research team was concerned. One of these was an appeal by a religious group at Cornell for permission to send a few students up for the summer to do good works. The first summer, three students came and helped a black community set up a nursery school, a sports program, and a community library in an abandoned school building. This went on to become a community center, which has helped the black community get itself together. After a year or two, one of the disintegrated communities requested its own team of students to help them start a similar program. This was surely a ripple effect.

The research team might, indeed, have objected to some kinds of promotional schemes or to rival research teams working on "our turf." However, we were as much interested in finding out what was good for mental health as we were in controlling our experiment—probably more so.

I believe that little impact on thinking or feeling would take place if you did a one-time survey that didn't take very long. However, if you stay around and continue to show interest in the area, you are almost bound to affect the people you talk to, although it might not be a very widespread or intense effect.

Muñoz: How long did this particular project go on altogether?

Leighton: Well, we first went up there with research in mind in 1948. We had hired two Cornell graduate students to interview people for a historical survey. Every summer from then until 1969 (and sometimes winters, too), varying numbers of people were working in the county. A lot of substudies were being done to fill in the picture that the surveys provided or to keep track of what was happening or to try something different. That's a good, long interaction. It wasn't so much that we gave the people great ideas to go ahead and develop; it is less definite and somehow deeper than that. It is the kind of thing that happens with successful community-development efforts, and, in this case, it happened to a whole county instead of a compact community. It seems somehow to give people heart to think that they really could do something themselves, which frees them to try.

Muñoz: We've been talking about the effect on the people of the community. I would like to hear your ideas on what effect this work has had in the field since 1948. What kind of things do you think have developed?

Leighton: To some extent, our research was part of a trend, and I guess this is usually the case. The first of this trend was Redlich's investigation of treated prevalence in New Haven. His study began to come out in 1953, before any of the other studies had gone very far, and its impact was tremendous. It was the first extensive study of people who, although in treatment, were not all residing in a hospital. Many were seeing private doctors in New Haven or other places. It served to bring the attention of psychologists and psychiatrists and the public to the etiological importance of various aspects of life. Unfortunately, it started a few misapprehensions, too, such as the general conclusion that rich people have neuroses, whereas poor people instead have schizophrenia, which is a false conclusion, in my view. You do find this relationship in a *treated* population, to be sure, but it is not the way the distribution of psychiatric problems turns out when you study everybody, irrespective of treatment status.

Our psychiatric report was a long time coming out—eleven years from the first survey to date of publication (1963). Meantime, our sister Midtown study ended and published its findings the year before. It was most interesting to see how closely our findings agreed and how they differed. The Stirling County Study contains much more psychiatric input and more sociocultural detail than the Midtown Study (Srole and others, 1962).

I have found that people who will take the trouble to really comprehend our findings appear to benefit in a considerable increase in understanding of the interaction between mental health and sociocultural environment. This requires a really thoughtful perusal of the material, not just a look at tables.

I feel that the intimacy of our contact with our site and subjects was very enlightening and is the kind of thing that is very difficult to achieve in a site like New York City. You can easily get statistical relationships in the big city, but, for instance, you do not find the kind of resources for corroborative or corrective information that we had with the doctors. We found later, to be sure, that New York doctors seemed to know more about their patients than we had expected. However, they rarely have the social interactions with them that were universal in the rural setting. I think that we really understood a lot about the county in the way of probable cause-and-effect (or at least coincidental) relationships, which are not available in a big, complicated place like New York. It was quite possible in Stirling, for example, to visit subjects where they worked and to talk to the boss about them. Moreover, we could discuss some of the findings with local people to see if they made sense to them.

I don't really know, of course, how effective our study has been. The three-volume report was a drug on the market for quite a while—because of its bulk and its price, perhaps. Partly, also, it was because they had striking titles, which gave little hint of content. However, in the past several years, I have had many requests regarding how to find a copy of any of them, for they have been out of print for many years. I have never heard any plans for reissuing them in any form. The requests seem to indicate to me that, belatedly, people have looked at the reports more closely and seen their value.

There have been other studies done, too, that have drawn attention to our work, like that of the Dohrenwends. Bruce Dohrenwend was on our staff for a couple of years and went on thinking along similar lines, to some extent. They have done much useful work, comparing various studies around the world and trying to study the essence of interrelationships in a way that most epidemiologists don't want to bother with and lack the skills to do. Our books certainly get referred to by everybody writing in the field, but whether they have been carefully read is hard to tell.

Muñoz: One of the things of importance about your study was that it was multidisciplinary. Could you comment on some of the advantages and disadvantages of that?

Leighton: Well, I think that you need to have a great many specialized people to get the meat out of such a situation as we were working in. To be sure, you have to spend a considerable amount of time finding out how to work together effectively. I don't remember exactly how this was in the beginning. We were all new to it, of course, and perhaps we wore the rough edges off each other without thinking much about it. Later, however, it was quite striking that, whenever some staff member left, it would always take about six months or so to break in his replacement. This wasn't a matter of breaking him in technically, but rather of getting him to a point where he didn't have to defend his position all the time, so he didn't have to talk in his own jargon and could listen effectively to other disciplines. It was interesting to watch sometimes, and some newcomers never made it. I really don't see how you can do much research of value in the field of personality and psychiatry without a wide representation of disciplines or even subdisciplines, such as both psychologists who do testing and those who are social psychologists.

Muñoz: If you had a chance to tell students who are preparing themselves to work in such endeavors, what would you recommend to them today? What kinds of ideas and skills do they need?

Leighton: One very helpful idea for someone who plans to work in a multidisciplinary group is to know not only his own discipline well but also at least one other. This is tremendously useful for cross-disciplinary communication. If all you can do when you first come into a multidisciplinary situation is to say your particular disciplinary piece, nothing much happens—no one wants to hear your piece. They want to hear what your *kind of thinking* can contribute to the problems the group is trying to handle.

I believe, too, that you need a broad social experience. I don't really think that anyone who has spent all his life on the educational treadmill is very much use. You need to make an active effort to do something to broaden your scope, if you want to work in interdisciplinary areas. Otherwise, you get an exaggerated notion of the importance of your own thoughts. Surely, one of the most important things for me was the year we spent with the Navajos and Eskimos. The experience of going from our own culture to two others was extraordinary. We learned immensely more about the Navajos by exposing ourselves to the Eskimos than by our months spent in a hogan, although that was, of course, a necessary preliminary. Some of the understandings would never have developed without the contrasts.

Naturally, it is not necessary to visit those particular cultures. The point is to take a searching look at more than one group of people that is very different from yourself. Close contact and systematic enquiry pay off, as compared with reading about them or touring through their area. This type of exposure would help offset the tendency to let the computer do all the work, once the data are collected. The broader the researcher's experience, the more fertile will be his background for thinking of all the possible outcomes and relationships his data might show. He will then be able to ask the indispensable computer some questions about his ideas that he wants to prove or disprove. All too often, data are fed into the computer with the expectation that *it* will do the thinking.

At the time we were engaged in all the experiences that I have described, it was exhilarating work. We were exploring new frontiers (with a good deal of company, to be sure). Statistics were of less interest than meaning of relationships, although the importance of numbers increased rapidly as various mechanical devices like calculators and computers were improved or invented. We felt our minds expanding, as previously unrecognized correlations appeared in our data. I'm not sure how these aspects are right now. The importance of numbers and of statistical significance seems to have overwhelmed the kind of intimate, detailed focus on people in life situations that seemed so fruitful. The academic pressure for publication has caused too much hurry in conducting research and particularly in thoughtful considerations of findings. Even so, I'm sure it is still possible to find and explore frontiers, and there is still a great deal left unexplained that can gradually be elucidated.

10

Experimental Development and Dissemination of an Alternative to Psychiatric Hospitalization: *Scientific Methods for Social Change*

George W. Fairweather

To understand the effects of social change from social experimentation, it is necessary to understand the process of social change and the roles that scientists play in this process. Much has been written and done about social change from a revolutionary perspective, but very little is known from a scientific perspective (Fairweather, 1972). This is probably due to the fact that revolutionaries have been motivated to change their societies when intolerable conditions have been endured by their fellow members, whereas scientists have viewed social change from an intellectual point of view. Thus, historically, scientists have thought and observed but not acted. In fact, there has been a norm established among the scientific community that equates objectivity with lack of action and nonintervention in social processes.

The notion of a relationship between social inaction and objectivity appears to have developed mainly from social scientists' fears of retaliation from politicians for actively espousing a particular social position (Gouldner, 1961). This is not the place for an extensive discussion and justification of a more active role for social scientists (which has been presented elsewhere, see Fairweather, 1967, 1972; Fairweather and Tornatzky, 1977), but it is important to understand the different roles required by problem-solving, naturalistic field experiments, where social intervention is necessary, and laboratory experimentation, observation, and survey research, which require less active roles by the social scientist. The contemporary role for problem-solving social scientists working in naturalistic settings involves a combination of political and scientific action in collaboration with persons who are suffering from a particular social problem.

The role model of the social problem-solving scientist is roughly similar to that of the agronomist, although there are great differences in subject-matter complexity, theory, research, and implementation. The similarity lies in the attempts by social scientists and agronomists to find a beneficial product and to disseminate it to the members of the problem population for their use. The differences result from the products that are to be disseminated and the audience. The agronomist typically has a physical object, such as a seed or a fertilizer, that needs to be disseminated to an audience of farmers, who, by this time in our history, have an excellent knowledge of the need for experimentally valid seeds and fertilizers. By contrast, a social innovation usually involves the creation of a new social program, which a large number of individuals have to promote if it is to be tried and evaluated.The process does not stop here, however; once a beneficial new social program is discovered, it is then necessary to involve an even more extensive audience of service personnel, social administrators, problem population groups, and other scientists in the spread of the innovation. This basic difference in complexity raises a series of social issues that differentiate social problem-solving research from agricultural product research. Thus, social scientists who attempt to find solutions for social problems in their natural setting find themselves in a fairly similar position to that of the agricultural scientists in both their scientific and change-agent roles, but in quite a different position with regard to the dissemination products and audiences.

Let us briefly explore what happens to agronomists when they are searching for new agricultural products that will benefit the farmer. First, extensive experimentation is done with the particular product—a highbred seed corn, for example. When a new seed is found that significantly improves corn production, the county agents, acting in consort with their agronomy counterparts, attempt to persuade farmers to use the new seed. If the new seed does not give the yield shown in the developmental experiments, this negative outcome becomes very obvious to the farmer after the first crop. The county agent as well as the agronomist then have to begin again exploring the reasons for the failure and attempting to develop new and improved seeds. Thus, the agronomist strives for the most accurate and objective results possible because of the loss of money and time that will accrue to the farmers when experimental results are in error. The agronomist and county agent are thus accountable to the problem population (farmers) as well as to their scientific colleagues.

The naturalistic social-change researchers find themselves in much the same role position. If the social program that is created and evaluated does not solve the problem of the population for which it is intended, the negative outcomes become painfully obvious from the very first replication. It is thus absolutely essential that such social scientists gain the most accurate information possible about the outcomes of any social program prior to its dissemination, since the ethical researcher would not want to create and replicate social programs that do not benefit the problem population. As with the agricultural researcher, the process of creation of a new social program, evaluation, and dissemination must be accurately done. Thus, problem-solving social scientists must take the most objective stance possible, so that valid information about social programs is obtained and the problem population will benefit once such programs are adopted.

This crucial aspect of public accountability makes the need for objectivity pronounced in problem-oriented field research. Social-action problem-solving research is done for an improvement in the quality of life for the problem population. For this reason, it is not only necessary but essential to include on the research team both social administrators and representative members of the problem population. A social innovation can only meet the needs of the problem population when the researchers know what those needs are, and this comes about when the problem population has a voice in determining the alternatives that might be most beneficial to them.

Even so, a social innovation that is valid and meets the needs of the problem population will not be spread throughout the society without the aid of social administrators. Because of these contingencies, all three parties (scientists, problem population, and social administrators) must work closely together in the design and implementation of social innovations.

In laboratory research, scientists ordinarily have other scientists as their audience. Their concern about lack of involvement stems from an attentiveness to the feedback from this scientific audience relative to the validity of the subject matter or the outcomes of such experiments. Such a situation is totally different for the problem-solving social scientists, since only one of their audiences is other scientists. The others are social administrators and the problem population, but the problem population is the most important of these.

With this cursory discussion of differences in roles, it should be clear that the difference between active and inactive scientific role behaviors is essentially attributable to audience differences and *not* to differences in scientific methodology. Scientific experiments are conducted by both groups using the logic of science embodied in its methodology. The creation of an actual social model and implanting it in a naturalistic setting for evaluation is one of the primary requisites for adequate social experimentation, just as creating an experimental condition is in the laboratory.

Since the social-change process rests on the assumption that social change is comprised of innovation creation and innovation dissemination (La Piere, 1965; Barnett, 1953; Rogers and Shoemaker, 1971; and Havelock, 1969), it is now necessary to turn our attention to establishing and evaluating both of these processes, so that social programs and their use can be assessed for their social benefit.

The Social-Change Process

Social change can be divided into two change processes. To make this clear, one needs only to think for a moment about the invention and spread of the electric light, the wheel, and the automobile as examples of technological change. Change in the social realm also occurs with such innovations as the public school and the mental hospital, which have been disseminated throughout our society to such an extent that they are now an intimate part of our educational and health systems. These two processes of technological change and institutional change have changed the entire course of our society.

Social change can occur in the future through these same two processes. But social innovations and their dissemination not only need to be created, they also need to be evaluated through scientific experimentation. The total process should go something like this: When it becomes obvious in a society that social programs are not serving the function for which they were designed, it becomes necessary to create new social models that do solve the problem. Although innovation in its broadest context often occurs as a result of an accidental observation or as an unplanned research outcome, from a social science perspective new social models can be planned by social innovators or groups of innovators. The process of innovation dissemination, which is the second element of the social change process, can also occur from a scientific perspective. The change process therefore is: defining the problem → creating the social innovation to solve the problem → implanting the social innovation in a natural setting → evaluating the innovation → replicating the beneficial innovation and evaluating it → experimentally valid social program. To disseminate the program, one must complete the following dissemination processes: identifying the dissemination target → approaching the target population about adopting the innovation target → persuading the target population to accept the innovation → activating the innovation by those who have been persuaded → helping the adopters learn techniques of dissemination, so that they can become disseminating agents → evaluating their dissemination effort, so that the valid dissemination techniques can be applied to the residual population → creating a second dissemination experiment for those individuals or organizations that have not adopted it yet → continuing to create new dissemination experiments until a critical mass of adopters has occurred → at this point, sufficient change should have occurred that the ongoing social-change process eventually spreads throughout the society.

At any moment, there are always a series of human problems facing a society that must be solved for that society to continue to exist as a cultural entity. Currently, overpopulation, environmental deprivation, and unjust human relations are examples of these problems.

When problems are recognized, individuals representing the three groups of society need to be involved in planning a solution. The representatives of the problem population itself, social administrators representing the society, and social scientists with the skill and knowledge to help these two groups create and evaluate social models need to begin planning alternative social solutions (models). These three groups are essential, because any solution found for a particular problem cannot be adopted as a solution unless all three aid in its development and dissemination. The problem population for whom it is intended needs to be involved in the planning, because whatever solution is found should be one that the problem population perceives as desirable. Social administrators must also agree that the social models designed as solutions to a contemporary problem are administratively feasible. Such elements as cost and responsiveness to society's needs are considered by such social planners. Finally, it is important that scientists become involved in the planning, so that they will have a stake in the models that will provide them with the motivation to design and evaluate the models without bias.

Regardless of the type of innovation involved, planning must be a democratic process that involves adequate representation from the three groups—problem population, social administrators, and researchers.

It may be important to look more closely at these three groups and the relationship that they have to the entire process of social innovation. First, it should be very obvious that any solution to a particular social problem that does not meet the needs of the problem population is, in fact, no solution at all. This should be obvious, because the adoption of any social innovation occurs only when individuals from the problem population participate in the new social program. Most social programs are planned by social administrators and never involve the problem population at all. When this is the case, the program either fails immediately or is discontinued later.

But involving the problem population alone is not sufficient. Social administrators, who have been charged by the society with creating new social programs for a particular human problem, also need to be involved in the planning of such solutions. Extensive experience with such human problems in actual field settings will often permit social administrators to have knowledge that is not available to anyone else, particularly from the point of view of what is financially and socially feasible. In the bargaining endeavors that go on in planning for problem-solving social innovations, it should be clear that, in the final analysis, there must be agreement between the problem population representatives and the social administrators before a particular solution can be considered as helpful to the society. Of course, this may eliminate programs that are perceived as valid only by the problem population but that would have no chance of implementation at this point in history. It may also eliminate programs that social administrators believe are solutions but that problem population representatives reject as unfeasible. However, this process should also reveal those models about which there is agreement and which could be considered by both groups as solutions, provided they are demonstrated to be solutions from a scientific point of view.

This points up the need for the third group. Scientists too should have an interest in the problem and a deep concern for the problem population, but what they bring to this bargaining arena that is unique is knowledge about how social models can be established and evaluated. From this perspective, information can be fed back to the members of the problem population and the social administrators about the validity of the social programs. This will involve comparing new social programs with those in existence. Only in this way can all three groups be assured, at a high level of probability, that social programs are doing what they are intended to do.

Thus, the planning of innovations by these three groups helps to ensure that, if a model is demonstrated to be more beneficial to the problem population than the current social practice, the participative ground work for disseminating the model has been started.

Once the initial discussions have resulted in agreement on one or more social models that need to be innovated, it then becomes necessary to define the social models in terms of their three basic elements—participants and internal and external social situational variables. Table 1 presents a list of the participant variables and social situational variables that the researcher needs to consider in planning an innovation. The participant variables listed here, such as age, sex, race, and the like, have been shown by several social researchers to affect the outcomes of social models. Similarly, the social situational variables have also been shown to affect outcomes. Since social-model outcomes are some function of the participants and social situational variables, it is necessary to consider the variables in Table 1 for their impact on any social innovation. The variables listed under both participants and social situations can affect outcomes and therefore must either be varied, matched across conditions and in that sense controlled, or monitored, at the very least, in each social experiment, so that the experimental conditions can be adequately evaluated.

The important point to understand here is that each of these variables must be considered in terms of the design of the social model and in terms of those who will participate. Only when all relevant variables have been considered and models are constructed in terms of each variable (or each variable is treated as an experimental condition or outcome) can a social model truly be established as an experiment. Even so, there are some unknown sources of error that will arise during the longitudinal field experiment; these have to be recorded and later analyzed in the best way possible to reduce the effect of the interfering elements. Once the experimental aspects of the social model have been completed— that is, a complete definition has been made of the actual social model or models and who will participate in them—an experimental plan can be established.

It is then necessary for the experimenters to create the actual model by implanting it in a naturalistic setting, so that people can participate in it and it can be evaluated. This typically requires the integrated activity of a number of social agencies and institutions,

Table 1. Participant Variables and Social Situational Variables[a]

Participant Variables

Demographic
  Age
  Economic status
  Education
  Employment history
  Family history
  History of institutionalization
    (prison, mental hospital, etc.)
  Marital status
  Medical history
  Membership in organizations
  Military history
  National origin
  Race
  Religion
  Sex
  Social class

Personality characteristics
  Behavior description
  Ratings
  Test scores

Intelligence
  Educational achievement
    (grades and awards)
  Test scores

Social Situational Variables

Internal
Organizational Components
  Hierarchial structure
  Size
  Complexity
  Formality/informality

Group Dynamics
  Cohesiveness
  Norms
  Leadership
  Composition
  Morale
  Reinforcement

Fiscal Processes
  Income
  Costs
  Rate of pay
  Bookkeeping

Membership
  Voluntary/involuntary
  Turnover

External
  Social climate
  Socioeconomic indicators
    (general and specific)
  Measurement objectiveness
  Geographical location
  Folkways and mores
  Publicity and media
    exposure
  Relationship to other
    organizations
  Legal constraints
  Time

[a]From Fairweather and Tornatzky, 1977.

so that funds and space can be set aside for the actual creation of the model.

In a more detailed discussion of the requirements for obtaining administrative agreements (Fairweather and Tornatzky, 1977), it was pointed out that one of the greatest difficulties the experimenter faces is that social administrators from whom they must receive support and help are often themselves out of step with the goals of the experimenters and the problem population. The social administrators are usually interested in obtaining publicity and promotion for their organizations as well as for themselves. This may make it difficult for the experimenters to get the needed agreements for establishing a social model. The administrators may not feel that a new, more beneficial model for the problem population is in their best interests or the best interests of their organizations. This entire process of bargaining for the administrative agreements necessary to create the models is a great stumbling block in community research. In fact, the research is more likely to be prematurely aborted at this level than at any other level in the longitudinal model-building and dissemination plan.

Let us, however, assume that the administrative agreements for creating the models have been obtained. Before the actual models can be created, it is necessary to develop a research team to implement the model and to evaluate it. Social administrators and the problem population as well as the initiating scientists will already have been involved in the planning and should continue to be members of the research team. In addition, certain specialists in both community action and social evaluation need now to be included, either as members of the research team or as consultants to it. These include experts from the various academic disciplines— sociology, education, biology, law, medicine, and the like—so that they can help develop more clearly and fully the social models and can evaluate the attempts that have been made to account for the different experimental variables found in Table 1. All these individuals—the initial planners, the disciplinary specialists, the social administrators, members from the problem population, and the consultants—comprise the research team. Such a research team, oriented toward the goal of solving a particular social problem, can bring a great deal of background information, planning skills, and knowledge to creating the new social model or models in the natural environment.

Assuming that the research team has been established and the experimental design has been approved by the operating research team, it now becomes important actually to create the models and to begin their operations, so that their outcomes can be perceived and evaluated. On a given day, the social models should be placed in operation, and the members should begin to participate in the models as planned. For a meaningful evaluation to occur, the social model will have to be in existence over a reasonably long period of time—somewhere from six months to four or five years, depending on the type of social model—for valid inferences about the value of the programs to be made. During this period of action, the data for evaluation are collected—usually every few weeks or months, so that the social processes can be studied—and stored for later evaluation.

The difficulties in administrating an actual model become most pronounced at this time. For example, interferences with models from overzealous administrators wishing to get their people into the program despite its temporary and unknown nature often occur. This is particularly true of innovations that gain widespread publicity. Of course, the experimental team must actively resist any attempt to destroy their meticulously planned sampling procedures, since, once this occurs, the social models cannot be adequately evaluated from a scientific perspective. Other sources of interference that can occur result from attempts on the part of the sponsoring agency or agencies to ignore the initial agreements, such as those for a random sample of participants or for continuing support of the model. Often, also, one or more of the research team members will need to leave for one reason or another, and the reseach team will have to replace that individual. Throughout all this, however, good administration and guidance by the research team can result in the generation of valid experimental data, so that the outcomes of the social model can be evaluated. For some social problems, such as drug addiction, follow-up studies may be needed for an adequate evaluation after the model has been discontinued.

Assuming that an adequate collection of data has been accomplished, it next becomes necessary to analyze the data to evaluate its outcomes. This often takes considerable time, because it is often necessary to take many measures over a long period of time. Usually, a much broader range of techniques is needed to evaluate the data than is common in other kinds of research.

Let us assume that the evaluation has resulted in the inference that a new model that significantly benefits the problem population has been found. It is then necessary for the research team to become accountable to the public and disseminate the new model. The dissemination process should be established as an experiment, so that the most effective dissemination techniques can be identified for promoting the new beneficial model.

Creating and Evaluating a Social Model

Here we will try to outline the thoughts and actions that were taken in the development and dissemination of an actual mental health model. Several researches completed over a fifteen-year period had convinced a group of researchers that the basic reason patients remained in the hospital for extensive periods of time, or returned to the hospital almost as quickly as they reached the community, was that no appropriate social role or social position was available to them in the community when they arrived there (Fairweather, 1964; Fairweather and others, 1960, 1969). Previous research had also shown that small groups of problem-solving mental patients, if organized around certain principles, could solve each other's problems and hence might be a vehicle to meet the daily tasks involved in leading an unsupervised life in the community. If this could be done, it would permit patients to live in the community rather than in the mental hospital. These researches also showed that, without such a vehicle, some persons would constantly return to the hospital, and others would remain there indefinitely. Thus, the basic problem for mental health planners was defined as creating appropriate social roles for chronically hospitalized mental patients and those patients who quickly return to the hospital once released.

A new model was needed to deal with this hospital chronicity associated with mental illness. It would first be necessary that the organization have self-government, if it was to meet the needs of all members. This would not only meet the democratic principles so revered in our society but would provide a more participative role for ex-patients, since previous studies had shown that, whenever mental health professionals were present with patients and ex-patients, the professionals remained dominant in the organization by filling the top administative positions. This, it was believed, could be circumvented by changing the professionals' roles to consultants, so that professionals would have a meaningful role in the creation of the new society, but they would leave the management and decision-making powers to the individuals living in that society. Thus, professionals would be on call but would not be supervisors of the individuals within the society, which was called *the lodge*.

Of course, for males in American society—and all who participated in the first lodge model were males—it was essential to have a work situation, which, at least in part, defines the social role and social position of males in our society. Men are considered quite successful in our society if they have their own business. It was therefore decided that a business would be established that the ex-mental patients would operate. This would also provide for another social-role aspect—vertical mobility would be possible within the organization itself. That is, individuals who began as workers could eventually become managers, if they showed the propensity to do so. They would also, obviously, have to demonstrate their managerial ability over a period of time, if the organization were to function properly. To accomplish the business mission, it was decided by the members themselves that a janitorial and gardening service could be established, which would fit the skills of individuals establishing the first small society.

There was concern about the acceptability of the community social climate. Some past studies, where chronic ex-mental patients had been introduced into middle-class neighborhoods, suggested that these areas would be more likely to sabotage the new organization than if it were implanted in a blue-collar working area, particularly when the incoming group had a racial mix. This was perceived as especially important, since the group of ex-mental patients was comprised of persons from different races. Accordingly, the social model was implanted in an area across the freeway (which has replaced the railroad track as defining social position in some contemporary American cities) in a neighborhood that was experiencing a shift from an all-white to a racially mixed population.

Open entry and exit were permitted by the group. They would admit new members from the hospital or old members returning from the community, who could stay indefinitely or until they were voted out of the organization because of infractions of the social rules (few were).

To accomplish the actualization of this small new society, it was necessary to make agreements with many organizations, neighbors, and others with whom these members would interact. There were primarily four organizations involved in the plan to create the new society.

The first was a university. This university agreed to provide legal council to the members of the lodge, to serve as the agency that would lease the grounds, buildings, and work equipment, to be responsible for their welfare and health, and to take the money from the granting agencies and make certain that it was spent properly in both the establishment and the evaluation of the new society.

A second agency involved was the National Institute of Mental Health. This agency provided the funding for the first lodge under a grant to the university (MH24230-03).

The third organization, a large Veterans Administration mental hospital, entered into the agreements with the university. The hospital agreed to permit volunteer mental patients to enter the lodge society. The hospital would, of course, be the society's owner and operator and would serve as a linkage organization with traditional community mental health programs (control model), to which persons who volunteered but did not attend the lodge were randomly assigned.

The fourth organization, a nonprofit corporation, served as the employing agency for the ex-mental patients. This nonprofit corporation was the organization to which the patients directly belonged. It took care of the legal aspects of the residency and business, workmen's compensation, income tax, and the like. It was linked to the university and the hospital by personnel who held joint membership—that is, persons from both the hospital and the university who belonged to the nonprofit corporation's board of directors. There were other linkages to the lodge that were primarily handled by individual consultants. A partial list included a physician, who was the medical consultant to the lodge;

psychologists, who were consultants to the lodge for organizational development, decision-making training, and the like; janitorial and gardening consultants, who helped the individuals at the lodge learn janitorial and garden skills; and a consultant to the lodge for nutrition.

There were also relationships with neighbors and other individuals and groups in the neighborhood where the lodge was located. A nearby store was often visited by the cook in the lodge, who purchased food there, and a service station, a greenhouse, and other businesses were close by.

After obtaining the grant to establish the lodge society and to hire the needed service and research personnel, one group on a ward in the hospital was trained in group decision making. Persons participating in this group had been randomly assigned from the volunteers and were later to comprise the first members of the lodge society. Two other groups of volunteers were created on the same ward. They were later to go to other community mental health services, and they served as the control group. While in the hospital, the future lodge group was given problems to solve that they would face once they arrived in the community. For example, they were taught about nutrition, how to prepare food, how to perform maintenance functions in a home, how to make decisions about each other in the group, how to activate democratic processes such as voting, and the like. After several weeks had passed, this group demonstrated proficiency in all these tasks and was judged ready for the move to the community.

An old motel had been leased for the group to live in, and they were given visitation privileges to the motel for several days prior to the move, so that they could get an understanding of the physical characteristics of their environment and how rooms might be assigned, food might be prepared, and so on. On a designated day, the patients and their belongings moved into their new home.

A detailed account of the early period of adjustment was presented in *Community Life for the Mentally Ill* (Fairweather and others, 1969). Suffice it to point out here that, through a period of trial-and-error experiences and continuous input from consultants about business, self-governance, and so on, the society eventually became self-governing, and its members were able to work actively in community settings doing janitorial and gardening work. Finally, the lodge became self-supporting. Supporting money was withdrawn, and those individuals who wished to remain in the society leased their own homes across the freeway, where they continued to live with their neighbors and where they made a reasonable community adjustment.

Over the five-year period of the research, a large number of measures were taken. Background information was obtained on everyone who entered the program; information about the processes in the lodge society was gained; social processes external to the lodge were measured; reactions of the participants and those with whom they interacted were secured; and follow-up information for everyone was gathered.

The first aspect of evaluation was to compare the background of the people who participated in the lodge with the control condition (usual community treatment) to test whether or not equivalency of sample had occurred through random assignment. The analyses of a number of comparative measures of pairs who had been matched in age, diagnosis, and length of hospitalization was completed. These analyses showed equivalence for the lodge and control group on socioeconomic status, education, race, marital life, and all other background historical measures of life adjustment. Various processes of the hospital and the lodge society were evaluated over time, so that the societies could be compared on social process.

Evaluation of the attitudes and actions of the neighborhood persons where the lodge was located showed an increasing respect for the members and positive attitudes toward the lodge society over time and a positive evaluation of the society from the participants themselves. In contrasting those who participated in traditional community programs with lodge members, the outcomes that the social administrators were most interested in were costs, duration of community residence, and employment. Comparative costs are shown in Figure 1, time in the community is shown in Figure 2, and employment is shown in Figure 3. It should be clear from these graphs that highly significant differences were obtained between the lodge society members and those who participated in traditional community programs. As shown in Figures 2 and 3 these differences continued over almost five years of follow-up of participation in both lodge and traditional program groups.

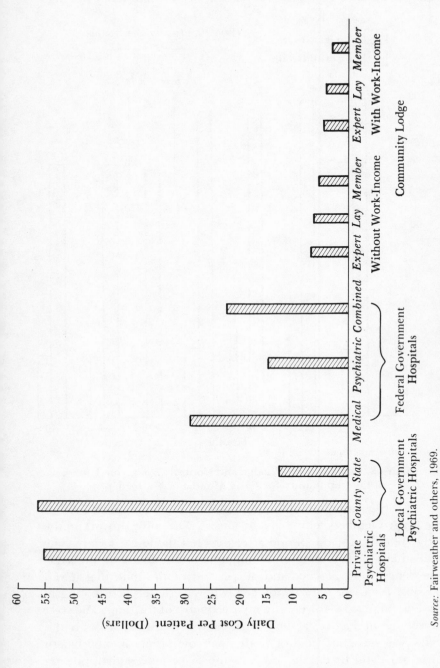

Source: Fairweather and others, 1969.

Figure 1. Mean Daily Cost per Person for Alternative Treatment Settings in California Bay Area

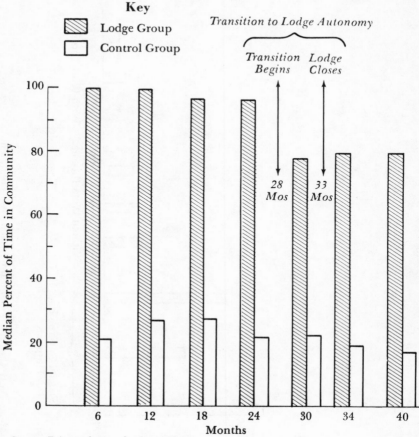

Figure 2. Comparison of Lodge and Control Groups on Time
in the Community for Forty Months of Follow-Up

Differences in employment and cost need elaboration. For the lodge members, employment consisted not only of work in the lodge but also for the period after they left the lodge society. The individuals participating in the lodge were employed on the average between 40 percent and 80 percent of the time that it was possible for them to be employed, whereas those participating in traditional programs were unemployed most of the time. The costs presented in Figure 1 show that, at the most, the cost to the lodge was one-third that of traditional community mental health programs, and finally the lodge members became self-supporting with no cost to the society at all.

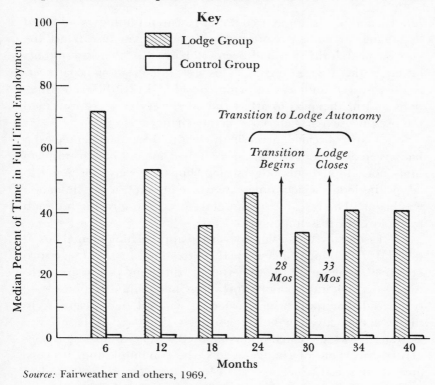

Key

Lodge Group

Control Group

Source: Fairweather and others, 1969.

**Figure 3. Comparison of Lodge and Control Groups on
Employment for Forty Months of Follow-Up**

Planning and Evaluating a Dissemination Effort

With such accurate information and clear superiority of one
treatment program over another, it might be expected that this
scientific data revealing the clear lodge success pattern would lead
to automatic adoption of the lodge society by mental health treatment centers. Nothing as rational as that occurred. Except for two
initial replicates that were started in different states and that continue operating to this day with equivalent or better results than the
prototype lodge, no other lodges were adopted. Without knowing
it, the experimenters had encountered the basic characteristic that
prevents organizational change—all organizations are established
to maintain the status quo (La Piere, 1965). The research function
has long been separated from the service function in these organi-

zations, and it was not expected that research findings would lead to a change in the service offered to ex-mental patients. In fact, the entire research division had been established so that it would *not* influence the service function. This basic organizational characteristic—research and service being considered two different functions and neither was to affect the other very much—prevented the use of research material to create change.

Thus, it became increasingly clear to the experimenters who had created the lodge that, not only had mental health problem units not adopted the lodge society, but they were not going to adopt the lodge society unless an active attempt at dissemination was begun. The researchers therefore prepared a research design to explore the dissemination process.

Essentially, the design concerned approaching mental hospitals and attempting to persuade them to adopt the new lodge society. In this phase of the experiment, different persuasive techniques (written information, workshops, and demonstrations) were compared. For those who decided to start a lodge society, techniques about activating the lodge society—what was the best way to activate it—were created and compared. Other comparisons concerned the value of change-agents, the communication process, and other social processes. Data were meticulously collected to evaluate the dissemination process over a period of five years with 255 mental hospitals—the total population of mental hospitals in the United States except for eight, which were discarded by random draw. The results of this extensive dissemination experiment can briefly be summarized as follows:

1. A group of persons working together is essential for lodge adoption. Such groups of change-agents support their members when institutional practices tend to destroy innovation.
2. It makes little difference about the social status of those one approaches in the hospitals. A nurse is as good as the manager. The most important factor is whether the individual approached has positive attitudes about the programs being promoted for adoption. For example, a nurse is a better disseminator than a superintendent, if the nurse is very positive about the program and the superintendent is either neutral or negative. The nurse will find a way to involve other members in

an attempt to persuade them to adopt a new program, if the nurse feels positively about the program.

3. No professional group is more innovative than any other professional group. Innovation adopters are just as likely to be ward aides as psychiatrists or psychologists. However, those who were given the task of establishing the lodge were usually in lower social positions, because persons higher in the social status hierarchy wanted to continue their traditional kinds of programs, and, even when they were positive, they assigned the actual activation of the lodge to a group of nonprofessionals.

4. Active demonstration of a program is a much better persuasive device then either the written word or presentation of the information by workshops. Simply put, cognitive understanding of an innovation generally will stop at cognitive awareness, unless specific attempts are made to bridge the gap between verbal behavior and performance.

5. Social-action consultants who are knowledgeable about the problem and who can help activate new programs are essential in the dissemination process. Without such outside consultation and help, no lodge was adopted by any hospital in this study.

6. Organizations with better communication tend to adopt more readily, particularly when the top persons in the organizations are not opposed to such an adoption.

Currently, another national study is under way to discover if other techniques can be helpful in persuading those hospitals who would not originally adopt the lodge to do so. This experiment involves an attempt to focus written material, workshops, and actual demonstration programs into an adoption activity that is smooth from the initial cognition of the problem to its adoption. There is a second planned experiment, which attempts to discover whether or not adoption groups such as those that were created in the hospitals that actually adopted the lodge can be formed through training in group process. And a further experiment is in the planning phase. It involves bringing together all the lodge adopters in the nation, so that they can plan a dissemination effort with their colleagues using the materials created by the research group for such purposes. The training of indigenous change-agents from those groups that initially adopted the lodge innovation should further our knowledge about lodge advocacy and adoption. It should be clear that other experiments can be done after these are finished, until either almost all hospitals have adopted the lodge innovation or the attainment of further adoptions is considered to be so costly that further intervention appears to be unwarranted.

The Future

I have tried to present here a cursory description of social change in which social scientists play a key and active role. Unlike the traditional inactive social scientist's role, this approach requires that the social scientist master a series of active techniques from social program development to dissemination, on the one hand, and of more traditional scientific methods on the other. Without the training of social problem-solvers, who are also experts in social action and scientific evaluation, it is highly doubtful that a program such as the one proposed here can be a valid alternative to contemporary decision processes. Attempts must be made to train social innovators who will, along with the problem population and social administrators, create new social programs, activate them, administer them, disseminate them, and evaluate the entire process. Such a role requires a fusion of humanitarian values and scientific methods in a social-action context. It appears to me that the future quality of life on this planet will depend on the degree to which such social roles and programs are initiated and promoted.

INTERVIEW WITH GEORGE W. FAIRWEATHER

Kelly: The first question I would like to ask you is, what were the factors that led you to become interested in the lodge?
Fairweather: The lodge experiment has to be viewed, of course, in its historical context. The lodge experiment was an experiment that was introduced as a logical sequence in a series of previous experiments, which had indicated the following: (1) Mental patients returned to the hospital at a rate of around 75 percent after being discharged; that is, the most chronic patients, within eighteen months after release, would return to the hospital, regardless of what was done for them in their previous hospitalizations; (2) the patients could become organized into groups, so that they could

solve their own problems; (3) the lack of social position in the community for the individual leaving the hospital was the single most important variable to be explored for its possible therapeutic contribution.

With those findings in mind, it seemed logical to take the next step in the experimental sequence—namely, to create a small society owned, operated, and governed by these members. The real trick of the research from a process point of view was to phase out the professional people as the lodge members demonstrated their willingness and their ability to carry out the tasks required in a self-governing society.

Kelly: The first lodge took place at the Veterans Administration Hospital in Palo Alto, California. Could you comment on the administrative context, some of the people at the hospital, and your own interests at the time? What were the conditions that helped you take on this work?

Fairweather: As you undoubtedly know, to start a project like the lodge was a very difficult task indeed, from both an experimental and logistical point of view. It required the creation of an entirely new small society, even though there were only fifteen original members. From an administrative point of view, probably the most important aspect of getting the lodge under way was the arrangements that were made with individuals and organizations in the Palo Alto area. From my own perspective, I will present them to you in sequence. I am not certain how they should be ranked in terms of their importance, since every one was so important. If they had not existed, the lodge would have failed before it started!

The first was a psychiatrist with whom we worked on the ward. In previous studies, we had demonstrated that small groups of mental patients could solve each other's problems. This particular psychiatrist was interested in that research and, more centrally, in social change. He was, in many ways, as interested as we were, from both a philosophical and humanitarian perspective, in creating a society or a community where ex-mental patients could live in an equivalent social position to other individuals in the society. His willingness to take on the legal and medical responsibility for this group as it went through the hospital process was essential.

The second group that was extremely important was the National Institute of Mental Health (NIMH), who agreed to fund the project from its very inception until its completion. I am not certain about whether or not this is the first project that did this, but it was one of the first. NIMH was willing to use research money to pay for the food, management, and building arrangements for individuals when a new social model needed to be created. The National Institute of Mental Health took on this innovative program with support and determination and a willingness to back up our program in any way that they could.

The third organization that was extremely helpful was the Veterans Administration Hospital itself. We were all convinced by this time that, to create a first-class citizenship role for ex-mental patients, you had to discharge them when they left the hospital and take them out of the traditional mental health system. This required administrative agreements by the director of the hospital and the physician I just mentioned, who took the responsibility for making those decisions both from a medical and legal point of view.

The fourth organization involved was Stanford University, who was the recipient of the grant and who helped us establish an entire program of consultation for the lodge in areas that appeared to be very important—legal and technical areas. For example, they wrote the contract with the organizations from which the work tools were rented; they wrote the lease for the motel; they provided legal and accounting counsel to the lodge to train lodge members to handle those matters themselves.

And last was a nonprofit corporation, which had been in existence for some time and had agreements with the local unions that work could be accomplished by ex-mental patients, if the work was to be of a rehabilitative nature. The unions supported rather than opposed such a work role.

So, a large number of people within these organizations were involved—I have no idea how many, but I think it's very clear that it was a rather massive effort, with a large number of individuals and organizations involved.

Kelly: One idea that struck me in terms of reading your work is that you were the right person with the right idea at the right time. Can you recall some of the interests of the hospital administration that helped these persons support you in this venture. Is this an apt hypothesis?

Fairweather: Generally, I think that's correct. That is, there was the halfway house movement in England; there were books like *The*

Mental Hospital (1954) by Stanton and Schwartz and numerous other sociological writings, particularly about the effects of institutionalization. In that sense, there was, we might say, a general cultural background, which, if it didn't provide support, certainly didn't provide strong resistance. That was an extremely important aspect. So there was, we might say, a readiness on the part of society to sanction this work.

The second aspect that was important was a beginning trend in the social, natural, and medical sciences to view experimentation done outside the laboratory as a possible and respectable avenue for scientific inquiry, even though the term *applied* was often used to separate it from what was sometimes called *true science*. There was an awareness on the part of the scientific community that supported research of this type, both administratively and professionally.

The third trend, I guess, and perhaps I and a few others were catalysts in that trend, was that the helping services of the mental health profession, including the work of psychologists, would eventually have to deal with the topics of social structure and social position. We couldn't ignore them any longer. One of the most paramount features of the patients' return to the hospital was their inability to obtain employment and acceptance in community settings. It was quite obvious that, unless the people who ran the service programs and we, as scientists, got interested in changing the social position of patients, we were not likely to get any further than we were at that point.

Kelly: Given that you were designing the experiment while also beginning to test how research ideas can be adopted, I am impressed at the amount of time, energy, persistence, and talent that you have given to this work. Were there personal or academic experiences that have helped you to sustain your efforts to integrate scientific research with social innovations?

Fairweather: As you might recall, I mentioned in the chapter some of the similarities and differences between the kind of research we were doing and agricultural research. I had taken my undergraduate training at Iowa State University, which was a land grant college. I had the great fortune of having as teachers some of the outstanding statisticians who were involved in both agricultural and sociological field experiments at that time. It seemed to me that there was a great parallel between the fact that these faculty were using scientific techniques to gain information that could be used by the society in the form of products. There were very few people who seemed to be interested in doing that with social programs. So, that was one aspect, the sustenance. There was simply a knowledge that people had for some time used these techniques to gain information to create and pass the products on to society.

Another aspect, I suppose, and probably the reason that I was initially interested in clinical psychology, was that I had always felt that whatever information society has available should be used for the welfare of the people. It seemed to me that, as I got more and more knowledge of the mental patient, this was a minority group of the first order who had no advocacy group, by and large, and could not be organized readily—certainly not in those years. If we could provide information that showed society and our scientific brothers that we could in fact prepare programs with a benefit to those persons and society, we had a likelihood of changing their attitudes. I guess the other element is persistence that comes with a Scottish background—the notion that most human problems could be solved, if the right people and the right combination of people in a society would work together to solve them rather than fighting one another for resources. So, it was a combination of personality characteristics, my educational background, and also a notion that service for people in trouble was an obligation of the society, that it was not something that people should have to bargain for.

Kelly: Given that, did the concept of the design of the lodge evolve from these early experiences?

Fairweather: I have thought about it several times. I guess, if one were to go back to the roots, I would have to say that, very likely, it would have something to do with being brought up in a big family. If one wanted to look at personality factors, I still can hear my Scottish grandmother say from time to time, "Divide small and share all." I think that a philosophical position is essential to the establishment of this kind of organization. From that kind of thinking came my early interest in such organizations as the Hutterites, because I could see clearly the need for a society that was organized along some of those principles. By the time we got to the phase where we clearly had to bridge the gap between the hospital and community, we already knew that these individuals could work as groups, if they were given the proper tools and were established appropriately. It seemed then almost automatic that we should try this kind of society. Again, it's a multivariate topic. Without some of those elements in it, it probably wouldn't have occurred that way.

Kelly: In thinking about that early period, when you were at the Veterans Administration Hospital in Palo Alto in the design and inception of the lodge, could you comment on how you resolved the personal, situational, and methodological factors that had to be dealt with to start that first experiment?

Fairweather: Again, we have to consider this in historical context. I was quite convinced by that time, and had in fact written in an experimental methods book, about the need for planning cooperatively a social program, especially one that was to be innovative. So, part of that whole process was to provide a meaningful role for individuals who would be on the research team and also a role where they could share their ideas with the group and have them incorporated in the experiment itself. For example, I learned from the small-group work we had done and a previous book, *Social Psychology and Treating Mental Illness,* that some nurses and social workers were very interested in writing scientific articles and that indeed they do an excellent job. So, it was important to them and to the project that they have some voice in the hypotheses that were formulated and in the analysis of the data and in the writing. What we tried to do was to create a team where everyone had some role in all the activities. I think that a program like this, a program of any magnitude that operates in a naturalistic setting with the kind of motivation and interest and long-term pursuit one has to have, cannot be done without that kind of devotion. I think it's important here just to make this comment: One of the most difficult aspects for new social scientists to learn is simply that there is a set of interpersonal, social, and cultural processes that go along with this kind of research that one does not learn in the classroom. You cannot get these issues from statistics books. Nonetheless, if you don't have them, you're just as crippled as if you had never taken a course in statistics. So, that must become an integral part of any program of this kind.

Kelly: Were there other issues that had to be dealt with in terms of balancing the concerns about patients' rights and participating in an experiment?

Fairweather: Yes, because, in this kind of solution to a social problem and experimental work, one should ethically do all this work with volunteers. We had to have a group of volunteers matched in terms of key variables. One of the matched pair would go to the lodge, and the other would not go to the lodge. This required a considerable amount of explanation to the patients, in an attempt to make it very clear to them regarding the alternatives that they were volunteering for. Now, this kind of negotiation had to be placed before everyone. For example, it's very difficult to get administrators to understand the need for random assignment. I would say that any field experimenter might very well plan to devote several weeks of follow-up visits for what appears to us to be a very simple, logical concept.

However, translated into action for the administrator, that's a very difficult task indeed. The administrator, in addition, is always concerned that people will take this as his or her personal deficit or the organization's lack of interest in people rather than as an attempt to find out something that might be of value. In that context, I am of the opinion that a control group in a study like this is always a treatment group. I don't think there is any such thing in field research as a no-treatment group. By the very nature of social organization, you are required as an agent of that society to offer a program. Nor is there a program that is designed not to help people as much as possible. So, we're talking about a spectrum of alternatives that are all on the positive side. The important thing from an experimenter's point of view is to make that clear to the people who have to make the decisions. They must know that Program A may be superior to Program B, even though B sounds much nicer and may be much more in tune with the times, and so on. At almost every turn, you need to communicate with people; you need to communicate clearly. I can't overstress from my experience the need to be very frank and honest. I think the earlier notions that were applied in a lot of laboratory researches, if my memory is correct—what were then called the *stooges* and so on— would be absolutely fatal in this kind of research, should one try to use them.

Kelly: Could you comment on some of the most striking outcomes of the lodge experiment on the hospital organization structures, on the professional staff, and on the patients?

Fairweather: I think the most striking outcomes predicted by the hospital staff—that the program would fail, that we were headed for disaster, both in terms of actions that we couldn't control or actions patients might take, that we were unable to carry out an experiment—were just not realized. The truth was that, by the end of the experiment, many of those people who had been lukewarm or negative initially had received feedback from individuals around the community and had changed their opinion.

From the patients' point of view, I think the most important outcome is that the new social role worked, that the characteristics of the lodge society were such that an individual was much like a member of a minority group in our historical context. It became very clear to me why the so-called ghetto was established, because, when you get support from your peers, they might support different kinds of behavior than the broader society will accept. What one does then is to behave in the small society as if one is at home—one does the kinds of things that come naturally. The reciprocal of that is that one isn't criticized, one isn't browbeaten, one isn't made to sit in the corner, and so on. However, when one goes into the larger society, what one does is live by their code while one is there. This type of learning did not occur to me at the outset as one of the key characteristics, but it certainly was. Later, this point became quite clear.

From the scientist's point of view, I guess I would have to say that we were, of course, surprised at the activity level and input from our most chronic people, who lost their lowly hierarchical status and looked much more like the less chronic people. We had stratified the sample on the basis that we would get those status differences, of course, and we did not. I guess the final scientific point was that, in a longitudinal study of five years or even eight years, you can create a plan that, if followed, will usually yield valid results. I have listed these in my two methods books in one way or another. But, just to look at one of the problems, in five years, someone's going to leave the project, some key individual. This can be planned for initially by training persons for multiple roles. So, if one thinks ahead and tries to conceptualize the future, what probably will happen is that many of the stumbling blocks that ordinarily defeat field research can be worked out reasonably well.

Kelly: What led you to decide to adopt the diffusion phase?

Fairweather: I might just set that scene a little bit, because that's a very important part of the whole experiment. I guess after I and my colleagues worked as we did, this preceding phase (the lodge society) was a success by almost any criteria one wishes to use, particularly in view of the fact that social scientists very rarely have those kinds of findings. If one takes the socially responsible position of a social scientist seriously, then it seems to me that one ought to try to make these findings available to the entire society. Now, of course, the problem that we faced when we started the first dissemination study was that, despite wide reading of all the literature we could put our hands on, we could find very few experiments that had actually been done in social change. Most of the research up to that point had been surveys and matters of judgment. Many of these ideas had been borne out by later research, and many were discarded. We were in a position where we were going to try a national dissemination effort for the lodge society. Since we had invented the society, we already knew from relationships with other people that the inventors must be involved in the dissemination; otherwise, the model that gets transmitted will not fit with the original model. From our knowledge of statistics, it was quite obvious that, as we varied from the original experimental conditions, we would vary from our original hypotheses. This could become a problem to us from a logical point of view. So, putting both those needs together, it was inevitable that we had to become involved in the design as well as the administrative arrangements, the training procedures, and the dissemination. That's what we did. I think that period of my professional life led me into a much stronger interest in social change. The resistance of a social system to innovation is eye-opening, if you're immediately involved in trying to do it, even when that innovation is demonstrably very valid. It's one thing to look at it historically or from an office, but it's a totally different matter, if you're the one who's getting the door slammed in your face. So, as part of the whole process of developing social programs that could be useful to the society, it was inevitable that, somewhere in this formula (which goes from initial discovery to actual implantation of the model), the scientists had to become involved as scientists in the whole social-change process. So, that's what we did.

Kelly: As you look at the adoption at this time, do the principles that you have articulated in your writing still hold, or are you modifying some of them?

Fairweather: I'm trying to think if the principles have changed rather dramatically. I don't think so. As far as I can recall, the most important ones haven't. For example, we started out by finding that the amount of money was not related to adoption, and that still is the case. The education of the adopter is not related, unless it is an education in what I call *cosmopoliteness,* or knowledge of several different societies. Certainly, perseverance is required for change and for almost anything in the area of social experimentation.

What we have really been looking at is how you put these dimensions together in a more meaningful framework than we did earlier. In our early research, much of this information was correlative. Yet, we believed that some of it was causative, but we didn't know who or what was pulling the sled. For example, one of the current findings that seems extremely important for future research is that action may very well be the central dimension and that communication, small-group development, and all such social processes occur as a by-product of that action. This is still under investigation, but now it's appearing to be an increasingly interesting idea.

Essentially, in the process of moving from persuasion to adoption, you typically start with an inactive kind of approach, which is cognitive, to acquaint people with the model and its advantages and disadvantages. There comes a point where you have to bridge what I believe is the most understudied and underrated area in the field of psychology, and perhaps in all of the sciences, and that is the gap between cognitive information and action. In some ways, the biologists have been looking at it for years in terms of the use of muscles and synaptic junctions and so on; but, as social scientists, we have often made the assumption, which our experience shows is totally inaccurate, that, if you provide people, particularly those who are educated, with a great deal of information, they will become enlightened and will change in some active ways. That just does not happen!

We were trying in this study to find out, first, how we could bridge that gap. We stumbled on the idea of approaching the whole problem in what we might call *mini-steps,* so that you start with an introduction to the problem, and you make sure that everyone understands that before you go on to the next cognitive element. After you get accustomed to making these little jumps cognitively, you come to the action setting, and hopefully you'll make the jump before you realize you're into it. It's very easy to do with the lodge society—to set it up—because there is a series of behaviors that has to occur before a lodge can be established. For example, you have to get a building. You also have to set up legal procedures, and so on. That's one of the things we've been looking into.

Another thing that we felt was extremely important and that needed to be explored much further than we did in the first dissemination study was how to organize a group of social change-agents. Our original study showed that, in every instance where we had developed a group and the group was organized around the change task, that group moved to adoption. Wherever we didn't have adoption, we didn't have the group, and we began to believe that, sequentially, at least, the group was causative. We tried a series of techniques that have been used to create groups, some of which appear to have worked, at least at first blush. We're just now looking at this data, so I can't be too definitive here, but it looks like we should be able to set up a series of procedures to organize change-groups. I think that, if that can be done, it would be a major step forward in the diffusion of innovations, because those groups are in a way sort of the force generator. Once you get the generator going and moving, I've been impressed with the force and momentum. Most of my life I have been much less struck by principles of physics and chemistry and so on than I have by social principles. But this whole business of moving an inert object, the amount of force that is required to move something inert, how once it gets going it's difficult to stop, is pivotal. How it gets going down one path and is difficult to transfer to another is certainly a counterpart in the physical world to exactly what we're going through. Maybe one of our better concepts would be a critical mass of people who are goal directed. How do you create the goal-directedness, and so on? Those have been some of our real concerns.

Our thinking now is moving into another phase of the study, which is the notion that, perhaps the best way to approach this, or at least one way that would be very good, would be to train people who are in the adopting process to become diffusion agents themselves—to give them the tools and equipment to do that. We are going to try an experiment along that line and see what our results are, what training procedures might be the best, and so on. I think this is an area in which psychologists certainly can play a key role, if not *the* key role, particularly with their sociological and anthropological counterparts, in the dissemination and use of social models. This has to be an area of future vital importance.

Kelly: What, in your view, is the most important accomplishment that you've initiated in these activities?

Fairweather: If it is kept in mind that I've been dealing over the years both with service persons and researchers, I would say the most important aspect has been training. That might not sound all that important, but I think that in every young trained person who truly has the welfare of the residents of his society at heart and wants to be a scientist—a good scientist and a good provider of service—is where the future of our society rests, rather than totally in organizational structure. I think, of course, you must have a receptive organization; we all realize that, but, if you don't have the people to fill those roles, I don't think in the long run you can have a successful human services program.

Kelly: Bill, on the basis of your work, what do you recommend regarding the creation of experimental design? Have your ideas become more firm, or have you modified them? You are viewed as *the* passionate exponent of randomization at all costs.

Fairweather: Well, I don't know whether it's at all costs, but I guess we were talking earlier about persistence, the inability to change reactively with every fad. Now, having had a strong background in statistical methods, having been convinced over a long period of time in the logic of statistics, and seeing the need for their integration into social policy, it just occurred to me that it was rather foolish to settle for something less than we might be able to get. So, I suppose that, if I had started out and had never been able to perform an experiment with random assignment, I may have changed my mind. However, subsequent experiences, and also, now, those of our students—a total of seventeen have gone through our Ph.D. program, and almost all of them have employed randomized assignments to conditions—have further convinced me that this kind of research is possible.

The problem that social experimenters run into and the reason why they often don't do it is because of the length of time and persuasion that's required. I don't know to what extent other scientists understand this, but you know that, when you develop an experimental technique, it has a great impact on the sociology of the discipline. When we got involved in animal psychology, the rat maze became an enduring methodology, and it may have, in fact, determined more experiments than the ideas that generated the maze in the first instance. That applied across the board. I always try to give our students a full background in all current methodology, because I think this is important. But what I warn them about is not to settle for less unless you have to! And I am concerned— and deeply concerned—about the move toward program evaluation where, very often, social scientists who are entering the social-policy arena are simply looking at other people's results and trying to make sense of them, when there are serious questions about whether one can use statistical tables under those conditions. And a second product of this approach, and perhaps this even bothers me more, is that the scientist thereby gives up his or her role in innovation. Now, I can't imagine the laboratory scientist running around trying to find out whether someone would just give them their data. An innovative scientist might discover more about the problem than the original researcher knew; so, I think the aspect of adopting scientific methods that are less than one need settle for encourages persons other than scientists to design the program. And, although I'm the first one to question whether the scientist has all the knowledge, I think the scientist in cooperation with the clients and social administrators can contribute knowledge and can, in fact, contribute it not only in experimental design but also in the theory and design of social innovation.

I have a deep concern that we not get so methodologically oriented that we simply run out and do everyone's bidding, because what is likely to happen is that a large number of the programs we are investigating will not even be valid. Some may even be harmful to people and may very well be totally politically determined rather than determined on the basis of what a given group of people might need. My own feeling is that the randomized design goes along with a deep concern about what the social process is, and it puts the scientist in a responsible position. We do have to be responsible. It is now very common to use the term *accountability*. But, as I look back on my own career, both as a mental health professional and as a scientist, I can say I've been deeply concerned about that for many years. I think that, whether in service work or in scientific work, we often do the easiest kinds of things, which, in the long run, are not very helpful to us or anyone else. So I see the random assignment as being a part of a much broader kind of concern.

Kelly: The principle for randomization is a currency for how the citizen can join with the researcher for the search for a better standard. If the principle of randomization is adopted, we are increasing the chances of the people who are going to be working with us to understand what an experiment is. It's a collective, self-conscious investment in trial and error. We will be able to believe with more confidence in what we have found. If we do find something that's useful, there is more credibility for what we have found.

Fairweather: Yes, that's exactly true. I can't recall the exact articles and books, and that isn't important here, but, early in social research, large numbers of essays were written about the process of change. The process might be thought of as something like this — take three individuals from different backgrounds who get together and want to work on a mutual project; probably, the first thing they have to do, if they're to have a true collaborative effort, is to understand the other individual's point of view and to develop a trust in that individual in areas where it is impossible to know about a particular idea without extended experience.

I think that's what happens in the bargaining situation with the problem population, the scientist, and the administrator. First, the problem-population group understands the problem from their daily living experience, and, if they are involved deeply and totally and aren't treated simply as persons to be taken advantage of, they will discuss the problem from their perspective and acquaint other people with it. In this kind of work, as I've said many times before, a solution that is not acceptable to this group is not a solution at all, at least for this period in history. If you can't implement a solution, it's likely not to be very helpful. However, the scientist has to demonstrate and in fact teach the social administrators and the representatives of the client population what the value of scientific methods is. Random assignment is a very important technique in getting this message across. It is a logical process, which can be readily understood, if an individual is treated as a person for whom such information might be important. That's aside from whether they have an academic education beyond the third grade or not. The social administrators have to persuade both the experimenters and the problem population in the early meetings that they can carry out adequately the dissemination of a new social program, if one is found. This sort of cooperative venture is one that each of the parties must take very seriously, if problem solution is to be achieved.

I think, too, that the use of the best statistical methods we have is an obligation. I am absolutely certain that all understand it as it goes along. In fact, we've never seen any problem in that at all. For example, we have told the patients before they volunteered that they might not be able to enter the lodge and that they will be assigned to one or two programs at random, both of which were beneficial, as far as we knew. One might be more beneficial than the other. We hoped it was, but we couldn't guarantee that. As far as I can recall, in not one single instance did we get any negative opinion about this. The idea was that, from the problem population's point of view, if you (the scientist) in conjunction with a professional staff can come up with a better treatment program that can keep people from sitting in hospitals for seven or ten years like I have done, I'm willing to devote a lot of time and energy to that. So I don't think we have the same kind of frivolous approach that one can get in nonhuman, nonnaturalistic situations.

Kelly: I am impressed with your comment that you felt that one of the most important things you had accomplished was through the association of colleagues and students—the training function that you've provided through these many years of research. What recommendations do you have for educating people to do this type of work, where there's equal attention to rigor and innovation?

Fairweather: Let me just speak briefly about the general educational process and then some of the specifics. I think that one of the very poor things we've done in education in this society is to isolate individuals from the community and its problems. If I were only permitted to make one change in our entire educational process, I would insist that half of every school year be spent in real-life situations of one kind or another. I think that provides the leap conceptually, emotionally, and behaviorally between theory and reality. It provides an understanding at a very personal level of human problems.

Specifically, at the university level, taking a long leap here, I would organize a program along the lines, partly at least, of our ecological psychology program here at Michigan State University. There are some things I would do differently. One thing I would do that would be quite similar is to begin in the first term of graduate or undergraduate study to give the person a multidisciplinary orientation and to try to get the student to think beyond the single-variable conceptual level. I would also try to introduce better courses in logic. I think some students' failure to be able to conceptualize can be improved. I think the reason people don't conceptualize better is because they have been educated in a system that doesn't teach them how to think creatively. I would try to give everybody some training in science, but with the careful notion of teaching it in an integrated way, so it's seen as part of a larger survival process. I'm very concerned now in terms of the decisions our society has to make about matters like impure water, about matters that can destroy both the social and the natural environment. I believe our lawmakers need some understanding of the value and the limits of scientific knowledge in those areas; they should learn something about how to interpret scientific results.

If you've ever been to a public hearing, and I'm sure you have, you know you can hear anything you want to hear. Not only that, but all people, even scientists, are chosen to pick out studies that demonstrate a particular point of view. I think that if our legislators were better trained than they are now in scientific methodology, they would make much greater demands on the evidence presented. So that's something else that I would do.

In graduate training, as I mentioned earlier, I would try to teach methodology and innovation. I would offer a great deal more, both behaviorally and intellectually, about values and ethics. I'm constantly startled by the lack of concern that's shown by people for other people. And a tremendous amount of emphasis is placed on making money, as if that were an end-product. So I think that should be a part of the whole educational process. To accomplish this, research programs in the community should be established.

Some of the things that we did in the ecological program, as I just mentioned, I think are important. One is to treat the person in graduate school as if he or she were a colleague and let them experience the problems of getting into organizations, of persuading organizations, of making their agreements, and so on. Then, serve as a resource person for them, rather than taking them by the hand, leading them into the field, doing the work, and having them stand there as observers. I think this traditional kind of training typically results in creating unnecessary fear on the part of the individuals who want to try social intervention themselves.

Generally, I would broaden the whole spectrum of education. I would try, just to summarize, to get education to be multidisciplinary, to make research work a typical experience, to perceive the community as a laboratory, if we wanted to look at it that way, rather than the classroom—to combine different kinds of training and, above all, to begin emphasizing more ethics and human values. I think that would be helpful.

11

Characteristics of Community Research Projects and the Implementation Process

James G. Kelly
Ricardo F. Muñoz
Lonnie R. Snowden

The contributors to this book were chosen because their work self-consciously attends to the social context in which their research takes place. For them, research is not just a scientific task. The people and communities to be affected by their work are given careful consideration. Responsiveness to social circumstances is an expected and necessary part of their involvement.

In their chapters and interviews, the contributors have presented their basic theories, their interventions, their research methods, their major findings, and their personal views on what it takes to accomplish this type of work. Collectively, these eight chap-

343

ters illustrate varied ways in which research-oriented community interventions can be successfully carried out. This concluding chapter will underscore some of the similarities of the projects that we feel contributed to their success and some of the major differences in opinion regarding how community interventions should be studied and evaluated. In addition, we will comment on the different levels of social contexts addressed by the eight projects.

Some Basic Themes

Each of the contributors has explicitly or implicitly addressed issues that can be identified as basic themes. Three of these themes are described here to encourage and assist the continued design and execution of community-based research. They are: the ability to respond to the unpredictability of social events, the need for social support for the investigator, and the desirability of certain personal characteristics that are adaptive for community work.

Theme One: The Ability to Respond to the Complexities of Social Events.   None of the contributors was rattled for too long by the array of political and social factors that affected them. Instead, each took advantage of the social context to improve both the nature of the research and the relationship between the research staff and the local community.

The implications of unexpected incidents in the field are much greater than those confined to a laboratory setting. The hoax perpetrated on Moos by the high school students had to be responded to quickly and effectively to safeguard the project's relationship to the school system. Maccoby and Alexander had to enlist the aid of the mass media to reach their communities, and they had to fill in gaps that occurred when one of the communities' newspapers became less responsive than the other. Shure's ability to improvise, such as making substitute travel arrangements during a transportation strike, made it clear to the parents that she considered the project important.

The issues surrounding entry into a community present one of the most complex periods in the life of a project. Holahan describes the process well, including the value of past cordial relationships between institutions. Fairweather prescribes a particular approach, in which the administration and clients share with the researcher many of the planning functions. Thus, the three groups can feel a sense of ownership about the project and can assume responsibility for implementing it, adopting it (if effective), and disseminating it. The role of becoming a reliable presence in the community is richly illustrated by Leighton's chapter. She presents a portrait of the investigator as a scanner and peripatetic observer who welcomes opportunities to build informal relationships and to respond to them as a potential source of knowledge. Todd and Gottlieb also present a tone of collaboration and mutual learning in their approach to studying support networks.

As the entry process starts to jell, we begin to perceive another major issue: how to balance the need to inspire trust with the inevitability of exercising power. Before the relationship between the researcher and the community begins to be clarified, it is often advisable to begin contacts at a tentative, nonthreatening level. The usual approach is one of inquiring about how best to collaborate and how each party could benefit from cooperating. The intent is to project an image of openness, a willingness to listen, and a desire to be truly responsive to the community's perspectives. At some point, however, the intervention needs to be decided on, and the intervener must be able to exert influence on the decision and its implementation.

At that point, whatever trust has been built is put to a test. Two kinds of trust are at stake: trust in the scientist's professional competence and trust in his allegiance to the community's goals and values. Shure gained trust partly by being open to teachers' suggestions. Maccoby and Alexander enlisted enthusiastic cooperation from the television stations by providing them with TV spots of professional quality. Holahan had to respond quickly to the night shift's concerns. The small interventions made by Leighton's colleagues were successfully carried on by the community itself, suggesting that the researchers' choices were on target and that the way they presented them must have been sensitive and caring to be so easily accepted.

Another unpredictable element of social contexts is byproducts—that is, unplanned or unintended side effects that can add to or diminish the effect of the initial intervention. Perhaps the most provocative example of this is given by Leighton. The change in the mental health levels of The Road and the parallel changes in the physical appearance of the community were surprising and still remain somewhat of a mystery. Were they triggered by the influx of money, by the investigator's demonstrated interest in the welfare of the settlement, or by the new ideas brought back to The Road by the workers who went to the city? Could it be some synergistic combination of factors? Whatever the answer, it is clear that the process achieved the kind of impact that community developers dream about.

At times, the effects that follow an intervention disappoint the researcher. Rappaport, Seidman, and Davidson, for example, express the frustration of the careful innovators, who, after conscientiously tracking the continuation of their program, discover that it has been modified and is no longer the same program that was evaluated originally. Even here, however, one wonders whether the apparent acceptance and obvious modification of such programs by community agencies may not be positive signs of psychological ownership over them. Although a total distortion of well-planned interventions could defeat their purpose, it is possible that modifications may increase their practical utility without radically reducing their effectiveness. The ultimate questions are whether a strict adherence to the original philosophy makes it less likely that it would continue to be implemented and whether the changes made by the agency staff will maintain a net gain over the methods used before the original intervention.

The effects on the researchers and their future work must also be kept in mind. Moos, for example, began by trying to develop valid and reliable measures of the characteristics of environments. Interventions to change them were not a top priority for him. However, the interest generated in the study participants about the characteristics of their settings has impelled him toward conceptualizing practical applications of his work.

Even the rejection of an intervention prompted one of our contributors to engage in a still more ambitious project. Fairweather, when faced with lack of acceptance of the lodge by the very hospital where he had researched its effectiveness, undertook the dissemination of his innovation and simultaneously the study of the process of dissemination. In his typically experimental fashion, he approached mental hospitals throughout the country using one of several predetermined methods. His purpose was to identify the methods that achieve the greatest probability of acceptance.

The by-products of empirically evaluated community interventions are generally multifaceted. These by-products affect not only the target community and the staff involved in implementation but also the originator of the project and the project itself. Sometimes, they may affect public policy on a large scale.

The greatest factor that diminishes the momentum of community involvement is *burn-out*. The term brings to mind a hopefully felicitous analogy: just as the interaction of many community groups can generate power, it can also generate heat. Power occurs when the concentrated efforts of the parties involved propel movement in the intended direction. When external or internal factors impede movement, heat results. Enough exposure to heat produces burn-out.

Burn-out has been described in many ways. At best, it is characterized by loss of enthusiasm and motivation; at worst, by a feeling of hopelessness and even aversion to one's work. Work that involves a large amount of contact with people, especially in situations in which their behavior cannot be controlled or predicted, tends to produce the greatest amount of burn-out. Similarly, work in which the product of one's efforts is not readily ascertainable can lead to burn-out. Community interventions tend to embody both of these factors. Therefore, it is imperative that researchers in social contexts develop and use social supports for themselves. This is the second common theme we want to address.

Theme Two: Social Support for the Investigator.   The issue of social support for action research is a critical factor in ensuring that the research is done and that the research findings will have impact. The more complex, the more unorthodox, and the more unfamiliar is the research effort, the more active and continuous is the aid that is required for the organizations and staff when doing the research. Three kinds of social support are readily discernible: personal, intraorganizational, and extraorganizational. Personal support is most directly mentioned by Gottlieb, who credits his wife with helping him cope with the uncertainty of whether contact would be established with the mothers in his study. However, it is almost certain that the significant others in all community researchers' lives can be indispensable sources of motivation and strength. The fact that these acknowledgments have become almost automatic in the prefaces to books does not make them any less real.

Fairweather recalls the courage and vision of the administrator of the Veterans Administration Hospital in Palo Alto, who supported a radical departure in clinical practices when establishing the design for the lodge experiment. Maccoby recounts how Farquhar listened to and acted on Maccoby's suggestion for an extensive media intervention instead of just one film on heart disease prevention. Leighton describes the process of breaking in new members of disciplinary teams so that they feel more secure, stop defending their own positions, and get on with the business at hand. Each of these cases illustrates the facilitating effect of intraorganizational support, of feeling that one's ideas are accepted by one's colleagues. The process involved in building this type of support could itself be the target of study, of course. Once again, the activities and necessary elements in a community psychologist's work become part of the field's legitimate area of concern. Its findings in the community are relevant to its own functioning and vice versa.

Extra organizational support comes from many levels, starting with the participants in the study and going up to federal government support. Shure was able to convince teachers, mothers, and the school system to accede to her program. Rappaport, Seidman, and Davidson gained collaboration from the juvenile court system. Maccoby and Alexander were accepted by the media and the medical professionals in the three communities. Most of these studies received grant support, which implies that they went through a peer-review process and were found to be fundable.

It is a compliment for each of our contributors that they were able to receive the help needed so their research enterprise could expand. The multifaceted properties of such research projects certainly dictated that they could not be done by one person. It is essential, therefore, that such research be done by persons who have the commitment and capacity to seek out cordial, reciprocal relationships.

During our interactions with the researchers included in this book, we have noticed certain styles and attitudes that appear to have been useful in their work. We address these factors in the following section.

Theme Three: Personal Characteristics.   The most evident characteristic among the contributors is a clear commitment of time and energy. Flexibility ranks a close second. And, two attitudes that capture their philosophy are the active belief that people can use new ideas if given the chance and that science and social action can blend in a manner that benefits both.

The amount of time and energy that went into implementing the projects described in this book is staggering. It implies not only a sense of professional commitment but also of personal commitment; it is easy to imagine how the projects could have become a major part of the researchers' lives.

Leighton's chapter presents conspicuous evidence of decades devoted to this longitudinal epidemiological study. In addition to the calendar time, one is aware of the involvement of the research staff with the community to ensure that the epidemiological data were interpreted within their social context, thus creating an in-depth portrait of the community's development.

Maccoby and Alexander portray their commitment to the project when, having become cognizant of the original oversight of the Spanish-speaking population, they devote significant energy to obtaining funds and staffing to fulfill both their scientific and humanistic goals.

Fairweather, Moos, and Shure illustrate persistence and follow-through. Their work unfolds steadily and with purpose. There is a thread that clearly connects their efforts through time and gives witness to the importance they place on their work. Fairweather starts with an alternative to hospitalization and pursues his innovation well into the dissemination phase. Moos expands his study of social environments across a number of settings: classrooms, hospital wards, work settings, families, and so on. Shure begins with a theoretical study, devises an intervention, does a pilot study, moves to more classrooms, and then involves teachers, the school system, and the mothers.

Holahan and Rappaport convey a sense of conceptual follow-through. Holahan rethinks the process he experienced and creates a framework for describing stages of intervention. Rappaport wrestles with the changes that occur in one's intervention after one has bequeathed it to a community agency. Todd and Gottlieb share the uncertainty of attempting to study a tough problem from the beginning, of trying untested approaches, and of beginning a research track for themselves that may or may not prove fruitful.

The subjective feeling we found after interviewing these researchers was one of enthusiasm. Their commitment of time and energy is reflected in the way they think about their work. They find the questions they are trying to answer significant and worthy of discussion, and they convey a sense of curiosity and eagerness to test their ideas.

The characteristic flexibility of these researchers has been alluded to before. There is a decided flavor of give and take in dealing with their target communities, with neither a sense of being in control nor of being controlled by them but rather an interactional process in which both goals and methods are subject to modification. This kind of flexibility could also be described as creativity. The perspective these scientists have appears to be one of continued creative engagement with the evolving conditions in the field. They do experience changes and obstacles as frustrating events, of course, but they are able to surmount them and push forward.

Paradoxically, this flexibility is found within self-imposed boundaries. Certain conditions are nonnegotiable. The boundaries are defined by practical and theoretical interests, by value systems, and by personal priorities. Within this finite space, however, one perceives a facility to maneuver freely. Without this flexibility, it is doubtful that any of these projects could have been done.

Although none of the researchers explicitly stated this belief, their work is implicitly based on the optimistic notion that people can use knowledge to better their lot. There is little cynicism or defeatism evident in our contributors on this matter. Shure is confident that teaching children to think and solve problems can provide them with opportunities for growth and development. Maccoby and Alexander are convinced that media can be used to teach skills that can have a significant impact on people's lives. Rappaport, Seidman, and Davidson show that a different approach to juvenile law enforcement can avoid certain undesirable effects. Moos hopes that, by being able to capture the essence of environmental differences, we may be able to understand and possibly prevent their negative influences. Holahan expresses obvious pleasure in seeing that mental patients could understand the benefits of changing the physical environment and that staff could also see opportunities for positive change. Fairweather, Leighton, Todd, and Gottlieb share the idea that the context in which people live can affect their functioning and that beneficial contexts can be consciously encouraged.

This optimistic existential stance toward life is supplemented with the attitude that scientific methods can help humanity to discover and evaluate the most effective and efficient methods for its continued well-being. It is here, perhaps, that our contributors most clearly demonstrate the added dimensions that bring social action into the realm of social science. Their work in the service of communities is a clear example of social action. Their commitment to integrate research components into the very fabric of their endeavors identifies them as scientists and researchers.

Each chapter depicts the struggle to maintain a conscious balance between developing research procedures to create knowledge or to benefit participants. Attention was focused on minimizing spurious factors that could limit the interpretations of the research. But this was done away from strict laboratory conditions. By placing themselves in a social context, they forced themselves to adapt to the needs of the people with whom they worked. Thus, these researchers stand distinctly apart from investigators who are interested in creating knowledge but do not attend to impact. In fact, impact on people's lives is one of their major goals. Without always expressing it, the contributors are in agreement with Fairweather in the belief that, over the long haul, the best insurance for lasting influence is to do good research—research that will stand up to the criticism of interested colleagues. We believe that this faith in scientific method has been a powerful force in anchoring each of the research contributions in this book.

The Differences

From the many ways in which the contributions differ, we have chosen to underline five. These issues form continuums, along which the contributions fall. We shall describe the ends of each continuum and exemplify portions of it using the projects in the book.

Development of the Intervention.   Some researchers approach the community with a package, which they have reason to think can benefit its people. They see their work as testing the package and, if it shows promise, disseminating it. Shure's interpersonal problem-solving course; Rappaport, Seidman, and Davidson's juvenile court diversion project; and Fairweather's lodge are such packages. At the other end of the continuum are researchers who have no package but are conducting exploratory studies and evolve their interventions from the resulting interaction. Gottlieb's work with mothers and Leighton's efforts in The Road approach this end of the continuum.

Any project may very well develop from an almost intuitive grasp of a situation to ideas about improving it to a well-thought-out plan to do so efficiently. The danger of having such a plan is that of creating a false aura of wisdom and power, when many of the key factors are outside the realm of influence of the research. The benefits include the possibility of testing a specific program and thus being able to determine its effectiveness and being able to export it to other settings.

The dangers of evolutionary interventions are the lack of goal clarity on the part of both researchers and participants and the possibility of similarly unclear evaluation of one's efforts. Benefits include the potential for truly innovative interventions, which address precisely the needs of the community in question.

The Role of Participants in the Research Process.   The issue of decision-making power in community work is continually a source of controversy. One can imagine two extremes. At one extreme, communities can charge social scientists with carrying out their wishes, and final decision-making power remains with the community. At the second extreme, social scientists can place individuals in experimental conditions as required by their research designs without need to consult with them or inform them of their ultimate goals (this is standard practice in laboratory studies). Neither extreme is represented in this book. However, final decision-making regarding the experimental design is generally kept by the researchers. Fairweather, to be sure, counsels that a tripartite group be involved in specifying the intervention plans, but his goal is not to have this group decide how the experiment will be carried out but rather to help them understand what can be learned from such a method so that they can evaluate the intervention.

The pros and cons of the arguments involve such questions as: Will more involvement by the community in shaping the area of study, the format, the procedures, and the variables lead to greater immediate utility of the results? Would such a process reduce a study's wider theoretical appeal by tailoring the intervention too closely to local conditions? The obvious factor of having training in research techniques gives the investigator a greater duty to ensure quality work. If he or she must make final decisions, it may be confusing to present oneself as an open, compliant, and egalitarian resource.

From a purely descriptive point of view, it appears that social scientists will spend their time and energy doing what they find interesting. It may be futile to suggest that they take on the goals or interests of community groups, unless they are somehow identified with such groups. (This is one argument for advanced training of more members of minorities and other disenfranchised groups.) Perhaps, as the benefits of such work become more widely known, more communities will consider hiring social scientists to research carefully the areas decided on by their people. And, as such work gains recognition, perhaps good community-originated research articles will start appearing in our journals.

Experimental Versus Nonexperimental Designs. The controversy surrounding the necessity of using strictly experimental designs finds a natural arena in community-based research. The practical hurdles needed to carry out any kind of study serve to temper the enthusiasm for control-group random-assignment studies: Maccoby and Alexander, for example, inform us that they attempted to find ways to assign matched towns randomly for follow-up work in heart-disease prevention. They were able to show that this could not be done within California.

Yet, we have adherents of the true experiment even here. Fairweather was able to apply these methods both to the lodge and to the subsequent dissemination study. His preference for this method and his success in using it serve as a clear challenge to other researchers to follow his lead. Shure and Rappaport also were able to carry out this task.

When the question became one of doing a non- or quasi-experimental study or not doing a research study at all, most of our contributors chose to go ahead and obtain what information they could, given their limitations. They chose to study their interventions with limited methods rather than limit their interventions to those their methods could evaluate comfortably.

Use of Well-Developed Methods.   A similar question is at issue here: Should researchers wait until their instruments have been thoroughly tested before using them in the field, or should they improvise while intervening? Moos is the clearest example of the former side of the question. His efforts have been primarily focused on the development of his scales. He has consciously chosen to let others use them as tools for change. Maccoby and Alexander, although they pretested their media spots, engage in formative assessment of their campaign. Through the use of short surveys, they are able to modify their messages to increase effectiveness during the intervention phase. Todd and Gottlieb present the most open-ended approach, wherein the participants help develop the questions to be considered. Although the differences are partly due to the subject matter the investigators are dealing with, the deciding factor appears to be the relative commitment they have to well-validated tools versus immediate impact.

Documentation of Unintended Effects.   The breadth of the information-gathering process is a widely varying factor in the eight projects. The question here is whether a researcher should focus on very few variables or whether he or she should cast a wide net and note the positive and negative unintended effects of the project.

Documenting side effects requires a research staff to demonstrate qualities and interests more identified with journalistic or anthropological work than with psychological research. Issues of inference arise; there are added costs of time and money, and the risks may outweigh the benefits. If the research staff does not attend to side effects and does achieve the intended goals, it becomes possible to speak with authority; there are no other sources of information to question the validity of the findings. The investigator who takes the added responsibility of systematically studying other trends in the community provides more possibilities to question the data. Factors beyond research variables, such as social or political forces, can be viewed as sources of impact. This revelation can be disheartening to the ambitious social scientist.

The studies that attended to unplanned occurrences have a vivid tone, which speaks for doing so more often. Leighton's account of the processes occurring in The Road exemplifies this exploratory style and provides a rich source of hypotheses regarding the remarkable change. Rappaport, Seidman, and Davidson were able to address the issue of agency modifications of their project (manifest adoption) after their involvement ended by continuing to monitor it.

The final decision, as in most of these cases, will be a compromise between reality constraints and scientific values. By pointing out the possible stances one might take, future researchers will be able to choose consciously to act according to one or the other of these dicta and to know the pros and cons of their decision.

Varied Perspectives About Social Contexts

The distinctive characteristic of the research projects featured in this book is their engagement with social contexts outside laboratory settings. All the researchers had to deal with their respective social environments. In some cases, this interaction was an integral part of their work, and whatever effect it had was part of their intervention. In other cases, it was a necessary prerequisite to being allowed to intervene. Whether as a target of their efforts or as a broader milieu in which they functioned, the social context was seen in somewhat different ways by each researcher.

To better appreciate these varied viewpoints, let us examine the levels of interaction present in the studies. There are four distinguishable levels: persons, settings, systems, and communities. Although most social and community interventions probably touch on every level, they emphasize one or another as their primary target. For example, Shure had to deal with community events, the school system, and classroom settings, but her primary target for change was the individual student's ability to solve interpersonal problems—that is, the level of *persons*. Similarly, Rappaport, Seidman, and Davidson were attempting to divert teenagers from the judicial system. In both cases, the intent was to show how a certain specifiable intervention could produce beneficial results for individuals. These interventions were, at least initially, suggested as viable and possibly superior alternatives to existing ones, but the focus was not on basically altering the system within which the alternatives could exist.

Settings are the explicit research targets chosen by Moos. His goal is to develop valid and reliable methods to quantify the characteristics of environments. His level of analysis is definitely not that of individuals. And he interacts with systems (such as the school system) merely as a way to gain access to specific settings. Holahan focuses his intervention on modifying a particular setting, an inpatient ward. And Fairweather goes as far as creating a setting—the lodge—as his intervention. Whether measuring, changing, or creating a setting, these researchers choose to focus their attention on the influence of the environment—be it the social or the built environment—on its inhabitants rather than on teaching individuals specific skills.

The level of *systems* is addressed in the dissemination phase of Fairweather's chapter. His focus is on identifying variables that increase the probability of implementation of an innovation (in this case, the lodge) in U. S. hospital systems. The breadth of his intervention and its experimental rigor show how our methods can be of value in public policy. Todd and Gottlieb give us an example of researching informal systems—in this case, the elusive system of social supports. Here, we are not examining specific procedures or geographical or structured settings. Rather, we are looking at the yet nonspecific forces that lead to the formation of support systems and maintain actively nurturing informal ties. In both chapters, the formal or informal rules regarding growth and change are the focus of study.

The *community* as the social context is perhaps most directly targeted for intervention by Maccoby and Alexander. Although their approach is primarily individual skill-learning, they are interested in producing and assessing impact on the populations of entire towns. To do so, they have to collaborate with certain systems within the towns, such as the mass media, the existing health-care providers, and the Spanish-speaking cultural structures. But their efforts with such systems are designed primarily to gain access to the community at large. Leighton's chapter also describes a study in which the level of analysis is an entire community, in this case The

Road. Her interview describes the degree of intense encounter that the Stirling County staff experienced with their participants. The tone one receives from her account is one of allowing the communities' reality to permeate the investigators. Filled with both quantifiable and nonquantified information, the investigators responded in an improvised way to the needs they saw. Whether or not their limited intervention significantly affected the outcome, their long-range commitment to studying the county's mental health status allowed them to document a significant change in The Road. Both of these studies used epidemiological methods to measure change. Maccoby and Alexander tapped very specific behavioral, physiological, and risk factors. Leighton looked at more global mental health indexes. Both approaches show how community-wide interventions could be monitored and evaluated.

The eight projects we have examined exemplify four levels of engagement with the social context: persons, settings, systems, and communities. Although all these levels must be considered when engaging in social and community interventions, the researcher can make more efficient use of resources by consciously deciding which level he or she wants to affect.

Beyond the Present State of the Art

What is needed to improve research-oriented community interventions? A manifest concern should be to produce more of them. Perhaps owing to the complexities of social contexts, the steep requirements for support, and the demand for varied personal qualities, projects like those featured in this book are rare. As the number of projects increases, community psychologists will not only have an added number of valid interventions but also an expanded base of experience to identify the issues in carrying out such interventions. As the number of projects increases, analysts will be better able to appraise the strengths and weaknesses of distinct approaches.

Reflection on the present group of projects suggests several matters that bear further thought and study. First is the question of implementation. As we have seen in the presentations of Fairweather and Rappaport, Seidman, and Davidson, successfully installing proven interventions is not the self-evident process it perhaps was initially thought to be. We shall analyze this problem and suggest directions for further development. Second is the question of how to further our understanding of the research process. Throughout this book, we have been privy to an informal, insider's view. We should consider how these initial steps may develop into more systematic and precise accounts. Third is the question of the proper educational process for community work. And fourth is the issue of ethnic relevance. Each of these issues is developed in this concluding section.

On the frontier of community-oriented interventions lie the problems of dissemination. Fairweather has taken a major step by documenting that service systems do not embrace even proven innovations automatically and by studying empirically how to improve their chances for acceptance. However, onion-like, the problem reveals other layers. Rappaport, Seidman, and Davidson show that the idea of acceptance itself bears careful scrutiny. Adopting a set of procedures without their originating philosophy can produce unacceptable results. By contributing technology that perpetuates undesirable objectives more efficiently, implementation may backfire.

As stated earlier in this chapter, the real issue is one of ethical control and quality control versus ownership. On the one hand, innovators need to ensure that the adopted procedure is philosophically and technically true enough to original specifications that the expected effects, both ethical and empirical, are achieved. On the other hand, certain modifications may be desirable, both as accommodations to local conditions and as part of the agency's process of incorporating the intervention into its identity.

As yet unexamined is the question of changes in the agency that may result from effective implementation. Although Rappaport, Seidman, and Davidson caution us that an organization may not change enough, attaining only manifest acceptance of a new procedure, it is also possible that an organization may change too much, sacrificing in the process some essential element for its survival. Moos raised the possibility that planned organizational change might gather unplanned momentum and continue beyond the original objective. If out of control, this escalating process could become ominous. Clearly, some optimum degree of reorientation along clearly specified lines ought to be sought.

A more thorough understanding is needed of how organizations modify innovations, or assimilate them, and how organizations themselves are modified by innovations, or accommodate them. Conceivably, these processes will vary, depending on both the innovation and the organization. Such specificity would imply that particular innovations are best suited for particular organizations. In the future, this kind of information on the implementation process will help in the formulation of truly sophisticated approaches to dissemination.

A second concern for the future arises from our need to understand the research process. The discussions in this book are essentially case studies, as some contributors have noted. However, these are case studies in only a looser sense of the term, as they rely on reconstructions after the fact. A better strategy would involve incorporating at the outset formal case-study methods for exploring the process of community-based research projects. Applying more rigorous case methodology would include formulating theoretically based expectations to be tested by procedures involving measurement and control. In Chapter Seven, Charles J. Holahan partially illustrates a more explicit case-study approach. While implementing his program of ward remodeling, Holahan systematically collected data on investigator-staff transactions, meetings, role-enactment by staff, and critical incidents. Formally measuring these processes allowed Holahan to go beyond his impressions in documenting changes in ward functioning subsequent to redesign of the physical environment. Since controls were absent, it remains possible that some coincidental factor, unrelated to the process of redesigning the ward, produced the observed results. Nevertheless, Holahan's use of empirical indicators enables us to conclude with confidence that change did occur.

To establish that the observed change was more than just coincidence, quasi-experimental and case-study methodology may play an enlightening role. For example, if feasible, measuring of social processes repeatedly before and after the experimental intervention would provide the increased margin of control associated with time-series analysis (Cook and Campbell, 1975). An alternative appears, if the investigator can specify a social process that will be unaffected by the experimental intervention. Given such a social process to serve as a control, the investigator may consider the multiple-baseline design, which is part of the increasingly sophisticated methodology for the experimental study of single cases (Hersen and Barlow, 1976). When the investigator plans formal procedures of measurement and research design for studying the research process, he or she has moved toward a more rigorous approach to the case study. Another important step in this direction is to formulate the expected changes in accordance with social theory. Again, Holahan has pointed the way in his application of Lewinian principles of organizational change to explain a social reaction to his intervention. At some point, investigators may be confident enough in their knowledge of theoretical mechanisms to formulate hypotheses beforehand.

The particular innovations suggested here may be found to be unfeasible. Whatever procedures do indeed prove useful will originate in an orientation that takes seriously the idea of community-based research as an opportunity for case study. Encouraging this proactive, systematic stance is a major goal of this discussion.

Many educational issues were mentioned in the chapters. Interdisciplinary efforts are explicitly described by Maccoby and Alexander and by Dorothea Leighton. In both cases, the authors point out the need to abandon the defensive posture common to newly recruited researchers in favor of truly cooperative efforts, in which disciplinary orientations are subordinated to common project objectives. Experience in such arrangements seems to be the best predictor of adequate performance. This raises the possibility of making training in community-oriented fields include placements with professionals of at least one other discipline. In addition, the usual indoctrination into the paradigms and theoretical biases of one's profession should be consciously tempered to reduce disciplinary chauvinism.

The need for projects that can be done within the demands of undergraduate academic life are exemplified by the work of Rappaport, Seidman, and Davidson as well as that of Gottlieb and Todd. The secret seems to be short-term tasks within ongoing faculty research programs in which the students are true project participants and not only observers or extemporaneous experimenters. Longer-lasting projects can easily absorb graduate student or trainee participation. In addition to the two projects already men-

tioned, the Stirling County study was a source of many disserta-
tions. Careful preparation by the professor can make good use of
the great source of energy and commitment in students who want
to get involved in real-life nonlaboratory research.

The advisability of providing more postdoctoral opportunities is exemplified by Holahan's project, which was implemented during such a fellowship. Unfettered by either academic or job requirements, a trained investigator is able to devote
full time to an in-depth project. The special need for such time
investment is particularly crucial in community projects, where
time and geographical boundaries are often outside the researcher's control.

The investigators, particularly during the interviews, revealed commonly shared opinions when educating new investigators to carry out community-based research. For example, the
investigators emphasized the value of formal course work in logic
and the inductive and deductive processes involved in conceptualizing and designing research. They also encouraged in-depth attention to the study of the philosophy of science. Here, the investigators were pointing to an informed appreciation for the varied
approaches to scientific inquiry, so that, during the educational
period, the assumptions of different modes of scientific inquiry
can be grasped without sanctioning any one mode as the principal mode.

All the investigators emphasized, applauded, and advocated
the validity of deep and concentrated work experiences in community settings. They share a strong belief that any learning experience that is not intensive and does not take place within social
contexts outside the university laboratory will not be instructive for
the research topic or the development of the investigator's research
career. They also pointed out that new and aspiring investigators
require a collaborative learning relationship with senior investigators, particularly to experience in a supportive setting how
community research is designed, carried out, and evaluated.

There was also a shared opinion for new investigators to
become competent in the use of several research methods. The
contributors to this book agreed that, in doing community research, the investigator must learn to fit the method to the topic
and the context. If research methods are only contrived to fit a

particular topic, there is a compensating loss in both clarity and the utility of the research. Some of the investigators, in addition, personally valued the opportunities that multidisciplinary research gave them to expand their vision of methods and concepts and to understand better the intricacies and complexities of research, where the topics of community research go beyond the discipline of psychology. Other investigators added the observation that the design of community-oriented action research is conjoined with directing change. The research topic and the design of research must be conceived as a program of planned change. All these comments point to the axiom that, when empirical inquiry is carried out within a community, the research must be organic to the various social contexts, requiring the adaptation of both research methods and social processes to increase the level of impact.

A final issue is that of ethnic relevence. This issue is most directly addressed by Maccoby and Alexander. Their experience with first neglecting and then actively seeking to adapt their messages to Spanish-speaking populations is a case study on the importance of having assertive advocates within the decision-making ranks. The very existence of the issue is a sign of health within the research group, especially since the change in plans occurred as a result of internal and not external pressure. It should be emphasized here that Alexander's espousal of a Spanish-language campaign was not based solely on social consciousness but also on scientific grounds. That about 30 percent of their town's population was Spanish-speaking necessitated taking this factor into account in designing the project. This type of intellectual honesty is difficult to maintain in the face of limited financial support and impending deadlines. We hope that, as more top researchers actively respond to their communities' cultural realities, this issue will no longer be seen merely as a desirable addendum but rather as an essential part of the research design.

Minority professionals need to be attracted to research-oriented community work. At present, our feeling is that direct services and social-change efforts at the political level are the main focus of minority mental health personnel. Unless community psychology show that the community-research process can be beneficial to underrepresented groups, their efforts will not be shifted in that direction. Hopefully, minority researchers in the field will come to the forefront in evaluating whether this is a worthwhile use of their energies. We also hope that the examples in this book show the potential of this area of endeavor to identify, measure, and document change in community strengths and community problems. The paradigms demonstrated by such researchers as Fairweather, in testing specific interventions and then testing specific dissemination strategies, seem particularly relevant to the struggles of minorities. It would be particularly apt if these scientific methods could be used to make solid gains in living conditions for those who lack access to the resources of our society.

We have been impressed by the tenacity, originality, and improvisational ability of our contributors. Their personal commitment to breaking new ground in both research methodology and in social action has been impressive. Our contributors have also created new insights about the social processes of doing research. We hope that the individual chapters, supplemented by personal commentary, will give both encouragement and guidance for continued efforts to bridge the relationship between research and action.

Throughout these chapters, the technical difficulties, frustrations, setbacks, and ego-deflating bumps are readily apparent, but the satisfactions, the learnings, and the personal and social integration resulting from such research are a major source of health and growth. Pursuing research with a goal toward impact, as these contributors have exemplified, involves designing a new role for oneself and for one's clients. We hope that we have shown how these newly emerging styles of research can be rewarding for the investigator, the citizens, and the social institutions, and help us to better understand and bring about change.

References

Alden, L. "Factor Analysis of the Ward Atmosphere Scale." *Journal of Consulting and Clinical Psychology,* 1978, *46,* 175–176.

Alden, L., Rappaport, J., and Seidman, E. "College Students as Interventionists for Primary Grade Children: A Comparison of Structured Academic and Companionship Programs for Children from Low-Income Families." *American Journal of Community Psychology,* 1975, *3,* 261–271.

Alderfer, C. P. "Organizational Development." *Annual Review of Psychology,* 1977, *28,* 197–223.

Allen, G., and others. *Community Psychology and the Schools: A Behaviorally-Oriented Multilevel Preventive Approach.* Hillside, N.J.: Earlbaum, 1976.

Altrocchi, J. "Mental Health Consultation." In S. Golann and C. Eisdorfer (Eds.), *Handbook of Community Mental Health.* Englewood Cliffs, N.J.: Prentice-Hall, 1972.

American Heart Association. *Heart Facts.* Dallas, Tex.: American Heart Association, 1972.

Ayllon, T., and Azrin, N. *The Token Economy: A Motivational System for Therapy and Rehabilitation.* New York: Appleton-Century-Crofts, 1968.

Bailey, K. D. *Methods of Social Research.* New York: Free Press, 1978.

Bandura, A. *Principles of Behavior Modification.* New York: Holt, Rinehart and Winston, 1969.

Bandura, A. *Social Learning Theory.* Morristown, N.J.: General Learning Press, 1971.

Bandura, A. "The Self System in Reciprocal Determinism." *The American Psychologist,* 1978, *33,* 344–358.

Barker, R. G. "Explorations in Ecological Psychology." *American Psychologist,* 1965, *20,* 1–14.

Barnes, J. A. *Social Networks.* Reading, Mass.: Addison-Wesley, 1972.

Barnett, H. D. *Innovation: The Basis of Cultural Change.* New York: McGraw-Hill, 1953.

Bateson, G. *Steps to an Ecology of Mind.* New York: Chandler, 1972.

Bauer, R. "The Obstinate Audience: The Influence Process from the Point of View of Social Communications." *American Psychologist,* 1964, *19,* 319–328.

Bentler, P. M., Jackson, D. N., and Messick, S. "Identification of Content and Style: A Two-Dimensional Interpretation of Acquiescence." *Psychological Bulletin,* 1971, *76,* 186–204.

Berman, E. "Social Networks, Support and Coping in Older Students." Unpublished senior honors thesis, University of Massachusetts at Amherst, 1977.

Bliss, F., Moos, R., and Bromet, E. "Monitoring Change in Community-Oriented Treatment Programs." *Journal of Community Psychology,* 1976, *4,* 315–326.

Bloom, L. "Commentary." *Monographs of the Society for Research in Child Development,* 1974, *39,* 82–88.

Bott, E. *Family and Social Network.* New York: Free Press, 1971.

Brennan, G. T. "Work/Life Segmentation and Human Service Professionals: A Social Network Approach." Unpublished doctoral dissertation, University of Massachusetts at Amherst, 1977.

Bromet, E., and Moos, R. "Environmental Resources and the Posttreatment Functioning of Alcoholic Patients." *Journal of Health and Social Behavior,* 1977, *18,* 326–338.

Bronfenbrenner, U. "Toward an Experimental Ecology of Human Development." *American Psychologist.* 1977, *32,* 513–531.

Bross, I. D. G. "How to Use Ridit Analysis." *Biometrics,* 1958, *14,* 18–38.

Buros, O. K. "Fifty Years in Testing: Some Reminiscences, Criticisms and Suggestions." *Educational Researcher,* 1977, *6,* 9–15.

Camp, B. N., and Bash, M. A. *Think Aloud Program Group Manual.* Boulder: University of Colorado Medical Center, 1975. (Available from the authors at 4200 E. 9th Avenue, Denver, Colo. 80220.)

Campbell, D. T., and Stanley, J. C. *Experimental and Quasi-Experimental Designs for Research.* Chicago: Rand McNally, 1966.

Caplan, N., and Nelson, S. D. "On Being Useful: The Nature and Consequences of Psychological Research in Social Problems." *American Psychologist,* 1973, *28,* 199–211.

Caplan, S., and Grunebaum, H. "Perspectives on Primary Prevention: A Review." In H. Gottesfeld (Ed.), *The Critical Issues of Community Mental Health.* New York: Behavioral Publications, 1972.

Cartwright, D. "Some Principles of Mass Persuasion." *Human Relations,* 1949, *2,* 319–328.

Cherniss, C. "The Consultation Readiness Scale: An Attempt to Improve Consultation Practice." *American Journal of Community Psychology,* 1978, *1,* 15–21.

Cobb, S. "Social Support as a Moderator of Life Stress." *Psychosomatic Medicine,* 1976, *38,* 300–314.

Coché, E., and Flick, A. "Problem Solving Training Groups for Hospitalized Psychiatric Patients." *Journal of Psychology,* 1975, *91,* 19–29.

Cohen, S., Glass, D., and Phillips, S. "Environment and Health." In H. Freeman, S. Levine, and L. Reeder (Eds.), *Handbook of Medical Sociology.* Englewood Cliffs, N.J.: Prentice-Hall, 1977.

Cook, T. D., and Campbell, D. T. "The Design and Conduct of Quasi-Experiments and True Experiments in Field Settings." In M. D. Dunnette (Ed.), *Handbook of Industrial and Organizational Psychology.* Chicago: Rand McNally, 1976.

Cooper, L. "Staff Attitudes About Ideal Wards Before and After Program Change." *Journal of Community Psychology,* 1973, *1,* 82–83.

Corwin, R. "Strategies for Organizational Innovation: An Empirical Comparison." *American Sociological Review,* 1972, *37,* 441–454.

Cowen, E. L. "Social and Community Interventions." *Annual Review of Psychology,* 1973, *24,* 423–472.

Cowen, E. L., Lorian, R. P., and Dorr, D. "Research in the Community Cauldron: A Case History." *The Canadian Psychologist,* 1974, *15,* 313–325.

Craven, P., and Wellman, B. "The Network City." *Sociological Inquiry,* 1973, *43,* 57–88.

Curtiss, S. "The Compatibility of Humanistic and Behavioristic Approaches in a State Mental Hospital." In A. Wandersman, P. Poppen, and D. Ricks (Eds.), *Humanism and Behaviorism: Dialogue and Growth.* Elmsford, N.Y.: Pergamon Press, 1976.

Daher, D., Corazzini, J., and McKinnon, R. "An Environmental Redesign Program for Residence Halls." *Journal of College Student Personnel,* 1977, *18,* 11–15.

Davidson, W. S., and Rapp, C. "Child Advocacy in the Justice System." *Social Work,* 1976, *23,* 225–232.

Davidson, W. S., and Rappaport, J. "Toward a Model for Advocacy: Values, Roles, and Conceptions from Community Psychology." In G. H. Weber and G. J. McCall (Eds.), *Social Scientists as Advocates: Views From Applied Disciplines.* Beverly Hills, Calif.: Sage, 1978.

Davidson, W. S., and others. "Diversion of Juvenile Offenders: Some Empirical Light on the Subject." *Social Work Research and Abstracts,* 1977, *1,* 40–49.

DeShong, B. "Student Involvement in University Policy Groups and Resultant Attitude Change." *Research in Higher Education,* 1976, *4,* 185–192.

DeYoung, A. "Classroom Climate and Class Success: A Case Study at the University Level." *Journal of Educational Research,* 1977, *70,* 252–257.

Dorr, D. "Division 27 Growth and Attrition Trends." *American Journal of Community Psychology,* 1977, *5,* 491–499.

Dworkin, A. L., and Dworkin, E. P. "A Conceptual Overview of Selected Consultation Models." *American Journal of Community Psychology,* 1975, *3,* 151–159.

Edelson, R., and Paul, G. "Staff 'Attitude' and 'Atmosphere' Scores as a Function of Ward Size and Patient Chronicity." *Journal of Consulting and Clinical Psychology,* 1977, *45,* 874–884.

Eichel, E. "Assessment with a Family Focus." *Journal of Psychiatric Nursing and Mental Health Services,* 1978, *16,* 11–15.

Elardo, P. T., and Cooper, M. *Project Aware: A Handbook for Teachers.* Reading, Mass.: Addison-Wesley, 1977.

Ellsworth, R. "Consumer Feedback in Measuring the Effectiveness of Mental Health Programs." In M. Guttentag and E. Struening (Eds.), *Handbook of Evaluation Research.* Vol. 2. Beverly Hills, Calif.: Sage, 1975.

Espvall, M., and Astrom, M. "A Study of the Ward Atmosphere in a Psychiatric Unit for Short-Term Treatment." *Acta Psychiatrica Scandanavia,* 1974, *255,* 309–317.

Fairweather, G. W. (Ed). *Social Psychology in Treating Mental Illness: An Experimental Approach.* New York: Wiley, 1964.

Fairweather, G. W. *Methods for Experimental Social Innovation.* New York: Wiley, 1967.

Fairweather, G. W. *Social Change: The Challenge to Survival.* Morristown, N.J.: General Learning Press, 1972.

Fairweather, G. W., Sanders, D. H., and Tornatzky, L. G. *Creating Change in Mental Health Organizations.* Elmsford, N.Y.: Pergamon Press, 1974.

Fairweather, G. W., and Tornatzky, L. G. *Experimental Methods for Social Policy Research.* Elmsford, N.Y.: Pergamon Press, 1977.

Fairweather, G. W., and others. *Community Life for the Mentally Ill: An Alternative to Institutional Care.* Chicago: Aldine, 1969.

Fairweather, G. W., and others. "Relative Effectiveness of Psychotherapeutic Programs: A Multicriteria Comparison of Four Programs for Three Different Groups." *Psychological Monograph,* 1960, *74* (entire issue).

Farquhar, J. W. "The Community-Based Model of Life-style Intervention Trials." *American Journal of Epidemiology,* 1978, *108,* 103–111.

Farquhar, J. W., and others. "Community Education for Cardiovascular Health." *The Lancet,* 1977, *4,* 1192–1195.

Freymann, J. G. "Medicine's Great Schism: Prevention vs. Cure: An Historical Interpretation." *Medical Care,* 1975, *13,* 525–536.

Friis, S. *Evaluation of a Therapeutic Milieu in a Psychiatric Hospital.* Bergen, Norway: Psykiatrisk Institutit, Neevengarden, Sykelus, Universitetet i Bergen, 1974.

Fullan, M., and Pomfret, A. "Research on Curriculum and Instruction Implementation." *Review of Educational Research,* 1977, *47,* 335–397.

Gelinas, D. "Support Development Issues During Life Transitions: Bereavement of Young Adults." Paper presented at 85th annual meeting of the American Psychological Association, Chicago, Sept. 1975.

Gergen, K. J. "Social Psychology as History." *Journal of Personality and Social Psychology,* 1973, *26,* 309–320.

Gergen, K. J. "Social Psychology, Science, and History." *Personality and Social Psychology Bulletin,* 1976, *2,* 373–383.

Gesten, E., and others. "Peer Related Social Competence in School: The Development of Social Problem Solving." Paper presented at the 3rd Vermont Conference on the Primary Prevention of Psychopathology: Promoting Social Competence and Coping in Children, Burlington, June 1977.

Glaser, B. G., and Strauss, A. L. *The Discovery of Grounded Theory: Strategies for Qualitative Research.* Chicago: Aldine, 1967.

Glaser, E. M., and Taylor, S. H. "Factors Influencing the Success of Applied Research." *American Psychologist,* 1973, *28,* 140–146.

Glass, D., Snyder, M., and Hollis, J. "Time Urgency and Type A Coronary Prone Behavior Pattern." *Journal of Applied Social Psychology,* 1974, *4,* 125–140.

Goffman, E. "Asylums: Essays on the Social Situation of Mental Patients and Other Inmates." New York: Anchor, 1961.

Gold, M. *Delinquent Behavior in an American City.* Belmont, Calif.: Brooks/Cole, 1970.

Goldenberg, I. I. "The Relationships of the University to the Community: Implications for Community Mental Health Programs." In H. E. Mitchell (Ed.), *The University and the Urban Crisis.* New York: Behavioral Publications, 1974.

Gomes-Schwartz, B., Hadley, S. W., and Strupp, H. "Individual Psychotherapy and Behavior Therapy." *Annual Review of Psychology,* 1978, *29,* 435–471.

Gottlieb, B. H. "The Development and Application of a Classification Scheme of Informal Helping Behaviors." *Canadian Journal of Behavioural Science,* 1978, *10,* 105–115.

Gouldner, A. W. "Anti-Minotour: The Myth of a Value-Free Sociology." In W. G. Bennis, K. D. Benne, and R. Chin (Eds.), *The Planning of Change,* New York: Holt, Rinehart and Winston, 1961.

Griffiths, W., and Knutson, A. L. "The Role of Mass Media in Public Health." *American Journal of Public Health,* 1960, *50,* 4.

Gripp, R., and Magaro, P. "A Token Economy Program Evaluation with Untreated Control Ward Comparisons." *Behavior Research and Therapy,* 1971, *9,* 137–139.

Gruver, G. G. "College Students as Therapeutic Agents." *Psychological Bulletin,* 1971, *76,* 111–127.

Gurel, L. "The Human Side of Evaluating Human Services Programs: Problems and Prospects." In M. Guttentag and E. Struening (Eds.), *Handbook of Evaluation Research.* Vol. 2. Beverly Hills, Calif.: Sage, 1975.

Hall, G., and Loucks, S. "A Developmental Model for Determining Whether the Treatment is Actually Implemented." *American Educational Research Journal,* 1977, *14,* 293–305.

Hatch, F. T. "Atherosclerosis Calls for a New Kind of Preventive Medicine." *California Medicine,* 1968, *109,* 134.

Havelock, R. G. *Planning for Innovation for Dissemination and Utilization of Knowledge.* Ann Arbor: Institute for Social Research, University of Michicagn, 1969.

Healey, R. "An Investigation of the Relationship Between Certain Cognitive Abilities and Social Behavior and the Efficacy of Training in Social Cognitive Skills for Elementary Retarded Educable Children." Unpublished doctoral dissertation, Bryn Mawr College, 1977.

Hearn, J., and Moos, R. "Social Climate and Major Choice: A Test of Holland's Theory in University Student Living Groups." *Journal of Vocational Behavior,* 1976, *8,* 293–305.

Henry, J. "The Personal Community and Its Invariant Properties." *American Anthropologist,* 1958, *60,* 827–831.

Hersen, M., and Barlow, D. H. *Single Case Experimental Designs.* Elmsford, N.Y.: Pergamon Press, 1976.

Holahan, C. "Seating Patterns and Patient Behavior in an Experimental Dayroom." *Journal of Abnormal Psychology,* 1972, *80,* 115–124.

Holahan, C. "Environmental Change in a Psychiatric Setting: A Social System Analysis." *Human Relations,* 1976, *29* (2), 153–166.

Holahan, C. *Environment and Behavior: A Dynamic Perspective.* New York: Plenum, 1978.

Hollingshead, A. B., and Redlich, F. C. *Social Class and Mental Illness: A Community Study.* N.Y.: Wiley, 1958.

Hughes, C. C., and others. *People of Cove and Woodlot: Communities from the Viewpoint of Social Psychiatry.* New York: Basic Books, 1960.

Hyman, H., and Sheatsley, P. "Some Reasons Why Information Campaigns Fail." *Public Opinion Quarterly,* 1947, *11,* 412–423.

Institute of Judicial Administration/American Bar Association. *Standards Relating to Juvenile Delinquency and Sanctions.* Cambridge, Mass.: Ballinger, 1977.

Intagliata, J. "Increasing the Interpersonal Problem Solving Effectiveness of an Alcoholic Population." Unpublished doctoral dissertation, State University of New York at Buffalo, 1976.

Inter-Society Commission for Heart Disease Resources, Atherosclerosis Study Group. "Primary Prevention of the Atherosclerotic Diseases." *Circulation,* 1970, *42,* A55–A95.

Ittelson, W. H., Proshansky, H. M., and Rivlin, L. G. "Bedroom Size and Social Interaction of the Psychiatric Ward." *Environment and Behavior,* 1970a, *2,* 255–270.

Ittelson, W. H., Proshansky, H. M., and Rivlin, L. G. "The Environmental Psychology of the Psychiatric Ward." In H. M. Proshansky, W. H. Ittelson, and L. G. Rivlin (Eds.), *Environmental Psychology: Man and His Physical Setting.* New York: Holt, Rinehart and Winston, 1970b.

Ittelson, W. H., Rivlin, L. G., and Proshansky, H. M. "The Use of Behavioral Maps in Environmental Psychology." In H. M. Proshansky, W. H. Ittelson, and L. G. Rivlin (Eds.), *Environmental Psychology: Man and His Physical Setting.* New York: Holt, Rinehart and Winston, 1970.

Izumi, K. "Psychosocial Phenomena and Building Design." *Building Research,* 1965, *2,* 9–11.

Jeger, A. "The Effects of a Behavioral Consultation Program on Consultees, Clients, and the Social Environment." Unpublished doctoral dissertation, Department of Psychology, State University of New York, Stony Brook, 1977.

Jesness, C., and others. *The Youth Center Research Project.* Sacramento, Calif.: American Justice Institute and California Youth Authority, 1972.

Kardiner, A. *The Psychological Frontiers of Society.* New York: Columbia University Press, 1945.

Katz, D., and Kahn, R. L. *The Social Psychology of Organizations.* New York: Wiley, 1966.

Katz, E., and Lazarsfeld, P. F. *Personal Influence.* New York: Free Press, 1955.

Kelly, J. G. "Toward an Ecological Conception of Preventive Interventions." In J. W. Carter, Jr. (Ed.), *Research Contributions from Psychology to Community Mental Health.* New York: Behavioral Publications, 1968.

Kelly, J. G. "The Ecology of Social Support Systems: Footnotes to a Theory." In J. Rappaport (Chair), "Toward Understanding

Natural Helping Systems." Symposium at the 87th annual meeting of the American Psychological Association, San Francisco, 1977.

Kelly, J. G., Snowden, L. R., and Muñoz, R. F. "Social and Community Interventions." *Annual Review of Psychology,* 1977, *28,* 323–361.

Kern, J. C. "Sociocultural Aspects of Poverty; Springboard for Action." *Journal of Community Psychology,* 1972, *2,* 5–10.

Kinder, S. "Coping: The Application of a Conceptual Framework to a Case Study." Unpublished master's thesis, University of Massachusetts at Amherst, 1975.

Kirschenbaum, D., and others. *Social Skills Development Programs: Handbook for Helping.* Cincinnati: Professional Services Division, Department of Health, 1977. (Available from the author at 411 Oak Street, Suite 204, Cincinnati, Ohio 45219.)

Kish, G. "Evaluation of Ward Atmosphere." *Hospital and Community Psychiatry,* 1971, *22,* 159–161.

Klapper, J. L. *The Effects of Mass Communication.* New York: Free Press, 1960.

Klein, D. "Some Notes on the Dynamics of Resistance to Change: The Defender Role." In W. G. Dennis, K. D. Benne, and R. Chin (Eds.), *The Planning of Change.* New York: Holt, Rinehart and Winston, 1969.

Kohn, M., Jeger, A., and Koretzky, M. "Social-Ecological Assessment of Environments: Toward a Two-Factor Model." *American Journal of Community Psychology,* 1979.

Ku, R., and Blew, G. (Eds.). *The Adolescent Diversion Project: A University's Approach to Delinquency Prevention.* Washington, D.C.; National Institute of Law Enforcement and Criminal Justice, 1977.

La Piere, R. T. *Social Change.* New York: McGraw-Hill, 1965.

Langer, E., and Saegert, S. "Crowding and Cognitive Control." *Journal of Personality and Social Psychology,* 1977, *35,* 175–182.

Larcen, S. W., Spivack, G., and Shure, M. "Problem-Solving Thinking and Adjustment Among Dependent-Neglected Preadolescents." Paper presented at the annual meeting of the Eastern Psychological Association, Boston, April 1972.

Lawton, P., Lipton, M., and Cohen, J. "The Mental Hospital Treatment Milieu: Parents' Perceptions and Rated Treatment Quality." Norristown, Pa.: Norristown State Hospital, 1976a.

Lawton, P., Lipton, M., and Cohen, J. "Ward Size, Staffing Pat-

terns, and the Quality of Psychiatric Treatment Environments."
Norristown, Pa.: Norristown State Hospital, 1976b.

Lawton, P., and Nahemow, L. "Ecology and the Aging Process." In
C. Eisdorfer and P. Lawton (Eds.), *The Psychology of Adult Development and Aging.* Washington, D.C.: American Psychological
Association, 1973.

Lazarus, R. S., and Cohen, J. B. "Theory and Method in the Study
of Stress and Coping." Paper presented at the 5th World Health
Organization Conference on Society, Stress, and Disease, Stockholm, Sweden, 1976.

Leavy, R., and Lekisch, H. "Support Development Groups in a
High School." Paper presented at the 85th annual meeting of
the American Psychological Association, Chicago, Sept. 1975.

Leighton, A. H. *My Name is Legion: Foundations for A Theory of Man
in Relation to Culture.* New York: Basic Books, 1959.

Leighton, D. C., and Cline, N. "Use of a Stress Scale with Mental
Hospital Patients." *North Carolina Journal of Mental Health,* 1972,
6 (4).

Leighton, D. C., and Leighton, A. H. *The Navaho Door: An Introduction to Navaho Life.* Cambridge: Harvard University Press, 1944.

Leighton, D. C., and Stone, I. T. "Community Development as a
Therapeutic Force: A Case Study with Measurements." In P. M.
Roman and H. M. Trice (Eds.), *Sociological Perspectives on Community Mental Health.* Philadelphia: Davis, 1974.

Leighton, D. C., and others. *The Character of Danger: Psychiatric
Symptoms in Selected Communities.* New York: Basic Books, 1963.

Leviege, V. "Group Relations: Group Therapy with Mentally Ill
Offenders." *Corrective Psychiatry and Journal of Social Therapy,*
1970, *16,* 15–25.

Levine, M. "Scientific Method and the Adversary Model: Some
Preliminary Thoughts." *American Psychologist,* 1974, *29,* 661–677.

Lew, E. A., and Seltzer, F. "Uses of the Life Tables in Public
Health." *Milbank Memorial Fund Quarterly,* 1970, *48,* 15.

Lewin, K. "Frontiers in Group Dynamics." *Human Relations,* 1947, *1,*
5–41.

Lindheim, R. "Factors Which Determine Hospital Design." *American Journal of Public Health,* 1966, *56,* 1668–1675.

Lippitt, R., Watson, J., and Westley, B. *The Dynamics of Planned
Change: A Comparative Study of Principles and Techniques.* New
York: Harcourt Brace Jovanovich, 1958.

McClure, L. F. "Social Problem-Solving Training and Assessment: An Experimental Intervention in an Elementary School Setting." Unpublished doctoral dissertation, University of Connecticut, Storrs, 1975.

Maccoby, N., and Farquhar, J. W. "Communication for Health: Unselling Heart Disease." *Journal of Communication,* 1975, *25* (3), 114–126.

Maccoby, N., and others. "Reducing the Risk of Cardiovascular Disease: Effects of a Community-Based Campaign on Knowledge and Behavior." *Journal of Community Health,* 1977, *3,* 100–114.

McKeachie, W. "Psychology in America's Bicentennial Year." *American Psychologist,* 1976, *31,* 819–833.

Macmillan, A. M., and Leighton, A. H. "People of the Hinterland: Community Interrelations in a Maritime Province of Canada." In. E. H. Spicer (Ed.), *Human Problems in Technological Change.* New York: Russell Sage Foundation, 1952.

Malzberg, B., and Lee, E. S. *Migration and Mental Disease.* New York: Social Science Research Council, 1956.

Manderscheid, R. W., and Koenig, G. R. "Dimensions of Classroom Psychosocial Environment." *American Journal of Community Psychology,* 1977, *5,* 299–306.

Mehan, H. "Structuring School Structure." *Harvard Educational Review,* 1978, *48,* 32–64.

Mehan, H., and Wood, H. *The Reality of Ethno-Methodology.* New York: Wiley-Interscience, 1975.

Menard, R. *Le Climat Social dans Les Equipes de Reeducation de Boscoville.* Montreal: Groupe de Recherche Sur L'Inadaptation Juvenile, University of Montreal, 1974.

Mendelsohn, H. "Some Reasons Why Information Campaigns Can Succeed." *Public Opinion Quarterly,* 1973, *37,* 50–61.

Meyer, A. *Psychobiology, A Science of Man.* (Compiled and edited by E. E. Winters and A. M. Bowers.) Springfield, Ill.: Thomas, 1957.

Meyer, A. J., and Henderson, J. B. "Multiple Risk Factor Reduction in the Prevention of Cardiovascular Disease." *Preventive Medicine,* 1974, *3,* 225–236.

Mitchell, J. C. "The Concept and Use of Social Networks." In J. C. Mitchell (Ed.), *Social Networks in Urban Situations.* Manchester, England: Manchester University Press, 1969.

Moos, R. H. *Evaluating Treatment Environments: A Social Ecological Approach.* New York: Wiley, 1974a.

Moos, R. H. *The Social Climate Scales: An Overview.* Palo Alto, Calif.: Consulting Psychologists Press, 1974b.

Moos, R. H. *Evaluating Correctional and Community Settings.* New York: Wiley, 1975.

Moos, R. H. *The Human Context: Environmental Determinants of Behavior:* New York: Wiley, 1976a.

Moos, R. H. "Evaluating and Changing Community Settings." *American Journal of Community Psychology,* 1976b, *4,* 313–326.

Moos, R. H. (Ed.). *Coping with Physical Illness.* New York: Plenum, 1977.

Moos, R. H. "A Social-Ecological Perspective on Health." In G. C. Stone, F. Cohen, and N. E. Adler (Eds.), *Health Psychology—A Handbook.* San Francisco: Jossey-Bass, 1979a.

Moos, R. H. *Evaluating Educational Environments.* San Francisco: Jossey-Bass, 1979b.

Moos, R. H., and Brownstein, R. *Environment and Utopia: A Synthesis.* New York: Plenum, 1977.

Moos, R. H., and Van Dort, B. "Student Physical Symptoms and the Social Climate of College Living Groups." *American Journal of Community Psychology,* 1979, *1,* 31–43.

Mosher, L., Menn, A., and Matthews, S. "Soteria: Evaluation of a Home-Based Treatment for Schizophrenia." *American Journal of Orthopsychiatry,* 1975, *45,* 455–467.

Munōz, R. F. "The Primary Prevention of Psychological Problems: A Review of the Literature." *Community Mental Health Review,* 1976, *1* (6), 1–15.

Murray, H. *Explorations in Personality.* New York: Oxford University Press, 1938.

Nielsen, D., and Moos, R. "Student Environment Interaction in the Development of Physical Symptoms." *Research in Higher Education,* 1977, *6,* 139–156.

O'Connor, R. D., and Rappaport, J. "Application of Social Learning Principles to the Training of Ghetto Blacks." *American Psychologist,* 1970, *25,* 659–661.

O'Keefe, M. T. "The Anti-Smoking Commercials: A Study of Television's Impact on Behavior." *Public Opinion Quarterly,* 1971, 242–248.

Osmond, H. "Function as the Basis of Psychiatric Ward Design."

Mental Hospitals, 1957, *8*, 23–30.

Pace, C., and Stern, G. "An Approach to the Measurement of Psychological Characteristics of College Environments." *Journal of Educational Psychology,* 1958, *49*, 269–277.

Paige, M. "The Impact of the Classroom Learning Environment on Individual Modernity and Academic Achievement in East Java." Unpublished doctoral dissertation, Department of Education, Stanford University, 1977.

Pike. K. L. *Language in Relation to a Unified Theory of the Structure of Human Behavior.* The Hague: Mouton, 1967.

Platt, J. J., and Spivack, G. "Studies in Problem-Solving Thinking of Psychiatric Patients: Patient-Control Differences and Factorial Structure of Problem-Solving Thinking." Paper presented at 81st annual meeting of the American Psychological Association, Montreal, 1973. *Proceedings of the American Psychological Association,* 1973, *8*, 461–462.

Platt, J. J., and Spivack, G. *Workbook for Training in Interpersonal Problem Solving Thinking.* Philadelphia: Hahnemann Community Mental Health/Mental Retardation Center, Department of Mental Health Sciences, 1976.

Platt, J. J., and others. "Adolescent Problem-Solving Thinking." *Journal of Consulting and Clinical Psychology,* 1974, *42*, 787–793.

Price, R. H., and Cherniss, C. "Training for a New Profession: Research as Social Action." *Professional Psychology,* 1977, *8*, 222–231.

Proshansky, H. M., Ittelson, W. H., and Rivlin, L. G. "Introduction." In H. M. Proshansky, W. H. Ittelson, and L. G. Rivlin (Eds.), *Environmental Psychology: Man and His Physical Setting.* New York: Holt, Rinehart and Winston, 1970.

Rappaport, J. *Community Psychology: Values, Research, and Action.* New York: Holt, Rinehart and Winston, 1977.

Rappaport, J., Lamiell, J. T., and Seidman, E. *Know and Tell: Conceptual Constraints, Ethical Issues, and Alternatives for Psychologists in (and out of) the Juvenile Justice System.* Washington, D.C.: American Psychological Association, in press.

Reppucci, N. D., and Saunders, T. J. "Social Psychology of Behavior Modification: Problems of Implementation in Natural Settings." *American Psychologist,* 1974, *29*, 649–660.

Reppucci, N. D., and Saunders, J. T. "History, Action and Change." *American Journal of Community Psychology,* 1977, *5*,

399–412.

Rieken, H. W., and Borouch, R. F. *Social Experimentation.* New York: Academic Press, 1974.

Rogers, E. M., and Shoemaker, F. F. *Communication of Innovations: A Cross Cultural Approach.* New York: Free Press, 1971.

Rokeach, M. "Long-Term Value Change Initiated by Computer Feedback." *Journal of Personality and Social Psychology,* 1975, *32,* 467–476.

Rorer, L. G. "The Great Response-Style Myth." *Psychological Bulletin,* 1965, *63,* 129–156.

Roth, W. F., Jr., and Luton, F. H. "The Mental Health Program in Tennessee." *American Journal of Psychiatry,* 1942, *99,* 662–674.

Rubenstein, K. "Client Fee Payment as an Issue for Therapists-in-Training: An Analysis of the Institution of a Fee System in a Training Clinic." Unpublished master's thesis, University of Massachusetts at Amherst, 1976.

Runkel, P. J., and McGrath, J. E. *Research on Human Behavior.* New York: Holt, Rinehart and Winston, 1972.

Rutherford, A., and McDermott, R. *National Evaluation Program Phase I Summary Report.* Washington, D.C.: National Institute of Law Enforcement and Criminal Justice, 1976.

Ryan, W. *Blaming the Victim.* New York: Random House, 1971.

Sanoff, H., and Cohn, S. "Preface." In H. Sanoff and S. Cohn (Eds.), *Proceedings of the First Annual Environmental Design Research Association Conference.* Raleigh: North Carolina State University, 1970.

Sarason, S. B. *The Creation of Settings and The Future Societies.* San Francisco: Jossey-Bass, 1972.

Sarason, S. B. "The Nature of Problem Solving in Social Action." Paper presented at the annual meeting of the Eastern Psychological Association, April 1977.

Sarata, P., and Reppucci, N. "The Problem is Outside: Staff and Client Behavior as a Function of External Events." *Community Mental Health Journal,* 1975, *11,* 91–100.

Scari, R., and Hassenfeld, Y. (Eds.). *Brought to Justice? Juveniles, the Courts and the Law.* Ann Arbor, Mich.: National Assessment of Juvenile Corrections, 1976.

Schachter, S. *The Psychology of Affiliation.* Stanford: Stanford University Press, 1959.

Schneewind, K., and Lortz, E. *Familienklima und Elterliche*

Erziehungs-Einstellungen ["Family Climate and Parental Child-rearing Attitudes"]. Forschungbericht 9, Trier, Germany: Psychology Department, University of Trier, 1976.

Schroeder, C. "Designing Ideal Staff Environment Through Milieu Management." *Journal of College Student Personnel,* 1979.

Schroeder, C., and Griffin, C. "A Novel Living-Learning Environment for Freshman Engineering Students." *Engineering Education,* 1976, *67,* 159–161.

Schulz, R., and Hanusa, B. "Long-Term Effects of Control and Predictability Enhancing Interventions: Findings and Ethical Issues." Unpublished manuscript, Department of Psychology, Carnegie Mellon University, 1978.

Schur, E. M. *Radical Non-Intervention: Rethinking the Delinquency Problem.* Englewood Cliffs, N.J.: Prentice-Hall, 1973.

Segal, S., and Aviram, U. *The Mentally Ill in Community Based Sheltered Care: A Study of Community Care and Social Integration.* New York: Wiley, 1978.

Seidman, E. "Steps Toward the Development of Useful Social and Public Policies." Paper presented at the interdisciplinary faculty seminar on Public Policy in Industrialized Countries, University of Illinois at Urbana-Champaign, Sept. 1976.

Seidman, E. "Justice, Values and Social Science: Unexamined Premises." In R. J. Simon (Ed.), *Research in Law and Sociology.* Vol. 1. Greenwich, Conn.: JAI Press, 1978.

Seidman, E., and Rappaport, J. "The Educational Pyramid: A Paradigm for Research, Training, and Manpower Utilization in Community Psychology." *American Journal of Community Psychology,* 1974, *2,* 119–130.

Seidman, E., Rappaport, J., and Davidson, W. S. "Adolescents in Legal Jeopardy: Initial Success and Replication of an Alternative to the Criminal Justice System." Address to the American Psychological Association, 1976.

Seidman, E., Rappaport, J., Davidson, W. S., and Linney, J. *Changing Human Service Systems: Interventions with Children, Adults, and the Elderly.* In press.

Shure, M. B., Newman, S., and Silver, S. "Problem-Solving Thinking Among Adjusted, Impulsive, and Inhibited Head Start Children." Paper presented at annual meeting of the Eastern Psychological Association, Washington, D.C., April 1973.

Shure, M. B., and Spivack, G. "Cognitive Problem Solving Skills,

Adjustment and Social Class." Research Evaluation Report No. 26. Philadelphia: Department of Mental Health Sciences, Hahnemann Community Mental Health/Mental Retardation Center, 1970a.

Shure, M. B., and Spivack, G. "Problem Solving Capacity, Social Class and Adjustment Among Nursery School Children." Paper presented at annual meeting of the Eastern Psychological Association, Atlantic City, 1970b.

Shure, M. B., and Spivack, G. "Means-Ends Thinking, Adjustment and Social Class Among Elementary School-Aged Children." *Journal of Consulting and Clinical Psychology,* 1972, *38,* 348–353.

Shure, M. B., and Spivack, G. *A Mental Health Program for Kindergarten Children: Training Script.* Philadelphia: Department of Mental Health Sciences, Hahnemann Community Mental Health/Mental Retardation Center, 1974a.

Shure, M. B., and Spivack, G. *Preschool Interpersonal Problem Solving (PIPS) Test Manual,* Philadelphia: Department of Mental Health Sciences, Hahnemann Community Mental Health/Mental Retardation Center, 1974b.

Shure, M. B., and Spivack, G. "A Mental Health Program for Preschool and Kindergarten Children, and a Mental Health Program for·Mothers of Young Children: An Interpersonal Problem Solving Approach Toward Social Adjustment. A Comprehensive Report of Research and Training," No. MH-20372. Washington, D.C.: National Institute of Mental Health, 1975.

Shure, M. B., and Spivack, G. *Problem-Solving Techniques in Child Rearing.* San Francisco: Jossey-Bass, 1978.

Shure, M. B., Spivack, G., and Gordon, R. "Problem-Solving Thinking and Adjustment Among Disadvantaged Preschool Children." *Child Development,* 1972, *42,* 1791–1803.

Shure, M. B., Spivack, G., and Jaeger, M. A. "Problem Solving Thinking and Adjustment Among Disadvantaged Preschool Children." *Child Development,* 1974, *42,* 1791–1803.

Siegel, J. J., and Spivack, G. "Problem-Solving Therapy: A New Program for Chronic Schizophrenic Patients." Research and Evaluation Report No. 23. Philadelphia: Department of Mental Health Sciences, Hahnemann Community Mental Health/Mental Retardation Center, 1973.

Sivadon, P. "Space as Experienced: Therapeutic Implications." In

Proshansky, H. M., Ittelson, W. H., and Rivlin, L. G. (Eds.). *Environmental Psychology: Man and His Physical Setting.* New York: Holt, Rinehart and Winston, 1970.

Skalar, V. "Social Climate in the Experimental and Control Institutions." In K. Vodopivec (Ed.), *Maladjusted Youth: An Experiment in Rehabilitation.* P.C. Heath, Westmead, Farnborouth, Honts, England: Saxon House, 1974.

Snow, D. L., and Newton, P. M. "Task, Social Structure, and Social Process in the Community Mental Health Center Movement." *American Psychologist,* 1976, *31,* 582–594.

Sodano, A. G. "Issues of Challenge, Coping and Support for First Semester Clinical Psychology Students." Unpublished master's thesis, University of Massachusetts at Amherst, 1977.

Sommer, R. "Toward a Psychology of Natural Behavior." *APA Monitor,* 1977, *8,* 1.

Sommer, R., and Ross, H. "Social Interaction on a Geriatrics Ward." *International Journal of Social Psychiatry,* 1958, *4,* 128–133.

Spivack, G., "Problem-Solving Thinking and Mental Health." *The Forum* (Department of Mental Health Sciences, Hahnemann Medical College, 1973, *2,* 58–73.

Spivack, G., and Levine, M. *Self-Regulation in Acting-Out and Normal Adolescents.* Report M-4531. Washington, D.C.: National Institute of Health, 1963.

Spivack, G., Platt, J. J., and Shure, M. B. *The Problem-Solving Approach to Adjustment: A Guide to Research and Intervention.* San Francisco: Jossey-Bass, 1976.

Spivack, G., and Shure, M. B. *Social Adjustment and Young Children: A Cognitive Approach to Solving Real-Life Problems.* San Francisco: Jossey-Bass, 1974.

Srole, L., and others. *Mental Health in the Metropolis: The Mid-Town Manhattan Studies.* Vol. 1. New York: McGraw-Hill, 1962.

Star, S., and Hughes, H. M. "Report of an Educational Campaign: The Cincinnati Plan for the United Nations." *American Journal of Sociology,* 1950, *55,* 389–397.

Stern, G. *People in Context.* New York: Wiley, 1970.

Stern, M. P., and others. "Results of a Two-Year Health Education Campaign on Dietary Behavior: The Stanford Three Community Study." *Circulation,* 1976, *54,* 826–833.

Stern, M. P. "Prevalence of Cardiovascular Risk Factors and Morbidity in Mexican-Americans Compared with Other Whites in Three Northern California Communities." *Journal of Chronic Disease,* 1975, *28,* 623.

Strupp, H. "On the Basic Ingredients of Psychotherapy." *Journal of Consulting and Clinical Psychology,* 1973, *41,* 1–8.

Tichenor, P. J., Donohue, G. A., and Olien, C. M. "Mass Media Flows and Differential Growth in Knowledge." *Public Opinion Quarterly,* 1970, *34,* 1959.

Tolsdorf, C. "Social Networks and the Coping Process." Unpublished doctoral dissertation, University of Massachusetts at Amherst, 1975.

Tolsdorf, C. "Social Networks, Support and Coping: An Exploratory Study." *Family Process,* 1976, *15,* 407–417.

Triandis, H. C. "The Future of Pluralism." *Journal of Social Issues,* 1976, *32,* 179–208.

Trickett, E. "Towards a Social-Ecological Conception of Adolescent Socialization: Normative Data on Contrasting Types of Public Schools." *Child Development,* 1978.

Trickett, E. J., Kelly, J. G., and Todd, D. M. "The Social Environment of the High School: Guidelines for Individual Change and Organizational Redevelopment." In S. E. Golann and C. Eisdorfer (Eds.), *Handbook of Community Mental Health.* New York: Appleton-Century-Crofts, 1972.

Trickett, E. J., and Quinlan, D. "Three Domains of Classroom Environment: An Alternative Analysis of the Classroom Environment Scale." College Park: Department of Psychology, University of Maryland, 1977.

Trickett, E. J., and Todd, D. M. "The High School Culture: An Ecological Perspective." *Theory into Practice,* 1972, *11,* 28–37.

Truax, C. B., and Mitchell, K. M. "Research on Certain Therapist Interpersonal Skills in Relation to Process and Outcome." In A. E. Bersin and S. L. Garfield (Eds.), *Handbook of Psychotherapy and Behavior Change.* New York: Wiley, 1971.

Truett, J., Cornfield, J., and Kannel, W. "Multivariate Analysis of the Risk of Coronary Heart Disease in Framingham." *Journal of Chronic Disease,* 1967, *20,* 511–524.

Udry, J. R. "Can Mass Media Advertising Increase Contraceptive Use?" *Family Planning Perspectives,* 1972, *4,* 3–7.

Walberg, H. "Psychology of Learning Environments: Behavioral,

Structural or Perceptual." In L. S. Shulman (Eds.), *Review of Research in Education.* Vol. 4. Itasca, Ill.: Peacock, 1976.

Walker, D. "Informal Helpers: An Exploratory Study of a Role and Its Contexts." Unpublished doctoral dissertation, University of Massachusetts at Amherst, 1976.

Wallack, L. M. *An Assessment of Drinking Patterns, Problems, Knowledge and Attitudes in Three Northern California Communities.* Berkeley: University of California Social Research Group, 1978.

Wanous, J. "Organizational Entry: Newcomers Moving from Outside to Inside." *Psychological Bulletin,* 1977, *84,* 601–618.

Watson, D. "Modeling the Activity System." In H. Sanoff and S. Cohn (Eds.), *Proceedings of the First Annual Environmental Design Research Association Conference.* Raleigh: North Carolina State University, 1970.

Watson, G. "Resistance to Change." In W. G. Bennis, K. D. Benne, and R. Chin (Eds.), *The Planning of Change.* New York: Holt, Rinehart and Winston, 1969.

Watzlawick, P., Weakland, J. H., and Fisch, R. *Change: Principles of Problem Formation and Problem Resolution,* New York: Norton, 1974.

Wellman, B. "The Community Question: The Intimate Networks of East Yorkers." *American Journal of Sociology,* in press.

Wilcox, B., and Holahan, C. "Social Ecology of the Megadorm in University Student Housing." *Journal of Educational Psychology,* 1976, *68,* 453–458.

Wilkinson, L. "An Assessment of the Dimensionality of Moos' Social Climate Scale." *American Journal of Community Psychology,* 1973, *1,* 342–350.

Willems, E. "Behavioral Ecology." In D. Stokols (Ed.), *Perspectives on Environment and Behavior.* New York: Plenum, 1977.

Name Index

Alden L., 112, 150, 364
Alderfer, C. P., 23, 364
Alexander, J., 6, 24, 69–100, 344, 345, 348, 349, 350, 353, 354, 356, 357, 360, 362
Allen, G., 31, 364
Altrocchi, J., 21, 364
Astrom, M., 152, 368
Attneave, C., 231
Aviram, U., 169, 378
Ayllon, T., 104, 364
Azrin, N., 104, 364

Bailey, K. D., 15, 364
Bandura, A., 73, 88, 364–365
Barker, R. G., 243, 365
Barlow, D. H., 360, 370
Barnes, J. A., 203, 365
Barnett, H. D., 308, 365
Bash, M. A., 31, 365–366
Bateson, G., 131, 132, 365
Bauer, R., 73, 365
Bentler, P. M., 149, 365
Berman, E., 214, 365
Bieman, I., 109
Blew, G., 107, 116n, 372
Bliss, F., 154, 161, 365
Bloom, L., 130, 365
Borouch, R. F., 29, 377
Bott, E., 203, 365

Boudreau, F., 296
Breitrose, H., 82, 88–89
Brennan, G. T., 211, 234–235, 237, 365
Bromet, E., 154, 161, 167, 365
Bronfenbrenner, U., 146, 192, 365
Bross, I. D. G., 283, 365
Brown, B. W., Jr., 71
Brownstein, R., 375
Buros, O. K., 151, 365

Camp, B. N., 31, 365–366
Campbell, D. T., 71, 85, 86, 359, 366
Caplan, N., 16, 366
Caplan, S., 6, 366
Cartwright, D., 73, 366
Chatlos, R., 207n
Cherniss, C., 15, 21, 22, 366, 376
Chinskey, J., 133
Cline, N., 290, 373
Cobb, S., 183, 366
Coché, E., 31, 366
Coelho, G., 174
Cohen, J., 150, 372–373
Cohen, J. B., 29, 373
Cohen, S., 168, 366
Cohn, S., 243, 377
Cook, T. D., 86, 359
Cooper, L., 162, 366

383

Subject Index

P9-ARI-718

THE TRVSTEES OF THE PVBLIC LIBRARY OF THE CITY OF BOSTON · 1852 · 1878

DIABETES

A Guide to Living Well

A Program of Individualized Self-Care

ERNEST LOWE & GARY ARSHAM M.D., Ph.D.

Foreword by Peter Forsham, M.D.

DIABETES:
A Guide
to Living Well

A Program
of Individualized Self-Care

Ernest Lowe
and Gary Arsham, M.D., Ph.D.

Foreword by Peter Forsham, M.D.

Diabetes: A Guide To Living Well

Copyright © 1989 by
Ernest Lowe
Gary Arsham, M.D.

All rights reserved. Except for review purposes, no part of this publication may be reproduced, stored in a retrieval system or transmitted, in any form or by any means, electronic, mechanical, photocopying, recording, or otherwise, without the prior written permission of Diabetes Center, Inc.

Printed in the United States of America.

ISBN 0-937721-51-4

Cover & text design: Terry Dugan Design

Editor: Carol Danielson

Typesetting: Dahl & Curry

Published by:
Diabetes Center, Inc.
P.O. Box 739
Wayzata, Minnesota 55391

Library of Congress Cataloging-in-Publication Data

Arsham, Gary M.

  Diabetes: a guide to living well.

  Bibliography: p.

  Includes index.

  1. Diabetes—Popular works. I. Lowe, Ernest. II. Title.
RC660.4.A77   1988   616.4'62   88-31040
ISBN 0-937721-51-4

RC660
.4
.A77
1989x

Table of Contents

Dedication

To Diana Silver Arsham and Grace Lowe
who could easily write a sequel to this book called
Diabetics: A Guide to Living Well with Them

To my parents, Florence and Sanford Arsham and my physician
while growing up, Max Miller, who gave me the guidance and
freedom to live well. — *Gary*

To John Menscher and Michael Barricks, whose skilled laser treatment enabled me to keep 20/20 vision. — *Ernest*

Acknowledgments

Many people have made valuable contributions to **Diabetes: A Guide to Living Well** — fellow diabetics (patients and friends) and professional colleagues.

We wish to thank Everett Ai, Carol Alston, Robert Barnes, Peter Barrett, Patrick Bean, Ken Burke, Philip R. Calanchini, Larry Catus, Cathy Corum, Leona Dang, Wayne Davis, Joan Enns, Fran Fernandez, Betty Fukuyama, Diana Guthrie, Dwight Holing, Peggy Huang, Larry Hulbert, Chris Kilduff, Barry S. Levin, Maureen McGrath, Fran Nereu, Jan Norman, Linda Parker, Sheila Perez, Donna Radcliffe, Vicky Sears, Nanci Stern, Wendy Ullman-Duarte, Helen Wall, Ben and Bonnie Weyhing, Seena Wolf, patients of the Early Treatment Diabetic Retinopathy Study, and the many others who supported our work with their knowledge and experience.

Special thanks go to George Cleveland of Diabetes Center, Inc., and Caroline Danielson, our editor, for helping to bring this book to completion.

Foreword

by Peter Forsham, MD, Professor of Medicine and Pediatrics, Emeritus and former Director, Metabolic Research Unit, University of California San Francisco. (Dr. Forsham has had diabetes for 64 years.)

Diabetes: A Guide to Living Well is one of the few books to acknowledge a difficult fact of life. There are three kinds of diabetics: those who cooperate completely in maintaining a normal blood glucose range; those who do this part time; and those who never do it. The authors, all type I diabetics for many years, provide guidance appropriate to all three groups.

This book covers all the modern ways of maintaining a normal blood sugar level (not usually exceeding 130 mg/dl) and introduces in a philosophical way the persuasive reasons for doing this. At the same time, the authors support the individual's right to choose his or her level of self-care and they recognize that many choose a level far below the standard now attainable. Their unique contribution is to offer alternative strategies for increasing the reader's willingness to follow regimens valuable in diabetes management. Throughout, the hope is expressed that through lifelong learning and adequate teaching by his or her medical team the reader will become increasingly wise.

The authors write from a powerful combination of personal and professional experience. Not only have they lived with diabetes for many years, but they've also surveyed advanced research in diabetes and medical education to uncover the most effective techniques for improving self-care and adherence to reasonable regimens. They dismiss ignorant old beliefs, some harking back to the days before insulin, when diabetics were absolutely forbidden sugar and were told to stay in a mild state of ketoacidosis to survive. Unfortunately, such misinformation from the past still fills some diabetes texts. This book makes little of the old prejudices, introducing instead the latest concepts in treatment of diabetes.

Beginning with tips on mastering the challenge of learning a complex regimen, the book is an operating manual for the individual who wishes to maintain the best possible level of diabetic control. It wisely charts alternative paths for those prepared to quickly gain this goal and those who prefer to move more gradually.

The authors accept the concept that hyperglycemia (or high blood sugar level) is what I once called toxic. Today we know that the prevention of general vascular disease in diabetes is a function of the control of blood glucose, cholesterol, and fat levels in the blood. This is an essential component in the reduction of the risk of diabetic complications involving the eyes, kidneys, nerves, and circulatory system. This Guide to Living Well imparts knowledge enabling the reader to manage fat intake on the one hand and to prevent hyperglycemia on the other.

The crowning achievement of this book, however, is its full synthesis of all factors affecting blood sugar level. On the deficit side, mental instability, stress, lack of exercise or rest, and dietary excess, each through different mechanisms, raise the blood sugar level and accelerate the degenerative processes of diabetes. But when a diabetic assumes a regimen integrating mental balance, stress management, dietary moderation, and exercise he or she is reducing long-term risks and insuring more immediate well-being.

The authors realistically offer routes to this ideal of self-management suited to a broad range of personalities, not just those immediately capable of strong discipline.

In the 1860s Claude Bernard observed that the condition for a free existence is the constancy of the internal environment. Now people with diabetes can hope to approach this metabolic constancy by controlling the multiple factors that are abnormal in the average patient. This aim is deeply supported by this very practical yet highly philosophical newcomer to the diabetes information scene.

Preface

We wrote **Diabetes: A Guide to Living Well** to give you (1) a command of one of medicine's most demanding regimens; (2) mastery over the threats diabetes presents; and (3) strength to meet its emotional challenges. Throughout the book, we encourage you to choose a regimen individualized to your personal needs and preferences. Most important,we present strategies empowering you to follow the regimen you choose.We wrote this book so that you can learn to live well with diabetes.

The **Living Well** approach is based upon the dual experience each of us brings to the book. We know diabetes professionally and personally. (Your writing team has logged a total of 170 years of living with diabetes!) We temper medical experts' views with first hand knowledge of the challenges, threats, and gifts of diabetes.

The basic diabetes life-style is a thorough program with a strong unity. Control of blood sugar levels is important in avoiding short-term crises, in maintaining a feeling of well-being, and in reducing your risk of long-term diabetic complications. Blood-sugar control, along with an active life, balanced diet, and effective stress management, work together to reduce your risk of complications. Emotional balance and self-esteem contribute to stress management and aid you in following your self-care program. Remembering this unity is central to the **Living Well** approach.

While we devote many pages to the question of blood glucose control, we emphasize throughout the book that you live well by balancing metabolic control with all other aspects of your life-style.When you do this, you integrate diabetes into your life and keep it from dominating you.

Individual choice is central to the **Living Well** approach and can easily be applied while using this book. It is not necessarily a book to be read from front to back. You know better than anyone else what you need to learn first. We encourage you to follow your own sense of priorities.

You may have much to learn, many skills to gain, and behaviors to change as you adopt the **Living Well** approach, especially if you are new to diabetes. Throughout this book, you will find ideas for making this process of learning and changing easier to handle. You will also find many techniques for increasing your willingness to follow this life-enhancing and demanding self-care regimen.

Ingredients of the Living Well with Diabetes Life-style

Find a balance between meeting your needs as a diabetic and the other needs in your life. Chapters 1 and 4 offer guidance on striking this balance.

- Know how to avoid the acute, life-threatening crises of diabetes. We have highlighted basic life-saving guidelines at the back of this book. Chapter 8 contains a thorough discussion of insulin reactions.

- Know the measures you can take to reduce the risk of developing diabetic complications. Preventive measures are discussed in Chapters 15 and 17.

- Maintain the best control of blood glucose levels you can achieve without damaging the quality of your life. Chapters 4 through 7 offer a choice of regimens and instructions for each.

- Meet your emotional needs, not just your physical needs. Chapter 14 presents a variety of techniques for maintaining emotional well-being. Chapter 3 describes techniques for dealing with crisis.

- Manage stress effectively. Chapter 11 describes the impact of stress in diabetes and techniques for coping with it.

- Maintain an active life-style, adjusted to your physical condition. Chapter 10 explores the role of exercise in diabetic management.

- Follow a balanced and moderate diet. Chapter 9 gives tips on making your diet delicious as well as healthy.

- Work to increase your willingness to follow this life-style, and continue learning about it. Chapter 1 surveys actions and beliefs that support continuing adherence to the self-care program you choose. Chapter 3 includes techniques to help you handle the times when you want to rebel.

A fundamental guideline to using this book

Diabetes is a condition requiring a balance between your own day-to-day decision making in self-care and your doctor's guidance on basic regimen decisions. We include detailed information on three regimens so you can work with your physician in making decisions about insulin dosage; overall balance between insulin, diet, and exercise; or treatment of acute crises like ketoacidosis. *In no way do we encourage you to make these fundamental medical decisions on your own.*

In writing this book, we have deepened our own capacity for living well with diabetes. We hope reading it helps you do the same.

Gary Arsham   Ernest Lowe

TO THE PHYSICIAN AND OTHER MEMBERS OF THE HEALTH CARE TEAM

Diabetes: A Guide to Living Well is intended to help your patient to not only live well with diabetes, but also to be a better, more informed, more responsible patient. As you know, with a chronic illness like diabetes, what patients do outside your office is critical to their medical care. You can recommend, monitor, guide, encourage, and exhort, but it is your patient who does or does not follow what the two of you agree is an appropriate regimen.

This book provides considerable information that should make your patient much more informed and motivated to work with you and other members of the health care team. It encourages the patient to examine the options available, consider the risks and benefits as we understand them today, and, in collaboration with you, choose a level of diabetes management and control that fits the individual situation. We hope that this book will help your patient and also make your tasks more satisfying and rewarding.

TO INCREASE YOUR CHANCES FOR A LONGER, MORE HEALTHFUL LIFE

Living well with diabetes means preserving your health and vitality and reducing your risk of developing future diabetic complications. Improving blood sugar control is just one of the things you can do to achieve these goals. The complete **Living Well** life-style asks you to

- Improve your control of blood glucose and continue improving it to the best level you are comfortable with (Chapters 4–7).
- Learn to handle stress well (Chapter 11).
- Follow a diabetic diet that features low animal fat and high fiber as well as limited sweets and rapidly absorbed carbohydrates (Chapter 9).
- Exercise regularly (Chapter 10).
- Lose weight if you are overweight.
- Act to prevent high blood pressure by controlling stress, weight, and salt consumption. Seek treatment for hypertension if your blood pressure is high (above 140/90) (Chapter 17, hypertension section).
- Get the amount of sleep and rest that you need.
- Know the warning signs for each complication. Begin treatment early if symptoms appear (Chapter 17).
- Consider taking a multivitamin pill daily.

These preventive measures are discussed in detail in Chapter 17. You should also skim through that chapter to find the sections describing what you can do to prevent individual complications.

A note on style: Although the noun *diabetic* has become controversial, we have chosen to use it in *Living Well*. We find nothing negative in the word itself. Being a diabetic is but one of the many roles we fill in life. Naming that role when it is appropriate does not make that our sole identity.

The information in this book, based on the knowledge and experience of the authors, is believed to be medically accurate at the time of publication. Information and recommendations change as new information is discovered. The authors, reviewers, and publisher disclaim all liability arising from any adverse effects or results that occur or might be construed to occur as a result of the application of any of the information or recommendations in this book. If you have questions or concerns about the appropriateness or application of the advice in this book, and how it may apply to you, consult your physician or other health care professional. The information in this book is not intended to replace health professional advice specifically tailored to you as an individual, but rather to complement it.

Section I
LEARNING TO LIVE WELL

Introduction

"Nobody asked me if I wanted to have diabetes. I just started feeling lousy, losing weight, and getting thirsty. And there I was—diabetic. I thought my life was ruined. But then I said,'No, dammit! This may not go away, but I'm going to call the shots. My life is more than a defective pancreas.'"

— John, 45 years old, twenty-five years diabetic

"The anger, the frustration, and all of these feelings aren't going to take the diabetes away. You have to find a level ground and decide,'Okay, this is the way I am now and I'd better learn what I'm supposed to do and what I'm not supposed to do and live with it, because that's the way it's going to be.'"

—Norma, 58 years old
(In Focus on Feelings, *from Pyramid Films.*)

We can choose how to live with diabetes. We can't decide not to have it, but we can decide to live a full and satisfying life, rejecting all images of ourselves as ill or disabled. No matter what our physical condition is, we can choose to live well. The act of choosing becomes the foundation of our ability to manage diabetes effectively.

Living well depends less on how we care for our diabetes than on how we care for ourselves. Each of us has a whole pattern of living that includes our individual needs, style, abilities, and physical characteristics. The diabetic regimen we choose will work only if it fits with this pattern. We cannot make decisions about diabetes care as if diabetes is the only thing we have to consider in life.

For this reason, the authors of *Diabetes: A Guide to Living Well*—insulin-dependent diabetics themselves—emphasize your right to select a self-care program, in conjunction with your physician and health care team, that will work for you as an individual. We encourage you to read this book in whatever order feels right to you. Work on the subjects that appeal to you the most. Find the level of regimen you believe you can follow faithfully. Work to find the right balance between quality of life and care of diabetes. When you exercise this freedom of choice, you are likely to arrive at a program you can live with.

Throughout this book, we have interwoven advice on how you can build willingness to follow the regimen you choose with information on the physical and emotional care of diabetes. In the last five years, dramatic improvements have been made in diabetes care, changes that have made the state-of-the-art regimen more complex. Taking full advantage of these breakthroughs may require you to pay attention to the feelings, beliefs, and patterns of behavior that sometimes divide your will.

Living well with diabetes is easier if you are willing to continually learn about the rapidly changing field of diabetes control. There are many new skills to be gained and, often, behaviors need changing as information is updated. We have included hints and strategies in the book to make the learning process easier.

WHICH REGIMEN?

If you elect anything less than the strictest regimen, you may feel guilt, anxiety, or conflict for making a "bad" choice. On one hand, these feelings are important to consider in your decision-making process. You must accept your level of care, or the quality of your life will suffer from the conflict you feel. However, to live well with diabetes, once you understand the risks and benefits of the different options and have made an informed choice, you must shed all feelings of conflict. Accept your decision. Realize that it is the best one for you.

Of course, we want to be certain that what we do to take care of ourselves will actually work. But the only certainty we can gain at this point is statistical: Excellent diabetic control reduces the risk of complications. A large percentage of us who maintain good control will escape blindness, kidney disease, nerve damage, and so on. But any one of us may do everything possible to control our diabetes and still experience some degree of disability because of the disease.

So, living well with diabetes calls for accepting uncertainty and staying motivated in the face of it. This is such a central issue that we ask you to explore your reactions to it in this questionnaire.

QUESTIONNAIRE: A CERTAIN UNCERTAINTY

1. As you read the last three paragraphs, how did you feel?____
   _____

2. How do you handle uncertainties in areas of your life outside diabetes?_____
   _____

3. What attitudes or beliefs could you adopt that would help you deal with the uncertainties about your future that diabetes imposes?_____

_____

4. What do you think would help motivate you to follow your diabetes management program, even though you have no guarantee that the program will prevent complications?_____

_____

There are no simple formulas for handling these basic questions. Yet it is dangerous to avoid them. Negative reactions to uncertainty range from abandoning all efforts to manage diabetes to caring for it so compulsively that life holds little joy. Clearly, managing diabetes is a matter of balance—doing the best you can and then living as fully as you can, without dwelling on possible future misfortunes.

One way of neutralizing uncertainty about the future is to make the present moment rewarding. Learn to accept each moment as a source of benefit, no matter what happens. Then you are prepared for whatever the future may bring. How do you learn such a profound lesson? Perhaps diabetes itself is the teacher.

Because we believe that diabetes is a teacher about living, we have chosen to make this book more than a manual on testing blood, taking shots, and balancing rutabagas against radishes. Having diabetes is a challenge, a burden, a transformation, a robber, a blessing, and sometimes a bitch. So let's accept its gracious gift and let it teach us to live the years we do have well.

Willing To Live Well

Although a cure for diabetes is probably many years away, fundamental breakthroughs in diabetes care have been made in recent years. These breakthroughs include

- Home blood glucose tests that give immediate and accurate feedback on your blood sugar levels whenever you need it.
- New approaches to the use of insulin that enable you to maintain better control of blood sugar.
- Better information about the steps you can take to reduce the risk of developing diabetic complications.
- Improved treatments for complications, which have allowed thousands of diabetics to save their vision, avoid impotence, survive kidney disease, and reduce the effects of heart disease.
- Greater awareness of the emotional and behavioral implications of diabetes.
- New knowledge about nutrition and diet.
- Recognition of diabetes education as a lifelong learning experience.

These are significant improvements and ones that may enable you to normalize many of your body functions (such as blood sugar, blood fats, cholesterol, hormones). There is strong evidence that controlling blood sugar level and other aspects of body chemistry greatly reduces the risk of developing diabetic complications. Studies are underway to test this hypothesis further.

The best level of diabetic self-care now available may enable you to keep blood sugar levels close to the normal range. Achieving this highly desirable goal requires that you learn and follow the most demanding regimen medicine offers (what we and others call the *Intensive Regimen*). More modest levels of control still call for education and the willingness to use what you learn.

LEARNING TO DO WHAT YOU CHOOSE TO DO

If you have had diabetes for some time, some items on this list are probably a part of your life already. Adding others may make living with diabetes much easier for you. You might check off the ones you already practice and note those you would like to add. Later, if you encounter difficulties, it may help you to see if something from this list offers a solution.

1. Believe that treatment for diabetes is effective. If you doubt that this is so, try to understand the basis for your doubt.
2. Recognize that diabetes is a serious condition worthy of respect, even if it presents few symptoms at present.
3. Balance seriousness with lightness, humor, and detachment.
4. Believe that you are capable of learning and following any regimen you adopt.
5. Recognize that you are the one who chooses how you will care for yourself. Make your choices consciously.
6. Make decisions about diabetes self-care in the context of your other life needs. Don't neglect other important aspects of your life or the overall quality of your life.
7. In choosing how you will care for yourself, find a balance between your subjective preferences and your objective needs.
8. Watch your stress level as you work on diabetes care. Use stress-management tools to keep the experience from becoming an additional source of strain.
9. Offer yourself healthful rewards for both the efforts and the achievements you make. Recognize that feeling better is itself a reward for improved self-care.

10. Define the tasks required by the regimen you choose. Divide the tasks and the behavioral changes into small, concrete steps. Set goals so you understand clearly what will demonstrate your success. Create a realistic time schedule for the learning or change.

11. Explore possible difficulties you may encounter in the process of change you are entering. Plans ways of dealing with them in advance.

12. Make a solid commitment to changing your behavior and learning the new skills and information you need.

13. When you feel reluctant to take on a particular change, try it for a short, predetermined time and see how it affects your life.

14. Give yourself positive feedback as you learn and support yourself when you have difficulty learning. Don't cling to feelings of guilt or failure.

15. When obstacles arise, deal with them and learn from them.

16. Evaluate your efforts and achievements objectively, without self-condemnation.

We will briefly discuss each of these factors affecting learning and sticking with your self-care program. Why are they important? What is there about diabetes that makes them especially relevant?

1. Believe that treatment for diabetes is effective. If you doubt that this is so, try to understand the basis for your doubt.

Obviously, if you don't believe treatment will do much good, you will have difficulty sticking with any regimen. This issue becomes complex with diabetes. As we have said, there is no guarantee that excellent self-care will prevent long-term complications. Effective treatment is a matter of improving your odds, but you cannot eliminate the risk of developing complications.

However, when you improve blood sugar control to moderate or tight levels, you get a short-term demonstration of effectiveness: You feel better, both mentally and physically.

Gary's Experience

"As my control improves, I feel leaner and healthier. I'm less sluggish, as though my blood has become less viscous with the reduction of excess sugar. I sleep better because I don't have to get up two or three times a night to go to the bathroom.

I was concerned that I might become preoccupied with diabetes as I tightened up my control. Actually, I find I can be less aware of it because there are fewer symptoms of high blood sugar to remind me."

If you choose loose control, you may still experience the short-term disadvantages of high blood sugar, depending on how high your tests run. But there is a level of effectiveness even here. By maintaining a limited regimen and remaining committed to learning more from it, you keep a positive attitude. You will be in a better position to improve physical control if and when you choose to.

2. Recognize that diabetes is a serious condition worthy of your respect, even if it presents few symptoms at present.

When you exercise a moderate degree of control, you may experience few symptoms of diabetes. Even when blood sugar levels are fairly high, it is possible to grow accustomed to the short-term symptoms: thirst, frequent urination, sluggishness, and susceptibility to infection and illness.

Unless complications develop, it's not easy to feel the seriousness of diabetes through your direct experience with it. Unlike people with arthritis, for instance, you have few immediate and painful reminders. You have to create your own personal way of remembering that diabetes is a crucial aspect of your life.

Respecting Diabetes

Writing your thoughts down can help you define the significance of diabetes in your life. Answer the questions spontaneously, even if the ideas that first come to mind seem inappropriate.

1. What aspects of diabetes make it a serious condition, one that may have a major impact on your life?

2. Do you tend to feel you have no future because of diabetes?

3. Do you avoid looking at problems and difficulties that arise because of your diabetes?

4. Do you sometimes take diabetes too seriously? If so, how?

5. Do you have any doubts about the long-term significance of diabetes? If so, quickly read Chapter 17, where complications are described.

---

3. Balance seriousness with lightness, humor, and detachment.

Diabetes is, at this point, a lifelong companion. You might as well make it an agreeable one, threats and all.

You can invoke lightness and humor when you are in a difficult spot by telling the story of your serious situation as though you were speaking of a third person, someone you are fond of but whom you find gently amusing. (You might even try telling the story of the person in the mirror.) Or look back from a decade in the future. See yourself and your dilemmas from a time when you have long since resolved them. Note the clever ways you avoided the obvious solutions back then.

The detachment we speak of here is not indifference, but rather a viewing of yourself and the problems you face from a larger perspective. From this point of view, you are not attached to the feelings and beliefs that often appear to trap you. You experience and acknowledge them, but you realize that you are more than these limitations. You can draw on your full resources to break through the limits.

Humor is a powerful way of breaking attachments. When you can laugh at habitual behavior, you feel less allegiance to it.

4. Believe that you are capable of learning and following any regimen you adopt.

Feeling competent may come naturally to you, or you may be one of the many people who learned to doubt that you can do what you set out to do. *Learned* is the key word here. Whether your doubts stem from feeling you are dumb, contrary, or stuck for life, they are aspects of self-image that you can unlearn. Diabetes itself tends to make us feel like dummies, even when we have no difficulties with learning or changing in other areas. This was especially true before the recent breakthroughs in self-care.

Ernest's Experience

"Out of 40 years of living with diabetes, I spent 30 of them resolving to try to make an effort to get it under control. I thought I knew what I should do. Actually doing it seemed harder than climbing Mount Everest. For one thing, I didn't feel I could ask my doctor for help. That would mean I'd have to tell him how out of control I was! At least I always tried to look like a good patient.

So I'd study my 1954 Joslin's Diabetes Manual. I'd measure the food I ate. I'd pee in the test tube. And I'd get more and more uptight. Nothing made any sense to me. I couldn't predict when I would or would not spill sugar. What an incredible sense of frustration and failure came with that stinking orange color foaming up at me in the test tube!

Of course, I always felt that I'd done something wrong, no matter how hard I'd tried. No one had ever mentioned that emotional stress affects blood sugar levels strongly; or that the urine test is very imprecise, measuring only moderately high, very high, and very very high; or that one shot a day of intermediate insulin couldn't possibly prevent large ups and downs in blood sugar level.

In short, I didn't know that I was in a double bind, being expected to do something but not having the tools necessary to do it. It was like being asked to build a house with bent nails and a hammer without a handle and feeling incompetent because the task seemed impossible."

Today the diabetes tool kit is full of new tools for both physical and psychological self-care, but diabetes is still not necessarily easy to master. If you choose to work for the tightest level of control, your ability to learn and to change behavior will be challenged. And even with the best effort, in some cases a moderate level of control is the best that can be achieved because of hormonal factors or high levels of stress.

Whenever you achieve less than your goal, don't label yourself a failure. Give yourself credit for what you have achieved, and look to see what you still have to learn or change to reach your goal. (This may be something other than what you set out to learn.) With this point of view, you learn from whatever happens, and you continue to believe in your capacity to learn. (Chapter 14, "Living Well with Yourself," contains ideas on freeing yourself from the limits described here.)

5. **Recognize that you are the one who chooses how you will care for yourself. Make your choices consciously.**

Your doctor, nurse, dietitian, social worker, or diabetes educator cannot make the actual choices for you. Only you can make them. You are the only one who can integrate prescriptions, recommendations, and external pressures into your life.

Sometimes you may find it difficult to accept the responsibility of making choices, especially when the choices conflict with professional recommendations. Then it is easier to say, "I don't have time to do all this testing," or "The cafeteria doesn't have the right kind of food for my diet," or "It's too much hassle to test my blood when I'm at work," or "I carry enough stuff around with me already."

If you make your choices consciously and accept them, you gain power. ("I prefer to sleep an extra few minutes rather than get up to test," or "I don't want to bother fixing a bag lunch.") You also make clear to yourself what the alternatives are, and you may find it easier to make more healthful decisions.

As we said at the beginning of this book, the realization of your power to choose all aspects of your regimen is fundamental to your following it. Your life is under your control. You make the important decisions. If you rebel against your own authority, then learning to stop doing that simply becomes one more item on your learning agenda.

Your medical team can do more than recommend a self-care program. Your physician and other professionals can also help you understand the alternatives available to you, and you can ask them

13

to work with you on identifying and overcoming barriers you encounter. Don't be afraid to say, "That's going to be hard for me to do because . . ." In fact, they'll appreciate it.

6. Make decisions about diabetes self-care in the context of your other life needs. Don't neglect other important aspects of your life or the overall quality of your life.

Health professionals naturally place top priority on your diabetes care and may even forget that you have other concerns. Diabetes itself sometimes urgently demands that you deal with it before all else. But most of the time, you must balance your needs as a diabetic with a host of other issues. If you don't, you may run into difficulties in many areas of your life. Use the following table to catalog your various needs and sort out your priorities.

In the following table, note specific important needs in any of the areas on the left, then use the other categories to help you rank them according to the amount of attention they demand from you.

Diabetes Care	Specific Need	Actions Called For	Difficulty	Urgency	Rank
Work					
Family					
Leisure					
Other Issues					
Education and Intellectual Growth					
Spiritual Concerns					

If this exercise suggests that you have enough concerns to keep a whole regiment busy, don't despair. See what can possibly be postponed or dealt with gradually. Reserve at least a few minutes each day to improving your diabetes care. Then set a date to review your priorities in a month or two.

Often several needs can be satisfied by a single, well-chosen activity. Dancing or sports, for instance, can help you improve metabolic control while providing enjoyment and social interaction. Better relations with your spouse and mutual support around diabetes

14

issues could both be served by participation in a support group or communications workshop. When you find connections between your different needs in this way, you won't spend nearly as much time dealing with them separately.

7. **In choosing how you will care for yourself, find a balance between your subjective preferences and objective needs.**

You can't ignore your feelings, but you also can't let them dominate your decisions about self-care. The best choices come out of an inner dialogue between your emotional and rational sides, with intuition helping. This dialogue may happen spontaneously with you, or you may need a structure to guide your decision making.

One simple way of opening this inner dialogue is to write it out, with your emotional self discussing the issue in question with your rational self.

8. **Watch your stress level as you work on diabetes care. Use stress-management tools to keep the experience from becoming an additional source of strain.**

It is possible to work at learning diabetes care with so much anxiety and tension that blood sugar levels shoot up solely because of the stress you are generating. In this area of your life, it is especially important for you to work with an awareness of the cues of stress. Let your body remind you when it's time to slow down and relax. (Chapter 11 contains many techniques for dealing with stress.)

9. **Offer yourself healthful rewards for both the efforts and the achievements you make. Recognize that feeling better is itself a reward for improved self-care.**

Rewards are a very important part of diabetes care because our condition deprives us of some old pleasures. People often reward themselves with sweets or extra food, for instance, but for people with diabetes, this is a penalty, not a prize. You may benefit from creating a positive reward system to offset possible feelings of deprivation.

As you work on learning and changing behavior, rewards also help reinforce the effort you make and the changes you achieve. The most substantial rewards, of course, come from feeling better physically, and from feeling more powerful and optimistic mentally. But there is good evidence that additional bonuses help keep motivation high.

Take a few minutes now to jot down a variety of rewards you would appreciate: gifts, good times, experiences, or even things it would be nice *not* to do. Then, at the start of any particular diabetes learning project, promise yourself one reward for effort after a certain period and another reward when you have successfully completed the learning project.

You May Have Already Won . . .

1. Gifts I can give myself:_____

_____

2. Celebrations and other good times I'd enjoy:_____

_____

3. New experiences I would value:_____

_____

4. Some things I'd like not to have to do:_____

_____

---

10. **Define the tasks required by the regimen you choose. Divide the tasks and the behavioral changes into small, concrete steps. Set goals so you understand clearly what will demonstrate your success. Create a realistic time schedule for the learning or change.**

It may seem to you that learning to manage diabetes is a full-time job. That's why this item is so important. When you divide a large project into its individual steps and schedule the steps over a realistic period, the project seems—and becomes—much more manageable. However much urgency you may feel, you simply cannot learn it all yesterday. Once you have mastered the basic survival skills (detecting and treating reactions, taking your shot, dealing with infections and illness, etc.), you can proceed with other learning and changing at a reasonable pace.

By setting reasonable and specific goals, you give yourself a much better chance of experiencing success as you progress. If you have been very poorly controlled, saying "I'll get my diabetes under control sometime" is too vague. Aiming at an average blood test of 180 milligrams of glucose per deciliter of blood (mg/dl) in a month gives you a manageable target, and you will clearly know whether you have attained it.

11. **Explore possible difficulties you may encounter in the process of change you are entering. Plan ways of dealing with them in advance.**

You may be one of the blessed who never have trouble doing anything. Or you may be like most of us, sometimes running into blocks. If the latter is true, you probably know what your typical difficulties are and ways you have dealt with them in the past. By making some notes on escape routes at the beginning, you will be able to draw on more creativity than you usually have available when you hit a stumbling block.

TROUBLE SPOTS

In the past, I have gotten stuck learning or following a diabetes regimen because_____

_____

I have run into trouble in areas other than diabetes because

_____

I have moved (or could move) through the difficulty by_____

_____

---

12. **Make a solid commitment to changing your behavior and learning the new skills and information you need.**

For some people, the matter of commitment falls into place easily, without being formalized. But others like to state their intentions in a way that helps them strengthen their will to change, in some cases even making a contract with themselves. If this appeals to you, you can use the following form.

A Contract with Myself

I commit myself to changing this behavior or learning this aspect of diabetes care (be as specific as possible):_____
_____

I believe this will improve my diabetes self-care by_____
_____

I believe I am capable of doing this, although I may need assistance in the form of_____
_____

If I experience difficulties in completing this task, I will use the help processes in Chapter 3 to help me overcome them.
I will learn from the whole experience—setbacks as well as achievements.
(Optional)

I will receive the following reward for effort by (specify date)_____
_____

I will receive the following reward for achievement upon completion_____
_____

If I do not fulfill this contract I will (specify penalty)_____
_____

I can reasonably expect to complete this by_____

Signature_____
Date _____

---

13. **When you feel reluctant to take on a particular change, try it for a short, predetermined time and see how it affects your life.**

Some alterations in life-style suggested by diabetes may arouse resistance in you. When this happens, it helps to remember that we often tend to exaggerate the consequences of changes we don't wish to make. In our imagination, we see only the negative and blow that up to monumental proportions.

If you tend to do this, you can suspend negative expectations and do a trial run. For instance, test your blood sugar four times a day for a few days, if that's what you're resisting. (Even a commitment a day at a time can help.) In this case, make no commitment beyond that period. Then contrast what you actually experience with your prior expectations. Whatever the specific change is, you are likely to find that it's not as bad as you thought it would be.

(If you still have trouble beginning, see if you can break the task down into smaller steps and try just the first step for a while, then try the second, and so forth.)

14. Give yourself positive feedback as you learn, and support yourself when you have difficulty learning. Don't cling to feelings of guilt or failure.

Just having diabetes is enough of an emotional load. You don't have to make it a bigger burden by telling yourself you are a "bad" diabetic. You improve your willingness to manage the illness well by accepting yourself when you have trouble learning about or following a regimen.

As you learn, notice the improvements, the changes, and the efforts you make, and consciously acknowledge them. Don't ignore your mistakes or your tendencies to hold back, but observe them without blame. They are simply areas requiring further attention. (Chapter 14, "Living Well with Yourself," includes ideas for supporting yourself and dealing with guilt.)

15. When obstacles arise, deal with them and learn from them.

An obstacle that you can't seem to push through is really a new learning assignment. Say you have started to learn home blood testing, but you are afraid to prick your finger, even with one of the automatic devices. Then your new assignment is learning to deal with fear of physical discomfort or negative expectations or whatever is at work in you.

Or perhaps the obstacle is total resistance to learning about diabetic complications. You break into a cold sweat every time you think of looking at that subject. In this case, you recognize an opportunity to learn about your feelings of vulnerability or mortality. Before—and probably while—studying complications, you need to work with these very human emotions. Perhaps you could enlist a friend or relative to help. Other diabetics who have dealt with these issues can also give valuable support.

16. Evaluate your efforts and achievements objectively, without self-condemnation.

Each time you complete an aspect of your diabetes learning program, take a moment to evaluate your work in a nonjudgmental manner. Look at both how you worked on it and what you accomplished. Give yourself credit for what you did achieve, even when you have not yet reached your final goal. Be honest with yourself about the shortcomings of your work, but don't view the shortcomings as a sign of weakness.

This clear process of evaluation is especially important in learning to manage diabetes well. Our condition demands a great deal from us. There are many variables affecting diabetic control. Sometimes we can make the best possible effort and still find blood sugar outside the limits we try to attain. It is important not to add negative judgments to the frustration we naturally feel. If we are to continue with the project, we must congratulate ourselves for hanging in there and look carefully to see what to do next.

Living Well At The Beginning Of Diabetes

"**I** really felt sorry for myself [when I found out I had diabetes]. I still want to know 'Why me?' I never did anything to deserve this. Why all of a sudden do I have to stick to a diet and take shots for the rest of my life?"

—*Carol, 17 years old*
(*In* Focus on Feelings, *Pyramid Films*)

If you have only recently discovered that you have diabetes, take a deep breath, sigh, and relax for a moment. You are going through a crisis. You may be handling the challenges of this time well, or you may feel overwhelmed by them. In either case, it is a difficult, demanding situation, and you need all the breaks you can get.

At the beginning of diabetes, you have three basic demands to handle:

1. *Practical tasks.* You must learn new skills, absorb new information, make decisions, and change aspects of the way you live.

2. *Emotional tasks.* You need to deal with the emotional impact of being told that you have a lifelong chronic disease that as yet has no cure.

21

3. *Support tasks.* You need to mobilize internal and external sources of support.

You may find yourself trying to meet all three needs at the same time, as well as dealing with the other needs in your life. It is very easy to feel overloaded in this initial period. So remember, *you can't do everything at once.* Set priorities, with the help of your doctor and the medical staff.

PRACTICAL TASKS
The practical demands of diabetes begin very quickly, much sooner than you feel ready for them. Even if you have gone into the hospital to get your system under control, you soon find that you are not allowed to play the role of the passive patient. You realize your life depends on learning a dizzying amount of information very quickly. Your learning may be marked by a bit of anxiety, since it is difficult to understand initially which information is of life-or-death importance. You are still dealing with the emotional shock of the diagnosis, as well as with the physical stress of diabetes out of control, so your mind may be functioning with less clarity than usual.

This is an excellent time to learn the fundamental lesson of diabetes education: When you don't understand something or when you feel overloaded with information, tell your doctor firmly and clearly. Ask for a restatement or a pause. Don't just nod your head so the doctor won't think you are stupid. Some health professionals are very good communicators, but others don't notice if you are suffering from information overload.

Sometimes your physician will involve other health professionals. In this case, your basic care will be supervised by the doctor, but the specific educational aspects may be handled by a nurse, dietitian, or diabetes educator.

Acute Versus Chronic Health Care
Until recently, newly diagnosed diabetics were usually hospitalized to get their blood sugar under control. Now this process is often accomplished through office visits and phone contact, so long as the initial symptoms are not too extreme. In either case, you will experience a combination of acute and chronic medical care, which may be confusing.

Before beginning treatment for diabetes, many people know only acute care. Acute care is that in which a doctor steps in to deal with a short-term illness or some other emergency. A patient in this situation usually has relatively little involvement other than following a few instructions. At the beginning of diabetes, your physician has to act quickly to restore order to a system seriously out of control.

But from the very beginning in diabetes, your doctor and the other health professionals are initiating you to a radically different style of medicine: chronic medical self-care. You are given extensive training to take care of yourself for the rest of your life. Within a few years, health professionals may be telling you that you know more than they do about diabetes. They are there to assist you in this process and to take charge when an acute crisis (such as diabetic coma) occurs. But you are the only one who can be responsible for your day-to-day care.

Your Treatment Program

Being in charge of your diabetes care may seem to be an enormous responsibility at first, but thousands of diabetics assume it and live well every year. Your medical team will provide lots of hand holding in the beginning, so you can always call for help when you can't figure out what to do. If you have some other diabetics to consult on the many smaller practical questions that arise, you can avoid feeling that you are bothering your medical team with too many queries.

If you feel able to meet the challenge, there are strong arguments for adopting an intensive treatment program right at the beginning. This will be the most intense period of diabetes learning you will go through. What you learn in the beginning tends to stick with you for years. If you begin with a fairly loose level of management, you may have a hard time tightening up on your regimen later. Maintaining excellent patterns of self-care from the first also strengthens your chances of benefiting from any future advances in research, such as beta cell transplants.

Some people are able to begin diabetes self-care at this level very easily. Others feel too overwhelmed by the shock of diagnosis to begin with such a detailed program. If you feel it is more than you can handle at this time, start with a more moderate regimen, but think of it as a temporary decision. When you have adjusted to the initial demands of diabetes, reconsider the intensive regimen.

Another factor affecting the standard of care you adopt at the beginning is the experience and attitude of your physician. As a whole, the profession is moving toward tighter control, but there is still a great variety of opinions on this matter. If you wish to maintain fairly strict control and your doctor doesn't strongly support this choice, you may need to find one who does. On the other hand, if your physician urges strict control and you do not feel ready for it, you can probably negotiate for looser control. Create a plan for moving in the direction your doctor recommends over the next few months. If a difference of opinion remains, you may need to find a new doctor.

Diabetes: A Lifelong Learning Experience
Living well with diabetes requires learning well for the rest of your life. You have probably already started discovering what a powerful teacher diabetes is, with its many challenges and surprises. You are in the midst of absorbing many practical details of care, some of which have life-or-death significance. At this stage, you need to determine which aspects of care have such vital importance. (See "Diabetes Survival Kit" at the back of the book.) You are probably changing aspects of your life-style and you are dealing with (or avoiding) the emotions that occur when diabetes is diagnosed.

Diabetes treatment is continually evolving, so you can expect to continue learning about it for many years. As you grow older, you may find that you are learning some of life's important lessons sooner and more deeply than your nondiabetic friends. Our physical condition calls on us to make peace with vulnerability and mortality and to value the preciousness of life. The depth of experience that accompanies such learning can be seen as a powerful benefit of this condition.

Learning About Diabetes
To avoid feeling overwhelmed by the amount you have to learn in the first months of diabetes, divide the learning into manageable lessons. Work out a time schedule. Identify the resources that can assist you. There may be a series of classes at a local hospital or clinic. A diabetes educator (usually a nurse or dietitian) may be available. Your local chapter of the American Diabetes Association

24

may offer educational programs and support groups. Don't worry if you find that your doctor seems to play a relatively minor role in the educational process. In many cases, other members of your health care team will have more time and training in this field.

EMOTIONAL TASKS

Ask a dozen of us how we reacted to being told we have diabetes and you will probably hear a dozen different stories: "It really scared me. My uncle had diabetes and he died when he was 40." "No big deal. I don't let things like that get to me." "I was angry for months. I thought it would destroy all of my plans." "I just pulled the covers over my head and felt numb."

There is no "right" way to feel, only the way you are feeling. Give yourself time, in the midst of learning countless practical details, to experience your particular emotions. If your style is to deal with feelings on your own, be sure you set aside periods to do this. Some people use writing, some take long solitary walks, others pray or meditate. (See Chapter 14 "Living Well with Yourself," for ways of handling your feelings.)

If you prefer to have assistance, remember that it is available, even if you think you are relatively isolated. There may be people available in your present support network; if not, you have guaranteed membership in the community of people with diabetes. Some people may also find value in a few sessions with a counselor, psychologist, or social worker.

Some common reactions to being told you are diabetic are described in the following paragraphs. To some extent, these feelings can be countered by information at a rational level; but you may find that the feeling persists even when you "know better." It may be simply your familiar way of reacting to situations—an old habit. The section on emotions in Chapter 14 offers means of dealing with such emotional habits.

You may feel helpless or unable to assume the new responsibilities diabetes assigns to you. With this response, it helps to discuss your feelings with other diabetics. Their reassurance comes from knowing that these feelings of being overwhelmed diminish as you actually start taking care of yourself.

You may be depressed, fearful, or angry over the many changes in life-style you are expected to achieve. Some of the changes are specific to diabetes, but it is useful to recognize that the majority of them are the basics of healthful living for anyone. Regular exercise and a balanced, moderate diet are the requirements of any human body. Even the scheduling required by diabetes can be much more flexible now, with multiple daily insulin injections or the insulin pump.

Perhaps you are anxious or depressed over the possibility of developing complications and dying early. Grim stories and statistics of the casualties of diabetes may lead you to believe you are doomed to disability and an early grave. Actually, recent advances in diabetes care offer the means of preventing or delaying the onset of diabetic complications. (See Chapters 15–17, "Living Well With Complications.")

You may feel frustrated over the changes in life goals you believe diabetes imposes. Actually, diabetes closes very few doors to you. You are not allowed to fly a plane solo. You would probably find it impossible to get some jobs where an insulin reaction would threaten the safety of others. But most roles you might seek are open to you, including the role of mother or father.

One reaction to diabetes that may appear completely positive is *doing everything right,* but doing it with so much anxiety that you feel terrible. If you are caught in this pattern, make relaxation and other stress management techniques a high priority. You will also benefit from sorting out which aspects of diabetes care are most critical. Until you do this, the slightest mistake in self-care may seem threatening.

The opposite reaction is to be "unconcerned," insisting that diabetes will have no effect whatsoever on your life. At some level, you may even believe that you don't really have the disease. Once you get your blood sugar under a moderate degree of control, diabetes has few outward signs. What a "nice" disease it seems to be. The temptation to do as little as possible to control it may be strong, especially when you seem to be getting away with "murder." In type I diabetes, there is even a "honeymoon period," a few months during which insulin requirements temporarily decrease. However, after this period, they do go up again.

Living well with diabetes calls for accepting it as a fact of life, a fact of major significance. The more you try to ignore it through minimal self-care, the greater the impact it can have. If, on the other hand, you follow a full regimen, you will lessen the risks and ensure that your body will be in shape to benefit from future advances in treatment or a cure.

SUPPORT TASKS

At the beginning of diabetes, you can find strong support for dealing with both the practical and the emotional issues. Relatives, friends, other diabetics, and professionals may be called upon at this time. You may need comfort, encouragement, or honest feedback on how you are handling things. You may have hundreds of questions that seem too minor to take to your doctor. You may need information on cutting the costs of the supplies you need.

Some people know that they are blessed with abundant support networks at times like this. Others feel isolated and don't know where to turn. If you tend to feel there is little support available to you, give yourself a chance to be surprised. You may have more resources than you think. Even if you know few people, you are probably no more than two or three phone calls away from dozens of people who are ready and willing to help you cope.

Wherever you live, there are other people nearby with diabetes who are well informed, positive, and helpful. You can make contact with other diabetics through your physician, your pharmacist or other health professionals, through the American Diabetes Association or Juvenile Diabetes Foundation, or through people you already know. Let them know you are looking for people who have a positive outlook and who don't mind talking with others who have diabetes. If you encounter people who only like to complain or tell horror stories, steer clear of them. You need support, not discouragement. (See Chapter 13 for more on networking.)

***

Beginning Well

This questionnaire is designed to help you bring order to the process of adjusting to diabetes. Use your answers here to guide you in sorting out your new priorities. See what requests you need to make of your health care team and support network. What immediate changes do you need to make in your own life to help you handle this crisis well? If the challenge of diabetes feels overwhelming, identify small first steps you know you can handle. The most important thing is getting started.

1. *Your Support Network*

   The people I can count on for emotional support include_____

   _____

   The people who will help me with practical problems (getting to an appointment with the doctor, bringing food when I'm ill, etc.) include_____

   _____

   (If you have trouble asking for help) I wouldn't want to ask for help because_____

   _____

   How would you answer a friend who gave you this reason?__

   _____

   (If you feel you need more support) I could enlarge my support network by
   ___Contacting the American Diabetes Association or the Juvenile Diabetes Foundation.
   ___Joining a support group (either general or diabetic).
   ___Asking my minister for help.
   ___Asking my doctor or pharmacist to help me get in touch with other people with diabetes.
   ___Going to a social worker or psychologist.
   ___Other.

(If there are people in your life who are discouraging or otherwise negative) I can neutralize this "antisupport" by

___Asking the person involved to change.

___Changing how I respond.

___Avoiding the person.

___Having more contact with people who show a positive attitude.

___Other.

The personal strengths I can call on within myself at this time include_____

A past crisis I handled well was_____

2. *Your Physical Care*

___I know which aspects of diabetes management have life-or-death significance. (See "Diabetes Survival Kit" at back of book.)

___I feel satisfied with my physician.

___I feel my physician is adequate, but I would like him/her to _____

___I feel I need a different doctor because _____

___I feel most certain about the aspects of diabetes care I've checked below:

___Insulin dosage

___Insulin reactions

___Blood testing

___Urine testing

___Diet and meal planning

___Exercise

___The effect of stress on control of diabetes

___The interactions among all of these

(If your budget is limited) Have you located the least expensive source for diabetes supplies? A local ADA chapter might be able to refer you to medical discount shopping services. Or refer to the Appendix.

3. *Your Emotional Care*

My emotional reactions to the diagnosis of diabetes include the items I've checked below:

___Anger

___Fear

___Anxiety

___Depression

___Guilt

___Lack of feeling

___Calm

___Other

I am dealing with these reactions by_____
_____

My overall response to the diagnosis of diabetes includes the items I've checked below:

___I feel overwhelmed by the whole thing and find it difficult to handle.

___I am upset because I have to make too many changes in my life.

___I feel anxious about the things I have heard about complications.

___I am concerned that diabetes will make it impossible to achieve my life goals.

___I am very worried about doing all the diabetes procedures right.

___I have withdrawn into myself.

___I don't believe that diabetes is any big deal or that I have to change much.

___I am dealing well with my feelings and with the practical challenges that diabetes has presented.

___Other.

30

I can reduce the negative side of my overall response to diabetes by_____

_____
_____

4. *Your Diabetes Learning Program*

___I have a good sense of what I know and what I still have to learn.

___I feel confused and need help figuring out what is important to learn.

___I have enrolled in a diabetes instruction class.

___I have subscribed to

___*Diabetes Forecast*

___*Diabetes Self-Management*

___*Diabetes in the News*
    (See Appendix for addresses.)

Help!

You may have noticed there are times when life gets difficult. And then diabetes has a way of adding its distinctive difficulties to those we already face as human beings. Our self-care regimen is demanding both to learn and to practice. We meet a variety of unique health crises, both immediate and long term. We are threatened by insulin reactions, delayed meals, lost insulin, forgotten injections, coma, runaway infections, depression, anxiety, denial, difficulties in relationships, and an amazing array of diabetic complications. Yes, there are times when life gets difficult.

You may have come to this chapter because you are in one of those times. You may be in the midst of a diabetes crisis and need help handling your feelings and actions. Or you may feel unable (or unwilling) to continue learning what you need to know to care for yourself well. Here you will find a number of tools to help you understand what is happening. You will also find what you need to do to move on.

While you can do much to help yourself, you may need help from your medical team or personal support network. Don't be afraid to give yourself permission to ask for that help. *If the specific crisis you are handling is an aspect of your physical care, do not fail to call your doctor or nurse practitioner for help.*

We offer a variety of methods to suit different individual styles and situations. You may want to work through the whole sequence laid out here, or you may need to use only one or two of the methods. Choose the course that is right for you.

We recommend beginning with relaxation and detachment. This will help you gain perspective and work more effectively.

TOOLS FOR RESCUING YOURSELF FROM A CRISIS

Relaxation

When you have trouble—especially when your health is at stake—a natural response is to become uptight and frustrated. The more tense you become, the harder it is to see a way out. We get tunnel vision when we're nervous, anxious, or scared. So you are wise to begin the process of rescuing yourself by relaxing as deeply as possible before doing anything more. This will broaden your vision.

If you have healthful techniques for relaxing that work for you, use them. Eating, drinking, watching television, and other common distractions don't count as healthful techniques. You may already be using practices described at the end of the chapter on stress management or ones that you learned elsewhere.

If you need a new means of relaxing right now, try this:

Begin by slowly saying something like: "My only job right now is to relax." For the moment, put all other concerns aside.

• Then, focus awareness on your breath, especially the feeling of it as you exhale. You can even sigh as you breathe out, if you like.

• Your body will respond now, if you talk with it. Say, "My right arm is growing heavier." Repeat it slowly in your mind, four or five times, or as many times as it takes to feel heavier.

• Now, repeat the same thing for your left arm: "My left arm is growing heavier," then your right leg, and after that, your left leg.

• Within five to ten minutes, the feeling of heaviness you are describing will have been translated by your body into a greater sense of relaxation. You can help the process by focusing your mind on whatever heaviness develops as you go along, rather than on the tensions that remain.

If you are familiar with spiritual practices, prayer or meditation may be the most effective means of relaxation you can use. These practices may also help you gain insight into the problem you are dealing with. Learn to pay attention to that kind, supportive voice inside you guiding you toward better health decisions. (Other techniques of relaxation are described at the end of Chapter 16, "Living Well With Stress.")

Detachment

When difficulties arise, we often feel closed in, limited. We lose both clear perception and creativity because we are so focused on what is wrong. Finding solutions is much easier if we can gain some distance from the difficult situation. This is especially true when a great deal is at stake, as with a pregnant woman trying to gain optimal control over diabetes, or with someone who has major diabetes complications developing. No matter how urgent the need to achieve a particular goal, it is more likely to be attained if the sense of anxious need can be suspended.

Following are a few of the many ways you might gain detachment from your reactions in a difficult situation. Once you have the basic idea, you will probably be able to find a way particularly suited to your style.

- Adopt an attitude of curiosity. Look at your situation as an artist or scientist who says, "Hmmm, very interesting. Let me explore what is happening."

- Remember a time of success, a time when things were going well for you, or when you felt very calm and peaceful. See or feel the places, happenings, or people that were part of this special time. Let the remembrance of positive feelings come into the present, reminding you that you are more than someone having a problem.

- Think of another area of your present life in which you are successful. Appreciate the strengths and skills that you demonstrate here. Imagine what it would mean to act with these qualities on the problem you are now facing.

- Speak in the past tense when describing the difficulties you are working on now. Look back on them from a time in the future when they have all been overcome and you have made great progress. See this immediate time as only one of many steps you needed to take to reach your goal.
- Describe your problems as those of someone else, someone you care for and understand and whom you see very clearly. Give this person credit for the effort he or she has made and assurance that the challenge will be met.
- Find a humorous point of view for perceiving the situation you are in. Laughter is itself a healing agent as well as a good lubricant for the imagination.

Central to this idea of detachment is letting go of any judgments about yourself and your ability to handle the problem that has arisen. Even if you are dealing with total rebellion against the whole diabetes regimen, suspend the self-condemnation that often goes along with it. You are acting with great power. You just haven't learned how to use that power to support living well.

FINDING OUT WHAT IS GOING ON NOW

You may already have full understanding of what is causing your present crisis and your difficulty in dealing with it. Or you may only have a vague sense of what is happening and why. If you need to develop more awareness of your problem and its source, the following exercise may help you.

Write a brief statement summarizing what you now know about the problem you are facing. This summary will help you clarify the problem and identify the solution. Draw on your answers to any of the following questions in the analysis.

- What are the objective facts of your situation? Which aspects appear to be outside your control? Which ones are within your control?
- When you examine how you are feeling about the problem, what are your strongest emotions? Where in your body do you feel them?
- Consider your thoughts. Are there beliefs or attitudes that make you feel unwilling or unable to deal with this situation? (Typical

limiting beliefs here would be: "I can't cope with crisis," "I can't learn this," "It won't do any good, anyway," "It's too late for me to change," "It's not fair," "I shouldn't have to," "I don't want to."

• In your behavior, what is it that you find difficult to do (or to stop doing)? Break down the behavior into small parts or steps. Figure out which are the most difficult. What pictures come to your mind when you consider the problem? Do they help you understand what is happening?

• Is there something you are holding onto by having this problem—some positive benefit, such as increased attention from someone you care about?

• Is there something you are avoiding? What undesirable result might come if you were free of this crisis?

• Is something else happening in your life that needs your attention or that is distracting you from what you are trying to accomplish with diabetes?

Some people are most comfortable doing this sort of work on their own, perhaps by writing notes in a journal. Others appreciate talking through a crisis with a friend or relative who is a good listener. A diabetes support group is another good setting for exploring such issues. If no progress is made in any of these ways, a few sessions with a counselor may be in order to sort things out.

CREATING YOUR SOLUTIONS

At times, a clear understanding of what is happening is all that we need to get past an obstacle. "Oh, I was hung up on that old belief 'I'll die by the time I'm 50,' just like Mom. No wonder I was stuck. It's time to get on with learning to live!" When this happens, tension is released and we are restored to full energy.

This may be a time when you need action, not just understanding. If so, take the role of creator, designing the solutions to your present problem. See the situation in its wholeness without blame or judgment. In the work you have just done, identify the specific beliefs, feelings, and behaviors interacting to produce your distress. Then generate a variety of options for dealing with these specifics.

Some guidelines for this process include the following:

- Affirm your ability to handle the situation. Recognize that you choose your responses to what is happening and can make new choices.

- Keep alive to your feelings throughout the process, but do not be trapped by them. Use the techniques for detachment described above when dark feelings seem to dominate. Remember, your feelings are created within you, and you have the power to change them. Ask yourself, "Is this how I want to feel?" If it isn't, create new feelings or attitudes.

- Work with the information about your situation you generated in the previous sections to help define your next steps.

- Identify the specific goals you wish to reach. What changes would let you know you were out of the crisis?

- Brainstorm a list of specific actions that will help you start moving forward. Write down any ideas that come to mind, then search the list for those you feel prepared to take right now. Choose the one that will enable you to take a first step.

- Use your imagination to see or feel yourself taking the actions you need to overcome your problem. In a relaxed state, let scenes unfold in your mind in which you discover new answers. (Also use this visualization to reinforce actions you chose in the previous step.)

- Take a first step, no matter how small. Action restores your confidence to take further action. Action is also an antidote to anxiety.

- Give yourself space for breaks, relaxation, exercise, and entertainment. In most crises, some time off increases your capacity for finding solutions.

If you do everything possible and still feel that you are getting nowhere, look for further help from your health care team and personal support network. Let go of any feeling that you must do this all on your own. Some challenges in living well with diabetes can be met only with outside support.

(See Chapter 14, "Living Well With Yourself," for more on working with feelings and beliefs. Chapter 11, "Living Well With Stress," can also be of aid in a crisis. If you are dealing with the threat or diagnosis of complications, see Section V.)

Section II
LIVING WELL WITH DIABETIC CONTROL

CHAPTER 4

Diabetes—Defining The Choices

Before we developed diabetes, our bodies performed a number of vital functions spontaneously, without our ever having to give a thought to them. The pancreas released insulin whenever it sensed that our blood sugar level was above a certain point. The hormones from other glands kept insulin from lowering blood sugar too much. (These counter-regulatory hormones inhibit insulin action or stimulate the release of sugar into the bloodstream.) We maintained a delicate balance, with blood glucose usually between 60 and 120 mg/dl. We enjoyed a natural control of our sugar metabolism and, as a result, other factors such as blood fats (including cholesterol and triglycerides) remained at normal levels.

When we developed type I diabetes, insulin production from our pancreas was reduced or eliminated. Blood sugar soared to readings two to five times the normal level, or maybe higher. Blood fats increased. Counter-regulatory hormones such as adrenalin—released in flight, fright, fight, or illness—increased because of physical stress and drove blood sugar level even higher. Our whole system was out of control.

When we started taking insulin, we regained a semblance of control, but with an enormous difference: *We had to be consciously involved in the metabolic control process.* We had to make decisions about many things that we had never had to worry about before: the amounts of insulin and food to take, the timing of meals and insulin injections, and the effects of exercise or stress on our blood sugar level.

Making metabolic decisions that result in normal blood glucose levels requires information and skill. We need to be able to measure our specific blood sugar level at any moment; we need to know what factors are determining that level (diet, activity medication, stress, etc.); and we need to know how to vary those factors to regain balance when tests are too high or too low. Finally we need support—from within or from outside—to maintain the regulated life-style that makes real control of diabetes possible.

Until the last few years, most of us were unable to achieve a good level of control. Only in mild cases of diabetes was it possible to avoid swings in blood sugar level far outside the normal range. Urine tests gave imprecise information abut the actual blood glucose level at the time of testing. Once-a-day injections of intermediate or long-acting insulin could not provide the insulin activity needed to handle blood sugar increases after each meal. We knew little about the way emotional stress raises and lowers blood sugar. And the need for emotional support was barely recognized.

All of this has now changed. Home blood glucose testing gives fairly precise readings of blood sugar level any time we need them. An insulin pump or two or more injections of insulin each day can provide a supply of insulin that more closely matches our hour-to-hour need for it. Physicians are encouraging us to learn to make the alterations in insulin dose, diet, and exercise necessary to keep blood glucose levels close to normal. Recognition of the effect of emotional stress on diabetic control has brought a new emphasis on learning means of dealing with stress more effectively; and we are finally admitting the need for emotional support, something required by anyone living with a chronic medical condition.

It is now possible for diabetics who need to develop optimal control rapidly (because of pregnancy, for instance) to do so. Within four to eight weeks, many of us have learned to achieve an average blood sugar level that was impossible five years ago. Even without an urgent short-term need, many of us have gained this level of control simply because we want to live well with diabetes.

The level of regimen needed to maintain optimal control of diabetes is demanding and liberating at the same time. This book outlines a step-by-step process for learning this regimen in an organized and safe fashion. This path is appropriate for people who are prepared to move to a style of intensive diabetes management. This level of management takes commitment, effort, time, a modest amount of money, and close teamwork with your health professionals.

Not everyone is prepared to follow this path. Some people like to move more gradually or are less motivated than others. Some have major concerns other than diabetes competing for their energies. Others may be held back by certain beliefs and emotional reactions that make them feel unable to change. For one reason or another, many diabetics choose to remain at a level of moderate or even loose management.

Although many powerful reasons favor the path of intensive management, we feel it is important not to bias this choice. If diabetics who do not adopt this type of program come to feel that anything less rigorous than the most intensive management is ineffective and futile, they may abandon all efforts to control their metabolism.

You may believe that you have no control at all; your blood sugar levels may soar and plummet crazily. Even so, it is vitally important that you do not condemn yourself as weak or incompetent. By accepting yourself and your past choices, you gain the power to make new, more healthful decisions about self-regulation. If your present choice is a moderate or loose regimen, give yourself credit for what you are doing and continue doing it. You will feel better, and this alone may help you decide to improve your level of management.

If the Word "Control" Sounds Like Fingernails
On a Blackboard . . .

Most of us believe that living well is living with freedom. Yet when we have diabetes, we are told that we must control our metabolism, our blood sugar, and our eating. Sometimes it seems as though every aspect of our lives requires some kind of control.

There is a basic problem with the word *control* itself. In *Roget's Thesaurus,* the synonyms for *control* include *whip hand, subjugation, domination, suppression, oppression,* and *tyranny.* Verbs associated with control include *browbeat, bully, restrict,* and *corner.* It doesn't sound like a very pleasant place to visit, much less live. No wonder controlling our diabetes often feels like a burden. Yet *control* is one of the most frequently used words in articles discussing diabetic management, and we have not been able to come up with many adequate substitutes.

We can purge *control* of its negative associations by evoking the image of metabolic order it really represents. When we work to gain control of diabetes, we are seeking deliberately to take over a task our bodies previously handled automatically. If anything, this opportunity of exercising control is a challenge. We are cooperating with and helping direct our life processes. We are not simply managing diabetes; we are managing our lives.

LEVELS OF CONTROL

We are considering two aspects of control here: the level of regimen you follow to control your metabolism and the actual level of control you achieve. The level of regimen is defined by what you do. The actual level of control you achieve is measured by home and lab tests and the way you feel. Before telling you about the different possible levels, we are going to suggest that you find out about them by determining what your own level is at present. The following questionnaire helps you to do this.

Finding Your Level
Circle the number following the statement that is most true for you. Your doctor's office can supply results of your lab tests if you have had tests done.

A. Level of Control
  1. My last fasting blood glucose test in the lab or doctor's office was

less than 120 mg/dl.	**3**	Don't know or NA (not ap-
between 120 and 180	**6**	plicable). **7.5**
between 181 and 240	**9**	
higher than 240	**12**	

2. My last hemoglobin A_1c test was

less than 8%	**3**	higher than 12%	**12**
between 8 and 9.9%	**6**	Don't know or NA	**7.5**
between 10 and 12%	**9**		

3. My last test for total cholesterol was

less than 201	**2**	higher than 240	**8**
between 201 and 225	**4**	Don't know or NA	**5**
between 226 and 240	**6**		

4. The average of all my home blood glucose tests for the last seven days is

less than 120 mg/dl.	**3**	higher than 240	**12**
between 120 and 180	**6**	Don't know or NA	**7.5**
between 181 and 240	**9**		

5. The approximate percentage of all my home blood glucose tests for the last seven days that were between 60 and 140 mg/dl was

more than 75%	**3**	less than 25%	**12**
between 50 and 75%	**6**	Don't know or NA	**7.5**
between 25 and 50%	**9**		

6. If you do not test blood or urine, or if you do so less than twice a week, circle 12 here, and skip to question 8.   **12**

7. I test urine for sugar regularly, and I almost never have a positive urine test (one or more +).   **2**

My tests are negative (−) at least half the time and usually not higher than 1/4%   **4**

My tests vary greatly, sometimes negative, sometimes 1 or 2%   **6**

My tests are usually over 1%   **8**

Not applicable, because I test only blood sugar.   **5**

8. When you test for ketones in your urine, the test is

always negative	**2**	frequently positive (1 + times a week)	**8**
always negative unless I am ill or under stress	**4**	NA	**5**
occasionally positive (1–3 times a month)	**6**		

45

9. I have had severe insulin reactions in the last month (severe = strong symptoms such as confusion, shakiness, sweating, pounding heart, etc.).

Never	2	5–10 times	6
1—4 times	4	More than 10 times	8

10. I have been unconscious from a reaction or failed to awaken to a reaction occurring during sleep in the last year. If yes, circle 16. If no, skip to question 11. **16**

11. I have had symptoms of high blood sugar (frequent urination, nighttime urination, thirst, and lethargy) in the last month.

Never	2	4–10 times	6
1–3 times	4	More than 10 times	8

12. I have normal weight. **3**

I am slightly overweight (up to 10% above normal) **6**

I am moderately overweight (10–20% above normal) **9**

I am seriously overweight (more than 20% above normal). **12**

13. I seldom have illness or infections, and I recover or heal easily when I do. **1**

I have occasional illness or infection, and I recover somewhat slowly. **3**

I frequently am ill or have infections, and I heal slowly. **4**

14. My energy level is good and I recover from exertion easily. **1**

I occasionally feel lethargic. **2**

I tire very easily and need to rest frequently during the day. **4**

15. In the last year I have been hospitalized because my diabetes was out of control.

Never	4	More than once	16
Once	9		

B. Level of Regimen
(These questions cover only the aspects of diabetes regimen that relate to metabolic control.)

1. I am on an intensive insulin regimen (2 or more injections per day, using both regular and intermediate or long-acting insulin or the insulin pump) and vary dosage according to blood sugar tests.   **3**

   I take two injections per day but rarely vary dosage from day to day.   **6**

   I take only one injection of insulin each day.   **9**

   NA   **6**

2. In the last two months I have forgotten or deliberately not taken insulin.

   Never   **4**

   1–2 times   **12**

   More than twice   **16**

   NA   **10.5**

3. I test blood glucose levels two or more times a day.   **3**

   I test blood glucose levels at least twice a week, or urine at least once a day.   **6**

   I test blood or urine at least twice a week.   **9**

   I seldom (or never) do any home urine or blood tests.   **12**

4. When my control is off (high or low blood sugar) or when there are changes in my routine (schedule, activity, food, or stress), I know how to alter insulin, diet, or activity to compensate for the changes. I can return to normal quickly.   **2**

   I make some general adjustments but sometimes don't get completely back to normal for a few days.   **4**

   I know when my control is off but rarely do anything to compensate.   **6**

   I don't know anything about adjusting insulin, food, or activity to maintain good control.   **8**

5. I measure or accurately estimate the amounts of food I eat and keep the prescribed balance of carbohydrate, protein, and fat.   **3**

   I usually eat in moderation and have a general awareness of the balance of carbohydrate, protein, and fat.   **6**

   I eat pretty much what I want to, but not to excess.   **9**

   I frequently eat excessively or irregularly.   **12**

6. I seldom eat sweets, and I minimize use of other simple carbohydrates (such as dried fruits and fruit juices). **3**

   I eat small portions of sweets and other simple carbohydrates. **6**

   I usually eat small portions, but at least once a week I binge. **9**

   I eat all the sweets and fruit I want, sometimes a lot. **12**

7. I eat as little animal fat as possible (butter, fatty meat, luncheon meat, high-fat cheese). **3**

   I eat small amounts of animal fat and rarely eat excessive amounts. **6**

   I usually eat only small amounts of animal fat, but at least once a week, I eat a lot or binge. **9**

   I eat all the animal fat I want. **12**

8. I eat complex carbohydrates and high-fiber foods (whole grains, vegetables, etc.)

   at most meals. **2**

   about half the time. **4**

   rarely. **6**

   never. **8**

9. When I have overeaten or know that a large meal is coming, I use extra insulin or exercise to compensate for the extra calories

   nearly always. **2**

   usually. **4**

   rarely. **6**

   never. **8**

10. I have moderate to full physical activity regularly (the equivalent of 20 minutes of exercise with heart rate 120+).**2**

    I have moderate physical activity but it usually varies quite a bit from day to day. **4**

    I am relatively inactive or irregular in my level of activity. **6**

    I am very inactive or very irregular in my level of activity. **8**

11. When I am under emotional stress,

    I feel able to cope well, and the stress does not seriously affect my blood sugar level. **2**

    I try to cope, but my control may be off for the next few tests.**4**

I don't cope too well, and my blood sugar level may be high
for a day or more.   **6**

I forget everything I know about coping, ignore my
diabetes, and my blood sugar stays high.   **8**

Add up the numbers you circled for parts A and B and enter your
totals here:

Part A: Level of Control _____

Part B: Level of Regimen _____

Now see what your level of control and level of management are.

Level of Control	Score	Level of Regimen	Score
Optimal	34–42	Intensive	28–42
Moderate	43–65	Moderate	43–63
Loose	66–90	Loose	64–84
Minimal	91+	Minimal	85+

These general ranges are derived from the authors' experience and
have been pilot tested, but they have not yet been fully validated.
However, your score should give you a sense of where you are and
what you need to work on.

Completing this exercise can be challenging, maybe even down-
right unpleasant. If your results were not as positive as you thought
they would be, don't blame yourself. Acknowledge the choices you
have been making and the reasons you have been making them.
Give yourself room to begin making new choices. You might go
through the regimen part of the questionnaire and check the places
where you marked the higher numbers. These will indicate areas
for needed improvement in management that you may feel willing
to begin at this time. A little later in this chapter, there is another
exercise that will help you choose the overall level of management
you wish to exercise at this time.

In your answers to this questionnaire, you have a general profile of
your current metabolic control regimen and your level of control.
You may feel comfortable with this level of management, or other
concerns may take priority. On the other hand, you may wish to
improve control as your next step in living well with diabetes. You
may wish to assume the intensive regimen. Or you may prefer to

make the change in stages, working first to gain loose or moderate control.

BENEFITS OF ACHIEVING OPTIMAL CONTROL

The first thing you need to consider in choosing your level of diabetic regimen is what you can gain from the best level of control. You know achieving it will take effort. What will it give you?

Just beginning the learning process necessary to achieve optimal control often brings an immediate emotional benefit to many people with diabetes. We report a sense of greater power, less depression, less anxiety. This emotional high helps us through the initial period of greater regulation required until we have learned the regimen. Once we have done so, we will experience greater freedom. We can deal with irregularities of diet, mealtimes, activity, and stress, and still obtain greatly improved blood sugar tests.

The first physical benefits start soon after control is improved. When blood sugar level is closer to normal, we simply feel better. We have more energy; we need to sleep less; we are less likely to grow fatigued. Our immune system works more effectively, so we are less likely to become ill or have infections that get out of control. When we do become seriously ill, we are more able to compensate for the effect of the physical stress on blood sugar, and we are less likely to develop ketoacidosis, a condition that can lead to diabetic coma. In formal studies, diabetics who maintained good control had many fewer hospitalizations, a considerable economic benefit.

Women who improve metabolic control develop fewer vaginal and urinary tract infections and consequently find greater enjoyment of sex. In addition, their menstrual periods became more regular. Adolescents are less likely to experience a delay in reaching menses. With strict control leading up to and continuing during pregnancy, the risks for both mother and child are greatly reduced. (In diabetes, very careful management of pregnancy is necessary. See Chapter 18, "Living Well As a Diabetic Woman.)

For children, optimal control encourages normal patterns of growth and development. (Growth is sometimes stunted when blood sugar is poorly controlled in childhood.) Fluctuations in insulin requirements caused by growth spurts and the hormonal changes during puberty are more easily handled with the intensive regimen. Parental awareness of the emotional side of diabetes can help children live well with the more demanding regimen.

These are the short-term benefits we can experience directly, but that's only half the story. Laboratory tests of diabetics in good control show that several important measures of physiological balance are brought to normal values. These include factors in the blood that are responsible for clotting; the levels of certain fats (cholesterol and triglycerides) that contribute to heart and circulatory disorders when they are high; the release of a variety of hormones; and even the thickness and fragility of capillaries (the thinnest blood vessels). All of these factors tend to be abnormal when blood sugar is high.

Although we don't experience symptoms from these abnormalities in the short run, their presence is not healthful. They are the basic building blocks from which diabetic complications are constructed over time. In the long run, high blood sugar levels increase the chance of developing heart disease, circulatory problems, blindness and other vision problems, kidney disorders, and neuropathy (nerve malfunctions).

These future possibilities support us in following a demanding regimen in the present. We work most effectively when this takes the form of healthy concern, not chronic anxiety.

Optimal control of diabetes has been possible for only a few years, not enough time to determine scientifically whether it will lower the chance of developing these long-term complications. But studies are now accumulating that document the effect of improved control in the short run. Capillary thickness, growth hormone levels, excessive fats in the blood, and factors affecting clotting have been normalized when blood sugar levels were brought under control. In this way, a major, but subtle, aspect of the *illness* of diabetes can be erased. We can live well with diabetes now and provide a basis for a future without major complications.

What if complications have already set in? Is it too late to bother with control? No. Even at this stage, one may benefit from improved control. In some cases, complications may be reversed or their impact lessened by careful management. Whether or not existing complications can be reversed, one's chances of avoiding or slowing the development of other complications are improved. The immediate physical benefits and the emotional lift gained by taking control help one deal more effectively with the fears that usually accompany the diagnosis of a complication. *(One caution: Control must be improved gradually if retinopathy or kidney disease has already started. See Chapter 17, "Complications Simplified," for details.)*

Optimal control of diabetes offers powerful benefits immediately and over the long run. But there is no guarantee that it will prevent future complications or reverse them once they have started. What it does do is improve our odds, reducing the risk of having complications. We feel that the decision to gain optimal control must be made in terms of the present benefits, which include having a body that functions more healthfully right now and that has less risk of developing complications later.

THE COSTS OF GAINING OPTIMAL CONTROL

What are the costs of better control? Economically, there is a moderate cost, one that more insurance companies are now covering. Blood test strips are still much more expensive than urine test materials, but there are ways of cutting corners (and the strips) to save money. At the time of most intensive testing (four to six times a day for the first weeks), the cost would be $15 to $25 a month by the economy route, but up to $100 a month without cutting costs. Some people need to use a meter for reading the strips, at a cost of $50 to $200. With most meters, it is also necessary to use the full strip. The only other piece of equipment is an automatic finger-pricking device that lessens the chance of pain. It costs around $15.

During the first months of intensive control, there is a significant cost in time and energy. Collecting information, testing, keeping records, figuring out what the records mean—all this becomes a major project. But probably it is no more complex than learning to drive. Depending on how much new information you have to acquire, the task could take anywhere from three to ten hours a week.

Another cost at the beginning: You need to regularize all aspects of life that affect blood sugar, making changes that may or may not be simple. The more you do this, the more quickly you will reach the point where you do not have to be so regular. It is much easier to learn how to keep your blood sugar within limits if you follow fairly set routines during the training period. Without this regularity, it is difficult to know what is causing tests to be too high or too low. Once you know the ropes, you'll enjoy much more freedom.

One potential liability when maintaining strict control: You are likely to have more insulin reactions. This is especially true if you have usually had high blood sugar levels or have been irregular in activity or diet. (Often, fear of reactions is one of the reasons a diabetic will keep blood sugar high.) Once control is well established, diabetics usually experience fewer severe reactions. Meanwhile, you will need to sharpen awareness of the cues indicating that a reaction is on its way and be sure to always have some form of sugar with you. With home blood testing, you can easily check whether those "funny feelings" are the result of low blood sugar or some other cause, like anxiety.

Testing is especially important if you find that your reaction symptoms have become more subtle. After years of having diabetes, some people experience a decrease in the output of stress hormones that signal the appearance of an insulin reaction. When this develops, blood sugar can drop quite low without triggering the usual alarms—shakiness, sweating, increased pulse rate, and so forth. This also may result from some forms of neuropathy. If you feel it has become difficult to tell when an insulin reaction is occurring, talk with your doctor. It is an important consideration when determining the level of control you will try to maintain.

We have included in the following pages many safeguards against insulin reactions. In Chapter 8, we give comprehensive information on reactions, including tips on recognizing and treating them.

Weighing the Costs and Benefits

Take a moment to consider how these benefits and costs of optimal control balance out for you.

- What value do you place on the benefits we have described?_____

_____

- Which are most important to you?_____

_____

- Do any of the costs seem particularly heavy to you?_____

_____

- If so, what could you do to lighten them?_____

_____

A CHOICE OF REGIMEN

Given the benefits of optimal control, one might conclude that the treatment plan designed to bring it about should be the only one offered to people with diabetes. This would be a profound mistake. We cannot ignore the obvious fact that diabetes care is just one of the many items we must manage in our lives. Until the next set of technical breakthroughs, optimal control will depend on a set of life-style changes and an educational process requiring time and intense effort. Those of us who are not prepared to make these changes or those with extraordinary demands on time and energy might choose to ignore our diabetes if we feel we cannot follow the optimal path.

Therefore, it makes more sense to offer a choice of alternative regimens—a continuum of self-care. This choice, made consciously or subconsciously, is reflected in our day-to-day actions. And there is an infinite range of actions along the continuum from intensive to loose. We do what we do, with or without the knowledge and support of our physician or health care team. It makes sense to us to recognize this and support each person in the choices made. With this approach, you can begin at the level where you feel willing to work and proceed at a pace that is right for you.

54

The Intensive Regimen

The first choice we will consider is the regimen that allows you to gain nearly normal blood sugar values in a few months. This optimal control of diabetes depends upon a number of innovations in self-care, knit together into a state-of-the-art management program. We call this the intensive regimen.

The Intensive Regimen

1. Home blood sugar testing (blood glucose monitoring) two to four times a day (as many as six times a day at the beginning).
2. Insulin injections two to four times a day, usually using both rapid-acting and intermediate or long-acting insulins, or continuous insulin delivery by insulin pump.
3. Knowledge of food values and ability to follow a diet that ensures normal body weight, diabetic control, and reducing risks of complications.
4. An active life-style, an exercise program, or both, followed regularly.
5. Ability to alter insulin dosage, food intake, and activity level to compensate for irregularities and the effects of stress.
6. Knowledge of the role of physical and emotional stress in diabetes and the ability to manage both.
7. Commitment to continuing diabetes learning, maintaining motivation, and meeting one's emotional needs.

The old staples of diabetes care are all here—insulin, diet, exercise—but we've added several new ingredients. In this approach, home blood glucose monitoring allows precise feedback about blood sugar level, information that enables you to make more precise decisions about insulin dosage, activity, and diet. When you test your blood several times a day, multiple injections or the pump can provide a pattern of insulin action closely matching the peaks of blood sugar following meals.

Awareness of the effect of stress on diabetic control helps you understand many puzzling swings in blood sugar level. More effective management of stressful situations helps to reduce the metabolic effect of these swings. Furthermore, the intensive regimen recognizes that the demands of the regimen itself may become a source of stress. So it includes work to make these demands less burdensome and to help you stay motivated. For the regimen to work in the long run, it must serve as a foundation for the rest of your life, not as a substitute for living.

Who Needs the Intensive Regimen?

Some people will choose this path simply because they tend to do their best in everything they do or because they have strong motivation to live as healthfully as possible. However, others will make this choice because of a specific and immediate health need.

The intensive regimen is especially recommended for

- Women who are pregnant or are planning to become pregnant.
- Patients with diabetic complications developing (nerve and kidney disorders, circulatory problems, heart disease, retinopathy, and other eye disorders.) (If retinopathy or kidney disease has started, you may need to proceed gradually. See Chapter 17, "Complications Simplified.")
- Children whose growth is significantly behind schedule.
- Patients with other chronic illnesses or conditions.

People in these categories often choose to make optimal control a high priority and to reorder other aspects of their lives that might interfere. If personal obstacles are making it hard for you to make this level of commitment, you may wish to seek assistance in the form of individual counseling or a support group. If you decide to continue with a moderate or loose regimen because other problems are more pressing, you can review your decision periodically to see if a new choice seems possible.

You may need to adopt a somewhat less strict version of the intensive regimen if you have difficulty recognizing the symptoms of an insulin reaction. After many years of diabetes, the usual signs of low blood sugar sometimes diminish or disappear because of hormonal changes. Your doctor can order tests to determine whether this has happened to you. If your hormonal output is normal, then you need to sharpen your awareness of the physical cues of low blood sugar. Medicines for some other conditions (typically beta blockers for high blood pressure) can also blunt your recognition of symptoms.

The Moderate Regimen

If we discussed only the intensive regimen, some of you, unable or unwilling to devote yourself to diabetes care in such a concentrated fashion, would be left out in the cold. These people include the young man who still feels invulnerable, except when shaken by an insulin reaction; the single mother fighting to keep her job; the student scraping through grad school with just a few extra dollars per month, or the welfare recipient who can barely afford the cost of insulin; the person with weighty emotional problems; or the pleasure seeker who fears losing the things that "make life worth living."

If you are facing extraordinary demands, if you have little motivation or a highly individualistic style, or if you have many emotional obstacles, you may need a regimen that respects your particular needs: a slower, less concentrated pace; a freer structure allowing you more room for dealing with your concerns; and a periodic review of your choice of regimen. It is possible to include in the moderate regimen many innovations of the intensive regimen so that you can significantly improve your control.

The Moderate Regimen

1. Regular home blood glucose testing (at least two to four times a week, best daily) combined with daily urine tests.
2. One or two insulin injections daily, usually with a combination of rapid-acting and intermediate or long-acting insulins. (The insulin pump is not recommended with this regimen.)
3. Knowledge of food values and ability to follow a diet that ensures normal body weight and moderate diabetic control.
4. An active life-style, a regular exercise program, or both.
5. Ability to make cautious adjustments in insulin dosage, food intake, and activity level to compensate for changes and the effects of stress.
6. Knowledge of the role of physical and emotional stress in diabetes and the ability to manage either.
7. Commitment to continuing diabetes learning, maintaining motivation, and meeting your own emotional needs.

The moderate regimen differs from the intensive regimen in the level of feedback and control it provides. Testing is less rigorous and, as a result, the style of insulin dosage cannot be so finely tailored. Without frequent blood tests, you have too little information to make precise daily adjustments in insulin dosage, food, or activity. Caution is recommended. For this reason, the insulin pump or more than two insulin injections a day are not recommended for anyone on either the moderate or the loose regimen.

Home blood sugar testing is an important part of the moderate regimen, even when it is done only a few times a week. The accuracy of the results, compared with urine tests, helps to build motivation to improve control. Having the strips on hand means that you can easily see how stress, a large meal, or an unusual level of exercise affects blood sugar. When you are ill, you can handle blood sugar and ketone problems more accurately. If you have difficulty detecting insulin reactions, you can use the tests to confirm hypoglycemia and to help develop more awareness of symptoms.

Sometimes, success in improving control has the unexpected effect of increasing your motivation dramatically. If you feel now that you could never handle the intensive regimen, you may find that the act of beginning to improve management gives you greater willingness later. Whether or not this occurs, you will feel much better about yourself than if you just continued in your old ways, believing that you cannot control your diabetes. You will be dealing with one of the most important issues in your life—living well with diabetes.

The Loose Regimen

For those of you who may feel that even the moderate regimen is too restrictive or too demanding, you have a third choice. In the loose regimen, the focus is on identifying whatever you are willing to do to start improving control, and then doing it. In this regimen, we emphasize building willingness and a positive attitude, even though you may be living with a low level of control now. One important element for many diabetics who maintain this level is to face the fact that loose control is a choice they have made consciously or unconsciously. It is not something that just happens to them.

It is useful to define this as a level of regimen rather than as a rebellion against or neglect of regimen. Both authors have managed their diabetes at this level in the past. Each of us has the right to choose how we live with our bodies. Learning to accept the choices we make helps us move on to more healthful choices.

The Loose Regimen

1. Knowledge of blood testing technique, even though tests may be done infrequently. Urine testing several times a week.
2. One or two insulin injections daily. (More injections or the insulin pump are not recommended without regular blood sugar testing.)
3. Eating a healthful diet, usually in moderation.
4. Caution in adjusting insulin dosage, food intake, and activity level.
5. Commitment to continuing diabetes learning, maintaining motivation, and reviewing obstacles to improving control.

You may choose the loose regimen because your attention is focused on problems in other areas of your life. If you do choose this level, remember that the time you do give to improving your diabetes management will probably help you manage the rest of your life better.

CHOOSING YOUR REGIMEN LEVEL
If you still have not decided which level of regimen to follow, answering these questions may help you to do so.

1. I need to achieve improved control soon because
   ___I have diabetic complications.
   ___I am pregnant.
   ___I am planning to become pregnant.
   ___I am a child whose growth is significantly below normal.
   ___I have another major illness.
   ___I have no immediate physical condition requiring optimal control.

2. It is difficult for me to detect insulin reactions, because I do not experience the usual symptoms of low blood sugar_____

3. The reasons I have for wishing to improve my control of diabetes include_____

4. a. Other major problems that need my attention now are____

   b. I could gain assistance and support in dealing with these issues by_____

   c. Could I postpone working on any of these to gain time for diabetes?_____

5. The external support I now have for dealing with diabetes is abundant _____ adequate _____ inadequate _____ .

6. In making this decision, I also have to consider_____

Review your answers, discuss them with your physician and people close to you, and then make a decision you are happy with.

7. Given the above, my choice of regimen is
   intensive _____ moderate _____ loose _____ .

The Intensive Regimen

You learn much more easily when you divide large projects into manageable steps. You can see each task more clearly, and you can see the progress you make toward your overall goal. This definition of steps is doubly important when the project is learning the intensive regimen and making significant changes in life-style. The sequence in which you learn can make the enterprise safer and quicker. You may already have some of the required skills or knowledge, but we urge you to review all of the information we provide in this book. You may learn some facts you haven't seen elsewhere.

Eleven Steps to Optimal Control

1. Create a positive foundation. Be sure you have a positive setting for learning the intensive regimen, a physician who agrees with your goals, and support from family, friends, and other people with diabetes.

   Review the tools available to help you if you become frustrated or discouraged along the way. (See Chapters 3 and 14.)

2. Under your doctor's supervision, have lab tests of hemoglobin A_1c and blood lipids (triglycerides and cholesterol) done to indicate your present level of control.

   This gives you a benchmark with which to measure the effect of your new regimen.

3. Learn the skills and information basic to the intensive regimen:
   a. Learn how to test blood sugar and urine.
      The criteria of diabetic control.
      An effective record-keeping system.
      The meaning of each laboratory test relevant to diabetic control.
   b. Review Chapter 8, "Living Well with Insulin Reactions." It is important to review this because you may experience different signs of reaction when your metabolism is under better control.
   c. Survey the basics of diabetic metabolism (how your system processes food and liquids to produce energy).
   d. Understand all of the different factors that determine blood sugar level.

4. Regularize diet and activity or exercise as much as possible during this period of learning. Later on you will have greater freedom.

5. Begin the period of intensive testing and record keeping without making any changes in regimen (unless your doctor requests changes). Keep careful records, and observe how you respond to your present regimen.

6. With your doctor's guidance, select the intensive insulin regimen best suited to you (two or more shots a day or the insulin pump). Begin this regimen and make the adjustments in it needed to obtain the best possible level of control.

7. Observe the variations in blood sugar level caused by stress, illness, changes in food and exercise, and other factors.
   a. Learn to vary insulin dosage, diet, and exercise to compensate for high or low tests and to deal with changes in routine.

8. Have new lab tests done after two to three months to determine the effect of your new regimen and to establish your ongoing regimen.

9. Assess your progress and determine what, if anything, is needed to further improve control.
10. Take steps to maintain your motivation for continuing at this level of management.
11. Celebrate!

Step 1: Create a positive foundation

You are starting one of the most positive and challenging things you can do for yourself to deal with your diabetes. The rewards at physical and emotional levels are profound. You may have to overcome many obstacles to gain these rewards. So your first step is making sure that the foundation for this work is also positive. This includes creating realistic expectations, neutralizing past failures at improving diabetes management, lining up professional and personal support, and becoming familiar with the things you can do if progress grinds to a halt.

One of the most useful expectations to have about this process is that it will take time. You can't just flip a switch and gain instant control. People who are willing and able to focus energy on gaining control quickly will find that the process takes one to two months and sometimes longer. It is possible to meet with repeated discouragement, even when committing to an all-out effort. This is particularly true for people with physiological problems such as partial immunity to insulin, and those with a high level of emotional or environmental stress. These people may follow the diabetic regimen perfectly and gain improved control, but still experience large fluctuations in blood sugar level.

If at first you don't succeed, find out what else you need to do. Discuss what is happening with your doctor, be patient with yourself, and keep giving yourself credit for what you have achieved. Sometimes improving diabetic control calls for a prescription of a stress-management class, couples counseling, or transfer to a less stressful job. Or a more highly purified insulin may be needed to overcome immunity that can develop after years of injections.

Occasionally, it becomes necessary to accept a lesser degree of control than you would like to have because, at the time, you are unwilling to make the changes called for. If so, spare yourself the

63

additional stress of feeling guilty. Respect your decision and keep the postponed changes on your agenda.

We discussed in the Introduction ways to safeguard against failure. There is probably no more important place to apply them than when learning the intensive regimen. If you start down this path and then feel you are failing, it is time to use Chapters 3 and 4, the "Help!" and "Living Well with Yourself" chapters, designed to help you overcome the obstacles you have encountered. You are not really failing; you just have something else to learn before you can succeed. Although you may feel a sense of urgency about the learning, it is helpful to drop your judgments. Transform obstacles into a natural part of the learning process, letting them define the next lessons you must master.

Those of us who have tried many times to improve our metabolic control may have to set aside a history of frustration and lack of success. In the past, we simply did not have adequate tools to achieve our goal. Now, it is important to let go of that old feeling, "I'll never get this right." It is time for a completely fresh effort.

The fear and sense of urgency that inspire many who decide to learn the intensive regimen need to be balanced with more positive motivation. Fear is a powerful feeling. It can move us for a time, but our progress is steadier and more enduring when it is grounded in a positive sense of oneself—in our basic wellness.

Ernest's Experience

I'm afraid I have to confess, I didn't really start to take control of diabetes until the ophthalmologist told me I had a high risk of going blind. I learned fast then. I enjoy the world's beauty too much to lose my vision of it.

But soon I realized that everything I was doing was for all of me, not just to save my eyes. I was giving myself a degree of love and respect that I'd always withheld before.

After a few months, I had the first hemorrhage in my left eye. And then, after laser treatment, another, and yet another. I could see only a blur through that eye. I had to face the strong possibility of losing vision in both eyes. When the difficulties started, I half expected to give up on my intensive regimen with the childish feeling, "It didn't do any good, anyway." Why didn't I? It's simple:

I feel better loving and respecting myself, no matter what the outcome of my actions may be. I am living well, despite the possibility of losing my sight.

As I'm writing, I'm watching cows switching their tails in the shade of a large oak, against golden hills. Above my typewriter there's a lovely bronze statue of Krishna, a flute-playing god who herds cows in Indian mythology. Once, when I asked my eye doctor what he thought would happen with my eyes, he answered with an unconscious pun, "We'll just have to wait and see." I replied, "I certainly hope so." I waited, and I'm still seeing. The laser treatment was successful.

Another important part of this first step is reviewing and strengthening your support system. A key element is, of course, your physician. You need one who is well informed about the newer approaches to diabetes care and who endorses your increased role in managing your condition. Discuss what you are doing thoroughly with your doctor and work out ground rules for the management decisions you are to make at each step. Most physicians working with diabetics are very pleased when they see their patients taking greater responsibility, and they support their independence fully. Often they make it possible for you to discuss test results and special problems by phone between office visits and provide twenty-four-access in case of emergencies. Ask about this is your doctor doesn't suggest it.

The encouragement of your family can help a great deal during that time. Let the people close to you know what you are working on and what it means to you. Share your concerns and expectations. Ask for the help you need or for changes in any family patterns that interfere with your efforts to improve management. If you are in a negative family situation, you may need to take action to neutralize your family's influence and look for more support from others.

You should also let your friends know about your project and ask them for assistance. This can be very helpful when you are attempting to make basic life-style changes. Friendships often revolve around habitual behavior and may be threatened when you start changing habits. You can reduce the threat and gain valuable aid if you communicate the importance of the changes you are making. Realize, though, that some friends may be too attached to their old image of you. If they offer little support, let that be their problem, not yours.

Support from other diabetics, especially those who are also learning the intensive regimen, is second only to the guidance of your physician during this period. Individual contacts or a support group can offer excellent encouragement and reinforcement, as well as sharing of practical tips on many details of management. Some physicians even organize a buddy system or support group for people working on improving control. Such groups could be organized by a few diabetics working through their local ADA chapter, or on their own, if necessary. It would probably be possible to contract with a physician to provide medical guidance.

The last task in this initial phase is remembering the support and guidance you can give yourself when you feel stuck, frustrated, confused, blocked, or otherwise discouraged. Chances are very good that you will reach this point one or two times in the coming months. It is a natural part of the process. Now, when you are still full of enthusiasm, is a good time to plant the seeds for the times when you may forget how creative you are. Glance through "Help!" and "Living Well with Yourself" (Chapters 3 and 14). Review your strengths and skills. You might even write a note to yourself to be opened when you feel that you can't go on. Remind yourself of all the things you can do at a time when you feel there is nothing you can do.

Summary of step 1
Begin by creating a positive foundation for the work of learning the intensive regimen. Review your support system and strengthen it where it is weak. This includes support from yourself as well as from your doctor, family, friends, and other diabetics. Remember that this is a fail-safe process designed to help you overcome any obstacles that may arise.

Step 2: Have laboratory tests done to provide a benchmark of control
Discuss with your physician the tests that will provide an accurate indication of your present level of control. The ones usually used include hemoglobin A_1c, fasting or random glucose, and blood lipids (the fats, triglycerides, and cholesterol). (These are described in step 3.) The results of these tests, along with your other records, tell you how far you have to go to obtain optimal control. But, more im-

portant, they will tell you how far you have come after a few weeks of learning. The objective feedback you receive when you compare the next set of lab tests with these may be very encouraging. Or, if there is little improvement, the new tests (together with your records of home tests, diet, stress, and exercise) will help you determine what to do next.

Step 3: Learn the skills and information basic to the intensive regimen

3a. Learn How to Test Blood Sugar and Urine.

Learn how to test your own blood for glucose (the type of sugar predominant in human blood), the relationship of this test to urine tests, the meaning of the different laboratory tests your physician requests, and a record-keeping method that makes it easy to measure your day-to-day control.

Self blood glucose testing is possibly the greatest advance in diabetes care since the discovery of insulin. It is a powerful feedback system that gives accurate information about the level of your blood sugar. On the basis of this data you can make decisions regarding precise insulin dosage, exercise, diet, stress, and reactions. It is one of the keys you can use to achieve both optimal metabolic control and greater freedom in your life.

You can understand the importance of this tool if you consider the automatic "testing" process in a person who does not have diabetes. There is a continuous, unconscious monitoring of blood sugar level, with feedback to the pancreas and other organs releasing hormones that maintain a normal level. The control information is available within seconds; insulin and other hormones regulating blood sugar level begin acting immediately. When blood sugar level rises after a meal, the pancreas releases insulin into the bloodstream. If the nondiabetic feels under attack or if blood sugar falls because of exercise, glucose is released by the liver, and adrenalin and other hormones inhibit the action of insulin. Through these processes, blood glucose levels are kept between 60 and 120 in the nondiabetic.

As you know, when you developed type I diabetes, you lost all or part of your ability to produce insulin. You still generate the other hormones that cause blood sugar to rise and fall, but the key hormone that allows cells to utilize blood sugar is missing. The inner testing signals high blood sugar, but there is little or no response from the pancreas.

So you have to enter into the control process consciously, injecting insulin and monitoring blood sugar level by tests and by how you feel. Your feelings tell you when blood sugar level is too low and you are having an insulin reaction; and they tell you when you have very high blood sugar. But you cannot feel the difference between normal (70–120 mg/dl), slightly high (121–180 mg/dl), and moderately high (181–240 mg/dl) levels. Until recently, the only day-to-day tests available were urine glucose sticks or tablets that give only a rough idea of blood sugar level. They do not give up-to-the-minute feedback; they only indicate whether you are a little out of control or very out of control. They do have their use in diabetes care, but it is limited.

Self blood glucose testing, on the other hand, gives information on your level of control at the time of the test. You can get a relatively accurate reading (within 10 to 20% of the actual value) in the critical area where urine tests only read "negative" (below 180 mg/dl). With this feedback, you can tell when you need extra insulin (or less food) and how much. You know when you are having an insulin reaction and you do not mistake the symptoms of an anxiety attack for those of low blood sugar. You know the precise effect on blood sugar level of a particular meal or snack or of a period of exercise. By making conscious decisions about all of this information, you can guide your body to a level of metabolic control that is more nearly normal.

This precise feedback of blood sugar level has a strong impact on the behavior of most diabetics who do blood testing. It becomes easier to deal with the craving for a hot fudge sundae when you've seen your blood sugar shoot up to 450 mg/dl upon eating one. That much-postponed stress-management class becomes a high priority when you've seen a distressing day at work produce a record high in blood sugar. With home blood glucose testing, you have a tool for understanding in detail exactly how you live with diabetes. You start to understand the reasons for the highs and lows, and you gain increasing ability to do something about them. That's living well!

Supplies You Will Need for Self Blood Glucose Testing

- Blood glucose testing reagent strips: Appropriate strips for visual reading or the strips used in the blood glucose meter you use.
- Lancets: Monolet by Monoject Division of Sherwood Medical (or other manufacturers, or the needle of a disposable syringe).
- Alcohol and cotton balls or tissue.
- An easy-to-read watch with a second hand or timer.
- A log for record keeping.
- *(Optional)* A small device that pricks fingers automatically. Monoject makes one called the Autolet, Bio-Dynamics makes the Autoclix and Palco makes the auto-Lancet. Several others are also available.
- A meter for reading the strips is advisable for many people. Ones that "speak" the blood sugar reading are now available for people with impaired vision. Your pharmacy can order one with a prescription from your doctor. Mail-order diabetes supply centers sell them at a discount. (See Appendix.)

    Testing equipment and supplies may be covered by your health insurance.

Using a blood glucose meter gives more exact results than can be obtained from visually reading Chemstrips or Visidex strips. For this reason, pregnant women and those using the insulin pump should use meters. People with color blindness or other visual impairment need them as well. Anyone fascinated with gadgetry may find that the little machine boosts their motivation to test.

Since a variety of strips and meters are available, and new ones keep appearing, we will not give specific testing instructions here. The new meters are even smaller and much easier to use than the older meters. We encourage you to attend a class in blood glucose testing at a diabetes clinic or to have your procedures and interpretation checked by your physician or nurse. Frequently, training is provided by the meter vendor. We will, however, offer some tips and cautions that will help you with your home blood testing.

To ensure the accuracy of your readings, test in a space that is at least 60 degrees F, or breathe gently on the strip while the blood is on it to keep it warm. Never use too small a drop of blood that you have to smear on the strip (the blood should stay liquid during the whole minute). Never use gauze to remove the blood (it may scrape off the test material). Keep your timing to within 3 to 5 seconds of 60 seconds (don't estimate). Never use test strips after they have expired. Do not match your test strip with a color chart other than the one on the container in which it came.

If you visually read the test strips, be sure to estimate blood sugar level when the colors fall between the ones on the container. A chief source of error is automatically choosing one of the "official" scores when the colors are actually midway between the colors given.

Here are a few of the objections and concerns about home blood testing that are raised by users.

"I'm afraid it'll hurt." We already stick ourselves at least once a day to take insulin, yet fingertips seem more sensitive, somehow, than thighs and upper arms. Actually, there is usually little pain, especially along the sides of the fingertips. Often you hardly feel the prick. With the automatic devices adjusted to the proper depth, you almost never notice when the lancet strikes. The anticipation of the pain is far worse than anything you actually experience. Also, your fingertips do not become sore or tender from repeated pricks. (It is a good idea to rotate from finger to finger, just as insulin shots are given in a different site each time.)

"Won't it be terribly expensive if I start testing several times a day?" Costs can be cut in two ways. First, you can cut the strips lengthwise in two with scissors. If you have sharp eyes, you can cut them into three or four strips, once you have learned to interpret the readings accurately. (Be sure to put unused strips back into the container right away. Cut strips have been tested and found to give reliable results, even when stored cut for a month. Some meters allow for using a half strip, but with most you must use a whole one.)

Second, you can buy the strips from a discount mail-order firm (see Appendix). At the time of this writing, each test costs about 12 cents if discounted strips are cut four ways. Uncut, the cost of each strip is 48 cents. If you have health insurance, check to see if it covers testing equipment and supplies. More and more medical plans are covering these costs.

"Won't I get discouraged if I see too many high tests?" Probably you will, and you can deal with the discouragement by remembering that this is only one of several steps in learning to control your blood sugar. High tests indicate only that you have more to learn, not that you are weak or unable to learn. You can use these tests to increase your motivation to master the regimen.

"Can children handle home blood testing?" Children can do it, with the proper support and guidance of adults. (It helps if the adults stick their own fingers and test their own blood a few times to offer encouragement and a good example.) Four- and five-year-olds have learned the testing procedure, though usually they are a few years older before they start doing their own tests. In fact, once they are trained in testing, children become excellent instructors of their peers.

"How often do I have to test?" Curiosity may lead you to do fairly frequent testing at first. It is very satisfying to be able to determine the exact impact of a given food, activity, or stress on your blood sugar level. For the first month or two of the intensive regimen, you may need to test up to six times a day to get a clear picture of your pattern of response. This would include tests before each meal, at bedtime, and, at least part of the time, one or two hours after a meal.

"I can tell by how I feel whether I'm high or low." This is true only if you are very high or very low. Usually, you cannot sense much without actual symptoms. You may be able to learn to sense blood sugar level in the midrange (70–200 mg/dl) by using the feedback from your home blood tests. You might try jotting down your guess-timate before testing for a few weeks. Write down the level you think you are at (given what you know about what you have eaten and done since the last test), and also write down the first number that pops into your mind. See if you come close to your actual test using either method.

Interpreting Blood Glucose Tests

With optimal control of diabetes, the test values you attain can be close to the blood sugar levels of a person who does not have diabetes. The following table gives the target glucose levels recommended by Jay Skyler, one of the leading diabetologists in the United States.

Intensive Regimen Target Glucose Levels

Time	Ideal	Acceptable Level
Fasting	60–90 mg/dl	60–105 mg/dl
Before meal	60–105 mg/dl	60–130 mg/dl
1 hr after meal	140 mg/dl or less	180 mg/dl or less
2 hr after meal	120 mg/dl or less	150 mg/dl or less

These are demanding standards, requiring full practice of the intensive regimen. If you can achieve them, fine. If not, keep working to improve your control. And remember that *you* are acceptable even when your test results are not. You and your doctor may agree on a higher set of target levels to begin with if these seem too difficult to attain. Or you may have to shift your targets up if you have too many insulin reactions.

By checking your blood sugar one to two hours after a meal, you will begin to learn how the food you have just eaten is affecting your sugar level. This information will greatly refine your skill in using your intuition, symptoms, general feelings, and blood tests to predict how different foods affect your control. Knowing this, you will be in a better position to choose the target blood sugar levels appropriate for you.

Urine Testing
In the intensive regimen, urine testing is still very useful for checking for ketones in the urine. You should keep ketone test supplies on hand, especially for when you are ill or stressed. Both tablets and strips are available.

The traditional test for sugar in the urine is useful chiefly in the moderate and loose regimens. For anyone on the intensive regimen, the test does not offer the precise feedback needed to maintain optimal control. For this reason, it is covered in the section on the moderate regimen.

Metabolic Record Keeping
Keeping clear records that you and your doctor can learn from is as important as doing the testing itself. At the beginning, we recommend that you log your tests, diet, activity level, and stress. (Once control is established, less detailed records will be sufficient.) During this initial period, you are a scientist studying your own me-

tabolism. The information you gather will help you learn more quickly about your individual patterns of response.

Here are forms you can photocopy for a daily log and for a periodic summary of your records. For the daily log, you can choose between a simple form that allows you to se the pattern of test results easily but that does not allow detailed recording of food and activity, and a more elaborate one that provides space for more detailed record keeping. (See pp.108 for examples of filled-in logs in step 7 below.) Some meters now have memories to record test results. They can also be hooked to computers for printouts and analyses.

Daily Diabetes Log I

DATE TIME	INSULIN DOSE	BREAK-FAST TEST	LUNCH TEST	DINNER TEST	BED TEST	COMMENTS: Ill-ness, change of pattern, stress

Daily Diabetes Log II

DATE TIME	BLOOD TEST & REACTIONS	INSULIN DOSAGE	ACTIVITY & EXERCISE	FOOD COMMENTS: Stress, illness, etc.

When you miss a test, indicate your estimate: "est. high" or "est. 150." Include reactions in the blood sugar test column, with the amount of food used to treat it in the food column. Grade reactions as mild (1), strong (2), or severe (3). Indicate the type of insulin if more than one type is used.

Grade activity for each period of the day relative to what is normal for you at that time: 1 = minimal activity, 2 = less activity than usual, 3 = your normal level, 4 = more activity than usual, 5 = maximum activity. Include length of time of activity or exercise.

Under "Food," indicate calories or exchanges and anything out of the ordinary. If you calculate only carbohydrates, indicate over- or underconsumption. You may wish to note the particular foods consumed.

Under "Comments," include any stressful events, whether or not you sensed having an emotional response. Note difficulty with sleeping, times of special tension or relaxation, good feelings, and any physical occurrences such as illness, the beginning of menstruation, low energy—anything that might help to explain the variations in your tests.

Remember, these records are not just for your doctor. Useful as they are to your physician, they are even more valuable to you. Analyze them, learn from them, and make changes based on what you learn from them. By writing down this information, you give yourself a tool for seeing the patterns of your life with diabetes. (The interpretation of these records is discussed in step 7.)

Lab Tests Your Physician May Order
When you are testing your own blood sugar regularly at home, the traditional fasting blood glucose test at the lab becomes less important. It can give you a quality check on your testing technique. (Bring your testing materials and do your own test at the same time your blood is drawn at the lab.) If there is a significant difference (more than 10%), ask your doctor or nurse to review your procedure.

The lab is able to make other important tests with the same sample of blood. A relatively new one, hemoglobin A_1c, gives an overall evaluation of blood sugar control. This test measures the amount of glucose that has bound to the hemoglobin in the red blood cells. Since the average blood cell lasts for two to three months, the test results give an approximate summary or average of our blood sugar levels over that period. Higher readings usually indicate need for a change in regimen or in your level of adherence.

Hemoglobin A₁c and Control	
4.0–8.2	Normal in nondiabetics
Less than 8.2	Good control of diabetes
8.2–10	Fair control
More than 10	Poor control

(Slightly different test methods are used in each lab, so different values may be used to evaluate your test. Ask your doctor or the lab technician for those being used in your test.)

A home test for hemoglobin A_1c is now available so you can test yourself between lab visits. It is called Self Assure GHb and can be obtained from the diabetic discount supply houses listed at the end of the book. A new lab test, not yet widely accepted or available, gives a measure for average blood glucose level over a three-week period. It's called a Fructosamine Assay and is marketed under the name RoTag. Check with your doctor.

Another set of blood tests reflects overall control. These tests measure certain blood fats (or lipids). High levels of cholesterol or triglycerides are commonly associated with high blood sugar values in diabetes. Their presence over long periods contributes to the development of diabetic complications. These blood lipids should be tested every year or two if they are in the normal range. If your tests are high and you are working to reduce them with diet and control, it is helpful to have the tests done every two or three months. It is also useful to measure high-density lipoprotein cholesterol (HDLC), the "good" cholesterol (the more you have, the better).

Normal Values for Blood Lipids
The National Institutes of Health Expert Adult Treatment Panel has made simplified recommendations on cholesterol and triglyceride levels. (Formerly they were determined according to age and sex.)

Total cholesterol below 200 mg/dl is considered desirable; between 200 and 240, borderline high; and greater than 240, high.

Those with levels over 240 should have their low-density lipoprotein (LDL) and HDL cholesterols and triglycerides measured. LDL levels of 160 mg/dl or greater are considered high risk; 130–159, borderline high risk; and less than 130, desirable. Although desired HDL levels are somewhat controversial, levels less than 35 mg/dl are considered a risk factor, and those greater than 60 are considered protective. Rather than looking at absolute levels of HDL, others consider the ratio of total cholesterol to HDL cholesterol a better measure of risk: The higher the HDL, the lower (and more desirable) the ratio, with ratios of 3.5–4 to 1 considered satisfactory. Triglycerides should probably be less than 250 mg/dl and treated with medication if greater than 500.

CAUTION: All of these numbers are subject to your specific situation, and how they apply to you should be discussed with your physician.

Tests and Our Emotions

It is natural to feel discouraged, and perhaps even guilty, when home or lab tests show that you are not in very good control. If the tests are high enough, you may despair and feel like throwing in the towel. At times like this, it is important to remember that you don't have to feel guilty about your errors and limitations. Use them to guide your next steps of learning. The energy of discouragement and guilt can be recycled into new motivation for change.

3b. Learn How to Recognize and Treat Insulin Reactions

This step is so important that we have given it a whole chapter, a chapter you should read even if you've had diabetes for years and think you know everything there is to know about insulin reactions. The symptoms of reactions change, becoming more subtle, when our metabolism is well controlled. Since our blood sugar is closer to normal, irregularities in food, activity, or schedule may cause reactions to occur more frequently at first.

In addition, some of us find it difficult to recognize the symptoms of a reaction. Sometimes this is because of changes in the output of hormones that signal low blood sugar. Review Chapter 8 for information on these subjects and other new ideas on increasing awareness of the early symptoms of a reaction and ensuring that you wake up to nighttime hypoglycemia.

3c. Survey the Basics of Diabetic Metabolism

Diabetes is a disorder of metabolism, the complex set of processes through which the food we eat becomes energy and replenishes our tissues. When we have diabetes, we play an active role in these processes, guiding things that happen automatically in non-diabetics. So we need to learn about our metabolism, especially as it relates to blood glucose.

Let's begin with some praise for blood glucose. We spend so much time trying to control it that we may forget how vital it is to our lives. Glucose is a major fuel for all of our cells and the only source of energy for the brain and nerve tissue. We have direct experience of this important function in the confusion we sometimes experience with an insulin reaction; it is a sign that not enough glucose is reaching the brain. We can respect our blood glucose, even as we work to keep it within acceptable limits.

The carbohydrates we eat are the main source of blood glucose. The different forms of starch and sugar in fruits and vegetables, beans and grains, and dairy foods are all transformed into glucose through the digestive process. (A small amount also comes from protein and fat digestion, but these foods go through their own metabolic cycles and do not contribute as much directly to the production of glucose.) Once in the bloodstream, glucose is either used directly to provide energy for our life processes and activities, or it is stored in several ways. It may be stored as glycogen in the liver or in the muscles, or it may be converted to fat and stored as adipose tissue.

The level of glucose in the circulating blood is maintained very precisely in nondiabetics by the interaction of a number of hormones. They increase or decrease the blood sugar level to keep it between 60 and 120 mg/dl. These hormones act in response to a variety of factors, primarily food or lack of food, exercise, and stress (including illness and emotional stress). When the pancreas senses an increase in blood sugar, it releases insulin, which in turn enables glucose molecules to enter cells that would remain closed without it—closed and without fuel.

This spontaneous release of insulin is what we lose when we develop type I diabetes. Blood sugar goes to very high levels (sometimes up to ten times the normal level) because the pancreas releases too little insulin or no insulin. Without adequate insulin, the glucose molecules are unable to pass through the cell walls, and the cells start burning fats instead. This is not as efficient a process as sugar metabolism, and the by-products—ketones—contribute to the ill feelings usually present when diabetes is first diagnosed. Once discovered, type I diabetes must be treated with injected insulin to supplement or replace the insulin from the pancreas.

But insulin is only one of the hormones affecting blood sugar level. Several others work to raise and lower the amount of circulating glucose. Glucagon, also produced by the pancreas, stimulates the release of glucose from the liver. (This substance is available for treatment of reactions when a person is unconscious.) Low blood sugar or stress hormones cue the pancreas to discharge glucagon into the bloodstream. The hormones released when we are under stress include cortisol and epinephrine, both from the adrenal gland. In addition to stimulating glucagon, they have a direct effect of inhibiting the action of insulin. A fourth major factor that also opposes the action of insulin is growth hormone, released by the pituitary gland.

In a nondiabetic, these various hormones work together, raising and lowering blood sugar from moment to moment, so that the proper level is maintained. When activity increases, they increase the glucose available to support it. When a person is under stress, they ensure that the muscles and nervous system are supplied with enough glucose to function at peak. After eating, the balance shifts so the influx of glucose will be assimilated.

When diabetes develops, insulin, the hormone most important in lowering blood sugar, is no longer available in adequate supply. The others continue to flow freely, however, and contribute to the dramatic increase in blood sugar level. Even when insulin therapy is begun, there isn't the same spontaneous interaction between insulin and the other, glucose-increasing, hormones. The insulin is usually given in fixed amounts rather than in the minutely measured doses the body delivers in response to moment-to-moment need. The automatic feedback loop between blood sugar level and insulin release is broken. The only thing that can begin to replace it is a conscious feedback process requiring external testing of blood (or, a poor second, urine), and decisions about insulin dosage, food, and activity based on test results.

Research scientists and medical engineers are attempting to create devices that will artificially restore the automatic loop. But they are probably years from the necessary breakthroughs. For now, we have the challenge of playing an active and conscious role in one of nature's more elegant processes. We could do worse.

3d. Understand the Factors Determining Blood Sugar Level

Metabolism is an internal process that is continually responding to external factors. Diet, activity level, insulin dosage, emotional stress, and physical stress all have a powerful influence on our sugar metabolism and the resulting blood sugar levels. Before we can effectively control these levels, we must know why they go up and down as they do. We will review each of the factors influencing blood sugar level and then explore how they work together. (Here we discuss only their effect on blood sugar. Later we discuss other ways they are important in diabetes management.)

Knowledge of how these factors influence blood sugar level allows us to analyze a given test result and understand why it was unexpectedly high or low. In the following discussion, we describe the common, day-to-day aspects of each factor; then we consider the aspects that come into play only occasionally or that affect only some of us.

Major Influences on Blood Sugar Level In Insulin-Dependent Diabetes

Universal (These factors affect all diabetics.)	Particular (These factors are temporary or affect only certain people.)
1. Insulin	1. Insulin
Types	Immunity to insulin action
Dosage	Interaction with other drugs (medicine, alcohol, marijuana, etc.) High
Site of injection	blood sugar levels inhibit action of
Schedule	insulin
Rebound from reactions	Overinsulinization
2. Diet	2. Diet
Total calories	High fat consumption inhibits insulin action
Distribution of calories among fat, carbohydrate, and protein	
Rate of absorption (glycemic index)	
Fiber	

3. Activity

Typical level

Frequency and level of exercise (There is a delayed lowering of bg as well as the immediate effect with strenuous exercise.)

4. Stress

Physical tension/relaxation

Possible increase or decrease caused by emotional stress

5. Other

Overall degree of regularity

Menstruation, menopause and pregnancy all affect control.

Socioeconomic—Not having enough money for insulin, testing supplies, and proper diet.

3. Activity

Exercise increases blood sugar when it is higher than 250 mg/dl

4. Stress

Infection, illness, fever, and other physical stresses raise blood sugar

Growth spurts

Over- and undereating when stressed

5. Other

Effects of marijuana, cigarettes, alcohol and other recreational drugs

---

Insulin

The effect of injected insulin on blood sugar level depends upon the type(s) of insulin used, the level and schedule of dosage, the site of injection, the timing of injection in relation to meals, the level of blood sugar, and a number of other factors. Variation of any of these factors can be responsible for changes in blood sugar level you observe.

The *type(s) of insulin* you take determines the pattern of insulin activity in your body throughout the day. A rapid-acting insulin, such as regular, can begin acting as soon as thirty minutes after injection and reaches its peak of action in two to four hours. Its effect is over in six to eight hours. NPH, on the other hand, starts acting in one to four hours, peaks in six to twelve hours, and may be exhausted after twelve to fourteen hours. Each type of insulin has its characteristic profile of action. Often a rapid-acting insulin is combined with an intermediate or long-acting insulin to create a series of insulin peaks matched to mealtimes.

(Human insulin, now available because of genetic engineering, appears to act sooner, peak earlier, and have a shorter duration of action than animal insulin. This is particularly true for the duration of action of human ultralente.)

In addition, each person has an individual pattern of response to insulin. This is why the times in the following table have so much variation. One may find regular insulin taking effect in thirty minutes; another person may wait an hour. The onset of action, peak of action, and duration all vary from one person to another.

You should know the daily pattern of insulin action your present regimen provides. When does each insulin peak for you? How long is it active? Do your mealtimes coincide with the times of maximum insulin activity? (Your physician can help you understand your insulin profile.) Blood sugar testing allows you to adjust insulin dosage and scheduling to obtain excellent matching between your hour-to-hour need for insulin and its availability. In most cases, this requires at least two shots a day.

Timing of Insulin Action (in hours)

Type	Regular	Semilente	NPH	Lente	Ultralente	Protamine
Onset	1/2–1	1–3	1–4	1–4	4–8	4–8
Peak	2–4	2–8	6–12	6–12	16–24	14–24
Duration	4–8	8–16	12–24	18–28	24–36	24–36

Note: Table derived from several sources, each of which gives different figures. Insulin activity varies greatly from person to person and between animal insulin and human insulin, so these times should be used only as guidelines.)

The effectiveness of insulin to lower blood sugar is dramatically decreased by *high blood sugar levels*. At normal levels (70–140 mg/dl), one unit of insulin will usually lower blood glucose around 30 mg/dl. With a high level (such as 300 mg/dl), it might take three units of insulin to lower it by the same amount. This is one of the reasons blood sugar levels sometimes skyrocket and remain high for several days. If stress or a food binge pushes tests to high levels and the usual insulin dose is still taken, its effect is inhibited by the excess sugar. Extra insulin at times like this enables you to regain balance.

High fat levels in the blood also reduce the power of insulin to lower blood sugar. In the short run, you may experience a high test after a meal unusually rich in fats but not necessarily high in carbohydrates. The insulin is just not able to do the same amount of work in the presence of excess fat. If your diet is usually high in fat, you might want to consider lowering it to increase the effectiveness of your insulin as well as to improve your general cardiovascular health.

A frustrating fact of insulin therapy is the high blood sugar level that often results from having low blood sugar. This is the rebound from an *insulin reaction.* One of the body's responses to the stress of a reaction is to pump out glucagon, which releases glucose from storage in the liver. We may find high blood sugar levels within an hour of hypoglycemia. This can happen even if we don't overeat when treating the reaction. (This spontaneous rebound can be a lifesaver if one passes out from very low blood sugar.) Hypoglycemia caught in an early stage usually doesn't produce this increase.

Occasionally, the rebound effect becomes a regular part of a diabetic regimen. This can occur when an excessive daily dose of insulin results in regular periods of low blood sugar that are not sensed as reactions (usually occurring during sleep). The body's natural defenses bring blood sugar to a point above normal by the morning test, and insulin may be mistakenly increased. (This Somogyi reaction is discussed in Chapter 8.) High levels before breakfast may also be due to a normal physiologic predawn rise in blood sugar (recently called the "dawn phenomenon"). If this is the case, before-dinner or before-bed insulin should be increased. Near-normal 3:00 A.M. blood sugars paired with high before-breakfast sugars suggest the dawn phenomenon. Near-normal bedtime and low-normal or hypoglycemic 3:00 A.M. levels with high prebreakfast levels suggest the Somogyi reaction. If all three levels are high, more insulin in general is probably needed.

Two other variables of insulin usage have a subtler effect: the part of your body where you inject and the timing of the injection relative to when you eat. Being aware of these increases your ability to fine-tune control after you have mastered the basics, but they are not nearly as important as the factors described above, especially in the beginning of your effort to improve control.

The *site of insulin injection* affects the timing of its action. Insulin injected into the abdomen is absorbed most rapidly, in the thigh, most slowly, and in the arm, at a moderate rate. In one experiment, the time of absorption was approximately 60 minutes for the abdomen, 75 minutes for the arm, and 90 minutes for the thigh. These different absorption times can be used practically: Injection in the abdomen when blood sugar is on the high side or when you want to eat soon; in the leg when a meal may be delayed or when blood sugar is quite low. (The usual rotation of injection site is also necessary. Within any area of the body, change the location you give your shot each day.)

If the site of injection is exercised vigorously, absorption is hastened. An arm swinging a tennis racquet or legs pumping while running will quickly activate insulin injected into them. If you are about to exercise and have recently taken an injection, you should be sure to eat before such activity unless blood sugar is high. If you wish to bring down high blood sugar, giving your shot in the part that is exercised will hasten the process.

The *timing of injection* in relation to mealtime is another subtle variable of insulin therapy. Unless blood sugar is below 80 mg/dl, insulin should usually be taken one-half hour to an hour before meals. This allows the insulin to start working about the time your blood glucose starts to increase from the meal. If you wait until just before the meal or after it, blood sugar is already high by the time the insulin starts to take effect. Shorten the wait if you have reactions before or during the meal.

Both *recreational and medical drugs* can have a significant effect on blood sugar level, either increasing or decreasing the effectiveness of insulin or the other hormones that regulate metabolism. Alcoholic beverages, especially when taken on an empty stomach, increase the ability of insulin to lower blood sugar. Alcohol also interferes with the liver's production of glucose. So drinking before a meal, especially if insulin has just been taken, can lead to reactions. After a drink or two, it may become difficult to notice the symptoms of a reaction. Drinking enough to become fully drunk increases risks further. The reduced awareness, nausea, vomiting, and dehydration play havoc with diabetic control and can lead to ketoacidosis or severe reactions.

Clearly, *alcohol* is to be used by a diabetic in moderation and with awareness. Avoid drinking on an empty stomach, or when blood sugar is relatively low, or after strenuous exercise. Accompany the predinner drink with some carbohydrate snacks. Know the carbohydrate content of your favorite beverages and take it into account in your diet. In some cases, alcohol must be avoided completely. This is an important issue to discuss with your doctor.

Marijuana may have a direct effect on blood sugar by breaking down glycogen, a form in which the body stores sugar. Its release increases blood glucose level. There is no doubt about marijuana's other effect: inducing the "munchies." This drug-induced hunger combines with a weakening of inhibitions to wreak havoc with a pot smoker's diet. As with alcohol, pot increases the risk of not noticing the symptoms of an insulin reaction until it is far advanced, because the sensations of the high mask them. The more powerful forms of marijuana carry the added risk of dependency.

Prescription Drug Interactions with Insulin

Many common prescription drugs can have a serious effect on blood sugar level by their interaction with insulin. Some reduce its power to lower blood sugar or otherwise increase blood glucose. These include diuretics such as Lasix or Thiazide, often used to rid the body of excess water for weight reduction. (They should be used in diabetes for heart disease or high blood pressure only.) Isoniazid (an antituberculosis drug) and estrogens or steroids that increase glucose production in the liver are others.

Other drugs add to the hypoglycemic (blood sugar–lowering) effect of insulin, sometimes causing serious insulin reactions. These include anticoagulants (Coumadin); sulfa (Gantrisin); tranquilizers (Thorazine); MAO inhibitors (Nardil and Parnate); and propranolol (Inderal). Propranolol and other "beta blockers" are potentially very dangerous because it minimizes the usual signs of an insulin reaction—sweating and rapid heartbeat. It is used primarily to treat high blood pressure.

The over-the-counter drugs most likely to influence blood sugar are decongestants and antihistamines.

You should ask whether any drugs prescribed for you affect insulin or blood sugar, especially when you go to a doctor other than the one who sees you for your diabetes. Use your blood test results to determine whether you should change your insulin dosage while you are on the medication prescribed.

One last special condition of insulin therapy: Some diabetics develop *resistance to injected insulin,* resulting in decreased effectiveness. (In extreme—but rare—cases, insulin dosage has been increased to hundreds of units per day.) Resistance is caused by antibodies the immune system creates in response to impurities in insulin or to the insulin from a particular animal. Anyone who has been taking insulin for several years may have developed some degree of insulin resistance. It can usually be overcome by using human insulin, highly purified insulin, the insulin from a different animal, or any combination of these types. When the change to more highly purified insulin is made, insulin requirements may decrease by as much as one-third.

Summary
The types of insulin, dosage, schedule of injection, and blood glucose level itself are the most important factors influencing blood glucose level. With the intensive regimen, the central goal is having peaks of insulin activity coincide with the times immediately following meals. This is achieved by taking two or more injections of insulin daily, usually mixing rapid-acting and intermediate or long-acting insulins. Each person should be familiar with the pattern of insulin activity provided by his or her regimen.

The action of insulin is inhibited by high blood sugar levels (over 240 mg/dl) or by high fat consumption. When blood sugar is very high, each unit of insulin is less effective.

Because of the delay before insulin starts acting, injections should usually be taken 30 to 60 minutes before meals. The site of injection has a significant effect on the timing of insulin activity, with the abdomen providing the most rapid start, the arm moderate, and the thigh the slowest.

When insulin reactions occur, the low blood sugar level frequently triggers a stress response resulting in high blood sugar, even though one has eaten moderately to treat the reaction.

The action of insulin to lower blood sugar may be inhibited or increased by interaction with both recreational and prescription drugs. This can result in unexpected high blood sugar tests or reactions.

Diet

The composition and balance of diet is the second major factor affecting blood glucose level.

We can easily see the impact of the *total calories consumed* on a given day and how they are distributed between meals and snacks. A too-small lunch on the run or a missed snack may bring low blood sugar and a reaction a little later. Overindulgence at one meal results in high tests afterwards. Heavy eating throughout a day may drive blood sugar up for several days if adjustments are not made.

When you are first learning to manage diabetes, a relatively regular pattern of eating, with approximately the same number of calories consumed at the same time each day, is one of the fundamental ingredients. With regular home blood glucose testing, you can determine the results of departures from the norm, and you can learn to correct for them by adjusting day-to-day insulin dose and exercise. (Once you have mastered your regimen, it is possible to vary food intake and timing and still maintain good control.)

Another aspect of diet affecting control is the speed at which different foods are converted into blood sugar. Although its utility is still being debated, nutrition researchers have developed a *glycemic index* to measure the conversion rate for different foods. They have found, for instance, that potatoes eaten alone bring a rise in blood sugar as fast as does a drink of glucose syrup. Pasta and beans, on the other hand, are absorbed much more slowly and result in a smaller increase in blood sugar at any one time.

The main categories of food—carbohydrate, fat, and protein—show different absorption times. Simple carbohydrates (sugars and highly refined starches) usually reach the bloodstream quickly, peaking in fifteen to thirty minutes. Complex carbohydrates (most starchy vegetables, whole grains, and beans) take from thirty to ninety minutes to reach their maximum impact on blood sugar. Fats take around ninety minutes, and proteins, three hours. (These times, however, vary greatly among specific foods. Chapter 9 presents a more detailed discussion of this subject.)

A well-balanced meal provides a gradual, sustained input of nutrition, avoiding the sudden high peak of blood sugar that a meal of simple carbohydrates causes. The amount of fiber in our food also affects absorption rate. High-fiber diets tend to slow the rate. High fat content, as indicated above, tends to interfere with the action of insulin, causing a need for higher doses. On the other hand, fat tends to slow the absorption of other foods eaten at the same time.

Significant daily variations in any of these factors—overall calories or balance between different food categories—can result in unexpectedly high or low blood glucose readings. For instance, high blood sugar caused by eating mostly simple carbohydrates may be followed in a short time by a serious reaction. Not enough slowly absorbed food is in the intestine to provide continued, gradual input of blood sugar. Or an overdose of steak and potatoes with butter and sour cream may bring elevated blood sugar the next morning and midday because the food is digested slowly and the fat decreases insulin effectiveness. Knowing how these principles apply to you, supplemented by results of your self blood glucose testing, will help you adjust and fine-tune your control.

Summary

The total calories consumed, how the calories are distributed between meals and snacks, and the types and combinations of foods consumed determine the impact on blood sugar level. Until you have learned the whole management regimen, you should eat approximately the same amounts of food (in terms of calories or exchanges) at approximately the same times each day.

Simple carbohydrates (sugars, fruits, juices, milk) are converted to blood glucose within a few minutes; complex carbohydrates (starchy vegetables, whole grains, and beans) take from thirty to ninety minutes; fats, around ninety minutes and proteins, up to three hours. High-fiber foods are absorbed more slowly and tend to slow the absorption rate of other foods as well. Regular high fat consumption inhibits the action of insulin.

A diet high in fiber and relatively low in fat that minimizes consumption of simple carbohydrates results in more stable blood sugar levels, with less severe peaks following meals. This is probably the ideal diet for diabetic management.

Activity

This is the third major influence on blood sugar. Control is profoundly affected by the general pattern of movement and exertion we follow as well as any periods of special exercise or work. Changes in either type of activity usually bring increases or decreases in blood sugar level and may result in insulin reactions. As with the other major factors determining blood sugar level, the more regular you are in your daily activities, the easier it will be for you to achieve optimal control.

General physical activity and specific times of exercise affect blood sugar in several ways. There is the immediate lowering due to the energy spent. The more strenuous the exercise, the faster blood glucose goes down. If insulin has not been decreased or food increased, a reaction is likely to occur (unless blood sugar level is high to begin with). Furthermore, during and following exercise, additional decreases in blood sugar level occur as the muscles absorb and store glucose beyond what they are burning. This process may continue for several hours after you have exercised vigorously. For this reason, reactions may occur long after you have finished the activity. Glucose is being pulled out of the bloodstream by muscles that need to replenish their stores.

Once you have learned to adjust diet and insulin dose, it becomes easier to avoid heavy reactions caused by exercise. In fact, the increased glucose storage means you will enjoy more stability of blood sugar level. When it starts to fall, more glucose is available to bring it back up to normal spontaneously.

If you maintain an active life, especially if you are able to follow a consistent conditioning program, there is an added benefit: Your sensitivity to insulin is increased. This means that a given amount of exercise will lower blood sugar more and a unit of insulin will be more effective. Insulin dose can be cut by a few units, more if you were sedentary before. A conditioning program is an exercise regimen in which you reach your peak of physical functioning three times a week for at least twenty minutes. Breathing is full and pulse is at the level defined for your age.

You don't have to exercise strenuously to gain benefits from physical activity. Even moderate movement—a quiet walk or work in the garden—can have a significant effect on blood sugar levels, compared to sitting and reading or watching television. This is important, as you may need to avoid heavy exercise. If complications have developed, you may experience severe harm from exercise programs that fail to respect your physical limitations. Even if you have early signs of complications, you should discuss your exercise program with your doctor.

Ironically, the power of exercise to reduce blood sugar is destroyed when the level is higher than 250 or 300 mg/dl, especially if ketones are present. When we need it most, the effect of exercise is reversed and blood sugar increases. *If blood sugar is higher than 250 mg/dl, especially when acetone tests are positive, do not try to bring blood sugar down with exercise.* At this level your body doesn't perform well and you won't enjoy it, anyway.

Summary
Physical activity helps to lower and stabilize blood sugar levels, with the greatest benefits gained from regular exercise. Changes in activity level must be balanced by corresponding adjustments of diet or insulin dose in order to avoid serious reactions. When blood sugar level is high, exercise is not recommended. When complications are developing, medical guidance in choosing appropriate physical activity is absolutely necessary.

Chapter 10, "Living Actively," gives more detail on all of these subjects.

Stress
Stress is the fourth major influence on blood sugar level. When we are presented with any challenge, physical or emotional, we adapt to it through a complex set of chemical and muscular changes. This physical adaptation is what we call the stress response, something neither negative nor positive in itself. (The noted student of stress, Hans Selye, draws a distinction between *distress*, "negative" stress, and *eustress*, "good" stress.) We need the stress response to function; it mobilizes us for action and organizes our defenses to maintain vital functions when we are ill or injured. However, in diabetes one aspect of the stress response itself becomes a challenge. To protect the brain and ensure energy for action, stress produces a rapid change of blood sugar level, often an increase.

Perhaps you have experienced a severe flu in which your urine or blood sugar tests were high even though you ate little. This is a classic example of the diabetic stress response triggered by a physical disorder. Other *physical stressors* include injury, burns, infections, severe pain, dehydration, surgery, hypothermia (extreme chill), exhausting exercise, and insulin reactions. These triggers cause blood sugar to soar, insulin to be less effective, and, if the condition persists, toxic ketones to build up in the bloodstream.

If you experience any of these physical stresses, you should carefully monitor your response by frequently testing your blood sugar and urine ketones, continue taking insulin, with extra injections of regular as needed, and contact your physician if you do not return to normal blood sugar levels and absence of ketones within a day. You may be in danger of going into ketoacidosis (diabetic coma) if any serious physical disorder is not handled properly. The risk is small if you act immediately to compensate for the effect of these disorders on your control.

You don't have to feel seriously ill for a physical stress to have a strong effect on your blood sugar level; so when you have a high test that you can't explain, check to see if anything is happening with your body that might be causing the increase—an infected cut, a bad sunburn, or fatigue, for example.

Emotions, images, and ideas can trigger the stress response as surely as a physical disorder. In fact, the body can't really tell the difference. An argument, a disappointment, even a thrilling discovery may bring about release of hormones that raise or lower blood sugar, sometimes dramatically. A sense of frustration or depression that continues for days may mean elevated blood sugar throughout the period. (The effect we are describing here is independent of any nervous nibbling of extra food you may indulge in during stressful times. This habit adds to the hormonal effects of stress to produce even higher blood sugar levels.)

So stress is one more variable to help you understand why your test results change when you think you are following your regimen carefully. With an awareness of the role of stress in your life, you are equipped to adjust for its effects on your metabolism (and even control it).

Unfortunately, there have been few clear research findings on the way emotional stress affects diabetic management. Like many other aspects of our condition, stress appears to be highly individual in its effects. Some people show relatively little change in blood sugar level after stressful experiences. Others experience amazing increases in blood sugar, and some find that it drops when they are under stress. The effect may depend on the type of emotion aroused, the duration and intensity of the experience, one's ability to express the feelings through communication or action, and the level of blood sugar at the time the incident begins.

You can use your blood glucose testing to do your own research on emotional stress in diabetes. When you have had a difficult day at work or school, an argument, a fright, or a strong disappointment, check your blood sugar level. See if it is significantly higher or lower than what you would expect on the basis of the day's activity and food. Some find that a stressful experience can raise blood sugar to the 400s, even higher. Note, too, whether you tend to have reactions after particular kinds of stress, especially those in which you have expressed your feelings strongly. A decrease in blood sugar level is also possible. Keeping notes on your observations in a section of your diabetes log is helpful. After a while, you will have a clearer picture of how your system responds to emotional stress.

Diabetics who experience chronically high stress levels in daily life often find that their blood sugar level decreases when they give themselves permission to relax. A holiday or vacation may bring more insulin reactions, not only because of increased exercise, but also because greater calmness means that fewer stress hormones (which counteract insulin) are at work. Studies are beginning to demonstrate that regular periods of relaxation can lower insulin requirements for many diabetics.

Summary
Severe physical stress, occurring as the result of illness, infection, injury, and so forth, increases blood sugar level and the development of ketones in the blood and urine. Careful monitoring of blood sugar and urine ketone levels and consultation with a physician are recommended when a person with diabetes encounters such stress.

Emotional stress may raise or lower blood sugar levels, depending on a number of factors. (It can also stimulate the development of ketones.) Each diabetic needs to observe his or her own pattern of response to stress and learn to adjust insulin, food, and exercise accordingly. Stress management and relaxation training can reduce the impact of stress on diabetic control.

Hormonal Changes in Women

Menstruation, pregnancy, and menopause trigger changes in hormone levels that in turn affect control for diabetic women. Variations in control during a woman's menstrual period have only recently been noted in diabetes care books. Unfortunately, little systematic research has been done. It appears from personal reports that the impact on blood sugar levels varies from woman to woman and at different phases of a woman's period. So this is another place in which the woman with diabetes becomes her own researcher. Use your blood sugar tests to see whether there are changes just before and during your menstrual period. You may need to make modest changes in insulin or food intake to compensate.

The many physical changes occurring in the pregnant woman with diabetes include an initial reduction in insulin requirement, and, after the first two or three months, an increase. Every stage of pregnancy should be supervised by a physician who has worked with diabetic pregnancies and is thoroughly committed to optimal control.

During menopause, profound hormonal changes occur that can affect blood sugar levels. Unfortunately, little research information is available, and the influences seem to vary from woman to woman. There is also the hazard of mistaking hot flashes for insulin reactions, and vice versa. This is a time when home blood testing can help a woman avoid confusion.

Puberty

During puberty, many physical and emotional changes affect blood sugar levels profoundly. In some cases, insulin dosage may have to be doubled to compensate for the impact of shifts in hormone levels. When teen rebellion is added to the mix, going through puberty calls for special strategies for teens with diabetes and their families.

Summary

All these factors work together. The interaction among them is, of course, what finally determines your blood sugar level at any time. Sometimes different factors balance each other, and sometimes they add to each other's effect, causing a steep rise or fall. After a period of intense jogging, you may still find a high blood sugar level if you were extremely stressed because someone almost ran over you. On the other hand, if you ate only quickly absorbed carbohydrates before jogging, you may have a severe reaction an hour or two later because the blood sugar was burnt up during exercise and no reserves remain. If you get depressed because blood sugar tests have been high, the emotional reaction may drive them still higher. If you don't adjust insulin dosage to deal with the high level, each unit is less effective and blood sugar may go up even more.

This all sounds very complex, but if you are willing to stabilize as many factors as possible during this period of learning the intensive regimen, you will soon be able to sort out which influences on blood sugar are at work at any given time. This is the reason for the next task.

Step 4: Regularize diet, activity, and schedules during the learning period

This temporary step of regularizing your life allows much more freedom in diabetes management in the long run. While learning the intensive regimen, you should eat more or less the same number of calories (or food exchanges) in each meal and snack; maintain a similar activity and exercise level from day to day; keep insulin dosage the same until instructed to alter it according to your tests; and not vary the timing of injections or meals by more than an hour.

Without this step, you will find it very difficult to understand how your system responds to the many variables affecting metabolic control. If diet, activity, schedules, and stress are all changing each day, you will lack the stability needed to establish the best insulin dosage or to learn how to vary insulin, diet, and activity to compensate for blood sugar levels that are too high or too low.

After a few months of following this routine carefully, it is possible to live with much less regularity and still keep blood sugar tests within limits. You will have learned how your system functions, how the different ingredients of your regimen affect you, and how to vary them to obtain good control. You may also have learned some internal cues that alert you to your level of control. You will understand what has caused a particular high test or insulin reaction; and you will have greater ability to make changes each day to even out the highs and lows. A relatively brief period of increased regularity will give you a life of greater freedom.

This step does not mean you should become rigid or compulsive and create a new source of stress in your life. Keep things as regular as you can from day to day, and see the times when diet or activity does change a lot as opportunities to study the effects of the changes on your blood sugar. (Remember, this is guilt-free learning.) Give yourself permission to take a day or two off from the routine now and then. You will return to it with renewed discipline. The changes you are making will last if you achieve them through willingness rather than force.

Some people may find it difficult to achieve greater regularity, either because of outside demands or because of their own emotional reactions. Work schedules and levels of activity may change frequently; regular daily exercise may not fit into already busy lives; or one may simply want to retain previous ideas of what freedom is.

If you do not find it easy to make your life more systematic, even for a few months, you can still improve control to an extent. Test as often as possible and record your results, together with notes on diet, activity, and stress. By reviewing the patterns in your records with your doctor, you will get a better idea of what makes blood sugar rise and fall in your case. You are also likely to become more willing to become more regular: you will have precise evidence of the effects of your lack of routine. (If you would like to explore the reasons for your reluctance, use the exercises in Chapters 3 and 14.)

One way of making this period of increased regularity more acceptable is to offer yourself a reward. For some people, the benefits of improved control are reward enough. But you may find it easier to reinforce your motivation by agreeing to give yourself some special experience or gift. After so many weeks of straight-arrow living, you become eligible for that trip or event or object you have been wishing for. Children like rewards, and we need to cooperate with the child within us to maintain discipline (see Chapter 2).

Step 5: Begin Period of Intensive Testing and Record Keeping
Many of us experience a sense of excitement as we begin testing blood sugar at home. For the first time, we are able to observe exactly how our system is affected by the food we eat, exercise (or inactivity), and the stresses we experience. We can find out if that queasy feeling is an insulin reaction or a stress response (or just an

unexplained queasy feeling). We can measure the effect of "just a few cookies" or extra slices of fresh bread and butter. We have the feedback essential to living well with diabetic control.

At the start, your doctor will probably ask you just to observe the pattern of blood sugar readings without making any changes in regimen. You will need to record tests for several days, along with detailed notes on food, exercise, stress, and any changes that might affect your tests. (Use one of the logs in step 3.) In this first period, your learning will be most rapid if you test before every insulin injection, before each meal, one to two hours after each meal, and at bedtime. In addition, test your blood sugar when you suspect that you are having an insulin reaction. If you show any signs of having reactions while sleeping, set the alarm and test around 2:00 or 3:00 in the morning (see Chapter 8 for signs of Somogyi reactions).

This may sound like a lot of finger pricks (up to seven or eight a day), but testing this often is necessary for only a few weeks, and the information you gain is pure gold. With it you and your physician will be able to tailor your insulin, diet, and activity to achieve great improvements in your level of metabolic control.

It is useful to assume the role of a scientific observer, not a judge of right and wrong, as you observe your test results. You are likely to find the jumps in blood sugar level puzzling at first. Many of us fall into the trap of believing that "I must have done something wrong." You will learn faster if you simply record the results (even if it is the result of a binge) and go on from there, without blame. Record all of your tests and don't neglect tests because you already know they will be high. It will help you to see how high they actually are. You are in the process of learning to control blood sugar. You can't possibly have it all under control yesterday.

Step 6: Selecting the Ongoing Insulin Regimen

With your initial blood tests in hand, you and your doctor are now ready to decide what (if any) changes are needed in your insulin regimen—the types, dosage, and timing of insulin you take. The insulin regimen chosen must be capable of meeting the following criteria.

Criteria for Insulin Regimen

1. Timing and dosage of insulin delivery provides for continuous, low-level availability of insulin throughout the twenty-four hours as well as peaks of insulin action following meals.
2. The majority of tests are between 70 and 150 mg/dl.
3. Hemoglobin A_1c is below 9.
4. Insulin reactions are not frequent, and their impact is minimized.
5. Normal body weight is maintained (excess weight is lost).
6. Flexibility in dealing with day-to-day changes and stress is ensured.
7. The convenience and preference of the individual diabetic are respected.
8. In children, normal growth and development are maintained.

A variety of insulin regimens are available that satisfy these criteria: two, three, or four injections a day, with or without mixtures of different types of insulin, or the continuous infusion of insulin provided by the pump. With these alternatives, it is possible to tailor the pattern of insulin action more precisely to meet your individual needs.

Your total daily insulin dosage is the first thing to be determined with your physician. When changing from a single daily injection to a more intensive treatment plan, insulin requirements change, usually downward. The total dosage of insulin you take each day is determined by your body weight and general level of activity.

For diabetics within 20 percent of ideal body weight and without illness or high levels of emotional stress, the daily dose varies between 0.5 and 1.0 unit of insulin for each kilogram of weight (1 kilogram = 2.2 pounds; 150 lb/2.2 = 70 kg).

Determining the total Insulin Dose
Recommended starting levels for intensive insulin regimens are as follows:

1. In newly diagnosed patients: 0.5 units of insulin per kilogram per day (a 132-pound person weighs 60 kg; 0.5 x 60 = 30 units of insulin per day).

2. During the "honeymoon" period, when insulin requirements temporarily decrease for the new diabetic: 0.4 unit per kg per day.

3. For established patients previously treated with more than 0.9 units per kilogram per day: reduce dose by 20 to 25 percent. (A 132-pound person taking 60 units would reduce dose by 12 to 15 units.)

4. For patients previously treated with 0.7 to 0.9 units per kilogram per day, use 0.7 unit per kilogram per day.

5. For patients previously treated with less than 0.7 units per kilogram per day, use old total dose unless it obviously is inadequate.

These are general guidelines, developed from averages for many patients. Your specific dosage will be worked out with your physician, taking your unique needs into account. We are providing the information so you will know what is happening, not because this is a do-it-yourself step.

After the daily dosage of insulin is determined, your physician will recommend one or two types of insulin, distributed into two or more injections a day. Many studies have been completed attempting to find the best style of treatment. So far it appears that the specific insulin regimen is not nearly as important as the total program of self-care. One research project in Florida compared the control of patients using the insulin pump, twice-a-day injections, and four-times-a-day injections. Their home and lab tests all indicated excellent control on all three regimens. The researchers concluded that selection of insulin regimen could be a matter of patient preference.

Their success was based on the full intensive regimen, not just the insulin regimen:

> It would seem that sustained glycemic (blood sugar) control requires (1) careful attention to all elements of the management routine: diet, exercise, and insulin; (2) patient self-monitoring of blood glucose; (3) defined treatment targets that are close to physiologic (near normal values); (4) a plan for adjustment of the treatment program to achieve the defined treatment targets; and (5) patient education and motivation.[1]
> —Jay S. Skyler

[1]From Jay S. Skyler, *Diabetes Care*, 4(2):313 (1981).

So it appears that you are free to choose the intensive insulin regimen that fits with your personal style if you are willing to follow all the other parts of the full intensive regimen. (In some cases, special factors may make one regimen more effective than another. Your physician will discuss these with you if any apply to you.) The critical elements are your awareness and willingness to make adjustments each day to maintain optimal control.

INSULIN REGIMENS FOR OPTIMAL CONTROL

1. Two injections of intermediate (NPH or Lente) and rapid-acting insulin taken before breakfast and before dinner.
2. Three injections, intermediate and rapid in morning, rapid before dinner, intermediate at bedtime.
3. Three injections: rapid and Ultralente before breakfast and dinner, rapid before lunch.
4. Four injections: rapid before meals and intermediate at bedtime.
5. The insulin pump provides both a continuous low-level flow of insulin and boluses or bursts of insulin before meals.

These regimens have been used and studied in research trials. Other dosage programs can be developed that may better suit your individual needs. The variety of insulins now available allows you to work with your doctor to find a mix that functions best for you.

(The convenience of the single-injection regimen is its only advantage, so it will be discussed later, in the sections on moderate and loose regimens. For anyone seeking optimal control, at least two shots a day with a mix of intermediate and rapid-acting insulins are required.)

Some people dislike injections and resist the idea of taking several a day. An alternative to injections with a syringe and needle is the jet, or needle-less, injection, using an instrument that injects insulin at high pressure through the skin's surface.

Gary Does Away with the Needle
I have been using a jet injector (Medijector) for over ten years. I began using it primarily because of curiosity and the hope that it would make my life somewhat easier. (I didn't particularly

99

dislike injections after twenty years of them.) I found this method of taking insulin faster and more convenient.

For people interested in avoiding the pain of the needle, jet injection is generally more comfortable. For me, the occasional discomfort is associated with larger volume of insulin, type of insulin, or tougher skin.

Another benefit of the jet injector is reduction in insulin dose due to improved absorption. When I switched to it, I could cut my dose in half. Most people don't experience such dramatic changes.

If you are thinking of switching to jet injection, you should consult your physician, because it requires a prescription. The relatively high price is covered by most medical insurance. But if it isn't, it can pay for itself over time, compared to the cost of disposable needles.

When two or more injections are taken each day, it is possible to adjust the peaks of insulin activity and the ongoing insulin availability to your individual life pattern. In fact, this individualization is essential. Your physician and you will use your home blood sugar tests to determine the best pattern for you. With care you can have near-normal blood sugar levels throughout the day. When tests are high, you can take action to bring blood sugar down.

The Regimens

1. The least demanding insulin regimen is the two-injection plan, in which rapid-acting (regular) and intermediate (NPH or Lente) insulins are taken thirty to sixty minutes before breakfast and dinner. (In the Florida study, two-thirds of the total dose was taken before breakfast, with two-thirds of the shot intermediate insulin, and one-third regular. The predinner shot was equal parts of the two insulins. Your doctor will select your dose according to your test results and your meal and activity patterns.) The peaks of the regular insulin handle the increase in blood sugar caused by breakfast and dinner. The peaks of the intermediate insulin cover lunch and the overnight need.

The more gradual action of the intermediate provides continuing low-level insulin activity. The greater convenience is the major advantage of this regimen. Its disadvantage is that one has less flexibility in the timing and size of lunch. If tests are high at midday, an extra shot of regular may be needed.

Two Injections Before Breakfast and Dinner

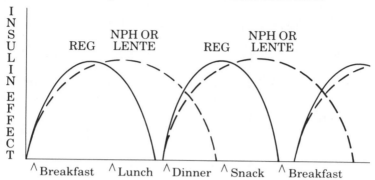

2. The second plan is essentially a variation of the first. The main difference is that the evening shot is divided, with rapid-acting insulin taken before dinner and intermediate at bedtime. This allows better overnight coverage for those who need more low-level insulin action while they sleep in order to wake up with a normal blood sugar level. It has the same disadvantage as plan 1.

Three Injections Intermediate and Rapid

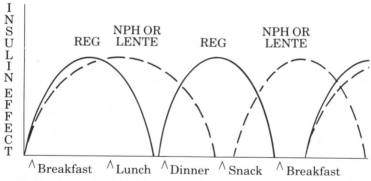

3. Plan 3 requires three injections daily, with mixtures of regular and Ultralente twenty to thirty minutes before breakfast and dinner, and regular only before lunch. (Here the long-acting Ultralente makes up 40 to 50 percent of the total dosage. The regular is divided equally between the three shots.) The regular insulin covers meals and the Ultralente ensures continuing low-level supply of insulin throughout the twenty-four hours.

101

This regimen provides a great deal of flexibility, allowing one to change mealtime or size and activity plans, and to correct for high blood sugar levels before each meal. (This is helpful for shift workers or people with schedules that change often.) The chief disadvantage lies with the very long time of action of each Ultralente injection. It takes approximately four days to determine the effect of a change in dosage. Furthermore, the rate of absorption of this insulin varies. which can result in periods of sustained hypoglycemia. Probably this regimen is advisable only when your physician has extensive experience with the ins and outs of Ultralente.[2]

Three Injections Rapid and Ultra Lente

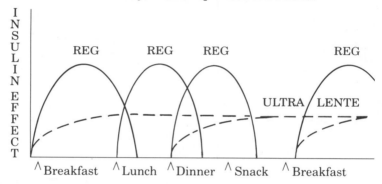

Gary's Ultralente Anecdote

  My personal experience using Ultralente is only a case history. There is little direct support for it in the diabetes literature.

  Currently I take one injection of Ultralente each morning. I supplement the Ultralente with regular insulin only when I am planning to have a large meal or otherwise find my blood sugar too high, and I have reasonably good control over twenty-four-hour periods. I have not been bothered by the reported unpredictable time of action of Ultralente, and I find the extra duration of coverage into the next day very helpful in preventing early-morning hyperglycemia. I like the combination of convenience and control that I can obtain with this regimen. It is certainly not for everybody.

[2]*From Jay S. Skyler, "Type I Diabetes...Regimens, Targets, and Caveats,: Diabetes Care,* 5(5):550 (1982).

I began using Ultralente insulin many years before it be-came medically fashionable. I found that I could obtain better control with fewer reactions (either late in the afternoon or early in the morning) using only Ultralente than with mixtures of Lente and Semilente. Since Lente insulin was at that time a fixed-ratio mixture of 30 percent Semilente and 70 percent Ultralente (currently, I believe Lente is formulated directly to produce that combination of activity, rather than as a mixture of the two), I started mixing Semi and Ultra to find the ratio that worked for me. As I adjusted the amounts, I found that I was gradually decreasing the Semi and increasing the Ultra. Finally, all I was taking was Ultralente. Thus, before anyone had written about using Ultra for "basal" insulin levels, I was using it as my only insulin. My own experience, personal and anecdotal, suggests that it is an underused insulin.

If one of you is interested in trying this, I suggest you discuss it with your physician and work out a program that you monitor carefully. Perhaps you will start with one of the more typical patterns, using Ultralente (once or twice a day with regular before meals, as needed). Home blood glucose testing makes it a lot easier to figure out what is working well for you.

One additional caution: The human Ultralente insulins have a shorter duration of action than the animal insulins. If you are presently taking human insulin and have never taken ani-mal, it's probably best to stick with human and see if the human Ultralente gives you long enough coverage. If you're taking an-imal insulin now or have taken it in the past, it's probably fine to try the longer-acting animal Ultralente. Discuss this with your doctor. Animal insulins are much purer now than they were several years ago, and the antibodies you may have to animal insulin will probably not be a factor for you.

4. The fourth insulin regimen includes three injections of rapid-acting insulin thirty minutes before meals and one of intermediate-acting (NPH or Lente) at bedtime. This plan allows one to adjust dose to meal size with every meal, but meals must not be greatly delayed or blood sugar may rise. This is because the regular dosage, which covers each meal, is declining in action by the next meal. The intermediate insulin before bed provides the additional low-level insulin action needed while asleep. The distribution of total insulin

dosage throughout the day is highly individualized and is best left to be determined by your physician and your blood glucose patterns.

Four Injections

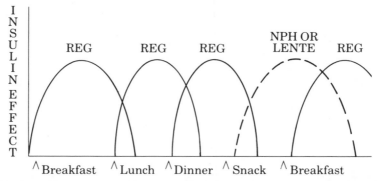

5. The insulin pump allows a fifth insulin regimen that comes closest to the natural pattern of insulin availability found in the nondiabetic. The device feeds a small amount of insulin at regular intervals into the abdomen through a tube and needle (or catheter) that remain implanted day and night. (The needle must be changed every one to three days. New devices allow the needle to be removed immediately after insertion, leaving behind a soft, flexible tube.) Before a meal or snack, the user triggers a measured bolus of extra insulin to handle the increase in blood sugar from the food. The most advanced models contain microcomputer chips that allow setting different rates of delivery for waking and sleeping hours.

Insulin Pump

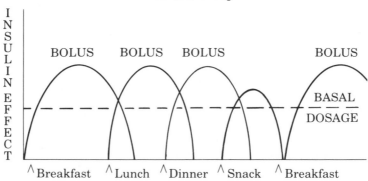

Even though the insulin-pump user may be wearing a tiny computer, this innovation still demands a very active role in management. Four to seven blood tests each day are recommended as standard procedure; these allow adjustment of the premeal boluses to actual blood sugar level. The person using the pump must also be especially aware of reactions (whose warning signs may become quite subtle) and the danger of fairly sudden rises in blood sugar through malfunction.

The insulin pump is still in the research and development phase. Many of us have willingly become pump guinea pigs, experiencing improved control and a wide range of side effects. Wearing a device that is plugged into one's belly (with some models that beep regularly) is a constant reminder of diabetes. This reminder can become physically painful if infection develops at the hookup site—not an unusual complication. The danger of hypoglycemia is greater because it is so easy to take extra insulin with the pump. This also results in a tendency for pump users to gain weight, especially at the beginning. Being a machine, the pump is subject to malfunction. Its foibles have caused both severe insulin reactions and ketoacidosis.

In spite of the side effects and the cost ($2,000 to $3,000), thousands are now using the insulin pump. Rapid progress is being made on overcoming its relatively infrequent technical failings, and greatly improved models will probably be on the market by the time you read this. It is clearly a viable choice for the person who wishes to maintain optimal control. If you are interested, discuss it with your physician and with people who are actually using a pump. But remember, it is not a replacement for your active participation in the management of your diabetes.

MAKING THE CHOICE

Now the art of medicine comes into play. There is no formula for prescribing insulin regimen. This is a highly individual process that takes into account the pattern of your test records, your personal style and preferences, your daily schedule, and even the style of your physician. Over the course of several weeks, you and your physician will work together, most likely with a phone consultation every few days, to adjust the initial dosage. Your test results and insulin reactions will provide the feedback needed to fine-tune the regimen and achieve blood sugar levels within the limits the two of you have agreed on. (If you are very loosely controlled to begin with, these may be higher than the optimal level for the first months and gradually brought down.) For many doctors and patients alike, the teamwork that develops at this stage is highly rewarding. If, on the other hand, your doctor gives little guidance at this stage, you may need to search for one who is either more knowledgeable or more cooperative.

The general guidelines for adjusting insulin regimen include the following:

1. Normalize the fasting blood sugar level first by adjusting the overnight insulin. Increase it only after determining that nighttime reactions are not the cause of high fasting BG tests. (See "Somogyi Reactions" in Chapter 8.)

2. When changes in dosage are needed, change only one type of insulin given at a particular time of day. (Determine the overall effect of changing morning NPH—for instance, before changing morning regular or dosage at other times.)

3. Wait two to three days to see the effect of the change before making any further change. (Wait three to four days with Ultralente insulin.)

4. Dosage should not be changed more than one unit at a time for anyone under 90 pounds.

5. For those over 90 pounds, increases of insulin should generally be one to two units at a time, although changes of two to six units may be made if your doctor advises.

6. Adjustments in dosage should be made on the basis of a pattern found over several days of testing, not just because of one high test or reaction.

7. Check for Somogyi reaction if results of changes are opposite what you would expect. If insulin is increased (or food decreased) and blood sugar goes up, high tests may indicate a rebound from too much insulin.

By the time you have established your ongoing insulin regimen, you will have some understanding of the timing of each insulin component—when it peaks and what meal it covers. The timing of reactions will help you sense this timing. You will also begin to know the art of making adjustments in dosage to keep your tests within the target range you are aiming for.

If your activity level changes significantly from weekday to weekend, you may need to adjust dosage regularly to account for the change. Women may need to make adjustments when menstruation affects blood sugar levels. Workers with swing or graveyard shifts may need regular shifts in insulin. In the beginning, check with your physician before making such changes. As you become experienced you will probably be encouraged to take the initiative.

If you experience a major improvement in control at this stage, with the majority of your tests in the target range, you may feel uncomfortable for a short time. At first, you may even have symptoms of hypoglycemia when your blood sugar level is normal. This is natural while you adjust to the new level of control. Discomfort can last up to two weeks. When your system gets used to the new level, you will feel better than you ever did when blood sugar was chronically high.

If, on the other hand, you find it difficult to bring your tests within the range you would like or if there is a great fluctuation in readings, don't despair. There can be many reasons for the frustration you experience, and there are just as many solutions. At this point, the next step is discovering the reason and defining what has to be done to correct the problem. Skip to step 9 at this point to clarify the cause of your difficulty and what you need to do to get past it.

Step 7: Observe the variations in blood sugar level caused by changes in food and exercise, stress, illness, and other factors

You will, of course, start to observe the causes of blood sugar variations as soon as you begin testing. But now it will be easier to sort out the factor or factors causing a particular high or low reading. In step 3, you reviewed all of the influences at work here, and this information will be put to work at this point. Your doctor may prefer that you spend some time just observing before you start making changes to compensate for levels outside your target range. Or you may begin making cautious changes right away, in which case you will be doing the two parts of step 7 at the same time.

Look through the sample logs that follow and see how many of the high tests or reactions you can explain. Then read the discussion of each log.

Daily Diabetes Log

Susan is on insulin regimen 1, with a regular dose of 15 NPH & 5 reg bf breakfast, 10 NPH & 5 reg bf dinner.

DATE & TIME	BLOOD TEST & REAC- TIONS	INSULIN DOSAGE	ACTIVITY & EXERCISE	FOOD	COMMENTS: Stress, illness, etc.
8-15 7 am	110	15 nph 5 reg	walk 30 min	8am 2 bread	
				1 oz cheese	
				orange	
10 am					My boss blew up at me for losing an im- portant account. I felt guilty & angry and just stewed.
11:45 am	240 (a)			green salad & ham	Cut the carbo for lunch.
4 pm	#2 react (b)			pack of choco- late cookies	
5:30 pm	200(c)	10 nph	walk 30 min	6:30 cup rice	
		7 reg		3 oz ham- burg	
				yel. squash	
				3 plums	quiet evening
10 pm	120			1 bread	
				1 oz peanut butter	

Before reading on, give your explanation of the high tests at (a) and (c) and the reaction at (b). What, if anything, could Susan have done to avoid them? What did she do to compensate?

Susan's high blood sugar level at lunch was probably caused by the emotional stress of being disciplined by her boss and not feeling able to express her feelings. Probably nothing short of a deep pool of inner peace could have spared her this high test. She then over-compensated for the high reading by avoiding carbohydrates alto-gether at lunch rather than just reducing them. Her roller coaster went from high to low, resulting in the reaction at 4:00 P.M. Rebound from the strong reaction (and probably an overdose of chocolate cookies) caused another high blood sugar level at 5:30. One can do nothing to avoid rebound, but not overtreating reactions helps lessen the rise in blood sugar. An additional two units of regular (over her usual five units) and a thirty-minute walk allowed Susan to return to a blood sugar level within her target range by bedtime.

Daily Diabetes Log

George is on regimen 3. His standard dosage is eight units of Ultralente and seven units of regular before breakfast and dinner, and seven units of regular before lunch.

DATE & TIME	BLOOD TEST & REAC-TIONS	INSULIN DOSAGE	ACTIVITY & EXERCISE	FOOD	COMMENTS: Stress, illness, etc.
Mar 5 6:30 am	90	8 ultr 7 reg		7 am cup oatmeal	
				cup milk	
				1 oz rai-sins	
				1 oz cashews	
7:30 am			jogging 45 min		
11 am	mild reac(a)			orange juice	
12 noon	140(b)	8 reg		egg sandw salad	Headache, sore muscles. Flu??
				med. apple	
3:30 pm				1 oz nuts & rai-sins	Feeling worse. Going home early
4:30 pm	240(c)	8 ultr		spltpea soup	
	11 reg			muffin	
5 pm				banana	
8 pm	150(d)				vomiting
				6 oz apl juic	
11 pm	100			6 oz apl juic	
2 am	120				vomiting
7 am	150	8 ultr 9 reg		6 oz orange j.	

You have probably already found the reasons for the reaction at 11:00 A.M. and the high blood sugar levels later. In spite of jogging in the morning, George missed his midmorning snack. It was a mild reaction because the action of the morning regular insulin was almost over. The slightly high test at noon might have been due to rebound from the reaction, but it is probably more likely that the developing illness was responsible. He took an extra unit of regular insulin before lunch, but by the time he tested at 4:30, his blood sugar had climbed to a fairly high level. Knowing that this was due to the physical stress of the flu, he took four extra units of regular before dinner and reduced the amount of carbohydrate eaten by 100 calories. Dinner was vomited by 8:00, so George tested to see how much more food seemed advisable. Blood sugar at 150, with extra regular still working, told him that some more carbohydrate was needed. The rest of the record shows him using frequent tests to stay in relative balance, despite the effects of the flu.

As you work with your own logs, you will gain skill at interpreting the results and understanding the reasons for high tests and reactions. You will also be able to see the effects of the actions you take to bring blood sugar back to normal as you begin the second part of this step.

7a: Learn to vary insulin dosage, diet, and exercise in order to compensate for high or low tests and to deal with changes in routine
The ability you learn in this step is central to improving blood sugar levels while living a life-style with a great deal of flexibility. When you are skilled in varying the ingredients of your regimen, you are able to live with a level of freedom previously associated with lack of control for a diabetic. You can usually bring blood sugar back to normal within a few hours when it is high. You can handle the effects of illness or emotional stress. You can change schedules, diet, and activity and still maintain acceptable readings. By your conscious decisions you are performing the balancing act that used to take place automatically before you had diabetes.

There are two types of changes you will be making on a day-to-day basis: those designed to correct for tests that are too high or too low, and those necessary to prepare for a change in routine. We can offer some general guidelines for making these alterations in regimen, but the feedback from your tests will help you learn exactly how much you should change insulin, food, or exercise to produce a given change in blood sugar level. At first, it is wise to change only one element at a time so you can see what the effect of the change is. Later you will be skilled enough to change more than one.

Use these target levels, or the specific ones you and your physician have agreed upon, to determine need for short-term changes in insulin, diet, or exercise. These target levels can be difficult to achieve even with dedicated effort. You may need to begin with less demanding goals if stress or other factors make it difficult to achieve this level of control. Negotiate a target you have a fair chance of hitting.

A menu of adjustments

If blood sugar is too high	Increase insulin (regular)	or	Increase exercise	or	Decrease carbohy-drates
To prepare for extra activity or exercise	Decrease insulin (regular or intermedi-ate)		or		Increase carbohy-drates

Insulin dosage is probably the easiest factor to change to correct for high readings. Extra insulin taken in this way is called supplemental. The general rule of thumb: If you are an adult of average weight, take one unit of additional regular for each 30 mg/dl above 120 that your premeal test shows. (If you are a child, or an adult under 100 pounds, take one unit for each 50 mg/dl above 150.) Thus, if your usual dose of regular is five units before dinner, take seven units to correct for a test of 180, or nine units if the test is 240. If the high test comes at a premeal time when you don't usually take a shot, go ahead and take a supplement, so long as you eat your usual meal. Usually you should not correct for high tests after a meal; wait to see what the next premeal test is.

It is best not to take supplements before going to bed. (When Ernest was a teenager, he woke up in the hospital after trying to balance a hot fudge sundae with a midnight injection of regular insulin. He overestimated the impact of the forbidden treat because blood glucose testing wasn't available then.)

Usually no more than four to five extra units of regular insulin should be taken at one time, even if blood sugar is very high. It is better to bring it down in steps, thus reducing the risk of severe reactions. *Children or lightweight adults should supplement no more than three units at a time.*

Similarly, you can take a supplement of insulin before a feast or other dietary indulgence to keep the excess from driving your blood glucose sky high. Be cautious here and, in general, increase regular only one or two units. Better to have a slightly high reading later than a heavy insulin reaction caused by too large a supplement. Also, be sure not to take the regular more than half an hour before eating, or you may need to ask for dessert before dinner.

Feedback from your blood tests (especially 1–2 hour postmeal tests) will tell you if you need larger or smaller supplements of regular insulin than the ones indicated here. This is a matter that has to be individually tailored.

You can also make small decreases in insulin dose to prepare for a period of exercise more strenuous than you would usually go through at a particular time. Regular should be cut for a shorter exercise period occurring two to three hours after injection. Intermediate insulin should also be reduced if you expect an extended period of exercise such as working in the garden or hiking all day. Approximate reduction should be at the rate of one unit for each thirty minutes of moderate exercise, or one unit for each fifteen minutes of heavy exercise. But do not decrease dose by more than one-third the total you normally would take at that time. Here, too, your test results and reactions will tell you if the reductions need to be smaller or larger for you.

If supplementing your insulin was the only thing you did to keep blood sugar normal, you would soon encounter a serious side effect: You would soon be putting on weight, because the blood sugar that used to be spilled into urine would be stored as fat. Extra insulin may be the easiest way to correct for high tests, but it definitely should not be the only one you use if you wish to avoid a steady weight gain.

So, after working with insulin supplements long enough to learn how to use them, start using the other two tools available for bringing down high blood sugar levels: reduction in meal size and exercise. When your test is high, cut back on carbohydrate (especially rapidly absorbed ones like fruit and white potatoes). Try one slice of toast instead of two, and no fruit if your morning blood sugar is between 150 and 200. Then test an hour after the meal and before lunch to see if this change was enough to bring you back on target. Through trial and error, you will soon see how much to cut back to normalize blood sugar and avoid a reaction.

Eating additional food to compensate for planned exercise is a well-established practice. The rule of thumb here is to add 10 to 15 grams of carbohydrate (such as a medium orange, a half-pint of milk, or a half-ounce of raisins) for each thirty to forty-five minutes of moderate activity. If the exercise goes on for an extended period, you may need additional, rapidly absorbed carbohydrates as you go along (dried fruit or juices). Reactions occurring during exercise and a blood test following exercise indicate just how much extra food you need for the kind of activities you engage in.

Exercise itself is the third tool for reducing blood sugar when it is too high. If the fasting test is between 150 and 240 mg/dl, a brisk walk or a half-hour of dancing between insulin injection and breakfast may be enough to bring blood sugar down to normal. There are so many levels of exercise that it doesn't seem wise to set guidelines here. Again, you have the feedback system necessary to find out how the kind of exercise you like works to reduce blood sugar. Test an hour after the meal and see if the result is back within acceptable limits. After a few trials you will know how much of a particular form of activity it takes to reduce blood sugar a given amount.

There is a limit to the usefulness of exercise in lowering blood sugar. In fact, at levels over 300 mg/dl, exercise will actually drive blood sugar still higher and is likely to produce ketones in your blood and urine. When blood sugar is this high, insulin supplements, moderation in diet, or both are the only ways to reduce it. When you find it necessary to deal with tests this high, it is important not to be excessive in treatment. Serious reactions have resulted from too-large supplements of insulin and decreases of food intake. It is better to come down in stages, taking no more than four or five extra units of insulin at a time (three units for a child or adult under 100 pounds), and never cutting more than half of any meal. It is a good idea to monitor your results by testing between meals when doing this.

While learning to make these day-to-day alterations in regimen, systematic record keeping will speed the process. On the basis of your logs, you will soon be able to set your own individual prescriptions for making changes. For each 30 mg/dl over 120, either take one extra unit of insulin or eat so many grams less carbohydrate or do so many minutes of moderate activity (using the values you discover work for you). You will gain a very precise ability to prepare for changes and deal with the results of changes after they occur.

Remember, you are an individual and these are only guidelines. You, in collaboration with your physician, now have the tools to tailor these guidelines precisely to yourself. You are a pioneer in a generation of diabetics who for the first time are able to live a flexible life and still keep blood sugar under good control.

Step 8: Have new lab tests done to measure the effect of your new regimen and establish an ongoing regimen

After you have been on the intensive regimen two to three months, your physician will order new hemoglobin A_1c and blood lipid (fats) tests and will probably also want to review your daily logs. This information will give an objective mirror of your level of control. With it, you and your doctor will be able to establish any further changes in ongoing regimen that may be needed.

At this point, you will establish how often to continue testing blood glucose and the level of record keeping to maintain. One study found that control suffered if subjects tested fewer than three or four times a day. Some doctors recommend testing each time insulin is taken and at bedtime. Others suggest at least two tests a day, one of them upon arising. One day a week test before every meal and at bedtime. Whatever the recommendations, many of us simply want to go on testing three to four times a day because the feedback is so valuable. Discuss this and the question of records with your physician.

Step 9: Assess your progress and determine what (if anything) is needed to further improve control

You may have made fantastic progress, with most tests within your target range. Or perhaps you have made significant improvements but are still testing higher than you would like. It may be that your tests show relatively little improvement, even though you have devoted yourself to doing everything the intensive regimen calls for. Your blood sugar level may have bounced up and down with frequent insulin reactions. Possibly you have been struggling just to become willing to follow the regimen.

No matter what you have achieved at this point, it is a time to pause reflectively and congratulate yourself. Even if you are still far out of control and fighting desperately against everything you know is good for you, it is time to retreat from the war with yourself. Whether you have much or little to accomplish, take time to define the progress you have made, what you still need to learn, what obstacles are holding you back, and what you can do to overcome them.

Assessing Your Progress
Give Yourself Some Credit.

1. No matter what you have achieved so far, the fact that you are still at work earns points for you. If you feel like it, collect a "Hanging-in-There" reward and give yourself some special treat.

2. Go through the list of eleven steps that you have been working on (at the beginning of Chapter 5); see which ones you have completed and which ones still need more work. Make sure you haven't missed any. Again, give yourself credit for what you have done and suspend any tendency to blame yourself for what is still to be done. (If you are one of those who was able to gain optimal control quickly, you are fortunate indeed.)

If You Choose to Make Further Improvements
in Control, Go Through the Following
Checklist and Find What You Still Need to Learn.

1. Do you understand your insulin regimen—what type of insulin you are supposed to take at what times and when each of them

peaks? If not, review this with your doctor and read the section in step 6 describing it.

Do you understand how the different factors determining blood sugar work? If not, go back to step 3 and review this information.

2. Is your blood glucose testing accurate? If you haven't taken a class or been instructed in the technique, ask your doctor or nurse to help you and review step 3.

3. Is your life filled with stress, or are you especially sensitive to stress? If so, read Chapter 11, "Living Well with Stress," and consider taking a stress-management class.

4. Are you finding it difficult to regularize diet, activity, or schedule for this learning period? Use Chapter 3 to help you discover the obstacles.

5. Do you understand your diet and follow it? Need some tips? Read Chapter 9, "Living Well with Your Diabetic Diet." See a nutritionist if you need more information.

6. Do you notice any signs of nighttime reactions or Somogyi effect? (See Chapter 8.) Have you tested blood sugar during the night (around 2:00 or 3:00 A.M.) to be sure you are not having reactions?

7. Are there any irregularities or imbalances in endocrine hormones other than insulin? Your doctor can determine whether this is likely and order tests.

8. Is any other physical condition affecting your control? Discuss this with your doctor.

9. Do you have strong doubts that optimal control is worth the work it takes to achieve it?

Do you believe that the intensive regimen intrudes on your life too much or creates too much inconvenience?

Review the section of Chapter 4 on the benefits of the intensive regimen and look at your answers to the guide to decision making at the end of that chapter.

Do the work in the next step: Maintaining Motivation.

Do you doubt yourself—either your ability to learn or your worth as a person? See Chapter 14, "Living Well with Yourself."

10. Are your trying to learn the intensive regimen at a time when too many other demands are being made on you? It may be that problems with school, work, family, relationships, or emotional difficulties are competing with your need to manage your diabetes well. If so, can you put any of the other challenges on hold? You may decide now to work with a moderate regimen.

11. Do you feel you have enough support and guidance from your physician and others?

Let your doctor and the other health professionals know what you need. If your requests are legitimate and they are unwilling to meet them, consider changing doctors. (See Chapter 12, "Living Well with Your Medical Team.")

Have you enlisted the support of other diabetics? (See Chapter 13, "Living Well with Other Diabetics.")

12. Is there anything else you think of that could be the reason for your difficulty?

If you feel tempted to throw in the towel because you've had a hard time gaining the level of control you hoped for, you may need a short breather. Back off from the thousand and one details you are trying to master and look at your whole situation. Even if your tests are not yet on target, you may find that you have made important progress in mastering some of the tasks of the intensive regimen. You haven't failed. It's just that there is more to be learned.

You may need to accept a higher blood sugar level while you work on motivation or on reducing your stress level or other issues outside diabetes. Or there may be physical conditions that make control more difficult to attain. You may need to find a physician who is better informed or more in sympathy with your goals.

If, after pinpointing the reasons for your frustration, you decide to put the intensive regimen on the shelf for a while, be kind to yourself. Make a commitment to reopen the subject at a scheduled date in the future. Understand the reasons you have made the decision and let them guide you to your next step in your ongoing diabetes education. Follow the moderate regimen, or at least the loose one, and work on the issues that have stopped you. There may be powerful negative beliefs or self-image issues (see Chapter 14, "Living Well with Yourself") that must be cleared up before you will be willing to accept a gift as valuable as optimal control. Or perhaps there are too many problems outside health that you are dealing with. Whatever the reason, if you discontinue the intensive regimen now without blaming yourself, you will find it much easier to begin again later.

You may also decide, on the basis of this experience with the intensive regimen, that you simply do not choose to manage diabetes at this level. As we have said before, you are the only one who can balance the questions of physical health and quality of life involved in this decision. Living well with diabetes is finding the balance that works for you.

Step 10: *Maintain motivation for continuing with the intensive regimen*
The intensive regimen becomes easier to manage once you know the basics. The testing schedule is not as demanding; you have the knowledge and skills you need to be fairly flexible in life-style and still maintain good control; and you have created a set of new habits that serve your purpose of living well with diabetes. Your regimen is easier, but it is not what most people would call easy. You have taken a position of responsibility, one calling for day-to-day awareness and decision making. It is advisable to take steps ensuring continuing motivation so that this responsibility does not begin to feel like a burden.

The immediate rewards of following the intensive regimen offer direct reinforcement of motivation. When you have immediate feedback on blood sugar level and the ability to do something about it, you enjoy a sense of power and control. (Anyone who has lived with diabetes for many years knows the frustration and sense of powerlessness that often accompanies attempts to gain control.) This emotional benefit is extended by the feeling of physical well-being that results from optimal control. Don't take these improvements in mind and body for granted. Remember that you have worked hard to achieve them and that you will continue to enjoy them by respecting your regimen.

You can also use the long-term benefits of optimal control as a way of remaining willing to adhere to regimen. You are increasing your chances of living a long and healthful life. Day by day you are maintaining a body that functions more like that of a nondiabetic. If you have children, you are more likely to be a fully active parent

119

throughout their childhood. If you are a woman who wants to become pregnant, you can be more sure of a safe pregnancy and a healthy baby. Periodically review what your personal reasons for living well are, and keep in mind how the intensive regimen will help you get what you want in your life.

Contact with others following the same regimen can also reinforce your motivation. Participation in a support group, or having friends with diabetes you can call on when you need understanding and encouragement, helps in a special way. You are talking with people who really know what you are dealing with. You are able to get practical tips from the old-timers and you yourself are soon giving valuable aid to the beginners. It is easier to stay involved with quality self-care when you know you are not alone.

Earlier we described the role of brief vacations from tight management as a way of lifting the sense of burden. With the skills in varying insulin, diet, and exercise you have learned, you can probably relax regimen for a day or two and not end up with severely elevated blood sugar levels. When doing this, it is wise not to set up conditions that might cause severe insulin reactions: too much added regular insulin, late meals, or "meals" of sweets unaccompanied by more slowly absorbed carbohydrates. It is much easier to continue with the intensive regimen if you do not think of it as a straitjacket that labels any departures as cheating. (That's a word we can do without!) Living well includes brief periods of relaxed control as part of the regimen itself.

If at any time you feel a strong resistance to continuing with the intensive regimen, remember that there are steps you can take to explore the causes and deal with them. Be aware of any rationalizations or denials that you use to justify the resistance. Don't accept, "I'm really too busy," or "I don't need to be so careful, I'm all right now," or "It won't do any good anyway." Use Chapter 3, "Help!" to gain awareness of what is happening and ask for personal help if you need to.

Step 11: Celebrate!

When you finish learning the intensive regimen, you have completed the most demanding set of learning tasks medicine has to offer its patient (and long-suffering) students. Celebrate your accomplishment. Let your family and friends know what it means to you and to them. After all, most of what you are doing to live well with diabetes would help them live more healthful lives, too. Share with them the joy of reaching your goal. It will help you to continue your new level of self-care not to keep it to yourself. You might take this task quite literally and have a party or a special dinner to announce your "graduation." It can be as subtle or as exuberant as fits your style.

If you have chosen to work with a reward system, now is the time to collect whatever external prize you contracted for. In fact, even if you haven't been working with this idea in mind, you might feel like giving yourself something very special, beyond the intrinsic and priceless prize of good control itself. It doesn't have to be a thing to buy. It might be an experience you have been postponing, a kind of relationship you have not felt ready for, or even a quiet time alone, away from all other demands. You will know what is right for you.

Next Steps

You will also know what more you need to learn about diabetes. Mastering the intensive regimen does not mean that you have finished with your diabetes education. Look through the other sections of the book to see what you need to study next. The pace will be much easier and you will be working on the basis of the solid learning that you have just completed.

Fortunately, you are engaged in a lifelong learning process, as there will always be new research and new techniques for diabetes care. Let us hope that the innovative self-care represented in this book is totally outmoded by new breakthroughs in a short time. To keep up with new developments, you can subscribe to such publications as *Diabetes in the News*, published by Ames, *Diabetes Forecast*, published by the ADA, or *Diabetes Self Management*. (See the Appendix at the end of the book for addresses.) If you are willing to wade through medical jargon, two excellent journals, *Diabetes Care* and *Diabetes Spectrum*, are available in medical libraries. Your local ADA chapter is another source of continuing diabetes education.

The Moderate Regimen

LEARNING THE MODERATE REGIMEN

1. Be sure you have a positive setting for your diabetes learning, a physician who agrees with your goals, and support from family, friends, and other people with diabetes.

2. Have lab tests of hemoglobin A_1c and blood lipids (triglycerides and cholesterol) done to indicate your present level of control.

3. Learn the skills and information needed for managing your diabetic control through the moderate regimen.

   a. Learn how to test blood sugar and urine.
      Understand the meaning of lab tests relevant to control.
      Know the criteria of control.
      Devise an effective record-keeping system.

   b. Review Chapter 8, on recognizing and treating insulin reactions.

   c. Survey the basics of diabetic metabolism (how your system processes food and liquids to produce energy and growth).

   d. Understand all the different factors that determine blood sugar level.

4. Determine the level of regularity of diet, activity, and schedule you are willing to follow. Establish a schedule of blood and urine testing that is acceptable to you.

5. With your doctor's guidance, establish your ongoing insulin regimen (no more than two injections of insulin per day. Use of the insulin pump is not recommended for the moderate regimen.) Set target levels for your tests and action to be taken when blood sugar level is high.

6. Observe the variations in blood sugar level caused by stress, illness, changes in food and exercise, and other factors. Learn to vary insulin dosage, diet, and exercise cautiously to compensate for high or low tests and to deal with changes in routine.

7. Have new lab tests done after two or three months to determine the effect of your new regimen.

8. Assess your progress. Find out what you need to do now to obtain further improvements in control or to maintain the level you have achieved. If you have not achieved all of your goals, determine the obstacles and how to overcome them.

9. Take steps to maintain your motivation for continuing to work on improving control.

10. Celebrate!

Step 1: Be sure you have a positive setting for your diabetes learning
There are many different reasons for choosing a moderate level of control. It may be the level that best balances the whole spectrum of needs in your life. For some, following the moderate regimen represents an enormous improvement in management. For others, it is a fall-back position chosen after attempting the intensive regimen and finding too many obstacles in the way. Some will be comfortable with this level of control until their motivation is boosted by an event like the onset of complications. Some will see it as only a temporary treatment plan until they have time and energy for learning the more disciplined approach.

Whatever your reasons for selecting the moderate regimen, it is important that you allow yourself the most basic ingredient of living well—accepting the choice you have made. The intensive regimen is praised so highly that you may feel a bit anxious, perhaps even guilty about choosing "second-best." Feelings like this are not good for your health.

Your decision about the regimen to follow was not made in isolation. You weighed your needs as a person and as a diabetic, your motivation, and the support available to you. The moderate regimen seems to you to be the wisest choice. Live well with it. (We have built into the regimen a periodic review of this choice—step 9.)

As you work with this regimen, you may find your interest in care of diabetes growing, or other concerns may diminish, allowing you to devote more time to diabetes care. Simply having the immediate feedback of blood glucose testing may improve your control and increase your motivation to manage your diabetes. Gradually you may find yourself moving toward improved control, learning the information and skills needed at the pace that is right for you.

You may feel anxious because you are not ready or willing to gain optimal control right away. Many of us have experienced a degree of anxiety connected with the possibility of developing complications. It was just something we lived with, consciously or unconsciously. It is natural to experience it, and there are positive things you can do to handle it (see Chapter 15).

We cannot yet say with certainty that the intensive regimen reduces the risk of complications. There are strong clues indicating that it will do so, but the research needed to prove this will not be completed for years. Furthermore, until the last few years, a moderate level of control was the very best one could attain. Past studies indicate that people who managed their diabetes at this moderate level had fewer complications than those whose blood sugar levels were higher. So you can find some reassurance in this: The moderate regimen is likely to reduce your risks, though possibly not as much as the intensive regimen.

All of the suggestions made in step 1 of the intensive regimen are applicable here, so you can continue by reviewing that information. See what you need to do to be sure you have adequate support: a physician you can work with effectively; family and friends acquainted with your project; and other diabetics with whom you can compare notes. *Go to Chapter 5, step 1.*

Step 2: Have lab tests done to determine your present level of control
Hemoglobin A_1c and the blood lipids (fats) tests will allow you to see how effective your previous regimen has been. You and your physician can set goals for these tests that are reasonable, given the

moderate regimen. Then new lab tests every three months, along with your own feelings of well-being, will be the best cue to how you are doing. You will find that the feedback from the tests will be very helpful, although at first you may need guidance from your doctor in interpreting them. *See Chapter 5, step 2* of the intensive regimen, for details.

Step 3: Learn the skills and information needed for managing your diabetic control through the moderate regimen.

3a: Learn how to test blood sugar and urine

A major difference from the intensive regimen emerges in this step. Although you will still be using home blood glucose testing, you will not be doing it as often and you will also be testing for glucose in your urine. (Possibly, one of the reasons you chose a moderate regimen was that you did not want to test your blood several times a day.) The best schedule of testing for this level of control would be to test blood glucose level before taking your morning insulin and to test your urine before meals and at bedtime. The daily fasting blood sugar test allows you to supplement your morning shot with regular to compensate for high readings when they occur. Starting the day in control helps you stay controlled throughout the day. The later urine tests give a very rough idea of how well you maintain control throughout the day. (Specifically, they tell whether blood sugar is staying over 180 mg/dl or so before meals. More on this later.)

If this is more testing than you are willing to do, determine a minimal schedule of testing that you feel able to follow consistently. Blood tests two or three times a week and urine tests once or twice a day are better than none. Schedule the urine tests at different times each day so you can see the pattern of results throughout the day, before and after meals, when you look at your log for several days.

By starting to test regularly, you will be creating a habit that you can expand on later. Even a few blood tests each week can help you improve control to some extent. Some people find it helpful to make a written contract with themselves or their doctor, stating the number of tests they will do. Then a report is regularly filed with the results.

You should do additional blood glucose tests when illness upsets your control and to check your perception of insulin reactions. Sometimes you may mistake symptoms of anxiety and stress for those of reactions to insulin. If you show any signs of Somogyi reactions during the night, you can find out whether blood sugar is low by testing around 2:00 or 3:00 in the morning. This special form of insulin reaction causes high fasting blood sugar tests that may mistakenly lead to increases in insulin dose. Whenever insulin dosage is more than 35 units a day, and morning blood sugar tests are high, you should check for low blood sugar during the night. It might also be the "dawn phenomenon." (See Chapter 8 for a full discussion of Somogyi reactions.)

It would help to go to a home blood glucose testing class if one is available, or to have your doctor or nurse instruct you in the correct testing procedures. A number of suggestions on home testing are given in Chapter 5, step 3a. Also, read the previous sections on laboratory tests and record keeping. With the moderate regimen, a different set of target values is necessary for evaluating your blood tests and urine tests than with the intensive program.

Moderate Regimen Target Glucose Levels

Fasting blood sugar test	70–150 mg/dl
Before meal blood sugar test	70–180 mg/dl
1–2 hr after meal blood sugar test	140–250 mg/dl
Before-meal urine test	Negative
Bedtime urine test	Negative or ¼%

We need to redeem the value of urine sugar testing. Blood sugar testing has offered such an improvement in accuracy that there is a tendency to dismiss the old urine test. This is a mistake for anyone who has not yet chosen the intensive level of diabetes management. While limited, the traditional test still provides useful information. It tells you if your blood sugar has been higher than about 180 mg/dl (the exact level varies from person to person) since you last urinated. This does not give adequate feedback for optimal control, but it can help you keep to a moderate level of control. If your tests are usually negative, you know that your blood sugar has been below 180 or so.

One of the shortcomings of urine testing is that the sample tested may reflect earlier blood glucose values. It is possible to have a positive test while undergoing an insulin reaction. For this reason, to get a current reading, you should empty your bladder completely and then urinate again in ten or twenty minutes. Testing this second sample gives a more up-to-date reading. (Testing the first sample gives you an idea of how much sugar was spilled during the whole time since you last urinated.)

Another problem with urine tests is that the level at which blood sugar spills into the urine varies from person to person. This level is called the renal threshold. Someone with a low renal threshold will show a positive urine test when the blood sugar is 140 or lower. Another person, with a high threshold, will not have a positive test until blood sugar is 200 or higher. (The average level at which sugar spills into the urine is 160–180 mg/dl.) The renal threshold may change over time, usually becoming higher with age or as kidneys function less well. Pregnancy also affects the renal threshold.

Finding your Renal Threshold

This variability makes it important for you to determine what your specific blood sugar spilling point is. This knowledge makes urine testing a much more effective tool. You can identify your renal threshold by testing both blood sugar and urine sugar at the same time. Probably the easiest way to do this is to test every thirty to forty-five minutes, beginning when urine sugar is positive and continuing until it is negative. Empty your bladder, test your blood sugar, and then urinate again a few minutes later and test this sample (using Testape, Diastix, or the Bm uG urine test, which are more sensitive than tablets). Drinking a glass of water each time you urinate will help. Record results of both tests until you can see the threshold level. A sample log illustrates this process:

Time A.M.	Blood Sugar Test (mg/dl)	Urine Test (%)
9:00	240	
9:10		2
9:45	200	
9:50		1
10:30	160	
10:35		1/4
11:00	140	
11:05		Negative

This person has a low renal threshold. A positive urine test here indicates that blood sugar is over 150. Another example shows a high threshold:

Time P.M.	Blood Sugar Test (mg/dl)	Urine Test (%)
6:00	300	
6:05		1
6:45	260	
6:50		1/4
7:30	220	
7:35		1/10
8:00	200	
8:05		Negative

In the second example, the threshold is somewhere between 200 and 220 mg/dl blood sugar. A negative test indicates only that blood sugar level is less than that. So it may be anywhere from very low (40 mg/dl) to fairly high (200 mg/dl) and still be negative.

Of the different products for testing urine, Clinitest tablets give results that are easy to read, but they are less sensitive and harder to use than the strips. Ames Diastix are easy to use, but the color continues to change after the required thirty seconds, so you must read your result quickly. Ames Clinistix show only if urine is positive or negative, with no percentage given. Boehringer Mannheim's uG strips give easy-to-read colors that do not continue changing. You can get a specific reading that shows whether you are negative, a little high, or very high. If your urine is positive, this test has to wait five minutes for a final reading. Test results can be affected seriously by large doses of vitamin C and some medications. Read the instructions to see if this is true with your product.

A second type of urine test, for urinary ketones, will provide very important feedback on certain occasions. Ketones in your urine indicate that your diabetes is getting out of control due to a relative insufficiency of insulin (too much food, not enough insulin, or too much physical or emotional stress). Both tablets and strips are available; you should know how to use both. It is especially important to check for ketones if you are ill (even with a bad cold) or experiencing high blood sugars (greater than 240 mg/dl) or 4+ urine sugars. (See end of book for more information on ketoacidosis.)

3b: Review the chapter on recognizing and treating insulin reactions
Anyone working on improved control of diabetes risks having more insulin reactions while establishing the new level of regimen. Handling reactions may seem like old news to you, but you will find some new approaches in Chapter 8. *Go to Chapter 8.*

3c: Survey the basics of diabetic metabolism
Go to Chapter 5, Step 3c.

3d: Understand all the different factors that determine blood sugar level
The information given on these subjects above will help you gain a general understanding of the ups and downs of your blood sugar level, even though you won't be working intensively to keep it close to normal range at this point. Later, if you decide to move to the intensive regimen, you can review it in more detail.

Go to Chapter 5, step 3d.

Step 4: Determine the level of regularity of diet, activity, and schedule you are willing to follow
With this step, we have come to one of the contradictions of the moderate regimen. On this treatment plan, you have a wider range

of acceptable blood sugar levels than on the intensive program, but you also have less capacity for adapting to irregularities. Without blood tests several times a day to guide you, you are more likely to have reactions or high blood sugar levels if you do not follow a fairly regular diet, activity plan, and schedule. (Some people prefer to keep blood sugar level a bit high to avoid reactions.) The intensive regimen, on the other hand, allows much more flexibility once you are past the first two or three months needed to learn it.

Ideally, your choice of moderate regimen means that you will stick to a fairly consistent healthful meal plan, either using exchanges or calorie count, with times of meals scheduled fairly closely (not more than an hour off schedule unless you know your blood sugar is high). When a meal must be delayed, you can eat a snack and deduct the calories or exchanges from the meal. Similarly, physical activities should be fairly regular from day to day, with adjustments in insulin dosage or food when there is an increase or decrease in the amount of exercise. As you gain experience with such adjustments, you may find it possible to increase the flexibility of this regimen.

It is up to you to decide just how regular you are willing to be in your management of diabetes. Fortunately, the combination of your home blood and urine tests and the hemoglobin A_1c test in the lab will tell you if your decision allows you to maintain a moderate level of control over a two- or three-month period. If the hemoglobin test is too high, you will know that you need greater regularity. Work with your doctor to find the places where your regimen needs to be tightened up.

Step 5: With your doctor's guidance, establish your ongoing insulin regimen

Your insulin regimen is the overall dosage of one or two types of insulin taken in a single morning injection, or a dose split between morning and predinner injections. To work with it well, you need to know the pattern of insulin activity—when it begins, when it peaks, and how long it is effective. Four insulin plans are available for the moderate regimen. (We do not recommend that people on the moderate regimen use more than two injections a day, nor should they use the insulin pump. These more intensive regimens require more frequent blood sugar tests and a stricter control program to be effective and safe.)

Moderate Insulin Regimens

Plan 1: A single daily dose of intermediate-acting insulin (NPH or Lente), taken 20 to 60 minutes before the first meal of the day.

Plan 2: A single daily dose of intermediate and rapid-acting (regular or Semilente) insulin mixed, taken 20 to 60 minutes before the first meal.

Plan 3: A split dose of intermediate-acting insulin, part taken before breakfast, part before dinner.

Plan 4: A split dose mixing intermediate- and rapid-acting insulins before breakfast and dinner.

Plan 1

The single daily shot of NPH or Lente insulin was the standard insulin regimen for many years. This was a convenient breakthrough in the beginning, compared to the earlier multiple-dose plans using regular alone. Only one injection a day! It must have felt like an enormous improvement, especially since we had only urine testing to show how well controlled we were each day.

Unfortunately, for most insulin-dependent diabetics, convenience is the only strength of this regimen. One shot of intermediate insulin has an extended peak, usually not beginning until the afternoon and lasting through early evening. (Thus, morning high blood sugar levels and afternoon reactions are common.) By evening, the insulin action is waning and often there is insufficient insulin to prevent high blood sugar levels overnight. Since there is only one long peak of activity, it is difficult for you to make adjustments to keep your tests within the moderate target range. Probably only a person whose pancreas still produces a substantial amount of insulin can maintain a moderate level of control on this treatment plan. A single dose of long-acting Ultralente insulin may also work for you. See Chapter 5, p 102 for Gary's Ultralente anecdote.

Single Injection NPH

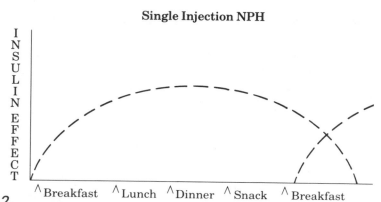

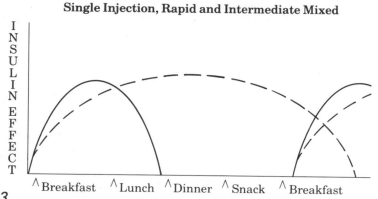

Plan 2

The single injection here mixes rapid-acting insulin with intermediate to cover the need for insulin during the time between breakfast and lunch. The regular dosage can be increased to reduce high blood sugar or reduced if there will be added exercise in the morning. Morning control is improved, but care must still be exercised to avoid afternoon reactions. With most people, it is still likely that blood sugar will rise during the night.

Plan 3

With intermediate insulin (NPH or Lente) taken twice a day, there is a better overall distribution of insulin activity, with peaks in the early afternoon and around bedtime. Overnight coverage is improved, and you are more likely to arise with blood sugar within your target range. Small doses of regular can be added to the intermediate when tests show high blood sugar. Since each of the

NPH injections is smaller, the effective duration of action is shorter. The overlap between the two shots helps to handle the mealtime insulin need following breakfast and dinner.

If one is taking two shots of insulin a day, anyway, plan 4 provides much better coverage and flexibility.

Two Injections a Day of Intermediate

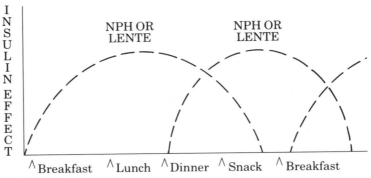

Plan 4
Two injections of rapid- and intermediate-acting insulin, one before breakfast and one before dinner, provide the most effective distribution of insulin activity available under the moderate regimen.

Two Injections with Rapid and Intermediate Mixed

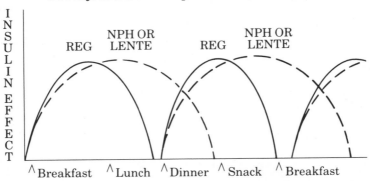

With this plan, a peak of insulin activity follows each meal and an adequate supply of insulin through the night. (The same schedule is used in the intensive regimen. Combined with frequent blood glucose testing, it allows normal or near-normal blood sugar levels for some.) It is possible for you to learn to vary the amounts of either kind of insulin cautiously to prepare for changes in routine, and to vary the regular to correct for high blood sugar levels. In this way you gain more flexibility than the other moderate insulin regimens offer.

These four insulin regimens are described in terms of idealized patterns of insulin activity. In any specific case, each type of insulin may have a pattern of activity that is very different from the averages. This is the reason you will be working closely with your physician at this stage, identifying the pattern at work in your case by studying your test logs. Your physician may recommend a variation on one of these plans, or even a plan not mentioned, to give you insulin activity that will match your life-style and physical needs.

Step 6: Observe the variations in blood sugar level caused by stress, illness, changes in food and exercise, and other factors
Earlier you studied the different influences on blood sugar level—insulin, diet, exercise, and physical and emotional stress. Now you can apply that information to understand your daily and weekly diabetes records. Seeing your blood or urine glucose levels swinging up and down and not knowing why they change can be very frustrating. But if you keep thorough records for a few weeks, you can quickly learn to read the reasons for your fluctuations. With understanding, you gain more power to control blood sugar levels.

We will illustrate this process by looking at several sample logs of people on the moderate regimen.

Daily Diabetes Log
Bill takes two shots of NPH insulin daily, twenty units before breakfast, and twelve units before dinner. He records only carbohydrates under the "Food" heading and usually eats snacks midmorning, in the afternoon, and at bedtime. His urine tests begin to show sugar when his blood sugar is around 200 mg/dl.

135

DATE & TIME	BLOOD OR URINE TEST & REACTIONS	INSULIN DOSAGE	ACTIVITY & EXERCISE	FOOD	COMMENTS: Stress, illness etc.
5-12 7 am	150 mg/dl	20 NPH	30 min bike	2 toast grpft	
11 am	strong re-act. (a)			roll of hard candies	
12 noon	2% urine gl (b)			cut 1 bread & fruit	
3 pm				cut snack (c)	
5:30 pm	neg	12 NPH		normal din	
8 pm					Big fight with Sue. She yelled. I bit my tongue.
10 pm	300 mg/dl (d)			no snack	
5-13 7 am	180 (e)	20 NPH	30 min bike	2 toast	
10 am				crackers	
12 noon	neg			normal lunch	
3 pm					
5 pm	neg			nuts & raisins	knew dinner wd be late
7:30 pm		12 NPH		Mexican din	extra carbo & 2 beers
10 pm	1%(f)				
5-14 7 am	150	20 NPH		usual brkf	

First, go through this log and explain the blood or urine sugar readings or reactions followed by a letter *(a)*. Then read the following paragraphs.

Bill's reaction at 11:00 A.M. (a) on May 12 occurred because he missed his midmorning snack, which was especially important, given the bike ride earlier.

The strength of the reaction caused him to overtreat it with a whole pack of hard candies. This, plus blood sugar rebound caused by the stress of the reaction, produced a 2 percent urine glucose test at noon. Since he starts spilling sugar into his urine only at 200 mg/dl, the 2 percent reading means blood sugar may have been as high as 300 mg/dl. He reduced carbohydrates at lunch to compensate and eliminated his snack when urine still tested positively at 3:00. His urine test before dinner was negative (which only shows that it was under 200 mg/dl) but the upsetting fight with his girlfriend caused another blood sugar peak by bedtime (d). He used a blood sugar test when he normally would have tested urine so he could see the impact of the strong emotional stress. He eliminated his evening snack.

His fasting blood test the next morning was down to 180 mg/dl, 30 above his target range for fasting tests, so he omitted fruit from breakfast and made his bike ride more energetic than usual to compensate. (Note: A urine test would have been negative for him because of his slightly high renal threshold.)

These changes in diet and activity balanced blood sugar enough that urine tests were negative at lunch and at 5:00 P.M. Knowing that dinner would be late, he ate an extra snack to avoid reactions. Bill overate at dinner, which produced a 1 percent urine test at 10:00. This would probably indicate that his blood sugar was over 240. By omitting his late night snack on the basis of this test, he was able to return to his target range for fasting tests by the next morning.

Daily Diabetes Log
Sandra, a working mother with two children, takes 40 units of NPH before breakfast. She records only carbohydrates in the food column and usually snacks in the afternoon and before bed. Her urine tests begin to show sugar when her blood sugar is around 160 mg/dl.

DATE & TIME	BLOOD OR URINE TEST & REACT	INSULIN DOSAGE	ACTIVITY & EXERCISE	FOOD	COMMENTS: Stress, illness, etc.
2-5 6:30 am	180 mg/dl	40 NPH		cut 1 bread	kids wild!
				no fruit (a)	
11:30 am	reaction (b)			2 donuts	too much but I've got to be sharp for noon meeting
			missed jazz dance class		
12:15 pm				2 rolls, bean soup 1/2 piece choc cake	Client insisted I share cake
3:00 pm	peeing a lot! (c) thirsty			skip snack	Must be high
5:30 pm	4 + urine 1 + ketones (d)			raw veggie salad & broth	
				took kids for 40 min walk	
9:30 pm	still peeing xtra (e)			skipped snack	
2-6 6:30 am	4 + urine but 150 mg/dl	40 NPH (f)		2 toast 1/2 orange	

Again, see how you explain the test results and symptoms marked by a letter *(a)*, and then read the following.

By cutting too much carbohydrate at breakfast (a), Sandra found herself with low blood sugar before lunch (b). Lunch was an important meeting with a business client, so she knowingly overtreated the insulin reaction to be sure she wouldn't have another one. Too many doughnuts, a usual amount of lunch, a missed exercise period, and the stress of the meeting conspired to increase her blood sugar to a symptomatic level (c) and (d). She knew from the excess urination and thirst that her blood sugar was fairly high, so she skipped her afternoon snack, and, finding ketones in her urine, ate a very light dinner. Sandra's blood sugar stayed high in spite of reduced carbohydrates and an evening walk with the kids (e). (Remember, when blood sugar is high, each unit of insulin is less effective at lowering it, and exercise may even cause it to increase.) Using frequent urination as her feedback, she skipped her bedtime snack. Her morning urine test was high (reflecting earlier high blood sugar), but her blood sugar test indicated she was within her target range (f). By cutting back on food, she had been able to cut the high blood sugar down to size.

Learn to vary insulin dosage, diet, and exercise cautiously to compensate for high or low tests and to deal with changes in routine.
Begin this step by reviewing Chapter 5, step 7b. The basic kinds of changes you can make are described there, although the amount of change advised is for the person on that regimen only. With fewer blood sugar tests to guide changes, you will have to work much more cautiously. After you read that material, come back to this point.

Moderate Regimen Target Glucose Levels

Fasting blood sugar test	70–150 mg/dl
Before-meal blood glucose test	70–180 mg/dl
1–2 hr after meal bG test	120–250 mg/dl
Before-meal urine test	Negative
Bedtime urine test	Negative or ¼%

Supplementary insulin can be used when tests are high or to prepare for a larger-than-usual meal. Supplements are always taken as regular insulin so the impact is over a limited period of time. Do not take extra insulin on the basis of tests of urine that has been in your bladder for more than fifteen or twenty minutes. (It may represent high blood sugar levels from hours ago.) Use urine samples collected a few minutes after you have completely emptied your bladder. Also, take into account what you have discovered about your renal threshold, the level at which you spill glucose from bloodstream into urine. If you have done the tests comparing urine and blood sugar readings described above under "Finding Your Renal Threshold" (step 3a in this chapter), you will have a better idea of what your urine tests actually mean.

You can make such supplements of insulin more accurate (and safer) if you usually base them on blood sugar tests rather than urine tests. More and more people on the moderate regimen are using blood sugar tests when they feel a need to, even though they use urine tests on a daily basis.

When your blood sugar control is upset by physical illness, emotional stress, or other factors, you may want to do more blood sugar tests than usual. The greater accuracy will help you deal with the unusual conditions.

A rule of thumb for supplementing insulin on the basis of urine tests is to use 5 percent of your daily dose if the reading is 1–2 percent, and 10 percent of daily dose if the reading is over 2 percent.

Urine Test (%)	Daily Total Dose	Extra Regular Units to Take	% of Total Dose
1–2	20	1	5
2+	20	2	10
1–2	50	2–3	5
2–5	50	5	10

If your supplement is based on a blood sugar test, take one unit of regular for every 30 mg/dl over 120 your test shows, up to five units. It is wise not to take more than five extra units of regular at a time (2-3 units if you are a child or small adult). If your blood sugar level is still high at the next test, you can take another supplement then. Avoid taking supplemental insulin at bedtime unless your doctor advises it because of severe illness and very high blood sugar.

If you are consistently spilling sugar into your urine (more than one test a day or even one test at the same time every day) you should discuss this with your doctor. You may need a larger standard dose of insulin or an adjustment in your diet.

Supplements of regular insulin can also be taken before a special meal that you know will be larger or richer than usual. How much extra to take depends, of course, on the size of the meal. At first, don't take more than one or two units extra and see what your next test is. By trial and error, you will learn how much to add, but it is better to err by adding too little than too much. Be sure not to take the supplement too early. Special meals have a way of being delayed.

When you are planning to be more active than usual, you can compensate by taking less insulin or eating more. If you take only NPH, reduce insulin only if the extra activity will last for an hour or more, or if you know it will be occurring around the time of your insulin peak (roughly 6–12 hr after injections). Otherwise it is better to eat extra food to cover the exercise period. Generally one extra serving of carbohydrate (a slice of bread, for instance) should be eaten for every 30 minutes of hard exercise.

Do not rely on increases in insulin only to correct for high blood or urine sugar tests. You should also bring blood sugar down by adjusting exercise and food. This is especially important in the moderate regimen, because generally you are likely to have more high blood sugar levels than the person on the intensive plan. If you use only insulin supplements to reduce these highs you will gain weight.

Remember that when blood sugar is quite high (over 250 or 300), exercise is not likely to lower it and may even cause an increase. Meals may be reduced by one or two carbohydrate servings, but you should not fast because of the risk of severe reactions if there is no food in your intestines. The safest way of reducing a very high blood sugar level is to take a series of small injections of regular (10% of daily dose), four to six hours apart until urine tests show less than 1 percent glucose or until blood sugar tests are under 200 mg/dl. (Someone with a daily dose of 40 units should take no more than four units at a time.) When you are lowering an extra-high blood sugar level in this way, it is wise to rely on the greater precision of the blood glucose tests to guide you. Urine tests can still be positive when blood sugar has already reached normal range. If you have high blood sugar and ketones in your urine or are ill, you probably should contact your physician for guidance.

Step 7: Have new lab tests done after two or three months to determine the effect of your new regimen

At this point, you will have solid feedback on the effectiveness of your regimen. Tests for hemoglobin A^1c and blood lipids, together with your home test records, will let you know if you have found the

141

right balance in your program of self-care. As you review the results with your physician, take an objective point of view. You have certain target levels you want to achieve. If you haven't reached them, suspend all judgments on yourself and simply look for the reasons. The next step will help you do this.

Step 8: Assess your progress and determine what (if anything) is needed to improve control further

Again, you can use the parallel step in the intensive regimen, with just a few changes. Where it refers to the eleven steps of the intensive, go to the beginning of this chapter instead, where the steps of the moderate learning process are listed. And, of course, substitute the word *moderate* for *intensive* throughout. *Go to Chapter 5, step 9.*

If you find that you have learned all you need to manage well at a moderate level of control, we suggest you take a moment to review the decision you made at the beginning. When you consider all factors, is a moderate regimen still your choice? You may feel content with the improvements in control you have achieved and prefer to give attention to other aspects of your life.

Or you may choose to move on to the intensive regimen. If so, you have already studied a major portion of what you need to learn, so it will be much easier to make the transition. Probably the main changes will be testing blood more frequently, possibly changing insulin regimen, and giving more attention to compensating for the variations you observe. Discuss the necessary changes with your doctor and review each step of the intensive regimen.

Step 9: Maintain motivation for continuing to work on improving control

If you choose to continue managing your diabetes at the moderate level, or if you still have more to learn about this level, keeping your motivation high is important. It may have been an easy process so far, or it may have been intensely frustrating. Either way, you will need to take steps to ensure that you remain willing to continue.

Rereading step 1 at the beginning of this chapter may be useful. All of the things said about building a positive foundation for this work continue to be relevant now. You might find elements you neglected the first time around but now feel like putting into effect.

Support from other diabetics working on improving control is one of the most important ways of keeping motivation strong. If you have not yet found ways of obtaining this, it may be time to do so. Support groups or individual contacts can give valuable emotional support and encouragement. You can receive practical guidance from people who have overcome many of the obstacles you may still be struggling with. You may also be able to help others with problems you have already solved. Serving someone else in this way keeps your motivation high. (See Chapter 13, "Living Well with Other Diabetics.")

Living on a regimen is easier if you do not feel you are in a regiment on active duty every day of the year. Occasional leaves or vacations should be part of your regimen; don't feel that you are cheating at these times. A day or two of relaxed management can make it much easier for you to continue with your usual level of control. If you take supplements of regular insulin to handle any feasts, keep them moderate to avoid severe reactions. (Such vacations are not advisable if you have any infection or a complication that could be made worse by higher blood sugar levels.)

If you have made significant improvements in control, you are probably feeling better, both physically and mentally. This immediate payoff makes it easier for you to continue following your regimen. It also becomes an inspiration for continued learning. This is reinforced by the blood testing process itself. When you can see exactly what your blood glucose level is and do something about it, you gain power over diabetes, instead of feeling controlled by it. It is natural to want to extend this sense of power by learning more about managing your condition well.

If you feel at any time a strong resistance to continuing with your regimen, remember that there are steps you can take to explore the causes and neutralize them. Be aware of any rationalizations or denials that you use to justify the resistance. Don't accept "I'm really too busy" or "I don't need to be so careful, I'm all right now," or "It won't do any good anyway." Use the Help processes in Chapter 3 to gain awareness of what is happening and ask for personal help, if needed.

Step 10: Celebrate!

When you finish learning the moderate regimen, you have completed a challenging assignment. You may feel like honoring yourself for your achievement, personally or even publicly, with a party, a dinner, or a picnic. Whether you invite a small group or a large one, give yourself credit for the many things you have learned. What you are doing to live well with diabetes can be generalized. Other than taking insulin and testing blood, the basics of your regimen would give good health to anyone. So share the health.

Now is the time to collect a reward if you promised yourself one to build motivation at the beginning. In fact, even if you didn't make that agreement with yourself then, you might feel that you deserve some special thing, event, or experience now. Living well is its own reward, but there is nothing wrong with bonuses from time to time.

Next Steps

You may have chosen to stay at a moderate level of control while you deal with other aspects of having diabetes. Review the Table of Contents to see what else you would like to work on now. You may find that you have learned enough to continue gradually improving your blood sugar management while you focus on other issues.

Possibly, there are problems or challenges in your life that you need to handle while you take an intermission in your diabetes learning (perhaps applying in other areas what you have learned about yourself here). If so, make a date with yourself to reopen the subject in three months or so. Mark the calendar: TIME TO START LEARNING MORE ABOUT DIABETES? Diabetes is a lifelong companion, so you will benefit from also seeing it as a lifelong teacher.

On the other hand, now that you have mastered the moderate regimen, you may be eager to go right on to the intensive program. You have a solid foundation in what you have learned up to now, so it will be much easier than it would have been a few months ago.

(Whatever your next steps, you might consider a subscription to the publications *Diabetes Forecast*, published by the ADA, *Diabetes in the News*, published by Ames, or *Diabetes Self-Management*. They are good sources for news on the latest developments in diabetes research and care. See resources in the Appendix.)

The Loose Regimen

"*It sure would have helped if someone had told me I was in control, even though my diabetes was out of control. I never saw that I was the one who went on binges or 'forgot' my shot. It just happened, like somebody else was doing it to me.*"

—*Ernest*

LEARNING THE LOOSE REGIMEN

1. Review the survival issues at the end of the book—insulin reactions, diabetic coma, and infections.

2. Learn to do home blood and urine glucose testing. Do tests occasionally, especially when you are ill or have an infection. Do urine ketone tests when you are ill or experiencing high stress.

   Test urine several time a week.

3. Take one or two insulin injections daily. (More injections or the insulin pump are not recommended without regular blood sugar testing.)

4. Eat a healthful diet, usually with moderation. Learn how to

increase the pleasure of eating without increasing the sugar and fat content.
Observe great caution in adjusting insulin dosage.
Make a commitment to continuing diabetes learning, maintaining your motivation, and reviewing obstacles to improving control.

The basic belief we assume in this book is that all people who have diabetes are on a controlled regimen, no matter how wildly their blood sugar levels rise and fall. Consciously or unconsciously, you make a series of self-care choices each day. Taken together, they are the regimen you live by. Not taking insulin, missing meals, overeating, keeping an irregular schedule—there are many possible ingredients in the regimens that are usually considered rebellion against any treatment plan.

We prefer to acknowledge the power that you wield if you are at this level of management. If you accept that you do, in fact, control the choices you make, you are more likely to realize that you can make other choices. You can live well while you find ways of using your power to adopt an approach more in tune with your physical needs as a diabetic.

So we have outlined a loose regimen, with recommendations for certain minimal self-care standards. It is a fairly simple approach, without elaborate lists of tasks. We go to the heart of our philosophy of diabetes care here. This regimen is far from the standards of control recommended for diabetes today. But you can still live well by doing what you can (or will) and not condemning yourself for what you can't (or won't) do. You can live well by finding whatever it is you are willing to do to begin improving control and making a start.

Step 1. Review the survival issues at the end of the book

The highest priority in your diabetes education goes to these three life-or-death issues: insulin reactions, diabetic coma, and infections. Ignorance of these could cost you your life.

If you have insulin reactions often (more than a couple of times a week), you may need more information on avoiding them. Chapter 8, on reactions, could be a lifesaver for you.

Step 2. Learn to do home blood and urine glucose testing

We would also like to suggest that one of your early actions be learning to do home blood glucose tests. Even if you use this skill infrequently, it is one of the most valuable things you can learn. As few as two tests a week have proven effective in helping diabetics to improve their metabolic control. Keep the test strips available so you can easily test when you want to know how changes in diet, activity, or stress have affected your blood sugar level. If you think your blood sugar becomes high, check it and validate your perception. When you become ill, home blood testing makes it much easier to keep blood sugar from skyrocketing. This can hasten your recovery.

If you wish to learn more about home blood testing, go to Chapter 5, step 3a. You may find it useful to take a class or ask your doctor or nurse to show you test techniques.

If you have not been doing urine glucose testing, you might also consider this as part of your regimen. Although not particularly useful in the intensive regimen, urine tests still give useful feedback with the less strict treatment plans. You can tell if your blood sugar is more or less controlled, and when it is quite high, you can take cautious action to bring it down.

The test for ketones in the urine is especially important because it indicates when your control is significantly off, because of physical illness or emotional stress or very high blood sugar levels. Information on making the feedback from urine tests more meaningful is in Chapter 6, step 3a.

Step 3. Take one or two insulin injections daily

(More injections or the insulin pump are not recommended without blood sugar testing.)

Without frequent blood sugar testing, you should not take more than one or two injections of insulin a day. Your physician will help you determine the types of insulin and dosage that will best suit your schedule.

Step 4. Eat a healthful diet, usually with moderation

If you overeat, binge eat, and generally ignore your diet, you might

147

find reading Chapter 9 on nutrition rewarding. It contains tips on ways to enjoy food while eating more healthfully.

Step 5. Observe great caution in adjusting insulin dosage

Be cautious in adjusting insulin dosage to compensate for changes in diet and level of activity. You need the feedback of regular blood sugar and urine tests to do this safely. If blood sugar is high because you are ill, consult with your doctor on any changes in the amount of insulin you take.

Step 6. Make a commitment to continuing diabetes learning, maintaining your motivation, and reviewing obstacles to improving control

Explore what commitment you are prepared to make to continuing learning about diabetes self-care. Determine for yourself the aspects of diabetes management that you can willingly choose to work on. By proceeding in this way, you are likely to learn much faster.

Scan the sections of the moderate and intensive regimens and see if you are attracted to learning about any of this material. And look again through the Table of Contents. Find what you are willing to learn about now. A conversation with your physician or nurse-practitioner might help you define your next steps.

Who chooses the loose regimen?

A variety of people may choose this level of diabetes management.

The loose regimen may be your choice if you are someone:

- Whose life is in turmoil or filled with external demands.
- Who values quality of life-style in the present over the possible reduction of future risks.
- Who feels rebellious and unwilling or weak and unable to change.
- Who has a poor self-image.
- Who has little money and cannot afford necessary supplies.

We can offer specific guidance to people in each of these groups.

1. If your life is filled with external demands or is in turmoil, set aside some minimum amount of time for learning to manage your diabetes better. As little as ten or twenty minutes a day can be a good beginning. The important thing is making a commitment in spite of a challenging schedule or an over-

148

whelming set of problems. Once you've made a beginning, it may be easier for you to give diabetes care a higher priority and give more time to it. You may find that some of those other tasks can be scaled down or put on hold for a while. If not, you will still be gradually learning information and skills vital to your well-being.

2. If you have chosen the loose regimen because you tend to live for the moment, valuing present pleasures over future risks, you may be surprised. Many people following more intensive regimens report no shortage of totally enjoyable experiences. For them, greater control is equal to greater freedom. Regular blood glucose testing and the ability to easily adjust insulin, diet, and exercise allow great flexibility in life-style, at a relatively small cost in time. This freedom in living carries with it less anxiety about the future. The person who is actively controlling diabetes is doing the best he or she can to reduce the risk of complications later.

   You might find it useful to review the leading pleasures in your life and ask yourself how they can be reconciled with improved diabetes care. There are relatively few absolute contradictions, so long as you are not attached to excess itself as a pleasure. It might help you to talk with others who are following more intensive regimens but who have found ways to respect the pleasure principle.

   Although you may feel rock-hard in your habits, you should remember that human beings are actually very adaptable. You can probably think of changes that have occurred in your own life that at first seemed very negative but soon proved to be definite improvements.

3. If rebelliousness or a sense of weakness and incapacity is your style, you may want to work on issues of power. Diabetes regimens are followed with greater ease when you find the source of authority within yourself, rather than in the medical system. You are the one who ultimately decides what you will or will not do, no matter what your doctor says. If you see doctors as authorities who give orders, and then you automatically do the opposite, your rebellion is hardly freedom. If, on the other hand, you feel weak and unable to do what your doctor says, this is often only a covert form of rebellion. Either way, you lose.

Real freedom and power come from consciously deciding what you will do in each situation you face and then leaving these automatic reactions behind. Even if your doctor does tend to give commands, hear them as intelligent advice. Make a conscious choice of what you will or will not do and give yourself room to make new choices. (See Chapters 3 and 14.)

4. Some of us feel that we don't deserve first-class care. "Why bother with me? I'm not worth it." If this is your reason for choosing a relatively casual approach to regimen, you may need to work on developing a more positive self-image. Unfortunately, negative beliefs about yourself tend to produce behavior that confirms them. Escape from this cycle can take place through work on the beliefs themselves or on the behavior. In some cases the assistance of a trained therapist is advisable, but many people have made changes at this level solely through their own efforts. (See the sections on self-image and beliefs in Chapter 14, "Living Well with Yourself." Chapter 3 also contains techniques you may find helpful.)

5. If you lack the money for home blood glucose testing or other diabetes care supplies, you may be able to gain assistance through your local ADA chapter. You may at least find a staff person there who can help you search for community resources that provide essential supplies. Some health insurance now covers testing supplies and equipment as well as diabetes education. (See the Appendix for discount mail-order supply houses offering significant savings.)

CHAPTER 8

Living Well With Insulin Reactions

"*There's nothing makes me feel more anxious than the idea that I may just lose it if I don't eat enough or if I jog too far. I've had one reaction I didn't wake up from and one where I got so confused I forgot I was looking for food. My son finally came home and had to tell me what to do. I don't ever want to go through that again!*"
—*Jan, a 35-year-old woman*

When psychologists ask us what bothers us about having diabetes, we usually cite insulin reactions as our top concern. When we don't respond adequately to this short-term complication of diabetes, we may find ourselves in an embarrassing situation because of things we did in a less-than-coherent state. We may even find ourselves waking up in the hospital or in jail. It's distressingly simple: A very low blood sugar level results in unclear thinking and emotional outbursts. If blood sugar falls too far, we can lose consciousness. No wonder we feel bothered by that one!

Because proper response to insulin reactions is such a vital part of living well with diabetes, this chapter reviews the traditional ways of treating these reactions. And we have added some new approaches to help people change some emotional and behavioral patterns that may cause frequent insulin reactions. There is also a section for the person working with optimal control, since hypoglycemia (low blood sugar) tends to work differently when blood sugar levels are usually near normal than when they are usually high. During the time when you are gaining optimal control, the risk of having reactions is higher than usual, and you need to know what to expect. This is true for people on the insulin pump as well as for those on multiple-injection regimens.

THE ACTION OF REACTION

When blood sugar falls below a certain point (usually around 60–70 mg/dl) our body signals red alert. The resulting stress reaction is to pump out adrenal hormones that produce the racing pulse, thumping heart, nervous feelings, and sweating indicative of a strong insulin reaction. This dramatic response is appropriate, because the situation is a serious one. If our blood sugar level goes too low, we lose consciousness. If it stays too low for too long, we risk brain damage. In as little as two to three minutes, some brain cells can die. Fortunately, we have a surplus of brain cells. Also fortunately, our bodies usually respond to the crisis if we do lose consciousness. One of the hormones released in a serious reaction is glucagon, a substance stored in the liver that helps raise blood sugar level. However, repeated insulin reactions can lower the amount of glucagon or glucose available to deal with hypoglycemia.

(The high blood sugar level that may follow a moderate to severe reaction is often caused by the glucagon stimulating more glucose release than is necessary. This is known as the rebound from a reaction. The effect is multiplied when the diabetic also eats more food than is necessary. More about this rebound effect later in the chapter under "Somogyi Reactions".)

Insulin reactions may be caused by several different factors: a delayed meal or missed snack; an unexpected period of strenuous activity; too much insulin because of a mistake in measuring dosage; a period of strong emotional expressions; even a time of relaxation after a week of high tension. In general, it's a matter of food too little or too late, or an excess of activity, insulin, or particular kinds of emotional stress. (Stress may lower or raise blood sugar, depending on the circumstances.)

152

This is really a matter of balance between the different factors affecting blood sugar level. Reactions occur because food, exercise, insulin, and possibly the results of stress are out of balance. As we learn to alter these factors, we learn to avoid reactions. We discover how different activities affect blood sugar and how to adjust food intake or insulin dosage to compensate for increased activity. We learn what kind of stress is likely to lower blood sugar for us and when to compensate.

Symptoms of Hypoglycemia

The symptoms of an insulin reaction vary from person to person and from reaction to reaction. Fortunately, home blood glucose testing provides one sure sign: If blood glucose is below 60 to 70 mg/dl, it's time to eat a snack that will be rapidly absorbed. Testing whenever a reaction is suspected or anticipated is excellent practice for the person new to diabetes as well as for the experienced diabetic who is tightening metabolic control. The objective feedback of the test helps you to develop and sharpen awareness of the particular set of symptoms signaling the onset of a reaction.

Other than blood sugar level itself, the particular symptoms of a reaction depend upon the severity of the reaction, the rapidity of onset, and other individual factors. The classic symptoms of a mild to moderate reaction include lightheadedness, dizziness, shakiness, sweating, increase in pulse rate, and hunger. As the reaction progresses, vision may become blurry, and the mind fuzzy. There may be mental confusion, emotional outbursts, or extreme anxiety. A person may forget that he or she is looking for candy, or become distracted by the search for the perfect candy bar. In some cases, a diabetic may even become angry or resistant if anyone else suggests eating something sweet.

Finally, if no food is taken, the diabetic loses consciousness and may experience convulsions. (The muscular movements may be imagined as the body's attempt to squeeze out any sugar the muscles might be storing.) If someone else knows what is happening, treatment can usually revive the person on the spot. Otherwise, it's time for the medic or the emergency room.

This sequence isn't always the same. Sometimes a reaction will approach very quietly, especially if the fall in blood sugar has been very slow. The first sign may be confusion or irritability. There may simply be a sense of unease or difficulty getting to sleep. Or in a time otherwise marked by anxiety or high stress, it may be difficult to notice that a particular bit of shakiness is indicating a reaction rather than more of the old stress. It is important that you know *your* reaction symptoms and variations in them that are likely to occur. Later we will describe ways of increasing your sensitivity to these signs so that you can treat reactions early.

Symptoms of Insulin Reactions

You will experience some, but not necessarily all, of these symptoms, and you may find a few unique to your own body.

- A *mild reaction*—Tiredness or weakness, hunger, sweatiness, chills, cold hands, increased pulse rate, shakiness (or shaky feeling), dizziness, lightheadedness, headache, pallor, difficulty getting to sleep.
- A *moderate reaction*—An increase in any of the above, anxiety, confusion, anger, unclear thinking, loss of emotional control, strange behavior, poor coordination, speech difficulties, blurred, spotty, or double vision.
- A *severe reaction*—Stupor, loss of consciousness, convulsions.

Both you and the people close to you should be familiar with these symptoms.

Some diabetics do not experience the usual reaction symptoms. Because of reduced production of the hormones that set off the alarm, blood sugar may fall very low, with little or no sign that it is happening. If you suspect that you are not experiencing the usual symptoms of a reaction, discuss this with your physician. Lab tests can determine if you have this type of hormonal lack.

To a large extent, the symptoms of an insulin reaction and those of several other conditions overlap. Anxiety or fear may cause a quickened pulse, cold hands, and shaking. Too many cups of coffee can produce a nervousness akin to the feelings of a reaction. The hot flashes of menopause or other hormonal changes may mimic hypoglycemia. And rapidly falling blood sugar level may bring the symptoms of a reaction long before blood sugar really is low. Treating a reaction when your symptoms are actually caused by anxiety may result in a high blood sugar level; so, at first, it is best to test your blood whenever possible to verify that the glucose level is really too low. *However, any time you are in doubt and cannot test, it is much better to eat some rapidly absorbed carbohydrate than risk experiencing a severe reaction.*

The symptoms of hypoglycemia can also be masked by the effects of alcohol or other drugs. A diabetic who becomes even moderately intoxicated or stoned may not notice a reaction until the blood sugar level is quite low. The need for caution is compounded with alcohol, because this drug lowers blood sugar when one has not eaten for some time. It also blocks the liver's ability to release glucose into the blood. So a couple of drinks before dinner can generate a severe insulin reaction that may not be discovered until the process is already far along. If you do choose to drink or use other drugs, it is best to check your blood sugar level and eat a moderate snack (unless your tests are high—over 180 mg/dl—to begin with).

Somogyi Reactions

One tricky form of insulin reaction has an exotic name, the Somogyi reaction (named for its discoverer, Dr. I. M. Somogyi). This is a prolonged insulin reaction that usually occurs during sleep as the result of too much insulin in the bloodstream. During this special type of reaction, the symptoms usually are not strong enough to wake you; on the other hand, blood sugar does not continue to go down. (Somogyi reactions are different in this way from typical nighttime insulin reactions in which you either wake up in a sweat or don't wake up until the medics pump glucagon into your arm.)

The low blood sugar level triggers the body's defense system, and glucose is released along with hormones that attempt to slow down the burning of glucose. A side effect of this process is the burning of fat, resulting in some degree of ketosis (reflected in a positive test for ketones in the urine). Because of the rebound effect, one may find blood sugar at a relatively high level in the morning and ketones in the urine. If the doctor responds by giving you more insulin, a vicious cycle is started that leads to more and more severe Somogyi reactions. The appropriate response is either a reduction in total insulin dose or an adjustment in the timing of insulin action.

Signs of a Somogyi reaction:

1. Ketones in the urine, with blood sugar under 250 mg/dl.
2. Evidence of night sweating (wet bedclothes).
3. Low temperature in the morning (body temperature may be low for as long as six hours after an insulin reaction).
4. Bad dreams or nightmares.
5. Grumpiness, abdominal pain, or headache upon awakening.
6. An apparent need for high insulin dosage (more than 50–60 units a day).

If you suspect that you are having Somogyi reactions, discuss your symptoms with your doctor. But first, you should do a bit of research by setting the alarm for a time midway through your sleep period and then testing your blood for several different nights to see if your blood sugar is at hypoglycemic levels (below 60 mg/dl). If so, the component of your insulin dose active during the night will need to be decreased. Usually only a few units are cut, although sometimes the overall insulin dose may be excessive and larger cuts may be needed. (Almost normal bedtime sugars with low or low normal 3:00 A.M. levels and high prebreakfast levels suggest the Somogyi reaction.) *Do not make changes in your basic insulin dosage without talking with your physician.*

A diabetic on the metabolic roller coaster produced by Somogyi reactions is likely to experience strong emotional swings. Such a person may have periods of irritability, depression, or anxiety, together with a sense of fatigue. These feelings are likely to clear when blood sugar levels even out.

Reactions and Optimal Control
In a person who manages diabetes with moderate or loose control, an insulin reaction may represent a very large fall in blood sugar level, and sometimes a very rapid one. The symptoms are usually strong and easily recognized. When stricter control is gained on the intensive regimen, the fall in blood sugar to reaction level may be as little as 20 or 30 mg/dl, and the change may take place very gradually. As a result, the symptoms are often much subtler. Slight confusion or vaguely unclear vision may be the only signs that blood sugar has dipped to 50 or 60 mg/dl. It is clear that those of us who

maintain this level of management need to heighten our awareness and not expect all reactions to sound a strong alarm. Again, the ability to check blood sugar level allows verification of hypoglycemia. In this way, we can learn what our new, subtler set of signals is.

In addition, during the time of switching over to the intensive regimen, reactions are likely to occur more frequently. The cushion against hypoglycemia provided by high blood sugar levels is gone, and it takes time to gain the skills and knowledge necessary to stay in balance. This is one reason for keeping schedules, diet, and exercise as regular as possible during this time. Once you've learned to play the game, you can make changes easily and still stick to the golden mean.

A diabetic who is first gaining optimal control may find that even normal blood sugar levels feel rather uncomfortable and trigger symptoms of hypoglycemia. This is especially true if blood sugar levels have been chronically high earlier. This is a brief occurrence, usually lasting no more than a week or two. The symptoms fade after adjustment to a more normal metabolism.

TREATING INSULIN REACTIONS

You now have a choice between making diabetes care a "treat" or a treatment. When blood sugar is too low, the sweets you usually avoid are prescribed medicine. Some of us use this opportunity to satisfy our craving for candy, cookies, and ice cream. Eating these foods is perfectly acceptable as long as you are able to control the amount you eat and not end up bingeing. On the other hand, pharmaceutical companies are now making products designed to treat insulin reactions. These are made of straight glucose—sugar in its most rapidly absorbed form. The advantage of using glucose lies in its somewhat quicker absorption rate, the precisely measured dose, and the fact that glucose products are less likely to lead to overdose or to indiscriminate use when blood sugar is not low. The flavor is rather bland. The disadvantage: They cost more than candy and they're difficult to carry in the pocket.

So long as the sugar is in a form that can be absorbed quickly, the amount used is more important than the kind. The usual recommendation is to eat a food containing 10 to 15 grams of concentrated carbohydrate. Some foods that satisfy this requirement are listed in the accompanying table. For comparison, we also list some dessert servings that would be overkill if taken for a moderate reaction.

Some Appropriate Treats for Insulin Reactions

One-half cup (4 ounces) orange juice — 13 grams carbo
One-half cup apple juice — 15 grams carbo
Six ounces (½ can) cola — 15 grams carbo
One cup milk — 12 grams carbo
One fig bar — 10 grams carbo
Two 2-inch chocolate chip cookies — 12 grams carbo
One tablespoon of granulated sugar — 12 grams carbo
Two teaspoons jam — 14 grams carbo
One-half-ounce raisins (half a small bag) — 10 grams carbo
One-half-ounce caramel or peanut brittle — 12 grams carbo
One ounce milk chocolate — 16 grams carbo
Five Lifesavers — 10 grams carbo

(The wise diabetic carries a couple of servings of these items and keeps a stash in the glove compartment, desk, or locker. A role of Lifesavers is especially convenient and inconspicuous.)

Some Excessive Treats

One slice apple pie — 60 grams carbo (four times as much as you need)
One piece of cake with frosting — 60 grams carbo
12 ounces of cola (a full can or bottle) — 30 grams carbo (three times the necessary amount)
One jelly doughnut — 48 grams carbo (three times as much as you need)

When you are in the throes of a full-tilt insulin reaction—confused, pulse racing, anxious, and extremely hungry—the temptation to overdose is powerful, to say the least. (This is especially true in the middle of the night, when blood sugar may fall to a very low level before you wake up.) If you wish to avoid an enormous leap in blood sugar level, however, you are advised to learn to eat moderately. Treat reactions in stages, first eating a sweet in the category of 10 to 15 grams of carbohydrate, waiting ten or fifteen minutes, and then taking another sweet only if the symptoms have not disappeared. (The obvious exception to this practice would be when you are experiencing a very severe reaction following heavy exercise or a missed meal. At such a time, you may need to double the amount of sugar to bring blood glucose back to normal.) Remember that you are likely to have a rebound effect, with the glucose from your liver increasing blood sugar, along with the sugar you use to treat the reaction. If you overeat, your next blood test may be up in the 300s.

Unless the reaction occurs within an hour of mealtime, you should have a moderate snack of longer-acting food—whole grain bread, crackers and cheese, nuts—after you have eaten a sweet. This will tide you over to the next meal and prevent another reaction.

As an insulin-dependent diabetic, you run the risk of not waking up when a reaction occurs, or of becoming unconscious because hypoglycemia is not treated in time. The people close to you should know what to do if they find you unconscious, so ask them to read this next section and take notes.

To the Person Who May Need To Treat an Unconscious Diabetic . . .
If you find that you cannot rouse your sleeping beauty, it is most likely that he or she is in insulin shock (severe hypoglycemia or insulin reaction), the result of very low blood sugar. The accompanying table compares the outward symptoms of insulin shock and diabetic coma (the result of very high blood sugar), so you can know for sure what is happening.

Outward Signs of Insulin Shock and Diabetic Coma

Shock	Coma
Sudden onset (minutes to hours)	Gradual onset (days)
Pale, moist, sweaty skin	Flushed, dry skin
Shallow breathing	Deep, labored breathing
Normal breath	Fruity smell on breath
Rapid pulse	Usually rapid pulse
Low blood sugar	Very high blood sugar

If it looks as if your friend is in a diabetic coma, the only treatment you can institute is calling a physician and getting him or her into the hospital immediately. If the doctor is not available, get your friend to an emergency room. Probably he or she will not have been feeling well for the last half-day or more. Diabetic coma is gradual in onset, and usually one feels ill, is thirsty, and has to urinate frequently as the process unfolds.

If the patient is in insulin shock, you may be able to help him or her regain consciousness on your own. Provide sugar in a form that he or she won't choke on. The best possible treatment is glucagon, a substance injected just like insulin. If you're lucky, there is a kit around and you have been instructed in its use. There are two vials—one containing the dry glucagon and the other, sterile water. You mix the two with the syringe and inject the mixture under the skin in a fleshy spot like the thigh or back of the arm. The glucagon encourages the liver to release glucose.

If there is no glucagon, jam or jelly is the treatment of choice, or a tube of frosting, or one of the jellied glucose products like Glutose or Monojel. Rub a bit on your friends's lips and into the mouth with your fingers, and he or she may start sucking. Stroke the throat to encourage swallowing. Provide a couple of tablespoons or more. (Ernest's wife, Grace, revived him once with an appropriately named preserve—Hero's Jam.)

If nothing is available in jellied form, see if you can get your friend to swallow very small sips of any fruit juice or soda pop (not diet soda!). Be cautious—you don't want to cause choking. Don't try any solid sweet unless you can get enough response to be sure that it will be chewed and swallowed and not cause gagging.

The scarcity of blood sugar reaching the diabetic's brain may produce antagonism and uncooperativeness as he or she starts to revive. It may seem like poor thanks for all you've just been through, but don't be alarmed. It's a natural result of a serious insulin reaction.

If you're not sure whether it's diabetic coma or insulin shock, it's best to try giving a sweet (as above) to see what happens. Low blood sugar can cause harm more quickly than high blood sugar.

If your patient doesn't start to recover consciousness within five minutes by the clock, call the medic team or get him or her to an emergency room. You've done everything you can. Thank you for your loving care.

To the Person with Diabetes . . .

Show your love for the people close to you by not putting them through the process just described. It is one of the most terrifying events that can be inflicted on someone. Study the next section on preventing reactions carefully, and practice what you learn here. If you have had more than one reaction that you did not awaken from in recent years, we suggest that you do the exercise on page 156.

PREVENTING INSULIN REACTIONS

The most fundamental way to avoid reactions is to be willing to keep a corner of your awareness devoted to diabetes. Don't obsess about it, but simply acknowledge that it is a companion who refuses to be left behind. People who suffer from frequent insulin reactions are often the ones who try to pretend that they do not have diabetes. This clearly doesn't work, and they often end up with vivid reminders of their illness.

You are more likely to have an insulin reaction in certain situations. When you have been more active, when a meal is delayed, or when you have eaten lightly, it is easy to predict that hypoglycemia will occur if you don't compensate for the change in routine. If these situations become cues to awareness, like little alarm clocks, you will find that you automatically take the appropriate action. The light meal or the delay becomes a signal for an added snack (unless blood sugar tests are high).

To deal with an increase in activity level, you can either take less insulin (cutting dose by two or three units, up to one-third the total dose, depending on the amount of the increase in exercise), or you can increase your food intake. A good rule of thumb is to eat 10 to 15 grams additional carbohydrate for each thirty minutes of extra physical activity (a slice of bread, a whole double graham cracker, one-half-ounce of raisins, or a medium orange).

Through trial and error you will find the amount that's right for the kinds of activities you are involved in. You will be able to hike or work all afternoon in the garden and keep in balance, avoiding both reactions and high blood sugar. The chart of calorie expenditures in Chapter 10, "Living Actively with Diabetes," gives you an idea of how much food you burn up with different activities. Note that vigorous activities (digging with a shovel, playing tennis, or hiking uphill) can use close to a whole meal's worth of calories in one hour.

Remember that vigorous exercise continues to lower blood sugar for as much as four to six hours after you finish; you may need an extra snack or a larger meal after a period of prolonged or intense activity. This happens because well-exercised muscles absorb more sugar from the bloodstream, even after the activity stops. Exercising regularly in itself helps you avoid reactions; the glucose stored in the muscles can be drawn on when the blood sugar level goes down.

Diet is another factor that helps to stabilize blood sugar levels and prevent hypoglycemia. If you tend to eat the slower-burning foods, you will have a more continuous supply of glucose entering the bloodstream. This is one reason the high complex carbohydrate, high fiber (HCF) diet is being recommended by many nutritionists. Protein burns even slower, but it is usually accompanied by more fat than we need.

As you become more aware of the physical sensations that precede an insulin reaction, you will find that you can often eat just enough simple carbohydrate to stay at normal blood sugar level and neither fall into hypoglycemia nor jump up to a high level. You gain a sense of "dosage" with foods like raisins, prunes, and fresh fruit. ("There's that feeling. I could test, but there's no reason to think that I have anything but normal or low blood sugar. Let's see, four prunes should see me through to lunch.") Sometimes this becomes a matter of shifting the order of a meal, eating the fruit or other simple carbohydrate at the beginning of the meal rather than at the end. Anyone who has experienced the frustration of a reaction occurring while gulping down a meal that won't be absorbed for an hour, knows the value of this practice.

Developing an Early Warning System
Sensitivity to the symptoms of insulin reactions varies greatly from person to person. One may be very aware of bodily states, noting the beginning of hypoglycemia at a very early stage. Another may be so absorbed in day-to-day activities that he or she recognizes a reaction only when sweat is already pouring down the brow and

speech is slurred. You can take steps to increase your bodily awareness and thereby your chances for survival. Diabetic neuropathy (see Chapter 17) and certain prescription drugs (such as beta blockers prescribed for high blood pressure or heart disease) can also block the typical symptoms.

Also, a few diabetics have rare hormone deficiencies that mask or even eliminate the symptoms of hypoglycemia. Blood sugar may fall to very low levels before any symptoms are experienced. Unfortunately, the symptoms that do occur are likely to be confusion or emotional instability caused by the brain's receiving too little glucose. Frequent blood testing and meticulous adherence to regimen is especially important for anyone in this category.

Many of us can sense the approach of an insulin reaction before blood sugar reaches a hypoglycemic level. It is possible to cultivate sensitivity to the subtle cues your body gives that indicate you are about to bottom out. This calls for deepening physical awareness, something that many diabetics avoid. When blood sugar is chronically high (200+ mg/dl), we tend to be mildly uncomfortable. (Ernest describes his discomfort as the feeling of having fine sand or granules of sugar in his muscles.) Rather than experience this vague distress, many of us ignore our bodies and live in our heads. Reactions have to be thundering before we notice them. If you spend much time out of touch with your body, there are ways you can increase your bodily awareness.

One way is to make routine physical activities like brushing your teeth, shaving, or showering occasions for *feeling* your body rather than thinking about other things. Become aware, for instance, of the sensation of temperature in various body parts, muscle tension, the texture of whatever surface is in contact with you skin, the feeling of your breath or pulse. (When you are relatively quiet you can sense the pulsing of your whole circulatory system.) A particularly good time for this casual survey is when you have time available because you are waiting for something to happen. Your body is always happening—no waiting necessary!

A more direct way of heightening physical awareness is to focus closely on everything you experience in your body as you become hypoglycemic (and, of course, as you eat something). See how many different sensations you can notice. Make mental notes. See how the sensations may differ from time to time. (More techniques are described in Chapter 11, "Living Well with Stress.")

Along with generally increasing body awareness, you can use blood testing to help identify the early cues that a reaction is near. When you note a physical change that might be signaling the approach of low blood sugar, check to see what your level actually is. If you are still in the normal range (70–120) wait a few minutes and see if more distinct reaction symptoms develop. (A reaction is more likely to follow a normal blood sugar reading of 80 than a reading of 120.) If you do this occasionally and write down the cues that are followed by a reaction, you will soon find that you can act to bring blood sugar level up before the stronger symptoms have developed. A real advantage here is that you avoid the rebound to high blood sugar levels produced by the stress of a full-scale reaction.

If you have difficulty waking up at night when blood sugar plummets, there are two solutions, one mental and one mechanical. The first is a matter of suggesting to yourself that you are ready and willing to learn to pay attention to the alarm your body rings, no matter what time it sounds. This can be done as a gentle talk with your body while you are relaxing into sleep, a time when your mind is very open to suggestion. You can find your own words to express thoughts such as these: "Body, I know that you send me signals when a reaction is happening and I want you to know that I am willing to hear them, no matter how deeply I am sleeping. I don't want to put you through the stress that occurs when I fail to wake up. I want to live well with you and our special needs. I'm willing to hear your call for help." You can reinforce the message by remembering the sensations that usually tell you a reaction is beginning and seeing an image of yourself awakening, getting out of bed, and going to the kitchen for a 3:00 A.M. snack. You can also use this sort of process to reinforce your awareness of daytime hypoglycemia.

The mechanical solution to not waking up when reactions occur is based on the wet bedclothes that we have all discovered in the middle of the night. The sweat of a strong reaction triggers a mechanical moisture sensor under the bedding that sets off an alarm. There is also a sweat sensor called The Sleep Sentry that can be worn on the wrist. (Ask your pharmacist or the diabetic supply firms listed in the Appendix about these products.)

As we mentioned earlier, certain types of stress can have a hypoglycemic effect. Relatively little is known about stress and diabetes, but it may be true that active expression of emotion, especially strong anger, tends to lower blood sugar. (The opposite—silent stewing and depression—appear to raise blood sugar.) What we can say with certainty is that you should study the effects on you of different kinds of stress so you will know which ones might cause insulin reactions. Then you will know when you may need to take preventive steps.

With A Little Help. . .

There is a social side to preventing insulin reactions. People close to you and those with whom you work have a right to know that you have diabetes and what the outward signs of hypoglycemia are for you. It is unwise to risk a situation dangerous for you and difficult for others because of pride. There are times when one is concentrating strongly on an activity or when confusion is the first symptom to appear. At such times, someone else may notice the signs of hypoglycemia long before you do. Make it easy for anyone to ask if you are having a reaction if they think this might be happening.

Another social aspect of reactions is that some of us feel embarrassed and a bother to others when we need food fast, especially if this interrupts or changes planned activities. It can be difficult to say, "I can't wait until we get to the beach to eat. Can we stop now? I have a reaction." But you will be putting your friends to much greater bother if you pass out on them while trying to remain "inconspicuous." You will find that if you state your needs directly, most people will be understanding. A variation on this pattern of embarrassment is feeling self-conscious about eating in front of others who are not eating, especially when they think of you as someone who "shouldn't" eat sweets.

If you are about to engage in a public performance, such as giving a talk or making a long sales call, you may feel anxious about the possibility of becoming hypoglycemic. The anxiety may even feel like a reaction. If possible, test your blood sugar beforehand and eat enough to get you through if it is not already high. If you can't test, go ahead and have a moderate snack. The risk of one high test is certainly less than the risk of falling apart at an important moment. (The precaution here is doubly important when the performance involves physical activity.)

We hope that the practice of wearing a diabetes I.D. bracelet or necklace and carrying a card with details of insulin dosage can be taken for granted. Unfortunately, some of us are afraid to have our friends or co-workers identify us with diabetes, and neglect to wear this basic bit of jewelry. In an episode of insulin shock or an accident, it could save your life.

SOME QUESTIONABLE BENEFITS OF REACTIONS

If you seem to resist doing anything to reduce the number of reactions you have, you may be gaining hidden benefits from them. The simplest example of this: When you are hypoglycemic, it is medically prescribed to eat something you are normally discouraged from eating ("Oh boy, a sweet treat! This is a pretty strong one. I must need a hot fudge sundae or apple pie à la mode"). Children are not the only ones to cultivate reactions as an excuse to indulge. As we mentioned before, when the sugar of the food joins with the rebound effect, you are likely to end up with a blood sugar level much higher than if you had eaten the candy without having a reaction.

The solution is also simple: Don't use the reaction to gain something you can just go ahead and do. In this case, give yourself a vacation once in a while and eat something sweet. It will help if you do it when your blood sugar level is near normal or when you are planning to be more active than usual. If you're going to be really outrageous (hot fudge sundae level), you might take an extra unit or two of rapid-acting insulin just before you gorge (but not at bedtime!). So long as this doesn't happen too often or lead to a binge, your control will be much steadier than if you go on having reactions in order to eat sweets. It is best not to use a big dessert as a substitute for a meal. It's possible you'll end up with a major reaction because the concentrated carbohydrate is absorbed rapidly and you have no continuing source of glucose.

Some of us use hypoglycemia as permission to express hostility we normally keep bottled up. Some of the sweetest diabetics rant and rage when their blood sugar level falls too low. Anyone who suggests that they may need a few chocolate chip cookies becomes a target for their abuse. When it is all over, the insulin reaction, not the person is held responsible. If this is your pattern, the direct approach to living is the key to living well. Learn to express your anger directly.

There are other ways some diabetics use reactions to escape responsibility. Not waking up from a reaction at night is practically a guaranteed method of getting someone else to take care of you. When you are knocked out by hypoglycemia, someone else has to play Mother to bring you out of it. It can become a way of testing a mate or a parent: "If you really love me, you'll save my life." It can also be a form of revenge, given the amount of stress the rescuer must go through to revive you. Ironically, the diabetic who fails to wake up at night may be the very one who fights off all assistance when he or she is hypoglycemic during the day, saying, "Don't you think I can take care of myself?"

An Anecdote

Two couples in one of the support groups Ernest ran in California played identical games around reactions. Each of the two men had experienced repeated nighttime hypoglycemia that had to be treated by their wives or the medic team. The men insisted they couldn't do anything about it. The wives were growing increasingly frustrated and angry.

When reactions occurred during the day, the men insisted on their independence and ability to take care of themselves. They were very reluctant to pay attention to the reaction cues their wives would point out in the evening, often waiting until they were deep into hypoglycemia to eat something. It took the feedback of the whole support group to help the men see the pattern of dependence they were caught in. They and their wives had to work to form a more balanced relationship.

This is a delicate issue to work with. We want to be independent, yet we must depend on food as well as insulin. We depend on regularity of meals. We depend on doctors to help us handle our condition and its complications. And, worst of all, in a very fundamental way, we cannot depend on our own bodies as others do. No wonder we sometimes bounce back and forth between declaring our independence and acting very dependent.

If you suspect that a desire to be taken care of is at the root of your difficulties with insulin reactions, you might explore the question with those who are important to you. In what ways can you be more direct in asking for care and support? What can you give in return? And, most important, what can you give yourself to increase your sense of being well cared for?

REACTIONS AND SEX

One of the peak frustrations in a diabetic's life occurs when the passion drains away while making love, and an insulin reaction takes the place of an orgasm. The wisdom of the body makes the wise choice of preservation over reproduction and pleasure; but sometimes that's not easy to explain to your partner. So this is one more time when a pre-event blood test and a little extra food may be in order, especially if you tend to be an athletic lover.

Section III

LIVING WELL WITH THE KEYS TO CONTROL

Living Well With Your Diet

"**T**ell me what you eat, and I shall tell you what you are," wrote Brillat-Savarin in 1825. This applies especially to people with diabetes: Most of us are very conscious of how particular foods (and the quantities we eat) affect how we feel. But now we are discovering that we aren't what we thought we were! Nutritional research has radically revised our understanding of the effects of various foods on our metabolism.

In this chapter, we highlight how the recommended "diabetic diet" has changed over the years, describe new findings, and integrate these into guidelines for healthy, appealing meals. We will also share some personal tips on ways to enjoy food and eating within these guidelines. In the process, we will watch old nutritional dogma become myth.

THE SO-CALLED DIABETIC DIET
Before insulin was discovered, diabetics were instructed to completely avoid carbohydrates (starches and sugars). After insulin was discovered, diabetics were usually put on low-carbohydrate diets with moderately high fat and protein. (Paradoxically, in the 1920s and 1930s, some research showed that high-carbohydrate

diets may be more advantageous than low-carbohydrate ones, but this work was largely ignored.)

The exchange system, based on the number of grams (weight) of the carbohydrate, protein, and fat in each food, became the basis for determining the proper diet for an individual diabetic. Usually the patient's physician would decide how many calories seemed appropriate, refer the patient to a dietitian skilled in teaching patients about exchange groups, create a diet prescription, tailor it to the patient's preferences, and issue warnings about which foods to avoid.

By the 1960s and 1970s, many physicians were recommending diets that were more flexible and less rigid, basing this recommendation mainly on the experiences of their patients. Little new research was being done, and different doctors perpetuated different truths—and myths—to their patients. However, by the mid-seventies, Americans were becoming more food conscious, and the effects of various foods on health were becoming more widely known. Along with growing interest in nutrition, sophisticated research was adding new and better data, which was widely disseminated to the general public.

Recommendations included decreasing the cholesterol and animal or saturated vegetable fats in our diets, increasing the proportion of unsaturated fats and mono-unsaturated fats (like olive oil) to saturated fats, and increasing the amount of fruit, vegetables, and fiber in our daily meals. Not surprisingly, these guidelines are totally appropriate for diabetics.

What was new and especially important for diabetics was research on the effect of specific foods on blood sugar levels in healthy people. This research turned up some surprising findings. Certain foods that diabetics had always been told to avoid, like ice cream, raised the blood sugar only half as much as "good" foods like whole wheat bread. Nutritionists were finding that the glycemic effect (speed of impact on blood sugar level) of a particular food was determined by a variety of factors, not simply by the number of grams of carbohydrate. The physical form of the food and the amount of fat eaten with it seemed to make a major difference in the food's effects.

Before we look at these recommendations in more detail, you might want to answer the following questions.

1. Among the foods you eat regularly, which do you enjoy the most?_____

   _____

2. Which of the above foods, if any, do you consider healthy? Which do you consider unhealthy?_____

   _____

3. What foods would you like to eat more of, but don't, because you feel they are unhealthy?_____

   _____

4. What foods do you eat too much of?_____

   _____

Review your answers to these questions. You may change some of your judgments about "good" and "bad" foods as you learn new information in this chapter.

NEW FACTS ABOUT FOOD

Fat and Cholesterol

Most scientists and health professionals now agree that everyone would be better off if we decreased the total fat in our diets, increased the ratio of polyunsaturated and mono-unsaturated fats to saturated fats, and reduced our cholesterol intake. (Polyunsaturated fats include most liquid vegetable oils; a major mono-unsaturated fat is olive oil; saturated fats are all animal fats, including dairy, and coconut and palm oil.) These changes have been linked to reduced risk of heart disease in nondiabetics. Since diabetics have twice the risk of heart disease as the general population, these dietary guidelines are especially important.

The American Diabetes Association, as well as the British and Canadian diabetes associations, have recommended lowering the fat content of diabetic diets from the usual 40 to 45 percent of total calories to less than 30 percent. The gap needs to be filled with more calories from either carbohydrate ("carbo") or protein. Recent studies generally have shown no serious adverse effects from high-carbo diets, especially when most of the calories come from complex carbohydrates (starches) with associated fiber. The ADA recommends 50 to 60 percent of calories from carbohydrates, minimizing simple sugars. (That leaves 15 to 20 percent from protein.) More about carbos later when we discuss the glycemic index.

What about cholesterol? Doctors are increasingly recommending that everyone limit intake of cholesterol. A large-scale study called "The Lipid Research Clinics Coronary Primary Prevention Trial" looked at middle-aged men who had no evidence of heart disease but did have cholesterol levels of 265 mg/dl or higher. This study showed that diet and the drug cholestyramine not only lowered cholesterol levels, but also reduced the risk of heart attack. This research provided strong evidence, for the first time, that decreasing cholesterol may directly prevent the development of coronary heart disease.

This report and a growing body of other evidence prompted the National Institutes of Health to convene a conference with a panel of fourteen experts to examine cholesterol and heart disease. This panel made the following recommendations:

1. All Americans over age 2 should adopt a diet limiting total fat to 30 percent (just as in the American Diabetes Association's plan). No more than one-third of the fat should be saturated, and cholesterol should be limited to 250–300 mg a day. (A large egg yolk, a very concentrated form of cholesterol, has 270 mg.)

2. Target levels for normal values among adults should be: under 30 years old, blood cholesterol no higher that 180 mg/dl; over 30, blood cholesterol no higher than 200 mg/dl. (These levels are below what many physicians consider acceptable, and are probably below the actual average levels for Americans.)

What does this mean for us? Probably that it will become increasingly easy for diabetics to eat lowfat, low-cholesterol diets. More attention will be given to labels on foods. Manufacturers and restaurants will offer more lowfat products. There will be more support for these practices among the general population. The "diabetic diet" is good for everyone.

Fiber

Food scientists and health professionals have increasing evidence that dietary fiber is good for diabetics. High fiber intake lowers cholesterol levels, lowers the usual rise in blood sugar following meals, and decreases insulin requirements.

The fiber we are talking about is plant fiber, the kind found in vegetables, fruits, grains, and legumes (beans). It is useful to divide fiber into two types: soluble (guar and pectin) and insoluble. The soluble is found in fruits, dried beans, and oat products (or in a pure form extracted from them); insoluble fiber is in other grains, wheat (cereal) bran, and vegetables. Soluble fiber lowers cholesterol.

How does fiber work? In general, the water-soluble fibers slow down the time food, particularly glucose, takes to leave the stomach, pass through the intestine, and be absorbed into the bloodstream. Soluble fiber increases the viscosity (thickness) of food in the digestive tract. On the other hand, insoluble fibers act like roughage and increase the bulk of our stool. Soluble fiber has a more acute effect on our blood sugar, smoothing out the response to food, whereas the insoluble fiber has a more longer term effect (two to three weeks) on glucose tolerance. Thus, it's wise to eat both kinds of fiber.

We can increase our fiber intake simply by eating more fresh fruits and vegetables, beans, bran, and whole grain. Many health food products are available to add purified fiber to the diet, but these must be mixed into the food in order to affect the glycemic response. We favor the fiber found in natural plant sources rather than these supplements. (An Israeli physician recently reported achieving beneficial effects similar to the high-carbo high-fiber diets using 2 or 3 tablespoons of a fiber-protein soy supplement. All fats and oils are removed from this specially processed soy preparation. It is not presently available in the United States, but it may well be on the market by the time you read this book.)

The Glycemic Effect

Traditionally, carbohydrates have been divided into simple and complex groups. Simple carbos consist of refined sugar and the unprocessed sugar found in fruits and vegetables; complex carbos consist of starches found in potatoes, rice, other grains, and beans. Diabetics were taught to avoid simple sugars, in the belief that they were absorbed more quickly and raised the blood sugar higher and faster than starches. Recent research has shown that the biologic effect of food on blood sugar is much more complex.

Under test conditions, researchers have found that some foods earlier thought to have less rapid effects on blood sugar (like potatoes) raise blood sugar as rapidly as a Mars bar. And others foods, like ice cream, raise blood sugar half as fast as a starchy staple like bread. Various foods have been studied and compared to the effect on blood sugar of pure glucose. Glucose was assigned a glycemic index of 100, and all other foods received a score proportional to the pure glucose effect. More recently, the standard has been changed to one slice of white bread equal to 100, and the scores adjusted appropriately (see Table 1 at the end of this chapter). Foods with a low glycemic index are called slow releasers.

What have these studies taught us? First, that pure sugars are high, but table sugar (sucrose) is less than bread (only 86), and fructose a low 30. (You still need to limit them, however, because of their high concentration.) High-fat foods, like ice cream and pastry, have relatively low indices, whether they are simple or complex carbos. (Fat is thought to slow absorption of carbohydrates.) Grain products varied widely, but there was little difference between whole grain and white bread, or whole grain and white pasta (spaghetti, noodles, etc.). The difference between pasta and bread is considerable. Pasta is a very slow releaser, thus raising blood sugar level much less than most other grain products.

The physical form of the food appears to explain the differences between pasta and bread. The starch in the pasta is more compact and perhaps less accessible to digestive enzymes. Similarly, rice ground into flour results in higher glycemic levels than does rice as a whole grain. Legumes (beans and peas), as a food group, have the lowest index. Presumably, their soluble fiber increases food viscosity, slows movement through the gut, and slows absorption. Finally, most cooked root vegetables, like white potatoes, beets, and carrots, have a very high index as a group. However, an average serving of cooked carrots has only 5 grams of carbo. Surprisingly, sweet potatoes and yams (not candied) have relatively low glycemic indices.

A few words of caution here: Although a food like ice cream has a low glycemic index, it should not be eaten in large quantities or substituted for potatoes. The fat and cholesterol in ice cream must also be considered. Also, the high candy content of some flavors takes them out of acceptable range: Their sugar content and glycemic index are both too high. So skip the English toffee and raspberry jamocha fudge ripple unless you have an insulin reaction. (Tastes are okay.)

Researchers are still disagreeing on how this new information should be applied. Nevertheless, we believe that we can offer reasonable guidelines on the basis of experience. Suggestions on how best to use the glycemic index are incorporated into the recommendations in the next section.

NUTRITION GUIDELINES
These guidelines are based on the preceding information, current ADA recommendations, and our own and others' experiences. Under each guideline, we will add tips that make the recommendation easier to follow.

Work with your physician or a dietitian to establish a general plan for total calories, distributed as mentioned earlier among carbos, mono-unsaturated, polyunsaturated, and saturated fat, protein (and alcohol, if desired). One gram of carbo or protein equals 4 calories, one gram of fat equals 9 calories, and one gram of alcohol about 7 calories.

Use Moderation
This principle is a guiding rule that will almost always keep you out of trouble.

1. Even slowly absorbed foods such as pasta should be eaten in the proper amounts. Too large a serving will produce high blood sugar tests later in the day. Be moderate also with high-fat foods, such as nuts and nut butters or potato chips. An ounce of peanuts has 165 calories, even more when cooked in oil.
2. Become a taster. Eat just a bite or two of a food that would greatly raise your blood sugar if you ate the whole thing.
3. Share sweet desserts with friends when you want a treat. Satisfy your craving without overloading your system. (You may have to explain to people that small servings of desserts are not poison to a diabetic.)
4. You may fear that sugar lust will overcome you, and one bite will lead to a binge. Since binges are usually a secret activity, you can learn to control this urge by eating sweets only when

you are with other people. Say, "I'm going to eat three bites of this pie and then it's all yours."

Decrease Total Fat, Cholesterol, and Saturated Fat

1. Eat less red meat. When you do eat it, choose cuts that have little fat. Limit your consumption of fast-food hamburgers.

2. Eat more poultry, but don't eat the skin and fat (except for a small taste). You can broil or grill chicken with the skin removed if you baste it with vegetable oil or an oily marinade.

3. Substitute turkey or chicken products for beef and pork hot dogs, bologna, and ground meats. Also, try Morningstar Farm products, made from soy. It may take some time to get accustomed to these soy products, but they are worth the effort. Taste preferences are surprisingly changeable.

4. Use lowfat or nonfat dairy products. Certain cheeses, like hoop or farmer cheese and skim milk mozzarella, are lower in fat than others. Sour cream and cream cheese substitutes can be made from tofu and lowfat yogurt (see recipes at the end of this chapter).

5. Substitute fish, beans, or tofu for fatty red meat. Fish oil, contained in all fish, is the most unsaturated oil you can eat (about twice as beneficial as vegetable oils).

A *word of advice here:* Don't take fish oil capsules. They are expensive, they offer no obvious benefit, and they may be harmful. Eat fatty cold-water fish like salmon, trout, haddock, and mackerel instead. They also contain the largest quantity of fats, known as omega-3 fatty acids, that help lower cholesterol and triglycerides and prevent blood clots by thinning the blood.

Furthermore, most seafood is now thought to be relatively low in cholesterol. Although most researchers now believe that what was thought to be cholesterol also includes similar appearing fish sterols, it is still unclear just how much cholesterol is in shellfish like shrimp, lobster, and crab. Most researchers now believe these are fine to eat in moderation, particularly since they are low in saturated fat. Mollusks, like scallops, clams, and oysters, are even lower in cholesterol.

Tofu is rapidly becoming a staple of delicious, healthy cooking. This soybean product is itself quite bland, so you can bestow many different flavors on it by your choice of recipes. With the water pressed out, tofu can be grilled (prepared in your favorite marinade first) or crumbled, sautéed, and substituted for ground beef in Mexican and Italian recipes. It is high in protein and contains little fat and no cholesterol. In the blender, tofu becomes the base for lowfat "mayonnaise," "sour cream," and "cream cheese." (See the end of this chapter for recipes.)

6. Eat egg yolks and organ meats (liver, kidneys, sweetbreads, etc.) no more often than once a week. These are extremely high in cholesterol. The yolk of the egg contains all of the cholesterol. You can safely eat egg whites, which are all protein.

7. Use margarine instead of butter. Choose a diet or imitation margarine—one that lists liquid vegetable oil as the first ingredient. (Ingredients are listed on product labels in order of amount of the whole product. Liquid is better than partially hydrogenated oil). If you prefer to use butter on some foods, use whipped butter in moderate amounts, or mix butter and margarine together.

8. Use noncaloric sprays (Pam and others) when you sauté or fry foods. Two new noncaloric fat substitutes, Simplesse and Olestra, are likely to be approved and released soon. Their effect on prepared foods may be similar to the effect of NutraSweet.

9. Try Butter Buds, Best O' Butter, or similar products (available in your grocery store), sprinkled on dry or dissolved in water for adding a buttery flavor to vegetables or popcorn. They have no fat or cholesterol.

10. Use olive oil in salad dressings and for sautéing. Nutritionists once considered mono-unsaturated fats like olive oil to be "neutral" compared to polyunsaturated (good) and saturated fats (bad). Newer research has determined that olive oil is a good fat, particularly in terms of lowering the bad cholesterol (LDL) and raising the good cholesterol (HDL).

11. Eat less total fat. The total fat you eat—particularly saturated fat—is the major dietary factor in determining your cholesterol level.

12. Limit your intake of saturated vegetable fats like palm and coconut oil. These are used in preparing canned nuts, cheap

179

cookies and candy, and other processed foods. Check labels for them.

Eat Foods with High Fiber and Low Glycemic Index

Don't eliminate foods solely because of their high glycemic index, but do shift the balance. Eat pasta, beans, and fresh fruit more often than potatoes, rice, and bread.

As you increase the carbo in your diet, it is important also to increase the fiber to gain the full beneficial effect: High fiber may be more beneficial when eaten in a high-carbo diet (see Table 2 at the end of this chapter).

Finally, using the tool of home blood glucose testing, you can determine your own glycemic responses to various foods by measuring your blood glucose one or two hours after eating. Let your home tests and blood lipid (fat) levels, as determined by your physician, be your guide in balancing your diet.

Here are some ideas on using fiber and glycemic index in your diet:

1. Begin to eat more pasta and beans in all their various forms. Choose a slow-release over a fast-release carbo.

2. Eat more fresh fruits and cut down on fruit juices, particularly frozen ones. Juices are great for insulin reactions because of their high glycemic index, but they're not so great otherwise.

3. Popcorn is a wonderful high-fiber, low-calorie food, especially without butter or margarine. To season it, use herbs or spices instead of salt.

4. Look for packaged or processed foods that use fructose instead of sugar or corn syrup. Fructose has a lower glycemic effect. But don't substitute granulated fructose for sugar. It is still too concentrated.

5. Use nonnutritive sweeteners and products that contain them. Aspartame (NutraSweet or Equal) is now widely available. Use the powdered form very lightly instead of powdered sugar on berries or pancakes, for instance. But use it sparingly, as it's highly concentrated. *Do not cook with Equal. It deteriorates when heated to boiling.*

6. Try tofu ice cream (Tofutti) or low-fat frozen yogurt. These have little fat or cholesterol and contain less sugar than ice cream. Several frozen desserts are sweetened with Nutrasweet instead of sugar. The lowfat products may have a higher glycemic index than ice cream.

7. Eat more whole grain breads, cereals, crackers, and pasta.

8. Use the glycemic index only to choose between one carbo and another, not between carbos and fats or proteins. Don't substitute ice cream for potatoes, or sausage for toast.

Moderate Alcohol Use

Alcohol is no longer prohibited for diabetics and can be used in moderation, with a few precautions. (Alcohol does not need insulin to be metabolized.)

Alcohol can lower blood sugar. Drinking before dinner may move you into an insulin reaction at the same time that it masks the signs of low blood sugar.

The consequences of intoxication are more significant in diabetics, since getting drunk might lead to skipping a meal or an insulin injection.

On the positive side, in a study of 480 randomly selected Italian and Italian-American adults, 73 had overt or borderline diabetes. All 73 were total abstainers or drank wine in small amounts. The remaining 407 drank wine on a regular basis. Other studies have suggested that a 1 to 2 ounces of alcohol daily has a protective effect against heart disease. (Abstainers and heavy drinkers had higher incidences of heart disease than moderate drinkers). The ADA now approves limited alcohol use with your physician's approval.

Needless to say, the consequences of alcohol abuse are just as serious for the diabetic as for the nondiabetic. Follow these guidelines when you decide to imbibe:

1. Remember to figure the calories of the carbohydrate as well as the alcohol in your drink.

2. Dry wines (most table wines, not dessert wines) have very little carbo in them.

3. Avoid sweet mixers. Use diet soft drinks and diet tonic.

4. You can check the effects of different alcoholic beverages on

your metabolism by checking your blood sugar one to two hours after drinking.

Moderate Salt Use

Evidence shows that avoiding salt will lower high blood pressure after it develops. No research has proven that minimizing salt intake will decrease your risk of becoming hypertensive if you do not already have high blood pressure. However, hypertension greatly increases the risk of other complications for a person with diabetes, so prudence argues for restraint with the salt shaker. Less than 2,000 mg a day is low (see Table 3 at end of this chapter for a table listing the salt content of various foods.) You can decrease your craving for salt. Begin at home by following these suggestions:

1. Learn to appreciate the flavors of fresh foods without additives.
2. Add only a small amount of salt to the foods you cook.
3. Avoid canned vegetables and other processed and packaged foods, which usually are very high in salt.
4. Use alternative seasonings, such as lemon juice, garlic, and onion as well as flavored powders (not salts), other herbs and spices, and wine or flavored vinegars.
5. Limit your use of soy sauce. Even the new low-salt "lite" soy sauce has a lot of salt.

EATING WELL WITH DIABETES

Both of the authors of this book love good food. With creativity and moderation, and using the ideas in this chapter, we have eaten our way healthfully through a variety of restaurants and cuisines. In addition to reading the tips in this chapter, we suggest that you find a nutritionist or dietitian who can tailor some specific diets or menus to your needs and preferences.

At the end of this chapter, we have listed books and other references we have found helpful, along with some recipes. If you don't have a book that lists food values, we recommend you obtain one; you may be surprised.

Finally, remember that the best way to find out how different foods affect you is to try them and measure their effect on your blood sugar one or two hours after you've eaten. This feedback helps motivate you to change your diet when the tests are high. And it helps you to know the types and amounts of food that are appropriate for you.

Additional Resources: Recipes, Tables, & Books

I. LOWFAT, LOW-CHOLESTEROL RECIPES

The following three recipes are from *The Book of Tofu*, Vol. I, W. Shurtleff and A. Aoyagi, published by Autumn Press, Inc.; distributed by Random House, 1975. This is a comprehensive book covering basic preparation methods as well as recipes.

TOFU SOUR CREAM
Real sour cream is high in fat and cholesterol, but this provides a pleasant substitute, with one-third the fat and none of the cholesterol.

Yield: 1½ cups
Nutrient value per tablespoon: 14 calories, .9 grams fat

12 ounces tofu, parboiled and
  squeezed (p. 15)

2 tablespoons lemon juice
¼ teaspoon salt

Combine ingredients in a blender or food processor and puree until smooth.

TOFU CREAM CHEESE
This can be used in any recipe calling for cream cheese as long as it is not reheated.

Yield: 1 cup
Nutrient value per tablespoon: 23 calories, 2.8 grams fat

12 ounces tofu, squeezed
(See below)
2 tablespoons vegetable oil
⅜ teaspoon salt

Dash white pepper
1 teaspoon lemon juice
  (optional)

Combine ingredients in a blender or food processor and puree until smooth.

TOFU MAYONNAISE

Use this mayo substitute as a sandwich spread or in any recipe calling for mayonnaise.

Yield: 1 cup
Nutrient values per tablespoon: 16 calories, .7 grams fat

6 ounces tofu, drained or pressed, if desired	2 tablespoons oil
1½ – 2 tablespoons lemon juice or vinegar	Salt and pepper to taste

Combine ingredients in a blender or food processor and purée until smooth, about 30 seconds.

TOFU TECHNIQUES

These are two of the many methods used to prepare tofu, each providing a different consistency and texture. The procedures below are used in one or more of the above recipes.

TO PARBOIL TOFU:

Bring 2 cups of water to a boil. Add a 12-ounce tofu cake and ½ teaspoon salt. Return water to a boil. Remove pan from heat, let stand 2–3 minutes; remove tofu.

TO SQUEEZE TOFU:

Place in center of a clean, lint-free dish towel. Gather corners and twist closed, squeezing and kneading as much of the water from the tofu as possible.

The following two recipes are alternative recipes for substitute sour cream and cream cheese, which use low-fat yogurt and cheese instead of tofu. Pick your favorites; all are healthy. The recipes below are from "Where's the Fat?" by Martha Wagner: Medical Self Care, Winter 1984.

ALMOST SOUR CREAM
Yield: 1 cup
Nutrient value per tablespoon: 14 calories, .3 grams fat

1 cup lowfat cottage cheese
2 tablespoons buttermilk or
  plain, lowfat yogurt

1 tablespoon lemon juice

Combine ingredients in a blender or food processor and blend until smooth.

CREAM CHEESE SUBSTITUTE
Yield: 1 cup
Nutrient value per tablespoon: 24 calories, 1.2 grams fat

1 cup part-skim ricotta
  cheese

2 tablespoons plain,
  lowfat yogurt

Combine ingredients in a blender or food processor and puree until smooth. Refrigerate for several hours before serving.

YOLKLESS EGGS
Although these eggs should be made without whole yolks, you can add a small amount of yolk to give the dish a yellow color and improve its texture.

Omelets and fried eggs can be made with yolkless eggs. Whole eggs can also be fried, boiled, or shirred, and the firm yolk removed after cooking. For fried egg whites, separate the whites and fry them as you would a whole egg. For an omelet, separate the whites into a mixing bowl, season with garlic, pepper, and herbs to taste, and mix gently (do not beat them). The pan should be hot enough that a drop of water vaporizes immediately. Use a nonstick pan that is large enough so that the white will cover the bottom and firm up almost immediately throughout. A fat-free nonstick cooking spray can also be used.

For slightly more elaborate (but not necessarily better) scrambled eggs or omelets, you can use the whites and replace each yolk with 1 teaspoon olive or polyunsaturated vegetable oil and ½ teaspoon of lowfat dry milk. Yellow food coloring can be added if desired.

Bon appetit!

II. USEFUL TABLES

Table 1
GLYCEMIC INDEX

Grain Foods		Fruits	
White bread	100	Raisins	93
Whole meal bread	99	Banana	79
Brown rice	90	Orange juice	67
Sweet corn	87	Grapes	62
White rice	83	Apple	53
White spaghetti	66	Pear	47
Whole wheat spaghetti	64	Peach	40
Whole grain rye bread	58	Plum	34
Breakfast cereals		**Sugar**	
CornFlakes	119	Maltose	152
Weetabix	109	Glucose	138
Shredded Wheat	97	Honey	126
All-Bran	73	Sucrose	86
Root vegetables		Fructose	30
Baked potato (russet)	115	**Dairy products**	
Instant potato	116	Ice cream	52
Boiled potato (new)	81	Yogurt	52
Sweet potato	70	Whole milk	49
Dried peas and beans		Skim milk	46
Baked beans (canned)	60		
Dried green peas	56		
Kidney beans	54		
Chick peas	49		
Soy beans (canned)	20		

Note: All foods in this table are standardized against one slice of white bread, assigned a value of 100.

The lower the index the better: the food is absorbed more slowly.

From Phyllis Crapo, R.D., *Clinical Diabetes,* Jan/Feb 1985, American Diabetes Association.

Table 2
Fiber Content of Selected Foods

Food	Portion Size	Plant Fiber (grams)
Breads, Cereals, and Starchy Vegetables (cooked/prepared)		
Beans, kidney	½ cup	4.5
Bran (100 percent), cereal	½ cup	10.0
Bread		
Rye	1 slice	2.7
White	1 slice	0.6
Whole grain wheat	1 slice	2.7
Corn, kernels	⅓ cup	2.1
Parsnips	⅔ cup	5.9
Peas	½ cup	5.2
Potatoes, white	1 small	3.8
Rice, brown	½ cup	1.3
Rice, white	½ cup	0.5
Squash, winter	½ cup	3.6
Sweet potatoes	¼ cup	2.9
Fruit (uncooked)		
Apples	1 small	3.9
Banana	½ small	1.3
Blackberries	½ cup	2.6
Grapefruit	½	1.3
Orange	1 small	2.1
Peach	1 medium	1.0
Pineapple	¾ cup	1.3
Strawberries	¼ cup	2.4
Vegetables (cooked unless indicated by plus sign)		
Asparagus	½ cup	1.2
Beans, string	½ cup	1.7
Beets	½ cup	1.5
Broccoli	½ cup	2.6
Carrots	½ cup	2.2
Cauliflower	½ cup	0.9
Cucumbers +	½ cup	0.8
Lettuce +	½ cup	0.5
Squash, summer	½ cup	2.3
Turnips	½ cup	1.3

Note: J.W.Anderson, K. Ward. Long-term effects of high-carbohydrate, high-fiber diets on glucose and lipid metabolism: A preliminary report on patients with diabetes. Diabetes Care *1978, 1:77-82, as adapted for Physician's Guide to Type II Diabetes: Diagnosis and Treatment, American Diabetes Association 1984.*

Table 3
Salt Content of Common Foods

Fresh/Minimally Processed Foods		Prepared Foods		"Fast Foods"	
1 cup orange juice	2 mg.	1 cup tomato		1 Arby's Turkey	
1 cup apple juice	2 mg.	juice	640 mg.	Sandwich	1,060 mg.
1 cup long-		1 cup Puffed Rice	1 mg.	3 pcs. Arthur	
cooking oatmeal	10 mg.	1 cup Corn		Treacher's Fish	675 mg.
3 ounces ground		Flakes	305 mg.	1 Burger King	
beef	60 mg.	3 ounces corned		Whopper	990 mg.
3 ounces pork	65 mg.	beef	1500 mg.	1 Dairy Queen	
1 cup fresh		1 cup canned green		Hot Dog	830 mg.
green beans	5 mg.	beans	320 mg.	Kentucky Fried	
1 cup frozen		1 cup chicken noodle		Chicken:	
green beans	2 mg.	soup	1050 mg.	3 pieces chicken,	
1 cup whole		3 ounces bacon	1400 mg.	mashed potatoes,	
milk	120 mg.	1 dill pickle	1930 mg.	gravy, cole	
1 large egg	70 mg.	1 slice white		slaw	2,285 mg.
1 lemon	1 mg.	bread	100 mg.	1 McDonald's Big	
1 head Boston		cooking oil	0 mg.	Mac	1,010 mg.
lettuce	15 mg.	1 cinnamon roll	630 mg.	1 Taco Bell	
1 peach	1 mg.	1 tablespoon		Enchirito	1,175 mg.
8 ounces		ketchup	155 mg.		
bluefish	170 mg.	1 cup all-purpose			
3 apricots	1 mg.	flour	2 mg.		
1 banana	1 mg.	1 cup self-rising			
1 carrot	35 mg.	flour	1565 mg.		
		1 beef frank-			
		furter	425 mg.		
		1 tablespoon Italian			
		dressing	250 mg.		
		1 cup instant			
		pudding	335 mg.		
		1 TV chicken			
		dinner	1400 mg.		
		1 olive	165 mg.		
		1 cup baked			
		beans	1000 mg.		

N.Kaplan, M.D., Clinical Diabetes, Mar/Apr, 1984, American Diabetes Association

Table 4
Fast Food Exchanges

Restaurant (Product) a	Serving Size	Calories (Serving)	Carb. (GM.)	Pro. (GM.)	Fat (GM.)	Sodium (MG.)	Exchange (1 Serving)
Arby's							
Roast Beef Sandwich	5 oz.	350	32	22	15	880	2 Bread, 3 Med.-Fat Meat
Junior Roast Beef Sand-wich	3 oz.	220	21	12	9	530	1½ Bread, 1 Med-Fat Meat, 1 Fat
Turkey Sandwich	6 oz.	410	36	24	19	1,060	2½ Bread, 2½ Med.-Fat Meat, 1 Fat
Arthur Treacher's							
Fish	2 pieces	355	25	19	20	450	1½ Bread, 2 Med.-Fat Meat, 2 Fat
Fish	3 pieces	533	38	29	30	675	2½ Bread, 3 Med.-Fat Meat, 3 Fat
Fish Sand-wich	1	440	39	16	24	836	2½ Bread, 1½ Med.-Fat Meat, 3 Fat
Chips	4 oz.	276	35	4	13	393	2 Bread, 3 Fat

Nutritive values supplied by company.
* For occasional use only, preferably before exercise.
NA = not available.
From Fast Food Facts, *Marion Franz, R.D., M.S., International Diabetes Center, Minneapolis, MN, as excerpted in Diabetes Forecast, 1983, American Diabetes Association.*

Restaurant (Product) a	Serving Size	Calories (Serving)	Carb. (GM.)	Pro. (GM.)	Fat (GM.)	Sodium (MG.)	Exchange (1 Serving)
Cole Slaw	3 oz.	123	11	1	8	266	1 Bread, 1 Fat
Chowder	1 bowl	112	11	5	5	835	1 Bread, 1 Fat

Burger King

Hamburger	3.9 oz.	290	29	15	13	525	2 Bread, 2 Med.-Fat Meat
Cheeseburger	4.4 oz.	350	30	18	17	730	2 Bread, 2 Med.-Fat Meat, 1 Fat
Whopper	9.2 oz.	630	50	26	36	990	3 Bread, 3 Med.-Fat Meat, 4 Fat
Whopper Jr.	5.1 oz.	370	31	15	20	560	2 Bread, 2 Med.-Fat Meat, 2 Fat
French Fries	2.4 oz.	210	25	3	11	230	1½ Bread, 2 Fat
Onion Rings	2.7 oz.	270	29	3	16	450	2 Bread, 3 Fat

Dairy Queen

Single Hamburger	5 oz.	360	33	21	16	630	2 Bread, 2 Med.-Fat Meat, 1 Fat
Hot Dog	3.5 oz.	280	21	11	16	830	1½ Bread, 1 Med.-Fat Meat, 2 Fat

Restaurant (Product) a	Serving Size	Calories (Serving)	Carb. (GM.)	Pro. (GM.)	Fat (GM.)	Sodium (MG.)	Exchange (1 Serving)
French Fries (regular)	2.5 oz.	200	25	2	10	115	1½ Bread, 2 Fat
Cone (small)*	3 oz.	140	22	3	4	45	1 Bread, 1½ Fruit
Chocolate Sundae (small)*	3.7 oz.	190	33	3	4	75	2 Bread, 1 Fat
"Dilly" Bar*	3 oz.	210	21	3	13	50	1½ Bread, 3 Fat
"DQ" Sand-wich *	2 oz.	140	24	3	4	40	1½ Bread, 1 Fat

Kentucky Fried Chicken

Original Rec-ipe Chicken (edible por-tion)

Wing (one piece)	1.5 oz	136	4	10	9	302	1½ Med.-Fat Meat
Drum-stick	1.6 oz.	117	3	12	7	207	2 Lean Meat
Side Breast	2.4 oz.	199	7	16	12	558	½ Bread, 2½ Med.-Fat Meat
Thigh	3 oz.	257	7	18	18	556	½ Bread, 2½ Med.-Fat Meat, 1 Fat

Nutritive values supplied by company.
* For occasional use only, preferably before exercise.
NA = not available.

Restaurant (Product) a	Serving Size	Calories (Serving)	Carb. (GM.)	Pro. (GM.)	Fat (GM.)	Sodium (MG.)	Exchange (1 Serving)
Keel (Extra crispy has more fat and approx. 50 cal. extra per piece.)	3.3 oz.	236	7	24	12	631	½ Bread, 3 Med.-Fat Meat
Chicken Breast Sand-wich	5.5 oz.	436	34	25	23	1,093	2 Bread, 3 Med.-Fat Meat, 1½ Fat
Mashed Po-tatoes	3 oz.	64	12	2	1	268	1 Bread
Gravy	1 Tbsp.	23	1		2	57	½ Fat
Roll	0.7 oz.	61	11	2	1	118	1 Bread
Cole Slaw	¾ Cup	121	13	1	7	225	1 Bread, 1 Fat
Kentucky Fries	3.4 oz.	184	28	3	7	174	2 Bread, 1 Fat

Long John Silver's

Restaurant (Product) a	Serving Size	Calories (Serving)	Carb. (GM.)	Pro. (GM.)	Fat (GM.)	Sodium (MG.)	Exchange (1 Serving)
Chicken Planks	4	457	35	27	23	NA[c]	2 Bread, 3 Med.-Fat Meat, 1½ Fat
Seafood Plat-ter							
Fish	1	183	11	11	11	NA	1 Bread, 1 Med.-Fat Meat, 1 Fat

Restaurant (Product) a	Serving Size	Calories (Serving)	Carb. (GM.)	Pro. (GM.)	Fat (GM.)	Sodium (MG.)	Exchange (1 Serving)
Scallops	2	94	10	4	5	NA	1 Bread, 1 Fat
Shrimp	2	89	10	3	4	NA	1 Bread, 1 Fat
Hush Puppies	2	102	13	2	4	NA	1 Bread, 1 Fat
Fryes	3 oz.	288	33	4	16	NA	2 Bread, 3 Fat
Cole Slaw	4 oz.	138	16	1	8	NA	1 Bread (or 3 Vegetable), 1½ Fat
Total		894	93	25	48	NA	6 Bread, 1 Vegetable, 1½ Med.-Fat Meat, 8 Fat
Clams on Clam Dinner	5 oz.	465	46	13	25	NA	3 Bread, 1 Med.-Fat Meat, 4 Fat
Clam Chowder	8 oz.	107	15	5	3	NA	1 Bread, 1 Fat

McDonald's

Hamburger	3.5 oz.	255	30	12	10	520	2 Bread, 1 Med.-Fat Meat, 1 Fat
Cheeseburger	4 oz.	307	30	15	14	767	2 Bread, 1½ Med.-Fat Meat, 1 Fat

Nutritive values supplied by company.
* For occasional use only, preferably before exercise.
NA = not available.

Restaurant (Product) a	Serving Size	Calories (Serving)	Carb. (GM.)	Pro. (GM.)	Fat (GM.)	Sodium (MG.)	Exchange (1 Serving)
Big Mac	7 oz.	563	41	26	33	1,010	3 Bread, 3 Med.-Fat Meat, 3 Fat
Quarter Pounder	5.8 oz.	424	33	24	22	735	2 Bread, 3 Med.-Fat Meat, 1 Fat
Filet-O-Fish	4.8 oz.	432	37	14	25	781	2½ Bread, 1 Med.-Fat Meat, 4 Fat
French Fries (regular)	2.4 oz.	220	26	3	12	109	2 Bread, 2 Fat
Egg McMuffin	4.8 oz.	327	31	19	15	885	2 Bread, 2 Med.-Fat Meat, 1 Fat
Scrambled Eggs (1 order)	3.4 oz.	180	2	13	13	205	2 Med.-Fat Meat, 1 Fat
Hash Brown Potatoes (1 order)	2 oz.	125	14	2	7	325	1 Bread, 1 Fat

Pizza Hut

Restaurant (Product) a	Serving Size	Calories (Serving)	Carb. (GM.)	Pro. (GM.)	Fat (GM.)	Sodium (MG.)	Exchange (1 Serving)
Thin 'n Crispy Pizza	½ 10" Pizza (3 slices)						
Beef	½ 10" Pizza (3 slices)	490	51	29	19	NA	3 Bread, 3 Med.-Fat Meat, 1 Fat
Pork	½ 10" Pizza (3 slices)	520	51	27	23	NA	3 Bread, 3 Med.-Fat Meat, 2 Fat

Restaurant (Product) a	Serving Size	Calories (Serving)	Carb. (GM.)	Pro. (GM.)	Fat (GM.)	Sodium (MG.)	Exchange (1 Serving)
Cheese	½ 10" Pizza (3 slices)	450	54	25	15	NA	3½ Bread, 3 Med.-Fat Meat
Pepperoni	½ 10" Pizza (3 slices)	430	45	23	17	NA	3 Bread, , 3 Med.-Fat Meat, 1 Fat
Supreme	½ 10" Pizza (3 slices)	510	51	27	21	NA	3 Bread, 3 Med.-Fat Meat, 2 Fat
Thick 'n Chewy Pizza	½ 10" Pizza (3 slices)						
Beef	½ 10" Pizza (3 slices)	620	73	38	20	NA	5 Bread, 4 Med.-Fat Meat
Pork	½ 10" Pizza (3 slices)	640	71	36	23	NA	5 Bread, 4 Med.-Fat Meat
Cheese	½ 10" Pizza (3 slices)	560	71	34	14	NA	5 Bread, 3 Med.-Fat Meat
Pepperoni	½ 10" Pizza (3 slices)	560	68	31	18	NA	4½ Bread, 3 Med.-Fat Meat
Supreme	½ 10" Pizza (3 slices)	640	74	36	22	NA	5 Bread, 4 Med.-Fat Meat

Nutritive values supplied by company.
* For occasional use only, preferably before exercise.
NA = not available.

Restaurant (Product) a	Serving Size	Calories (Serving)	Carb. (GM.)	Pro. (GM.)	Fat (GM.)	Sodium (MG.)	Exchange (1 Serving)
Taco Bell							
Beef Burrito	6.5 oz.	466	37	30	21	327	2½ Bread, 3 Med.-Fat Meat, 1 Fat
Beefy Tostada	6.5 oz	291	21	19	15	138	1½ Bread, 2 Med.-Fat Meat, 1 Fat
Enchirito	7 oz.	454	42	25	21	1,175	3 Bread, 3 Med.-Fat Meat, 1 Fat
Taco	3 oz.	186	14	15	8	79	1 Bread, 2 Med.-Fat Meat
Wendy's							
Hamburger	7 oz.	470	34	26	26	774	2 Bread, 3 Med.-Fat Meat, 2 Fat
Cheeseburger	8.5 oz.	580	34	33	34	1,085	2 Bread, 4 Med.-Fat Meat, 3 Fat
French Fries	4.2 oz.	330	41	5	16	112	3 Bread, 3 Fat
Chili	8.8 oz.	230	21	19	8	1,065	1½ Bread, 2 Lean Meat

III. USEFUL REFERENCES

1. *Cookbooks for People with Diabetes* (1981, with 1986 supplement), is a descriptive compilation available for $1.00 from the National Diabetes Information Clearinghouse, Box NDIC, Bethesda, MD 20892. Ask to be put on the mailing list for their newsletter, "Diabetes Dateline."

2. Any one of Nathan Pritikin's diet books (e.g. *The Pritikin Program for Diet and Exercise*). These books have good recipes for lowfat, low-cholesterol, high-fiber dishes. The full diet is very demanding for some to follow because of the lowfat content.

3. The *HCF Guidebook* and *Dr. Anderson's Life-Saving Diet* are two books developed by Dr. James Anderson and colleagues, leading researchers in the effects of such diets. The books are available for purchase from the HCF Diabetes Foundation, P.O. 22124, Lexington, KY 40522, for $8.00 and $7.00, respectively.

4. *Food Values of Portions Commonly Used*, by J. A. T. Pennington and H. N. Church (Harper and Row, 14th edition, 1985), is a handy reference giving grams of fat, carbohydrates, proteins, and other food values. A new edition is in preparation at the time of this writing (Fall, 1988).

5. The *New American Diet* (Sonja and William Connor, Simon and Schuster, 1988) and *Eater's Choice: A Food Lovers' Guide to Lower Cholesterol.* (R. and N. Goor, Houghton Mifflin, 1987) are both innovative and useful guides to healthy eating (not specifically for the diabetic).

6. *Fast Food Facts* (M.J. Franz, 1987) and *Convenience Food Facts* (A. Monk and M. J. Franz) contain useful lists of food values from fast-food chains and name-brand processed foods from 75 companies. Available from Diabetes Center, Inc. P.O. 739, Wayzata, MN 55391, 1-800-848-0614. Ask to be put on the mailing list, and request their newsletter, *Living Well With Diabetes*.

7. *Diabetes Forecast*, the monthly magazine of the American Diabetes Association, carries many helpful nutrition articles and recipes. The ADA offers several cookbooks for diabetics. The appendix at the end of the book gives addresses and telephone numbers for ordering Forecast and a catalog of ADA publications.

Living Actively With Diabetes

"**O**ne of the good things about diabetes is that it makes a virtue out of enjoying myself physically. The little doctor in the back of my head smiles when I go dancing or swimming, even when I make love. My prescription includes having fun!"

—*Linda*

In this chapter, we review the many ways that exercise improves your management of diabetes and reduces the risks of complications. We present an activity questionnaire that helps you assess your present exercise level and plan for improving it. We conclude with guidelines for staying motivated to follow your program.

With so many people jogging and working out, it may seem unnecessary to urge diabetics to exercise. Everybody knows the benefits of staying fit: Exercise decreases your risk of heart disease, lowers high blood pressure, improves general physical fitness, reduces anxiety and depression, and enhances your sense of well-being. As a person with diabetes, however, you enjoy an extra bonus from exercise: It helps you control blood sugar and it lessens the risk of some complications.

199

HOW PHYSICAL ACTIVITY HELPS YOU MANAGE DIABETES

1. Any physical activity lowers your blood sugar by burning it as fuel. You can use exercise to return your levels to normal when tests are high (if BG test is not higher than 300).

2. Steady exercise for more than twenty minutes enables your muscles to store glucose, further lowering blood sugar after you've stopped exercising. Your body draws on this store when your blood sugar drops too low. When you exercise regularly, your blood sugar levels will be more stable.

3. Consistent physical activity that is moderate or strenuous increases the cell's ability to use insulin. This allows a lower insulin dose.

4. Exercise builds physical fitness, strengthening the heart, circulatory system, and lungs, as well as the muscles. This reduces the risk of cardiovascular complications.

5. Exercise is a key to losing or controlling weight and is at least as important as diet.

6. You can neutralize the effects of emotional stress by energetic physical activity.

7. Exercising makes you feel good!

Regular physical activity is a key ingredient of your diabetes control regimen, especially if you want optimal control. Exercise reduces your overall insulin requirement, helps you correct for blood sugar highs, and gives you greater balance in blood sugar levels (once you have adapted to exercising). The cardiovascular gains are especially important to you because, as a diabetic, you have a higher risk of heart and circulatory difficulties. So, in addition to improving your metabolic control, a consistent exercise program makes a heart attack less likely and improves your circulation.

The physical benefits of exercise are echoed at an emotional level. The increased flow of blood and oxygen to the cells and the hormonal shifts that occur when we are physically active lift our spirits. A stressful day at work can be counteracted by a brisk walk or game of tennis. Mild depression may be lightened by an hour of working in the garden or riding a bicycle. When we feel energized, we find it much easier to handle difficult problems and mood swings.

How does all of this magic occur? As soon as we start walking, dancing, swimming, or even swinging our arms, our muscles demand more energy. Blood flow to the muscles increases and soon more oxygen and glucose are moving into the muscles cells. Blood supply to the skin also increases, so the heat generated can be radiated out of the body. As an exercise session progresses, the liver releases additional glucose to fuel the muscles. Fats are also burned to provide further energy.

During physical work or play, insulin and the counter-regulatory hormones (adrenalin, growth hormone, glucagon, etc.) interact to ensure an adequate supply of glucose to the cells. Without insulin, the process breaks down in an insulin-dependent diabetic. In spite of the activity level, blood sugar will rise steeply, and excessive burning of fats will produce ketones if insulin has been omitted. On the other hand, the effectiveness of insulin is increased by exercise. More insulin molecules can connect to the cells and enable glucose to pass through the cell walls.

After you stop exercising, the effects continue to accumulate if you have been playing or working at a moderate to strenuous level. The liver and muscles need to restore their supply of glucose, and they draw it from the bloodstream even when you are resting. This process can go on for several hours following heavy activity. This is why reactions sometimes occur a long time after you've stopped exercising.

Physical activity enables you to lose weight by burning fat and turning glucose into muscle instead of adding more fat. Combining exercise with the proper diet allows a degree of weight control that cannot be obtained by diet alone. In fact, many weight-control programs now recommend at least a week of exercise before you start to diet. The increase in activity level apparently makes appetite control easier.

The power of exercise to relieve stress symptoms is easy to explain: At the most basic level, the stress response is designed to prepare us to act physically. When stressed, we are ready for "fight or flight," so the most natural way to deal with stress is to move vigorously in order to use the hormones and glucose generated by it. This also allows us to release the physical tension that usually accompanies stress, assuming that the exercise includes a relaxed warm-up period.

The short-term effects follow any period of increased physical activity. When you continue the activity long enough to raise your pulse to the target range for your age for fifteen to twenty minutes or more a day, you achieve what is called "the training effect." If you do this regularly for a few weeks, you start to enjoy the long-term benefits of exercise. A consistent program of physical training gives you even greater sensitivity to insulin, usually allowing a significant decrease in insulin dosage. Your muscles store more glucose, which is readily available to spontaneously balance low blood sugar. Reactions may become less severe as a result. Your body performs better, your lungs breathe deeper, your heart is stronger, and you feel better. You are living well.

Before we discuss starting or improving your program of physical activity, you may gain some insight into your present activity level by answering the following questions.

MY ACTIVITY PROFILE

1. My typical day includes

   ___hours of sleep. (7–8 hours recommended)

   ___hours of low activity (riding in or driving a car, reading, watching television, eating, talking while sitting or standing, etc.).

   ___hours of moderate activity (moderate walking, moderate gardening, mopping, light labor, slow sports like golf or bowling, easy swimming, etc.).

   ___hours of vigorous activity (rapid walking or running, heavy bicycling, moderate to heavy labor such as digging or carrying heavy objects, climbing stairs, playing tennis or basketball, etc.).

2. At least _____ times a week I increase this to

   ___hours of moderate activity.

   ___hours of vigorous activity.

   ___This increase of activity happens only on weekends.

   ___This activity is distributed through the week.

   ___Although I am usually sedentary, I occasionally have bursts of heavy physical activity.

3. I do some form of stretching or limbering before physical activity _____ .

   I do stretching as a cooldown after exercise _____

4. The physical activities I enjoy most are _____

   _____

   Activities I would like to learn are _____

   _____

5. I have the following medical conditions, which need to be considered in designing my activity program:
   ___Difficulty sensing the signals of an insulin reaction
   ___Heart disease
   ___High blood pressure
   ___Poor circulation
   ___Retinopathy
   ___Neuropathy (especially if it involves decreased sensation in the feet)
   ___Nephropathy (kidney dysfunction)
   ___I tire quickly
   ___Back pain (or other muscular or joint discomfort)
   ___Foot problems
   ___Other
   (If you checked any of the above, you should discuss exercise with your physician. You may need tests to determine the level of activity advisable.)

6. I see the following obstacles to exercising:
   ___I don't feel I have enough time for it.
   ___I'm afraid I'll have too many reactions.
   ___I feel clumsy and uncomfortable with my body.
   ___I'm bored by physical activities. I prefer using my mind.
   ___I don't have much energy.
   ___Other _____

7. I could overcome these obstacles to exercise by_____
   _____

8. I would like to increase my level of activity by_____
   _____

9. I would like to begin

   today _____ this week _____ this month _____

BEGINNING YOUR ACTIVITY PROGRAM

Without fail, wear a diabetes I.D. bracelet or necklace and inform any gym personnel, coaches, or fellow participants that you have diabetes and may need sugar for an insulin reaction.

We advise you to begin any program of exercise gradually. You need to build strength, endurance, and flexibility so that you will be comfortable exercising. You also have to discover your particular balance between increased activity, insulin, and diet in order to avoid serious reactions. If you have diabetic complications or other physical conditions, you will need to proceed cautiously and with guidance from your doctor. If you are over 35, you should probably have a physical stress test to determine the level of exercise appropriate for you.

Choose activities that you enjoy. You should look forward to your exercise times as positive experiences, not dreaded ordeals. In the following list are several physical activities, ranked according to calories burned. If you have several favorite activities, you will be able to choose among them to deal with changes in weather, mood, and physical state. Although you may prefer to have a partner in exercise, you should also have activities you can do by yourself. If your only physical activity tends to be your work, either on the job or at home, you will gain more benefit from it if you find new ways to enjoy it. Focus on your bodily movements as though they were a dance or a sport. Don't be so fixed on the end product that you ignore your body.

Let Me Count the Ways . . .

(The category an activity falls into depends on how energetically you do it. A * indicates that activity is good aerobic exercise.)

Light Activity (50–200 calories burned per hour)

Stretching	Yoga
Slow t'ai chi chaun	Light housework
Slow walking	Slow social dancing

Moderate Activity (200–400 calories per hour)

Moderate to fast walking*	Golf
Gardening	Calisthenics
Mopping	Horseback riding
Tennis (doubles)	Canoeing and rowing
Bowling	Trampolining
Stationary bicycle*	Square dancing or folk*
Swimming*	dancing
Ice skating	Fencing
Ping-Pong and badminton	Aerobic dancing*
Making love	Gymnastics
Slow jogging*	Walking up stairs
Volleyball	Roller skating
Jumping rope*	Whirling
Bicycling *	

Vigorous Activity (400–900 calories per hour)

Digging and shoveling	Football
Moderate to rapid jogging*	Racquetball
Hiking*	Skiing (downhill and cross-
Chopping wood	country)*
Tennis (singles)	Moving furniture
Waterskiing	Ice skating
Running up stairs*	Hill climbing*
Basketball	Squash and handball
Bicycle racing	Soccer

You should always warm up before vigorous activity. More importantly, though, you should cool off afterwards. Stretching and limbering muscles for five minutes beforehand and beginning exercise at a moderate pace allows pulse and blood pressure to increase slowly. Cooling down with five or more minutes of slower activity allows your body to return to normal gradually. Neglecting to warm up or cool down can cause risky, abrupt shifts in pulse and blood pressure.

Although any activity helps you become more fit, you will receive the greatest benefit from exercise that requires a fairly steady level of exertion and movement (such as jogging, dancing, or swimming). Stop-and-start activities (such as tennis and volleyball) and static straining (weight lifting) do not build the same level of fitness in your cardiovascular system.

How to know when you are exercising beyond your limit

- If you become faint, dizzy, or nauseated, if you experience severe shortness of breath or tightness or pain in your chest, or if you lose control of your muscles, stop immediately, rest, and discuss these symptoms with your doctor.

- If your pulse or rate of breathing does not return to resting level within three minutes of stopping exercise, you are probably pushing yourself too hard. Take this as a sign to ease up.

- If you are fatigued by moderate activity, and especially if you continue feeling worn out in the hours following, you are doing more than your current condition will support. Cut back in duration or intensity of exercise until you feel stronger. (If this tiredness begins abruptly, it may indicate that you are coming down with a cold or the flu.)

Be sure that you get enough water during exercise. You need regular drinks every fifteen to twenty minutes during strenuous activity.

Exercise and Blood Sugar Levels

Home blood glucose testing and knowledge of your insulin regimen will help you avoid heavy insulin reactions. If you test blood sugar before exercise, ten to fifteen minutes after you stop, and one hour after that, you will see how different types and amounts of activity affect you. (The ten- to fifteen-minute delay after exercising is necessary because sugar from the liver may temporarily raise blood sugar during vigorous activity.) You will have a rough idea of how much exercise it takes to lower a high blood sugar level and when you need extra food or reduced insulin.

If blood sugar is under 120 before moderate to heavy activity, be sure to eat food that is absorbed quickly (fruit juice dried fruit, etc.). By trial and error, you will discover how much you need to eat before a given amount of exercise to avoid a reaction or a high blood sugar level. (See Chapter 5, step 7a for suggestions on changing food and insulin to prepare for extra activity.) Keep in mind when your insulin tends to peak, and either eat food if you are exercising at that time or try to match your activity to the times when insulin is not so active. The ideal time for exercise is about one hour after a meal. Blood sugar is at a peak and reactions are less likely to occur then. If you wait two hours or more, you should have a snack before physical activity, unless blood sugar is high.

When you exercise the place where you injected the insulin, the insulin goes to work faster. This can be an advantage if you need to bring down a high blood sugar level, or a disadvantage if you are at a normal level to begin with. If the level is normal, you should avoid legs as an injection site before a hike, or your racquet arm before a tennis match.

When you exercise fairly heavily or over a long period (over an hour), your blood sugar will continue to decrease after you stop. The muscles and liver are replenishing their stores. You may need a larger meal or extra snacks to avoid reactions in the hours following a time of high or extended exertion.

Keep in mind the overall interaction between insulin, diet, and activity. You can vary any one or a combination of these factors to compensate for high blood sugar levels or changes in routine. This allows you a high degree of flexibility while maintaining good metabolic control.

If blood sugar is high (over 300 mg/dl), exercise is not an effective way to lower it. Insulin action is inhibited, and vigorous activity may even cause blood sugar to rise. If ketones are present, they will also increase. Extra insulin or less food are the best ways to reduce very high blood sugar levels.

Similarly, if you are ill, you should avoid all but the mildest activities. Your body needs energy to deal with the stress of the illness. Exercise only adds to this physical stress and may even worsen the condition.

The Training Effect

The greatest benefits of exercise occur when you regularly reach the training effect. This is achieved through sustained activity that raises your pulse to your target level for at least twenty minutes. If you do this at least three times a week (every other day), both your heart and your metabolic system will function better, assuming you have no major diabetic complications.

You have a built-in meter right at your fingertips for measuring the effectiveness and the safety of any type of physical activity. Count the number of heartbeats you can feel at your wrist or throat (just above the collarbone toward the center of your throat) for fifteen seconds, multiply by 4, and you have your pulse rate. Do this when resting and then during and immediately following exercise. The following table gives the meaning of different pulse rates, in terms of exercise intensity.

Pulse Rate (beats per minute)	Degree of Exertion You Feel	Comments
60—80	Very, very light	Of little value as exercise
80—100	Very light	Useful if condition is very poor
100—120	Moderate	Intensity just right
120—140	Somewhat hard	
140—160	Very hard	Stop! unless you are an athlete in top condition.

Those of you reluctant to stop and measure your pulse can simply use the degree of exertion that feels right to you as your guide. If you are unable to talk to a fellow exerciser, you are probably overdoing it. If you work in the Moderate to Somewhat Hard range, you will probably be at the level you need.

Another indication of your ability to handle exercise is the time it takes for your pulse to return to your resting rate after exertion. Measure it after you have been sitting quietly for fifteen minutes, move vigorously for as long as it takes to get your pulse over 120, then rest and measure your pulse again at one-minute intervals. If it takes more than three minutes to return to your resting rate, you are in poor shape and need to proceed cautiously with your exercise program. A more precise way of assessing your condition is to undergo an endurance or stress test at your doctor's office or at the local YMCA.

If you have been fairly sedentary, you may find that even relatively mild activity will bring your pulse up to a high level quickly. Your body is out of condition, and your heart has to work hard to handle any increased exercise. Recognize that your limits will gradually expand, and don't push yourself too hard. Twelve to twenty minutes a day at a pulse rate of 100 to 120 is a good beginning. (If you are over 60 and have not been very active, start with five minutes a day.) Stay at this level for a couple of weeks, and increase the duration and intensity of activity only when you feel your endurance growing.

As you get in better condition, you will find that you are exerting yourself harder before you reach the same pulse rate. The flight of stairs that left you breathless and your heart pounding a few weeks ago will be handled with ease. *If you don't experience improved endurance, be sure to discuss this with your physician.*

As you experience progress in endurance and performance, you will be able to gradually raise your sights. If your doctor approves, you can increase the duration and intensity of exercise every two or three weeks, until you are at your peak. For a younger person without complications, peak performance would allow a pulse rate of 140 to 160 beats per minute for sessions of thirty to sixty minutes. It can take up to six months to reach this level of conditioning, depending on where you start. If you are older, a lower pulse rate goal should be set, depending on age.

Pulse Rate by Age

Age	Recommended pulse	Pulse rate if you have history of heart disease, not to exceed:
20	130—170	150
30	124—162	143
40	117—153	137
45	114—149	134
50	111—145	131
55	107—140	128
60	104—136	120
65	101—132	113

How often do you need to exercise?

Three workout sessions a week can be enough to build conditioning. However, if you have diabetes, you benefit from the blood sugar–lowering effects as well. Ideally, you should include some physical activity in your schedule every day. This regularity helps you maintain good blood sugar levels consistently. You can't always meet this ideal, but fortunately you can use your skill at varying the ingredients of your regimen to deal with varying levels of activity. Diet or insulin dosage can be tailored to the kind of day you plan. A few more units of insulin or smaller meals will help maintain balance on the sitting-around-and-reading-or-watching-television kinds of days.

You should avoid concentrating all of your major exercise on weekends. If your job is fairly sedentary during the week, try to mix in some physical activity during the day: Take the stairs rather than using the elevator, walk the long way around, exercise at lunchtime, take a stroll after dinner. It is much easier on your body to maintain a steady pace through the whole week.

What if you have an active job?

Your work may be vigorous enough to keep you physically fit without further exercise. It depends upon the degree of exertion and the variety of movements you use. If your pulse stays in the range of 100 to 140 for extended periods during the day, you are working at a level that satisfies conditioning requirements. However, if your

210

pulse is usually below 100 even when active on the job, you may need to add more active movement. If your job keeps you moving in the same repetitive patterns, you may need limbering and loosening exercises to avoid sore muscles and maintain full flexibility.

GUIDELINES FOR DEVELOPING AN ACTIVITY PROGRAM YOU WILL FOLLOW

1. Build on the physical activities you already enjoy doing. Your exercise program may take several hours a week for the rest of your life. Start with the activities that give you real pleasure, and then learn some of the ones you've always wished you could do. Avoid boredom by using several different forms of active exercise.

2. If you feel short of time, do things simultaneously: Socialize and exercise at the same time (friends don't always have to sit down!); ride the exercise bicycle while watching television or listening to music; hold business discussions as you walk.

3. Keep a balance between developing more endurance and staying comfortable. You need time to strengthen your heart and muscles and to learn how to adjust diet and insulin to your new level of exercise. If you go too fast, pain and insulin reactions may discourage you from continuing. This is especially important if you are over 35, if you have any signs of heart trouble, or if other complications have started to develop.

4. Use your knowledge of changing diet and insulin dosage to prepare for increased physical activity. You are probably better off having a few high blood sugar tests from eating a little more than you need than risking serious reactions. Feedback from your tests will soon tell you how much is enough. Exercise beginning thirty to sixty minutes after a meal is least likely to cause reactions. If activity comes two or more hours after eating, you should have a snack unless blood sugar is over 150 mg/dl.

5. If you have a distaste for exercise because you are a "mental" type, use the "inner-sports" approach. Techniques such as visualization, affirmation, and meditation help many people understand the strong relationship between mind and body. Another possibility is to keep an exercise log and calculate your progress.

6. If you are anxious about exercise because of limiting physical conditions, ask your doctor for guidelines to ensure safety. You might consider joining a class specifically designed for people with physical limitations. Your YMCA, March of Dimes, or adult-education school may have a program taught by someone trained to help you exercise safely and monitor your special condition. Organizations for the visually handicapped may also be of help.

7. If you are reluctant to move because everyone will see how clumsy and awkward you are, try starting with walking. It's hard to look so clumsy while walking that anyone notices, and you can use walking exercise to develop your sense of grace. The trick is to pay attention to your body as you walk. Keep your attention turned to the sensations in your feet, legs, hips, arms, back, and shoulders. Let go of any tightness you notice. Then apply this same awareness to any form of motion. You are likely to find any awkwardness decreasing as you learn to be conscious of your body and release its tensions.

8. If competitive activities make you anxious, avoid them. The stress they create for you will tend to offset the benefits of the exercise. (Others may find the spirit of competition necessary to maintain motivation and avoid boredom.)

9. If you exercise outside, do it away from busy streets. Deeper breathing isn't so healthful when the air you breathe is full of carbon monoxide.

Living Well With Stress

I n recent years, a distressing amount of information has been spread about the effects of stress on health. As people with diabetes, we have reasons to take special interest in the subject of stress:

- Simply having diabetes generates stress-inducing events.
- Either physical or emotional stress can play havoc with our blood sugar levels.
- Chronic stress can contribute to the development of diabetic complications.

These three facts alone make an effective stress-management program a high priority for anyone with diabetes. If you follow such a program, you will be stabilizing your blood sugar levels by reducing the effect of stress on your metabolism. You will be lowering the risk of developing complications, and you will find it easier to live well with diabetes as you neutralize the distress of having it.

Let's examine the three ways that stress affects diabetics.

Simply having diabetes generates stressful events.
How many simple events become stressful for us because we have diabetes? "Sorry, dinner's going to be a bit late." "I'm afraid your

bag got put on another plane." "Look's like that blister on your foot has gotten a little infected." "No, there's no drugstore open on Sunday here." Our sense of security depends upon an amazing number of routines functioning smoothly. We are vulnerable to happenings that to others may be trivial.

In almost every hour of the waking day, we must consider some aspect of our self-care, and we may be confronted with a significant diabetes problem to solve. Even our sleeping hours may be shattered by the shaking cold sweat of an insulin reaction (itself an event of powerful physical stress.)

These day-to-day stresses of diabetes can build strong feelings of guilt and anxiety because they remind us of a deeper fear: the fear of diabetic complications. No matter how much we may try to forget the possibility of blindness, kidney failure, or heart disease, our mind remembers at some level that we are at risk. Anything that suggests this risk becomes a source of further stress.

Now is probably an excellent time to practice some stress management. Check yourself to see how you responded to the statements you just read. What changes can you detect in your body? Do you feed edgy, tense, nervous, suddenly tired? How did your mind respond? Did you want to stop reading, to deny that you are at risk?

Close your eyes and say to yourself slowly, "I am learning to take better care of myself. I am reducing the risks." Let the words relax you as you repeat them several times. If any other words try to deny what you are affirming, just hear them as static.

This illustrates one way of reducing stress: working to replace the thoughts that trigger it with more reassuring thoughts.

Either physical or emotional stress can play havoc with our blood sugar levels.
Diabetes gives us added sources of stress. And, adding insult to injury, diabetics are more vulnerable to its effects. Physiologically, the stress response is a powerful shift in hormone levels. It can raise, and sometimes lower, blood sugar levels to two or three times the normal level. Ironically, a botched and painful drawing of blood by an incompetent lab technician can result in an artificially high test result because of the emotional stress. Similarly, a bad scare while driving or a frustrating put-down by the boss can send blood

sugar soaring. Many so-called brittle diabetics are probably simply people who don't know how to manage the stress in their lives.

Similarly, physical stresses such as infections, wounds, or burns are likely to have a powerful effect on metabolism, raising both blood sugar and ketone levels. These high levels, if uncontrolled, slow down healing and can result in medical emergencies and hospitalization. The skills of blood glucose testing and adjusting insulin dosage can be lifesavers when we suffer severe physical stress.

Chronic stress can contribute to the development of diabetic complications.

High blood sugar levels are usually thought to be the primary cause of complications, but there is growing evidence that stress also plays a role here. Heart disease, for instance, is strongly associated with poorly managed stress in the general population. With diabetes, high levels of stress hormones may contribute to such conditions as retinopathy. Stress definitely is a factor in hypertension (high blood pressure), which in turn contributes to the development of a number of complications. Clearly, effective management of stress is an important component in any program to reduce the risk of complications.

Poorly managed stress has a major impact on the health of everyone—not just the health of diabetics. Many books, magazines, television shows, and classes have been detailing this impact and offering suggestions for handling stress. Stress is believed to contribute to heart disease, hypertension, and cancer. Although other factors also play a role in any of these conditions, reducing your stress level is likely to increase you chances of living well.

UNDERSTANDING THE STRESS RESPONSE

Stress is an inherent part of living. When a change in our environment demands something of us, our bodies react, preparing to meet the demand. There are similarities to this reaction no matter what the external stimulus (called the stressor): a threat of physical attack, an emotional blow, a joyous event, a burst of energetic activity, or an actual injury or illness. The stress response is our body's attempt to maintain or restore healthful conditions in all our physical systems.

You can appreciate the great value of the stress response simply by remembering the last time you had a strong insulin reaction. You probably felt shaky and nervous, your pulse speeded up, your blood pressure increased, and you may have become sweaty and emotional. These outward cues were responses to the physical emergency of low blood sugar. The adrenal hormones released as the result of this physical stress caused the symptoms you experienced. (They also signaled the liver to release glucose and glucagon into your bloodstream in an attempt to correct the low blood sugar.) The same hormones also tend to neutralize the effectiveness of insulin so it will not lower blood sugar any further.

If you had become unconscious, this automatic system might have been enough to bring you around, if you were lucky. The body treats this situation as an emergency because the brain needs a certain level of glucose to function effectively and may be damaged if blood sugar falls to very low levels.

Now, if the stressor was the threat of a mugging or negative criticism from a fellow worker or a bad fall, you would probably experience the same stress response. The hormones flow, blood sugar goes up, insulin becomes less effective, and you are ready for "fight or flight." Your energy is mobilized for an all-out effort.

You can see what a negative effect this mobilization has on metabolic control, unless the appropriate response to the situation is a major physical effort. Your pancreas is unable to contribute enough additional insulin to burn all that extra blood sugar stimulated by the stress. Your next test would be high, and, if you didn't know about the effects of stress, you might be shaking your head in puzzlement, saying, "But I didn't eat any more than usual!" You might not even be conscious of the source of distress, and the symptoms of the stress response may sometimes be subtle enough to escape notice, though blood sugar still rises.

Ernest's traffic with stress

I'm generally very polite and restrained, earnest even, but in traffic I used to express myself rather emphatically when other drivers treated me unkindly ... until the last and absolutely final time I ever made an obscene gesture on the freeway. I was chased down Interstate 5 through Seattle, onto city streets, and back on to the freeway for seven miles before I finally ditched my offended pursuer. I did my best to meditate while weaving in and out of traffic, but I still ended up with blood sugar at 500 mg/dl by the time I got home.

The threat doesn't have to be so real, though, to raise my blood sugar. A number of times I have found that my emotional participation in a movie I'm watching has been enough to produce similar increases.

On the other hand, there have been times when blood sugar has gone down to a reaction level after I got angry and expressed it strongly.

One other aspect of the stress response has a special importance for people with diabetes. Both physical and emotional stress can have a powerful effect on blood ketone levels. In some adolescents, ketones have increased tenfold during family arguments.

Stress does not stop with these effects that relate directly to diabetes. Your muscles tense, preparing for action and expression. When you are unable to release this tension, headaches, back pain, and other muscular disorders may occur. Your digestive system becomes involved, with changes in secretion of stomach acids, digestive hormones, and the muscle tone of the alimentary canal. Blood fat and cholesterol levels increase to provide additional energy for action. Pulse and blood pressure increase. The whole body participates in the stress response. If the cycle is not completed by action, the tension, hormones, glucose, fats, and other stress products stay at unnaturally high levels. If the stress is chronic and poorly managed, your health suffers.

> From the point of view of its stress-producing activity, it is immaterial whether the agent or situation we face is pleasant or unpleasant; all that counts is the intensity of the demand for readjustment or adaptation . . . [We need] to distinguish between distress, which is always unpleasant, and the general concept of stress, which . . . also includes the pleasant experiences of joy, fulfillment, and self-expression.
>
> —Hans Selye *in Stress Without Distress*

Although stress has powerful effects on diabetes control, it still is not a major subject of research. On the basis of existing studies, it is not even clear whether stress is more likely to raise or lower blood sugar in a person who has diabetes.

This gap in scientific knowledge is based, in part, on the difficulty of doing reliable stress research. (One study in the late 1940s would probably be rejected today by research review committees on the grounds of cruelty. In it, the doctor tested his subjects' blood sugar level and then berated them for being weak and spineless for controlling their diabetes so poorly. Then he tested again and found higher blood sugar. He apologized.)

Although scientists are not totally certain about anything concerning stress and diabetes, you do not have to wait for their conclusions on the subject. Armed with your blood glucose test kit, your urine ketone test strips, and your log, you can do the research that is most important for you: Determine how stress affects you as an individual. (Apparently the impact of stress is highly individual.)

Note distressing or exciting events and periods; study your test results in terms of these events. See if there is a difference in blood sugar level during a week when you are depressed and during a week when you are happier than usual. What happens after a quarrel or a frightening episode? The following list of questions can help you discover how stress effects your diabetes.

Some questions to guide your research on stress

1. Does stress seem to have much effect on your blood sugar level? If so, is your blood sugar level increased or decreased?

2. Does the type of emotion aroused influence the direction or amount of change in blood sugar?

3. What difference do you see between short, intense moments of distress and long, drawn-out episodes? What impact do you find from stress that extends for days or weeks at a time?

4. Is the effect on blood sugar level different when you express feelings fully rather than holding them in? (One classic study found blood sugar in one woman unaffected after she became angry and hit her mother-in-law over the head. We hope that more modest forms of expression prove adequate!)

5. Do you have positive tests for ketones in your urine after stressful incidents? If so, when?

6. How do any attempts to cope with stress through self-gratification (such as overeating, drinking, and not exercising) disrupt control?

7. What overall patterns do you see in the ways you responded to stress?

As you understand more about how stress affects your control of diabetes, you will be better equipped to handle it. You will know that you need to check blood sugar level after certain kinds of experiences to see whether you need extra insulin. You will know whether you need to modify your insulin dose during times of increased (or decreased) stress. And you will have evidence of the kinds of stressful experiences you need to learn to manage more effectively.

Recognizing the symptoms of stress

Acute symptoms
Pounding heart, rapid pulse
Trembling, shaky
Dry throat and mouth
Hard to concentrate
Change in blood sugar level
Emotional and physical tension
Sweating
Easily startled
Diarrhea or frequent urination
Indigestion
Tension headaches
Compulsive eating

Chronic symptoms
General irritability
Depression
Easily fatigued
Loss of appetite
Anxiety
Insomnia
Missed menstrual periods
Nervous tics
Stuttering
Migraines
Chronic muscular pains
Nightmares
More accidents and
    mistakes than usual

—adapted from *The Stress of Life* by Hans Selye
(McGraw-Hill, 1976)

Some of us are open to feelings and physical sensations and have no difficulty spotting the signs of stress. If this is not true for you, you may need to spend time developing more awareness of this side of your life. Ignoring the effects of stress does not decrease the impact of stress. If you know when stress is building, you are better able to do something about it. With more awareness of your body, you are also able to detect the onset of an insulin reaction sooner.

219

At times, you may mistake an insulin reaction for a general stress response, or vice versa, because the symptoms overlap. You may have some clear signs of low blood sugar: blurred or double vision, tingling or metallic taste on the tongue. If in doubt (and if you cannot test your blood at the time), eat a moderate amount of something sweet and see if the symptoms decrease at all.

DOING SOMETHING ABOUT STRESS
There are four main styles of managing stress:
1. Reduce the frequency of stressful incidents by
   a. Making changes in your family, social, or work situation.
   b. Changing beliefs and emotional reactions that trigger stress for you.
   c. Gaining skills that allow you to function more effectively.
   d. Preparing for events likely to be distressing.
2. Reduce the intensity of your stress response by
   a. Learning to relax.
   b. Meditating.
   c. Praying.
   d. Using bio-feedback.
3. Put the stress response to work by becoming more active physically.
4. Decrease your consumption of stimulants.

As with other aspects of the diabetes regimen, coping with stress is a highly individual matter. Vulnerability to stress, the level of arousal, the effectiveness of any particular coping technique, all vary from person to person. Fortunately there are many different approaches to stress management, so you can find at least one that works for you. The only formula is this: Whatever you do should not increase your stress level. Find an approach that suits you.

1. Reduce the frequency of stressful incidents
   a. Make changes in your family, social, or work situation.

You may find it easiest to act on your environment, demanding or requesting changes in the people and conditions that produce stress for you. Or, for the less assertive, you may be able to withdraw from whatever is distressing to you. For instance, you might have a doctor who doesn't listen to you or who tries to motivate you with fear. You could let him know how that approach affects you and ask for changes. If your physician doesn't respond, or if you do not care to confront him, you could change doctors.

b. Change beliefs and emotional patterns that trigger stress for you.

You may prefer to work on yourself, using the source of stress to show you the areas of your personality that need change. With the same insensitive doctor, you might discover that the root of your stress is a belief such as "No one thinks anything I say is important." By neutralizing this belief, you would reduce your stress and probably find it easier to speak with more strength.

Similarly, you could work with the feeling of stifled anger triggered when an authority figure ignores you. By learning to express or become detached from such responses, you gain power to use the energy they release. (See Chapter 14 for more on working with beliefs and feelings.)

c. Gain skills that allow you to function more effectively.

Often the source of distress is a sense of inadequacy that can be corrected by learning to perform tasks that are important to us. This might involve skills of learning, working, relating, or even of simply enjoying life. You might overcome your physician's resistance to listening by taking a workshop in assertiveness training or communication skills (assuming this was not the only relationship in which you had difficulty getting your point across).

d. Prepare for events likely to be distressing.

We often do this negatively, imagining everything that can possibly go wrong, sometimes in great detail. This skill of visualization can be turned into a positive resource in the following way: Relax deeply and then imagine living through the event. Imagine yourself performing with calm, strength, and clarity, no matter what others do. Go through the experience in detail several times if you see yourself faltering. Then forget about it so you won't try to use the visualization as a map when you get to the actual event. Real life calls for spontaneous, not rehearsed, action.

2. Reduce the intensity of your stress response by learning to relax

Your body knows how to relax, but sometimes your mind forgets to use this essential skill. When you practice it in the midst of a distressing incident, you can lessen the physical impact of the event. When you forget to relax until afterward, you still benefit from releasing the tensions that develop under stress. A relaxed body deals with stress more effectively and also provides the best conditions for creative problem solving. Some studies have also indicated that diabetics who regularly practice relaxation improve their metabolic control. It also just feels better to be relaxed!

There is a wonderful variety of relaxation techniques: visualization, music, autogenics, meditation, prayer, and biofeedback. If you learn several ways of relaxing, you will have one to use no matter what external situation you have to face. (This chapter contains several examples of relaxation techniques.)

One tip: Whatever relaxation techniques you choose, practice them while sitting, standing, or moving, as well as while lying down. It is important to learn that you can lose tension in any position, especially since it is more likely to strike when you're up and about.

Visualization involves using mental imagery in any sense mode (not just visual) to produce relaxation. Examples are imagining warm water flowing gently across tense muscles; imagining each breath carrying tension out of your body; or imagining warm light moving through your body. Your body releases tension in response to this visualization process.

Autogenics, on the other hand, uses words to instruct the body to relax. By telling yourself that your arms and legs are becoming heavier, and then warmer, you are suggesting that the results of relaxation are beginning to take effect. As you repeat the phrases, you body responds by relaxing deeply. Physicians in Europe have reported decreased insulin requirements in diabetics who regularly practice autogenics.

Quiet and peaceful music can be used to shape special periods of relaxation and is also effective as background sound. (In fact, relaxing music might help you as you work with this book.) Our bodies respond to excess noise with tension, but they tend to relax when the sounds around us are tranquil. (The resource list at the end of the chapter lists records and tapes that can be used.)

Meditation is a centuries-old means of contacting inner sources of strength and calmness. The physical effects of meditation have been shown to quiet the ravages of stress in our bodies.

Prayer may be seen as a meditation of words directing awareness to a sense of unity and connectedness. Some envision their words being received by a personal deity; others imagine them simply joining the wholeness of the universe.

Biofeedback enables us to know exactly when we are relaxing (or tensing). By helping us become sensitized to subtle cues, the electronic feedback helps us learn to attain very deep levels of relaxation.

3. You put the stress response to work by becoming more active physically

Since the stress response is designed to prepare us for maximum physical activity, exercise is ideally suited to using the physical changes produced by stress in a positive way. Try running up and down stairs after you learn you will not get that hoped-for promotion. Jog or dance after a quarrel with your lover. Thirty to sixty minutes of exercise at a moderate to brisk level will use the adrenalin and start to bring down the blood sugar. (If you have very high blood sugar because of stress, you may need extra insulin.)

4. Decrease your consumption of stimulants

Caffeine in coffee and tea and nicotine in cigarettes, along with their other negative effects, add to stress. Although they are advertised as calming, their actual effect is just the opposite.

Any one of these techniques for managing stress will benefit your health. If you have a fairly stressful life, you may need to combine several of them to cope with the demands on you. Find the right combination for you, and be gentle in its application. Don't make stress management one more source of stress in your life.

RELAXATION EXERCISES

First, remember to practice relaxation in a variety of situations— while sitting, standing, and moving, as well as lying down. You can relax anywhere, not just when you're flat on your back. (If you are usually tense, though, you may want to start learning to relax when lying down, with your eyes closed.)

Give up the waste of time called *waiting*. No matter where you are, you can use those in-between times to let go of tensions and notice what's happening with your body. As long as you don't start snoring, no one will notice or care what you are doing.

Breathe away tensions

Begin by just noticing how you are breathing. What part of your torso are you using? How deep or shallow is your breathing? How fast?

Then, focus on the feeling of air moving in and out of your nostrils for a minute. Follow the air down into your lungs and feel your chest and stomach expand and contract with each breath.

Focus now on each exhalation, imagining that the air is carrying tension out of your body. If you are alone, sigh or hum gently with each breath.

Finally, focus on each inhalation, imagining new energy coming into your body with the air.

Visualize with any or all of the senses

A simple visualization to use for relaxation is to imagine yourself immersed in a sensory bath—fragrant, warm breezes, tropical showers, glowing light, gentle, natural sounds . . . . Sense warm water and breezes flowing over each muscle of your body, even through the muscles, opening and relaxing them.

An alternative visualization: Let your mind return you to a specific time when you felt happy and deeply relaxed. Relive the event in as much detail as you can recall.

Talk your body into relaxing

When our minds talk, our bodies listen. European doctors have created a whole discipline of relaxation on the basis of this simple truth. Called autogenic training, this approach uses repeated phrases to suggest to the body that it is experiencing relaxation . . . and it does.

Repeat each phrase slowly (and silently) five or six times:

"My right arm is growing heavier."
"My left arm is growing heavier."
"My right leg is growing heavier."
"My left leg is growing heavier."
"My right arm is growing warmer."
(and so on through the other limbs).

Meditate

Among the hundreds of meditations, one of the easiest to learn is called mindfulness. With this, you step back from the constant flow of thoughts and sensations and simply watch the parade.

Find a posture you can maintain comfortably without moving for ten to twenty minutes. Balance your body so you are not leaning forward or backward or to the side. (Or lie down if you can stay awake.)

Begin with awareness of the breath passing through your nostrils, and use this sensation as an anchor. Each breath can be a reminder that all you have to do is watch the flow of thoughts, feelings, perceptions, and body sensations. Just watch, without commenting on or judging what you see.

Naturally you forget to "just watch" and you become immersed time and again in the process of thinking, feeling, and so on. You forget even the simple task of sensing each breath. But soon your breath itself reminds you that you can detach and step back again.

You move back and forth between just watching and marching along in the parade of your mind. Then gradually the periods of watching grow longer and the mind grows quieter.

RESOURCES FOR STRESS MANAGEMENT
Books on Relaxation
Herbert Benson, *The Relaxation Response,* Avon, 1975
Patricia Carrington, *Freedom in Meditation,* Anchor Books, 1978
Daniel Girdano and George Everly, *Controlling Stress and Tension,* Prentice-Hall, 1979
Joseph Levine, *A Gradual Awakening,* Doubleday, 1984
Hans Selye, *Stress Without Distress,* Signet, 1975
Norman Shealy, *90 Days to Self-Health,* Dial, 1978

Music to Help You Relax
Gregorian Chant and other early church music (before Baroque)
William Ackerman, *Passages,* Windham Hill Records
Brian Eno, *Music for Airports* or *Plateaux of Mirrors,* ECM
Steve Halprin, *Spectrum Suite,* SRI Records
Georgia Kelly, *Seapeace,* Global Pacific
Deuter, *Silence, Ecstasy, and Celebrations,* Kuckkuck
Environments (natural sound recordings—waves, bird song, country streams, and the like) Cyntonic Research, 175 5th Ave., New York, NY

Guided-Relaxation Tapes
Emmett Miller, *Letting Go of Stress* and *Health and Wellness*

Classes on Stress Management
Your local chapter of the American Diabetes Association may offer or know of a stress-management class especially designed for people with diabetes.

YMCA and high school or college adult-education programs usually have general stress-management classes.

Section IV
SUPPORT FOR LIVING WELL

| C H A P T E R | 12 |

Living Well With Your Medical Team

O f all the chronic medical conditions, diabetes probably has the most sophisticated, well-developed team of health professionals dedicated to helping you learn about and manage the disease. There is even an American Association of Diabetes Educators (AADE) with several thousand members. Membership includes a wide variety of professionals all interested and involved in working with diabetes. Who are they?

DIABETES HEALTH PROFESSIONALS
Physicians

Most likely, your primary physician is either a family physician or an internist. The physician may or may not have special interest or expertise in diabetes. There are also subspecialists—endocrinologists and diabetologists—who have special training in diabetes. Any of these physicians can help you live well with your diabetes. You may find one who is more responsive to your individual needs, more knowledgeable about the options available, more willing to work with you, than another. These qualities may well be more related to the physician's personal characteristics than to training. You have the right to choose a physician with whom you have a mutually rewarding relationship. You need not feel guilty if you decide to change doctors because you want a better relationship.

If complications develop, your physician may refer you (or you may ask for a recommendation) to a specialist or subspecialist in the area of your complication: for skin problems, a dermatologist; for nerve problems, a neurologist; for kidney problems, a nephrologist; for problems with digestion or bowels, a gastroenterologist or neurologist (since these problems in a diabetic are usually due to neuropathy); and for eye problems, an ophthalmologist. We recommend that you see an ophthalmologist at least once a year on a preventive basis.

Podiatrists and Dentists
Diabetes can affect you from head to toe. It is wise to have regular (yearly, and more often, if recommended) preventive maintenance on your teeth and gums and your feet. You should be sure that your dentist and podiatrist are aware that you have diabetes. It will affect the signs and symptoms they look for and the kind of treatment they may give you.

Diabetes Educators
In this category, we include nurses, nurse educators, nurse practitioners, dietitians, nutritionists, patient educators, and exercise specialists. Diabetes educators know that the knowledge, skills, and attitudes involved in living well with diabetes require someone who is well trained to help the patient learn them. The nurse or patient educator may teach most areas and may refer you to a dietitian if you need detailed information in the areas of food, nutrition, and weight. An exercise specialist can help you design a program of sports or exercises suited to your level of fitness.

The AADE has recently instituted a program of certification for diabetes educators. Educators who pass a comprehensive exam become Certified Diabetes Educators and are entitled to put the initials "CDE" after their names. A CDE is likely to be well informed about the latest and best methods of diabetes management, although many excellent diabetes educators are not certified.

Psychologists, Psychiatrists, Counselors, and Other Psychotherapists
These professionals are available to help you with crises or difficult changes that you wish to make in your life. They can help you

230

overcome resistance to following the diabetes regimen you choose, if you need more than the techniques presented in this book. They are also very useful in helping you deal with the emotional and the problem-solving aspects of crises like the onset of complications. You may be able to find someone who specializes in diabetes or other chronic illnesses through your local chapter of the American Diabetes Association. (See Chapter 13 for more on the times when professional psychological support may be needed, as well as some powerful sources of lay support.)

Pharmacists

Pharmacists can be extremely helpful in providing information on insulin, other medications and their effect on your diabetes, and the selection and use of a wide variety of diabetes products.

WORKING WITH THE TEAM

The idea of a team implies coordination of roles and responsibilities to accomplish a mutually shared goal. You are the focus, and the team's general goal is helping you to live well with diabetes.

It is your responsibility to convey to individuals on the team your needs, concerns, questions, and problems. As health professionals ourselves, we urge you to speak up

• When you do not understand something you are told;

• When too much is being told you at once;

• When you think you will have difficulty carrying out a recommendation;

• When you may not agree with something you are told to do; or

• When you want to know if there are alternatives to the plan recommended.

Most health professionals prefer that you voice lack of understanding or disagreement from the start rather than not say anything because you may feel awkward or embarrassed. Otherwise, you're both wasting time. Health professionals realize that *you* make the ultimate decisions about your care, and they want you to understand their recommendations fully and be willing to follow them.

It is the health professional's responsibility to communicate clearly to you about your care and the options available to you. They should use words you understand, speak slowly enough for you to follow, and write down or provide printed information about their recommendations. They should outline the risks and benefits of alternative courses of action and explain any side effects of recommended tests, medications, procedures, or treatment.

As you read this book and work with members of the diabetes team, you may wish to bring this book with you. With the health professional, go over parts of the book that are particularly relevant to you at the time, ask questions about what might not be clear to you, and show them this chapter, if desired. In particular, you may with to show them the special note in the Preface.

The basic tool of your diabetes care team is communication. We hope that this book will help support the communication between you and the members of your team.

CHAPTER 13

Living Well With Other Diabetics

"**I** always felt lonely and a little weird, like I was the only diabetic in the world who lied to her doctor or ate lemon meringue pie. The only thing worse than my guilt was my depression over feeling so out of control. I didn't think anyone could understand what I was up against, until I went—not very willingly—to a diabetes support group. For the first time I got to talk to people who were struggling with the same issues that had me down. They taught me I could do something to get myself under control."

—Jean

CREATING A DIABETIC SUPPORT NETWORK

Diabetes is a demanding companion that tends to isolate us from others. Our friends and relations may have little understanding of the frustrations and challenges we face. We may believe we would only bore them with the countless details of regimen we stay aware of every day. We need a special quality of support that depends upon living knowledge of diabetes: support for coping with our feelings, support for solving the many practical questions we need answered, support for improving our ability to follow our complex regimen.

Contact with others who are attempting to live well with diabetes is a vital ingredient in our program of self-care.

Support from other diabetics is especially important when you decide to improve your level of management. The experiences, practical knowledge, and understanding of someone else who has gone through this process make the path much easier. Other diabetics can help you see when you are trying to move too fast or when you are forgetting important aspects of regimen. They can offer encouragement and practical tips. This level of support is a beautiful complement to the direction you obtain from your medical team.

Support is especially important when diabetes is first diagnosed or when complications first appear. These are times of crisis when we may be filled with strong feelings and countless questions. Other diabetics can help us deal with these challenges and learn the lessons of living well.

Those who are close to us need support as well. Being the mate or parent of a diabetic has its own unique demands. Just ask a person who has found a loved one unconscious or who watches one of us consistently overeating. Our close friends can learn from and be encouraged by other diabetics and their families.

Anyone with diabetes may encounter problems that require professional mental health assistance. Our support system may be weak, or the particular challenges we meet may require the aid of someone with professional training. Some of the signs of needing to see a psychotherapist, counselor, or social worker include

1. Chronic depression.
2. Repeated self-destructive behavior such as "forgetting" insulin, going on frequent eating binges, and not learning to handle insulin reactions.
3. A sense of helplessness that blocks learning and action.
4. Unwillingness to ask for help from an informal support system.
5. Participation in a negative family or in social situations that detract from self-care.

If you feel you need more support than your network or group can give, take this as a sign of healthful perception, not as evidence that something else is wrong with you.

SETTING UP YOUR SUPPORT NETWORK

In some areas of the country, you can find an abundance of diabetes support activities. Local ADA chapters, hospitals, clinics, or individual physicians may sponsor continuing support groups that you can attend. Your local ADA office should know if anything is available in your area. You may find that there are only general educational meetings. Although not specifically devoted to emotional support, these events are good places to meet other people with diabetes and their families and thus start building your diabetes network.

Cultivating this network—the informal cluster of people who share your interest in diabetes—is an effective and relatively easy way to develop your support system. You may find people who are already functioning as diabetes networkers, and they are often storehouses of information on people, resources, and meetings. "You're trying to get control of your eating? Talk to Joe Dodds. He's winning that battle and can really help you." "You're afraid of laser treatment and keep putting it off? Joan Mason can tell you how she overcame her fear." Don't feel that it is an imposition to ask for help. Most people genuinely enjoy an opportunity to help someone, especially when they share a condition as significant as diabetes. Networkers themselves are a special breed who love the process of making connections. As you gather your own information, you may find that you would like to serve in this way, too.

Talk to your friends and relatives, your druggist, your doctor and nurse, clinics or hospitals with diabetes education programs, and the nearest ADA chapter. Indicate that you want to get in touch with diabetics who have fairly positive attitudes and who could encourage you. If you need support, it doesn't help to begin networking with people who will make you feel worse.

You may run into some dead ends as you begin, so be prepared to persevere in building your network. Some doctors may feel very protective of you and may discourage you from learning from others with diabetes. And some people with diabetes avoid other diabetics like the plague. You may have to make a number of calls before you start getting positive responses, or you may find enthusiastic support right from the beginning.

Soon you will have several people you can call on when you need support or information. Perhaps there will be a person who shares a compulsive eating pattern with you, and you agree to call each other when the urge strikes. If you have a complication developing, you may want a buddy who has dealt with the same problem. Or you may just want a sympathetic ear when it all feels like too much.

Occasional telephone contact or conversation over a diet soda or cup of coffee may satisfy your need for support. You'll go through a sorting process, dropping out of contact with people who just complain and turn away from any encouragement. You may find friends of friends calling you because they have heard you are interested in mutual support.

You will soon be giving support to others, offering resources you know about: a new development in diabetes care you have just read about, a drugstore that sells insulin at a discount, a doctor who works well with patients. When you encourage another, you encourage yourself. A basic principle in mutual aid is that giving and receiving are really the same.

Sometimes you will be able to offer guidance or information well suited to someone else's needs. But there will be times when there is little you can do. Don't feel that you always have to have an answer. Your responsibility is to listen, to show that you care, and to share what you know. "You'd better talk to your doctor about that" may be the most useful thing you can tell someone. As your network grows, you will also be able to suggest talking with other diabetics who can help with particular problems.

DEVELOPING A SUPPORT GROUP

Informal networking can provide very effective support, especially for people who are uncomfortable in groups. A regular group, though, offers certain bonuses. You can obtain feedback from a variety of points of view, and you have a larger body of experience to draw upon. A group can bring in guest speakers or even set up a training program in different aspects of diabetes management. People working together are usually more effective than individuals in handling the needs of members going through a crisis such as occurs when complications develop.

A support group is most effective when it is one activity of an ongoing network. If members feel free to contact each other between meetings, support is always available. Members maintain continuity of contact even though they may not be able to attend every meeting. The meetings themselves are more relaxed, since they are only one of several ways of sharing.

If you find no existing diabetes support group to join, you can start one by following the networking steps just described. Ask the people you contact if they are interested in helping to create the group. Find out what they are willing to do, what they want out of the meetings, and how often they would like to get together. You will find some who enjoy organizing and leading meetings, and others with practical skills like typing or access to copying machines. Assume that the work load will be shared and that you do not have to carry the whole burden. It helps to be clear about the tasks people take on and to specify when they need to be completed. "You're willing to call Sarah, Phil, Joan, and Larry? The meeting is on the tenth, so can you do that by the second?"

You may want to proceed informally, or you may prefer to set up a coordinating committee right at the beginning. Two or three other members are enough to work with you in organizing the group, planning meetings, and developing any other activities. It will become clear which decisions need to be made by the whole group and which by the committee. Some groups want to share in the organizational tasks and decisions, and others prefer to use most of their meeting time for support and learning. In your initial conversations with potential members, you will begin to get a sense of how they feel about this question. It can be explored at length in the first meeting.

The First Meeting
It is important to establish a positive tone at the first meeting, for without it, there may not be a second meeting. The details of this first meeting depend upon your style and that of the people you are working with. We will describe three alternative ways of conducting this session, but there are many others.

Shared leadership
Everyone shares in the creation of the group. At the beginning, the facilitator or discussion leader asks the group to work together to develop guidelines, structure, and topics. Everyone in the group should answer the following questions:

• What do you want out of the group?

• What do you want to avoid?

• How do you want the group to operate—no leader, rotating leaders, professional facilitators?

• What guidelines for discussion are important to you?

• What are you willing to do to help the group function?

The leader encourages everyone present to describe his or her preferences. After discussion of each question, agreement may be reached, a vote may be taken, or further discussion may uncover solutions that satisfy conflicting views.

The strength of this approach is that it encourages a high level of participation and responsibility. In this way, it reflects the level of individual responsibility demanded by diabetes itself. However, if some group members are dealing with major problems, they may find it difficult to give their attention to discussion of organizational questions. If you know you have someone in crisis, find out—before the meeting—how they feel about this way of beginning the group.

There should be a definite cutoff point for the organizational discussion, and at least half of the meeting should be devoted to talking about living well with diabetes.

Committee Leadership
A coordinating committee is responsible for defining initial guidelines and structure of leadership. This style may be appropriate if you sense that the people coming to the first meeting are on the shy side. The discussion leader briefly describes the proposed structure and asks for approval or recommendations for change. Then it is possible to move right into the support work. With good topics for initiating discussion, group members can quickly experience the value of being in a support group. But it may take more effort to involve them in keeping the group going.

Outside Leadership
If you find that you or the potential members lack confidence in a self-directed group, a counselor or social worker might be hired to lead the first few meetings. You would need to look for someone experienced at facilitating groups and willing to build the group's capacity for functioning on its own. A local college, hospital, or

public health department could help you find such a person, who might even be willing to volunteer the time. If not, the group would have to be willing to pay fifty to one hundred dollars for each meeting.

Any of these structures can be effective. Choose the one that feels most appropriate to the people in your group. For more information on conducting this first support meeting, see the general comments on meetings that follow, especially the sections on guidelines, stress level, and evaluation.

Conducting Successful Support Meetings

A clearly stated set of guidelines for meetings helps to instruct new members and remind old ones of the group's basic values and meeting style. The list can be printed or read at the beginning of the first few meetings. This helps to keep discussion within bounds and avoids pitfalls of discussing individual regimen in a group setting. Your group can create its own guidelines from scratch or use the following as a model.

Guidelines for a Diabetic Support Group

1. We are here to support each other in facing the challenge of living well with diabetes. By helping each other, we help ourselves. We intend to maintain a positive climate for discussing our experiences, feelings, problems, and solutions.

2. We will feel free to share any information about ourselves within the group, but we will not disclose anything we hear to people outside the group.

3. We will respect each other's right to remain silent as much as his or her right to speak. And we will be sure to leave openings for the silent to speak.

4. The proper care of diabetes differs from person to person. We will remember that regimen is individual and not try to advise someone else on the basis of our own practice.

5. If we hear something that suggests possible changes in our own regimen of physical care, we agree to discuss such changes with our physician before acting.

6. If we feel anyone is passing on misinformation, we will not be afraid to challenge the information. When there is a difference

of opinion or doubt, we will check out the facts with a health professional.

7. One of our functions is to share feelings. When we do this, we will give support but avoid interpretation and analysis. If any of us opens to deep emotions during the meeting, we will allow room for this. At the end of the meeting, one of us will check with the person to be sure he or she is all right.

8. We will feel free to express anger but not to direct it at other group members.

9. Many of the topics we discuss at an informational level may arouse strong feelings and stress reactions. When any of us senses stress and tension growing, we will feel free to ask for a moment of silence to check our feelings. When the group stress level is high, we will take time for guided relaxation or another stress-reduction technique.

10. When one person is discussing a problem, we will encourage that person to find his or her own answers before offering ours. When we make suggestions, we will do it gently, without pushing.

11. If any of us is an alcoholic or a drug user, we agree to come to meetings only when we are sober or straight.

12. If any of us decides to stop coming because we can't handle the issues the group discusses or the way the group functions, we will discuss our reasons in the meetings or contact someone in the group and give feedback on what is causing the difficulty.

13. Having diabetes is a challenge to learn the lessons of life it brings to us. We are together to support this learning.

Leading Effective Meetings

These suggested guidelines imply that many of the leadership functions in a group can be shared by all the members. If each person takes responsibility for maintaining orderly discussion, awareness of stress levels, respect for feelings, and other questions of process, the meetings will practically run themselves. When there is clear understanding of the group's guidelines, it is even possible to function without a formal discussion leader.

However, it may be more effective to designate one person as facilitator or discussion leader for each meeting, with the role rotating to another member each time the group meets. This is especially true if new people come regularly.

The facilitator will do the following:

1. See that the group's guidelines are read at the beginning of each meeting.
2. Mention any departures from the guidelines if they occur.
3. Lead introductions and collect the subjects people wish to bring up.
4. Gently steer discussion, quieting side conversations and opening new subjects when the last has been completed.
5. Stay attentive to stress levels and call for relaxation when the level is high.
6. Reserve space for discussion of any group business, such as change in meeting place.
7. Conclude each meeting with a time of evaluation and appreciations.

When a different member handles this job at each meeting, the whole group becomes experienced in the skills required. It becomes natural for everyone to share the leader's tasks. Then, when the evening's facilitator fails to notice the high level of stress caused by a description of his or her own problems, for instance, anyone can call for a relaxation break.

Introductions

You can ask members to introduce themselves, describing their relationship to diabetes as well as saying something about their life outside diabetes. If they also mention any subjects they would like to discuss during the meeting, the evening's agenda is developed by the time they are finished. (The facilitator should list subjects, perhaps on a chalkboard or a large pad of paper.) Knowing who has type I or type II diabetes and who is a parent or spouse of a diabetic helps keep information relevant. The information about one's life outside diabetes helps group members see each other as complete persons, not just as people who have diabetes.

Starting Discussion

Reviewing the subjects people mention during introductions may be all that is needed to begin a flow of discussion that lasts all evening.

The facilitator can read the list and ask the group which topic to take up first. Another way of beginning is to assign a subject that establishes a positive mood: "The most useful thing I've learned about living with diabetes is . . ." or "How has diabetes improved my life?" It is surprising how easily most people talk when such simple questions are presented.

Guiding Discussion

Sometimes meetings flow spontaneously, with little need for guidance from the facilitator. But there are times when some gentle steering is helpful. One person may be cut off prematurely. A quiet "I'm not sure Francis was finished speaking" will return the floor to the speaker.

There may be shy members in the group who will say little or nothing during the meetings. You can open space for them by saying, "Do any of the people who've not been saying much want to speak?" Allow them time to speak up, but do not pressure them. They may prefer to just listen for a while, and they will be able to learn from other people's experiences.

Setting a Positive Tone

A support group is more attractive if members emphasize abilities rather than disabilities, and solutions rather than problems.

Members need room for describing the difficulties they experience, but they should be encouraged to overcome these difficulties rather than be a victim to them. Pose questions in such a way that they elicit positive responses. Ask: "How do you deal with your feelings about diabetes?" instead of "What psychological problems does diabetes cause?"

Awareness of Stress and Feelings

Many of the things we need to discuss at a support group may raise the stress level for some or all of the people present. Feelings of vulnerability will be aroused by even the most boring and technical description of laser treatment: "My doctor shot this blue beam through a thick contact lens. The flashes were really bright. He said he did 800 zaps the first session." When the group is discussing highly charged subjects such as complications, it is important that the facilitator and group members watch for signs of rising stress. Some of these signs include a tendency to change subjects too quickly or to give in to nervous laughter.

It is always appropriate for any group member to ask, "Is anyone else feeling anxious?" and call for a stress check—a moment of silence in which people sense how they are reacting to the subject under discussion. If enough of the group shares the discomfort, the facilitator can lead a guided relaxation session. In this way, members learn to be aware of and manage stress as it occurs. This also makes participation in the group a more positive experience. A diabetes support group should reduce, not increase, the stress level.

Avoiding Misinformation

Members must feel free to challenge any information they believe to be inaccurate or incomplete. Keeping the facts straight is so important that a self-led group might enlist a physician or nurse practitioner to be a resource person who can be contacted by phone between meetings about questions that arise.

Handling "Difficult" Members

You may feel you lack the necessary assertiveness to confront the person who talks all the time, or the one who drains the group with chronic complaints and discouragement, or the one who sarcastically criticizes others. As facilitator, one thing you can do is refer the difficulty to the group as a whole: "Jim seems to have a lot to say tonight. Does anyone else want to say anything?" Or suggest doing something that will change the tone: "Betty has pointed out quite a few of the things she doesn't like about doctors. I'd like to hear if any of you have anything good to say about your doctor." Or just say what you are feeling: "I'm frustrated. It sounds like everyone's doing everything wrong, according to Cliff."

Evaluation

At the end of the meeting, each member describes what he or she most appreciated about the evening's discussion (and other members' contributions) and mentions any changes that would improve the sessions. This regular feedback helps keep the group on course.

Meeting Format

Support group meetings can follow a variety of formats. Each encourages a different style of discussion, so it is a good practice to vary the format occasionally. Some of the possibilities include the following:

1. General discussion following from the questions and concerns members bring up at the beginning of the meeting.

2. Sessions organized around a specific topic. The coordinating committee might choose the topic in advance, or the group could decide on one at the beginning of the meeting.

3. Discussion in subgroups: insulin dependent and non-insulin dependent; diabetics and nondiabetic family members; married and single people. With this format, people are able to spend more time on questions unique to being the spouse of a diabetic, a single diabetic, and so on.

4. Discussion in pairs. The group can break up into pairs occasionally, either to discuss an assigned topic or just to get better acquainted. This is an important variation for people who are more comfortable talking one-to-one than in groups. When the group reassembles, members may summarize their learning from the more intimate conversation.

5. Question-and-answer or instructional periods with a guest speaker. A nurse practitioner or psychologist might give instruction in stress management for diabetes. You might ask a physician to answer questions such as "How can we make the most effective use of our office visits?" A nutritionist might be asked to describe new research affecting diabetic diet. (Guest speakers can be effective early in the development of a group to enlist new members.)

6. Films related to diabetes as a way to focus discussion. *Diabetes—Focus on Feelings,* for instance, is an effective tool for a group exploring feelings about having diabetes.

7. Social events. Potlucks to share favorite dishes, parties, and picnics.

Some Topics for Discussion

• How has diabetes been my teacher, helping me learn about living?

• What attitudes, beliefs, or skills have helped me cope with diabetes?

• What do I wish I had known about living with diabetes at the beginning?

• What benefits do I receive from diabetes?

• What are three things I like most about myself? How do they (or how could they) help me deal with diabetes?

- What attitudes and skills do I need to learn to deal with diabetes better? How can I learn them?
- How does diabetes affect my relationships, both intimate and casual?
- How did I feel when I first learned I had diabetes?
- What can I do to create a more effective relationship with my doctor and health care team?
- Given my need to respect the demands of diabetes, what can I do to improve the quality of my life?
- How can we cut the costs of managing diabetes?

The elements you select for your diabetes support group and the ways you combine them are up to your particular group. There is no universal formula for support groups, just as there is no universal regimen for diabetes care. Feel free to experiment until you find the combination that works for all your members.

The following is a description of how one group met in Seattle.

A MEETING OF A DIABETIC SUPPORT GROUP

Five of the regulars are present at the agreed-upon meeting time, so they begin with guided relaxation and introduce the topics for the evening. Three more people, one of them new, come in during the introductions and join in. The newcomer says she wants to find out about blood glucose testing, so this is discussed first. The three members who are doing blood glucose testing talk about how it has improved their control. They recommend that the newcomer attend a class at a diabetes clinic. Later in the evening, the hostess, brings out a blood test strip and a lancet, and the woman tests her blood, with participation of the others.

A man with type I diabetes and his wife arrive late because the man had a serious insulin reaction just before dinner. As he described what happened, it becomes evident that he is on a metabolic roller coaster. Group members emphasize the importance of working closely with one's doctor to get regulated. They also suggest some specific actions that would help: making his schedule more regular, keeping detailed records, handling stress more effectively, and sharpening his awareness of reaction cues. A young woman who has

245

had diabetes most of her life says with conviction, "It is possible to learn to control diabetes."

The man's wife describes her distress over the difficulties she goes through with her husband. Others acknowledge that it can be as difficult to live with a diabetic as it is to be one. Another spouse offers to get together with the woman for coffee and share some of the things that have helped her live with her husband's diabetes.

One member notes that the stress level seems high after talking about personal relationships. She asks if others would enjoy a relaxation break. Many people nod, and the facilitator reads a guided relaxation exercise, going through the steps of the relaxation as she reads.

A 32-year-old woman who works in an office says that she has been using the relaxation technique she learned at the previous meeting. She says she does it several times a day at her office, and she believes that her blood sugar control has improved. She suggests relaxation to the man who had the reaction.

The facilitator notes that only 30 minutes of the meeting are left, and she asks how the group wants to end the meeting. The man who had been delayed by the reaction says he had been wondering if his difficulty with control had something to do with his beliefs. He asks people in the group to talk about the beliefs that help them maintain control. A thoughtful discussion follows in which people describe the beliefs that help them. The ones who feel they have very little control speculate on the beliefs they think might help them.

A coordinating committee member asks about the possibility of shifting the meeting to another night because of conflicts in several members' schedules. Another evening is found. Everyone agrees to meet on a different night next time. She also asks for a volunteer to type up a new membership list.

The meeting ends with the facilitator and other members expressing appreciation to individuals and to the group as a whole.

SUPPORT GROUP HOUSEKEEPING
Several practical aspects of an ongoing support group need to be handled. The two to four members of the coordinating committee can work with the group as a whole on these matters.

Information System

Coordinating committee members can be the ones who talk to potential new members and whose phone numbers are listed on any printed announcements. A membership list can serve as the basis for a phone chain that allows easy communication with the group between meetings. Each committee member calls two people, who each call two people, and so on through the list. The phone list indicates clearly who calls whom.

If the group wishes to grow larger, information can be distributed by networking through doctors, nurses, pharmacists, dietitians, friends, and relatives, as well as the local ADA chapter. If these channels fail to bring in the flocks, you can send press releases to neighborhood newspapers and make spot announcements on radio and television stations.

Group Size

This depends on space available and flexibility about meeting format. Large groups (more than ten members) can work effectively if they use subgroups and pairs fairly often to give everyone a chance to participate. Small groups can function well because of their close or personal nature.

Meeting Frequency

Every other week is probably the best schedule for the meetings. A weekly meeting may feel burdensome. Gathering once a month may not allow the group to develop momentum.

Meeting Place

Private homes, schools, churches, community centers, and bank meeting rooms are some potential meeting places. Some support groups meet in hospitals or public health buildings, but the association with illness may discourage some diabetics from coming. Using homes gives a more informal atmosphere. So long as the site is changed every month, meeting in homes does not become a burden on any one member.

Attendance

Some members may come regularly; others may drop in on the group only when they feel a special need. If the group is seen as only one function of a diabetes network, irregular attendance becomes

247

less frustrating to the people organizing it. They can stay in touch with members by phone. People who do not appear regularly will know that they can always get support by calling or visiting another member.

Screening and Referring

Occasionally, a diabetic who clearly needs professional physical or psychological assistance may come to a support group. This might be someone who simply does not have a physician, someone dangerously out of control metabolically, or someone with serious mental problems. Only people who seriously disrupt meetings process should be screened out. But the group should not try to solve problems that call for skilled help. Members should clearly indicate that professional guidance is needed and, if necessary, help the person find a physician or mental health professional.

OTHER ACTIVITIES OF THE SUPPORT NETWORK

Many other support activities can be initiated by your diabetes network. Your network may or may not be related to the local ADA chapter. Some chapters are fairly conservative, and diabetics may find independent organization more creative than working through the official group. The power of your network can be directed to opening such chapters to more input from diabetics. If your local ADA already has a good level of participation, any of the following activities might be easily accepted.

Training for Support Giving

Diabetics and family members can learn communication skills, stress management, problem-solving techniques, and guidelines as to the limits of peer support. Such a training program might be developed with the aid of mental health professionals from a local college or community clinic. (Crisis clinics often have volunteer training workshops that could be adapted to the needs of diabetics.)

Support for New Diabetics or Diabetics in Crisis

Beginning with visits to new diabetics still in the hospital after diagnosis, or at home if the person has not been hospitalized, network members can provide desperately needed encouragement and practical information to patients and their families. They can also visit people in the hospital after a major emergency such as diabetic coma, insulin reaction, or treatment for complications. This is a time when one's motivation to improve self-care is high. Contact with a fellow diabetic who has gone through similar crises and learned from them can be inspiring. Many ADA chapters have a special program for newly diagnosed diabetics.

Study Groups

People who are interested in learning about a particular subject might form a study group. For instance, three or four people interested in learning the intensive regimen might work together, helping each other master information they need to attain optimal control. This would make the learning process easier and ensure the emotional support needed to make such basic life-style changes. Or people with retinopathy could work together collecting and sharing information on the condition and its treatment.

Residential Houses

A live-in treatment center for adolescent diabetics was operated in Gainesville, Florida. This was available for children who had serious difficulties managing diabetes. The program included individual and family psychotherapy and intensive instruction in diabetes care. When families were willing to participate in the center activities, the children showed a significant improvement in management. A diabetes network could take the lead in developing profession and community support for the creation of such a center.

SUMMARY

We can draw powerful support from the community of people who have diabetes—the people who best understand the meaning of living with diabetes. We can work together to deal with feelings, to share information, and to learn the new skills needed for diabetic management. This can happen individually, through personal networking, or in support groups that meet regularly. Both styles of giving and receiving support are effective. If diabetes networks or groups do not exist in your area, you can create them using the information in this chapter.

Living Well With Yourself

Y ou are one of the best available sources of support for living well with diabetes. You are always there. You know yourself well. No one else can take care of you as well as you can.

The way you feel about yourself affects your willingness to live healthfully. And having diabetes can affect how you feel about yourself. The goal of this chapter is to help you become aware of the personal strengths and resources within you and to learn how to neutralize patterns that weaken your ability to care for yourself well.

You are resourceful. You are stronger, more creative, and more able than you usually realize. Some of these strengths may be hidden, some may be used in only one corner of your life, some may be expressed in negative ways. All your strengths can be redirected to increase your ability to live well with diabetes.

For example, the teenager who refuses to test or to follow diet or schedule is showing great strength of character. This strength is focused on rebellion and denial, but it is a valuable resource. This teen can learn to turn "won't power" into "will power" and improve his or her self-care.

After months of receiving support, a man acts the weak and pathetic victim of diabetic complications. He is overwhelmed, helpless, and depressed. Where is his strength now? Perhaps he is very strong in the tenacity with which he holds onto his role as victim, refusing to adapt to his situation. Feeling sorry for oneself consistently takes enormous energy. The self-image of weakness can be recycled into the true flexibility that a person needs to live well with the changes being experienced. The source of many negative feelings can be redirected into positive action. This redefinition of apparent flaws reveals a surprising new set of resources to apply in a healthy way.

Often you develop skills in one realm that you never use in the rest of your life. A photographer, for instance, learns about tests, measurements, precision, and combining a complex series of actions to achieve a given result. This person clearly has the basic skills needed for learning a diabetic regimen. A salesman is skilled at communication and persuasion. Perhaps he could use these strengths to sell himself an improved regimen.

Let's explore the store of resources you can use to live well with diabetes.

GOING INTO YOUR STOREHOUSE

Do this exercise in a quiet place where you won't be disturbed. At each step, close your eyes and allow both words and images to come to mind to help you find answers. Then make notes before you go to the next step.

1. Think of three areas of your life in which you are successful. See yourself in action. What strengths do you demonstrate here?
2. Think of three activities you truly enjoy. See yourself enjoying them. What personal qualities do you have that allow you to enjoy these activities?
3. What do you believe about yourself that enables you to act with success? With enjoyment?
4. Remember one of the best times in your life. Tell yourself the story of that time or recall scenes from it. What qualities of yours made this such a good time?

5. What strengths do you draw on in your work (or schoolwork, if you are a student)?

6. What personal strengths do you express in your relationships with friends?

7. What special qualities do you experience only when you are alone?

8. If you were to fulfill your true potential, what hidden qualities would you feel free to express?

9. What qualities would you like to develop?

10. What are some of your most negative traits or limitations?

11. Can you find a strength that each of these limitations contains? Can you think of a way to turn it to serve you?

12. Now, review your answers and examine how these qualities can:

    • Help you deal with diabetes.

    • Enable you to improve your physical self-care.

    • Help you feel better about having diabetes.

    • Assist when you are fearful or unwilling to do what you know you should do.

    • Allow you to resolve problems in relationships with others.

In the days after you first do this exercise, observe your life with these questions in mind. See what other traits you can find that could help you live well with diabetes. Continue exploring how the qualities you have just identified could improve your self-care.

Recognizing your inner resources will help you feel you have the power to deal with diabetes creatively. You can support this positive step by learning to overcome whatever negative self-image, limiting beliefs, self-judgments, emotional reactions, and behavioral patterns you experience because of diabetes.

A CASE OF MISTAKEN IDENTITY

Beliefs, feelings, and actions work together in a system that forms your sense of who you are. You tend to become closely identified with this system, forgetting that it is only a set of patterns you learned. Many of your limitations seem so real and deeply rooted that you can't imagine being anything more. You forget that you *learned* to see yourself as inadequate or helpless or rebellious or sick.

This mistaken identity become self-perpetuating. When you believe you are weak and unable to follow regimen, you act weak and unable. Then you may feel depressed and eat a pint of ice cream. Now even your sugar-clogged body feels uncomfortable. The evidence grows. Beliefs, feelings, and actions interact to reinforce each other and strengthen your negative self-image.

Responses to the threat of diabetic complications illustrate the way false identity functions as a circular system of beliefs, feelings, and actions.

If you believe that diabetic complications and an early death are inevitable, you are likely to feel anxious and fearful or possibly depressed. Or you may bury your feelings and live for the moment, hurrying heedlessly or ignoring the actions that could improve your odds. The idea creates the feeling. The idea and the feeling together lead to action. When you believe nothing will do any good, you may do little or nothing to manage diabetes. Or, with great anxiety, you may manage so compulsively that your stress level decreases the benefits of a tighter regimen.

On the other hand, if you believe you can reduce the risk of complications and early death, you become more hopeful. Anxiety may still be with you, but you learn to handle it and return to positive feelings. When you do, it is much easier to follow regimen and do the things that reduce your risks. Following regimen encourages positive feelings, and the immediate benefits support the belief that it does make a difference.

In both cases, beliefs affect feelings, beliefs and feelings affect actions, and the actions then affect the beliefs and feelings. Neither pattern is an inevitable response to having diabetes. Either way, you choose, consciously or unconsciously, the way you respond. You can choose to become aware of any of your beliefs, feelings, and actions relating to diabetes and to change them when they lead to negative results.

Change comes from seeking a deeper identity and detaching from seeing ourselves as our limitations. Not, "I am weak, sick, and unable," but, rather, "I am the person who can see without judgment these negative patterns. I am the person who chooses the life I live. I am the person who learns, who grows, and who changes. With this image of myself, I find it easier to use the strengths implicit in all I have learned."

With this self-image as a foundation, you can work for specific change at the level of belief, feeling, or behavior, whichever suits your style best. Or you may move from one level to another, integrating changes in beliefs, emotions, and actions.

CHANGING BELIEFS

A belief is a statement about yourself or about the world that shapes your life. It may be conscious or unconscious. Some beliefs give you power; some make you feel weak.

I am capable of learning to manage diabetes; or
I just can't manage; it's all too complex.

Diabetes is a teacher, challenging me to be my best; or
Having diabetes is a punishment.

People accept me as I am; or
People judge me for having diabetes and think I'm a bother.

Some beliefs are limiting, restricting your ability to act and producing feelings of hopelessness. Others are enabling, giving more power and encouraging positive feelings. The limiting beliefs are often so deeply ingrained that you believe them to be absolutely true. They tend to be reinforced by the feelings and actions that result from them.

If you believe you cannot control the amount you eat, your actions keep proving you to be correct. Then you feel depressed and eat even more to bury your feelings. Such vicious cycles can be broken by recognizing that beliefs like these are not truths but only learned habits of thinking. When you view them as mental habits rather than facts, you begin to reduce the power they have over you.

Of course, many of your beliefs will be related to factual knowledge. It is a fact that diabetics have a higher risk of kidney failure than nondiabetics. It is a mistake to build on this fact the belief: "I will have kidney failure." A more appropriate belief is "I can act to reduce my risk of kidney failure." This one gives you power and also has a factual basis, because most diabetics do not develop kidney disease.

UNCOVERING YOUR BELIEFS ABOUT YOU AND DIABETES

Watch for hidden beliefs as you work on diabetes learning, especially at times when you feel stuck. Catalog the major beliefs that both empower you and limit you in your life with diabetes.

Some techniques for uncovering beliefs are as follows:

1. Ask yourself a repeating question: "What do I believe about _____ (diabetes, home blood testing, complications, my diabetic regimen, how diabetes affects my relationships, my doctor, my old age, etc.)?"

   Another way of doing this is to alternate between "What do I believe about _____ ?" and "What should I believe about?"

   Repeat the question for each topic a dozen or so times, writing down whatever beliefs come to mind.

   Example: What do I believe about myself as a diabetic?

   Beliefs: I am more vulnerable than other people. I should get special consideration. I will probably die in my sixties. My problems are a bother to others. I am unwilling to follow a strict regimen; this is a sign of weakness. Others should take care of me. I really want to be fully responsible for myself. I have learned to live better because of diabetes. I value my life because I know how vulnerable I am.

2. In a concrete situation — especially at a time of distress, frustration, or failure — ask "What beliefs have created this problem?"

   Example: I have "forgotten" to take my morning dose of insulin and don't notice the signs of high blood sugar until late afternoon. (I am scheduled for a job interview that day.)

   Beliefs: If I'm sick, I won't be held responsible for anything. Diabetes isn't really serious. I'm invulnerable. Hurting my body is better than facing difficult challenges. I'm weak and deserve to be hurt. I want someone to take care of me.

3. Choose an enabling belief you would like to adopt. Calmly repeat it, holding out one hand as though it were speaking the belief. Let the other hand state the limiting beliefs that oppose it. Keep repeating until you understand the conflicting beliefs and the conflict starts to dissolve.

   Example: Right hand: A blood sugar test is free of judgments.
   Left hand: It shows I've eaten like a pig.
   Right: A blood sugar test is free of judgments.
   Left: Big Brother is watching me.
   Right: A blood sugar test is free of judgments.
   Left: It just makes me worry to see how high the test can be.
   Right: A blood sugar test is free of judgments.
   Left: Can I ever learn to control myself?
   Right: A blood sugar test is free of judgments.
   Left: I'd like to stop worrying so much.
   Right: A blood sugar test is free of judgments.
   Left: I really want to know the truth.

4. Write or speak a fantasy in which you are easily doing something that now feels difficult or impossible. Write down all the reasons the fantasy could not come true. Then write down the beliefs that would enable you to make the fantasy real.

After completing any of these exercises, underline the beliefs that seem most powerful, indicating the ones that limit you and the ones that free you. Then choose the limiting ones you would like to change.

Bringing limiting beliefs into the open is a first step toward changing them. Sometimes the new awareness itself is enough to dissolve the power a belief has over your feelings or behavior. Or you may have to take further steps to replace the belief with one that enables you to live as you wish.

There are many techniques for changing beliefs. Some are developed by behavioral psychologists, others by people in the human potential movement. (Techniques 3 and 4 in the preceding section are good for changing as well as uncovering beliefs.) A few techniques for changing beliefs are as follows:

1. Create a positive phrase in present tense that clearly states the belief you want to adopt. Use your own words. Find ways of reminding yourself that this new belief is entering your life (for example, put signs around the house and repeat the phrase with feeling every day).

   Example: To replace the phrase "I am unable to follow diabetic regimen" try "I am improving my regimen step by step. I am able to continue until I have excellent control." The new belief is encouraging but not overwhelming.

2. Relax and imagine yourself doing the specific things that would indicate you are living according to the new belief. Let a concrete scene unfold in your mind where you see (or feel) yourself acting as you wish to.

   Example: With "I am improving my regimen . . ." I see myself testing blood, keeping records, rejecting extra food, exercising, and doing the other things that mean improvement for me.

3. Recycle scenes from your life in which a powerful limiting belief was active. Recall the scene in detail, noting how the belief was expressed in your feelings and actions. Then imagine how you would have lived the scene if you had held the new belief at that time.

   Example: My old belief is "I must keep my diabetes a secret. I'll be rejected if people know."

   I'm embarrassed at lunch because a friend keeps insisting I eat her cake and I don't want to tell her I have diabetes. I'm afraid she won't go out with me if she knows. I get angry and uptight. She is hurt.

   I want to adopt the new belief "I am open about having diabetes. Anyone who rejects me isn't worth having around anyway."

   I see myself at lunch, smiling when my friend presses me to eat the cake. I say, "I've got a little secret I'm going to let you in on. I'd love to eat that cake but I really can't. I have diabetes." I sigh as she responds with surprise and caring. I answer her questions without embarrassment and feel deeply relieved to have torn down that wall between us.

4. Trace the roots of beliefs and cut them. You learn your beliefs. The strongest ones you learn from your parents or other people who have had a parental influence. When you have trouble weakening a particular belief, it helps to determine who you learned it from. You can even see yourself giving it back to the source, or cutting the connection. With a belief specific to diabetes, you may have to look for a generic idea underneath it.

Example: I have a set of related beliefs: "I am more vulnerable than other people. I should get special consideration. I will probably die in my sixties." These beliefs are clearly from my father, who had rheumatic fever as a child. He was sure he had cancer years before it finally developed. He was 67 when he died.

I would rather believe: "I am both vulnerable and strong. I will give myself special consideration by living well. I will die when I die, and I can't predict when that will be."

I see myself telling my father why I won't follow his example anymore. I give him a box containing his old beliefs and he throws it into the fire. He smiles at me and says, "Go ahead. You are free to outlive me."

Beliefs are closely related to emotions. Working at the level of beliefs can help relieve negative feelings. And it helps to have tools for working directly at the emotional level.

DEALING WITH FEELINGS

Living with a complex, life-threatening condition like diabetes adds many emotional triggers to our lives. The threat of long-term complications creates an underlying anxiety for many of us. A delayed meal, a cut foot, or having no sweets available when blood sugar swoops low can become major emergencies. Diabetes even affects our relationships with others.

Our feelings have very direct effects on diabetic control through the stress response and through their effect on our willingness to follow regimen.

Throughout the book, we have examined a number of the emotional issues specific to diabetes. We focus here on ways of gaining awareness of and handling your feelings as they relate to your self-care.

The following exercises will help you sharpen your emotional awareness and capacity for more effectively working with your feelings.

In this work, you may find strong emotions coming to the surface (particularly if you are in the midst of dealing with a tough situation). If you are not used to feeling things very deeply, this can be an alarming experience. You may want the aid of a friend, support group, or professional.

What am I feeling?

1. Breathe. A very simple way of finding out what you are feeling is to sit quietly and breathe a bit more deeply than usual. Feel your stomach, your chest, your throat, and your face. Relax and breathe and allow the feelings to emerge.

2. Imagine. Visualize in whatever sense you use (sight, sound, body movement, smell, or taste) to form images of what you are feeling. Let scenes unfold in your mind that act out your feelings.

3. Move. Let your body tell you what you're feeling by moving or dancing. Allow the movements to come spontaneously, without worrying about appearing graceful.

4. Descend. Often there are layers of feeling below the emotion you're conscious of, all crying to come into awareness. The experience of being stuck in a feeling may stem from there being deeper feelings underneath it. Breathing, relaxing, and visualizing are ways to sink into these deeper layers. After you've experienced each level, ask yourself, "What feeling is below this one?" Then sink down, as though going through the floor.

(The exercises for getting in touch with beliefs in the previous section are also likely to bring feelings to the surface.)

Just getting in touch with an emotion often will be all you need to do about it. You feel it for a time, you may express it, and then go on with life. At other times, a feeling may seem eternal and inescapable. Perhaps you've just seen a diabetic relative who has recently become blind, and you feel down for a week. You've been on a food binge for two days and are filled with guilt and anger at yourself. You can probably supply your own examples all too well.

What you can do about feelings

1. **Accept what you are feeling and experience it.**
   Don't compound the problem by chastising yourself for feeling the way you do. You have every right to feel whatever you are feeling. Use the techniques described above to explore this experience with a sense of curiosity.

2. **Express the feeling.**
   With the mode of expression that feels most appropriate, communicate the emotion that you feel stuck in. Draw or paint, write poems, speak to a friend (or into a recorder), sing, or dance. Communication often enables you to let go of a feeling that seems endless.

3. **Detach from the feeling.**
   Detachment is not suppression of emotion. It is a refocusing of awareness to a broader sense of yourself. The emotion is there, along with the detailed experience of your bodily sensations, your perceptions of the world around you, and a center of awareness that observes your feeling, sensing, and perceiving.

   Example: I am feeling hopeless. Depressed. Black. I can't escape this feeling. I sense my feet on the rug, the texture of the rug. My breath is shallow. My nose is dry as I breathe. I want to escape, go to sleep. I've never felt such deep despair. I see wind blowing trees outside the window. I hear the wind in the leaves. My stomach is tight. I smell the rose across the room. I hear music from downstairs. It's a song I like. My chest relaxes when I think of the words. Depression seems like a ball inside of me instead of me locked inside it. The ball is dissolving. My breath is deep now. I have tears in my eyes. I'm alive again.

"It should recompense us well to study the qualities of our emotional spectrum, studying them not as a pathologist dissects but as an artist cares for his materials. Or perhaps as one who loves. For the quality of our emotions belongs to ourselves perhaps more than any other aspect of being. To love ourselves, then, means to love these pure qualities. In a strange way purely expressed emotions engender a degree of empathy and love as part of our interrelatedness. 'Seeing' them as they are eases the burden and boundary that separates man from man."

— Dr. Manfred Clynes

Changing behavior

Discussion of the third area of change important to living well with diabetes, how we act, extends throughout this book. The introduction and Chapter 1 in particular explore the techniques and attitudes that support changing our behavior. Rather than repeating any of these themes we ask you to review the introduction.

TELLING THE STORY OF YOURSELF

Earlier in this chapter, we emphasized the interaction between the three levels of life: beliefs, feelings, and behavior. Now we would like to explore the integration of the three. Work on any one of the levels produces change, and at some point you will want to bring them all together. This may be after you've gained greater clarity or it may be when you are feeling so stuck you don't know what else to do.

A powerful way of integrating levels is to simply tell your story. See your whole situation by telling yourself what is happening. Move back and forth between what you are feeling, the beliefs and mental images that surround your feeling, and the things you are doing. See how the different levels reinforce each other. Identify the specific limiting beliefs that have gotten you stuck, if that's where you are. Recognize how your actions feed the feeling and demonstrate the truth of the beliefs.

You can write this narrative or say it aloud to a friend or into a tape recorder. Use the most direct language you can.

Example: I'm frustrated, angry, and guilty. I've been on a binge for two days and can't stop. I have no self-control. I'm probably taking years off my life when I do this. I must hate myself. I started eating Tuesday morning, just after Dr. Blast told me my tests were lousy and that I really had to take better care of myself or I'd be in for real trouble. I've been trying so damned hard and it just doesn't do any good. Nothing I do works out right. Why can't he understand how hard I've been trying?

Now I'm poisoning myself with candy and pastries. My blood sugar must be 500! Every time I eat something I feel worse. I'm angry at how weak I am. Afraid I'll never learn how to take care of myself. Afraid of what this is doing to me.

Oh! There's a blind woman at the newsstand in the lobby of Dr. Blast's building. I never even noticed her before Tuesday. I forgot about her right away, but now I can see her face so clearly. I'm terrified I'll go blind like her. I don't believe there's anything I can do. I can't do anything right.

No wonder I'm in such a pit. I must be stronger than I think if I can keep myself feeling this bad and acting so stupid for so long. My eyes are still fine. There's still lots I can do to keep them that way. Dr. Blast was worried and doesn't know how to be gentle. I can be gentle. Gentle and strong.

This example focuses on a specific situation. You can also gain great insight by telling your story in a more expansive fashion. Describing your life with diabetes through the years can give you extraordinary perspective, balance, and understanding. You might do this with a friend who has diabetes or another medical condition, swapping stories at length.

When you have reached a point of achievement, narrating the tale of how you got there both rewards and reinforces the changes you have made. You need not be bashful about giving yourself credit for the work of living well with diabetes.

Living well with yourself is, finally, a matter of balance — balance between emotions, intellect, body, and spirit; balance between the needs of diabetes and the other demands in your life; and balance between acceptance and reaching out for something better. As this sense of equilibrium grows, you will find that it endures even in times of turbulence and upset as a deep source of inner support.

Section V

LIVING WELL WITH DIABETIC COMPLICATIONS

Neutralizing The Threat Of Complications

"*C*omplications?! I don't want to hear about them. That's too depressing.*"*

If that's the way you're feeling when you turn to this section, we can sympathize. After living with diabetes for about forty years each, your authors have experienced all the fears and uncertainties you may feel. One of us, Ernest, has experienced a major complication — temporary loss of vision in one eye and then when that cleared, a temporary loss of vision in the other. Treatment was successful, and Ernest's vision is still clear six years later. So we know there is hope to counterbalance the threats implicit in this subject.

Absorb the challenging information contained in the next three chapters, and you will have the ability to improve your odds for avoiding complications. You may limit, postpone, or even avoid altogether the effects of diabetic complications on your future health. You will know what you can do to increase your chances of preventing them. You will know what their early warning signs are so you can seek treatment in time. If you are already dealing with their unwelcome arrival, you will have tools to avoid their dominating your life, no matter what disabilities they bring.

267

Complications are not an inevitable process in diabetes. How we live with diabetes can slow and even reverse the development of its side effects. So make a date with these chapters — today, tomorrow, next week, next month, whenever you're ready, but soon!

Roget's Thesaurus comes close to capturing the emotional quality of the word *complication* when it gives *entanglement, snag, snarl,* and *difficulty* as synonyms. Diabetes by itself is a relatively friendly condition. But when we consider its potential complications, it can become intensely threatening.

An essential part of the diabetes self-care package is staying open to new information about this topic we love to avoid. Face the fears that it brings up, and go ahead and face the facts. This doesn't mean studying every last detail of what can go wrong, but you do need to know the following:

• Changes in regimen and life-style that will reduce your risk.

• Early warning signs that enable you to seek prompt treatment if a complication starts to develop (both laboratory test results and signs that you can recognize yourself).

• Treatments now available and under research for each complication.

• Ways of reducing anxiety over the possibility of developing diabetic complications (or of dealing with feelings that come up if they do begin).

• When you know these things, you have the power to turn the odds in your favor. You may be able to avoid complications altogether, or if they do develop, escape their more serious consequences.

In these three chapters:

• We examine recent developments in diabetes care that can reduce the risk of complications emerging.

• We offer attitudes and techniques for dealing with the anxiety, fear, and uncertainty engendered by the threat of major complications.

• We explore the physical and emotional needs of the person who is experiencing the onset of a major complication of diabetes.

• We discuss the specific long-term complications of diabetes and the steps you can take to improve your chance of escaping them.

Taking It Easy

No other aspect of diabetes education is as promising — or as threatening — as the subject of diabetic complications. We want you to live well while you work with these chapters. That means taking it easy, pausing, relaxing, using other techniques for reducing stress, and remembering that the very act of reducing stress is likely to reduce your risk of developing complications. Our purpose is to convey the idea that you can do many things to reduce this risk, not to overwhelm you with the risk itself.

Special care must be taken in discussing complications with diabetic children.

NEUTRALIZING THE THREAT

We are at risk for serious disabilities and early death, yet we can live well with the risks and the anxiety they evoke. What could better express the central concept of this book? We can reduce both the risk and the anxiety. Even if we are disabled by one or more complications, we can still go on living well.

We have said many times that diabetes is a teacher. Here the lessons are powerful: living peacefully with physical and emotional risk; accepting vulnerability while living a full life; coming to terms with aging and mortality; identifying with inner healthfulness, no matter what the state of your body. When you deal with the questions raised by complications, you can't help but grow as a human being.

A medical dictionary defines *complication* as a disease process that may or may not accompany a primary disease. Possibly you have had a doctor who warned you of your higher risk of stroke or heart attack. Or you may have diabetic friends or relatives who have become blind or whose kidneys have failed. You may have read of the diabetic nerve disorders that can result in loss of feeling, in pain, or in impotence.

The possibility of developing these complications is the most serious consequence of diabetes, so serious that many of us avoid facing it. (Avoidance has been reinforced by the tendency of some parents and doctors to use the threat of complications as a motivation-through-fear device.)

269

"I ignored my fear of complications. I felt good so I didn't give them a thought. I knew that complications existed for other people —but not for me. "Then all of a sudden I was realizing, I'm a little lazier, more lethargic. I feel drained. It gradually got worse, to the point of my kidneys failing."

— Jim

We feel that hope is a much better motivator than fear. You have a solid new basis for hope — you can limit or avoid the effects of complications. To do this you need to be informed, and you need to find the willingness to act on what you learn.

Three Anxiety-Reducing Ideas Concerning Complications

1. Complications are not inevitable. You have a risk but, fortunately, no guarantee that you will develop major complications of diabetes.
2. You can reduce your level of risk by improving your diabetes self-care program, maintaining better control of blood sugar and blood pressure, practicing stress management, and exercising regularly.
3. Treatment for most complications is becoming more and more effective. In many cases their negative results can be reversed or reduced, especially when detected early enough.

These three ideas provide an essential context for considering diabetic complications, so we will examine them here in detail.

Complications are not inevitable.

When you read statistical reports on diabetic complications, you may believe you cannot escape them. "Blindness is 25 times more common in individuals with type I diabetes" is a typical statement. Those are dramatic odds, but actually, less than 1 percent of us loses our vision. The majority of diabetics do not become blind. Even without doing anything special, you have a good chance of escaping a major handicap.

Statistics are misleading — if not terrifying — for a very fundamental reason: They are based on an earlier era of diabetes care when the medical knowledge and tools we have now were not available. It was a time when individuals were much less interested in a healthy life-style. Some important research questions are still unanswered, but the statistics for the present generation of diabetics will be improved.

Michael and Cousin Melvin

Ernest counseled a 13-year-old boy named Michael who had developed diabetes six months earlier. Michael's doctor had asked him to test his blood sugar, but he seldom did so. "It reminds me of being in the hospital at the beginning. They were testing me all the time," Michael complained. Ernest asked what the tests had meant to Michael. "They remind me I'm diabetic. I want to forget it. I don't care." Michael talked more about being in the hospital. "I kept hearing about my uncles and how they died of diabetes when they were in their forties."

"Michael, I think it's time you heard about my cousin Melvin. He became diabetic the year after they first used insulin with people. He's almost 80 now and he's still going strong. No complications most of that time. What happened to your uncles doesn't happen to all of us!"

Ernest asked Michael if he'd like to adopt a cousin. Melvin agreed to this, and the next week Michael said he'd told everyone about his new cousin Melvin. He wanted them to know he had a chance.

You can reduce your risk by improving your management of diabetes.
You can tip the odds in your favor by the way you live. Older studies of people maintaining a moderate level of control showed they were less likely to develop major complications. Now that a near-normal level of control is possible, you can reduce your risk even more. The risk is still there, but it is much smaller. Diet, exercise, blood pressure control, and stress management also make complications less likely to occur.

(The development of complications is determined by a number of factors other than metabolic control. Inheritance, stress, and other matters of life-style may also play significant roles in any particular case. So it is possible to be well controlled and still experience a serious impairment.)

271

Treatment for most complications is becoming more effective.
If a complication does develop, you are more and more likely to find a treatment that will reverse or limit its advance. This is especially true if you are aware of early warning signs and seek treatment promptly. Thousands of diabetics are escaping disability thanks to laser treatment, kidney transplantation, early treatment of foot disorders, and other new developments.

But There Are No Guarantees
In spite of all these advances, real risks are still present for you. There are many variables: how long you have had diabetes, at what age it began, the kind of life-style you have had, your genetic makeup, and other individual factors still poorly understood. You can do everything possible to reduce your risks of developing complications, and they may still occur.

So diabetes makes a clear demand: Learn to do your best and at the same time live well with uncertainty. Learn to cope with anxiety and return to hope, no matter what happens. This is not too different from the demand the world at large makes upon us all.

You and Diabetic Complications
This exercise will help you see how you relate to the possibility of diabetic complications developing. Answer spontaneously, even though the feeling or belief that comes may seem "wrong."

1. **What did you feel as you read the beginning of this chapter?**_____

   _____

2. **Which of the following statements describe(s) the way you have dealt with complications in the past?**

   ____I don't want to think about the possibility of complications.

   ____I worry about them quite a bit.

   ____It makes me angry that diabetes could do that to me.

   ____I do everything I can to reduce the risk.

   ____I could do more to reduce the risk.

   ____I just do everything I want to, since I don't know how long I'll last.

___I probably spend too much time taking care of my diabetes.

___I feel depressed quite a bit.

___I feel guilty because I have not taken good care of myself.

3. **I believe I will probably live to the age of**_____
4. **The complication I fear the most is**_____
5. **I tend to believe**

___I will escape major complications.

___I will certainly develop a major complication.

___There is nothing I can do to change what will happen.

___Complications are punishment for not taking care of myself.

___If one complication develops, others will surely follow.

___If I become (or am) disabled in any way, my life will be damaged beyond repair.

___I will be able to learn to live well with the disability.

___I will be a burden on others.

Other beliefs I hold about complications include_____
_____

Positive beliefs that would neutralize any negative beliefs listed above include_____
_____

6. **Is there anyone close to you who keeps reminding you of what can go wrong? Who uses threats to motivate you? Have any of your doctors done this?**_____
7. **My present level of control is** _____ . **My level of regimen is** _____ . **(See your questionnaire results in Chapter 4.)**
8. **I intend to make the following improvements in self-care in the next months** _____
9. **I can get support for my feelings about complications and for making changes from** _____

10. **I do not intend to make any changes in self-care at this time because**

___I am already doing everything possible.

___I do not believe it would do any good.

___I do not feel I have the time and energy needed.

___I feel the changes would reduce my freedom or pleasure.

___I feel overwhelmed by the demands of diabetes.

___Other_____

___If someone you loved gave the reason(s) checked above for not improving his or her care of diabetes, what would you say to that person?_____

Make an appointment with yourself to reopen this question in a few months. Mark it on your calendar.

Reflect on your answers to these questions. Look for changes in beliefs or behavior that will help you to lessen the threat of complications. For example, if you do not feel you have the time and energy needed to improve your self-care program, ask yourself what changes in your life would give you that time.

DEALING WITH ANXIETY ABOUT COMPLICATIONS

Undoutedly the best way to deal with anxiety about diabetic complications is to do as much as possible to reduce your risk of developing them. A complete diabetic regimen makes complications less likely at the same time that it handles your day-to-day need for metabolic control. The following list indicates the things you can do.

WAYS YOU CAN REDUCE YOUR RISKS

1. Improve your metabolic control and continue improving it to the best level you are comfortable with.
2. Learn to handle stress well.

3. Follow a diabetic diet that features low fat and high fiber, as well as limited sweets and rapidly absorbed carbohydrates.

4. Exercise regularly.

5. If you are overweight, lose weight.

6. Act to prevent high blood pressure by controlling stress, weight, and salt consumption. Seek treatment for hypertension if your blood pressure is high (above 140/90).

7. If you smoke, quit.

8. Get the amount of sleep and rest that you need.

9. Know the warning signs for each complication.

10. Consider taking a multivitamin pill even though there is no compelling evidence that this will do more good than a balanced diet.

Except for item 1, this is the same prescription for good health doctors give nondiabetics. It is especially important for you because each item on it will improve your odds of avoiding other diseases as well as escaping diabetic complications (or of limiting them if they have already started.)

You may have already adopted some of the measures and need to make only a few changes. Or you may need to alter your life in every area. Begin where you feel most willing to change; or, if your sense of urgency is great, begin with metabolic control, the most fundamental way of reducing risk. You give yourself the best chance for a long and healthful life by following the complete preventive program as soon as you can. At least give yourself the benefit of some stress reduction and self-acceptance if you choose nothing else from this list. Only you can define the ingredients of a life-style that will work for you.

More on Reducing Anxiety

Assuming that you are doing everything on the preceding list or are in the process of learning to, you may still experience anxiety. So one of the useful skills to develop is the art of living well with uncertainty. For all the talk of risks and odds and possibilities, you simply cannot know if you will or will not end up with one or more diabetic complications. You can do your best to avoid them, and then a special sort of surrender to uncertainty is necessary. You squarely face the possibility that you will become disabled as a consequence of diabetes. And with equal power, you face the possibility that you will remain free of major complications. You decide you will live well with yourself, no matter which path is given to you. And you return to the immediate task of living well right now.

Learning about complications should be a gentle process in which you use stress-reduction techniques to their fullest: relaxation, meditation, prayer, and whatever else is effective for you. Take in information in small doses, and give yourself intermissions that allow you to focus on positive, optimistic aspects of life. Participation in a diabetes support group or one-to-one conversations with other diabetics can help you deal with the feelings that come up. Some diabetics will find a few counseling sessions helpful while they are dealing with this threatening subject.

Another way of dealing with your feelings at this point is to explore the beliefs and attitudes you have about the possible consequences of diabetes. Neutralizing crippling beliefs and adopting more positive ones can help relieve the anxiety, depression, or anger that you may experience. For instance, a typical belief is, "I've been so out of control that I can't possibly escape complications." In any individual case, this is a belief, not a fact. A more useful belief to replace it is, "If I improve control now, I may still escape major complications."

IF YOU DECIDE NOT TO ACT NOW TO REDUCE THE RISKS OF COMPLICATIONS

You may feel unwilling at this time to make the changes in your life that would lessen the risk of complications. If so, it is vitally important that you make this a conscious choice. Look at the reasons you give for maintaining your present level of self-care. Discuss them with someone you trust. Explore them fully within yourself, through writing, inner dialogue, prayer, meditation, or whatever means works for you.

See if you can find a new point of view that allows you to begin making the necessary changes while still dealing with whatever is valid in your reasons for not changing. For example, if lack of time is your main reason for not changing, find changes that do not require additional time, or learn to use your time more effectively.

276

And, if you consciously choose not to change, accept your decision and any anxiety that goes a long with it. You are increasing a set of risks in your life, but you are not guaranteeing the development of complications. We all make risk/benefit decisions about our lives each day. Self-acceptance is itself healthful for body and mind. And it gives you a positive foundation for making new decisions in the future.

We suggest you make a date with yourself a few months in the future to reopen the question of what you are then willing to do to reduce the risk of complications. Your life may or may not have changed enough that other choices are available.

If Complications Develop

"*How long can you mope and pine after disaster? You've got to ultimately pick up your life and sing.*"

Rev. Karl Baehr
(Diabetes Forecast, *Nov./Dec. 1983*)

"*When my kidneys started to go, it stimulated me to educate myself. I put time and energy into finding out what I could do to help myself. It was a great deal of motivation. It scared me a lot. I knew how sick I could become. That terrified me — what my body could do with me having no control over it. I also realized there was something I could do to gain control.*"

— James

THE EARLY SIGNS

Usually diabetic complications show early signs of development. They may appear in laboratory tests; you may notice the signs yourself, or your doctor may notice them during a routine exam. Your ophthalmologist may tell you that you have background retinopathy, a condition found in the majority of people who have had diabetes for ten years or longer. Or your physician may tell you the beginning signs of kidney disease are present, shown by protein in your urine.

You may shrug off the diagnosis, or you may find the news very disturbing. But this "bad news" can provide the motivation you may need to improve your regimen dramatically. Action now may enable you to delay or halt the progress of the disorder, and perhaps even reverse it. (The early signs of each complication are described in the next chapter. If you know these warning signals, you will be able to avoid delay in beginning preventive treatment.)

THE CRISIS BEGINS

The onset of a major diabetic complication is a crisis, no matter how well you handle it. It reminds you of your vulnerability. The beginning of one disorder may suggest that others will follow. You may feel guilty for the times you have neglected your diabetes. You may feel angry and frustrated if excellent self-care has not prevented complications. At the same time such feelings come up, you may have to make serious decisions about treatment and changes in life-style.

All of this adds up to a major life challenge that demands your time and energy and the support of others. You will live well through this crisis if you deal with the many practical, emotional, and social needs it generates.

At first, however, you may react to the crisis in a way that allows you to deal with the shock of diagnosis. Some people go through a stage of denying that anything is happening and try to ignore both the doctor's recommendations and their own feelings. Others enter a period of withdrawal and defeat while they absorb the impact of the news. Still others become convinced that the worst will happen to them. Some feel guilty. Others go on a food binge, believing that nothing does any good anyway.

Understand what your own pattern of response to diagnosis of a complication has been. If your response is negative, do not fault yourself for reacting in this way. You had to deal with a stressful piece of news. But recognize the limitations of this initial reaction and allow yourself to move on to a more functional response.

Treatment and Self-Care

You may have to absorb new information quickly, learn new skills, make important decisions, and change some basic elements of your life at this time. These changes may feel overwhelming, especially when you are still trying to deal with your feelings. You can regain control of the situation if you clearly define the tasks facing you. Break them down into manageable steps. Establish how much time is needed, what resources and support you must line up, and what information you must acquire. By organizing the demands, you tame them. (The questionnaire at the end of this chapter will help guide you through this process.)

You will probably be faced with decisions about treatment and regimen. In some cases, specialists may describe fairly complicated procedures that would be difficult to follow even if you were not under emotional stress. If you do not understand what is being recommended, say so, and ask for explanations in language you do understand. If you still don't understand, ask your internist or family practitioner to help you. Ask if there are written materials or audiovisual aids describing the treatment. You have a right to understand fully what you are being asked to undergo.

You should know what the risks of the recommended treatment are. What are the odds for success? For a negative outcome? What is likely to happen if you do nothing? Are any alternative treatments available? If you have any significant doubt about the course of treatment your doctor suggests, seek a second opinion from another physician with equivalent expertise. (For instance, do not go to a general practitioner or an internist for a second opinion about eye treatment. You need an ophthalmologist, preferably one who specializes in retinal diseases or even diabetic retinopathy.) If your doctor does not have much experience working with diabetes, you probably should find someone who does to guide treatment of the complications.

In addition to prescribing a specific treatment, your doctor may suggest that you improve your regimen of self-care at this time. Improvement in blood sugar control may help you handle the condition that has developed. It may also make other complications less likely to occur. You will need to *proceed cautiously in tightening metabolic control if you have advanced retinopathy or kidney disease.* In a number of studies, these complications worsened (at least initially) when good control was gained too quickly. When retinopathy (at the proliferative stage) or kidney disease is clinically evident, blood sugar levels must be lowered gradually, over a period of three to six months. This is true whether control is improved through multiple insulin injections or the insulin pump.

You may need to be cautious in your exercise and physical activity at this time, depending upon the specific complication you have. This is especially true if you are starting an exercise program after years of relative inactivity. You should discuss exercise and physical activity with your doctor. You may want to enroll in a medically supervised exercise program that monitors your physical condition.

This may also be a good time to improve your diet. You can begin by eating more fresh vegetables and fruits and cutting down on animal and saturated fats and salt. You could add more beans, pasta, and other high-fiber foods to your meals.

Coping with the Emotional Impact of Complications

Having a diabetic complication is inherently stressful, so this is an especially important time to manage stress well. Stress from any source interferes with your control of blood sugar, and it plays a role in the development of diabetic complications. Do your best to limit other sources of stress in your life. Learn to relax under anxiety.

The emotional impact of the changes in your body is a highly individual matter. You may feel overwhelmed, or you may come out swinging. You may feel frightened or depressed or angry. You may do your best not to feel anything at all. If a major body function is involved (loss of vision, amputation, or kidney failure), it is natural to go through a grieving process. In any case, you are likely to find yourself going through a series of emotional reactions, rather than experiencing just one. Allow yourself to feel what you are feeling, but if you become stuck or find that you are unable to act, ask for help.

Family and friends may be able to assist. Or a support group, guidance from others who have gone through what you are facing, or professional counseling may be required. This is a time when most people need some form of support. Immediate family members usually experience their own stress about what is happening to you, so it is best not to rely solely on them. (In some cases, their input may be so negative that it is better to seek all support elsewhere.)

Other diabetics who have weathered the storm will know what you are going through. They may be able to help you sort things out at a practical level and offer encouragement at the same time. If informal support is not enough, you may want to see a medical social worker or a psychotherapist who specializes in medical counseling.

The onset of a diabetic complication is a time when you may gain a new appreciation of your own internal resources for coping. Such a crisis often puts you in touch with your greatest personal strengths and spirituality. You may gain encouragement from remembering the resources that helped you through difficult times in the past. Chapter 14, "Living Well with Yourself," describes many techniques to help you handle your emotional responses at this critical time.

IF COMPLICATIONS DEVELOP

The diagnosis of a diabetic complication is a major life challenge. This questionnaire will help you clarify what is happening, how you are responding, and what you need to do.

1. What diabetic complication(s) has your doctor diagnosed?____

2. At what stage of development is the complication?_____

3. What treatment does your doctor recommend?_____

4. What risks are involved with this treatment?_____

5. What are the odds for a successful outcome?_____

6. What does your doctor think will happen if you do nothing?_

7. What changes in regimen or life-style does your doctor suggest?_

8. Do you think you will have any trouble making these changes?_

    (If so, go to Chapter 3, "Help!")

9. Outline the individual steps you need to take to make these changes. Also include any decisions you need to make about treatment or things you have to do to undergo treatment.___

_____

_____

_____

10. How are you coping with the diagnosis of the complication so far?

___I am trying to ignore what the doctor told me.

___I am ignoring my feelings.

___I am paying attention to my feelings.

___I am reading everything I can get my hands on about the complication.

___I am talking with people who have been through this.

___I am feeling withdrawn. I don't want to talk to anyone.

___I am worrying a lot and dwelling on the worst possible outcome.

___I am blaming myself and feeling guilty.

___I am living it up. I'll enjoy myself while I can.

___I am doing everything possible to take care of myself.

___I am becoming too dependent on my family or friends.

___I feel absolutely overwhelmed.

___Other_____

11. How would you like to change your reaction?_____

_____

12. How are you feeling about the diagnosis?

___Angry

___Frightened or anxious

___Guilty

___Depressed

___Hopeless

___Hopeful

___Grief-stricken

___Calm

___Other _____

13. What support can you count on? (Name the people.)

Family _____

Friends _____

Diabetes network _____

Other support network _____

Professional and religious counselors _____

Other _____

14. If you do not now have enough support, what steps can you take to find the help you need?_____

_____

FOR YOUR FAMILY OR FRIENDS . . .

Someone close to you is going through a crisis, and, most likely, you are too. Give him or her all the support and encouragement you can, and seek the same from others for yourself. This is a time when you will all be drawing on inner resources, and, with luck, becoming closer.

If, at first, you find your diabetic (or yourself) reacting negatively, understand that something shocking has occurred. If the negative reaction in your loved one persists, gently suggest some appropriate responses. If your own reactions remain negative, seek outside help for yourself and try to find others who can give support to your friend until you can.

Find a balance in the assistance you give. Issues of dependency may arise. Your friend may feel he or she is being a burden or may attempt to be overly independent. Help define where help is and is not needed. Don't reinforce feelings of inadequacy by doing things he or she would rather take care of. But also be realistic about any physical limits imposed by the disorder.

Complications Simplified

"I *want to know the risks I'm facing as a diabetic. Why stick my head in the sand and pretend I'm not worried? I tried that and it didn't work worth a damn. I kept hearing horror stories, anyway. I finally pushed through my fears and read about all the things that could happen to me. Glad I did. I found out what I could do to improve my odds for avoiding them."*

— *Marybeth, 50 years old,*
Forty years diabetic with only minor complications

In this chapter we review background information on the causes of diabetic complications and the possibility of reversing or preventing them. We also offer a comprehensive program for reducing your risks of developing complications. We review in detail the nature of the major disorders of diabetes, specific preventive measures, and the options for treatment.

If you feel tempted to skip this chapter, we suggest you read at least the sections describing what you can do to avoid the various complications. This is the most important reading you can do. Then, later, return to read the rest of the chapter.

WHY DO DIABETIC COMPLICATIONS DEVELOP?

Although medical library shelves bulge with studies trying to answer this question, it still is not fully resolved. Still, the broad outlines of an answer do exist.

One major explanation centers on the many abnormalities found in the system of a person with poorly controlled diabetes. The basic inner ecology is profoundly out of balance, especially in the circulatory and hormonal systems. When blood sugar is chronically high, excess sugar disrupts the structure and biochemical processes within the body's cells, particularly those of blood vessels, nerves, kidneys, and eyes. These repeated imbalances create the building blocks for diabetic complications.

One imbalance caused by high blood sugar is hormonal. When combined with the biological disruption of emotional or physical stress, the damage from this is compounded. This means that stress management can also play a vital role in reducing your risk of complications.

One crucial result of circulatory changes is a tendency for diabetics to develop high blood pressure. Though hypertension has no symptoms of its own, it contributes strongly to the development or worsening of retinopathy, kidney disease, and cardiovascular diseases. If hypertension is present, control of blood pressure may be as important in preventing complications as keeping blood sugar levels down. (The life-style factors associated with high blood pressure include obesity, high intake of salt, smoking, stress, and lack of exercise.)

Finally, recent studies show increasing evidence of the importance of genetic factors in complications. We inherit tendencies toward or resistances to some of the disorders related to diabetes.

So, in any individual case, the onset of a diabetic complication will be determined by a unique combination of past blood sugar imbalances, hormonal imbalances, hypertension, environmental influences, and genetic tendencies.

CAN COMPLICATIONS BE PREVENTED OR REVERSED?

This question has been a subject of medical controversy that is only beginning to be resolved. Some diabetic nerve disorders have been reversed through stricter control. Retinal disorders have shown mixed results, with improvements in some cases. Kidney disease in diabetes may be influenced more by high blood pressure than by high blood sugar.

While the evidence is still fragmentary, many researchers believe that tight blood sugar control can prevent or reverse some complications and delay the onset of others. But major questions remain unanswered: How early must one maintain this level of control in the course of diabetes? How do the different factors that cause complications interact? How do other aspects of self-care influence the risks? Are the benefits worth the costs in time and effort and risks of acute insulin reactions?

Diabetes research examines relationships among a limited number of factors — control of blood sugar levels and development of complications studied statistically in a group of people. But the situation of each of us as an individual is influenced by a whole life system generally outside the researcher's capacity for study. Diabetic control must be seen as one of a variety of factors determining our future — diet, exercise and activity level, patterns of managing stress, emotional life, immunological responses, heredity, and other influences yet to be discovered.

If we look at the question of preventing complications in this broader frame of reference, improving blood sugar control becomes one important part of a healthy, balanced life-style that is of immediate and long-term benefit to people with diabetes. In the face of researchers' specific uncertainties, the total benefits of improving diabetic control are well worth the costs. The degree of control you maintain, though, must be determined by your other life demands and the need to avoid acute insulin reactions. That is why we describe three levels of control to help in your decision making. Our goal is to help you be realistic in your choices and not fool yourself about what you are and are not willing to do to control your diabetes.

Diabetes Control and Complications Trial
A study of 1,400 diabetics will bring more understanding to some of these issues as results begin to be reported in the early 1990s.

The ten-year study is being conducted to determine the effect of strict blood sugar control: Can it control, prevent, delay, lessen, or reverse diabetic complications? What level of control is needed?

289

There is already a great deal of evidence on this question generally suggesting that strict control reduces the risk; but many details still need to be studied.

REDUCING YOUR RISK OF DEVELOPING COMPLICATIONS

If you believe the hoped-for cure for diabetes or breakthroughs in treatments of complications will allow you to forget about preventive measures, don't fall for this illusion. The building blocks for diabetes' side effects accumulate over time, cause deterioration of basic body systems, and, in many cases, are not reversible. If you just wait for discovery of the cure, it may not work for you because too much damage may have already occurred. Preventive measures, started as early as possible, are much more effective than later treatment.

We will expand upon the list of actions you can take to reduce the risk of complications that appears in Chapter 15. "Reducing the risk" does not necessarily mean "avoiding complications." This is not always possible. But by following these preventive measures, you will improve your odds. If complications develop, they are likely to appear later, progress more slowly, and be more treatable, perhaps with methods not yet perfected or discovered. It is also likely that there will be fewer of them to deal with.

Ways to Reduce Your Risk

1. Improve your metabolic control and continue improving it until you achieve the best level with which you can live well.

   While other factors play important roles, blood sugar control is clearly central to reducing your risks for diabetic complications.

   Improvements in your level of control will make complications less likely to develop or delay their onset and severity. As we have said before, there is no guarantee, simply improved odds.

2. Learn to handle stress well.

   In the short run, poorly managed stress interferes with blood sugar control, causing either high tests or swings between high and low. In the long run, excessive levels of stress hormones are probably a major contributor to many diabetic complications.

3. Follow a diet low in fat, high in fiber, and with controlled salt consumption, as well as limitation of sweets and rapidly absorbed carbohydrates.

   Low salt consumption helps control high blood pressure. Restriction of cholesterol and total fat, especially animal fat (and other saturated fats like coconut and palm oils) helps maintain a healthy circulatory system. In addition to having a beneficial effect on blood sugar, high-fiber diets have been associated with a lower incidence of colon diseases, including cancer.

4. Exercise regularly.

   Exercise provides a foundation for good metabolic control as well as helping control weight and stress. It also has significant benefits for cardiorespiratory fitness.

5. If you are overweight, lose weight.

   In addition to contributing to metabolic control, weight loss will decrease your risk for cardiovascular disease and hypertension.

6. Act to prevent high blood pressure by controlling stress, weight, and salt consumption. Seek treatment if your blood pressure is high (above 140/90).

   High blood pressure dramatically increases the risk of kidney failure and visual loss from retinopathy. As in people who do not have diabetes, it increases the risk of heart and circulatory illness. A program of prevention and treatment can be found in the section on hypertension later in this chapter. Following this program is one of the most important preventive actions you can take.

7. If you smoke, quit.

   Smoking usually increases the risk of vascular disorders and heart disease, risks already heightened in diabetes. Smoking has a negative effect on arteries, small blood vessels, blood pressure, and circulation, thus contributing to arteriosclerosis, hypertension, and coronary artery disease.

8. Get the amount of sleep and rest that you need.

   Adequate sleep and rest minimizes stress and contributes to good metabolic control.

9. Consider taking a daily multivitamin.

Scientific evidence supporting the preventive role of vitamin and mineral supplementation in diabetes is sketchy. Many claims for substances such as vitamins E and C, bioflavanoids, and brewer's yeast are made in health magazines, yet few reliable studies support these claims. There may be definite benefits in moderate vitamin·and mineral supplementation.

Large doses of vitamins C (thousands of units per day) and E (over 250 units per day) should be avoided if advanced retinal disorders (proliferative retinopathy) or kidney disease (nephropathy) have developed. Such megavitamin self-treatment may have a damaging impact on these conditions, involving capillary fragility.

This is not an all-or-nothing program. Each item on the list improves your chances. If you want to do more than you are now doing but have difficulty making all of the changes suggested, review the information on learning and change in Chapter 1.

THE MAJOR COMPLICATIONS OF DIABETES

The following catalog describes the conditions specific to diabetes or that take a special form in diabetics. We have not covered the cardiovascular complications whose course is similar indiabetics and nondiabetics. You can find good sources of information on heart disease at the end of the chapter.

As you read this part of *Living Well*, be aware of the stress it is likely to trigger. Don't just plow through it, ignoring the feelings that naturally arise as you study such threatening material. Pause often, relax, and reassure yourself. Talk about your feelings with someone close to you, or write them down. Live well, even with this very difficult information about diabetes.

Complications of the Eyes

Diabetic Retinopathy

What Goes Wrong?

Abnormalities in blood sugar level, blood chemistry, and hormone levels produce an oxygen or circulatory shortage in the eye's retina and blockages of small blood vessels. At first, this results in background retinopathy — minor changes in blood vessels of the retina.

292

When the process intensifies, new blood vessels form in the retina in an attempt to increase the supply of blood and oxygen. These vessels are weak and prone to leak   blood and fluid into the retinal tissue or the vitreous liquid (the jelly-like substance between the retina and the lens) of the eye. Together with other blood vessel abnormalities in the retina, these hemorrhages can lead to decreased or total loss of vision. These changes also create a risk of retinal detachment or macular edema (excess fluid in the portion of the retina used for sharp vision).

Signs and Stages of Development

Background retinopathy begins to develop after five to twenty years of diabetes. It is a mild condition characterized by small, scattered changes in the retina. Vision is not affected, and the disorder is no cause for alarm. The condition can be detected only through an ophthalmological examination by a doctor trained to recognize it.

Proliferative retinopathy may develop after fifteen years of diabetes, but it may develop sooner. New fragile blood vessels and fibrous scarring are found on the retina. Unless there is retinal detachment or hemorrhages interfering with vision, it can only be discovered through an eye examination. (Possible visual cues of this condition include the presence of flashing lights, floaters, and blurred vision.) Photos of your retinas may be taken, with and without a flourescein dye, to indicate points of leakage.

If proliferative retinopathy continues to develop, vision-blocking hemorrhages or retinal detachment may occur.

Macular edema is retinopathy that may result in thickening of the retina or the collection of fluid around the central part of the retina used for fine vision (the macula). This thickening results in blurring or fuzziness of vision.

The risk

More than 90 percent of type I diabetics have mild or background retinopathy after fifteen years of diabetes. By twenty years, 25 percent have developed some degree of proliferative retinopathy. Before laser treatment was introduced, many diabetics experienced severe visual loss or blindness from advanced retinopathy. This risk has been dramatically reduced by the laser. Relatively few diabetics now become blind from this condition.

Prevention

1. Have an ophthalmologist examine your eyes each year after you have had diabetes for five years. Even if your vision is normal, you may have changes that can benefit from laser treatment.

2. Check your own vision in each eye weekly (or even daily), looking for any changes: increased blurriness, floaters, fuzzy areas. (Good vision in one eye may mask worsening vision in the other, so make sure you close each eye to check the sight in the other.)

3. Report any changes in vision to your doctor immediately.

4. Keep blood sugar as close to normal as possible.

5. Maintain normal blood pressure. (Practice preventive measures for high blood pressure.) Adhere to treatment for hypertension, if prescribed.

6. Maintain normal weight.

7. Avoid smoking.

Treatment

Your internist or family physician is trained to examine your eyes for retinopathy, but after five years of diabetes, you should have a yearly examination by an ophthalmologist. All treatments for retinopathy are performed by ophthalmologists. Once the first stages of proliferative retinopathy are diagnosed, you may need examinations every three or four months.

Laser photocoagulation is the recommended treatment for retinopathy once a certain level of new vessel formation or macular edema is reached. This is an office procedure in which an ophthalmologist uses a laser to make hundreds of microscopic scars along the sides of the retina. A local anesthetic can be used, but usually the process causes only moderate discomfort. The treatment increases the oxygen available to the central area of the retina and promotes healing of the new vessel growth. This decreases the risk of blindness by 60 percent.

Risks of treatment, occurring very rarely, include further bleeding and inadvertent scarring of the central area of the retina.

Possible side effects include a moderate restriction of peripheral vision, a slight decrease in sharpness of vision, and decreased night vision.

A study about to end (the Early Treatment Diabetic Retinopathy Study) will determine if the use of a laser at an earlier stage of retinopathy further decreases the risk of blindness. This study is also exploring use of the anticlotting quality of aspirin as a treatment for early-stage retinopathy.

Initial findings have shown that "focal" laser treatment decreased visual loss by about 50 percent in those patients with clinically significant macular edema. This is defined very precisely for the ophthalmologist and requires a special, painless exam. You may have clinically significant macular edema that would benefit from treatment, but you may not know it because your eyesight is still normal. It is essential that you have your eyes checked even if your sight appears unaffected.

Vitrectomy is a surgical procedure used when retinopathy is too far advanced to be treated by laser (because extensive hemorrhages fill the vitreous fluid in the eye, blocking the retina). The fluid is removed and replaced with a clear saline solution. The operation may also remove scar tissue and fibers that can cause retinal detachment. This process is riskier than laser treatment, so ophthalmologists usually prefer to wait six to twelve months to see if blood in the vitreous will clear without treatment.

Cautions

If proliferative retinopathy has developed, you should avoid activities that cause a sudden rise in blood pressure or a sudden flow of blood to the head: straining with bowel movements, bending over quickly, high diving, scuba diving, lifting heavy weights, head stands, and so on. Hemorrhages in the eye can result from these activities as well as from blows to the head. Discuss the general level of physical activity appropriate for you with your ophthalmologist.

At the proliferative stage, you should not tighten control quickly. Control should be improved gradually, over a period of several months. A sudden change to tight control can cause retinopathy to worsen at this stage.

It is important to cope with the emotional stress accompanying this threat to your vision. Highlevels of stress can add to the threat through the periods of high blood pressure they may cause.

Chronic high blood pressure should be controlled with medication.

High doses of vitamin C (over 500 mg per day), used by some to treat colds, should be avoided. This vitamin in large doses affects blood clotting and thickness.

Diabetic Cataract

What goes wrong?

The lens of the eye becomes cloudy as an indirect result of high blood sugar. The immediate cause is an excess of sorbitol, the alcohol of glucose, in the lens. This changes the chemical balance of the lens because it tends to accumulate in the cells. (Diabetics may also be more likely to develop the more common age-related form of cataract.)

Signs and stages of development

Cataracts affect vision differently, depending upon the pattern of cloudiness that develops in the lens. Opacity may occur at the center, around the sides, or diffusely throughout the lens. The initial stage of development may be detectable only through ophthalmological examination. In the mature phase, a milkiness can be seen from the outside, and vision decreases, with fogginess and halos around lights.

Prevention

1. Maintain excellent blood sugar control.
2. Some biochemical research indicates that taking 1,000 mg of bioflavanoids daily may help. This food supplement may reduce sorbitol in body tissues.
3. Research is now being conducted on aldose reductase inhibitors, drugs such as sorbinil, which counter the action of the enzyme that converts sugars into the sorbitol causing cataracts. If successful, a drug may be available to prevent diabetic cataract formation.

Treatment

Cataract surgery involves the removal of the cloudy lens, replacing it with a plastic lens. This process is usually done under local anesthesia. It restores vision in 90 to 95 percent of patients. Surgery is really indicated only when the disruption of vision interferes with your daily life.

Risks

This procedure incurs the usual surgical risks of infection and bleeding that can further compromise vision. The risk is low.

Take a break
Especially if you are reading straight through this chapter, you need one. Relax, check your feelings, and give yourself some warm love and friendship. Taking in all this information is a difficult task. Do not imagine that you can just absorb it without emotional impact. After working with these hard facts for years, your authors still feel them deeply.

Kidney Disease (Diabetic Nephropathy)

What goes wrong?

The kidney filters blood, clearing out waste products and recirculating blood chemicals and proteins that are then reused. This is achieved by networks of capillaries (called the glomeruli), fine blood vessels that can become severely damaged by years of high blood sugar. A layer of the capillary — the basement membrane — becomes thickened.

With this thickening, kidney function is progressively altered. The selective filtering by the kidney is impaired. First, protein (albumin) that should be retained in the bloodstream is passed through the kidney into urine (a condition called microalbuminuria and albuminuria or proteinuria). Then, toxic waste products that should be filtered out of the blood remain in circulation (azotemia). Serum creatinine and BUN (blood urea nitrogen) levels become abnormally increased. (Creatinine and BUN are chemicals normally found in the blood and passed into the urine. Their levels rise if the kidney is not working well. Temporary increases may occur occasionally from causes such as eating a large quantity of meat.)

This stage eventually leads to a condition known as uremia: an excess of urea and other nitrogen wastes in the blood that produces

297

symptoms of kidney failure, such as fatigue, decreased appetite, nausea, and vomiting.

The good news is that for patients who have had diabetes for more than forty years and have not developed proteinuria, it is unlikely that nephropathy will develop. Moreover, it appears that 60 to 70 percent of patients with insulin-dependent diabetes will never develop clinical kidney disease.

Signs and stages of development

The early stages of kidney disease are revealed only by urine and blood tests. We provide technical information on these signs to help you understand the results of tests your physician may report. The early signs of kidney disease can be strong motivators for preventive action on your part.

Stage 1

Changes to the kidneys begin to develop slowly over many years, with no obvious clinical signs or symptoms. The normal kidney excretes a small amount of protein (albumin) in the urine (less than 30 mg in a 24-hour period). With new, more sensitive tests, it is now possible to measure such small amounts clinically (rather than in a research lab). A urine protein level between 30 and 300 mg per day is called microalbuminuria.

Substantial evidence now indicates that persistent microalbuminuria predicts the later development of diabetic kidney disease (particularly in patients with insulin-dependent diabetes). So urine protein in this range — 30 to 300 mg per day — along with the typically increased blood flow and filtration rate through the kidneys, can now be considered Stage 1. If nephropathy is going to develop this stage may last an average of fifteen to seventeen years and has traditionally been considered the silent period of nephropathy.

Stage 2

The next development may occur after fifteen to seventeen years of diabetes on average. Standard urine tests may show abnormally increased albumin excretion, greater than 250–300 mg per day. At this stage, the kidney is leaking out protein, but BUN and creatinine — other indicators of disease detected through blood tests — have not yet started to rise. If Stage 2 is reached, development of further disease is highly likely. Proteinuria may be present in urine for several years without other evidence of kidney disease. (Remember, there is great individual variation for these statistics, and many diabetics never develop kidney disease.)

Stage 3
In this stage, BUN and serum creatinine levels slowly begin to rise. Once an individual's creatinine exceeds 2 mg/dl (milligrams per deciliter), it is possible to estimate roughly the time progression of disease and the percentage of kidney function remaining. Divide the creatinine level into 1 and multiply by 100 to get the percentage remaining. For example, a creatinine level of 4 gives approximately 25 percent remaining function. Most patients don't have symptoms until function drops to 5–15 percent.) Your physician can give you a rough estimate of the rate of progress of kidney disease.

Stage 4
At this point, the kidneys are failing. BUN and creatinine levels have risen high enough that symptoms of kidney failure are occurring. These symptoms include poor appetite, vomiting, ankle swelling or other signs of fluid accumulation, weakness, lethargy, drowsiness, fatigue, and nausea. Weight gain, mostly from excess fluid accumulation, is continuing to occur. Do not scare yourself with the presence of any of these symptoms. Individually they are signs of a large variety of low-threat disorders. Laboratory urine and blood tests interpreted by your physician are the only way to determine the presence of kidney disease.

In Stage 4 kidney disease, dialysis or kidney transplant is necessary to preserve life.

Monitoring and Prevention
Although no evidence suggests that improved blood glucose control will affect the course of disease progression once Stage 2 has begun, there is some initial evidence that action in Stage 1 may benefit you. Researchers recommend that you generally strive for control as good as possible when your tests show microalbuminuria (30–300 mg/dl).

The American Diabetes Association *(Physician's Guide to Insulin-Dependent Type I Diabetes: Diagnosis and Treatment,* Alexandria,

Va, 1988) has recommended these guidelines for monitoring kidney function:

In the first five years of diabetes, you should have a routine check for protein in the urine each time you visit your physician. BUN and creatinine should be measured at least yearly if proteinuria is present.

After five years or in the postpubertal patient, in addition to the above, you should have a 24-hoururine test yearly to measure total daily protein. If possible, tests for microalbuminuria should be done. (This may become increasingly common and easy to obtain. Ames, a pharmaceutical company, is releasing a simple office test which, if it proves reliable, will facilitate screening for the presence of microalbuminuria.)

Once overt (dipstick) proteinuria or elevated serum creatinine or BUN is detected, kidney function should be monitored at least two or three times a year. Consultation with a nephrologist (kidney specialist) is necessary to plot a long-term therapeutic strategy and to discuss the possibility and implications of renal failure with the patient.

Additional preventive measures in kidney disease

1. Maintain the best possible metabolic control.
2. Avoid ketoacidosis (diabetic coma) by careful management of infections and stress.
3. Avoid high blood pressure through weight control and limited intake of salt or sodium (i.e., no added salt). Adhere to any hypertension medication prescribed. (Hypertension promotes the development of diabetic kidney disease.)
4. Use relaxation techniques as a further way of lowering blood pressure.
5. Avoid urinary tract infections. (Know the symptoms: burning or pain on urination and cloudy urine.) Seek treatment promptly if they occur. Such infections can contribute to kidney damage.
6. To minimize the risk of infection, you should not be catheterized unless it is absolutely necessary.
7. Use of dye-contrast agents in X-ray or other radiological studies

should be avoided unless absolutely necessary. (They tend to be toxic to the kidney.)

Treatment

In the first stage, your internist or family practitioner is equipped to watch for signs of advancing kidney disease. By Stage 2, a kidney specialist (nephrologist) should be consulted to monitor your condition. Treatment in Stages 3 and 4 is by a nephrologist, preferably one experienced in diabetic kidney disease.

Stage 1

Strict adherence to preventive measures described above is likely to allow you to avoid or postpone diabetic kidney disease. The fact that you have an early warning sign in the microalbuminuria test gives you a valuable gift of motivation. The best possible self-care can keep your kidneys intact.

Stage 2

With excellent self-care — including all the preventive measures just described — you can probably extend the life of your kidneys by many years. Blood sugar control, weight control, and treatment for high blood pressure and urinary tract infections are the key ingredients of treatment here. Care at this stage is designed to extend kidney function by controlling hypertension and avoiding urinary tract infection and drugs toxic to the kidney (such as those used in some radiographic studies).

Stage 3

At this stage, your kidney function has deteriorated and toxic products are building up in the bloodstream. Blood sugar control may help other body systems, but it cannot reverse kidney disease at this stage. Dietary restriction of protein may be recommended, although this is still an area of controversy. Diuretic pills to help you lose any accumulated fluid may be prescribed.

Stage 4

Once kidney failure occurs, the two choices for treatment are dialysis or a kidney transplant.

Dialysis is a demanding procedure in which a machine performs the blood-filtering function of the kidneys. You are attached to the machine, using blood vessels in your arm, typically for four hours, three times a week. The experience is taxing, but it can add years to your life. Peritoneal dialysis uses the peritoneum (the lining of the abdominal cavity) to filter toxins out of the blood. It is possible to do this procedure at home or at work, and it may provide a motivated patient with more flexibility. Its long-term effectiveness is still being evaluated.

Kidney transplants allow a more normal life than dialysis. The technique is advancing rapidly, increasing the acceptance rate and long-term survival rate. Successful transplantation no longer depends on your having a kidney from a relative, since matching of cadaver kidneys has improved significantly. Five-year success rates range from 70 to 80 percent, depending upon the source of the kidney donated.

Cautions
Avoid ketoacidosis (diabetic coma), urinary tract infections, use of dye contrast agents in X-ray studies, and catheterization; follow treatment for high blood pressure.

Time for another break
Even if your kidneys are still completely healthy, what you have just read may be frightening and depressing. If you actually have signs of kidney disease developing, you will probably need to deal with strong emotional reactions. Chapters 3, 11, and 14 can help you handle these reactions. Don't be afraid to seek outside aid in a diabetes or kidney disease support group or from professionals.

Nerve Disorders (Diabetic Neuropathies)
What goes wrong?
Several families of nerve disorders may develop as complications of diabetes, producing pain, lack of sensation, digestive and urinary difficulties, and impotence. Fortunately, many of the disorders usually disappear after a few months to a year. Others are successfully treated with a variety of drugs. Good metabolic control probably reduces your risk of developing a neuropathy.

The reasons for the development of diabetic neuropathies is still not completely understood, but the overall cause is clearly higher-than-normal blood sugar. The ability of nerves to carry messages and the nature of the messages themselves may be altered by several chemical results of poor control. The insulation of the nerves (the myelin sheath) is damaged. Sorbitol (a glucose-related alcohol) and fructose accumulate in nerve cells. The speed at which messages travel is slowed. Myoinositol content of nerve tissue is reduced. (This deficiency may be corrected by drugs.) Glucose attaches to protein cells. The net result: a nerve disorder.

Neuropathies are caused by elevated blood sugar, so it is possible that good metabolic control will allow you to escape these complications and possibly reverse them if they develop. At this point, available evidence indicates that the possible benefits of optimal control are worth the cost.

The various forms of neuropathy are rare among young diabetics. They usually do not develop before fifteen years of diabetes. Generally, if the symptoms are mild in the first few years of neuropathy, they are unlikely to develop to an extreme degree.

Prevention
Maintain good metabolic control.

Under development is the use of sorbinil or other drugs that counter the build up of sorbitol in nerve cells, as well as drugs that help restore nerve tissue.

Peripheral neuropathy
In this disorder, impairment occurs in those nerves extending down the legs and arms — the peripheral nervous system. Two main forms of disorders occur: those that develop gradually, usually without pain, and those with rapid onset and significant pain.

Gradual peripheral neuropathy is marked by numbness, tingling, itching, burning, a decreased sense of touch, a decrease in deep tendon reflexes, or any combination of these. These symptoms are usually found on both sides of the body and occur more frequently in the feet and legs than in the hands and arms. (Your doctor is checking for this disorder when testing your reflexes and when using the tuning fork and sharp devices to test your sensations.) Another possible symptom is the loss of the sense of orientation (proprioception) in the feet and legs — not knowing by feel which way a foot is turned, for instance.

While not painful, this form of nerve damage can lead to serious foot problems.

Treatment seems to be limited to improving control of diabetes. Myoinositol and sorbinil may prove to be effective against this form of neuropathy.

Peripheral neuropathy with rapid onset and pain is a temporary complication, but the pain can be intense. It develops within a matter of days or weeks and generally lasts from six to eighteen months. The chief symptom, a burning pain like a "toothache" in the feet or legs, is usually worse at night.

Treatment focuses on reducing the pain, first with aspirin or acetaminophen. Narcotics such as codeine, or tranquilizers such as Elavil or Prolixin may be used to provide relief. The anticonvulsant drugs, phenytoin or carbamazepine, although not substantiated in controlled clinical trials, may be worth a therapeutic trial. Some larger medical centers now have pain clinics offering a wide choice of treatments beyond drugs.

Autonomic neuropathy
This disorder affects the nerves controlling internal organs, genitals, small blood vessels and sweat glands of the skin, bladder muscles, and gastrointestinal tract. Some of the conditions that can result include impotence, difficulty urinating or sensing when the bladder is full (which can lead to bladder infection), diarrhea, stomach upset due to retention of food, dizziness after standing up, loss of the normal sweating response, and weakening or disappearance of the symptoms of an insulin reaction.

The symptoms of autonomic neuropathy are usually not temporary, as with some other forms of neuropathy. However, effective modes of treatment are available for most of the specific disabilities. Impotence from neuropathy, for instance, can be effectively overcome by a surgical implant that allows full sexual functioning. Several nonsurgical approaches, including external vacuum aids and drug injections, are available at some clinics. Tests are often given to distinguish clearly between neuropathic impotence and impotence caused by psychological factors, tests essential to avoiding unnecessary surgery.

We do not know to what extent metabolic control can reverse any of these conditions caused by autonomic neuropathy. Evidence so far indicates that stricter control can reverse the other form of neuropathy: peripheral.

Complications of the Feet and Legs

What goes wrong?

Two diabetic complications join forces to threaten the feet and legs of a diabetic: peripheral neuropathy and peripheral vascular disease. With proper self-care and regular foot examinations, you can neutralize this threat and reduce or eliminate the risk of losing a limb.

When peripheral neuropathy (described above) causes numbness and lack of feeling, injuries to the feet may go unnoticed, leading to infection and amputation. Pressure sores and ulcerations can develop on the feet and not be discovered until severe infection has set in.

This risk is compounded by the presence of peripheral vascular disease, a common disorder that takes a unique form with diabetes (described in this chapter under "Complications of the Heart and Circulatory System"). This disorder causes decreased blood flow in the legs and feet. This, in turn, means a decreased flow of the oxygen, white blood cells, and nutrients needed to fight infection. Either of the peripheral disorders can lead to loss. Together, the two multiply the risk.

One other foot problem can develop from lack of sensation. If any bone or joint disorders begin, symptoms may not be evident until they reach an advanced stage (neuroarthropathy). You are able to go on walking and standing without pain on feet and ankles that need immediate attention. This is not a common condition, but it is one more argument for excellent daily foot care.

Prevention of complications of the feet and legs

1. Maintain the best possible blood sugar control.
2. Do everything possible to prevent peripheral neuropathy, peripheral vascular disease, and hypertension.
3. Wash and inspect your feet daily. (If you can't see clearly or get close enough, have someone else do it for you.)
4. Check for blisters, bruises, cracks, cuts, and scratches. A sore, scratch, or red area that could be ignored by someone without diabetes should be watched very carefully by someone with diabetes. Use mild antiseptic and antibacterial salve on minor injuries. See your doctor for any sore that does not improve or

heal within a few days. If the sore becomes infected or swollen, or if white or yellow pus appears, take no chances. See your doctor. You need to avoid serious infection, which can lead to gangrene and loss of a toe or foot.

5. Athlete's foot and fungal infections of the toenails should also be caught early and treated aggressively. Long-term care using antifungal creams or ointment may be necessary.

6. Massage your feet with lanolin or polysorb. Do not rub lotion between the toes. (Massage helps maintain good circulation. Foot cream prevents dry, cracked skin.)

7. Do not cut or use patent medicines on corns or calluses. File calluses gently with an emery board. See your physician or a podiatrist for any large or painful lumps on your feet or for any changes in the shape of toes, toenails, or other parts of the foot.

8. When trimming toenails, gently round them to follow the shape of the toe. Avoid creating sharp points that dig into the next toe or sharp angles that cause ingrown toenails.

9. Select shoes that fit well and feel good. Break them in gradually. Always wear soft, seamless socks with shoes. Avoid sandals with thongs between the toes.

10. Inspect shoes daily for rocks, nail points, or damage.

11. Avoid very hot or very cold water. Do not use heating pads or hot water bottles on your feet. Wear socks to bed if your feet are cold.

12. Do foot and ankle exercises to stimulate circulation. (Two good exercises: rotating your feet at the ankle with your leg raised when you first wake up; standing with the front one-third of your feet on the edge of a step and raising and lowering your body a dozen times.)

13. Do not smoke. Nicotine is very damaging to the circulatory system.

Treatment

Early treatment of any foot disorder is essential, because infections can advance rapidly when circulation is poor. The primary guideline is to be alert and call or see your doctor for what may appear to be minor blisters, cuts, or sores. The earlier these can be treated, the less likely they are to become serious.

Other Skin and Joint Complications
We want to mention briefly the thickening of the skin and possibly the connective tissue that may be present in up to one-third or more patients with insulin-dependent diabetes. It is usually painless and causes little if any disability. However, it can restrict joint movement, particularly in the wrists, hands and fingers, and may be the cause of otherwise unexplained musculoskeletal problems. It can also affect the shoulder and neck. Because it is believed to result from glucose attaching itself to tissue proteins, it may represent an early warning of other complications such as retinopathy, neuropathy, and nephropathy. The aldose reductase inhibitors may prove useful in relieving some of this limited joint mobility (LJM).

Complications of the Heart and Circulatory System
In most cases, the characteristics of the following disorders are not unique to diabetes. We differ from nondiabetics only in having a higher risk for these problems, a risk that begins earlier in life (about 10 years earlier). This risk can be reduced significantly by excellent self-care.

The primary risk factors for cardiovascular diseases (heart attack, stroke, arteriosclerosis, and peripheral vascular disease) are
• Smoking
• High fat and cholesterol levels in the blood
• Obesity
• Lack of exercise
• Family history of heart and circulatory disease
• High blood pressure

Prevention of cardiovascular disorders
A general preventive program for your heart and circulatory system includes many of the basic elements of the full diabetic regimen. Most of these are fundamental to a healthy life-style for anyone. They include the following.
1. Maintain normal body weight. If you are overweight, lose weight.
2. Limit sodium consumption to 2 grams per day.
3. Avoid foods high in saturated fat and cholesterol.

4. Learn and use effective techniques of relaxation and stress reduction.

5. Exercise regularly, at an aerobic level if your condition allows.

6. If you smoke, stop smoking.

Since information on stroke and heart attacks is widely available, we will discuss only high blood pressure and peripheral vascular disease. These conditions have unique significance in diabetes.

High Blood Pressure
Prevention of chronically high blood pressure ranks close to blood sugar control as a means of avoiding diabetic complications. It also plays a major role in treatment of complications; lower blood pressure helps to slow or reverse the progress of eye, kidney, and circulatory problems. So here is a keystone of living well with diabetes: Act to maintain normal blood pressure before it starts to climb, and begin treatment promptly if it does go up.

What goes wrong?
Hypertension is more common among diabetics, and it tends to begin at an earlier age. The condition has no symptoms that you experience and can be diagnosed only through a series of blood pressure readings (consistent readings above 140/90). The causes of high blood pressure are not completely known. Contributing factors include obesity, stress, smoking, lack of activity, and genetic tendency.

Hypertension occurs more often in diabetics because high blood sugar and fats contribute to its development. Once narrowing of arteries due to fat deposits (atherosclerosis) or kidney disease start, these disorders further heighten blood pressure.

Although you feel no immediate symptoms, hypertension has very serious consequences for diabetics and nondiabetics alike. In any person, hypertension

• Intensifies the buildup of fatty deposits, narrowing the blood vessels in a condition known as atherosclerosis, which increases all of the risks below.

• Causes your heart to work harder, enlarging it, and adding to your risk for heart attack.

• Increases your chances of developing peripheral vascular disease.
• Makes strokes more likely.

Diabetics have a higher risk for all of these disorders, a risk made even higher by hypertension. But there are further effects specific to diabetes. High blood pressure in diabetics also contributes to the development and progress of kidney disease and hastens the development of retinopathy.

Hypertension is called the silent disease, because its effects are not experienced directly. But it speaks loudly in its impact on our health.

Prevention

General preventive measures for circulatory disease are given at the beginning of this section. Following this set of recommendations is one of the greatest gifts you can give yourself, hundreds of times more valuable than the relatively small sacrifices involved.

Treatment

For a diabetic, when blood pressure consistently goes above 140/90, it is time to start treatment for hypertension. Fortunately, the first stage of treatment is to do the very things recommended for prevention, if you are not already doing them. You may not need medication, assuming that your blood pressure is only mildly elevated and that other complications do not require it. You might want to buy a blood pressure cuff (sphygmomanometer), the device for measuring your blood pressure, so you can monitor your pressure at home between medical appointments.

If an antihypertensive drug is prescribed at the first sign of high blood pressure (and if you are willing to follow the recommendations above), ask your physician if there is any special reason to go directly to medication. If there is not, you both can consider a six-month trial to determine whether relaxation, sodium restriction, weight reduction, and so forth will bring your blood pressure down. Most people with high blood pressure need antihypertensive drugs, but if you can control blood pressure without them, you avoid the potential side effects of the drugs.

Great care must be taken in choosing an anithypertensive medication, as many of the products available have side effects potentially harmful to diabetics. Don't be afraid to ask your physician to choose the drug with the fewest possible side effects for you and your diabetes.

There are more than twenty-five different drugs available to lower blood pressure, including many new ones particularly useful for diabetics. Some, however (propranolol and other beta blockers) eliminate the warning signs of an insulin reaction and block the release of the hormone that helps us recover from hypoglycemia. One of the most popular diuretics used for hypertension, hydrochlorothiazide, tends to increase both blood sugar and blood fat levels. Others reinforce the difficulties with impotence some diabetic men have. Adrenergic inhibitors are the worst offenders. These include reserpine, clonidine, and methyldopa.

You may feel uncomfortable raising the choice of drugs with your physician. We suggest that you say something like: "I've read that some of the common blood pressure drugs are not as good for diabetics as others. Can we discuss this? Which one(s) are you going to prescribe for me?" Most likely, the physician will respond with an explanation indicating an awareness of a considered choice and that more monitoring of blood sugar or potassium may be needed. Possible major side effects to watch for should be discussed.

If kidney disease has started, treatment for hypertension becomes more complex and even more important. High blood pressure hastens deterioration of kidney function. Kidney impairment further increases blood pressure. This vicious cycle can be slowed and possibly halted if medication and nondrug therapy are started early enough. Antihypertensive treatment is the only factor known to slow the advance of existing kidney disease. Under your physician's care, you should begin all of the measures listed in the general prevention of circulatory disease above. But you will need stricter control of salt in your diet (no more than 1 gram per day.) The selection of drugs at this point is crucial and should be made by a physician familiar with diabetic kidney disorders.

Peripheral Vascular Disease

What goes wrong?
Poor circulation develops in the legs and feet of diabetics, mostly through atherosclerosis. The decreased blood flow results in inadequate supplies of oxygen and nutrients reaching cells in the feet.

This is one of the major causes of the difficulties described under "Complications of the Feet and Legs." Disorders of this type can result in serious infection, gangrene, and amputation. For this reason, foot care is one of the most vital aspects of your regimen.

Symptoms

Aching, cramping, or pain sometimes occurs in the legs while walking. This pain usually subsides in a few minutes when you rest. (Its technical name is intermittent claudication.) Other symptoms are

- Cold feet.
- Aching in the legs or feet when lying down.
- Feet that become red or purplish when your legs hang down.
- Pulses in the feet that become weaker.
- Feet that become pale when raised above your body.
- Reduced blood pressure at the ankles.

Prevention

The basic cardiovascular preventive measures described all apply here. You should also review and follow the foot care recommendations given under "Complications of the Feet and Legs."

Treatment

Treatment of peripheral vascular disease seeks to avoid the consequences of poor circulation. Pentoxifylline may help to relieve symptoms. Surgery to bypass the diseased blood vessels or angioplasty to open them up may be necessary for severe persistent pain.

Summing Up

Complications are the most disturbing aspect of having diabetes. We face serious risks, and it is still unclear how much we can actually do to prevent complications from developing. Yet we can defy this uncertainty and face the consequences of diabetes bravely, even if we do develop a complication. We are free to reduce the risks and improve our odds.

We are, after all, individuals, each with our own unique history. Some of us will live long lives without major complications. Others will delay the onset and lessen the severity of the disorders that result from diabetes. Ever-improving treatment of these afflictions will enable us to limit their consequences in our lives. By learning to follow the balanced and healthy life-style this book presents, we will be able to live well with diabetes, even if its complications develop.

BOOKS ON DISEASES OF THE HEART AND BLOOD VESSELS

Stress, Diet and Your Heart. Dean Ornish. Holt, Rinehart, and Winston, New York (1982).

Heartcare, rev. ed. American Medical Association. Random House, New York (1984).

Your Heart: Questions You Have . . . Answers You Need. Ed Weiner. Peoples Medical Society, Emmaus, Penn. (1985).

Take Care of Your Heart: The Complete Book of Heart Facts. E. A. Amsterdam and A. M. Holmes. Facts on File Publications, New York (1984).

Heart to Heart: Cleveland Clinic Guide to Understanding Heart Disease and Open Heart Surgery. N. V. Richards. Atheneum, New York (1987).

Coming Back — A Guide to Recovering from a Heart Attack rev. ed. K. Cohn and D. Duke. Addison Wesley, Reading, Mass. (1987).

There is no single book that covers the entire field of heart disease adequately. Look for these or other books in your local library or bookstore.

Section VI

WOMEN AND CHILDREN LIVING WELL

Living Well As A Diabetic Woman

This chapter, was written by Cathy Feste. *Cathy is a nationally recognized health motivation specialist, president of her own wellness consulting business, and the author of the best-selling book* **The Physician Within.** *She has had insulin-dependent diabetes for more than thirty years.*

As a woman who has lived with diabetes for thirty-one years I know that it carries with it some special challenges. I have seen my blood sugars swoop when a period is approaching. I saw my insulin requirements nearly quadruple during my pregnancy. As I nursed my baby, I faced the additional challenges of low blood sugar as my body burned extra calories.

Those are physical issues. But there's another side to life with diabetes. Being unwilling to miss out on the fun and fulfillment of life has required extra creativity. As a teenager, I found that cheerleading and marching band worked out fine if I hid Lifesavers in my uniform. Girl Scout canoe trips were not a problem if I kept insulin, syringes, testing strips, and carbohydrates in airtight plastic containers that would float. These early successes gave me the confidence as an adult to ski in the Rocky Mountains.

Living well as a diabetic woman requires adapting to certain physical requirements without sacrificing the quality of life. It's a constant balancing act. This chapter discusses the major physical issues unique to women with diabetes. It also explores some emotional and spiritual concerns associated with the disease.

PHYSICAL ISSUES

Diabetes presents women with special challenges during pregnancy, menstruation, and menopause. The interactions between blood sugar and hormone levels during these times affect our blood glucose regulation. Control, in turn, has a profound effect on pregnancy. Awareness of these effects will help you to manage both your diabetes and these aspects of your womanhood.

Menstruation

Interviews with both diabetic women and doctors reveal that, although hormones affect blood glucose levels, the effect is not uniform in all women. Even more frustrating is the fact that the effect can vary in the same woman; some months the blood sugars may rise dramatically, and some months they fall. Living well with the hormonal challenge requires a team effort. It isimportant for you to have medical advisors on your team who are knowledgeable and experienced in diabetes as well as female issues. They will best understand the general effect of hormones on blood sugars. Your job as a member of the team will be to record blood glucose levels accurately before, during, and after your menstrual periods. If you find a definite pattern, then together you can determine an appropriate course of action. If, for example, your blood sugar levels are consistently high the week before your period begins, then you may be able to successfully anticipate the increased need for insulin. However, it may not be that easy if your needs cannot be anticipated. The hormonal impact may vary or your periods may be inconsistent.

There is an individualized and changeable hormonal impact on blood sugar levels. Your choices are as follows. (1) With the help of your medical advisors, make a monthly plan of action designed to anticipate and meet your needs. (2) Do nothing anticipatory, but deal with the fluctuating blood sugars with the same strategies you use to cope with any stress-related, unpredictable blood sugars.

In addition, remember the strategy used by every woman in dealing with a period: When you can't exactly predict when it's coming, you start carrying some form of protection with you toward the end of the month so that you're prepared when it starts. We get frustrated and angry about periods when we are not prepared for them. The same is true of diabetes. Insulin reactions or high sugar levels are far more frustrating to us when we are ill prepared to handle them. When we handle them well, we increase our entire sense of well-being.

Birth Control

Since blood glucose should be under control before a woman becomes pregnant, it is important that a woman with diabetes practice birth control as soon as she becomes sexually active. Various methods are available. The method of choice will be determined through careful consideration of its effect on the woman's health as well as her personal preference.

In her book *The Diabetic Woman,* Dr. Lois Jovanovic recommends that if a woman does not have high blood pressure, she may use low-dose birth control pills. Their impact on insulin doses is minimal. Dr. Jovanovic writes that research shows that birth control pills do not increase the risk of blood clots. (Women with diabetic retinopathy should seek the advice of a specialist in diabetic retinopathy.) Dr. Jovanovic further points out that some women will require higher-dose pills that do affect glucose and insulin requirements, however.

If birth control pills are not chosen, women can use barrier methods such as the diaphragm, condom, or cervical sponge. Talk this over with a trusted medical advisor.

Pregnancy

> "When I decided to get married, my physician said to me: 'I think it's fine if you get married. But don't ever have children. Don't spread your genes around.' Because I am an educator, I believe that people ought to be given information and then make their own decisions. I felt that this doctor was giving me his personal opinion rather than information upon which to make a very important decision. So, my husband and I saw a genetic counselor who gave us not only information, but also a great deal

of encouragement about the genetic issues involved. Appropriately informed about genetic issues and my good health, my husband and I chose to have a baby."

The outcome of diabetic pregnancies has improved dramatically. Many years ago, women with diabetes had miscarriages at an alarmingly higher rate than did their nondiabetic counterparts. Today, a healthy woman with diabetes can expect an outcome similar to that of the general population if

1. She is seen and closely followed by a knowledgeable medical team experienced in diabetic pregnancies. Teams vary from center to center, but they usually include specialists in endocrinology, diabetology, obstetrics, dietetics, nursing, psychology, and social work or family counseling.
2. She is educated about caring for diabetes and is motivated to act on what she learns.
3. Her diabetes is under control *before* she becomes pregnant.
4. She keeps blood glucose levels within normal limits throughout the pregnancy. Research indicates that babies in utero tolerate low blood sugars much better than they tolerate high blood sugars.

The mother's health should be assessed before she conceives. If she has existing complications, especially of the kidney and eye, she must be informed about what effects the pregnancy might have on her health and the health of her baby. After an evaluation by a doctor extensively educated and experienced in both diabetes and pregnancy, the potential mother can make an informed choice about whether or not to attempt a pregnancy.

Ask your physician how many diabetic pregnancies he or she has managed. Also ask for a description of how your physician manages diabetic pregnancies. You need to have an obstetrician and a diabetes care specialist who are knowledgeable and experienced with diabetic pregnancies. If you know of no such physicians, ask your local American Diabetes Association Chapter for a referral.

Another essential element of a successful pregnancy is good health insurance. Even an uncomplicated diabetic pregnancy includes extra tests and visits to the medical team. A complicated pregnancy could include a lengthy hospitalization as well as intensive neonatal care for the baby. Make sure you have good health insurance before you become pregnant.

Throughout pregnancy, you should keep your blood sugars as nearly normal as possible. Chapter 5 of this book provides detailed information for learning the intensive regimen needed for this level of control. Your doctor will adapt this regimen to your individual needs. Besides the impact on the overall successful outcome of a pregnancy, it is important to keep blood sugars in normal range for the sake of the baby's size. The pregnant mother's blood sugar crosses the placenta. When the sugars are high, the baby's pancreas produces insulin to normalize them. In the process of using the mother's blood sugar, the baby gains weight. The baby's weight is one of the factors that determines the method through which the baby is delivered. Babies of normal weight can be delivered vaginally if the health of both the mother and the baby is otherwise good. Large babies must be delivered by Caesarean section.

Close blood sugar control presents numerous challenges. Ironically, close control increases the risk of severe insulin reactions (hypoglycemia). Fortunately, this is not a great problem for the baby, since babies can tolerate low blood sugar much better than high. The risk of low blood sugar is to the mother and her diabetes management. One undesirable result of low blood sugar is a swing to high blood sugar (hyperglycemia) and a bouncing effect that can upset one's control for a day or longer. Testing blood sugars more frequently is an excellent strategy for avoiding hypoglycemia.

One reason blood sugars rise too high following a low-blood-sugar episode is that people sometimes eat more than they need to counteract the lower sugar level.

> *"While I was pregnant, I forced myself to drink four ounces of juice and then wait a full fifteen minutes before taking anything more if the symptoms had not subsided. To help me wait, I pretended that it was a middle-of-the-night feeding for the baby. I viewed this strategy of treating low blood sugar as good practice for motherhood."*

With self blood glucose monitoring, we now have tools to tell us the impact of the food we eat. This is especially helpful when we need to assess the impact on low blood sugar. After you have eaten, you should wait fifteen minutes before rechecking blood sugar. After fifteen minutes, if the reading is still low or has not moved toward normal levels, drink another glass of juice or milk and retest in another fifteen minutes.

Doing periodic 3:00 A.M. blood tests can help to prevent problems with very low blood sugars. Report middle-of-the-night low blood sugars to your doctor. A change in your insulin dosage may be required. You may already be doing 3:00 A.M. blood tests on days when you are unusually active and are more inclined to an ongoing blood sugar–lowering effect. Knowing your body and your unique responses to activity, food, and stress is extremely helpful.

Close control of blood sugars will mean that your life-style during pregnancy will be closely regulated. This may not be typical of your usual way of living. Most of us slide off our regimens occasionally, and some do so fairly frequently. Reflect carefully on your willingness to maintain tight control in order to have a responsible pregnancy. Although it does require effort on the part of the diabetic woman, many women have reported that it actually turned out to be less of a challenge than they had anticipated. A common comment from pregnant women with diabetes is that their growing abdomen serves as a constant reminder of why they're working so hard.

"I made a commitment to follow my diabetic regimen to a point of perfection. Neither birthday nor any other holiday succeeded in tempting me to deviate from my meal plan. I related to a cartoon I saw just before Christmas. Two little boys in a department store were standing before a Christmas display. One boy said to the other, 'I'm so good at this time of year I can hardly stand myself.' While I understood that feeling, I also made the surprising discovery that it actually became easier and easier simply to make no exceptions. And I had a tremendous amount of support from the medical team.

The team of mother, father, obstetrician, diabetologist, dietitian, and nurse worked hard to make my pregnancy successful. I was extremely thankful to have an upbeat, 'human' medical team whose humor and warmth reinforced the excitement of a pregnancy instead of treating it like a high-risk, complicated medical problem. Whenever the seriousness of the situation did arise, I felt supported rather than fearful. For example, my di-

abetes doctor told me that any sign of infection, high sugars, or ketones should be reported immediately and not be left until tomorrow. It wasn't frightening to hear him say that, just reassuring to know that he would be there to help.

Besides wonderful medical support, I was blessed with a supportive husband who gave me a steady diet of love and humor. As my abdomen increased, I began to wonder how much longer I should inject my insulin abdominally. Although my obstetrician gave me the answer 'as long as it is both physically and psychologically comfortable,' it was my husband's response that took the prize. He told me, 'Just keep injecting in your abdomen until you hear someone say 'ouch.' Humor gives wonderful perspective."

Laboratory tests are an important part of support in a diabetic pregnancy. Each test and each visit to your medical team is an excellent reminder that you are not alone. Skilled people are doing everything they can to help you.

The baby's birth does not signify the end of the close working relationship between the mother and medical team. If you choose to nurse your baby, you must be well informed about your caloric needs for milk production as well as the ongoing balancing act with insulin. Throughout pregnancy, insulin requirements increase. Toward the end of a pregnancy, a woman may be taking two to three times as much insulin as in her prepregnancy days. At the time of birth, insulin requirements drop dramatically and a woman becomes extremely sensitive to insulin. Some women require no insulin immediately following delivery. The nursing mother may drop bedtime insulin entirely as her body burns many calories overnight for the production of milk. The teamwork continues. The baby is its newest member.

Because information on diabetic pregnancies is continually changing and growing, we encourage you to rely more on your medical advisors than on any printed information. Reflect on the issues. Make informed, responsible choices.

To Pregnant Women Whose Diabetes Is Not in Good Control . . .
The advice given so far on preparing for a diabetic pregnancy may raise fears in anyone who is already pregnant and maintaining less-than-excellent blood glucose control. Have you endangered

either your baby's health or your own? There is no simple answer. You must discuss your situation with an obstetrician experienced in diabetic pregnancies.

In the past, when tight control was not yet possible, many women had successful pregnancies with only minor difficulties. Statistically, these women and their babies were at greater risk, but each individual pregnancy had its own outcome. Even if your control has been moderate to poor, you may still have few problems if you regulate your blood glucose levels now. Discuss this fully with your medical team.

Beyond this, you may want to explore the techniques for working through possible resistance to maintaining good control is Chapters 3 and 14.

Vaginitis

Some women report that their diabetes was diagnosed when they went to see their doctor about severe vaginal itching. This problem is usually due to yeast infection. Diabetic women have an increased incidence of yeast infections because yeast grows more rapidly in glucose. The infections occur more frequently when blood sugars are high enough that glucose is present in the urine. Your doctor can prescribe treatments for yeast infections, but prevention is better. Generally these infections can be prevented by keeping the urine free of sugar.

If you choose to keep blood sugars in a normal range, refer to Chapter 5, "The Intensive Regimen." Using this chapter as a guide, discuss improving your regimen with your physician.

Menopause

At some point in middle age, women cease having periods. Because certain hormones are no longer present, the need for insulin usually drops. However, if the hormones are replaced, then insulin requirements will be affected by the estrogen and the progesterone. According to Dr. Lois Jovanovic, a noted authority in diabetic women's issues and herself a diabetic, the insulin requirements with hormone replacement are determined by how closely the hormone doses match the woman's needs. Higher doses of hormones require higher doses of insulin.

Day-to-day variations during menopause are far easier to handle with blood glucose monitoring. Some women experience profuse sweating during menopause and wonder if it is caused by hypoglycemia or by their "change." With blood testing, a woman can generally figure out what's happening and get in control of her life.

Hormones do affect blood sugar levels. You can choose whether or not to take hormones. Since a history of cancer is another factor to consider in making this decision, it is best to discuss all the factors with your carefully selected medical advisors. Remember that you are a unique person, and the effect your hormones have on your blood sugar levels may be different from what you hear from other women or read about. When books describe what is *normal,* they are more accurately describing what is *average.* Since few of us are "average," you should work with your medical team to understand your unique reactions. Doing this is another leg of the journey toward personal growth and fulfillment.

It is comforting to have support for the physical needs of diabetes—the timing of meals, appropriate food, and time and space for monitoring blood glucose. But there is another type of support that is equally important, if not more so. That is emotional support.

EMOTIONAL ISSUES

I believe that women who have diabetes have a distinct advantage over men who have diabetes. Traditionally, women have found it easier to connect with friends on an emotional level. To receive emotional support, one needs to understand the language and be willing to engage in the process of both seeking and receiving it. The language of emotional support includes "I feel. . . I need . . . I am angry, fearful, lonely because . . . " "It makes me feel so good when . . ." Getting emotional support includes a willingness to begin conversations with phrases like these. The process also requires time and an appropriate setting. A fifteen-minute commute on the way to work won't do it. A meeting in a relaxed atmosphere like a restaurant or your home, with an hour's worth of time, is more likely to allow the process to work.

People who feel reticent to begin talking with their friends about the feelings they have about diabetes may find it very helpful to attend a meeting of the local American Diabetes Association. Meeting others who have diabetes often creates an instantaneous bond that connects people on an emotional level.

A variety of support groups are available to people who are interested in group interaction. At many ADA affiliates, visitation programs are now being offered. These allow people who have diabetes and are feeling "stuck" to meet one-to-one with others who have diabetes. This effective program provides two-way benefit, as both the giver and the recipient find support. If this type of program appeals to you, check with your local ADA chapter or affiliate. Whether it's through a formalized program of social support or the casual warmth of two friends having coffee, take the step toward connecting on a feeling level. It may seem awkward at first, but keep at it. The rewards are great.

Dating and Marriage

Some women are reluctant to tell their dates that they have diabetes. If you are dating, consider the following scenarios.

1. Which situation would be better?
   a. You have an insulin reaction when you are with a man who knows you have diabetes.
   b. You have a reaction when you are with someone who hasn't a clue as to why your behavior is changed.
2. You are dating someone who needs to eat at a particular time. Would you prefer to have your date tell you that? Or, would you prefer to have him jeopardize his health to eat a fashionably late dinner?
3. Do you really believe that diabetes is such an awful disease that someone would not want to date you because of it?
   a. If your answer is yes, you should talk to a diabetes educator who can help you to adapt to diabetes and have a fun and full social life.
   b. If your answer is no, remember that you can influence the way your date thinks about diabetes. Present it positively, as a disease that can be controlled through a healthy lifestyle.

"A touching and reinforcing moment for me came at a party one evening when I overheard my husband say to the group of people with whom he was visiting: 'The best thing that ever happened to me was marrying someone with diabetes. We live such a healthy life.'

Dating was not particularly problematic for me in terms of my diabetes until marriage became an issue. It is at major decision points in life — such as marriage, career, children — that one is confronted again with accepting the fact that diabetes, like any chronic disease, is unavoidably a part of life and of that decision."

While my husband and I were dating, I wondered about what diabetes would mean for him if we were married. But I did like his attitude. He was at ease — never treating me like a "diabetic," but rather as an attractive (to him) young woman. And he had just the right measure of concern; that is, he asked questions about appropriate restaurant choice, timing for meals, and what, if any, dessert I would eat when we ate at his parents' house for the first time. Humor helped us through the rough spots (and it still does!).

"But somewhere in my subconscious a shadow was lurking, and I couldn't quite make out what it meant. A wonderfully sensitive physician helped me bring it into the light so that I could see it and deal with it. It was this: Just before I became engaged, I visited my doctor. In the waiting room, I met a young woman exactly my age who was losing her sight as a result of diabetes.

Suddenly I had an urgent need to know the future. I wanted my doctor to look into a crystal ball and tell me what course my diabetes would take, so that I would have some idea of what 'for better or for worse' might mean to my husband. My doctor gently explained to me that no one knows what the future will bring. Perhaps the most profound lesson that diabetes has taught me is this: Diabetes does not make life any more uncertain. It simply makes us more aware of the uncertainty of life."

People blessed with the awareness that life is uncertain are in a unique position to enjoy life more fully. Time is more likely to be savored than wasted. All of life's experiences become a potential sorce of wonder. The embarrassment of saying "I love you" gives way to appreciation for having the courage to say it.

It is helpful to be able to identify what makes your life fulfilling, because that's what will motivate you to handle any challenge that threatens your enjoyment of life. Your desire to live fully will mobilize the great inner strengths that you have.

> *My husband and I wed and have enjoyed healthy, happy times. Four years after we married, we had a child. I knew that our son would never see his mother coping with stress by taking alcohol or drugs. My early experiences had already set healthy stress- management habits of diet and activity."*
>
> *Our family life has been full. I have felt great and participated actively and fully in my teaching career as well as having a social life of partying, cross-country skiing, and bicycling.*

Most women fully expect to enjoy retirement with their husbands. They also expect to watch every hockey game of their children as they grow up. They look forward to graduation, weddings, and grandchildren. Without the challenge of a chronic disease, it is easier to deny that untimely death could ever rob them of their lifelong plans. Besides a mighty important lesson about the uncertainty of life, diabetes can give one the gift of appreciating how precious life is. It's an odd and profound gift that is difficult to explain. It's like appreciating the fragile, exquisite beauty of a snowflake with the understanding that it may be the last one you'll ever see along with the faith that it isn't. Perhaps the oddest part of the gift is the realization that we receive this gift through suffering. The painful awareness of our mortality actually gives us the gift of appreciating life.

Balancing the Emotions
Although there surely are times when diabetes causes us to grapple with life's most profound issues, there are plenty of times when having diabetes is little more than a minor inconvenience. Balancing the emotions of those very different viewpoints is important to one's overall well-being.

> *"At about the six-week point in my pregnancy (before it had been confirmed), I attended a diabetes and pregnancy conference. It was directed to health professionals and contained (to me, because I suspected I was pregnant) a ton of horror. I heard someone talk about the possibility of brain damage to the baby if*

ketones were present in the early weeks of development. That horrified me because I had been experiencing fasting ketosis recently. I went to my doctor immediately following the conference. He explained that in the early weeks of fetal development the body's need for calories greatly increases, and that's why I had ketones in my urine. An increase in calories and insulin took care of the physical problems.

I resolved to avoid similar conferences during my pregnancy to alleviate my emotional discomfort. But this is not to recommend ignorance as bliss. Education is a most important ally. I sincerely believe that one must strive for the balance of knowing what you need to know and then avoiding a mental diet of facts that only frighten and immobilize the spirit. I knew that my carefully selected physicians knew the facts, dangers, and cautions of a diabetic pregnancy. I allowed them to do the worrying. I concentrated my efforts on doing all that they recommended and then did everything possible to keep mind and spirit positive and hopeful."

To follow a self-care regimen, we need to accept the seriousness of diabetes as well as our personal vulnerability. Then, we also need hope. We need to understand all of our options for health and act on them. Reflect on the issues that cause you emotional discomfort. Talk them over with a trusted advisor. Act to prevent problems, and promote health and well-being. By taking positive action, you will gain an overall sense of control over your life.

CAREER CONCERNS

Until the mid-eighties, women were bombarded with advice about what to do with their lives. We were urged to seek nontraditional careers. We were told to rebel against being "just homemakers." But now the pendulum seems to be swinging toward more reasonable advice: Women should be able to choose whatever they want to do—have a career, go to school, stay at home, do volunteer work, or combine any of these choices. If the choices they make are manageable and fulfilling, women can find satisfaction and harmony in their lives. If they undertake either too little or too much, the effects are negative and stressful. Balance is essential to anyone who wants a happy, healthy life. We need enough meaningful activity to give life excitement and a sense of purpose, but not so much

327

activity that we are overwhelmed by demands on us. All men and women struggle with this balancing of life. When diabetes is present, it is simply another ball to juggle.

Reflect on your own life challenges as I share a few of mine.

Diabetes goes with me:

- Into the hospital where I do volunteer work. I attend monthly meetings from 4:00 until 6:00 P.M. To keep balance, I do a blood test just before the meeting and then help myself to the fruit and crackers offered if I need them. My own supply of dried fruit is ever at hand should I need more.

- On national and international airplane flights. I juggle time-zone changes and insulin requirements according to my doctor's good advice. With snacks like dried fruit and granola bars in my purse or briefcase, I can cope when a meal flight ends up serving no food. I always carry my blood glucose meter with me on the plane. Extra tests reassure me that I am remaining in balance.

11 Up to the podium as I make presentations. A blood test before speaking tells me if my jitters are simply from nervousness or if I am hypoglycemic.

- Into those "one-hour" meetings that begin at 11:00 A.M. and end at 1:00 P.M. Inconspicuous snacks like Lifesavers keep me going without interrupting the meeting.

Diabetes is ever present when I'm working too many hours and forgetting to balance my work with exercise (for the body). I have seen tests of 400 as a result of the distress of imbalance. It is tempting to curse my diabetes, saying, "If it weren't for that darned diabetes, I could keep up the same pace as my friends do!" But then I look at the picture more carefully. What is really happening is this: Diabetes tells me when life is out of balance and my body is asking me not to abuse it. Diabetes, in this case, is a blessing in disguise. In fact, I often find myself cautioning my nondiabetic friends to take better care of themselves. Although they know the harmful effects of stress, they don't have a tool (like my blood glucose meter) to tell them that their stress is harming them.

IN MY HEART OF HEARTS . . .

The heart of life is neither male nor female, for it beats for all. The skills we need to live well with diabetes are the very same skills that anyone needs to meet the inevitable pain and challenges of life. To experience joy and soul-satisfying growth, we need to believe that diabetes has that gift to give. Great philosophers teach us that pain hollows us out, allowing us to hold more joy. They even suggest that pain holds as much wonder as joy. Indeed, joy and sorrow are inseparable in the same way that pain and growth often come together.

With maturity, we all become philosophers to some degree. If we can accept the philosophy that pain brings growth, then we have the foundation upon which to build a healthy life. Neitzche said that people who have a *why* to life can bear almost any *how*. With this belief, we accept diabetes as one more building block of life.

Living Young With Diabetes

Believe it or not, every grown-up has a child inside that remembers what being a kid is all about. The authors of this book asked the kids inside them to write about having diabetes when they were young. Cathy was 10, Gary was 12, and Ernie was 14 when their diabetes started.

You're really lucky to be a kid now. The doctors and nurses today know so much more about diabetes than when we were kids. They're good at helping you learn all the things you need to know about taking care of yourself. They've finally figured out that kids can do all kinds of complex things, like testing their own blood sugar. Children are a lot smarter than most grown-ups probably realize.

Having diabetes keeps us on our toes — more than most people. Some great entertainers and athletes have diabetes. Wade Wilson, Mary Tyler Moore, and Catfish Hunter have diabetes, and it hasn't stopped them. It doesn't have to stop you. With diabetes or without diabetes, there is a world of things we can accomplish if we really want to.

The kid inside Ernie says:

One dumb thing I had to get over when I was a kid was pretending not to have diabetes. For a long time, I ate whatever I wanted (usually when no one was looking). I even forgot shots and ended up in the hospital in a coma one time. I thought if I acted like I didn't have diabetes it would just go away. But it didn't.

I think I would have been a lot happier if I had taken better care of myself. I don't mean being perfect! But I wish I had remembered my shots, done my tests regularly, and not eaten sweets so often. I guess I thought the doctor and my mom and dad were the ones I did those things for, and I resented them for that. Now I know you do those things for yourself, not for anybody else.

Sometimes having diabetes makes me feel sad or angry or afraid. Don't ever think you shouldn't have these feelings. They are a natural part of you, and there's no reason to pretend you don't have them. When I kept my feelings inside, I ended up doing things that were worse than saying "I'm angry."

The kid inside Gary says:

My doctor wanted me to meet another diabetic while I was still in the hospital. (When I was a kid, you had to stay in the hospital for several days just to get regulated). I was embarrassed to meet this person who had diabetes. It was even worse because he was coming to the hospital just to see me. I don't remember his name, but he was just a little older than me, and I liked him a lot. I remember him telling me that taking your insulin gets to be a habit, like brushing your teeth. It helped me to talk to someone else who had diabetes. It took away some of my fear. At the time, I didn't think it was that important. But I still remember it.

In a way, diabetes really helped me grow up. I learned about taking responsibility. I learned how to talk about diabetes and even other things without being ashamed. I learned how to talk to the coaches at school and the dietitian in the school kitchen. I learned how to arrange my life so that diabetes didn't interfere too much. I learned how to go out with my friends and do what they did and still keep my diabetes under pretty good control.

The kid inside Cathy says:

When I was little, they didn't even have blood sugar testing you could do at home. Blood tests are a lot better than testing your urine. They help you know if you have enough energy for playing hard without having reactions. But remember, those test numbers are just facts to help you. They don't say whether you're a good person or a bad person. They just tell what your blood sugar is, so you can figure out how to change your insulin, food, or exercise.

It's a little like being a scientist. If your blood sugar is higher or lower than you want it to be, you can usually figure out why. Maybe you ran extra hard today. Maybe your snack was bigger than usual. Maybe you've got a bad cold. When you figure out the reason your blood sugars are off, you're not only a scientist, you're a detective, too!

My doctor first told me I had diabetes when I was in the hospital for a broken arm. A clown came to my room to cheer me up and give me a balloon. I said, "I just have a broken arm and diabetes. I'm not sick!" I went on feeling that way and never saw diabetes as a reason not to do anything. I did everything my friends did, except for eating lots of sweet things.

I asked my mom if having diabetes would make me different from the other kids. She told me, "You'll be stronger and more in charge of your life. You'll learn how to take care of yourself and eat the right things. That will mean our whole family will benefit because we'll learn to take care of ourselves from you.

All three of us say:

We know having diabetes is a problem sometimes, but we want you to remember that having diabetes doesn't mean you're sick. You just have to watch some things other kids don't ever have to think about. (Some people think that makes us smarter than other people.) But most of the things we are supposed to do are healthy for everybody.

You'll be learning about diabetes for a long time, probably the rest of your life. We hope there will be a cure for you to learn about someday. Scientists are working on it now, but nobody's sure when they'll find it. Until they do, take good care of yourself so the cure will work for you.

TO THE PARENTS OF A DIABETIC YOUTH . . .

Credo for the parent of a diabetic child

My child is an essentially healthy person who happens to have some qualities that need special attention, not a sick child who must be protected.

My child is capable of learning to handle all aspects of diabetes care over time, not someone who must remain dependent on me.

My child will learn to take good care of diabetes by following my model of healthful behavior and by receiving positive rewards, not from threats of the consequences of diabetes.

I will find the right balance between my responsibility as a parent and my child's growing responsibility for his or her own life, including the care of diabetes.

When I feel I can't cope, I will get the help I need to go on living well and aiding my child to live well. I do not need to sacrifice my life to diabetes.

To live well with childhood diabetes calls for a unique partnership between you and your child, one that can enrich and deepen your relationship. You can learn together, adapt together, and feel together as you meet the demands of this condition. With a preteen, especially, you become an authoritative source of information and guidance as you learn about diabetes. At the same time, you respect and support your child's growing capacity for self-management and participation in decision making.

Having a child with diabetes presents enough special challenges that you deserve a book specifically addressing your child's and your unique needs. Fortunately, there is an excellent one that we suggest you get if you are the parent of a diabetic youth. It was written by the founder of the Juvenile Diabetes Foundation, Lee Ducat, who is herself the parent of a diabetic. You can find a complete reference and description of this book at the end of this chapter, together with several other resources specific to parents and youth.

We begin with an often-neglected subject: your own needs as the parent of a youth with diabetes.

Take Care of Yourself!

Many of the techniques for living well described in this book apply to your life as well as your child's. Your maintenance of psychological health, good diet, and exercise programs become a model for your child. This is the very best way of teaching — to be what you want your child to become. With this understanding, taking care of yourself helps both you and your child. And you avoid the useless martyr role —sacrificing yourself for someone else's well-being.

Use the tips for stress management and coping included in Chapters 3, 11, and 14, and find a support group for parents of diabetics through your local chapter of the American Diabetes Association. Parents with experience can help you cope with your problems and guide you in handling the problems that come up with your child. (See Chapter 13 for more on support groups and networks for both you and your child.)

Adapting the Living Well Approach to Your Child's Situation

The underlying approach of this book is respect for the capacity of the individual diabetic to make wise choices in his or her self-care. We believe the diabetes regimen must be individualized; that adherence to it grows when parental attention is positive rather than threatening; and that living well is a matter of one's whole life, not just blood sugar levels.

As the parent of a child or teenager, you may wonder if these beliefs are fully applicable without risk to your child. Can a child of 5 or 6 make wise choices or handle precise techniques like insulin injections or home blood glucose testing? What will control the rebelliousness of your teen other than threats of future catastrophes if he or she doesn't shape up?

Many parents and diabetic youths have demonstrated this approach by sharing responsibility fully, discussing decisions together, and gradually passing responsibility on to the growing child. Children as young as 5 have learned to use meters accurately to test blood sugar levels and to give their own insulin. Rebelliousness may be an inevitable part of the teen years, but there is little evidence that coercion and threats are an effective way of handling it. The *Living Well* approach gives a teenage diabetic positive reinforcement and opportunities to learn to make more responsible choices.

Balance and Individualization

We have emphasized the need to design a diabetes treatment program specific to the needs and character of the individual throughout this book. Now we must consider two or three individuals — the child and the parents — as well as the rest of the family. Living well with youthful diabetes demands a balance between the lives of all the family members and an adaptation to the unique pattern of the individual family.

Different families have very different patterns concerning responsibility, decision making, participation, emotional support, health practices, and other areas important to diabetes care. You must find a way of dealing with the demands of diabetes that fits your family's patterns. But you may need to change patterns that unintentionally undermine your young diabetic's ability to live well. He or she may find it difficult to follow a healthful life-style if the rest of the family eats an unhealthy diet, doesn't exercise, and handles stress poorly. Becoming responsible for his or her own care will be hard if the parents are either too protective or too dominating.

My Family Profile

To identify your family's patterns, explore your answers to this questionnaire. You can gain insight into your own family's patterns and how they may affect your diabetic youth.

1. How are decisions made in your family?_____
   _____

   Do you discuss issues together?_____
   _____

   Do you explore alternative options to choose from?_____
   _____

Who participates in the actual decision making?_____

What matters do the children decide on their own?_____

In what areas are the children simply given orders?

2. How well do the children follow either their own decisions or suggestions and orders given by parents?

   Parent's opinions _____
   Children's opinions _____

   How well do the parents follow either their own decisions or directions given by external authority?_____

3. When a child disobeys or acts irresponsibly, how do the parents respond?_____

   What is done to help the child act differently?_____

   Do these things work?_____

4. In your family who has taken the responsibility to learn about diabetes?_____

   Mother_____ Father_____ Child_____

5. Does the family as a whole follow a healthful life-style?_____
   A moderate and balanced diet? _____
   Regular exercise and activity? _____
   Effective stress management? _____
   Emotional stability? _____

6. What major challenges other than diabetes face you and your
    family?_____

_____

Your answers may suggest areas where your family could
strengthen its ability to cope with diabetes and other life challenges. Parents can use the results of this exercise to discuss possible changes, first between themselves and then with the whole
family.

AGES AND PHASES OF YOUTHFUL DIABETES
The age of your child will determine how you adapt this book to your
situation. In this section, we will make a few suggestions for different ages.

Infancy to age 4 or 5
If you have a young child with diabetes, *Living Well* will be a major
educational source for you, but you will need detailed guidance in
many aspects of caring for and educating your child. Your health
care team and diabetes support network will play an important role,
even more than with older children. The Introduction and Chapter
1 offer basic attitudes and practices that you can draw on in your
parenting. Chapters 3, 11, and 14 will help you help yourself as well
as your child with the emotional challenges of diabetes. Toward the
end of this phase you can cautiously begin sharing responsibility for
day-to-day diabetes tasks. As the young one demonstrates expertise
under your supervision, you will gain confidence and a sense of
what he or she can handle.

Age 5 to Puberty
As your child matures, you will be able to start passing on more and
more responsibility for details of self-care. From this time, you will
be able to use diabetes classes, support groups, and camps to supplement your roles in education and emotional support. Use *Living
Well* as a source book for answering questions and offering guidance. You and your doctor will form a team determining regimen
choices for the child to consider. You will work together to build the
positive motivation needed for following the resulting treatment
program.

Teenage years

At this time, the basic approach of *Living Well* may be the most effective way of bypassing or quieting rebellion against diabetic regimen. See your child as capable of making responsible choices, as needing to participate fully in decisions about his or her health and life-style, and as the final authority over what he or she actually does with his or her life. With this point of view, there is a basis for negotiation that cannot exist if you hold onto this responsibility and authority. You are also more likely to keep communication open about what is going on with diabetes in your teen's life. Children who learn well from written material may be able to start working directly with *Living Well*, although you may need to help. (This book is written at the level of a high school graduate.)

CHOOSING THE LEVEL OF REGIMEN

For all but the very young, your doctor, your child, and you must work together to find a level of diabetic regimen and control that will work for all parties. Often the physician advises against the intensive regimen because of the greater dangers of insulin reactions in childhood. Children are usually much more active and engage in their activities with such intensity that the onset of reactions may be difficult to notice. Often they wish not to appear different because of their diabetes, and they may want to hide their vulnerability. The level of awareness demanded by the intensive regimen might cause some children to become preoccupied with their illness and some parents to become obsessive about it.

On the other hand, with the right combination of child, parents, and doctor, many children have learned to manage diabetes very carefully and live full, exuberant lives. The decision about the level of regimen a child is to learn to follow must be reached through thoughtful discussion between the whole family and the physician. The factors you will need to balance include

1. The likely long-term value of avoiding chronic high blood sugar levels
2. The need to avoid frequent insulin reactions;
3. The feelings of your child and yourself;
4. Your child's age and learning skills;
5. Your child's growth pattern and overall health (chronically high blood sugar can slow growth and the onset of puberty).

339

DIABETIC COMPLICATIONS

Diabetes carries with it the risk of secondary disorders that may develop later in your child's life. No subject in parenting requires more sensitivity than these possible complications. Along with insulin reactions and diabetic coma, they constitute a major threat and source of fear for parents and children alike. When your child begins to be aware of diabetic complications, you will need to convey carefully the nature of the threat and tell your child what to do to reduce the risk. (Your child may come to you in distress after hearing of a diabetic relative or friend of the family who has developed serious complications.) There are several important points to make:

- Some diabetics develop a complication, but many do not. The authors of *Living Well*, after 170 years of diabetes altogether, all see clearly, have no kidney disease, and have only minor complications.
- Diabetics can do many things to lessen their risk of developing complications.
- Treatment for diabetic complications is improving; in many cases, treatment enables the person with diabetes to avoid disabilities altogether.
- If your child is old enough, discuss the concept of risk, and how everyone is at risk and has to learn to deal with the fears this produces. Life has threats, but we live well by remembering life's promises more than the threats.
- In general, answer the questions your child brings up, but don't flood him or her with too much information. Keep a balance between the facts and the emotional reassurance you offer.

You should not force information about complications on your child, and, above all, you should never use threats of dire consequences to encourage your child to follow regimen. Either practice is likely to build more anxiety than adherence. Carefully inspect any booklets or audiovisual presentations on complications before using them. Old educational materials often use frightening, worst-case photos and threatening language. Even current publications on complications are seldom written with sensitivity to the emotional needs of the reader.

Before discussing complications with your child, read Chapter 15 and the sections on preventive measures in Chapter 17. Deal with your own feelings about these threats first, so you can be calm in helping your child.

DIABETES POWER STRUGGLES

Any parents and children may develop power struggles over the children's behavior. With diabetes, however, these conflicts can take on an extreme level of emotion when "not doing the right thing" appears to threaten the child's very survival. As the parent, you may feel anxious, frantic, and possibly angry when your child "forgets" insulin repeatedly or eats excessive amounts of sweets. If your anxiety causes you to try to force your child to follow regimen, you may simply incite your child to rebel even more.

You can do several things to avoid turning a matter of such genuine concern into a full power struggle:

- Deal with your own feelings apart from the situation. Don't dump them on your child.

- Ask your child to help you understand what is happening and what changes are needed to handle the problem. Work with your child rather than giving commands.

- Look at your child's behavior in terms of what is happening in his or her life. How does having diabetes function to reward the child with attention; to allow him or her to escape obligations or responsibilities; or to express feelings he or she can't express directly? How can you help satisfy these needs directly?

- Set goals together, with a clear understanding of how you will both know when they are met. If it fits your style of parenting, set appropriate rewards and penalties.

- Work with the basic understanding that you have a problem to solve together, not that your child is the problem.

Finally, understand that in some matters of regimen there is room for a few little vacations. Sweets, for instance, are not poison to a diabetic; they are simply something to be eaten with great moderation. Don't let your child think that the only time he or she can eat a dessert or piece of candy is during an insulin reaction. Dietitians have found that regular nondietetic ice cream at mealtime does not increase blood sugar level seriously, so long as it is not a candy flavor or covered with gooey toppings.

DIABETIC FOR A DAY

Parents and diabetes professionals have gained remarkable empathy by living as diabetics for a day or more. They test their blood several times a day, take injections of sterile water, watch their diet, and follow an exercise program. If you care to enter into your child's reality in this way, you will discover a new level of respect for what he or she must do each day. And your youngster will be delighted that you have taken this dramatic step to see the world in this new way.

The theme of empathy this simulation teaches is the foundation for good parenting. When your love for your child is supported by this sort of respect and understanding, you both find that you can live well with diabetes.

BOOKS FOR PARENTS OF A DIABETIC YOUTH

Diabetes. Lee Ducat and Sherry Suib Cohen. Harper and Row (1983). A complete guide to healthier living for parents, children, and young adults who have insulin-dependent diabetes.

The first author of this book, Lee Ducat, is the founder of the Juvenile Diabetes Foundation and the mother of a diabetic. She has drawn on her own experience as well as that of the patients, families, and doctors involved in JDF. The book is written as a "coping manual, a practical guide," with tips to help young diabetics and their families live well with diabetes.

It includes information on "how to deal with doctors, teachers, babysitters, and other children; how to set and achieve reasonable goals for testing, diet, and exercise; how to handle camp, birthday parties, school, sports, and travel; what to do in emergencies; advice on dating, sex, marriage, and pregnancy; and how to deal with the anger and depression this disease can cause." This valuable resource has chapters on the needs of diabetic babies, youngsters, teenagers, and young adults.

You can order a copy by calling 1-800- 242-7737.

Whole Parent/Whole Child, A Parent's Guide to Raising Children with a Chronic Health Condition. Broatch Haig and Patricia Moynihan. International Diabetes Center, Minneapolis, Minnesota (1989).

While covering a broader range of conditions than diabetes, the authors (a dietitian and a nurse specialist) are diabetes educators. Their book is based on years of helping parents and children deal with the demands of diabetes.

This book can be ordered by calling DCI's toll free number, 1-800-848-2793. In Minnesota, call 1-800-444-5951. Ask for a catalog of other publications on diabetes.

What Does It Feel Like to Have Diabetes? Denise J. Bradley. Charles C. Thomas, Springfield, Illinois.

This autobiographical book was written by a 27-year-old woman who has had diabetes since the age of 3.

The American Diabetes Association has a number of publications in its catalog, including *Especially for Parents,* a package of articles reprinted from *Diabetes Forecast* newsletter; cookbooks; pamphlets, and the following two books. You can order all of these and request the catalog by calling the ADA's toll free order number, 1-800-ADA-DISC.

Children with Diabetes. Linda M. Siminerio and Jean Betschart. For parents, teachers, and others who work with diabetic children.

This book covers all the details of diabetic management, takes a sensitive look at children's psychological needs, and offers suggestions for promoting a positive and supportive home environment. Order from the AOA.

Kid's Corner. For children with diabetes. Children aged 8 to 12 have fun as they learn about diabetes through this booklet of puzzles and games. Order from the AOA.

A Book on Diabetes for Brothers & Sisters. Linda Siminerio. Children's Hospital of Pittsburgh, Pennsylvania.

Resources For Living Well

DIABETES IDENTIFICATION

You should wear, at all times, a bracelet or necklace identifying you as having diabetes and giving a number to call for information in case of emergency. The following services maintain 24-hour hotlines, where details of your diabetes care are available to medical personnel from anywhere in the world. Medic Alert says, "This identification could save your life." Any diabetic who has passed out from insulin shock or coma will agree.

Medic Alert Foundation
P.O. Box 1009
Turlock, CA 95381
(209) 668-3333

Medic Alert Foundation provides attractive I.D. bracelets and necklaces and has a toll-free number with medical information.

Med-Fax
618 Venice Blvd.
Marina del Rey, CA 90291
(213) 821-1984

Med-Fax is a highly specialized emergency data system that allows one to store emergency medical information in the MED-FAX Voice

Computer. In an emergency, the computer speaks your medical file directly over the telephone to physicians or trauma centers worldwide.

ORGANIZATIONS AND SOURCES OF INFORMATION

American Diabetes Association
1660 Duke Street
Alexandria, VA 22314
1-800-ADA-DISC
The American Diabetes Association (ADA) supports research, education, and public awareness programs relating to both insulin-dependent and non-insulin-dependent diabetes. Membership for $20 a year provides monthly issues of *Diabetes Forecast* and automatic membership in a local chapter. Information on the *Diabetes Forecast* reprint series and other publications can be requested in writing.

Juvenile Diabetes Foundation Intl.
23 E. 26th Street
New York, NY 10010
(800) 223-1138
The Juvenile Diabetes Foundation (JDF) is a volunteer organization specializing in insulin-dependent diabetes. It has a network of chapters worldwide and raises funds for diabetes research. Chapters provide helpful brochures as well as personal contact. A quarterly newsletter is published for JDF members.

National Diabetes Information Clearinghouse
Box NDIC
Bethesda, MD 20205
(301) 468-2162
(301) 496-7433
The National Diabetes Information Clearinghouse (NDIC) works to increase knowledge and understanding about diabetes among patients, health professionals, and the public. It provides responses to inquiries, publications, professional and patient education programs, and an online data base. Call or write to request NDIC's publications list. *Diabetes Dateline* is the organization's newsletter.

American Association of Diabetes Educators

500 N. Michigan Ave. # 1400

Chicago, IL 60611

The American Association of Diabetes Educators (AADE) publishes a directory of diabetes education programs. (Diabetes Center Pharmacy will send you a list of qualified diabetes educators in your area. Call 1-800-848-2793.)

Joslin Diabetes Foundation, Inc.

One Joslin Plaza

Boston, MA 02215

Joslin Clinic was the pioneer treatment center for diabetes care. The Foundation provides information and literature concerning diabetes.

HCF Diabetes Foundation

P.O. Box 22124

Lexington, KY 40522

The HCF Diabetes Foundation publishes *Diabetes and Nutrition* ($6.00 per year), a newsletter based on the work of James W. Anderson, M.D. concerning the healthful benefits of high-carbohydrate, high-fiber diets. Other publications are available.

Sugarfree Center

P.O. Box 114

Van Nuys, CA 91408

1-800-972-2323 (Nationwide)

1-800-336-1222 (California only)

Health-O-Gram, and living-well information from "the diabetic's own service for living and learning." A $10 membership fee includes a one-year subscription to the newsletter and other special publications. (Also see listing under Diabetic Supplies.)

Other sources of information include companies that produce diabetic supplies. You may request specific booklets and catalogs of publications from the following:

Ames Division, Miles Laboratories, Inc.

P.O. Box 70, Elkhart, IN 46515

347

Becton-Dickinson
Rochelle Park, NJ 07662

Eli Lilly & Co.
Indianapolis, IN 46285

Monoject Division
Sherwood Medical
St. Louis, MO 63166

Pfizer Laboratories
New York, NY

Squibb-Novo
120 Alexander St.
Princeton, NJ 08540

DIABETES MAGAZINES

American Diabetes Association
General Membership
P.O. Box 2055
Harlan, IA 51593-0238
Diabetes Forecast is the most complete magazine for people with
diabetes. Published by the American Diabetes Association, it in-
cludes reports on new research, personal stories, practical tips on
diabetes care, and articles for children. Membership is $20 per year.

Center for Diabetes Education
Ames Division
Miles Laboratories, Inc.
P.O. Box 70
Elkhart, IN 46515
Diabetes in the News is a magazine featuring diabetes management
and life-style articles. It is published every other month by the
Ames Center for Diabetes Education. Subscription is $9 per year.

Diabetes Center, Inc. (DCI Publishing)
P.O. Box 739
Wayzata, MN 55391
Living Well with Diabetes is a quarterly magazine that includes informative articles on self-care and current research, as well as the catalog for discount supplies from the Diabetes Center Pharmacy. You can order a free two-issue trial subscription by calling 1-800-848-0614. Subscription is $6.

Diabetes Self-Management
42-15 Crescent St.
Long Island City, NY 11101
Diabetes Self-Management is a quarterly magazine containing practical self-care articles. Subscription is $8 per year.

SOME BOOKS ON DIABETES
The following books are available from DCI Publishing.

Learning to Live Well with Diabetes, by Donnell D. Etzwiler and others from the International Diabetes Center. This up-to-date, comprehensive and easy-to-understand manual helps people with diabetes work with their health care team to improve diabetes control and quality of life.

The Physician Within — Taking Charge of Your Well Being, by Catherine Feste. This book is about self-motivation for people who are trying to follow either a pattern of healthy living or a specific medical regimen.

Exchanges for All Occasions — Meeting the Challenge of Diabetes, by Marion J. Franz. This book helps everyone use the exchange system for meal planning in almost any situation.

DCI also has pamphlets from the International Diabetes Center available through their catalog. Order any of these DCI books or the catalog from DCI Publishing, P.O. Box 739, Wayzata, MN 55391. Or call 1-800-848-2793.

Diabetes, by Lee Ducat and Sherry Suib Cohen. A complete guide to healthier living for parents, children, and young adults who have insulin-dependent diabetes. Harper and Row (1983). You can order a copy by calling 1-800-242-7737.

Diabetic Child and Young Adult, by Mimi Belmonte (1983).

Diabetes: A Practical Guide To Healthy Living, by James W. Anderson. Arco, Inc., publishes this guide for general diabetes management written by Dr. Anderson, with a special section on the HCF diet plan. Warner Books (1983). Order from HCF Diabetes Foundation, P.O. Box 22124, Lexington, KY 40522

The American Diabetes Association publishes a large number of books, pamphlets, and reprints of articles from *Diabetes Forecast*. Below are some of the ADA titles available.

Family Cookbook—Volumes 1, 2, and 3.

Kid's Corner, ADA (1983). Children have fun as they learn about diabetes through this booklet of puzzles and games. For children ages 8 through 12 with diabetes.

Children with Diabetes, by Linda M. Siminerio and Jean Betschart. ADA (1986). For parents, teachers, and others who work with diabetic children. It covers all the details of diabetic management, takes a sensitive look at children's psychological needs, and offers suggestions for promoting a positive and supportive home environment.

Diabetes in the Family, ADA (1987). This book deals with day-to- day issues of diet and self-care as well as lifetime issues such as employment and marriage.

Diabetes: Reach for Health and Freedom, by Dorothea Sims. ADA (1984). Learn how a person with diabetes not only survives but excels. For both patients and professionals.

Diabetes A to Z, ADA (1988). An expanded and updated version of the former *Guide to Good Living*. Arranged in dictionary format for easy reference, this book covers the medical concerns of a person with diabetes, as well as some less conventional topics, such as tax tips, dealing with Halloween and Valentine's Day, dancing, driving, and handling feelings of loneliness.

Diabetes Forecast reprints and special topic reprint packages

The ADA publications listed can be ordered from

American Diabetes Association
National Service Center
1660 Duke St.
Alexandria, VA 22314
Or call 1-800-ADA-DISC.

Diabetes: Caring for Your Emotions As Well As Your Health, by Jerry Edelwich and Archie Brodsky (1986).

The Diabetic's Book: All Your Questions Answered, by June Biermann and Barbara Toohey. Tarcher, Santa Monica, CA (1981).

The Diabetic's Total Health Book, by June Biermann and Barbara Toohey. Tarcher, Santa Monica, CA (1988).

The Peripatetic Diabetic, by June Biermann and Barbara Toohey. Tarcher, Santa Monica, CA (1984).

The Diabetic Woman, by June Biermann, Barbara Toohey, and Dr. Lois Jovanovic. Tarcher, Santa Monica, CA (1987).

FILMS AND AUDIOVISUALS
Films, videos, and audiotapes are available on different aspects of diabetes care. Your library, local chapter of ADA, or your diabetes educator or doctor may have these resources. Some of the titles available are

Diabetes: Focus on Feelings
The Sugar Film
Gestational Diabetes — Great Expectations
Know Your Diabetes: Know Yourself

DISCOUNT DIABETES SUPPLIES
The following companies advertise in the ADA Diabetes Forecast magazine. They all have toll-free numbers, so calling to check on prices is free to the caller. Also inquire about any specials they may be offering.

Diabetes Center Pharmacy
P.O. Box 739
Minneapolis, MN 55391
1-800-848-2793

Diabetic Express
P.O. Box 80037
Canton, OH 44708
1-800-338-4656

Diabetic Promotions
P.O.Box 462
Cleveland, OH 44107
1-800-433-1477
1-800-334-1377 (In Ohio)

Diabetic Supplies
8181 N. Stadium Dr.
Houston, TX 77054
1-800-6-CALL US

H-S Medical Supplies
P.O. Box 42
Whitehall, PA 18052
1-800-344-7633

Hospital Center Pharmacy
433 Brookline Ave.
Boston MA 02215
1-800-824-2401
1-800-462-1122 (In Massachusetts)

Jocelyn Bischoff's Diabetic
464 Vista Robles
Ben Lomand, CA 95005
1-800-537-0404

SugarFree Center
P.O.Box 114
Van Nuys, CA 91408
1-800-972-7223
1-800-336-1222 (In California)

Thrif-Tee Home Diabetic Center
937 Apperson Dr.
Salem, VA 24153
1-800-847-4383
703-389-4195 (In Virginia,
    call collect)

A Diabetes Survival Kit

Living well with diabetes begins with staying alive. So this positive book on self-care highlights three potential threats diabetes presents and the things you can do to tame them. Being knowledgeable about these subjects is of the highest priority in your diabetes management.

1. *Insulin reactions.* Low blood sugar (hypoglycemia) can lead to confusion and unconsciousness. You need to know what causes very low blood sugar, the symptoms that you experience, and the treatment. Chapter 8 provides the details of insulin reactions and how to deal with them.

2. *Diabetic coma.* You also need to learn the causes and symptoms of diabetic ketoacidosis and coma, which can result from very high blood sugar (hyperglycemia), omitted insulin shots, poorly managed illness or infections, or extreme stress. The Diabetic Ketoacidosis and Sick Day Management sections on the inside back cover at the back of this book discuss diabetic coma.

3. *Handling infections.* Small infections can become severe, and severe ones can lead to diabetic coma. A section on the inside back cover at the back of this book and the foot-care section of Chapter 17 are good sources of information on handling infections.

353

These three threats require that you

- Never omit an insulin injection unless your doctor says you may
- Always carry candy, sugar, or glucose tablets with you to treat reactions
- Always wear a diabetes identification bracelet or necklace
- Treat all wounds, scratches, and punctures to prevent infections.

Report illness or infections to your doctor, especially when they increase blood sugar levels or when you have ketones in your urine. See your doctor without delay if you need treatment.

Diabetic Ketoacidosis and Sick Day Management

Diabetic ketoacidosis — or ketosis — is a condition of type I, insulin-dependent, diabetes in which blood glucose and ketones rise to high levels. This state can be dangerous for a person with diabetes, leading to diabetic coma if not treated. It usually responds to prompt treatment, however, so you should know the symptoms and steps you can take when the symptoms occur.

Causes

> The physical stress of illness or infected wounds
> Great emotional stress
> Chronically high blood sugar levels combined with stress
> Omitted insulin
> Any combination of the above

Initial Signs and Symptoms

> Positive urine ketone and glucose tests
> High blood sugar tests (above 240 mg/dl)
> Dehydration, thirst, dry mouth
> Excessive, frequent urination
> Nausea, vomiting, abdominal pain
> Fatigue or weakness
> Fever
> Blurred vision

354

Signs and Symptoms As Condition Advances Toward Diabetic Coma

Flushed, dry skin
Fruity odor on breath
Sunken eyes
Deep, labored breathing
Pulse usually rapid
Unconsciousness

You may need to be treated in the hospital if your condition advances toward diabetic coma or does not respond to home treatment. Stay in touch with your doctor from the very first signs of ketosis.

(Note that insulin reactions, which can also lead to unconsciousness, are marked by much more rapid onset than ketosis, shallow breathing, normal-smelling breath, and low blood sugar.)

Treatment of Ketoacidosis
Any level of ketosis marked by a positive test for ketones in your urine needs your immediate attention. (People with kidney disease, especially, should be aware of the symptoms and begin treatment immediately when urine tests show ketones.)

Test urine and blood frequently: When you are ill— especially when you are vomiting, have diarrhea, or are feverish— you should test your urine for ketones and test your blood glucose. Infected wounds also can produce ketosis. Test every two or three hours until the results are normal.

Confer with your doctor: When you are ill and have ketones in your urine, ask your doctor for guidance in handling the situation. Your doctor will usually suggest extra shots of regular insulin to bring blood glucose and ketone levels down. The amount of insulin needed will be determined according to your body weight, blood sugar level, and severity of illness.

(After you have dealt with this level of illness a few times, your doctor may tell you that you know enough to handle it with minimal medical guidance. But any time you do not see improvement within six or eight hours, ask for your doctor's help.)

Continue taking insulin: You should never omit insulin, even when you are ill and unable to eat solid food. The stress of illness itself raises blood sugar levels.

Continue eating: You need to continue eating and drinking foods and fluids with caloric value, even if your blood sugar is high and you are vomiting or have diarrhea.

Take in at least 10 to 20 grams of carbohydrate every one to two hours. (Possible sources include: 1/3 cup flavored gelatin, 1/2 cup vanilla ice cream, 1/2 cup custard, 1/2 cup orange juice, 3/4 cup ginger ale (not diet), 1/2 cup regular cola, or 1 cup Gatorade.

If you have trouble keeping food down, take smaller quantities every fifteen to thirty minutes.

Limit activity: Even if you feel able to exercise when you have high blood sugar and ketones in your urine, *don't*. Exercising at this time actually raises blood sugar.

INDEX

A

AADE, 230, 347
acetaminophen, 304
acetone tests, 90
activity profile, 202
adipose tissue, 78
adrenal gland, 79
adrenal hormones, 152, 216
adrenalin, 41, 67
adrenergic inhibitors, 310
albumin, 297, 298
albuminuria, 297
alcohol, 80, 81, 84, 181, 326
alcoholism, 84
aldose reductase inhibitors, 307
Almost Sour Cream, 185
American Association of Diabetes
    Educators, 230, 347
American Diabetes Association, 24, 27,
    28, 173, 174, 231, 299, 318, 323,
    346, 348, 351
Ames Clinistix, 129
Ames Diastix, 129
Ames Division, 347, 348
amputation, 282, 305, 311
Anderson, J., 197
anger, 165, 221, 276
animal insulin, 82, 103
animal Ultralente, 103
anticoagulants, 85
anticonvulsant drugs, 304
antihistamines, 85
antihypertensive drug, 309
anxiety, 15, 22, 26, 33, 38, 50, 51, 53,
    125, 154, 156, 199, 254, 274, 276
anxiety-reducing ideas, 270
arteriosclerosis, 291, 307
arthritis, 10
aspartame, 180
atherosclerosis, 308, 310
autogenic training, 225
autogenics, 222
Autolet, 69
automatic finger-pricking device, 52
autonomic neuropathy, 304
azotemia, 297

B

Background retinopathy, 293
Baehr, K., 279

Becton-Dickinson, 348
behavior, 37, 262
behavioral psychologists, 257
beliefs, 262
Best O' Butter, 179
beta blockers, 56, 163, 310
Betschart, J., 350
Biermann, J., 351
Bio-Dynamics, 69
biofeedback, 222
bioflavanoids, 292, 296
birth control, 317
birthday parties, 342
blindness, 51, 214, 270, 293
blood glucose meter, 69, 328
blood glucose test kit, 218
blood glucose testing reagent strips, 69
blood pressure control, 271
blood urea nitrogen, 297
Boehringer Mannheim, 130
books for Parents of A Diabetic Youth,
    342
books on diseases of the heart and blood
    vessels, 312
books on relaxation, 226
Bradley, D. J., 343
brewer's yeast, 292
British and Canadian diabetes
    associations, 173
Brodsky, Archie, 351
burns, 91
Butter Buds, 179

C

Caesarean section, 319
caffeine, 223
cancer, 215, 291, 323
capillary thickness, 51
carbamazepine, 304
cardiovascular diseases, 288, 307
cataract, 296
causes of diabetic complications, 287
Center for Diabetes Education, 348
Certified Diabetes Educators, 230
changing behavior, 262
changing beliefs, 255
Chemstrips, 69
children's behavior, 341
cholesterol, 41, 45, 51, 62, 76, 123, 172,
    307